# 2020 杭州统计年鉴

HANGZHOU STATISTICAL YEARBOOK

杭州

# 2020
# 统计年鉴

HANGZHOU STATISTICAL YEARBOOK

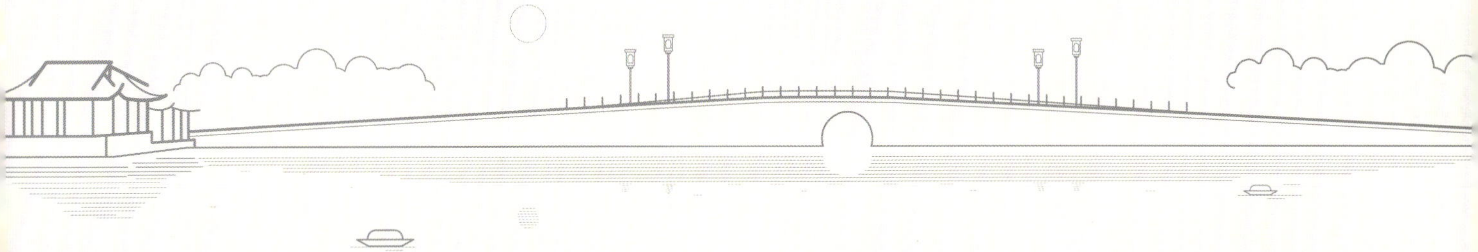

杭 州 市 统 计 局
国家统计局杭州调查队
杭州市社会经济调查队

中国统计出版社
China Statistics Press

图书在版编目（CIP）数据

杭州统计年鉴. 2020 = Hangzhou Statistical Yearbook 2020：汉英对照 / 杭州市统计局，国家统计局杭州调查队，杭州市社会经济调查队编. -- 北京：中国统计出版社，2020.9

ISBN 978-7-5037-9263-2

Ⅰ. ①杭… Ⅱ. ①杭… ②国… ③杭… Ⅲ. ①统计资料－杭州－2020－年鉴－汉、英 Ⅳ. ①C832.551-54

中国版本图书馆CIP数据核字(2020)第174149号

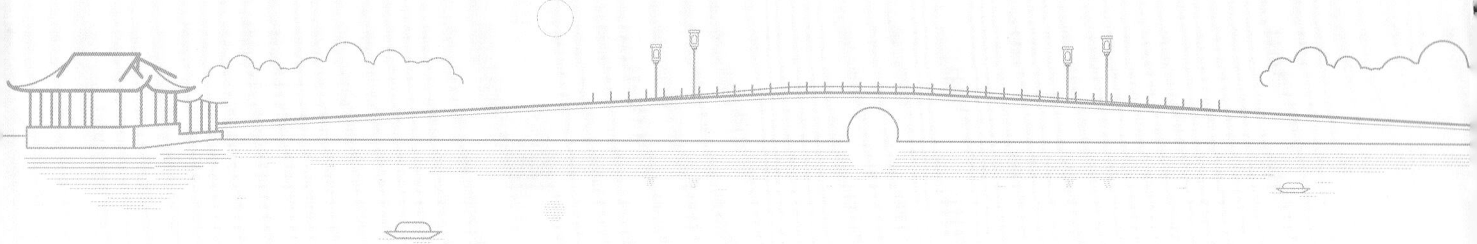

# 杭州统计年鉴 2020

作　　者/ 杭州市统计局
　　　　　国家统计局杭州调查队
　　　　　杭州市社会经济调查队
责任编辑/ 钟钰
装帧设计/ 张子杰
出版发行/ 中国统计出版社有限公司
地　　址/ 北京市丰台区西三环南路甲6号
邮政编码/ 100073
电　　话/ 邮购（010）63376909　书店（010）68783171
网　　址/ http://www.zgtjcbs.com
印　　刷/ 浙江新中商务印刷有限公司
经　　销/ 新华书店
开　　本/ 890mm×1240mm　1/16
字　　数/ 1017千字
印　　张/ 29.5
版　　别/ 2020年9月第1版
版　　次/ 2020年9月第1次印刷
定　　价/ 300.00元　Price: 300.00yuan(RMB)

# 统计年鉴

HANGZHOU STATISTICAL YEARBOOK

## 2020 编委会和编辑人员

统计年鉴

HANGZHOU STATISTICAL YEARBOOK

# 2020 Editorial Board and Staff

# 编者说明

一、《杭州统计年鉴—2020》是一部信息密集的资料性年刊。本年鉴系统收集了全市和各区、县（市）2019 年经济和社会各方面的统计数据，以及多个重要历史年份和近年全市主要统计数据。

二、本年鉴分为 13 个篇章：综合；人口和就业人员；农业；工业、能源；建筑业；交通运输、邮电；固定资产投资；批发、零售贸易和住宿餐饮业；对外经济、旅游；财政、金融、保险；城市建设、环境保护；科技、教育、文化、卫生、体育；人民生活、物价、民政。为便于读者使用，各篇章附有简要说明和主要统计指标解释。

三、本年鉴中涉及到历史数据，均以最新版本为准；本年鉴中部分数据合计数或相对数由于单位取舍不同而产生的计算误差，均未做机械调整。

四、2001 年起，萧山、余杭撤市建区，市区数据含萧山、余杭区；2014 年起富阳撤市建区，市区数据包括富阳区；2017 年起临安撤市建区，市区数据包括临安区。2019 年起区县分组新增钱塘新区，萧山区数据未做特殊说明的均含托管在钱塘新区的街道数据。

五、本年鉴表中符号使用说明：“－”表示这一栏没有数字；“…”表示该数字不足本表最小计量单位；“#”表示其中的主要项；“空格”表示该项统计数据不详或无该项数据；“＊”表示表下有注解。

六、本年鉴所使用的度量衡单位均采用国际统一标准计量单位，金额除特别标明外，均以人民币计量。

七、与 2019 年版《杭州统计年鉴》相比较，本年鉴在篇章结构和内容上主要做了以下修订：第一篇增加分地区数字经济核心产业增加值（2019 年）；第七篇增加高新技术产业投资指标（2011－2019 年）；第九篇增加进出口货物分贸易方式总值（2018－2019 年）；第十二篇增加规模以上工业企业 R&D 经费投入情况（2019 年）。

八、《杭州统计年鉴》公开出版以来，受到了社会各界的关心和支持，对此我们深表谢意。限于我们的水平，欢迎各界人士继续对年鉴的不足之处给予批评指正，帮助我们进一步提高统计年鉴的编辑工作，更好地为社会各界服务（网址：http：//tjj. hangzhou. gov. cn）。

# Editorial Note

Ⅰ. *Hangzhou Statistical Yearbook 2020* is an informative annual which contains very comprehensive statistics of Hangzhou's social and economic development in 2019, and selected data of recent years and some historically important years.

Ⅱ. This yearbook is composed of 13 chapters: 1. General Survey; 2. Population and Employment; 3. Agriculture; 4. Industry and Energy; 5. Construction; 6. Transportation, Post and Telecommunications; 7. Investment in Fixed Assets; 8. Wholesale and Retail Trade and Hotel and Catering Trade; 9. Foreign Economic Cooperation and Tourism; 10. Finance, Banking and Insurance; 11. Urban Construction and Environmental Protection; 12. Science and Technology, Education, Culture, Public Health and Sports; 13. People's Livelihood, Price Indices and Civil Administration. To facilitate readers, each chaper provides brief introduction and explanatory notes on main statistical indicators.

Ⅲ. Please refer to the newly published version of the yearbook for updated historical data. Statistical discrepancies on totals and relative figures due to rounding are not adjusted in the yearbook.

Ⅳ. Because of the change of urban administrative division, the data of Xiaoshan District and Yuhang District have been included into the urban districts since 2001, and it is the same for Fuyang District since 2014, Lin'an District since 2017. Qiantang New Area has been added into classification of districts and counties since 2019. Figures of Xiaoshan District without special explanation all include districts under administered by Qiantang New Area.

Ⅴ. Notations used in this Yearbook:"—" indicates that the column has no figure;"…" indicates that the figure is not large enough to be measured with the smallest unit in the table;"#" indicates that the date are unknown, or are not available;"blank" indicates the major items of the total;" * " indicates"see footnotes below".

Ⅵ. International standard units of measurement are applied in this Yearbook, all amounts are denominated in RMB, unless otherwise indicated.

Ⅶ. Compared with the 2019 edition of *Hangzhou Statistical Yearbook* , the revisions in structure and content made in this edition are as follows: The added value of core industries of digital economy by Region (2019) is added to Chapter 1; The investment index of high-tech industry (2011-2019) is added to Chapter 7; Total value of import and export goods by trade mode (2018-2019) is added to Chapter 9; R&D expenditure of industrial enterprises above designated size (2019) is added to Chapter 12.

Ⅷ. Since published openly, previous editions of *Hangzhou Statistical Yearbook* have been widely concerned and supported, for which we are very grateful. In order to get further improvement in the yearbook editing, we welcome all candid comments and criticism from our readers (website: http://tjj.hangzhou.gov.cn).

# 目　录
# Contents



## 一、综合
## Ⅰ. General Survey

## 二、人口和就业人员

## Ⅱ. Population and Employment

## 三、农业
## Ⅲ. Agriculture

## 四、工业、能源
## Ⅳ. Industry and Energy

## 五、建筑业
## Ⅴ. Construction



## 六、交通运输、邮电
## Ⅵ. Transportation, Post and Telecommunications

## 七、固定资产投资
## Ⅶ. Investment in Fixed Assets

## 八、批发、零售贸易和住宿餐饮业

## Ⅷ. Wholesale and Retail Trade and Hotel and Catering Trade

# 九、对外经济、旅游
# Ⅸ. Foreign Economic Cooperation and Tourism

# 十、财政、金融、保险

## Ⅹ. Finance, Banking and Insurance



# 十一、城市建设、环境保护

## Ⅺ. Urban Construction and Environmental Protection

## 十二、科技、教育、文化、卫生、体育

## Ⅻ. Science and Technology, Education, Culture, Public Health and Sports

## 十三、人民生活、物价、民政

## XIII. People's Livelihood, Price Indices and Civil Administration

# 2019年杭州市国民经济和社会发展统计公报

杭 州 市 统 计 局
国家统计局杭州调查队

（2020年3月20日）

2019年，全市坚持以习近平新时代中国特色社会主义思想为指导，深入贯彻党的十九大、十九届二中、三中、四中全会精神，坚持新发展理念，坚持稳中求进工作总基调，坚持“干好一一六、当好排头兵”目标，全力推动稳增长、调结构、促改革、惠民生、防风险、保稳定，着力提升城市能级和核心竞争力，经济社会发展实现稳中有进、进中提质，“十三五”规划主要指标进度符合预期，高水平全面建成小康社会取得新进展。

## 一、综　　合

### （一）经济增长。

初步核算，全年地区生产总值15373亿元，比上年增长6.8%，其中第一产业增加值326亿元，第二产业增加值4875亿元，第三产业增加值10172亿元，分别增长1.9%、5.0%和8.0%。三次产业结构调整为2.1∶31.7∶66.2（根据第四次全国经济普查结果和我国GDP核算制度规定，2018年杭州GDP修订为14307亿元，三次产业增加值结构为2.1∶32.8∶65.1）。全市人均地区生产总值达152465元（按年平均汇率折算为22102美元）。

数字经济持续引领。数字经济核心产业增加值3795亿元，增长15.1%，高于GDP增速8.3个百分点，占GDP的24.7%。数字内容、软件与信息服务和电子商务分别增长16.3%、15.7%和14.6%。

全年民营经济增加值9378亿元，占GDP的61.0%，比上年提高0.5个百分点。年末，全市私营企业63.2万户，比上年末增长14.0%；个体工商户61.0万户，增长19.6%。

### （二）财政收支。

全年财政总收入3650.0亿元，增长5.6%；一般公共预算收入1966.0亿元，增长7.7%，其中税收收入1791.2亿元，增长8.5%，占一般公共预算收入的91.1%。一般公共预算支出1952.9亿元，增长13.7%，其中民生支出1535.3亿元，增长15.2%，占一般公共预算支出的78.6%，比上年提高1个百分点。

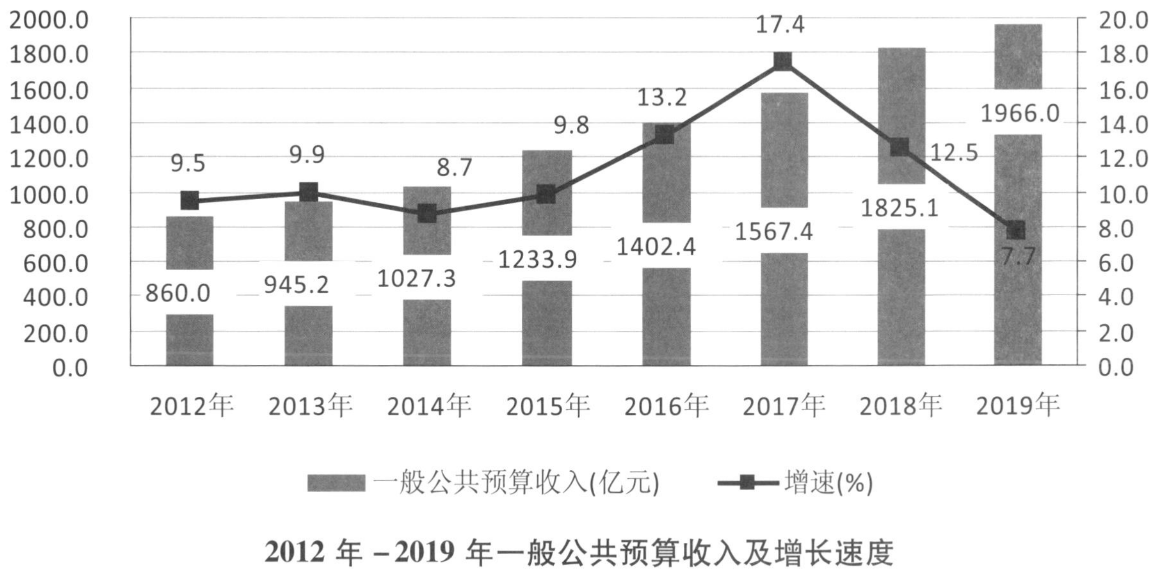


**2012年–2019年一般公共预算收入及增长速度**

## （三）市场价格。

全年市区居民消费价格比上年上涨3.1%，其中医疗保健类价格上涨7.0%、食品烟酒类价格上涨6.3%。商品零售价格上涨3.1%。工业生产者出厂价格下降1.0%，工业生产者购进价格下降3.2%。

**市区居民消费价格涨跌幅度（%）**

| 项　　目 | 2018年 | 2019年 |
|---|---|---|
| 市区居民消费价格 | 2.3 | 3.1 |
| 1.食品烟酒 | 2.7 | 6.3 |
| 其中：粮食 | 0.7 | 1.1 |
| 鲜菜 | 8.6 | 3.4 |
| 畜肉类 | -2.3 | 23.1 |
| 鲜瓜果 | 5.2 | 14.6 |
| 2.衣着 | 1.4 | 1.3 |
| 3.居住 | 3.7 | 0.9 |
| 4.生活用品及服务 | 0.6 | 3.0 |
| 5.交通和通信 | 1.3 | -1.0 |
| 6.教育文化和娱乐 | 1.5 | 4.3 |
| 7.医疗保健 | 2.0 | 7.0 |
| 8.其他用品和服务 | 0.0 | 2.8 |

## （四）人口就业。

年末全市常住人口1036.0万人，比上年末增加55.4万人，其中城镇人口813.3万人，占常住人口的78.5%，比上年末提高1.1个百分点；人口出生率为11.1‰，自然增长率为6.0‰。全市户籍人口795.4万人，人口出生率为11.65‰，自然增长率为6.97‰。全市新增城镇就业人员34.0万人，安置失业人员再就业6.4万人。年末城镇登记失业率1.8%。

**2019年末常住人口数及其构成**

| 指　　标 | 年末常住人口数（万人） | 比重（%） |
|---|---|---|
| 常住人口 | 1036.0 | - |
| 其中：城填 | 813.3 | 78.5 |
| 乡村 | 222.7 | 21.5 |
| 其中：男性 | 530.7 | 51.2 |
| 女性 | 505.3 | 48.8 |
| 其中：0-14岁 | 133.7 | 12.9 |
| 15-64岁 | 769.7 | 74.3 |
| 65岁及以上 | 132.6 | 12.8 |

## 二、农业和农村

全年农林牧渔业增加值 333 亿元，增长 2.1%，其中农业 210 亿元、林业 48 亿元、渔业 30 亿元，分别增长 2.7%、3.9% 和 0.7%；农林牧渔专业及辅助性活动 7.0 亿元，增长 9.2%；牧业 37 亿元，下降 4.8 %。

全年粮食总产量 49.6 万吨，蔬菜产量 340.1 万吨，水果产量 82.6 万吨，水产品产量 20.30 万吨，肉类产量 14.97 万吨。市级“菜篮子”基地 541 个，其中新建 27 个。新启动 4 个省级重点历史文化村、72 个市级精品村、7 个风情小镇、8 条精品示范线建设。农家乐（民宿）接待游客 8489.8 万人次，实现经营收入 80.8 亿元，分别增长 23.3% 和 18.5%。农村电商销售额 142.6 亿元，增长 18.8%。

全年培训农村实用人才 14426 人。累计创建省级“田间学校”51 家、市级农民教育培训实训基地 67 家。

## 三、工业和建筑业

全年工业增加值 4288 亿元，增长 5.3%，其中规模以上工业增加值 3482 亿元，增长 5.1%。规模以上工业中高新技术产业、战略性新兴产业、装备制造业增加值分别增长 8.5%、13.1% 和 7.9%，占规模以上工业的 62.6%、38.2% 和 47.1%；八大高耗能行业增加值占比 23.6%。新产品产值率 42.8%。规模以上工业企业实现利润 1126 亿元。规上工业全员劳动生产率 34 万元/人；规上工业单位增加值能耗下降 7.2%，降幅比上年扩大 1.3 个百分点。

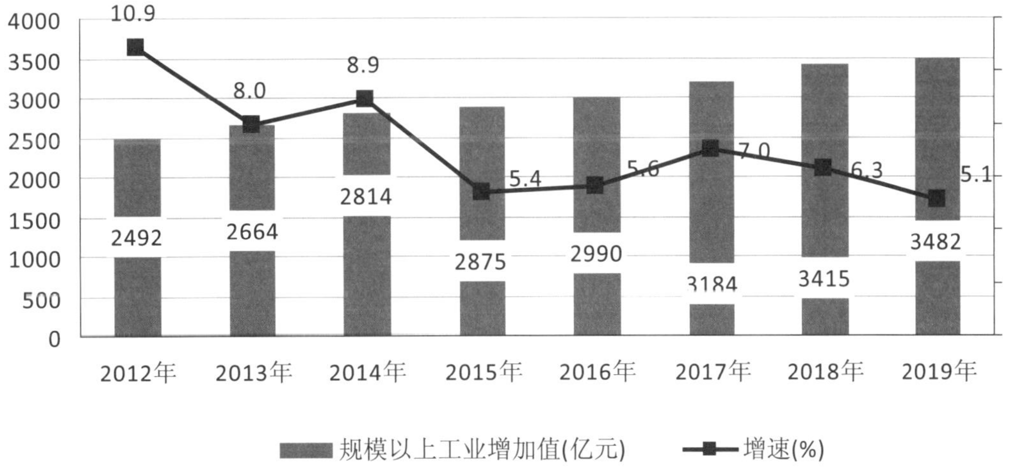


**2012 年 -2019 年规模以上工业增加值及增速**

全年建筑业增加值 588 亿元，增长 1.6%。

## 四、交通运输和邮电

全年交通运输、仓储和邮政业增加值 398 亿元，增长 4.4%。

全年货运量 3.6 亿吨，增长 3.2%。客运量 2.1 亿人次，增长 3.8%。至年末萧山国际机场开通航线 301 条，其中国际航线 63 条，港澳台航线 6 条。航空客运吞吐量达 4011 万人次，货物吞吐量 69.0 万吨，分别增长 4.9% 和 7.7%。地铁客运量 6.3 亿人次，增长 19.3%。

年末社会机动车保有量297.6万辆，增长3.3%。民用汽车保有量269.0万辆，增长12.7%，其中私人汽车216.2万辆，增长4.1%。

全年邮政企业和规模以上快递服务企业实现业务收入402.3亿元，增长10.3%，其中快递业务收入326.8亿元，增长10.2%。年末固定电话用户233.1万户；移动电话用户1817.9万户；宽带用户554.5万户。

**2019年各种运输方式完成货运量和客运量**

| 指　　标 | 绝对数 | 比上年增长(%) |
| --- | --- | --- |
| 全社会货运量(万吨) | 36384 | 3.2 |
| 铁路(万吨) | 537 | 35.8 |
| 公路(万吨) | 31732 | 3.7 |
| 水路(万吨) | 4073 | -4.0 |
| 航空(万吨) | 41 | 9.8 |
| 全社会客运量(万人次) | 20888 | 3.8 |
| 铁路(万人次) | 8874 | 17.8 |
| 公路(万人次) | 9360 | -6.7 |
| 水路(万人次) | 610 | 1.1 |
| 航空(万人次) | 2044 | 4.5 |

## 五、金融

全年金融业增加值1789亿元，增长9.1%。

年末金融机构本外币存款余额45287.0亿元，增长13.8%；贷款余额42245.2亿元，增长15.4%。

**2019年末金融机构本外币存贷款余额及增速**

| 指　　标 | 年末数(亿元) | 比上年末增长(%) |
| --- | --- | --- |
| 各项存款余额 | 45287.0 | 13.8 |
| 其中:住户存款 | 11901.3 | 16.7 |
| 非金融企业存款 | 20280.3 | 16.5 |
| 各项贷款余额 | 42245.2 | 15.4 |
| 其中:住户贷款 | 16518.0 | 18.5 |
| 非金融企业及机关团体贷款 | 25375.5 | 13.6 |
| 其中:短期贷款 | 8113.7 | 5.7 |
| 中长期贷款 | 14683.2 | 16.4 |
| 票据融资 | 1627.3 | 44.5 |

年末上市公司192家，其中境内上市146家；全年新增上市公司22家，IPO融资162.3亿元，增长64.6%。中小板上市公司34家，创业板上市公司43家。

全年保费收入846.3亿元，增长27.5%，其中财产险保费收入248.0亿元，人身险保费收入598.3亿元。支付各类保险赔款243.1亿元，增长19.9%，其中财产险152.6亿元，人身险90.5亿元。

## 六、固定资产投资和房地产开发

### (一)固定资产投资。

全年固定资产投资增长 11.6%,其中基础设施投资增长 5.2%,交通投资增长 16.9%;高新技术产业投资增长 8.4%。从产业投向看,第二产业投资增长 6.2%,其中工业投资增长 5.6%;第三产业投资增长 12.2%。

### (二)房地产开发。

全年房地产开发投资增长 10.7%,其中住宅投资增长 12.6%,办公楼投资增长 13.4%,商业营业用房投资下降 5.9%。年末房屋施工面积 11996 万平方米,增长 2.1%;新开工面积 2435 万平方米,下降 10.1%;竣工面积 1728 万平方米,增长 5.5%。商品房销售面积 1514 万平方米,下降 9.7%。

**2019 年房地产开发和销售主要指标**

| 指　　标 | 实绩数 | 比上年末增长(%) |
|---|---|---|
| 房地产开发施工面积(万平方米) | 11996 | 2.1 |
| 其中:住宅(万平方米) | 6263 | 1.7 |
| 房地产开发竣工面积(万平方米) | 1728 | 5.5 |
| 其中:住宅(万平方米) | 964 | 14.5 |
| 商品房销售面积(万平方米) | 1514 | -9.7 |
| 其中:住宅(万平方米) | 1284 | -3.4 |

## 七、国内贸易

全年批发和零售业增加值 1225 亿元,增长 3.3%;住宿和餐饮业增加值 234 亿元,增长 4.0%。

全年社会消费品零售总额 6188 亿元,增长 8.8%,按消费类型统计,商品零售 5110 亿元,增长 8.8%,餐饮收入 1077 亿元,增长 8.6%。限额以上批零单位可穿戴智能设备零售额增长 38.4%,智能家用电器和音像器材增长 21.7%;限额以上批零单位通过公共网络实现的商品零售增长 20.0%,占限额以上批零单位商品零售总额的 25.5%。

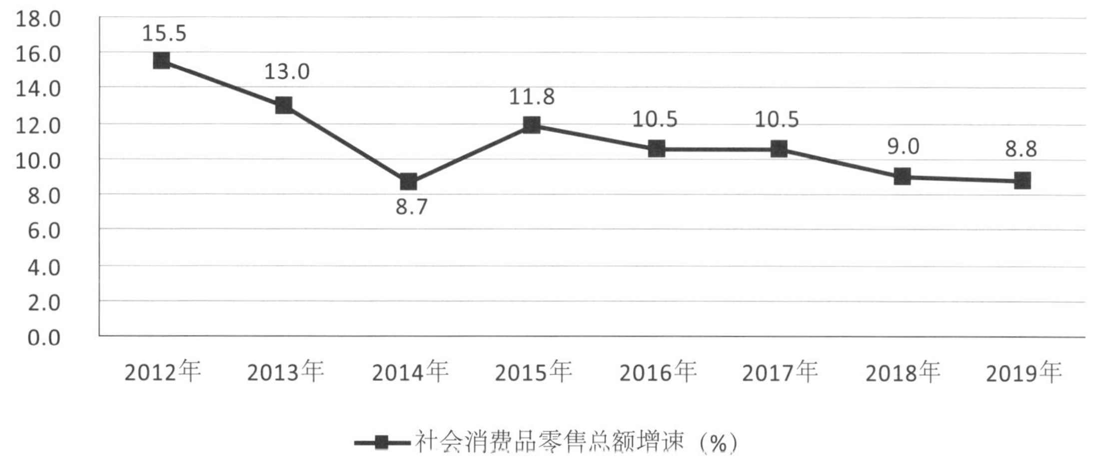


**2012 年 -2019 年社会消费品零售总额增速**

## 八、对外经济

### （一）对外贸易。

全年货物进出口总额5597亿元，增长6.7%，其中出口3613亿元，增长5.7%，进口1984亿元，增长8.5%。高新技术产品出口569亿元，增长9.7%，机电产品出口1550亿元，增长6.1%。对“一带一路”沿线国家出口1177亿元，占出口总额32.6%。服务贸易出口124.9亿美元，增长19.0%。

全年跨境电商进出口总额952.1亿元，增长28.8%，其中出口658.8亿元，进口293.3亿元，分别增长26.4%和34.6%。

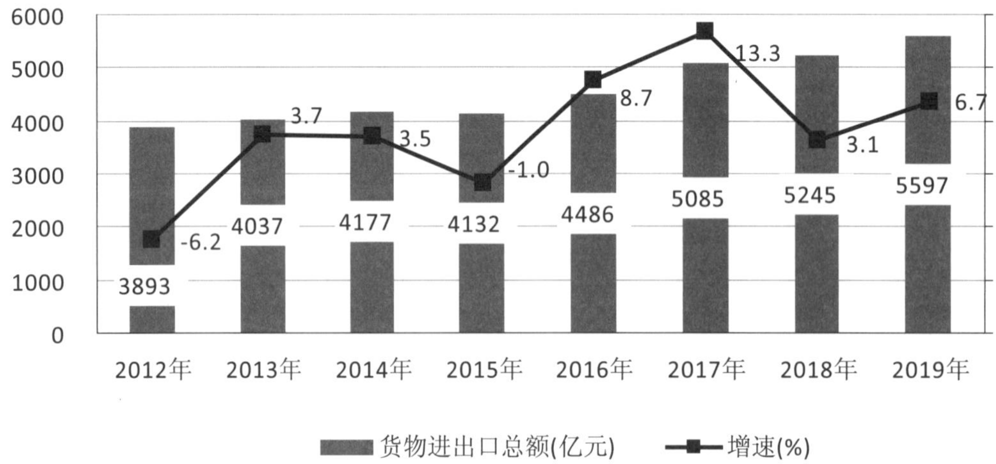


**2012年－2019年货物进出口总额及增速**

### （二）利用外资。

全年新引进外商投资企业736家，其中总投资3000万美元以上企业118家。实际利用外资61.3亿美元，增长14.0%，其中第二产业7.3亿美元，第三产业54.0亿美元。至年末，126家世界500强企业来杭投资219个项目。

### （三）对外合作。

年末全市设立各类境外投资企业（机构）2237个，增长11.4%。对外承包工程和劳务合作营业额27.4亿美元，增长6.0%。离岸服务外包合同执行额71.9亿美元，增长3.9%。

## 九、人民生活和社会保障

### （一）人民生活。

全年全市居民人均可支配收入59261元，增长9.0%，扣除价格因素实际增长5.7%。按常住地分，城镇、农村居民人均可支配收入分别为66068元和36255元，增长8.0%和9.2%，扣除价格因素增长4.8%和5.9%。

全年全市居民人均消费支出40016元，增长7.1％。按常住地分，城镇、农村居民人均消费支出分别为44076元和26296元，增长5.9%和8.6％，扣除价格因素增长2.7%和5.3%。

**2019 年全市城乡居民人均收支主要指标**

| 指标名称 | 全体居民 | | 城镇居民 | | 农村居民 | |
|---|---|---|---|---|---|---|
| | 绝对数(元) | 增速(%) | 绝对数(元) | 增速(%) | 绝对数(元) | 增速(%) |
| 人均可支配收入 | 59261 | 9.0 | 66068 | 8.0 | 36255 | 9.2 |
| (一)工资性收入 | 34136 | 8.9 | 37845 | 7.9 | 21601 | 9.1 |
| (二)经营净收入 | 6584 | 8.2 | 5849 | 10.4 | 9067 | 6.4 |
| (三)财产净收入 | 8111 | 12.6 | 10045 | 10.6 | 1574 | 14.1 |
| (四)转移净收入 | 10430 | 7.4 | 12329 | 5.3 | 4013 | 14.8 |
| 人均消费支出 | 40016 | 7.1 | 44076 | 5.9 | 26296 | 8.6 |

年末城镇居民人均住房建筑面积 38.2 平方米,每百户居民家庭拥有家用汽车 62.6 辆、空调 250.2 台,分别增长 4.9% 和 2.9%,每百户居民家庭拥有家用电脑 89.8 台,下降 10.6%。农村居民人均住房建筑面积 74.1 平方米,每百户居民家庭拥有家用汽车 52.7 辆、空调 211.4 台,分别增长 3.5% 和 2.4%,每百户居民家庭拥有家用电脑 60.2 台,下降 14.5%。

### (二)社会保障。

年末职工基本养老保险参保人数、城镇职工基本医疗保险参保人数分别为 704.7 万人和 671.1 万人,增长 5.0% 和 6.1%;年末失业、职工工伤保险参保人数分别为 486.7 万人和 556.7 万人,增长 5.9% 和 7.0%。主城区居民最低生活保障标准调整至每人每月 1041 元,增长 9.0%。年末全市最低生活保障对象 10.25 万人,全年发放困难家庭救助金 8.88 亿元,增长 3.6%。

**社会保障相关待遇标准**

| | 2019 年 | 2018 年 |
|---|---|---|
| 失业保险金最低标准(市区城镇居民) | 1608 元/月 | 1608 元/月 |
| 城乡最低生活保障标准(市区不含临安) | 1041 元/月 | 955 元/月 |
| 城乡最低生活保障标准(桐庐、淳安、建德) | 833 元/月 | 764 元/月 |
| 城乡最低生活保障标准(临安) | 989 元/月 | 860 元/月 |
| 职工最低工资标准(市区) | 2010 元/月 | 2010 元/月 |

### (三)社会福利。

年末全市拥有城乡社区居家养老服务照料中心 2898 个。拥有各类福利院、敬老院 328 所,床位 7.47 万张,收养人员 3.55 万人。儿童福利机构 8 个,床位 1040 张。全年发行各类福利彩票 30.27 亿元,下降 2.8%。

## 十、科学技术和教育

### (一)科学技术。

全年发明专利申请量和发明专利授权量分别为 43357 件和 11748 件,增长 18.7% 和 14.4%。累计拥有市级以上企业技术中心749家,其中国家级42家;国家技术创新示范企业11家,省级技术创新示范企业11家。科技企业孵化器178家,其中国家级41家,省级92家。众创空间180家,其中省级132家。全年签订技术合同总量15612项501.1亿元,分别增长12.7%和31.8%。

全年研究与试验发展(R&D)经费支出占地区生产总值比重3.45%。财政一般公共预算支出中科技支出148.2亿元,增长25.4%。

**(二)教育。**

年末全市拥有普通高等学校40所,在校学生51.8万人,增加2.2万人,其中研究生7.2万人,高等教育毛入学率67.3%;普通高中87所,在校学生11.8万人,增加0.4万人;职高和中等专业学校37所,在校学生6.1万人,与去年持平;初中269所,在校学生24.4万人,增加0.9万人,初中毕业生升入各类高中比例为99.75%;小学489所,在校学生61.7万人,增加2.6万人;幼儿园1020所,在园幼儿35.0万人,增加0.7万人,学前三年幼儿入园率为99.1%。累计解决义务教育阶段外来务工人员子女入学28.7万人。各级各类中外合作办学项目70个,其中市属高校项目8个,高中段学校项目7个。

## 十一、文化旅游、卫生健康和体育

**(一)文化旅游。**

全年文化创意产业增加值3735亿元,增长15.6%。年末全市拥有文化馆15个,公共图书馆16个。博物馆79个,全国重点文物保护单位48处。全年制作电视剧7部357集,网络电视剧6部,网络电影13部,网络动画片2部。放映电影274万场次,电影票款收入15.8亿元。年末有线电视注册用户298.1万户。"杭州刺绣"等24个非遗代表性项目入选首批浙江省传统工艺振兴目录。

全年旅游休闲产业增加值1191亿元,增长12.1%。旅游总收入4005亿元,增长18.3%;旅游总人数20813.7万人次,增长15.1%,其中接待入境过夜游客113.3万人次,增长5.7%。年末各类旅行社895家,增长5.5%。星级宾馆126家,其中五星级23家。A级景区103个,其中5A级3个。

**(二)卫生健康。**

全年健康产业增加值975亿元,增长12.5%。年末拥有各类医疗卫生机构5925个,其中医院343个,比上年末分别增长10.2%和8.5%。各类专业卫生技术人员12.7万人,其中执业(助理)医师4.9万人,注册护士5.5万人,分别增长8.2%、8.9%和10.2%。拥有床位8.6万张,其中医院床位8.0万张,分别增长5.5%和6.4%。全市医疗机构完成诊疗人数14640.7万人次,增长5.5%。全市婴儿死亡率和5岁以下儿童死亡率分别为1.65‰和2.35‰。孕产妇死亡率为2.75人/10万。

**(三)体育。**

全年运动员获得国际性比赛奖牌50枚,其中金牌23枚,银牌11枚;全国性奖牌410枚,其中金牌160枚,银牌114枚。十四届全国冬季运动会跳台滑草体能大比武单项第一名。举办杭州马拉松、国际(杭州)毅行大会、首届中国-新西兰青少年高尔夫球团体对抗赛、2019年杭州国际网球邀请赛等本土国际品牌赛事。

全年销售体育彩票33.97亿元,下降21.8%。

## 十二、城市建设

全年境内公路总里程达到16667公里,其中高速公路632公里。年末主城区公共交通运营线路402条,其中新辟线路15条,优化线路45条。地铁运营里程135.4公里,在建里程381公里。

全市用电量817亿千瓦时,增长2.5%,其中三次产业用电679亿千瓦时,增长1.6%;城乡居民生活用电138亿千瓦时,增长7.0%。

全市新建成停车泊位100021个,其中公共泊位11271个。

## 十三、环境保护和安全生产

全年市区空气优良天数287天,优良率78.6%。市区PM2.5平均浓度37.7微克/立方米,同比持平。二氧化氮年均浓度值41微克/立方米,上升2.5%;二氧化硫年均浓度值7微克/立方米,下降22.2%。市控以上断面达标率98.1%,提高1.9个百分点。全市森林覆盖率达66.84%。

全年共发生各类生产安全事故229起、死亡190人,分别下降27.3%和38.5%。

公报注释:

1. 本公报所列各项数据为年度初步数据。部分数据因四舍五入原因,存在分项与合计不等的情况。

2. 全市地区生产总值和各产业增加值绝对数按现行价格计算,增长速度按不变价格计算;三次产业划分执行国家统计局2018年修订的《三次产业划分规定(2012)》。

资料来源:

本公报中城镇新增就业、登记失业率、社会保障数据来自市人力社保局;私营企业、个体工商户、专利数据来自市市场监管局;财政数据来自市财政局;农业园区、美丽乡村、农家乐(民宿)数据来自市农业农村局;教育数据来自市教育局;货物进出口数据来自杭州海关;低保、社会服务和救助、福利彩票数据来自市民政局;公路里程、公交运营线路数据来自市交通局;航空客运吞吐量、货邮吞吐量、通航线路数据来自萧山机场;地铁运营数据来自市地铁集团;停车泊位数据来自市建委;生态建设、环境监测数据来自市生态环境局;各类事故发生起数、死亡人数来自市应急管理局;实际利用外资数据来自市投资促进局;对外承包工程、服务贸易数据来自市商务局;用电量数据来自国网杭州供电公司;户籍人口、机动车拥有数据来自市公安局;邮政业务数据来自市邮政管理局;货币金融数据来自人民银行杭州中心支行;保险业数据来自中国保监会浙江监管局;博物馆、纪念馆数据来自市园林文物局;科技创新、高新技术企业、研发中心、众创空间数据来自市科技局;旅游、艺术表演团体、公共图书馆、文化馆数据来自市文化广电旅游局;电影、动画片数据来自市委宣传部;上市公司数据来自市金融办;卫生数据来自市卫生健康委员会;医疗保险数据来自市医疗保障局;体育数据来自市体育局;建设用地数据来自市规划和自然资源局;森林覆盖率数据来自市林业水利局;价格、城乡居民收支、人均住房面积、百户居民耐用品数据来自国家统计局杭州调查队;其他数据均来自市统计局。

# Statistical Communiqué of Hangzhou on the 2019 National Economic and Social Development

Hangzhou Municipal Bureau of Statistics

Hangzhou Survey Office of National Bureau of Statistics

March,2020

In 2019,Hangzhou persisted in the guidance of Xi Jinping's Thought of Socialism with Chinese Characteristics in the New Era, thoroughly implemented the spirit of the 19th CPC National Congress and the 2nd, 3rd and 4th Plenary Sessions of the 19th CPC Central Committee. Adhered to the New Development Concept, adhered to the general keynote of seeking progress in stability, adhered to the goal of " Building a world famous city with unique charm; creating an important window to show socialism with Chinese characteristics in the new era; comprehensively promoting six actions as the development of embracing Qiantang River, the integration of digital industrialization, industrial digitization and urban digitization, the prosperity of cultural, the well - being of the people's livelihood, tackling key problems in reform, and strengthening the foundation; and being a good pacesetter". Made every effort to promote stable growth, adjust structure, promote reform, benefit people's livelihood, prevent risks and ensure stability. Strive to improve the city's function level and core competitiveness. Economic and social development achieved progress in stability and quality improvement in progress. The progress of the main indicators of the 13th Five Year Plan is in line with expectations, and new progress has been made in building a moderately prosperous society in an all - round way at a high level.

## I. General Outlook

### Economic Aggregate

The gross domestic product (GDP) of the year was 1537. 3 billion yuan, up by 6. 8% over the previous year. Of this total, the added value of the primary industry was 32. 6 billion yuan with an annual increase of 1. 9% , that of the secondary industry was 487. 5 billion yuan with an annual increase of 5. 0% , and the tertiary industry was 1017. 2 billion yuan with an annual increase of 8. 0%. The proportions of the three industries was adjusted to 2. 1:31. 7:66. 2 (According to the results of the fourth national economic census and the national GDP accounting system, the gross domestic product (GDP) of Hangzhou in 2018 was adjusted to 1430. 7 billion yuan, the proportions of the three industries was adjusted to 2. 1:32. 8:65. 1). The city's per capita GDP was 152,465 yuan (According to the average exchange rate in 2019 which published by the Central Bank, the per capita GDP was 22,102 U. S. dollars).

Digital economy continues to lead. The added value of digital economy core industry was 379. 5 billion yuan, up by 15. 1% ,which was 8. 3 percentage points higher than the GDP growth rate and accounted for 24. 7% of GDP. Digital content industry, software and information service industry and e - commerce industry increased by 16. 3% , 15. 7% and 14. 6% respectively.

The annual added value of the non - state - owned economy was 937. 8 billion yuan, accounting for 61. 0% of GDP which is 0. 5 percentage points higher than the previous year. At the year end, there were 632 thousand private enterprises and 610 thousand individual businesses, up by 14. 0% and 19. 6% respectively.

### Fiscal Revenue and Expenditure

The general fiscal revenue of the city reached 365 billion yuan, up by 5. 6%. The general budgetary revenue of the local government was 196. 60 billion yuan, up by 7. 7% ;of which, the tax revenue was 179. 12 billion yuan, up by 8. 5% , accounting for 91. 1% of the general public budget revenue. The fiscal expenditure of the local government was 195. 29 billion yuan, up by 13. 7% ; of which, the fiscal expenditure for promoting people's livelihood reached 153. 53 billion yuan, up by 15. 2% , accounting for 78. 6% of the fiscal expenditure of the local government, which was 1 percentage point higher than that of the previous year.

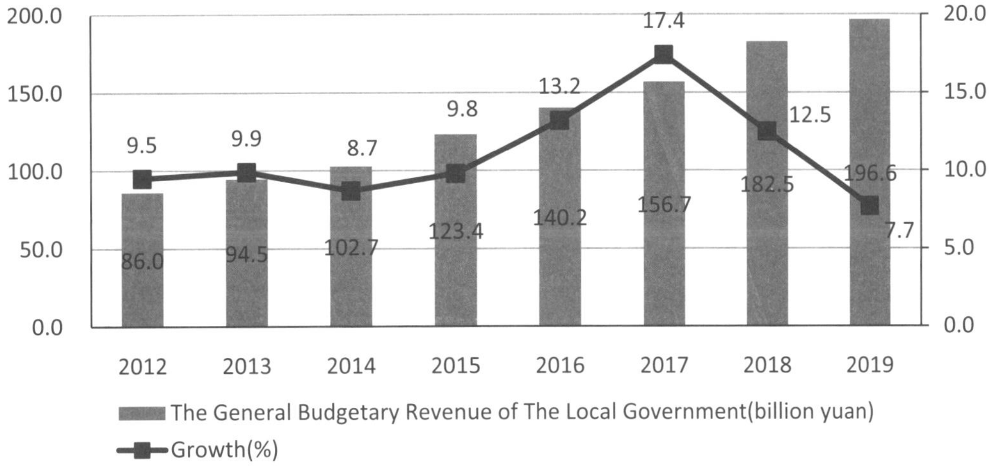


**The General Budgetary Revenue of The Local Government from 2012 to 2019**

## Commodity Price

The consumer price in urban area went up by 3. 1% over the previous year, the price of health care went up by 7. 0% , the price of food and tobacco went up by 6. 3%. The commodity retail price went up by 3. 1%. The producer price for industrial products went down by 1. 0% , the purchasing price for industrial producers went down by 3. 2%.

**The Changes of Consumer Price in Urban District ( % )**

| Item | 2018 | 2019 |
| --- | --- | --- |
| General level of consumer price in urban district | 2. 3 | 3. 1 |
| 1. FoodandTobacco | 2. 7 | 6. 3 |
| Of which: Grain | 0. 7 | 1. 1 |
| Fresh Vegetables | 8. 6 | 3. 4 |
| Meat | -2. 3 | 23. 1 |
| Fresh Fruits | 5. 2 | 14. 6 |
| 2. Clothing | 1. 4 | 1. 3 |
| 3. Residence | 3. 7 | 0. 9 |
| 4. Daily necessities and Services | 0. 6 | 3. 0 |
| 5. Transportation and Communication | 1. 3 | -1. 0 |
| 6. Education, Culture and Entertainment | 1. 5 | 4. 3 |
| 7. Health Care | 2. 0 | 7. 0 |
| 8. Other supplies and Services | 0. 0 | 2. 8 |

## Population and Employment

By the end of the year, the population of Hangzhou reached 10. 36million, an increase of 554 thousand over the previous year. Of this total, the urban population reached 8. 133 million, accounting for 78. 5%, increased by 1. 1 percentage points than last year; the crude birth rate was 11. 1‰, and the natural growth rate of population was 6. 0‰. The population of household registration reached 7. 954 million, the crude birth rate was 11. 65‰, and the natural growth rate of population was 6. 97‰. The newly employed people in urban area increased 340 thousand, and 64 thousand unemployed people were re – employed. The registered urban unemployment rate was 1. 8% at the year end.

**Population and Its Composition by the end of Year 2019**

| Item | Population(million) | Proportion(%) |
|---|---|---|
| Population | 10. 36 | – |
| Of which: urban | 8. 133 | 78. 5 |
| countryside | 2. 227 | 21. 5 |
| Of which: male | 5. 307 | 51. 2 |
| female | 5. 053 | 48. 8 |
| Of which: age 0 – 14 | 1. 337 | 12. 9 |
| age 15 – 64 | 7. 697 | 74. 3 |
| age 65 or above | 1. 326 | 12. 8 |

# II. Agriculture and Rural Area

The added value of agriculture, forestry, animal husbandry and fishery achieved 33. 3 billion yuan, up by 2. 1%. Of this total, the added value of agriculture was 21. 0 billion yuan, that of forestry was 4. 8 billion yuan, that of fishery was 3. 0 billion yuan, and that of agriculture & forestry & animal husbandry & Fishery Services was 0. 70 billion yuan, up by 2. 7%, 3. 9%, 0. 7% and 9. 2% respectively. The added value of animal husbandry was 3. 7 billion yuan, down by 4. 8%.

The total output of grain was 0. 496 million tons, the output of vegetable was 3. 401 million tons, the output of fruit was 0. 826 million tons, the output of aquatic products was 0. 203 million tons, and the output of meat was 0. 1497 million tons. There were 541 municipal vegetable bases in Hangzhou, of which 27 were newly built. Hangzhou newly launched the construction of 4 provincial – level key historical and cultural villages, 72 municipal – level boutique villages, 7 folk towns and 8 boutique demonstration lines. The farmhouse (home hostel) received 84. 898 million tourists and the business revenue was 8. 08 billion yuan, up by 23. 3% and 18. 5% respectively. The sales volume of rural e – commerce was14. 26 billion yuan, up by 18. 8%.

14426 rural practical talents were trained throughout the year. A total of 51 provincial "field schools" and 67 municipal farmer education and training bases have been established.

# III. Industry and Construction

## Industry Production

The added value of the industrial sector was 428. 8 billion yuan, up by 5. 3%. Of this total, the added value of industrial enterprises above designated size was 348. 2 billion yuan, up by 5. 1%. In the industrial enterprises above designated size, the added value of high - tech industries, strategic emerging industries and equipment manufacturing industries increased by 8. 5%, 13. 1% and 7. 9% respectively, accounted for 62. 6%, 38. 2% and 47. 1% of industrial enterprises above designated size respectively; the added value of eight high energy consuming industries accounted for 23. 6%. The output value ratio of new products was 42. 8%. The profit of industrial enterprises above designated size achieved 112. 6 billion yuan. The total labor productivity of industrial enterprises above designated size was 0. 34 million yuan per personnel; The unit added value energy consumption of industrial enterprises above designated size decreased by 7. 2%, the decline was 1. 3 percentage points greater than last year.

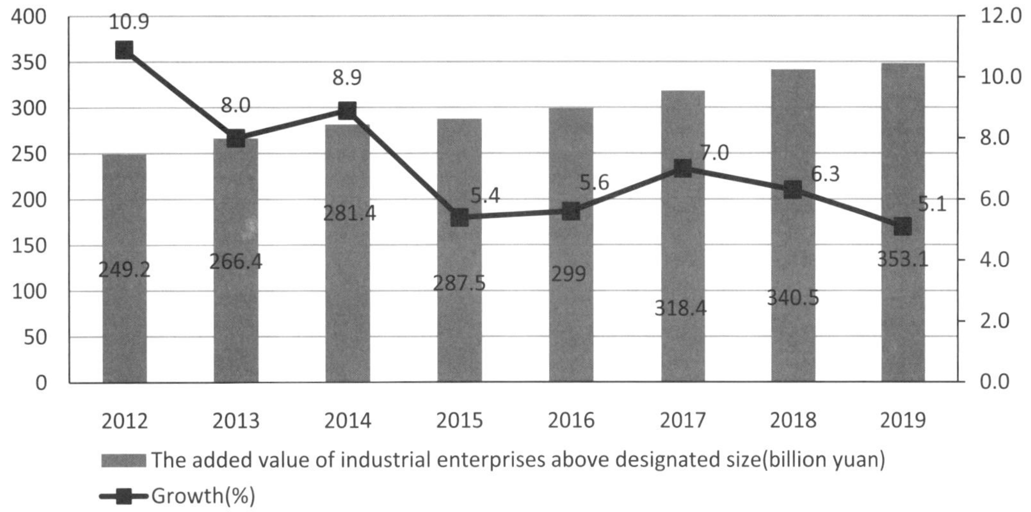


**The added value of industrial enterprises above designated size from 2012 to 2019**

## Construction

The added value of construction industry was 58. 8 billion yuan, up by 1. 6%。

# IV. Transportation, Post and Telecommunications

## Transportation

The added value of transportation, storage and post achieved 39. 8 billion yuan, up by 4. 4%. The annual total freight traffic was 0. 36 billion tons, up by 3. 2%. The total passenger traffic was 0. 21 billion persons, up by 3. 8%. By the end of 2019, 301air routes had been opened, including 63 international routes and 6 routes to Hongkong, Macao and Taiwan. The aviation passenger throughput was 40. 11 million persons, the cargo throughput was 0. 690 million tons, up by 4. 9% and 7. 7% respectively. The annual subway passengers were 0. 63 billion persons, up by 19. 3%.

The total possession of motor vehicles reached 2. 976 million, up by 3. 3%. The total possession of civil vehicles reached 2. 690 million, up by 12. 7%, of which private cars numbered 2. 162 million, up by 4. 1%.

## Post

The business income of postal enterprises and express delivery enterprises above designated size totaled 40. 23 billion yuan, up by 10. 3%, of which the business income of express delivery was 32. 68 billion yuan, up by 10. 2%. At the end of 2019, there were 2. 331 million fixed - line telephone subscribers, 18. 179 million mobile phone users and 5. 545 million broadband subscribers.

**Freight and Passenger Traffic Completed by Various Transport Modes in 2019**

| Item | Number | Growth(%) |
|---|---|---|
| Total Freight Traffic(million tons) | 363.84 | 3.2 |
| Railway (million tons) | 5.37 | 35.8 |
| Highway (million tons) | 317.32 | 3.7 |
| Waterway (million tons) | 40.73 | -4.0 |
| Aviation (million tons) | 0.41 | 9.8 |
| Total Passenger Traffic(million person) | 208.88 | 3.8 |
| Railway(million person) | 88.74 | 17.8 |
| Highway(million person) | 93.60 | -6.7 |
| Waterway(million person) | 6.10 | 1.1 |
| Aviation(million person) | 20.44 | 4.5 |

## V. Financial Intermediation

The added value of financial intermediation achieved 178.9 billion yuan, up by 9.1%.

The saving deposits of RMB and foreign exchange from all financial institutions in Hangzhou was 4528.70 billion yuan, up by 13.8%; and the loans balance was 4224.52 billion yuan, up by 15.4%.

**Deposit and Loan Balance in RMB and Foreign Exchange from All Financial Institutions at the End of 2019**

| Item | Year-end Figure (100 million yuan) | Growth(%) |
|---|---|---|
| Total Deposit Balance | 45287.0 | 13.8 |
| Of which: Household Deposit | 11901.3 | 16.7 |
| Non-financial Enterprise | | |
| Deposit | 20280.3 | 16.5 |
| Total Loan Balance | 42245.2 | 15.4 |
| Of which: Household Loans | 16518.0 | 18.5 |
| Non-financial Enterprise Loans | 25375.5 | 13.6 |
| Of which: Short-term Loan | 8113.7 | 5.7 |
| Medium and Long Term Loans | 14683.2 | 16.4 |
| Bill financing | 1627.3 | 44.5 |

There were 192 listed companies in Hangzhou at the year-end, of which 146 were listed domestically. There were 22 newly authorized listed companies in Hangzhou, and raised a total of 16.23 billion yuan, up by 64.6%. There were 34 companies listed on small and medium board, and 43 companies were listed on entrepreneurship board.

The premiums received by the insurance companies totaled 84. 63 billion yuan, up by 27. 5%. Of this total, the premiums of property insurance was 24. 8 billion yuan, and that of life insurance was 59. 83 billion yuan. The payments of insurance indemnity of various kinds totaled 24. 31 billion yuan, up by 19. 9%. Of this total, the payments of property insurance was 15. 26 billion yuan, and that of life insurance was 9. 05 billion yuan.

# VI. Investment in Fixed Assets and Real Estate

## Investment in Fixed Assets

The investment in fixed assets increased by 11. 6% over the previous year, the investment in infrastructure increased by 5. 2%, the investment in transportation increased by 16. 9%, the investment in high - tech industries increased by 8. 4%. Grouped by sectors, the investment in the secondary industry increased by 6. 2%, of which the industrial investment increased by 5. 6%; the investment in the tertiary industry increased by 12. 2%.

## Investment in Real Estate

The investment in real estate increased by 10. 7% over the previous year, of which residential investment increased by 12. 6%, the investment in office buildings increased by 13. 4%, and the investment in commercial business housing decreased by 5. 9%. At the end of the year, the floor space under construction was 119. 96 million square meters, up by 2. 1%; the newly started floor space under construction was 24. 35 million square meters, down by 10. 1%; the completed floor space was 17. 28 million square meters, up by 5. 5%. The sold floor space of commercial buildings was 15. 14 million square meters, down by 9. 7%.

**Main Indicators of Real Estate Development and Sales in 2019**

| Item | Number | Growth(%) |
|---|---|---|
| The Floor Space Under Construction(million square meters) | 119. 96 | 2. 1 |
| Of which: Residence (million square meters) | 62. 63 | 1. 7 |
| The Completed Floor Space(million square meters) | 17. 28 | 5. 5 |
| Of which: Residence (million square meters) | 9. 64 | 14. 5 |
| The Sold Floor Space of Commercial Buildings (million square meters) | 15. 14 | -9. 7 |
| Of which: Residence (million square meters) | 12. 84 | -3. 4 |

# VII. Domestic Trade

The added value of wholesale and retail sale was 122. 5 billion yuan, up by 3. 3%, the added value of accommodation and catering services was 23. 4 billion yuan, up by 4. 0%.

The total retail sales of consumer goods reached 61. 88 billion yuan, a growth of 8. 8% over the previous year. Grouped by consumption type, the retail sales of consumer goods reached 511. 0 billion yuan, up by 8. 8%; the revenue of catering services reached 107. 7 billion yuan, up by 8. 6%. Retail sales of wearable intelligent devices for wholesale and retail units above quota increased by 38. 4%, and that of smart home appliances and audio - visual equipment increased by 21. 7%. Retail sales through public network of wholesale and retail units above quota increased by 20. 0%, accounting for 25. 5% of the total retail sales of wholesale and retail units above quota.

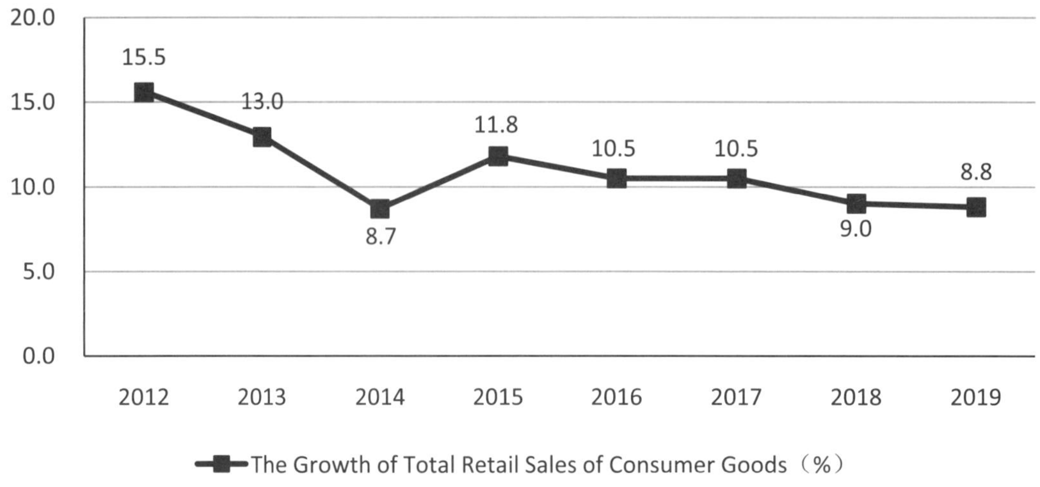


**The Growth of Total Retail Sales of Consumer Goods from 2012 to 2019**

# VIII. Foreign Economic Relations

## International Trade

The total value of import and export of goods in 2019 was 559. 7 billion yuan, up by 6. 7%. Of this total, the export was 361. 3 billion yuan, up by 5. 7% ; the import was 198. 4 billion yuan, up by 8. 5%. The export of high – tech products was 56. 9 billion yuan, up by 9. 7% , the export of electromechanical products was 155. 0billion yuan, up by 6. 1%. The export to the countries which along The Belt and Road was 117. 7 billion yuan, accounting for 32. 6% of the total export. The total export of service trade was 12. 49 billion U. S. dollars, up by 19. 0%.

The import and export volume of cross border e – commerce was 95. 21 billion yuan, up by 28. 8% , of this total, the export was 65. 88 billion yuan, and the import was 29. 33 billion yuan, up by 26. 4% and 34. 6% respectively.

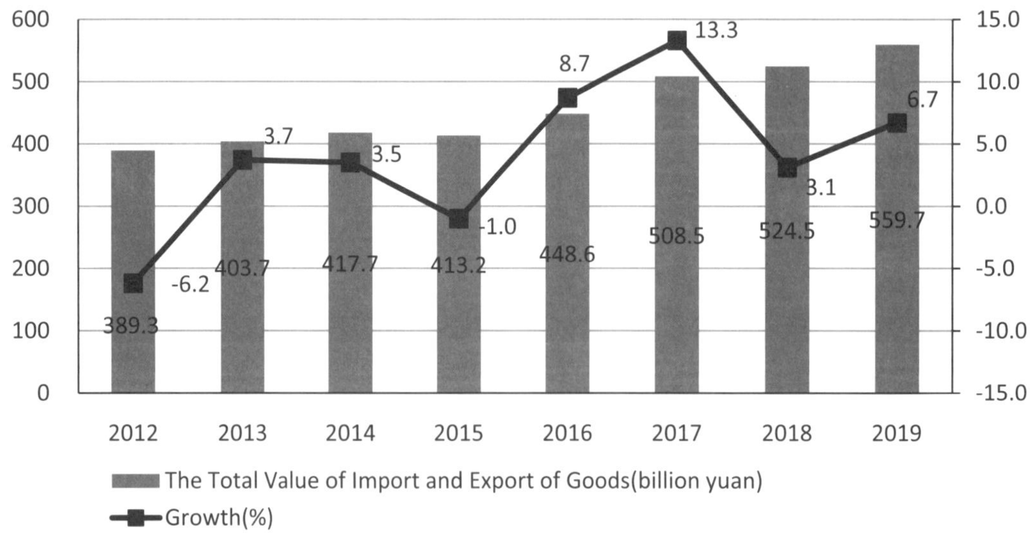


**The Total Value of Import and Export of Goods from 2012 to 2019**

## Utilization of Foreign Capital

In 2019,736 foreign – invested enterprises were newly set up, of which, the number of enterprises invested more than 30 million U. S. dollars reached 118. The actually utilized of foreign direct investment was 6. 13 billion U. S. dollars, up by 14. 0%. Of this total, the actually utilized of foreign direct investment in secondary industry was 0. 73 billion U. S. dollars; and that in tertiary industry was 5. 40 billion U. S. dollars. By the end of 2019, 126 companies of Global Fortune

500 invested 219 projects in Hangzhou.

### International Cooperation

By the end of 2019, the total number of overseas investment enterprises (Institutions) in Hangzhou was 2,237, up by 11.4%. The accomplished business revenue through oversea contract engineering projects and labor cooperation was 2.74 billion U.S. dollars, up by 6.0%. The contract execution amount of offshore service outsourcing was 7.19 billion U.S. dollars, up by 3.9%.

## IX. Living Conditions and Social Security

### Living Conditions

The annual per capita disposable income in Hangzhou was 59,261 yuan, up by 9.0% or a real increase of 5.7% after deducting price factors. In terms of resident area, the annual per capita disposable income of urban households reached 66,068 yuan, up by 8.0% or a real increase of 4.8% after deducting price factors, and the annual per capita disposable income of rural households was 36,255 yuan, up by 9.2% or 5.9% after deducting price factor.

The per capita consumption expenditure in Hangzhou was 40,016 yuan, up by 7.1%. In terms of residence area, the per capita consumption expenditure of urban households was 44,076 yuan, and that of rural households was 26,296 yuan, up by 5.9% and 8.6% respectively, after deducting price factors, the real increase was 2.7% and 5.3% respectively.

**Per Capita Disposable Income and Consumption Expenditure in Hangzhou in 2019**

| Item | All Residents | | Urban Residents | | Rural Residents | |
|---|---|---|---|---|---|---|
| | Absolute Number(yuan) | Growth (%) | Absolute Number(yuan) | Growth (%) | Absolute Number(yuan) | Growth (%) |
| Disposable Income | 59261 | 9.0 | 66068 | 8.0 | 36255 | 9.2 |
| 1. Income from Wages | 34136 | 8.9 | 37845 | 7.9 | 21601 | 9.1 |
| 2. Income of Staff & workers in Other – owned Units | 6584 | 8.2 | 5849 | 10.4 | 9067 | 6.4 |
| 3. Property Income | 8111 | 12.6 | 10045 | 10.6 | 1574 | 14.1 |
| 4. Transfer Income | 10430 | 7.4 | 12329 | 5.3 | 4013 | 14.8 |
| Consumption Expenditure | 40016 | 7.1 | 44076 | 5.9 | 26296 | 8.6 |

By the end of the year, the per capita floor space of residential building in urban areas reached 38.2 square meters, and every 100 urban households had 62.6 family cars, 250.2 air conditioners, up by 4.9% and 2.9% respectively, every 100 urban households had 89.8 home computers, down by 10.6%. The per capita floor space of residential building in rural areas reached 74.1 square meters, and every 100 rural households had 52.7 family cars, 211.4 air conditioners, up by 3.5% and 2.4% respectively, every 100 rural households had 60.2 home computers, down by 14.5%.

### Social Security

By the end of the year, a total of 7.047 million people participated in the basic social pension insurance for employees, up by 5.0%; a total of 6.711 million people participated in the basic medical insurance program for employees, up by 6.1%; a total of 4.867 million people participated in the unemployment insurance, 5.567 million people participated in the maternity insurance, up by 5.9% and 7.0% respectively. The minimum subsistence guarantee standard for residents in urban areas increased to 1041 yuan per person per month, up by 9.0%. By the end of the year, 102.5 thousand people were benefitted from the city's minimum living guarantee system, the annual payment of minimum living guarantee system reached 0.888 billion yuan, up by 3.6%.

**Social Security Related Treatment Standards**

| Item | 2019 | 2018 |
|---|---|---|
| Minimum Unemployment Insurance Standard (Urban Residents) | 1608 yuan/month | 1608 yuan/month |
| Urban and Rural Minimum Subsistence Guarantee Standard (Urban Areas Excluding Lin'an) | 1041 yuan/month | 955 yuan/month |
| Urban and Rural Minimum Subsistence Guarantee Standard (Tonglu, Chun'an, Jiande) | 833 yuan/month | 764 yuan/month |
| Urban and Rural Minimum Subsistence Guarantee Standard(Lin'an) | 989 yuan/month | 860 yuan/month |
| Minimum wage for employees(Urban) | 2010 yuan/month | 2010 yuan/month |

### Social Welfare

By the end of the year, the number of community home care service centers reached 2,898. There were 328 welfare institutions and nursing homes for the aged, providing 74.7 thousand beds, accommodating 35.5 thousand people. There were 8 child welfare institutions with 1,040 beds.

The fund raised by all kinds of welfare lotteries issued this year reached 3.027 billion yuan, down by 2.8%.

## X. Science & Technology, Education

### Science & Technology

In 2019, 43,357 invention patents were applied and 11,748 were authorized, up by 18.7% and 14.4% respectively. There were a total of 749 enterprise technology centers above city level, of which 42 at national level. There were 11 national technological innovation demonstration enterprises and 11 provincial technological innovation demonstration enterprises. There were 178 technology enterprise incubators, of which 41 at national level and 92 at provincial level. There were 180 public innovation spaces in Hangzhou, of which 132 at provincial level. The total number of technology contracts signed throughout the year was 15,612 and 50.11 billion yuan, an increase of 12.7% and 31.8% respectively. The expenditures on research and development activities (R&D) accounted for 3.45% of Hangzhou's GDP. The expenditure on science and technology in general public budget expenditure was 14.82 billion yuan, up by 25.4%.

### Education

At the end of 2019, there were 40 regular institutions of higher education with 518 thousand students, an increase of 22 thousand than last year, of which 72 thousand were postgraduates, with a gross enrollment rate of 67.3% for higher education; There were 87 ordinary high schools with 118 thousand students, an increase of 4 thousand ; There were 37 professional high schools and secondary technical schools with 61thousand students, same as last year; There were 269 junior high schools with 244 thousand students, an increase of 9 thousand, and the proportion of junior high school graduates entering into various kinds of high schools was 99.75%; There were 489 primary schools with 617 thousand students, an increase of 26 thousand; There were 1,020 kindergartens, with 350 thousand children, an increase of 7 thousand, and the enrollment rate of children who 3 years preschool was 99.1%. The number of migrant workers'children who were enrolled in the stage of compulsory education in Hangzhou was accumulated to 287 thousand. There were 70 home and abroad cooperative projects at all education levels, of which 8 projects were municipal colleges and universities, 7 projects were senior secondary schools.

## XI. Culture, Tourism, Public Health and Sports

### Culture and Tourism

The added value of cultural and creative industries was 373.5 billion yuan, up by 15.6%. By the end of 2019, there were

15 cultural centers, 16 public libraries, 79 museums, 48 national key cultural relics protection units. During the year, we produced 7 TV plays with 357 episodes, 6 online TV plays, 13 online movies and 2 online cartoons. There were 2.74 million times of all kinds of films, the ticket revenue was 1.58 billion yuan. At the end of the year, there were 2.981 million registered cable TV users. 24 representative intangible cultural heritage projects including "Hangzhou Embroidery" were selected into the list of the first batch of Zhejiang Provincial Traditional Craft Revitalization Catalog.

The added value of tourism and leisure industry in the whole year was 119.1 billion yuan, up by 12.1%. The total revenue of tourism reached 400.5 billion yuan, up by 18.3%. The total tourists were 208.137 million, up by 15.1%, of which 1.133 million were overseas visitors, up by 5.7%. At the end of 2019, there were 895 travel agencies, up by 5.5%; 126 star-rated hotels, including 23 5-star hotels. There were 103 A-rated scenic spots, including 3 AAAAA scenic spots.

### Public Health

The added value of health industry in the whole year was 97.5 billion yuan, up by 12.5%. At the end of the year, there were 5,925 medical and health institutions in Hangzhou, including 343 hospitals, up by 10.2% and 8.5% over the previous year respectively. There were 127 thousand professional medical personnel, including 49 thousand licensed (assistant) doctors and 55 thousand registered nurses, up by 8.2%, 8.9% and 10.2% respectively. There were 86 thousand beds, including 80 thousand hospital beds, up by 5.5% and 6.4% respectively. A total of 146.407 million patients received diagnosis and treatment in medical institutions, up by 5.5%. The infant mortality rate and the mortality rate of children under the age of 5 were 1.65‰ and 2.35‰ respectively. The mortality per 100,000 pregnant women was 2.75 persons.

### Sports

Hangzhou athletes won 50 medals in international competitions throughout the year, including 23 gold medals, 11 silver medals; won 410 medals in national competitions, including 160 gold medals, 114 silver medals; Won the first place in the competition of jumping platform and grass skiing in the 14th National Winter Sports Meeting. Hangzhou successfully held a series of local international brand events, such as Hangzhou Marathon, International (Hangzhou) Trailwalk, The First China-New Zealand Youth Golf Team Competition and 2019 Hangzhou International Tennis Invitational Tournament etc.

The annual sales of sports lottery reached 3.397 billion yuan, down by 21.8%.

## XII. Urban Construction

The total mileage of roads in the whole year reached 16,667 km, including 632 km of expressways. At the end of the year, there were 402 public transport lines in the main urban area, of which 15 were newly opened lines, 45 were optimized lines. The total operational metro mileage reached 135.4 km, and the metro mileage under construction was 381 kilometers.

The electricity consumption of the whole city was 81.7 billion KWH, up by 2.5%, of which the consumption of the tertiary industry was 67.9 billion KWH, up by 1.6%; the consumption of residents in urban and rural areas was 13.8 billion KWH, up by 7.0%.

A total of 100,021 parking spaces were newly completed, of which 11,271 were public parking spaces.

## XIII. Environmental Protection and Production Safety

### Environmental Protection

The total days of good ambient air accumulated to 287 throughout the year, the rate of good was 78.6%. The average concentration of PM2.5 in the urban area was 37.7 micrograms per cubic meter, same as last year. The annual average concentration of nitrogen dioxide was 41 micrograms per cubic meter, up by 2.5%; the annual average concentration of sulfur dioxide was 7 micrograms per cubic meter, down by 22.2%. 98.1% of the sections above the municipal level reached the standard, up by 1.9 percentage points. The forest coverage rate in the whole city reached 66.84%.

## Production Safety

The number of all kinds of production accidents were 229 throughout the year, the death toll was 190, down by 27.3% and 38.5% respectively.

## Notes:

1. Some data presented in this communiqu are preliminary data for the year. There may have a difference between sub item and aggregate, because some data were half adjusted.
2. GDP and absolute added value of various industries are calculated based on current price, whereas the growth rate is calculated based on constant price; the classification on primary, secondary and tertiary industries is subjected to the 《Classification on Primary, Secondary and Tertiary Industries(2012)》 which was revised by National? Statistics? Bureau in 2018.

## Source of Statistics:

Statistics on newly increased employed people in urban areas, registered urban unemployment rate and social security are from Hangzhou Municipal Bureau of Human Resources and Social Security; statistics on private enterprises, individual businesses and patents are from the Municipal Bureau of Market Supervision; fiscal statistics are from Hangzhou Bureau of Finance; statistics on agricultural park, beautiful countryside and happy farmhouse are from Municipal Bureau of Agriculture and Rural Area; statistics on education are from Hangzhou Municipal Bureau of education; statistics on import and export are from Hangzhou Custom; statistics on subsistence allowance, social services and assistance, welfare lottery are from Hangzhou Municipal Bureau of Civil Affairs; statistics on highway mileage, bus lines are from Hangzhou Transportation Bureau; statistics on air passenger throughput, freight and postal throughput, navigable routes are form Xiaoshan International Airport; statistics on passenger capacity of metro are form Hangzhou Metro Group; statistics on parking places are from Municipal Construction Commission; statistics on ecological construction and environmental monitoring are from Hangzhou Municipal Bureau of Environmental Protection; statistics on production safety are from Hangzhou Emergency Management Bureau; statistics on actually utilized foreign direct investment are from Municipal Investment Promotion Bureau; statistics on oversea contract projects and service trade are from Hangzhou Municipal Bureau of Commerce; statistics on electricity consumption are from State Grid Hangzhou Power Supply Company; statistics on household population, motor vehicle ownership are from Municipal Bureau of Public Security; statistics on post are from Postal Administration Bureau; statistics on money and finance are from Hangzhou Center BranchofPeople's Bank; statistics on insurance are from Zhejiang Bureau of China Insurance Regulatory Commission; statistics on museums, memorial halls are from Municipal Park and Cultural Relics Bureau; statistics on technological innovation, high - tech Enterprises, research center, public innovation spaces are from Municipal Science and Technology Bureau; statistics on tourism, art performance groups, libraries, cultural centers are from Hangzhou Municipal Bureau of Culture and Tourism; statistics on films and cartoons are from Hangzhou Municipal Party Committee Publicity Department; statistics on newly authorized listed companies are from Hangzhou Finance Office; statistics on healthcare are from Hangzhou Municipal Health Commission; statistics on medical insurance are from Hangzhou Medical Security Bureau; statistics on sports are from Hangzhou Municipal Bureau of Sports; statistics on construction land are from Municipal Bureau of Planning and Natural Resources; statistics on forest coverage are from Hangzhou Municipal Bureau of Forestry & Water Resoures; statistics on price, income and expenditure of urban and rural residents, per capita floor space, durable goods per 100 households are from Hangzhou Survey Office of National Bureau of Statistics; other statistics are from Hangzhou Municipal Bureau of Statistics.

# 一、综合

GENERAL SURVEY

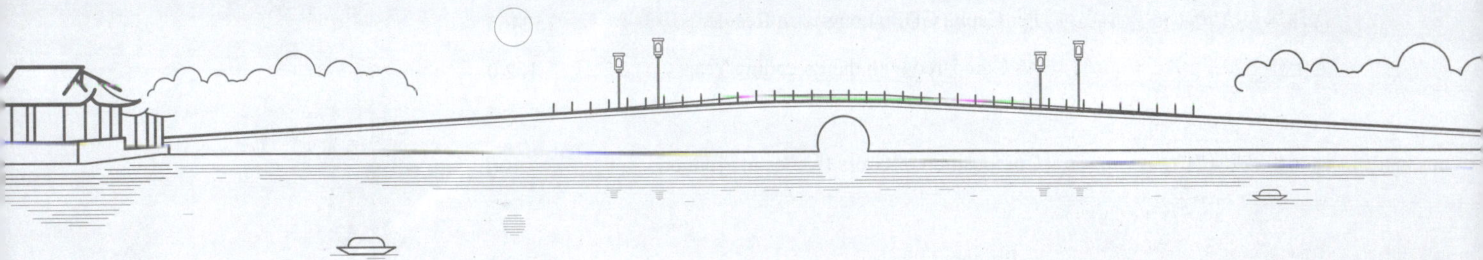

# 1 综 合
# General Survey

## 主要统计指标
## Major Statistical Indicators

| | | | | |
|---|---|---|---|---|
| 全市生产总值 | Gross Domestic Product | 15373.05 | 亿元 | ( 100 million yuan ) |
| 为上年 | As Compared with the Preceding Year | 106.8 | % | ( % ) |
| 第一产业 | Primary Industry | 325.70 | 亿元 | ( 100 million yuan ) |
| 为上年 | As Compared with the Preceding Year | 101.9 | % | ( % ) |
| 第二产业 | Secondary Industry | 4875.07 | 亿元 | ( 100 million yuan ) |
| 为上年 | As Compared with the Preceding Year | 105.0 | % | ( % ) |
| 第三产业 | Tertiary Industry | 10172.28 | 亿元 | ( 100 million yuan ) |
| 为上年 | As Compared with the Preceding Year | 108.0 | % | ( % ) |
| 常住居民人均生产总值 | Per Capita GDP (Long-term Residents) | 152465 | 元 | ( yuan ) |
| 为上年 | As Compared with the Preceding Year | 102.0 | % | ( % ) |
| 地区生产总值构成 | Composition of Gross Domestic Product | 100 | % | ( % ) |
| 第一产业 | Primary Industry | 2.1 | % | ( % ) |
| 第二产业 | Secondary Industry | 31.7 | % | ( % ) |
| 第三产业 | Tertiary Industry | 66.2 | % | ( % ) |

# 1－01　行政区划(2019 年末)

## Administrative Division( End of 2019)

单位:个　　　　　　　　　　　　　　　　　　　　　　　　　　　　(unit)

| 地　区 | Region | 街　道 Subdistrict Offices | 乡(镇) Towns and Townships | 镇 Towns | 村、社区 Villages and Communities | 村 Villages |
|---|---|---|---|---|---|---|
| **全　市** | **Whole City** | **92** | **98** | **75** | **3196** | **2011** |
| 市　区 | Urban District | 85 | 52 | 46 | 2299 | 1178 |
| 上城区 | Shangcheng | 6 | – | – | 54 | – |
| 下城区 | Xiacheng | 8 | – | – | 74 | – |
| 江干区 | Jianggan | 10 | – | – | 191 | 4 |
| 拱墅区 | Gongshu | 10 | – | – | 99 | – |
| 西湖区 | Xihu | 10 | 2 | 2 | 210 | 41 |
| 高新(滨江)区 | Hi－Tech( Binjiang) | 3 | – | – | 60 | – |
| 萧山区 | Xiaoshan | 14 | 12 | 12 | 610 | 411 |
| 余杭区 | Yuhang | 14 | 6 | 6 | 369 | 176 |
| 富阳区 | Fuyang | 5 | 19 | 13 | 326 | 276 |
| 临安区 | Lin′an | 5 | 13 | 13 | 306 | 270 |
| 桐庐县 | Tonglu | 4 | 10 | 6 | 203 | 181 |
| 淳安县 | Chun′an | – | 23 | 11 | 438 | 423 |
| 建德市 | Jiande | 3 | 13 | 12 | 256 | 229 |

注:西湖区含风景名胜区,江干、萧山含托管在钱塘新区的街道数据。

a) Figures of Xihu include the West Lake Scenic Zone, and Figures of Jianggan and Xiaoshan include districts which under administered by Qiantang New Area.

# 1-02 土地面积和人口密度(2019年末)

## Land Area and Population Density(End of 2019)

| 地　区 | Region | 土地面积<br>(平方千米)<br>Land Area<br>(sq. km) | 年末总人口<br>(万人)<br>Population<br>(10000 persons) | 人口密度<br>(人/平方千米)<br>Population Density<br>(person/sq. km) |
|---|---|---|---|---|
| **全　市** | **Whole City** | **16850** | **1036.0** | **615** |
| 市　区 | Urban District | 8289 | 911.9 | 1100 |
| 上城区 | Shangcheng | 26 | 34.5 | 13260 |
| 下城区 | Xiacheng | 29 | 52.6 | 17954 |
| 江干区 | Jianggan | 200 | 122.7 | 6126 |
| 拱墅区 | Gongshu | 69 | 57.9 | 8366 |
| 西湖区 | Xihu | 309 | 93.8 | 3031 |
| 高新(滨江)区 | Hi-Tech(Binjiang) | 72 | 45.5 | 6300 |
| 萧山区 | Xiaoshan | 1414 | 181.8 | 1286 |
| 余杭区 | Yuhang | 1228 | 189.1 | 1540 |
| 富阳区 | Fuyang | 1821 | 74.4 | 409 |
| 临安区 | Lin'an | 3119 | 59.6 | 191 |
| 桐庐县 | Tonglu | 1829 | 43.6 | 238 |
| 淳安县 | Chun'an | 4418 | 35.8 | 81 |
| 建德市 | Jiande | 2314 | 44.7 | 193 |

注:土地面积取自2017年土地变更调查成果数据,西湖区含风景名胜区,江干、萧山含托管在钱塘新区的街道数据。

a) Figures of Xiaoshan include Dajiangdong, Figures of Xihu include the West Lake Scenic Zone, and Figures of Jianggan and Xiaoshan include districts which under administered by Qiantang New Area.

# 1－03 平均每天主要社会经济活动(2012－2019 年)

## Selected Indicators on Average Daily Social and Economic Activities(2012－2019)

| 指 标 Item | 2012 | 2013 | 2014 | 2015 | 2016 | 2017 | 2018 | 2019 |
|---|---|---|---|---|---|---|---|---|
| 全市生产总值 (万元) Gross Domestic Product (10,000 yuan) | 217721 | 236710 | 260335 | 287542 | 319930 | 360568 | 391965 | 421179 |
| 工业增加值 (万元) Value－Added of Industry (10,000 yuan) | 85072 | 87282 | 94747 | 99774 | 101894 | 107739 | 113221 | 117491 |
| 规模以上工业企业利税总额 (万元) Total Pre－tax Profits of Industrial Enterprises above Designated Size (10,000 yuan) | 36711 | 39741 | 42139 | 42731 | 45236 | 48617 | 49322 | 50822 |
| 农林牧渔业总产值 (万元) Gross Output Value of Farming, Forestry, Animal Husbandry and Fishery (10,000 yuan) | 10530 | 10942 | 11468 | 12066 | 12268 | 12540 | 12770 | 13730 |
| 固定资产投资 (万元) Investment in Fixed Assets (10,000 yuan) | 101993 | 116818 | 135690 | 152228 | 159629 | 160456 | － | － |
| 住宅竣工面积 (平方米) Floor Space of Residential Buildings Completed (sq. m) | 18466 | 23154 | 25425 | 29323 | 30419 | 40297 | 30434 | 28301 |
| 社会消费品零售总额 (万元) Total Retail Sales of Consumer Goods (10,000 yuan) | 85123 | 96495 | 104899 | 117277 | 129180 | 143078 | 155885 | 169526 |
| 住户存款新增额 (万元) The Increased Amount of Household Deposits (10,000 yuan) | 14863 | 8729 | 9825 | 8739 | 23921 | 4858 | 41861 | 46066 |
| 财政总收入 (万元) Total Financial Revenue (10,000 yuan) | 44600 | 47534 | 52606 | 61335 | 69902 | 80036 | 94725 | 100001 |

# 1-04 国民经济

## Major Indicators of

| 指　标 | | Item | |
|---|---|---|---|
| 年末常住人口 | (万人) | Long-term Residents(End of 2019) | (10,000 persons) |
| 年末户籍人口 | (万人) | Household Registration Population(End of 2019) | (10,000 persons) |
| #城镇人口 | (万人) | Urban Population | (10,000 persons) |
| 年末从业人员数 | (万人) | Total Number of Employed Persons(End of 2019) | (10,000 persons) |
| 全市生产总值 | (亿元) | Gross Domestic Product | (100 million yuan) |
| 第一产业 | (亿元) | Primary Industry | (100 million yuan) |
| 第二产业 | (亿元) | Secondary Industry | (100 million yuan) |
| 第三产业 | (亿元) | Tertiary Industry | (100 million yuan) |
| 人均生产总值(户籍) | (元) | Per Capita GDP(Household) | (yuan) |
| 人均生产总值(常住) | (元) | Per Capita GDP(Long-term) | (yuan) |
| 主要农产品产量 | | Output of Major Farm Products | |
| 粮食 | (万吨) | Grain | (10,000 tons) |
| 棉花 | (吨) | Cotton | (ton) |
| 油菜籽 | (吨) | Rapeseeds | (ton) |
| 茶叶 | (吨) | Tea | (ton) |
| 蚕茧 | (吨) | Silk-worm Cocoons | (ton) |
| 生猪年末存栏 | (万头) | Hogs in Stock at Year End | (10,000 heads) |
| 肉类产量 | (万吨) | Output of Meat | (10,000 tons) |
| 淡水产品产量 | (吨) | Freshwater Aquatic Products | (ton) |
| 全部工业总产值 | (亿元) | The Total Output Value of Industrial Enterprises | (100 million yuan) |
| 规模以上工业总产值 | (亿元) | The Output Valne of Industrial Enterprises Above Designated Size | (100 million yuan) |
| 规模以上工业企业利税总额 | (亿元) | Total Pre-tax Profits of Industrial Enterprises Above Designated Size | (100 million yuan) |
| 客运量 | (万人次) | Total Passenger Traffic | (10,000 person-times) |
| 货运量 | (万吨) | Total Freight Traffic | (10,000 tons) |
| 固定资产投资 | (亿元) | Investment in Fixed Assets | (100 million yuan) |
| 社会消费品零售总额 | (亿元) | Total Retail Sales of Consumer Goods | (100 million yuan) |

注:1. 规模以上工业的计算口径,1997 年以前为乡及乡以上,1998 年-2010 年为主营业务收入 500 万元及以上,2011 年起为 2000 万元及以上的工业企业。

2. 从 2014 年起,粮食数据按粮食生产统计监测抽样调查口径。

# 主要指标(主要年份)
# National Economy(Main Years)

| 1985 | 1990 | 1995 | 2000 | 2005 | 2010 | 2013 | 2014 | 2015 | 2016 | 2017 | 2018 | 2019 |
|---|---|---|---|---|---|---|---|---|---|---|---|---|
|  | 583.21 |  | 701.70 | 771.30 | 870.54 | 884.40 | 889.20 | 901.80 | 918.80 | 946.80 | 980.60 | 1036 |
| 543.05 | 574.78 | 597.96 | 621.58 | 660.45 | 689.12 | 706.61 | 715.76 | 723.55 | 736.00 | 753.90 | 774.10 | 795.37 |
| 153.46 | 169.00 | 191.43 | 226.99 | 297.54 | 365.24 | 393.88 | 404.27 | 447.24 | 463.86 | 482.55 | 515.04 | 535.96 |
| 330.37 | 363.49 | 422.55 | 408.11 | 481.10 | 626.33 | 650.51 | 654.92 | 663.03 | 676.95 | 681.06 | 690.10 | 720.00 |
| 90.49 | 189.62 | 762.01 | 1395.67 | 2973.74 | 6049.56 | 8639.91 | 9502.21 | 10495.28 | 11709.45 | 13160.72 | 14306.72 | 15373.05 |
| 15.97 | 30.94 | 69.25 | 103.96 | 140.29 | 205.34 | 254.74 | 266.62 | 278.98 | 293.63 | 299.96 | 305.56 | 325.70 |
| 52.08 | 96.17 | 410.00 | 717.88 | 1524.25 | 2861.45 | 3649.62 | 3953.53 | 4133.92 | 4226.87 | 4453.44 | 4694.06 | 4875.07 |
| 22.44 | 62.51 | 282.76 | 573.83 | 1309.21 | 2982.77 | 4735.54 | 5282.07 | 6082.38 | 7188.96 | 8407.32 | 9307.10 | 10172.28 |
| 1675 | 3310 | 12797 | 22554 | 45327 | 88154 | 122802 | 133611 | 145838 | 160453 | 176668 | 187263 | 195897 |
|  |  |  |  | 38542 | 71007 | 97925 | 107152 | 117200 | 128633 | 141088 | 148456 | 152465 |
|  |  |  |  |  |  |  |  |  |  |  |  |  |
| 180.00 | 189.56 | 174.50 | 153.08 | 103.50 | 58.00 | 47.53 | 47.53 | 45.91 | 45.91 | 47.26 | 49.60 | 49.64 |
| 6704 | 6693 | 8038 | 2112 | 1038 | 704 | 509 | 426 | 378 | 300 | 255 | 240 | 292 |
| 51849 | 60683 | 61446 | 80436 | 70733 | 67946 | 64816 | 50181 | 51186 | 43526 | 47223 | 55584 | 59503 |
| 22742 | 26429 | 19824 | 24810 | 25551 | 30500 | 28503 | 26548 | 28139 | 28150 | 30103 | 30091 | 31342 |
| 7980 | 11085 | 13240 | 9308 | 16339 | 11700 | 8267 | 6364 | 4880 | 3482 | 3013 | 4564 | 3454 |
| 166.10 | 159.00 | 147.58 | 172.16 | 165.28 | 192.53 | 219.23 | 173.46 | 156.82 | 126.91 | 114.03 | 107.02 | 90.34 |
| 11.16 | 14.93 | 19.21 | 25.24 | 30.74 | 31.78 | 30.27 | 26.98 | 24.31 | 22.19 | 21.27 | 19.11 | 14.97 |
| 30400 | 47588 | 63294 | 91626 | 147800 | 208945 | 197992 | 186026 | 178880 | 173447 | 172845 | 166947 | 168042 |
|  |  |  |  | 6589.51 | 12810.52 | 15211.78 | 15851.40 | 15018.77 | 15054.78 | 15688.35 | 16087.41 | 16895.32 |
| 128.59 | 292.26 | 1020.03 | 1543.57 | 5441.13 | 11081.04 | 12418.00 | 12853.05 | 12415.68 | 12420.96 | 12963.76 | 14016.41 | 14585.45 |
| 24.81 | 31.54 | 63.05 | 161.61 | 450.68 | 1224.48 | 1450.55 | 1538.07 | 1559.68 | 1655.64 | 1774.52 | 1800.26 | 1854.99 |
| 6724 | 8119 | 16620 | 18607 | 24124 | 33772 | 36409 | 24070 | 23942 | 20541 | 22289 | 20121 | 20888 |
| 2488 | 6522 | 10347 | 11459 | 19909 | 25915 | 30734 | 29335 | 29384 | 30170 | 34785 | 35180 | 36384 |
| 14.19 | 22.92 | 156.63 | 376.65 | 1277.80 | 2651.88 | 4263.87 | 4952.70 | 5556.32 | 5842.42 | 5856.65 | - | - |
| 47.81 | 98.17 | 299.35 | 514.68 | 1036.96 | 2270.61 | 3522.05 | 3828.82 | 4280.61 | 4727.97 | 5222.33 | 5689.82 | 6187.70 |

a) The standard for above designated size of industry, before 1997, it was above the sub - district level; 1998 - 2010, it was the annual sales income over 5 million yuan; since 2011, it was the annual sales income over 20 million yuan.

b) The data of grain was obtained from the sampling survey of grain production in 2014.

1－04 续表

| 指 标 | | Item | |
|---|---|---|---|
| 境外旅游者人数 | （万人次） | Number of Foreign Tourists | （10,000 person－times） |
| 财政总收入 | （亿元） | Total Financial Revenue | （100 million yuan） |
| 一般公共预算支出 | （亿元） | General Public Budget Revenue | （100 million yuan） |
| 金融机构存款余额（本外币） | （亿元） | Deposits of Financial Institutions | （100 million yuan） |
| 住户存款余额 | （亿元） | Household Deposits | （100 million yuan） |
| 金融机构贷款余额（本外币） | （亿元） | Loans of Financial Institutions | （100 million yuan） |
| 非私营单位就业人员工资总额 | （亿元） | Total Wages of Employed Persons in Non－private Units | （100 million yuan） |
| 非私营单位就业人员平均工资 | （元） | Average Wage of Employed Persons in Non－private Units | （yuan） |
| 市区居民消费价格指数 | （以 1978 年为 100） | Consumer Price Index in Urban District | （Year of 1978＝100） |
| 市区商品零售价格指数 | （以 1978 年为 100） | Retail Price Index in Urban District | （Year of 1978＝100） |
| 全体居民人均可支配收入 | （元） | Per Capita Annual Disposable Income of Urban and Rural Residents | （yuan） |
| 城镇居民人均可支配收入 | （元） | Per Capita Annual Disposable Income of Urban Residents | （yuan） |
| 农村居民人均可支配收入 | （元） | Per Capita Annual Disposable Income of Rural Residents | （yuan） |
| 高等学校在校学生数 | （人） | Student Enrollment in Institutions of Higher Education | （person） |
| 中等专业学校在校学生数 | （人） | Student Enrollment in Secondary Specialized Schools | （person） |
| 普通中学在校学生数 | （人） | Student Enrollment in Secondary Schools | （person） |
| 小学在校学生数 | （人） | Student Enrollment in Primary Schools | （person） |
| 卫生机构数 | （个） | Number of Health Institutions | （unit） |
| #医院 | （个） | Number of Hospitals | （unit） |
| 卫生技术人员 | （人） | Number of Medical Technical Personnel | （person） |
| #执业（助理）医师 | （人） | Number of Lisensed（Assistant）Doctors | （person） |
| 床位数 | （张） | Number of Beds in Health Institutions | （unit） |
| #医院 | （张） | Beds in Hospital | （unit） |

continued

| 1985 | 1990 | 1995 | 2000 | 2005 | 2010 | 2013 | 2014 | 2015 | 2016 | 2017 | 2018 | 2019 |
|---|---|---|---|---|---|---|---|---|---|---|---|---|
| 23.84 | 38.83 | 44.13 | 70.71 | 151.36 | 275.71 | 316.01 | 326.13 | 341.56 | 363.23 | 402.23 | 420.51 | 113.31 |
| 18.65 | 25.25 | 55.13 | 142.85 | 520.79 | 1245.43 | 1734.98 | 1920.11 | 2238.75 | 2558.41 | 2921.30 | 3457.46 | 3650.04 |
| 5.77 | 11.82 | 24.91 | 73.43 | 238.33 | 616.58 | 855.74 | 961.18 | 1205.48 | 1404.31 | 1540.92 | 1717.08 | 1952.85 |
| 48.50 | 133.77 | 707.97 | 2088.47 | 6748.72 | 17084.35 | 22174.71 | 24450.51 | 29863.83 | 33386.04 | 36483.24 | 39810.50 | 45286.99 |
| 15.96 | 69.75 | 342.34 | 788.56 | 2191.66 | 4990.97 | 6408.59 | 6767.20 | 7617.75 | 8493.27 | 8670.60 | 10198.52 | 11901.30 |
| 58.01 | 180.33 | 567.20 | 1686.64 | 5545.30 | 15078.73 | 19350.46 | 21316.83 | 23327.95 | 26169.00 | 29270.94 | 36598.25 | 42245.17 |
| 13.01 | 27.79 | 89.05 | 126.75 | 297.02 | 933.06 | 1758.23 | 1982.27 | 2152.40 | 2417.60 | 2646.72 | 2864.69 | 3298.52 |
| 1266 | 2382 | 7156 | 14257 | 31069 | 48772 | 63664 | 69209 | 76073 | 85022 | 93891 | 103798 | 117339 |
| 140.21 | 246.68 | 503.06 | 611.07 | 623.07 | 701.33 | 772.19 | 787.63 | 801.81 | 822.66 | 843.23 | 862.62 | 889.36 |
| 142.61 | 256.45 | 476.99 | 504.42 | 470.47 | 526.76 | 568.80 | 573.35 | 574.50 | 583.12 | 588.95 | 600.73 | 619.35 |
|  |  |  |  |  |  | 35763 | 39237 | 42642 | 46116 | 49832 | 54348 | 59261 |
| 1026 | 1985 | 6301 | 9668 | 16601 | 30035 | 40925 | 44632 | 48316 | 52185 | 56276 | 61172 | 66068 |
| 624 | 1171 | 3012 | 4894 | 7655 | 13186 | 21208 | 23555 | 25719 | 27908 | 30397 | 33193 | 36255 |
| 36996 | 39866 | 63124 | 122386 | 351918 | 434811 | 471820 | 474652 | 485558 | 480953 | 484070 | 496383 | 518325 |
| 16527 | 23564 | 42784 | 45238 | 20344 | 3999 | 3656 | 3974 | 3968 | 4402 | 4566 | 4448 | 4535 |
| 244399 | 199940 | 257071 | 342533 | 362257 | 352997 | 327346 | 324414 | 321306 | 326187 | 337851 | 349327 | 362109 |
| 414839 | 460514 | 513988 | 485679 | 458942 | 453897 | 483489 | 502688 | 524513 | 543038 | 560411 | 590491 | 616929 |
| 1582 | 1738 | 1712 | 1599 | 2196 | 2819 | 4139 | 4198 | 4428 | 4691 | 4933 | 5377 | 5925 |
| 404 | 440 | 414 | 396 | 127 | 151 | 208 | 218 | 244 | 277 | 302 | 316 | 343 |
| 25593 | 30990 | 34245 | 35487 | 42353 | 61117 | 78340 | 85614 | 93036 | 101194 | 110395 | 117425 | 126995 |
| 11503 | 14483 | 16465 | 16317 | 17833 | 24345 | 29686 | 31977 | 34832 | 38172 | 41833 | 44896 | 48962 |
| 19637 | 24121 | 26684 | 27166 | 33251 | 42828 | 52056 | 55779 | 63632 | 69452 | 75948 | 81215 | 85708 |
| 15010 | 18879 | 21360 | 23303 | 25907 | 33611 | 46636 | 50805 | 58400 | 63994 | 70187 | 75186 | 79957 |

# 1－05　地区生产总值及发展指数(1978－2019年)

## Gross Domestic Product and its Indices(1978－2019)

单位:万元　　(10000 yuan)

| 年　份 Year | 地区生产总值(当年价格) Gross Domestic Product (Current Price) | | | | 人均生产总值(元)(按户籍) Per Capita GDP (Household Registered) | 人均生产总值(元)(按常住) Per Capita GDP (Long－term Residents) | 地区生产总值指数(%) Indices of Gross Domestic product(%) (1978＝100) | | | |
|---|---|---|---|---|---|---|---|---|---|---|
| | | 第一产业 Primary Industry | 第二产业 Secondary Industry | 第三产业 Tertiary Industry | | | | 第一产业 Primary Industry | 第二产业 Secondary Industry | 第三产业 Tertiary Industry |
| 1978 | 284046 | 63372 | 169344 | 51330 | 565 | － | 100.0 | 100.0 | 100.0 | 100.0 |
| 1979 | 335285 | 83852 | 194132 | 57301 | 659 | － | 113.3 | 114.2 | 114.0 | 110.0 |
| 1980 | 406508 | 81524 | 253545 | 71439 | 791 | － | 135.7 | 105.6 | 148.4 | 130.7 |
| 1981 | 468206 | 90955 | 287632 | 89619 | 904 | － | 154.1 | 108.7 | 169.2 | 162.3 |
| 1982 | 501854 | 108769 | 294725 | 98360 | 957 | － | 165.2 | 129.8 | 174.6 | 176.3 |
| 1983 | 558947 | 101106 | 334413 | 123428 | 1054 | － | 183.7 | 115.6 | 199.6 | 219.8 |
| 1984 | 694690 | 126443 | 405535 | 162712 | 1298 | － | 225.4 | 140.1 | 241.1 | 283.6 |
| 1985 | 904897 | 159684 | 520853 | 224360 | 1675 | － | 269.0 | 139.9 | 295.6 | 352.7 |
| 1986 | 1053589 | 177589 | 601277 | 274723 | 1917 | － | 300.0 | 145.0 | 329.4 | 409.8 |
| 1987 | 1260162 | 204366 | 718892 | 336904 | 2276 | － | 338.5 | 148.7 | 375.6 | 471.5 |
| 1988 | 1525427 | 256838 | 855305 | 413284 | 2717 | － | 363.4 | 145.5 | 412.5 | 497.0 |
| 1989 | 1662945 | 282746 | 896736 | 483463 | 2928 | － | 352.2 | 145.1 | 389.2 | 508.6 |
| 1990 | 1896216 | 309404 | 961673 | 625139 | 3310 | － | 372.6 | 154.5 | 414.6 | 527.8 |
| 1991 | 2279545 | 334024 | 1131088 | 814433 | 3952 | － | 439.9 | 161.3 | 483.6 | 670.5 |
| 1992 | 2900690 | 349033 | 1487838 | 1063819 | 4996 | － | 540.5 | 161.8 | 627.5 | 820.3 |
| 1993 | 4247094 | 419364 | 2264440 | 1563290 | 7263 | － | 703.1 | 171.3 | 867.8 | 1031.9 |
| 1994 | 5855239 | 575131 | 3143430 | 2136678 | 9924 | － | 888.1 | 185.2 | 1146.1 | 1258.4 |
| 1995 | 7620055 | 692510 | 4100008 | 2827537 | 12797 | － | 1065.2 | 198.3 | 1410.5 | 1479.6 |
| 1996 | 9066133 | 839985 | 4776225 | 3449923 | 15095 | － | 1204.2 | 209.0 | 1614.4 | 1659.4 |
| 1997 | 10363299 | 913611 | 5415017 | 4034671 | 17113 | － | 1361.4 | 223.2 | 1821.7 | 1905.0 |
| 1998 | 11348899 | 960558 | 5879589 | 4508752 | 18611 | － | 1514.6 | 244.2 | 2035.9 | 2108.1 |
| 1999 | 12252795 | 975821 | 6307510 | 4969464 | 19961 | － | 1668.6 | 257.7 | 2242.4 | 2343.0 |
| 2000 | 13956746 | 1039641 | 7178843 | 5738262 | 22554 | － | 1868.6 | 272.3 | 2523.7 | 2626.5 |
| 2001 | 15829368 | 1114569 | 8031554 | 6683245 | 25313 | － | 2097.0 | 292.5 | 2844.2 | 2954.8 |
| 2002 | 17989565 | 1146388 | 9127846 | 7715331 | 28421 | － | 2374.2 | 304.5 | 3222.4 | 3389.2 |
| 2003 | 21187148 | 1265890 | 10877415 | 9043843 | 33115 | － | 2735.8 | 322.8 | 3820.5 | 3814.9 |
| 2004 | 25664609 | 1322341 | 13349904 | 10992364 | 39653 | － | 3146.8 | 339.2 | 4458.5 | 4360.4 |
| 2005 | 29737445 | 1402851 | 15242521 | 13092073 | 45327 | － | 3559.0 | 350.8 | 4973.8 | 5078.7 |
| 2006 | 34834137 | 1498775 | 17636486 | 15698876 | 52510 | 44639 | 4066.9 | 365.1 | 5594.7 | 5964.4 |
| 2007 | 41558438 | 1628498 | 20851510 | 19078430 | 62090 | 52065 | 4666.5 | 375.2 | 6400.6 | 6934.1 |
| 2008 | 48505857 | 1784963 | 24190807 | 22530088 | 71861 | 59619 | 5178.1 | 389.3 | 6960.7 | 7904.6 |
| 2009 | 51818020 | 1884452 | 24049182 | 25884387 | 76146 | 62673 | 5695.2 | 401.4 | 7376.0 | 9068.4 |
| 2010 | 60495624 | 2053425 | 28614514 | 29827686 | 88154 | 71007 | 6381.1 | 411.5 | 8203.4 | 10292.4 |
| 2011 | 71530334 | 2323187 | 33263386 | 35943761 | 103306 | 82014 | 7025.3 | 421.8 | 8897.2 | 11546.9 |
| 2012 | 79685754 | 2494438 | 35531848 | 41659468 | 114144 | 90862 | 7656.5 | 432.2 | 9513.7 | 12851.9 |
| 2013 | 86399093 | 2547447 | 36496248 | 47355398 | 122802 | 97925 | 8268.5 | 438.1 | 10151.5 | 14075.1 |
| 2014 | 95022130 | 2666167 | 39535268 | 52820695 | 133611 | 107152 | 8945.0 | 446.3 | 10948.3 | 15314.1 |
| 2015 | 104952793 | 2789754 | 41339248 | 60823790 | 145838 | 117200 | 9854.2 | 454.5 | 11554.4 | 17542.9 |
| 2016 | 117094540 | 2936259 | 42268729 | 71889552 | 160453 | 128633 | 10808.8 | 460.8 | 12080.0 | 19921.5 |
| 2017 | 131607164 | 2999567 | 44534382 | 84073215 | 176668 | 141088 | 11691.7 | 468.7 | 12655.4 | 22025.9 |
| 2018 | 143067220 | 3055586 | 46940642 | 93070992 | 187263 | 148456 | 12476.7 | 477.4 | 13386.1 | 23668.0 |
| 2019 | 153730458 | 3256976 | 48750711 | 101722772 | 195897 | 152465 | 13319.3 | 486.7 | 14049.7 | 25556.5 |

注:1.根据第四次经济普查结果,对地区生产总值、三次产业及相关行业增加值的历史数据进行了修订。

2.2019年为初步统计数(后同)。

a) According to the results of the fourth economic census, the data of GDP、Three industries and some other relevant industries are adjusted.

b) It was preliminary statistics in year 2019.

# 1－06　市区生产总值及发展指数(1978－2019年)

## Gross Domestic Product and its Indices of Urban District (1978－2019)

单位:万元　　　　(10000 yuan)

| 年 份 Year | 地区生产总值(当年价格) Gross Domestic Product (Current Price) | 第一产业 Primary Industry | 第二产业 Secondary Industry | 第三产业 Tertiary Industry | 人均生产总值(元)(按户籍) Per Capita GDP (Household Registered) | 人均生产总值(元)(按常住) Per Capita GDP (Long－term Residents) | 地区生产总值指数(%) Indices of Gross Domestic product(%) (1978＝100) | 第一产业 Primary Industry | 第二产业 Secondary Industry | 第三产业 Tertiary Industry |
|---|---|---|---|---|---|---|---|---|---|---|
| 1978 | 141995 | 5215 | 106663 | 30117 | 1389 | － | 100.0 | 100.0 | 100.0 | 100.0 |
| 1979 | 167206 | 6527 | 126517 | 34162 | 1555 | － | 116.4 | 109.4 | 118.1 | 111.6 |
| 1980 | 208220 | 5943 | 159161 | 43116 | 1863 | － | 145.3 | 94.0 | 150.9 | 133.9 |
| 1981 | 229243 | 6165 | 171946 | 51132 | 2005 | － | 159.9 | 90.3 | 163.9 | 157.2 |
| 1982 | 248297 | 7327 | 183284 | 57686 | 2125 | － | 173.7 | 107.3 | 176.0 | 175.6 |
| 1983 | 282171 | 5938 | 200334 | 75899 | 2369 | － | 197.9 | 83.1 | 193.8 | 229.5 |
| 1984 | 353781 | 8469 | 244445 | 100867 | 2919 | － | 245.4 | 114.9 | 235.5 | 298.4 |
| 1985 | 448574 | 11233 | 293579 | 143762 | 3633 | － | 289.9 | 120.7 | 270.1 | 382.2 |
| 1986 | 513639 | 12245 | 324585 | 176809 | 4042 | － | 317.3 | 122.6 | 287.7 | 446.1 |
| 1987 | 605234 | 15408 | 370668 | 219158 | 4724 | － | 353.2 | 137.1 | 313.8 | 517.4 |
| 1988 | 708474 | 19602 | 425319 | 263553 | 5441 | － | 370.8 | 136.0 | 332.7 | 534.0 |
| 1989 | 772208 | 23869 | 435847 | 312492 | 5848 | － | 347.0 | 146.6 | 296.5 | 544.8 |
| 1990 | 896496 | 23919 | 470844 | 401733 | 6722 | － | 366.5 | 147.5 | 314.3 | 573.1 |
| 1991 | 1096628 | 25767 | 547949 | 522912 | 8158 | － | 426.0 | 151.3 | 356.0 | 690.6 |
| 1992 | 1413278 | 27611 | 712697 | 672970 | 10420 | － | 535.3 | 153.0 | 447.0 | 877.0 |
| 1993 | 2086571 | 36208 | 1052187 | 998176 | 15196 | － | 687.6 | 157.5 | 583.3 | 1116.5 |
| 1994 | 2788314 | 48257 | 1395127 | 1344930 | 19945 | － | 870.9 | 172.2 | 779.0 | 1334.2 |
| 1995 | 3697793 | 57784 | 1866784 | 1773225 | 25969 | － | 1041.7 | 183.4 | 944.9 | 1573.0 |
| 1996 | 4727377 | 110881 | 2356408 | 2260088 | 28552 | － | 1194.9 | 194.6 | 1102.7 | 1768.1 |
| 1997 | 5414265 | 130062 | 2630349 | 2653853 | 32227 | － | 1354.9 | 214.0 | 1229.3 | 2050.9 |
| 1998 | 5905726 | 134320 | 2786159 | 2985247 | 34620 | － | 1482.5 | 230.5 | 1336.1 | 2264.2 |
| 1999 | 6317335 | 145242 | 2915614 | 3256479 | 36394 | － | 1599.3 | 254.3 | 1429.9 | 2465.8 |
| 2000 | 7111585 | 145715 | 3278310 | 3687560 | 40127 | － | 1785.5 | 255.3 | 1595.4 | 2761.7 |
| 2001 | 12260890 | 582492 | 6026353 | 5652045 | 32607 | － | 2017.2 | 275.4 | 1803.8 | 3123.4 |
| 2002 | 14042278 | 605433 | 6901224 | 6535621 | 36640 | － | 2300.8 | 289.8 | 2036.9 | 3604.4 |
| 2003 | 16647332 | 665083 | 8343138 | 7639111 | 42675 | － | 2664.8 | 301.9 | 2446.4 | 4055.0 |
| 2004 | 20362738 | 664676 | 10368453 | 9329609 | 51241 | － | 3077.4 | 312.8 | 2871.6 | 4626.8 |
| 2005 | 23789254 | 682559 | 11800886 | 11305809 | 58659 | － | 3461.3 | 316.5 | 3125.6 | 5379.2 |
| 2006 | 27930116 | 728962 | 13551253 | 13649901 | 67816 | 51904 | 3950.8 | 320.3 | 3475.2 | 6348.1 |
| 2007 | 33296640 | 780966 | 15859466 | 16656208 | 79879 | 59911 | 4526.3 | 325.0 | 3933.7 | 7401.8 |
| 2008 | 38841136 | 838780 | 18288447 | 19713909 | 92062 | 68036 | 5013.2 | 327.9 | 4238.9 | 8442.8 |
| 2009 | 41615787 | 879676 | 18119189 | 22616921 | 97491 | 71325 | 5534.9 | 337.5 | 4507.0 | 9657.4 |
| 2010 | 48718469 | 920654 | 21638629 | 26159186 | 112740 | 80409 | 6195.6 | 342.1 | 4985.8 | 10952.7 |
| 2011 | 57405621 | 1019227 | 25002422 | 31383972 | 131189 | 91740 | 6814.7 | 348.7 | 5375.7 | 12275.2 |
| 2012 | 64206239 | 1083214 | 26609724 | 36513301 | 144973 | 101991 | 7425.1 | 355.9 | 5712.4 | 13665.1 |
| 2013 | 70003793 | 1108054 | 27286186 | 41609552 | 156215 | 110439 | 8004.4 | 353.9 | 6081.4 | 14903.3 |
| 2014 | 83305362 | 1506729 | 33190100 | 48608533 | 159934 | 117294 | 8658.9 | 357.3 | 6560.8 | 16192.3 |
| 2015 | 92269251 | 1589108 | 34672097 | 56008046 | 174434 | 128726 | 9556.0 | 362.7 | 6907.0 | 18561.2 |
| 2016 | 103682893 | 1664265 | 35642963 | 66375666 | 192444 | 142100 | 10492.4 | 362.9 | 7189.5 | 21087.3 |
| 2017 | 122414796 | 2100929 | 40378589 | 79935278 | 201827 | 151042 | 11355.1 | 367.1 | 7534.8 | 23293.0 |
| 2018 | 133519062 | 2123934 | 42866281 | 88528847 | 213540 | 158847 | 12125.3 | 372.7 | 7986.0 | 25011.0 |
| 2019 | 143489200 | 2269869 | 44349935 | 96869397 | 222140 | 162236 | 12948.1 | 378.3 | 8357.7 | 27038.5 |

# 1-07　地区生产总值指数（1978-2019年）
# Indices of Gross Domestic Product（1978-2019）

（上年=100）　　　　　　　　　　　　　　　　　　　　　　　　　　　（Preceding Year=100）

| 年　份<br>Year | 地区生产总值<br>Gross Domestic Product | 第一产业<br>Primary Industry | 第二产业<br>Secondary Industry | 第三产业<br>Tertiary Industry | 人均生产总值(元)（按户籍）<br>Per Capita GDP(yuan)（Household Registered） | 人均生产总值(元)（按常住）<br>Per Capita GDP(yuan)（Long-term Residents） |
|---|---|---|---|---|---|---|
| 1978 | 120.2 | 119.1 | 123.7 | 111.6 | 119.0 | |
| 1979 | 113.3 | 114.2 | 114.0 | 110.0 | 112.1 | |
| 1980 | 119.7 | 92.5 | 130.2 | 118.8 | 118.4 | |
| 1981 | 113.6 | 102.9 | 114.0 | 124.2 | 112.6 | |
| 1982 | 107.2 | 119.4 | 103.2 | 108.6 | 105.9 | |
| 1983 | 111.2 | 89.1 | 114.3 | 124.7 | 109.9 | |
| 1984 | 122.7 | 121.2 | 120.8 | 129.0 | 121.6 | |
| 1985 | 119.4 | 99.9 | 122.6 | 124.4 | 118.2 | |
| 1986 | 111.5 | 103.6 | 111.5 | 116.2 | 110.3 | |
| 1987 | 112.8 | 102.5 | 114.0 | 115.1 | 111.3 | |
| 1988 | 107.4 | 97.8 | 109.8 | 105.4 | 105.8 | |
| 1989 | 96.9 | 99.8 | 94.4 | 102.3 | 95.8 | |
| 1990 | 105.8 | 106.4 | 106.5 | 103.8 | 104.9 | |
| 1991 | 118.1 | 104.4 | 116.6 | 127.0 | 117.3 | |
| 1992 | 122.9 | 100.3 | 129.7 | 122.3 | 122.1 | |
| 1993 | 130.1 | 105.9 | 138.3 | 125.8 | 129.1 | |
| 1994 | 126.3 | 108.1 | 132.1 | 122.0 | 125.2 | |
| 1995 | 119.9 | 107.1 | 123.1 | 117.6 | 118.8 | |
| 1996 | 113.0 | 105.4 | 114.5 | 112.2 | 112.0 | |
| 1997 | 113.1 | 106.8 | 112.8 | 114.8 | 112.1 | |
| 1998 | 111.2 | 109.4 | 111.8 | 110.7 | 110.5 | |
| 1999 | 110.2 | 105.5 | 110.1 | 111.1 | 109.4 | |
| 2000 | 112.0 | 105.7 | 112.5 | 112.1 | 111.1 | |
| 2001 | 112.2 | 107.4 | 112.7 | 112.5 | 111.1 | |
| 2002 | 113.2 | 104.1 | 113.3 | 114.7 | 111.8 | |
| 2003 | 115.2 | 106.0 | 118.6 | 112.6 | 114.0 | |
| 2004 | 115.0 | 105.1 | 116.7 | 114.3 | 113.7 | |
| 2005 | 113.1 | 103.4 | 111.6 | 116.5 | 111.6 | |
| 2006 | 114.3 | 104.1 | 112.5 | 117.4 | 113.0 | |
| 2007 | 114.7 | 102.8 | 114.4 | 116.3 | 113.7 | 112.2 |
| 2008 | 111.0 | 103.8 | 108.8 | 114.0 | 110.0 | 108.9 |
| 2009 | 110.0 | 103.1 | 106.0 | 114.7 | 109.1 | 108.2 |
| 2010 | 112.0 | 102.5 | 111.2 | 113.5 | 111.1 | 108.7 |
| 2011 | 110.1 | 102.5 | 108.5 | 112.2 | 109.1 | 107.5 |
| 2012 | 109.0 | 102.5 | 106.9 | 111.3 | 108.1 | 108.4 |
| 2013 | 108.0 | 101.4 | 106.7 | 109.5 | 107.2 | 107.3 |
| 2014 | 108.2 | 101.9 | 107.8 | 108.8 | 107.0 | 107.6 |
| 2015 | 110.2 | 101.8 | 105.5 | 114.6 | 108.9 | 109.1 |
| 2016 | 109.7 | 101.4 | 104.5 | 113.6 | 108.2 | 107.9 |
| 2017 | 108.2 | 101.7 | 104.8 | 110.6 | 106.0 | 105.6 |
| 2018 | 106.7 | 101.8 | 105.8 | 107.5 | 104.1 | 103.3 |
| 2019 | 106.8 | 101.9 | 105.0 | 108.0 | 103.9 | 102.0 |

注：本表按可比价格计算。

a) The indices in this table are calculated at comparable prices.

# 1－08 市区生产总值指数(1978－2019年)

# Indices of Gross Domestic Product of Urban District (1978－2019)

(上年＝100) (Preceding Year＝100)

| 年 份<br>Year | 地区生产总值<br>Gross Domestic Product | 第一产业<br>Primary Industry | 第二产业<br>Secondary Industry | 第三产业<br>Tertiary Industry | 人均生产总值(元)(按户籍)<br>Per Capita GDP(yuan)(Household Registered) | 人均生产总值(元)(按常住)<br>Per Capita GDP(yuan)(Long－term Residents) |
|---|---|---|---|---|---|---|
| 1978 | 120.1 | 118.8 | 122.3 | 113.6 | 118.0 | |
| 1979 | 116.4 | 109.4 | 118.1 | 111.6 | 111.4 | |
| 1980 | 124.8 | 85.9 | 127.8 | 120.0 | 119.7 | |
| 1981 | 110.1 | 96.1 | 108.6 | 117.4 | 107.6 | |
| 1982 | 108.6 | 118.8 | 107.4 | 111.7 | 106.3 | |
| 1983 | 113.9 | 77.5 | 110.1 | 130.7 | 111.7 | |
| 1984 | 124.0 | 138.2 | 121.5 | 130.0 | 121.8 | |
| 1985 | 118.2 | 105.0 | 114.7 | 128.1 | 116.0 | |
| 1986 | 109.4 | 101.6 | 106.5 | 116.7 | 107.4 | |
| 1987 | 111.3 | 111.8 | 109.1 | 116.0 | 109.4 | |
| 1988 | 105.0 | 99.2 | 106.0 | 103.2 | 103.3 | |
| 1989 | 93.6 | 107.8 | 89.1 | 102.0 | 92.2 | |
| 1990 | 105.6 | 100.6 | 106.0 | 105.2 | 104.6 | |
| 1991 | 116.2 | 102.6 | 113.3 | 120.5 | 115.3 | |
| 1992 | 125.7 | 101.1 | 125.6 | 127.0 | 124.5 | |
| 1993 | 128.5 | 103.0 | 130.5 | 127.3 | 126.9 | |
| 1994 | 126.6 | 109.3 | 133.6 | 119.5 | 124.4 | |
| 1995 | 119.6 | 106.5 | 121.3 | 117.9 | 117.4 | |
| 1996 | 114.7 | 106.1 | 116.7 | 112.4 | 105.3 | |
| 1997 | 113.4 | 110.0 | 111.5 | 116.0 | 104.7 | |
| 1998 | 109.4 | 107.7 | 108.7 | 110.4 | 107.8 | |
| 1999 | 107.9 | 110.3 | 107.0 | 108.9 | 106.0 | |
| 2000 | 111.6 | 100.4 | 111.6 | 112.0 | 109.3 | |
| 2001 | 113.0 | 107.9 | 113.1 | 113.1 | 111.2 | |
| 2002 | 114.1 | 105.2 | 112.9 | 115.4 | 111.9 | |
| 2003 | 115.8 | 104.2 | 120.1 | 112.5 | 113.8 | |
| 2004 | 115.5 | 103.6 | 117.4 | 114.1 | 113.4 | |
| 2005 | 112.5 | 101.2 | 108.8 | 116.3 | 110.2 | |
| 2006 | 114.1 | 101.2 | 111.2 | 118.0 | 112.4 | |
| 2007 | 114.6 | 101.5 | 113.2 | 116.6 | 113.2 | 111.0 |
| 2008 | 110.8 | 100.9 | 107.8 | 114.1 | 109.4 | 107.9 |
| 2009 | 110.4 | 102.9 | 106.3 | 114.4 | 109.1 | 108.0 |
| 2010 | 111.9 | 101.4 | 110.6 | 113.4 | 110.6 | 107.5 |
| 2011 | 110.0 | 101.9 | 107.8 | 112.1 | 108.6 | 106.5 |
| 2012 | 109.0 | 102.1 | 106.3 | 111.3 | 107.7 | 108.3 |
| 2013 | 107.8 | 99.4 | 106.5 | 109.1 | 106.5 | 107.1 |
| 2014 | 108.2 | 101.0 | 107.9 | 108.6 | 106.7 | 107.6 |
| 2015 | 110.4 | 101.5 | 105.3 | 114.6 | 108.7 | 109.3 |
| 2016 | 109.8 | 100.1 | 104.1 | 113.6 | 107.8 | 107.9 |
| 2017 | 108.2 | 101.2 | 104.8 | 110.5 | 105.6 | 105.3 |
| 2018 | 106.8 | 101.5 | 106.0 | 107.4 | 103.6 | 103.0 |
| 2019 | 106.8 | 101.5 | 104.7 | 108.1 | 103.4 | 101.5 |

# 1-09 分行业

## Composition of

单位:万元

| 行业 | Sector | 全 Whole 2019 | 为上年(%) As Compared with the Preceding Year(%) |
|---|---|---|---|
| 全市生产总值 | Gross Domestic Product | 153730458 | 106.8 |
| 按行业分 | Grouped by Sector | | |
| #农、林、牧、渔业 | Farming, Forestry, Animal Husbandry & Fishery | 3327177 | 102.1 |
| 工业 | Industry | 42884161 | 105.3 |
| 建筑业 | Construction | 5882963 | 101.6 |
| 批发和零售业 | Wholesale and Retail Trade | 12245813 | 103.3 |
| 交通运输、仓储和邮政业 | Transportation, Storage and Post | 3978788 | 104.4 |
| 住宿和餐饮业 | Hotels and Catering Services | 2342506 | 104.0 |
| 信息传输、软件和信息技术服务业 | Information Transmission, Software and Information Technology Services | 27721488 | 115.9 |
| 金融业 | Financial Intermediation | 17893907 | 109.1 |
| 房地产业 | Real Estate | 10570408 | 99.5 |
| 租赁和商务服务业 | Leasing and Busyness Service | 4535669 | 101.6 |
| 科学研究、技术服务业 | Scientific Research, Technical Service | 4735176 | 107.8 |
| 水利环境和公共设施管理业 | Management of Water Conservancy, Enviroment and Public Facilities | 1151397 | 80.7 |
| 居民服务、修理和其他服务业 | Service for the Residents, Repair and Others | 892438 | 106.4 |
| 教育 | Education | 5512318 | 108.1 |
| 卫生和社会工作 | Health Care and Social Work | 4611059 | 117.5 |
| 文化、体育和娱乐业 | Culture, Sports and Entertainment | 1136942 | 91.1 |
| 公共管理、社会保障和社会组织 | Public Administration ,Social Security and Social Organization | 4308249 | 104.5 |
| 第一产业 | Primary Industry | 3256976 | 101.9 |
| 第二产业 | Secondary Industry | 48750711 | 105.0 |
| 第三产业 | Tertiary Industry | 101722772 | 108.0 |

# 生产总值构成(2019 年)

# Gross Domestic Product(2019)

(10000 yuan)

| 市 City | | #市 区 Urban District | | | |
|---|---|---|---|---|---|
| 比 重 (%) Proportion(%) | | 2019 | 为上年(%) As Compared with the Preceding Year(%) | 比 重 (%) Proportion(%) | |
| 2019 | 2018 | | | 2019 | 2018 |
| 100.0 | 100.0 | 143489200 | 106.8 | 100.0 | 100.0 |
| | | | | | |
| 2.2 | 2.2 | 2323066 | 101.7 | 1.6 | 1.6 |
| 27.9 | 28.9 | 39434459 | 105.1 | 27.5 | 28.5 |
| 3.8 | 3.9 | 4930582 | 100.6 | 3.4 | 3.6 |
| 8.0 | 8.0 | 11555847 | 103.2 | 8.1 | 8.1 |
| 2.6 | 2.6 | 3502508 | 104.2 | 2.4 | 2.5 |
| 1.5 | 1.5 | 2126611 | 103.9 | 1.5 | 1.5 |
| 18.0 | 16.6 | | | | |
| 11.6 | 11.2 | 17354865 | 109.1 | 12.1 | 11.6 |
| 6.9 | 7.9 | 9836003 | 99.6 | 6.9 | 7.9 |
| 3.0 | 3.1 | | | | |
| 3.1 | 2.9 | | | | |
| 0.7 | 1.0 | | | | |
| 0.6 | 0.6 | | | | |
| 3.6 | 3.4 | | | | |
| 3.0 | 2.6 | | | | |
| 0.7 | 0.9 | | | | |
| 2.8 | 2.8 | | | | |
| 2.1 | 2.1 | 2269869 | 101.5 | 1.6 | 1.6 |
| 31.7 | 32.8 | 44349935 | 104.7 | 30.9 | 32.1 |
| 66.2 | 65.1 | 96869397 | 108.1 | 67.5 | 66.3 |

# 1－10 分地区和产业生产总值构成(2019 年)

## Gross Domestic Product by Region and Industry(2019)

单位:万元 (10000 yuan)

| 地 区 | Region | 地区生产总值 Gross Domestic Product | 第一产业 Primary Industry | 第二产业 Secondary Industry | 第三产业 Tertiary Industry | 工 业 Industry | 建筑业 Construction | 户籍人口人均 GDP(元) Per Capita GDP (yuan)(Household Registered) | 常住人口人均 GDP(元) Per Capita GDP (Long－term Residents) |
|---|---|---|---|---|---|---|---|---|---|
| **全 市** | **Whole City** | **153730458** | **3256976** | **48750711** | **101722772** | **42884161** | **5882963** | **195900** | **152465** |
| 市 区 | Urban District | 143489200 | 2269869 | 44349935 | 96869397 | 39434459 | 4930582 | 222144 | 162236 |
| #上城区 | Shangcheng | 11714081 | － | 3999993 | 7714089 | 3805052 | 194972 | 367376 | 339539 |
| 下城区 | Xiacheng | 10495999 | － | 420842 | 10075157 | 143887 | 277064 | 251643 | 199544 |
| 江干区 | Jianggan | 9493736 | － | 1341430 | 8152305 | 487507 | 854924 | 196342 | 120098 |
| 拱墅区 | Gongshu | 6621610 | － | 1395613 | 5225997 | 1092470 | 307726 | 170292 | 114859 |
| 西湖区 | Xihu | 14158253 | 25826 | 1240629 | 12891797 | 869026 | 372742 | 192725 | 160161 |
| 高新(滨江)区 | Hi－Tech (Binjiang) | 15922036 | 7219 | 7435951 | 8478866 | 7295352 | 140709 | 590123 | 375963 |
| 萧山区 | Xiaoshan | 21985106 | 716581 | 10390291 | 10878234 | 9459943 | 934280 | 164745 | 124315 |
| 余杭区 | Yuhang | 28240220 | 533118 | 6522505 | 21184597 | 6039963 | 485149 | 249870 | 161650 |
| 富阳区 | Fuyang | 8204686 | 493055 | 3739223 | 3972408 | 3335087 | 405511 | 119643 | 110426 |
| 临安区 | Lin'an | 5729427 | 458604 | 2572754 | 2698069 | 2151296 | 421490 | 106389 | 96374 |
| 钱塘新区 | Qiantang New Area | 11002380 | 136220 | 7618580 | 3247580 | 7257171 | 363118 | 371951 | 171510 |
| 西湖风景名胜区 | The West Lake Scenic Zone | 473645 | 9491 | 1033 | 463121 | 106 | 929 | 243069 | 157882 |
| 桐庐县 | Tonglu | 3863850 | 250273 | 1775952 | 1837626 | 1499486 | 277449 | 92439 | 89029 |
| 淳安县 | Chun'an | 2544966 | 381430 | 779570 | 1383966 | 497734 | 282071 | 55426 | 71088 |
| 建德市 | Jiande | 3832442 | 355404 | 1845255 | 1631783 | 1452482 | 392861 | 75008 | 85833 |

# 1－11 分地区和产业生产总值指数(2019 年)

## Indices of Gross Domestic Product by Region and Industry(2019)

(上年＝100) (Preceding Year＝100)

| 地 区 | Region | 地区生产总值 Gross Domestic Product | 第一产业 Primary Industry | 第二产业 Secondary Industry | 第三产业 Tertiary Industry | 工 业 Industry | 建筑业 Construction |
|---|---|---|---|---|---|---|---|
| **全 市** | **Whole City** | **106.8** | **101.9** | **105.0** | **108.0** | **105.3** | **101.6** |
| 市 区 | Urban District | 106.8 | 101.5 | 104.7 | 108.1 | 105.1 | 100.6 |
| #上城区 | Shangcheng | 106.1 | – | 102.8 | 108.2 | 103.0 | 97.7 |
| 下城区 | Xiacheng | 106.8 | – | 102.2 | 107.0 | 94.1 | 109.7 |
| 江干区 | Jianggan | 105.1 | －100.0 | 100.1 | 106.0 | 93.1 | 105.3 |
| 拱墅区 | Gongshu | 108.3 | – | 111.0 | 107.5 | 114.2 | 99.4 |
| 西湖区 | Xihu | 108.0 | 79.9 | 108.2 | 108.0 | 112.9 | 96.9 |
| 高新(滨江)区 | Hi－Tech(Binjiang) | 108.2 | 91.1 | 109.4 | 107.2 | 110.6 | 69.4 |
| 萧山区 | Xiaoshan | 105.1 | 101.6 | 103.6 | 107.4 | 103.6 | 103.7 |
| 余杭区 | Yuhang | 108.6 | 102.6 | 105.0 | 110.0 | 105.5 | 99.1 |
| 富阳区 | Fuyang | 106.0 | 102.6 | 103.9 | 109.1 | 102.5 | 121.3 |
| 临安区 | Lin'an | 108.0 | 102.8 | 107.8 | 109.5 | 108.4 | 103.2 |
| 钱塘新区 | Qiantang New Area | 102.1 | 101.8 | 99.6 | 109.7 | 99.7 | 97.5 |
| 西湖风景名胜区 | The West Lake Scenic Zone | 103.5 | 105.0 | 81.8 | 103.7 | 100.1 | 52.6 |
| 桐庐县 | Tonglu | 106.8 | 102.5 | 108.6 | 105.1 | 108.2 | 111.9 |
| 淳安县 | Chun'an | 104.6 | 103.8 | 102.6 | 106.2 | 103.4 | 100.7 |
| 建德市 | Jiande | 107.0 | 102.5 | 109.0 | 105.2 | 109.0 | 109.1 |

# 1－12　主要指标占全省比重(2019 年)
## Proportion of Main Indicators in Whole Province(2019)

| 指　标<br>Item | | 全　省<br>Zhejiang Province | 杭州市<br>Hangzhou City | 杭州市占全省(%)<br>Proportion of Hangzhou in Zhejiang(%) |
|---|---|---|---|---|
| 年末常住人口<br>Long－term Residents(End of 2019) | (万人)<br>(10000 persons) | 5850.0 | 1036.0 | 17.7 |
| 年末户籍人口<br>Household Registration Population(End of 2019) | (万人)<br>(10000 persons) | 5038.91 | 795.37 | 15.8 |
| 年末就业人员数<br>Total Number of Employed Persons | (万人)<br>(10000 persons) | 3875.10 | 720 | 18.6 |
| 地区生产总值<br>Gross Domestic Product | (亿元)<br>(100 million yuan) | 62351.74 | 15373.05 | 24.7 |
| 第一产业<br>Primary Industry | (亿元)<br>(100 million yuan) | 2097.38 | 325.70 | 15.5 |
| 第二产业<br>Secondary Industry | (亿元)<br>(100 million yuan) | 26566.6 | 4875.07 | 18.4 |
| 第三产业<br>Tertiary Industry | (亿元)<br>(100 million yuan) | 33687.76 | 10172.28 | 30.2 |
| 常住人口人均生产总值<br>Per Capita GDP of Long－term Residents | (元)<br>(yuan) | 107624 | 152465 | － |
| 农林牧渔业总产值<br>Gross Output Value of Farming, Forestry, Animal Husbandry and Fishery | (亿元)<br>(100 million yuan) | 3355.25 | 501.15 | 14.9 |
| 主要农产品产量<br>Output of Major Farm Products | | | | |
| #粮食<br>Grain | (万吨)<br>(10000 tons) | 592.1 | 49.64 | 8.4 |
| 蚕茧<br>Silk－worm Cocoons | (万吨)<br>(10000 tons) | － | 0.35 | － |
| 生猪年末存栏<br>Hogs in Stock at Year End | (万头)<br>(10000 heads) | 427.30 | 90.34 | 21.1 |
| 肉类产量<br>Output of Meat | (万吨)<br>(10000 tons) | － | 14.97 | － |
| 淡水产品总产量<br>Freshwater Aquatic products | (万吨)<br>(10000 tons) | 133.11 | 16.80 | 12.6 |

1－12　续表1　continued 1

| 指　　标<br>Item | 全　省<br>Zhejiang Province | 杭州市<br>Hangzhou City | 杭州市占全省（%）<br>Proportion of Hangzhou in Zhejiang（%） |
|---|---|---|---|
| 规模以上工业增加值（亿元）<br>Value－added of Industrial Enterprises above Designated Size（100 million yuan） | 15786.03 | 3481.89 | 22.1 |
| 规模以上工业企业利税总额（亿元）<br>Total Pre－tax Profits of Industrial Enterprises above Designed Size（100 million yuan） | 7860.71 | 1854.99 | 23.6 |
| 主要工业产品产量<br>Output of Major Industrial Products | | | |
| #发电量（亿千瓦时）<br>Electricity（100 million kwh） | － | 160.00 | － |
| 氢氧化钠（烧碱）（折100%）（万吨）<br>Caustic Soda（100% discount）（10000 tons） | 200.77 | 24.60 | 12.3 |
| 碳酸钠（纯碱）（万吨）<br>Soda Ash（10000 tons） | 31.74 | 31.74 | 100 |
| 合成氨（万吨）<br>Synthetic Ammonia（10000 tons） | 61.21 | 23.51 | 38.4 |
| 水泥（万吨）<br>Cement（10000 tons） | 13399.94 | 1663.39 | 12.4 |
| 钢材（万吨）<br>Steels（10000 tons） | 3468.2 | 392 | 11.3 |
| 化学纤维（万吨）<br>Chemical Fiber（10000 tons） | 2822.84 | 975.55 | 34.6 |
| 纱（万吨）<br>Yarn（10000 tons） | 149.09 | 39.27 | 26.3 |
| 自行车（万辆）<br>Bicycles（10000 units） | 407 | 95 | 23.3 |
| 电冰箱（万台）<br>Household Refrigerator（10000 units） | 568 | 77 | 13.6 |
| 洗衣机（万台）<br>Washing Machine（10000 units） | 1118 | 244 | 21.8 |
| 客运量（万人次）<br>Volume of Passenger Transport（10000 person－times） | 105259 | 20888 | 19.8 |

1－12 续表2 continued 2

| 指 标<br>Item | | 全 省<br>Zhejiang Province | 杭州市<br>Hangzhou City | 杭州市占全省(%)<br>Proportion of Hangzhou in Zhejiang (%) |
|---|---|---|---|---|
| 货运量<br>Volume of Goods Transport | (万吨)<br>(10000 tons) | 288550 | 36384 | 12.6 |
| 社会消费品零售总额<br>Total Retail Sales of Consumer Goods | (亿元)<br>(100 million yuan) | 27343.81 | 6187.70 | 22.6 |
| 出口额<br>Total Exports | (亿元)<br>(100 million yuan) | 23069.77 | 3612.66 | 15.7 |
| 实际利用外资<br>Foreign Capital Actually Used | (亿美元)<br>(100 million USD) | 135.59 | 61.28 | 45.2 |
| 财政总收入<br>Total Financial Revenue | (亿元)<br>(100 million yuan) | 12267.66 | 3650.04 | 29.8 |
| #一般公共预算收入<br>General Public Budget Revenue | (亿元)<br>(100 million yuan) | 7048.00 | 1965.97 | 27.9 |
| 一般公共预算支出<br>Financial Expenditure | (亿元)<br>(100 million yuan) | 10052.99 | 1952.85 | 19.4 |
| 金融机构存款余额(本外币)<br>Deposits of Financial Institutions | (亿元)<br>(100 million yuan) | 131298.5 | 45287.0 | 34.5 |
| 住户存款余额<br>Deposits of Households | (亿元)<br>(100 million yuan) | 53733.3 | 11901.3 | 22.1 |
| 金融机构贷款余额(本外币)<br>Loans of Financial Institutions | (亿元)<br>(100 million yuan) | 121750.6 | 42245.2 | 34.7 |
| 非私营单位就业人员平均工资<br>Average Wage of Employed Persons of Non－private Units | (元)<br>(yuan) | 99654 | 117339 | 117.7 |
| 全体居民人均可支配收入<br>Per Capita Annual Disposable Income of Urban and Rural Residents | (元)<br>(yuan) | 49899 | 59261 | 118.8 |
| 城镇居民人均可支配收入<br>Per Capita Annual Disposable Income of Urban Residents | (元)<br>(yuan) | 60182 | 66068 | 109.8 |
| 农村居民人均可支配收入<br>Per Capita Annual Disposable Income of Rural Residents | (元)<br>(yuan) | 29876 | 36255 | 121.4 |
| 高等学校在校学生数<br>Number of Institutions of Higher Education | (万人)<br>(10000 persons) | 116.7 | 51.83 | 44.4 |
| 普通中学在校学生数<br>Number of Secondary Schools | (万人)<br>(10000 persons) | 242.1 | 36.21 | 15.0 |
| 小学在校学生数<br>Number of Primary Schools | (万人)<br>(10000 persons) | 367.1 | 61.69 | 16.8 |

# 1－13 国民经济主要指标人均水平(2012－2019年)
# Major Per Capita Indicators of National Economy(2012－2019)

| 指标 Item | 2012 | 2013 | 2014 | 2015 | 2016 | 2017 | 2018 | 2019 |
|---|---|---|---|---|---|---|---|---|
| 全市生产总值 (元) Gross Domestic Product (yuan) | 90862 | 97925 | 107152 | 117200 | 128633 | 141088 | 148456 | 152465 |
| 规模以上工业总产值 (元) Gross Industrial Output Value above Designatted Size (yuan) | 147773 | 140746 | 144937 | 138645 | 136449 | 138977 | 145444 | 144654 |
| 农林牧渔业总产值 (元) Gross Output Value of Farming, Forestry, Animal Husbandry and Fishery (yuan) | 4382 | 4526 | 4720 | 4918 | 4933 | 4907 | 4837 | 4970 |
| 社会消费品零售总额 (元) Total Retail Sales of Consumer Goods (yuan) | 35524 | 39919 | 43176 | 47801 | 51939 | 55986 | 59041 | 61368 |
| 财政总收入 (元) Financial Revenue (yuan) | 18562 | 19664 | 21652 | 25000 | 28105 | 31318 | 35877 | 36199 |
| #一般公共预算收入 (元) General Public Budget Revenue (yuan) | 9806 | 10713 | 11585 | 13779 | 15406 | 16803 | 18938 | 19498 |
| 一般公共预算支出 (元) General Public Budgetary Expenditure (yuan) | 8966 | 9699 | 10839 | 13462 | 15427 | 16519 | 17818 | 19368 |
| 全体居民可支配收入 (元) Annual Disposable Income of Urban and Rural Residents (yuan) | － | 35763 | 39237 | 42642 | 46116 | 49832 | 54348 | 59261 |
| 全体居民消费性支出 (元) Annual Living Expendituer of Urban and Ruarual Residents (yuan) | － | 26827 | 28492 | 30181 | 31905 | 34146 | 37369 | 40016 |
| 城镇居民可支配收入 (元) Annual Disposable Income of Urban Residents (yuan) | 37511 | 40925 | 44632 | 48316 | 52185 | 56276 | 61172 | 66068 |
| 城镇居民消费性支出 (元) Annual Living Expenditure of Urban Residents (yuan) | 22800 | 30659 | 32165 | 33818 | 35686 | 38179 | 41615 | 44076 |
| 农村居民可支配收入 (元) Annual Disposable Income of Rural Residents (yuan) | 17017 | 21208 | 23555 | 25719 | 27908 | 30397 | 33193 | 36255 |
| 农村居民消费性支出 (元) Annual Living Expenditure of Rural Residents (yuan) | 13612 | 16021 | 17816 | 19334 | 20563 | 21983 | 24203 | 26296 |

# 1－14　数字经济主要指标(2018－2019年)
## Digital Economy(2018－2019)

| 指　　标 Item | 2018年 | | | | 2019年 | | | |
|---|---|---|---|---|---|---|---|---|
| | 营业收入(亿元) Revenne from Principal Business (100 million yuan) | 增速(%) Growth (%) | 增加值(亿元) Added Value (100 million yuan) | 增速(%) Growth (%) | 营业收入(亿元) Revenne from Principal Business (100 million yuan) | 增速(%) Growth (%) | 增加值(亿元) Added Value (100 million yuan) | 增速(%) Growth (%) |
| **数字经济核心产业 Digital Economy Core Industry** | **－** | **－** | **3356** | **15.0** | **11296** | **19.4** | **3795** | **15.1** |
| **相关产业** | | | | | | | | |
| 电子商务产业 E－commerce | 2777 | 18.6 | 1529 | 17.5 | 3197 | 23.6 | 1847 | 14.6 |
| 云计算与大数据产业 Cloud Computing and Big Data | 2461 | 19.4 | 1332 | 16.5 | 2948 | 16.0 | 1381 | 6.0 |
| 物联网产业 Internet of Things | 1716 | 22.5 | 492 | 21.0 | 2040 | 14.1 | 582 | 13.6 |
| 数字内容产业 Digital Content | 6100 | 24.5 | 2098 | 15.8 | 7576 | 24.5 | 2505 | 16.3 |
| 软件与信息服务产业 Soft－ware and Information Service | 7189 | 21.5 | 2508 | 17.0 | 8898 | 21.4 | 2889 | 15.7 |
| 电子信息产品制造产业 Electronic Information Products Manufacturing Industry | 3124 | 14.2 | 847 | 10.0 | 3641 | 11.3 | 911 | 10.6 |
| 集成电路产业 Integrate Circuit Industry | 191 | 6.2 | 65 | 8.1 | 282 | 8.8 | 84 | 7.4 |
| 机器人产业 Robot Industry | 82 | 17.4 | 24 | 16.9 | 95 | 10.6 | 27 | 11.3 |

注:2018年起采用浙江数字经济口径,之前为杭州信息经济口径。

a) Since 2018, the statistical caliber was zhejiang Digital Economy, it was Hangzhou Information Economy before.

# 1－15　分地区数字经济核心产业增加值(2019年)

# Added Value of Core Industries of Digital Economy by Region(2019)

| 地　区 | Region | 增加值(亿元) Added Value (100 million yuan) | 比上年增长(%) Increase over the preceding year(%) | 占地区生产总值(%) Proportion in Gross Domestic Product(%) |
|---|---|---|---|---|
| **杭州市** | **Hangzhou** | **3795** | **15.1** | **24.7** |
| #上城区 | Shangcheng | 26 | 6.0 | 2.2 |
| 下城区 | Xiacheng | 24 | 15.3 | 2.3 |
| 江干区 | Jianggan | 39 | 3.0 | 4.1 |
| 拱墅区 | Gongshu | 32 | 10.0 | 4.8 |
| 西湖区 | Xihu | 309 | 20.4 | 21.8 |
| 高新(滨江)区 | Hi－Tech(Binjiang) | 1202 | 16.5 | 75.5 |
| 萧山区 | Xiaoshan | 76 | 21.5 | 4.1 |
| 余杭区 | Yuhang | 1649 | 15.2 | 58.4 |
| 富阳区 | Fuyang | 78 | 20.3 | 9.5 |
| 临安区 | Lin'an | 59 | 10.1 | 10.2 |
| 钱塘新区 | Qiantang New Area | 111 | 17.5 | 10.1 |
| 西湖风景名胜区 | The West Lake Scenic Zone | － | － | － |
| 桐庐县 | Tonglu | 49 | 21.3 | 12.6 |
| 淳安县 | Chun'an | 8 | 7.8 | 3.3 |
| 建德市 | Jiande | 8 | 6.0 | 2.2 |

注:快报未经省局核定,且萧山区不含托管在钱塘新区的街道数据。

a)The preliminary statistics has not been approved by the Provincial Bureau, Figures of Xiaoshan District don't include districts which under administered by Qiantang New Area.

# 1－16 “1＋6”产业集群主要指标（2018－2019 年）
# “1＋6” Industrial Cluster（2018－2019）

| 产业分组 Industry Grouping | 2018 年 | | 2019 年 | |
|---|---|---|---|---|
| | 增加值（亿元） Added Value （100 million yuan） | 速度（％） Growth （％） | 增加值（亿元） Added Value （100 million yuan） | 速度（％） Growth （％） |
| 数字经济核心产业 Digital Economy Core Industry | 3356 | 15.0 | 3795 | 15.1 |
| 文化创意产业 Cultural and Creative Industry | 3347 | 11.6 | 3735 | 15.6 |
| 金融产业 Financial service Industry | 1205 | 8.8 | 1791 | 9.1 |
| 旅游休闲产业 Tourism Leisure Industry | 1038 | 13.0 | 1191 | 12.1 |
| 健康产业 Health Industry | 809 | 10.0 | 975 | 12.5 |
| 时尚产业（制造业） Fashion Industry （Manufacturing） | 195 | 8.2 | 213 | －1.5 |
| 高端装备产业（制造业） High－end Equipment Industry（Manufacturing） | 643 | 3.5 | 653 | 1.2 |

# 1－17　按机构类型和登记注册类型分组的法人单位数(2019年)

## Number of Corporation Units by Types of Organization and Registration(2019)

单位:个　　　　(unit)

| 指标名称 | Item | 法人单位数 Number of Corporation Units | 单产业法人单位 Containing Single Industrial Activity | 多产业法人单位 Containing Multiple Industrial Activity |
|---|---|---|---|---|
| **总计** | **Total** | **436425** | **425339** | **11086** |
| **按机构类型分组** | **By Type of Organization** | | | |
| 企业 | Enterprises | 410451 | 399650 | 10801 |
| 事业单位 | Publlic Institution | 5350 | 5214 | 136 |
| 机关 | Office | 1202 | 1096 | 106 |
| 社会团体 | Social Group | 4100 | 4098 | 2 |
| 民办非企业单位 | Private Non－enterprise Unit | 6827 | 6826 | 1 |
| 基金会 | Foundation | 244 | 244 | － |
| 居委会 | Neighborhood Committees | 1167 | 1157 | 10 |
| 村委会 | Villagers Committees | 2108 | 2097 | 11 |
| 农民专业合作社 | Specialty Cooperative of Peasants | 2764 | 2755 | 9 |
| 农村集体经济组织 | | 887 | 879 | 8 |
| 其他组织机构 | Other | 1325 | 1323 | 2 |
| **按登记注册类型分组** | **Grouped By Registered Type** | **436425** | **425339** | **11086** |
| 内资企业 | Domestic－funded | 431188 | 420533 | 10655 |
| 国有企业 | State－owned | 7737 | 7428 | 309 |
| 集体企业 | Collective－owned | 2894 | 2854 | 40 |
| 股份合作企业 | Cooperative | 380 | 365 | 15 |
| 联营企业 | Joint Ownership | 37 | 36 | 1 |
| 国有联营企业 | State Joint Ownership | 3 | 3 | － |
| 集体联营企业 | Collective Joint | 6 | 6 | － |
| 国有与集体联营企业 | Joint State－collective | 11 | 11 | － |
| 其他联营企业 | Other Joint Ownership | 17 | 16 | 1 |

| 指标名称 | Item | 法人单位数 Number of Corporation Units | 单产业法人单位 Containing Single Industrial Activity | 多产业法人单位 Containing Multiple Industrial Activity |
|---|---|---|---|---|
| 有限责任公司 | Limited Liability Corporations | 12691 | 11590 | 1101 |
| 国有独资公司 | State - funded Corporations | 707 | 602 | 105 |
| 其他有限责任公司 | Other Limited Liability Corporations | 11984 | 10988 | 996 |
| 股份有限公司 | Share - holding Corporations Ltd. | 1092 | 800 | 292 |
| 私营企业 | Private | 391197 | 382336 | 8861 |
| 私营独资企业 | Private - funded | 12730 | 12566 | 164 |
| 私营合伙企业 | Private Partnership | 7759 | 7731 | 28 |
| 私营有限责任公司 | Private Limited Liability Corporations | 369911 | 361336 | 8575 |
| 私营股份有限公司 | Private Share - holding Corporations Ltd. | 797 | 703 | 94 |
| 其他企业 | Other Domestic - funded | 15160 | 15124 | 36 |
| 港、澳、台商投资企业 | Enterprises With Investment from Hong Kong, Macao and Taiwan | 2085 | 1902 | 183 |
| 合资经营企业(港或澳、台资) | Joint - venture Enterprises with funds from Hong Kong, Macao and Taiwan | 719 | 649 | 70 |
| 合作经营企业(港或澳、台资) | Cooperative Enterprises with funds from Hong Kong, Macao and Taiwan | 12 | 11 | 1 |
| 港、澳、台商独资经营企业 | Enterprises With Sole Investment from Hong Kong, Macao and Taiwan | 1337 | 1229 | 108 |
| 港、澳、台商投资股份有限公司 | Share - holding Corporations Ltd. With Investment from Hong Kong, Macao and Taiwan | 9 | 8 | 1 |
| 其他港、澳、台商投资企业 | Other Enterprises With Investment from Hong Kong, Macao and Taiwan | 8 | 5 | 3 |
| 外商投资企业 | With Foreign Investment | 3152 | 2904 | 248 |
| 中外合资经营企业 | Joint - venture | 1235 | 1144 | 91 |
| 中外合作经营企业 | Cooperation Enterprises | 35 | 31 | 4 |
| 外资企业 | With Sole Foreign Investment | 1792 | 1642 | 150 |
| 外商投资股份有限公司 | Share - holding Corporations Ltd. With Foreign Investment | 45 | 43 | 2 |
| 其他外商投资企业 | Other Enterprises With Foreign Investment | 45 | 44 | 1 |

# 1－18 按行业和地区分组的法人单位数(2019年)

## Number of Corporation Units by Sector and Region(2019)

单位:个 (unit)

| 指标名称 Item | 法人单位数 Number of Corporation Units | 单产业法人单位 Containing Single Industrial Activity | 多产业法人单位 Containing Multiple Industrial Activity |
|---|---|---|---|
| **合计 Total** | **436425** | **425339** | **11086** |
| **一、按国民经济行业分组 Grouped by Sector** | | | |
| 农、林、牧、渔业 Farming, Forestry, Animal Husbandry and Fishery | 5778 | 5742 | 36 |
| 农业 Agriculture | 3375 | 3361 | 14 |
| 林业 Forestry | 912 | 907 | 5 |
| 畜牧业 Animal Husbandry | 587 | 579 | 8 |
| 渔业 Fishery | 619 | 613 | 6 |
| 农、林、牧、渔、服务业 Services for Farming, Forestry, Animal Husbandry and Fishery | 285 | 282 | 3 |
| 采矿业 Mining and Quarrying | 137 | 134 | 3 |
| 煤炭采选业和洗选业 Coal Mining and Processing | 2 | 2 | - |
| 黑色金属矿采选业 Ferrous Metals Mining and Processing | 4 | 4 | - |
| 有色金属矿采选业 Nonferrous Metals Mining and Processing | 10 | 9 | 1 |
| 非金属矿采选业 Nonmetal Minerals Mining and Processing | 117 | 115 | 2 |
| 开采专业及辅助性活动 Supplementary Activities for Mining | 3 | 3 | - |
| 其他采矿业 Other Minerals Mining | 1 | 1 | - |
| 制造业 Manufacturing Industry | 50100 | 49228 | 872 |
| 农副食品加工业 Agricultural Products Processing | 804 | 786 | 18 |
| 食品制造业 Food Manufacturing | 708 | 665 | 43 |
| 酒、饮料和精制茶制造业 Wine, Beverage and Tea Manufacturing | 563 | 537 | 26 |
| 烟草制品业 Tobacco Processing | 1 | - | 1 |
| 纺织业 Textile Industry | 4258 | 4192 | 66 |
| 纺织服装、服饰业 Textile Products and Costune Indnstry | 4460 | 4391 | 69 |

单位:个　　　　1-18　续表1　continued 1　　　　(unit)

| 指标名称　Item | 法人单位数 Number of Corporation Units | 单产业法人单位 Containing Single Industrial Activity | 多产业法人单位 Containing Multiple Industrial Activity |
|---|---|---|---|
| 皮革、毛皮、羽毛及其制品和制鞋业 Leather. Furs. Downand Related and Shoes Products | 957 | 944 | 13 |
| 木材加工和木、竹、藤、棕、草制品业 Timber Processing, Bamboo, Cane, Palm Fiber and Straw Products | 937 | 930 | 7 |
| 家具制造业 Furniture Manufacturing | 974 | 959 | 15 |
| 造纸和纸制品业 Paper Making and Paper Products | 2153 | 2135 | 18 |
| 印刷和记录媒介复制业 Printing and Record Media | 1254 | 1239 | 15 |
| 文教、工美、体育和娱乐用品制造业 Cultural, Educational. Industrial Arts. Sports and Entertainment Goods | 2194 | 2171 | 23 |
| 石油、煤炭及其他燃料加工业 Petroleum, Coal and other Fuel Processing | 78 | 76 | 2 |
| 化学原料和化学制品制造业 Raw Chemical Materials and Chemical Products | 1701 | 1660 | 41 |
| 医药制造业 Medical and Pharmaceutical Products | 298 | 287 | 11 |
| 化学纤维制造业 Chemical Fiber | 336 | 332 | 4 |
| 橡胶和塑料制品业 Rubber and Plastic Products | 3201 | 3165 | 36 |
| 非金属矿物制品业 Nonmetal Minerals Products | 2306 | 2265 | 41 |
| 黑色金属冶炼和压延加工业 Smelting and Processing of Ferrous Metal | 258 | 254 | 4 |
| 有色金属冶炼和压延加工业 Smelting and Processing of Nonferrous Metals | 326 | 319 | 7 |
| 金属制品业 Metals Products | 5411 | 5355 | 56 |
| 通用设备制造业 Ordinary Machinery | 5366 | 5264 | 102 |
| 专用设备制造业 For Special Purpose Equipment Manufacturing | 2760 | 2702 | 58 |
| 汽车制造业 Automobile Manufacturing | 1694 | 1674 | 20 |
| 铁路、船舶、航空航天和其他运输设备制造业 Railway. watercraft. Avigation spaceflight and other Equipment Manufacturing | 457 | 452 | 5 |
| 电气机械和器材制造业 Electric Equipment and Machinery | 3053 | 2989 | 64 |
| 计算机、通信和其他电子设备制造业 Computers. Telecommunications and Other Electronic Equipment Manufacturing | 1777 | 1722 | 55 |
| 仪器仪表制造业 Instruments and Meters Manufacturing | 981 | 941 | 40 |

单位:个　　1－18　续表 2　continued 2　　(unit)

| 指标名称 Item | 法人单位数 Number of Corporation Units | 单产业法人单位 Containing Single Industrial Activity | 多产业法人单位 Containing Multiple Industrial Activity |
|---|---|---|---|
| 其他制造业 Other Manufacturing | 378 | 376 | 2 |
| 废弃资源综合利用业 Multiple Utilization of Waste Resouces | 133 | 130 | 3 |
| 金属制品、机械和设备修理业 Metal Products, Machinery and Equipment Repair | 323 | 316 | 7 |
| 电力、热力、燃气及水生产和供应业 Produotion and supply of electricity, gas & water | 684 | 653 | 31 |
| 电力、热力生产和供应业 Production and Supply of Electric Power and Hot Water | 425 | 417 | 8 |
| 燃气生产和供应业 Production and Supply of Gas | 56 | 48 | 8 |
| 水的生产和供应业 Production and Supply of Tap Water | 203 | 188 | 15 |
| 建筑业 Construction | 19087 | 18375 | 712 |
| 房屋建筑业 Housing | 2349 | 2155 | 194 |
| 土木工程建筑业 Civil Engineering | 4329 | 4106 | 223 |
| 建筑安装业 Installation | 2190 | 2080 | 110 |
| 建筑装饰、装修和其他建筑业 Building Decoration and Others | 10219 | 10034 | 185 |
| 批发和零售业 Wholesale and Retail Trade | 139990 | 137286 | 2704 |
| 批发业 Wholesale | 87044 | 85825 | 1219 |
| 零售业 Retail Trade | 52946 | 51461 | 1485 |
| 交通运输、仓储和邮政业 Transportation, Storage and Post | 8143 | 7840 | 303 |
| 铁路运输业 Railway Transport | 6 | 6 | – |
| 道路运输业 Highway Transport | 5878 | 5708 | 170 |
| 水上运输业 Water Transport | 102 | 95 | 7 |
| 航空运输业 Air Transport | 67 | 62 | 5 |
| 管道运输业 Pipeline Transport | 1 | 1 | – |
| 多式联运和运输代理业 Multimodal Transport and Transport Agency | 1102 | 1053 | 49 |

单位：个 1－18 续表3 continued 3 (unit)

| 指标名称 Item | 法人单位数 Number of Corporation Units | 单产业法人单位 Containing Single Industrial Activity | 多产业法人单位 Containing Multiple Industrial Activity |
|---|---|---|---|
| 装卸搬运和仓储业 Carrying and Storage | 580 | 563 | 17 |
| 邮政业 Postal Services | 407 | 352 | 55 |
| 住宿和餐饮业 Lodging and Catering Services | 10031 | 9368 | 663 |
| 住宿业 Lodging | 3314 | 3175 | 139 |
| 餐饮业 Catering Services | 6717 | 6193 | 524 |
| 信息传输、软件和信息技术服务业 Information Transmission，Software and Information Technology Services | 43072 | 42388 | 684 |
| 电信、广播电视和卫星传输服务 Telecommunication, Radio and Television, Satellite Transmission Services | 494 | 448 | 46 |
| 互联网和相关服务 Internet and Related Services | 2958 | 2903 | 55 |
| 软件和信息技术服务业 Software and Information Technology Services | 39620 | 39037 | 583 |
| 金融业 Banking and Insurance | 3301 | 3037 | 264 |
| 货币金融服务 Monetary and Financial Services | 354 | 271 | 83 |
| 资本市场服务 Capital Market Services | 2268 | 2223 | 45 |
| 保险业 Insurance | 233 | 122 | 111 |
| 其他金融业 Others | 446 | 421 | 25 |
| 房地产业 Real Estate | 16122 | 15311 | 811 |
| 房地产业 Real Estate | 16122 | 15311 | 811 |
| 租赁和商务服务业 Renting and Business Service | 59914 | 58184 | 1730 |
| 租赁业 Renting | 3617 | 3508 | 109 |
| 商务服务业 Commercial Service | 56297 | 54676 | 1621 |
| 科学研究和技术服务业 Scientific Research and Technical Service | 30631 | 29824 | 807 |
| 研究和试验发展 Research and Experiment | 3639 | 3589 | 50 |
| 专业技术服务业 Technical Services | 15295 | 14678 | 617 |

单位:个　　　　1－18　续表4　continued 4　　　　(unit)

| 指标名称　Item | 法人单位数 Number of Corporation Units | 单产业法人单位 Containing Single Industrial Activity | 多产业法人单位 Containing Multiple Industrial Activity |
|---|---|---|---|
| 科技推广和应用服务业 Promotion and Application of Service and Technology Services | 11697 | 11557 | 140 |
| 水利、环境和公共设施管理业 Water Conservancy, Environment and Public Utility | 2113 | 2013 | 100 |
| 水利管理业 Water Conservancy | 158 | 151 | 7 |
| 生态保护和环境治理业 Ecological Protection and Environmental Management | 388 | 369 | 19 |
| 公共设施管理业 Public Facilities | 1466 | 1405 | 61 |
| 土地管理业 Land Management | 101 | 88 | 13 |
| 居民服务、修理和其他服务业 Service for the Residents , Repair and Others | 10116 | 9740 | 376 |
| 居民服务业 Resident Services | 5441 | 5184 | 257 |
| 机动车、电子产品和日用产品修理业 Motor Vehicles , Electronics and Household Goods Repair Industry | 3221 | 3149 | 72 |
| 其他服务业 Other Services | 1454 | 1407 | 47 |
| 教育 Education | 9462 | 9153 | 309 |
| 教育 Education | 9462 | 9153 | 309 |
| 卫生和社会工作 Health Care, Sports & Social Welfare | 3701 | 3398 | 303 |
| 卫生 Health Care | 1964 | 1676 | 288 |
| 社会工作 Sports & Social Welfare | 1737 | 1722 | 15 |
| 文化、体育和娱乐业 Culture, Sports and Entertainment | 12055 | 11812 | 243 |
| 新闻和出版业 News and Publishing | 212 | 205 | 7 |
| 广播、电视、电影和录音制作业 Television, Radio, Film and Television Sound Recording Production | 2173 | 2149 | 24 |
| 文化艺术业 Culture and Arts | 2551 | 2524 | 27 |
| 体育 Sports | 1330 | 1236 | 94 |
| 娱乐业 Recreation | 5789 | 5698 | 91 |

单位:个　　1-18　续表5　continued 5　　(unit)

| 指标名称　Item | 法人单位数 Number of Corporation Units | 单产业法人单位 Containing Single Industrial Activity | 多产业法人单位 Containing Multiple Industrial Activity |
|---|---|---|---|
| 公共管理、社会保障和社会组织 Public Administration ,Social Security and Social Organization | 11988 | 11853 | 135 |
| 中国共产党机关 Communist Party Agencies | 131 | 131 | - |
| 国家机构 Government Agencies | 2585 | 2473 | 112 |
| 人民政协、民主党派 The CPPCC, Democratic Parties | 50 | 50 | - |
| 社会保障 Social Security | 36 | 36 | - |
| 群众团体、社会团体和其他成员组织 Mass Organizations,Social Groups and Other Members of Organization | 5114 | 5112 | 2 |
| 基层群众自治组织及其他组织 Basic Level Mass Autonomous Organization and Other Organizations | 4072 | 4051 | 21 |
| **二、按地区分组** | | | |
| 杭州市 HangZhou | 436425 | 425339 | 11086 |
| 上城区 Shangcheng | 15089 | 14333 | 756 |
| 下城区 Xiacheng | 28632 | 27574 | 1058 |
| 江干区 Jianggan | 55614 | 54147 | 1467 |
| 拱墅区 Gongshu | 31384 | 30354 | 1030 |
| 西湖区 Xihu | 46079 | 44421 | 1658 |
| 滨江区 Binjiang | 25789 | 25090 | 699 |
| 萧山区 Xiaoshan | 80665 | 79267 | 1398 |
| 余杭区 Yuhang | 71911 | 70324 | 1587 |
| 富阳区 Fuyang | 25696 | 25257 | 439 |
| 临安区 Lin'an | 14862 | 14590 | 272 |
| 桐庐县 Tonglu | 16829 | 16600 | 229 |
| 淳安县 Chun'an | 12788 | 12478 | 310 |
| 建德市 Jiande | 11087 | 10904 | 183 |

注:建筑业单位按地区分组汇总按照注册地行政区划代码进行,因此与分机构类型、登记注册类型及行业汇总数据有差异。

a) Construction enterprises grouped by region is according to the code of administrative division of the registered area, therefore the data is different to grouped by organizations, groupe by registration types and industry aggregate.

# 1－19 新中国成立以来主要指标之一：全市生产总值

## Main indicators since the founding of PRC: The city's GDP

| 年 份<br>Year | 地区生产总值(亿元)<br>Gross Domestic Product<br>(100 million yuan) | 第一产业<br>Primary Industry | 第二产业<br>Secondary Industry | 第三产业<br>Tertiary Industry | 人均地区生产总值(元)常住<br>Per Capita GDP(yuan)<br>Long－term Residents | 人均地区生产总值(元)户籍<br>Per Capita GDP(yuan)<br>Household Registered |
|---|---|---|---|---|---|---|
| 1949 | 2.55 | 1.43 | 0.38 | 0.74 | | 89 |
| 1950 | 2.99 | 1.73 | 0.48 | 0.79 | | 102 |
| 1951 | 3.76 | 1.94 | 0.86 | 0.96 | | 125 |
| 1952 | 4.47 | 2.28 | 1.05 | 1.14 | | 145 |
| 1953 | 5.02 | 2.32 | 1.32 | 1.37 | | 159 |
| 1954 | 5.17 | 2.28 | 1.50 | 1.40 | | 160 |
| 1955 | 5.37 | 2.43 | 1.49 | 1.45 | | 161 |
| 1956 | 6.20 | 2.50 | 1.94 | 1.76 | | 181 |
| 1957 | 7.04 | 2.33 | 2.61 | 2.10 | | 198 |
| 1958 | 9.91 | 2.55 | 5.28 | 2.07 | | 268 |
| 1959 | 12.50 | 2.63 | 7.20 | 2.71 | | 330 |
| 1960 | 13.39 | 2.49 | 7.74 | 3.16 | | 345 |
| 1961 | 10.70 | 2.70 | 5.16 | 2.84 | | 273 |
| 1962 | 9.94 | 3.04 | 4.24 | 2.67 | | 249 |
| 1963 | 10.32 | 3.28 | 4.39 | 2.64 | | 252 |
| 1964 | 11.56 | 3.39 | 5.49 | 2.68 | | 274 |
| 1965 | 12.77 | 3.56 | 6.38 | 2.83 | | 296 |
| 1966 | 13.91 | 3.82 | 7.10 | 2.99 | | 317 |
| 1967 | 13.27 | 3.72 | 6.49 | 3.05 | | 298 |
| 1968 | 13.06 | 3.77 | 6.26 | 3.03 | | 288 |
| 1969 | 15.13 | 3.81 | 8.09 | 3.23 | | 332 |
| 1970 | 16.73 | 4.07 | 9.25 | 3.42 | | 366 |
| 1971 | 19.10 | 4.74 | 10.59 | 3.77 | | 412 |
| 1972 | 19.92 | 5.19 | 10.83 | 3.90 | | 423 |
| 1973 | 20.75 | 4.99 | 11.72 | 4.04 | | 435 |
| 1974 | 18.98 | 5.14 | 9.80 | 4.04 | | 393 |
| 1975 | 18.63 | 4.88 | 9.62 | 4.13 | | 381 |
| 1976 | 19.04 | 5.00 | 9.87 | 4.17 | | 386 |
| 1977 | 23.06 | 4.91 | 13.59 | 4.56 | | 463 |
| 1978 | 28.40 | 6.34 | 16.93 | 5.13 | | 565 |
| 1979 | 33.53 | 8.39 | 19.41 | 5.73 | | 659 |
| 1980 | 40.65 | 8.15 | 25.35 | 7.14 | | 791 |
| 1981 | 46.82 | 9.10 | 28.76 | 8.96 | | 904 |
| 1982 | 50.19 | 10.88 | 29.47 | 9.84 | | 957 |
| 1983 | 55.89 | 10.11 | 33.44 | 12.34 | | 1054 |
| 1984 | 69.47 | 12.64 | 40.55 | 16.27 | | 1298 |
| 1985 | 90.49 | 15.97 | 52.09 | 22.44 | | 1675 |
| 1986 | 105.36 | 17.76 | 60.13 | 27.47 | | 1917 |
| 1987 | 126.02 | 20.44 | 71.89 | 33.69 | | 2276 |
| 1988 | 152.54 | 25.68 | 85.53 | 41.33 | | 2717 |
| 1989 | 166.29 | 28.27 | 89.67 | 48.35 | | 2928 |

# 1-19 全市生产总值(续)

## The city's GDP(continued)

| 年 份<br>Year | 地区生产总值(亿元)<br>Gross Domestic Product<br>(100 million yuan) | 第一产业<br>Primary Industry | 第二产业<br>Secondary Industry | 第三产业<br>Tertiary Industry | 人均地区生产总值(元)常住<br>Per Capita GDP(yuan)<br>Long-term Residents | 人均地区生产总值(元)户籍<br>Per Capita GDP(yuan)<br>Household Registered |
|---|---|---|---|---|---|---|
| 1990 | 189.62 | 30.94 | 96.17 | 62.51 | | 3310 |
| 1991 | 227.95 | 33.40 | 113.11 | 81.44 | | 3952 |
| 1992 | 290.07 | 34.90 | 148.78 | 106.38 | | 4996 |
| 1993 | 424.71 | 41.94 | 226.44 | 156.33 | | 7263 |
| 1994 | 585.52 | 57.51 | 314.34 | 213.67 | | 9924 |
| 1995 | 762.01 | 69.25 | 410.00 | 282.75 | | 12797 |
| 1996 | 906.61 | 84.00 | 477.62 | 344.99 | | 15095 |
| 1997 | 1036.33 | 91.36 | 541.50 | 403.47 | | 17113 |
| 1998 | 1134.89 | 96.06 | 587.96 | 450.88 | | 18611 |
| 1999 | 1225.28 | 97.58 | 630.75 | 496.95 | | 19961 |
| 2000 | 1395.67 | 103.96 | 717.88 | 573.83 | | 22554 |
| 2001 | 1582.94 | 111.46 | 803.16 | 668.32 | | 25313 |
| 2002 | 1798.96 | 114.64 | 912.78 | 771.53 | | 28421 |
| 2003 | 2118.71 | 126.59 | 1087.74 | 904.38 | | 33115 |
| 2004 | 2566.46 | 132.23 | 1334.99 | 1099.24 | | 39653 |
| 2005 | 2973.74 | 140.29 | 1524.25 | 1309.21 | | 45327 |
| 2006 | 3483.41 | 149.88 | 1763.65 | 1569.89 | 44639 | 52510 |
| 2007 | 4155.84 | 162.85 | 2085.15 | 1907.84 | 52065 | 62090 |
| 2008 | 4850.59 | 178.50 | 2419.08 | 2253.01 | 59619 | 71861 |
| 2009 | 5181.80 | 188.45 | 2404.92 | 2588.44 | 62673 | 76146 |
| 2010 | 6049.56 | 205.34 | 2861.45 | 2982.77 | 71007 | 88154 |
| 2011 | 7153.03 | 232.32 | 3326.34 | 3594.38 | 82014 | 103306 |
| 2012 | 7968.58 | 249.44 | 3553.18 | 4165.95 | 90862 | 114144 |
| 2013 | 8639.91 | 254.74 | 3649.62 | 4735.54 | 97925 | 122802 |
| 2014 | 9502.21 | 266.62 | 3953.53 | 5282.07 | 107152 | 133611 |
| 2015 | 10495.28 | 278.98 | 4133.92 | 6082.38 | 117200 | 145838 |
| 2016 | 11709.45 | 293.63 | 4226.87 | 7188.96 | 128633 | 160453 |
| 2017 | 13160.72 | 299.96 | 4453.44 | 8407.32 | 141088 | 176668 |
| 2018 | 14306.72 | 305.56 | 4694.06 | 9307.10 | 148456 | 187263 |
| 2019 | 15373.05 | 325.70 | 4875.07 | 10172.28 | 152465 | 195897 |

# 1-19 新中国成立以来主要指标之二:全市生产总值发展指数

## Main indicators since the founding of PRC: The developing indices of the city's GDP

(上年=100) (Preceding Year=100)

| 年 份<br>Year | 地区生产总值(%)<br>Gross Domestic Product(%) | 第一产业<br>Primary Industry | 第二产业<br>Secondary Industry | 第三产业<br>Tertiary Industry | 人均地区生产总值(%)常住<br>Per Capita GDP(%)<br>Long-term Residents | 人均地区生产总值(%)户籍<br>Per Capita GDP(%)<br>Household Registered |
|---|---|---|---|---|---|---|
| 1949 | 100.0 | 100.0 | 100.0 | 100.0 | | 100.0 |
| 1950 | 116.4 | 119.9 | 116.8 | 105.8 | | 113.0 |
| 1951 | 118.3 | 112.9 | 165.8 | 111.0 | | 115.4 |
| 1952 | 119.0 | 114.7 | 135.3 | 120.4 | | 116.1 |
| 1953 | 108.9 | 103.4 | 115.9 | 119.9 | | 106.2 |
| 1954 | 101.9 | 99.5 | 111.7 | 100.4 | | 99.5 |
| 1955 | 105.6 | 106.9 | 104.4 | 103.3 | | 102.3 |
| 1956 | 111.2 | 103.1 | 124.0 | 121.9 | | 108.4 |
| 1957 | 113.6 | 99.9 | 144.4 | 116.2 | | 109.4 |
| 1958 | 132.2 | 105.7 | 204.0 | 99.2 | | 127.6 |
| 1959 | 118.9 | 101.9 | 129.4 | 129.8 | | 116.1 |
| 1960 | 105.4 | 91.8 | 110.1 | 117.2 | | 102.8 |
| 1961 | 76.7 | 94.6 | 61.8 | 87.6 | | 76.0 |
| 1962 | 91.3 | 104.5 | 77.6 | 94.6 | | 89.7 |
| 1963 | 105.3 | 109.4 | 104.5 | 101.3 | | 102.5 |
| 1964 | 111.5 | 105.4 | 126.0 | 107.6 | | 108.4 |
| 1965 | 112.3 | 106.5 | 120.9 | 105.8 | | 109.7 |
| 1966 | 107.0 | 103.8 | 110.5 | 101.5 | | 105.3 |
| 1967 | 96.6 | 94.4 | 96.1 | 99.3 | | 95.0 |
| 1968 | 99.2 | 105.5 | 93.9 | 106.4 | | 97.6 |
| 1969 | 114.1 | 96.9 | 130.3 | 105.8 | | 113.3 |
| 1970 | 109.8 | 110.3 | 114.8 | 110.1 | | 109.6 |
| 1971 | 100.3 | 100.9 | 96.0 | 103.4 | | 99.0 |
| 1972 | 114.4 | 109.1 | 123.1 | 103.6 | | 112.5 |
| 1973 | 103.6 | 96.4 | 108.2 | 100.2 | | 102.2 |
| 1974 | 92.9 | 103.6 | 84.3 | 100.2 | | 91.9 |
| 1975 | 98.7 | 95.7 | 99.1 | 102.4 | | 97.7 |
| 1976 | 102.4 | 102.9 | 102.7 | 101.0 | | 101.2 |
| 1977 | 118.8 | 98.3 | 136.7 | 109.3 | | 117.9 |
| 1978 | 120.2 | 119.1 | 123.7 | 111.6 | | 119.0 |
| 1979 | 113.3 | 114.2 | 114.0 | 110.0 | | 112.1 |
| 1980 | 119.7 | 92.5 | 130.2 | 118.8 | | 118.4 |
| 1981 | 113.6 | 102.9 | 114.0 | 124.2 | | 112.6 |
| 1982 | 107.2 | 119.4 | 103.2 | 108.6 | | 105.9 |
| 1983 | 111.2 | 89.1 | 114.3 | 124.7 | | 109.9 |
| 1984 | 122.7 | 121.2 | 120.8 | 129.0 | | 121.6 |
| 1985 | 119.4 | 99.9 | 122.6 | 124.4 | | 118.2 |
| 1986 | 111.5 | 103.6 | 111.5 | 116.2 | | 110.3 |
| 1987 | 112.8 | 102.5 | 114.0 | 115.1 | | 111.3 |
| 1988 | 107.4 | 97.8 | 109.8 | 105.4 | | 105.8 |
| 1989 | 96.9 | 99.8 | 94.4 | 102.3 | | 95.8 |

# 1－19　全市生产总值发展指数(续)

## The developing indices of the city's GDP( continued)

(上年＝100)　　(Preceding Year＝100)

| 年　份 Year | 地区生产总值(％) Gross Domestic Product (％) | 第一产业 Primary Industry | 第二产业 Secondary Industry | 第三产业 Tertiary Industry | 人均地区生产总值(％)常住 Per Capita GDP(％) Long－term Residents | 人均地区生产总值(％)户籍 Per Capita GDP(％) Household Registered |
|---|---|---|---|---|---|---|
| 1990 | 105.8 | 106.4 | 106.5 | 103.8 | | 104.9 |
| 1991 | 118.1 | 104.4 | 116.6 | 127.0 | | 117.3 |
| 1992 | 122.9 | 100.3 | 129.7 | 122.3 | | 122.1 |
| 1993 | 130.1 | 105.9 | 138.3 | 125.8 | | 129.1 |
| 1994 | 126.3 | 108.1 | 132.1 | 122.0 | | 125.2 |
| 1995 | 119.9 | 107.1 | 123.1 | 117.6 | | 118.8 |
| 1996 | 113.0 | 105.4 | 114.5 | 112.2 | | 112.0 |
| 1997 | 113.1 | 106.8 | 112.8 | 114.8 | | 112.1 |
| 1998 | 111.2 | 109.4 | 111.8 | 110.7 | | 110.5 |
| 1999 | 110.2 | 105.5 | 110.1 | 111.1 | | 109.4 |
| 2000 | 112.0 | 105.7 | 112.5 | 112.1 | | 111.1 |
| 2001 | 112.2 | 107.4 | 112.7 | 112.5 | | 111.1 |
| 2002 | 113.2 | 104.1 | 113.3 | 114.7 | | 111.8 |
| 2003 | 115.2 | 106.0 | 118.6 | 112.6 | | 114.0 |
| 2004 | 115.0 | 105.1 | 116.7 | 114.3 | | 113.7 |
| 2005 | 113.1 | 103.4 | 111.6 | 116.5 | | 111.6 |
| 2006 | 114.3 | 104.1 | 112.5 | 117.4 | | 113.0 |
| 2007 | 114.7 | 102.8 | 114.4 | 116.3 | 112.2 | 113.7 |
| 2008 | 111.0 | 103.8 | 108.8 | 114.0 | 108.9 | 110.0 |
| 2009 | 110.0 | 103.1 | 106.0 | 114.7 | 108.2 | 109.1 |
| 2010 | 112.0 | 102.5 | 111.2 | 113.5 | 108.7 | 111.1 |
| 2011 | 110.1 | 102.5 | 108.5 | 112.2 | 107.5 | 109.1 |
| 2012 | 109.0 | 102.5 | 106.9 | 111.3 | 108.4 | 108.1 |
| 2013 | 108.0 | 101.4 | 106.7 | 109.5 | 107.3 | 107.2 |
| 2014 | 108.2 | 101.9 | 107.8 | 108.8 | 107.6 | 107.0 |
| 2015 | 110.2 | 101.8 | 105.5 | 114.6 | 109.1 | 108.9 |
| 2016 | 109.7 | 101.4 | 104.5 | 113.6 | 107.9 | 108.2 |
| 2017 | 108.2 | 101.7 | 104.8 | 110.6 | 105.6 | 106.0 |
| 2018 | 106.7 | 101.8 | 105.8 | 107.5 | 103.3 | 104.1 |
| 2019 | 106.8 | 101.9 | 105.0 | 108.0 | 102.0 | 103.9 |

注:本表按不变价格计算。

a) This table was calculated at comparable prices.

# 1－19　新中国成立以来主要指标之三：全市年末总人口（户籍）

## Main indicators since the founding of PRC: The total population of the city at the end of the year (household registration)

单位：万人　　　　(10000 Persons)

| 年　份<br>Year | 总户数<br>Total Households | 总人口<br>Total Population | 城镇人口<br>Urban Population | 按性别分 By Sex 男<br>Male | 女<br>Female |
|---|---|---|---|---|---|
| 1949 | | 288.08 | 68.67 | 152.99 | 135.09 |
| 1950 | | 297.64 | 70.08 | 158.74 | 138.90 |
| 1951 | | 304.89 | 73.10 | 163.27 | 141.61 |
| 1952 | | 318.97 | 75.18 | 164.60 | 147.52 |
| 1953 | | 328.63 | 77.17 | 168.69 | 150.28 |
| 1954 | | 339.29 | 82.71 | 173.67 | 154.96 |
| 1955 | | 346.57 | 85.27 | 179.25 | 160.04 |
| 1956 | | 365.64 | 86.97 | 182.86 | 163.71 |
| 1957 | | 372.75 | 99.49 | 192.46 | 173.18 |
| 1958 | | 384.41 | 108.15 | 198.82 | 173.93 |
| 1959 | | 391.16 | 117.88 | 204.89 | 179.52 |
| 1960 | | 391.16 | 126.55 | 207.87 | 183.29 |
| 1961 | | 393.79 | 119.23 | 207.15 | 186.64 |
| 1962 | | 403.74 | 108.96 | 211.02 | 192.72 |
| 1963 | | 416.36 | 108.83 | 217.15 | 199.21 |
| 1964 | | 426.76 | 104.96 | 222.66 | 204.10 |
| 1965 | | 435.66 | 107.29 | 226.56 | 209.10 |
| 1966 | | 441.84 | 106.64 | 229.25 | 212.59 |
| 1967 | | 449.35 | 107.92 | 233.27 | 216.18 |
| 1968 | | 456.39 | 107.14 | 236.76 | 219.63 |
| 1969 | | 455.58 | 104.49 | 235.77 | 219.81 |
| 1970 | | 458.82 | 101.94 | 237.09 | 221.73 |
| 1971 | | 467.81 | 105.98 | 241.93 | 225.88 |
| 1972 | | 474.06 | 109.08 | 244.68 | 229.88 |
| 1973 | | 480.62 | 110.10 | 248.06 | 232.56 |
| 1974 | | 485.68 | 109.87 | 250.73 | 234.95 |
| 1975 | | 491.68 | 110.87 | 253.71 | 237.97 |
| 1976 | | 495.91 | 112.05 | 255.78 | 240.10 |
| 1977 | | 499.96 | 112.14 | 257.75 | 242.20 |
| 1978 | 117.89 | 505.55 | 116.06 | 260.74 | 244.81 |
| 1979 | 116.61 | 511.83 | 124.60 | 263.97 | 247.86 |
| 1980 | 119.11 | 515.53 | 128.88 | 266.02 | 249.51 |
| 1981 | 125.96 | 520.73 | 134.56 | 268.69 | 252.04 |
| 1982 | 131.53 | 528.06 | 139.94 | 272.72 | 255.34 |
| 1983 | 135.55 | 533.05 | 143.34 | 275.64 | 257.41 |
| 1984 | 139.24 | 537.49 | 147.46 | 278.04 | 259.45 |
| 1985 | 145.23 | 543.05 | 153.46 | 281.11 | 261.94 |
| 1986 | 151.59 | 549.53 | 157.19 | 284.57 | 264.96 |
| 1987 | 157.66 | 557.63 | 161.12 | 288.70 | 268.93 |
| 1988 | 164.41 | 565.04 | 164.87 | 292.21 | 272.83 |
| 1989 | 169.09 | 570.98 | 167.28 | 295.15 | 275.83 |

# 1－19 全市年末总人口(户籍)(续)

The total population of the city at the end of the year (household registration) (continued)

单位:万人 (10000 Persons)

| 年 份<br>Year | 总户数<br>Total Households | 总人口<br>Total Population | | 按性别分<br>By Sex | |
|---|---|---|---|---|---|
| | | | 城镇人口<br>Urban Population | 男<br>Male | 女<br>Female |
| 1990 | 171.94 | 574.78 | 169.00 | 297.02 | 277.76 |
| 1991 | 174.78 | 578.73 | 171.25 | 298.85 | 279.88 |
| 1992 | 177.68 | 582.40 | 174.03 | 300.63 | 281.77 |
| 1993 | 179.17 | 587.10 | 179.11 | 303.03 | 284.07 |
| 1994 | 180.65 | 592.93 | 186.50 | 306.00 | 286.93 |
| 1995 | 182.55 | 597.96 | 191.43 | 308.25 | 289.71 |
| 1996 | 184.33 | 603.22 | 196.68 | 310.76 | 292.46 |
| 1997 | 186.28 | 607.96 | 204.39 | 313.02 | 294.94 |
| 1998 | 187.80 | 611.64 | 210.52 | 314.69 | 296.95 |
| 1999 | 191.60 | 616.05 | 219.05 | 316.63 | 299.42 |
| 2000 | 193.48 | 621.58 | 227.00 | 319.09 | 302.49 |
| 2001 | 195.56 | 629.14 | 237.77 | 322.78 | 306.36 |
| 2002 | 198.27 | 636.81 | 252.02 | 326.62 | 310.19 |
| 2003 | 201.12 | 642.78 | 263.67 | 329.04 | 313.74 |
| 2004 | 204.52 | 651.68 | 282.58 | 332.62 | 319.06 |
| 2005 | 207.42 | 660.45 | 297.54 | 336.12 | 324.33 |
| 2006 | 209.91 | 666.31 | 309.78 | 338.23 | 328.08 |
| 2007 | 211.99 | 672.35 | 323.75 | 340.50 | 331.85 |
| 2008 | 213.74 | 677.64 | 340.76 | 342.45 | 335.19 |
| 2009 | 215.28 | 683.38 | 354.48 | 344.51 | 338.87 |
| 2010 | 216.51 | 689.12 | 365.24 | 346.56 | 342.56 |
| 2011 | 218.26 | 695.71 | 376.03 | 349.09 | 346.62 |
| 2012 | 218.95 | 700.52 | 384.09 | 350.90 | 349.62 |
| 2013 | 220.66 | 706.61 | 393.88 | 353.32 | 353.29 |
| 2014 | 222.35 | 715.76 | 404.27 | 357.26 | 358.50 |
| 2015 | 225.79 | 723.55 | 447.24 | 360.68 | 362.87 |
| 2016 | 229.57 | 736.00 | 463.86 | 366.47 | 369.53 |
| 2017 | 235.26 | 753.88 | 482.55 | 374.75 | 379.12 |
| 2018 | 241.84 | 774.10 | 515.04 | 384.20 | 389.90 |
| 2019 | 248.14 | 795.37 | 535.96 | 394.26 | 401.11 |

## 1－19 新中国成立以来主要指标之四:全市人口自然变动情况(户籍)

## Main indicators since the founding of PRC: Natural changes of population in the city(household register)

| 年 份<br>Year | 人口自然变动人数(人) | | | 人口自然变动率(‰) | | |
|---|---|---|---|---|---|---|
| | 出生人数<br>Birth Population | 死亡人数<br>Death Population | 自然增长人数<br>Natural Growth Population | 出生率<br>Birth Rate(‰) | 死亡率<br>Death Rate | 自然增长率<br>Natural Growth Rate |
| 1949 | - | - | - | - | - | - |
| 1950 | 101227 | 41810 | 59417 | 34.56 | 14.28 | 20.28 |
| 1951 | 116825 | 43156 | 73669 | 38.78 | 14.32 | 24.46 |
| 1952 | 120319 | 45073 | 75246 | 39.00 | 14.61 | 24.39 |
| 1953 | 124863 | 44777 | 80086 | 39.57 | 14.19 | 25.38 |
| 1954 | 130491 | 45526 | 84965 | 40.30 | 14.06 | 26.24 |
| 1955 | 130236 | 43984 | 86252 | 39.00 | 13.17 | 25.83 |
| 1956 | 111440 | 30537 | 80903 | 32.50 | 8.90 | 23.60 |
| 1957 | 142406 | 34673 | 107733 | 39.99 | 9.74 | 30.25 |
| 1958 | 137238 | 35642 | 101596 | 37.17 | 9.65 | 27.52 |
| 1959 | 102030 | 40031 | 61999 | 26.95 | 10.57 | 16.38 |
| 1960 | 108282 | 34569 | 73713 | 27.92 | 8.91 | 19.01 |
| 1961 | 83206 | 34361 | 48845 | 21.20 | 8.75 | 12.45 |
| 1962 | 155335 | 32116 | 123219 | 38.95 | 8.05 | 30.90 |
| 1963 | 170431 | 30884 | 139547 | 41.59 | 7.54 | 34.05 |
| 1964 | 146073 | 36868 | 109205 | 34.62 | 8.74 | 25.88 |
| 1965 | 137319 | 32585 | 104734 | 31.85 | 7.56 | 24.29 |
| 1966 | 120047 | 31509 | 88538 | 27.36 | 7.18 | 20.18 |
| 1967 | 107577 | 28248 | 79329 | 24.14 | 6.34 | 17.80 |
| 1968 | 111134 | 28303 | 82831 | 24.55 | 6.25 | 18.30 |
| 1969 | 109723 | 26956 | 82767 | 24.06 | 5.91 | 18.15 |
| 1970 | 101075 | 27768 | 73307 | 22.08 | 6.08 | 16.00 |
| 1971 | 96497 | 28571 | 67926 | 20.83 | 6.17 | 14.66 |
| 1972 | 85188 | 27890 | 57298 | 18.09 | 5.92 | 12.17 |
| 1973 | 81414 | 28144 | 53270 | 17.06 | 5.90 | 11.16 |
| 1974 | 70353 | 29723 | 40630 | 14.56 | 6.15 | 8.41 |
| 1975 | 74209 | 29655 | 44554 | 15.19 | 6.07 | 9.12 |
| 1976 | 71064 | 30053 | 41011 | 14.39 | 6.09 | 8.30 |
| 1977 | 73471 | 33239 | 40232 | 14.76 | 6.68 | 8.08 |
| 1978 | 73550 | 29928 | 43622 | 14.63 | 5.95 | 8.68 |
| 1979 | 71442 | 29500 | 41942 | 14.04 | 5.80 | 8.24 |
| 1980 | 52145 | 30727 | 21418 | 10.15 | 5.98 | 4.17 |
| 1981 | 73015 | 31352 | 41663 | 14.09 | 6.05 | 8.04 |
| 1982 | 82910 | 30805 | 52105 | 15.81 | 5.87 | 9.94 |
| 1983 | 69940 | 33598 | 36342 | 13.18 | 6.33 | 6.85 |
| 1984 | 60091 | 33070 | 27021 | 11.23 | 6.18 | 5.05 |
| 1985 | 66757 | 33715 | 33042 | 12.36 | 6.24 | 6.12 |
| 1986 | 84702 | 33576 | 51126 | 15.50 | 6.15 | 9.35 |
| 1987 | 94127 | 33238 | 60889 | 17.00 | 6.00 | 11.00 |
| 1988 | 85472 | 35356 | 50116 | 15.23 | 6.30 | 8.93 |
| 1989 | 81048 | 34031 | 47017 | 14.27 | 5.99 | 8.28 |

# 1－19 全市人口自然变动情况(户籍)(续)

## Natural changes of population in the city(household register)(continued)

| 年 份<br>Year | 人口自然变动人数(人) | | | 人口自然变动率(‰) | | |
|---|---|---|---|---|---|---|
| | 出生人数<br>Birth Population | 死亡人数<br>Death Population | 自然增长人数<br>Natural Growth Population | 出生率<br>Birth Rate(‰) | 死亡率<br>Death Rate | 自然增长率<br>Natural Growth Rate |
| 1990 | 76579 | 34977 | 41602 | 13.37 | 6.11 | 7.26 |
| 1991 | 66144 | 33534 | 32610 | 11.47 | 5.81 | 5.66 |
| 1992 | 61708 | 34681 | 27027 | 10.63 | 5.97 | 4.66 |
| 1993 | 62465 | 34127 | 28338 | 10.68 | 5.84 | 4.84 |
| 1994 | 63580 | 35099 | 28481 | 10.78 | 5.95 | 4.83 |
| 1995 | 62586 | 36186 | 26400 | 10.51 | 6.08 | 4.43 |
| 1996 | 63680 | 35417 | 28263 | 10.60 | 5.90 | 4.70 |
| 1997 | 58471 | 34663 | 23808 | 9.65 | 5.72 | 3.93 |
| 1998 | 53951 | 38302 | 15649 | 8.85 | 6.28 | 2.57 |
| 1999 | 59085 | 36866 | 22219 | 9.63 | 6.01 | 3.62 |
| 2000 | 62300 | 40218 | 22082 | 10.07 | 6.50 | 3.57 |
| 2001 | 52088 | 33827 | 18261 | 8.33 | 5.41 | 2.92 |
| 2002 | 53064 | 35867 | 17197 | 8.38 | 5.67 | 2.72 |
| 2003 | 51420 | 36662 | 14758 | 8.04 | 5.73 | 2.31 |
| 2004 | 59940 | 34078 | 25862 | 9.26 | 5.27 | 3.99 |
| 2005 | 57233 | 35417 | 21816 | 8.72 | 5.39 | 3.33 |
| 2006 | 57790 | 38892 | 18898 | 8.71 | 5.86 | 2.85 |
| 2007 | 60296 | 37833 | 22463 | 9.01 | 5.65 | 3.36 |
| 2008 | 61332 | 42648 | 18684 | 9.09 | 6.32 | 2.77 |
| 2009 | 62441 | 39159 | 23282 | 9.18 | 5.76 | 3.42 |
| 2010 | 69606 | 46193 | 23413 | 10.14 | 6.73 | 3.41 |
| 2011 | 70337 | 38225 | 32112 | 10.16 | 5.52 | 4.64 |
| 2012 | 77349 | 49789 | 27560 | 11.08 | 7.13 | 3.95 |
| 2013 | 70850 | 37544 | 33306 | 10.07 | 5.34 | 4.73 |
| 2014 | 89743 | 40415 | 49328 | 12.62 | 5.68 | 6.94 |
| 2015 | 70617 | 40326 | 30291 | 9.81 | 5.60 | 4.21 |
| 2016 | 90896 | 35614 | 55282 | 12.46 | 4.88 | 7.58 |
| 2017 | 109496 | 63366 | 46130 | 14.70 | 8.51 | 6.19 |
| 2018 | 94713 | 46525 | 48188 | 12.40 | 6.09 | 6.31 |
| 2019 | 91450 | 36774 | 54676 | 11.65 | 4.68 | 6.97 |

# 1-19 新中国成立以来主要指标之五:全市农林牧渔业总产值

Main indicators since the founding of PRC: Total Output Value of Agriculture, Forestry, Animal Husbandry and Fishery in the City

单位:亿元 (100 million yuan)

| 年份 Year | 合计 Total | 为上年(%) | #农业 Agriculture | #林业 Forestry | #牧业 Husbandry | #渔业 Fishery |
|---|---|---|---|---|---|---|
| 1949 | 3.38 | - | 2.34 | 0.47 | 0.47 | 0.10 |
| 1950 | 4.03 | 119.3 | 2.85 | 0.55 | 0.52 | 0.11 |
| 1951 | 4.57 | 113.3 | 3.27 | 0.61 | 0.58 | 0.11 |
| 1952 | 5.16 | 112.9 | 3.71 | 0.65 | 0.69 | 0.12 |
| 1953 | 5.33 | 103.2 | 3.77 | 0.66 | 0.78 | 0.13 |
| 1954 | 5.24 | 98.5 | 3.58 | 0.73 | 0.80 | 0.13 |
| 1955 | 5.67 | 108.1 | 4.10 | 0.72 | 0.70 | 0.14 |
| 1956 | 5.99 | 105.7 | 4.15 | 0.80 | 0.89 | 0.15 |
| 1957 | 6.40 | 106.8 | 4.34 | 0.78 | 1.13 | 0.15 |
| 1958 | 6.76 | 105.6 | 4.97 | 0.80 | 0.86 | 0.13 |
| 1959 | 6.89 | 101.9 | 4.93 | 0.95 | 0.86 | 0.15 |
| 1960 | 6.32 | 91.8 | 4.53 | 0.86 | 0.80 | 0.13 |
| 1961 | 5.97 | 94.5 | 4.53 | 0.65 | 0.67 | 0.11 |
| 1962 | 6.24 | 104.4 | 4.63 | 0.71 | 0.80 | 0.09 |
| 1963 | 6.74 | 108.1 | 4.97 | 0.64 | 1.03 | 0.09 |
| 1964 | 7.20 | 106.8 | 5.24 | 0.66 | 1.19 | 0.11 |
| 1965 | 7.86 | 109.1 | 5.67 | 0.66 | 1.36 | 0.17 |
| 1966 | 8.10 | 103.1 | 5.82 | 0.67 | 1.47 | 0.14 |
| 1967 | 7.94 | 98.1 | 5.81 | 0.53 | 1.50 | 0.10 |
| 1968 | 7.98 | 100.5 | 5.92 | 0.59 | 1.35 | 0.11 |
| 1969 | 8.06 | 101.0 | 5.96 | 0.59 | 1.39 | 0.12 |
| 1970 | 8.40 | 104.7 | 6.15 | 0.56 | 1.61 | 0.13 |
| 1971 | 8.44 | 100.1 | 6.21 | 0.38 | 1.74 | 0.11 |
| 1972 | 9.16 | 108.5 | 6.85 | 0.43 | 1.79 | 0.11 |
| 1973 | 8.79 | 98.9 | 6.43 | 0.44 | 1.80 | 0.12 |
| 1974 | 9.05 | 103.0 | 6.61 | 0.46 | 1.87 | 0.11 |
| 1975 | 8.62 | 95.2 | 6.29 | 0.45 | 1.74 | 0.13 |
| 1976 | 8.85 | 102.7 | 6.72 | 0.49 | 1.53 | 0.12 |
| 1977 | 8.90 | 100.5 | 6.73 | 0.46 | 1.58 | 0.13 |
| 1978 | 8.59 | 114.0 | 6.74 | 0.34 | 1.45 | 0.07 |
| 1979 | 11.56 | 115.0 | 8.47 | 0.46 | 2.52 | 0.11 |
| 1980 | 11.24 | 92.3 | 7.90 | 0.73 | 2.50 | 0.11 |
| 1981 | 12.08 | 105.9 | 8.74 | 0.83 | 2.38 | 0.13 |
| 1982 | 15.06 | 116.5 | 10.76 | 0.89 | 3.18 | 0.23 |
| 1983 | 14.89 | 95.7 | 10.37 | 0.98 | 3.27 | 0.27 |
| 1984 | 17.70 | 113.5 | 12.26 | 1.48 | 3.59 | 0.38 |
| 1985 | 21.30 | 98.3 | 13.69 | 1.90 | 5.01 | 0.69 |
| 1986 | 23.83 | 105.8 | 15.08 | 2.00 | 5.82 | 0.93 |
| 1987 | 28.13 | 104.4 | 17.31 | 2.64 | 7.01 | 1.17 |
| 1988 | 35.85 | 101.0 | 20.88 | 3.14 | 10.10 | 1.72 |
| 1989 | 38.68 | 100.3 | 22.60 | 2.79 | 11.40 | 1.90 |

# 1－19　全市农林牧渔业总产值(续)

## Total Output Value of Agriculture, Forestry, Animal Husbandry and Fishery in the City (continued)

单位:亿元　　(100 million yuan)

| 年　份 Year | 合计 Total | 为上年(%) | #农业 Agriculture | #林业 Forestry | #牧业 Husbandry | #渔业 Fishery |
|---|---|---|---|---|---|---|
| 1990 | 42.10 | 103.3 | 26.00 | 2.70 | 11.34 | 2.06 |
| 1991 | 46.36 | 104.4 | 28.43 | 3.78 | 11.75 | 2.41 |
| 1992 | 49.79 | 104.7 | 30.08 | 3.56 | 13.39 | 2.76 |
| 1993 | 60.08 | 106.7 | 36.51 | 4.75 | 15.48 | 3.34 |
| 1994 | 81.25 | 106.6 | 49.64 | 5.86 | 21.72 | 4.02 |
| 1995 | 99.64 | 105.2 | 62.01 | 8.13 | 24.41 | 5.10 |
| 1996 | 117.33 | 104.7 | 74.02 | 9.57 | 27.17 | 6.57 |
| 1997 | 128.77 | 106.2 | 79.78 | 11.45 | 29.42 | 8.12 |
| 1998 | 136.76 | 105.2 | 84.51 | 12.12 | 28.91 | 11.22 |
| 1999 | 141.47 | 103.4 | 87.67 | 12.60 | 29.35 | 11.86 |
| 2000 | 152.65 | 107.9 | 90.33 | 13.68 | 33.16 | 15.48 |
| 2001 | 165.00 | 108.1 | 96.50 | 14.93 | 36.23 | 17.34 |
| 2002 | 168.50 | 102.1 | 93.30 | 16.22 | 39.19 | 19.80 |
| 2003 | 189.01 | 112.2 | 99.16 | 18.26 | 41.78 | 23.26 |
| 2004 | 198.27 | 104.9 | 101.09 | 20.68 | 45.76 | 23.41 |
| 2005 | 219.48 | 110.7 | 113.66 | 23.30 | 49.59 | 27.08 |
| 2006 | 225.38 | 102.7 | 122.48 | 26.77 | 49.04 | 20.61 |
| 2007 | 247.14 | 109.7 | 130.80 | 29.47 | 58.55 | 22.26 |
| 2008 | 273.76 | 110.8 | 140.81 | 32.02 | 63.66 | 30.93 |
| 2009 | 289.74 | 105.5 | 149.74 | 36.23 | 64.29 | 32.56 |
| 2010 | 316.34 | 109.2 | 169.88 | 32.93 | 70.56 | 34.90 |
| 2011 | 357.07 | 112.9 | 190.79 | 34.85 | 83.65 | 39.00 |
| 2012 | 384.34 | 107.6 | 207.72 | 38.18 | 86.85 | 42.00 |
| 2013 | 399.37 | 103.9 | 216.11 | 40.82 | 91.13 | 40.73 |
| 2014 | 418.58 | 104.8 | 233.38 | 47.02 | 82.82 | 44.20 |
| 2015 | 440.41 | 105.2 | 252.42 | 49.81 | 80.70 | 45.23 |
| 2016 | 449.01 | 102.0 | 262.15 | 53.05 | 76.88 | 43.61 |
| 2017 | 457.70 | 101.9 | 273.88 | 54.91 | 68.58 | 45.32 |
| 2018 | 466.10 | 101.8 | 282.71 | 57.30 | 61.85 | 47.47 |
| 2019 | 501.15 | 107.5 | 295.33 | 61.89 | 76.77 | 48.57 |

# 1－19 新中国成立以来主要指标之六:全市工业总产值

## Main indicators since the founding of PRC: Total Industrial Output Value of the City

单位:亿元 (100 million yuan)

| 年 份<br>Year | 规上工业总产值<br>Industry above Designated Size | 轻工业<br>Light Industry | 重工业<br>Heavy Industry | #国有经济<br>State－owned | #集体经济<br>Collective－owned |
|---|---|---|---|---|---|
| 1962 | 9.96 | | | 8.93 | 1.02 |
| 1963 | 10.35 | | | 9.40 | 0.95 |
| 1964 | 12.40 | | | 11.29 | 1.12 |
| 1965 | 14.70 | | | 13.35 | 1.35 |
| 1966 | 17.42 | | | 15.84 | 1.58 |
| 1967 | 16.22 | | | 14.57 | 1.65 |
| 1968 | 15.35 | | | 13.67 | 1.67 |
| 1969 | 20.17 | | | 18.02 | 2.15 |
| 1970 | 23.49 | | | 20.63 | 2.87 |
| 1971 | 26.48 | | | 22.98 | 3.51 |
| 1972 | 27.75 | | | 23.72 | 4.03 |
| 1973 | 30.73 | | | 26.02 | 4.71 |
| 1974 | 25.56 | | | 20.78 | 4.79 |
| 1975 | 24.33 | | | 19.08 | 5.25 |
| 1976 | 25.39 | | | 19.45 | 5.93 |
| 1977 | 35.09 | | | 27.37 | 7.71 |
| 1978 | 42.96 | | | 33.48 | 9.48 |
| 1979 | 49.58 | | | 37.89 | 11.69 |
| 1980 | 61.79 | | | 45.13 | 16.66 |
| 1981 | 68.99 | | | 48.24 | 20.51 |
| 1982 | 73.50 | | | 50.98 | 22.07 |
| 1983 | 83.00 | | | 55.29 | 27.18 |
| 1984 | 100.84 | | | 43.43 | 36.70 |
| 1985 | 128.59 | 79.38 | 49.21 | 72.62 | 54.66 |
| 1986 | 153.48 | | | 84.25 | 67.80 |
| 1987 | 190.01 | | | 100.36 | 86.34 |
| 1988 | 245.67 | | | 124.10 | 116.32 |
| 1989 | 274.03 | | | 141.56 | 124.74 |
| 1990 | 292.26 | 184.89 | 107.37 | 153.29 | 130.09 |
| 1991 | 352.49 | 220.18 | 132.31 | 177.94 | 160.14 |
| 1992 | 452.74 | 273.52 | 179.22 | 214.10 | 208.40 |
| 1993 | 637.99 | | | 250.54 | 287.48 |
| 1994 | 843.37 | | | 313.82 | 379.09 |
| 1995 | 1020.03 | 560.07 | 459.96 | 358.53 | 399.96 |

# 1－19 全市工业总产值(续)

## Total Industrial Output Value of the City (continued)

单位:亿元 (100 million yuan)

| 年 份<br>Year | 规上工业总产值<br>Industry above Designated Size | 轻工业<br>Light Industry | 重工业<br>Heavy Industry | #国有经济<br>State－owned | #集体经济<br>Collective－owned |
|---|---|---|---|---|---|
| 1996 | 883.12 | 460.67 | 422.44 | 290.56 | 332.08 |
| 1997 | 911.47 | 487.19 | 424.28 | 318.59 | 297.16 |
| 1998 | 1109.94 | 572.64 | 537.30 | 342.23 | 282.48 |
| 1999 | 1200.08 | 613.00 | 587.08 | 316.46 | 254.40 |
| 2000 | 1543.57 | 762.33 | 781.24 | 186.03 | 269.84 |
| 2001 | 1919.51 | 995.70 | 923.81 | 178.88 | 191.13 |
| 2002 | 2400.30 | 1243.55 | 1156.75 | 214.71 | 215.15 |
| 2003 | 3202.52 | 1565.25 | 1637.28 | 248.42 | 244.40 |
| 2004 | 4486.58 | 1976.19 | 2510.38 | 342.00 | 55.89 |
| 2005 | 5441.13 | 2405.97 | 3035.16 | 605.43 | 60.34 |
| 2006 | 6975.46 | 2909.35 | 4066.11 | 677.68 | 66.76 |
| 2007 | 8351.40 | 3587.84 | 4763.56 | 768.89 | 51.79 |
| 2008 | 9379.58 | 3873.53 | 5506.05 | 744.07 | 38.61 |
| 2009 | 9390.73 | 4011.60 | 5379.14 | 757.65 | 35.47 |
| 2010 | 11081.04 | 4576.47 | 6504.57 | 905.05 | 30.03 |
| 2011 | 12352.92 | 4866.08 | 7486.84 | 1022.05 | 17.19 |
| 2012 | 12959.68 | 5137.76 | 7821.92 | 1150.72 | 16.73 |
| 2013 | 12418.00 | 4866.38 | 7551.63 | 714.09 | 3.98 |
| 2014 | 12853.05 | 4997.92 | 7855.13 | 692.22 | 3.22 |
| 2015 | 12415.68 | 4820.80 | 7594.88 | 230.94 | 1.41 |
| 2016 | 12420.96 | 4693.99 | 7726.97 | 553.41 | 1.23 |
| 2017 | 12963.76 | 4711.50 | 8252.27 | 187.04 | 0.59 |
| 2018 | 14106.41 | 4882.08 | 9134.33 | 169.11 | 0.24 |
| 2019 | 14585.45 | 5221.27 | 9364.18 | 177.62 | – |

# 1-19 新中国成立以来主要指标之七:金融机构存贷款余额

## Main indicators since the founding of PRC: Deposit and loan balance of financial institutions

单位:万元 (10000 Yuan)

| 年份<br>Year | 各项存款合计<br>Deposits Total | #住户存款<br>Household Deposits | 各项贷款合计<br>Loans Total |
|---|---|---|---|
| 1949 | 241 | | 131 |
| 1950 | 2044 | | 63 |
| 1951 | 5475 | | 2214 |
| 1952 | 7727 | | 4533 |
| 1953 | 7806 | | 7693 |
| 1954 | 7358 | | 14900 |
| 1955 | 8996 | | 10697 |
| 1956 | 8751 | | 9674 |
| 1957 | 14878 | | 11494 |
| 1958 | 10898 | | 26220 |
| 1959 | 17912 | | 46141 |
| 1960 | 17303 | | 61064 |
| 1961 | 18943 | | 45856 |
| 1962 | 22739 | | 33740 |
| 1963 | 21725 | | 24558 |
| 1964 | 23522 | | 24721 |
| 1965 | 25415 | | 29611 |
| 1966 | 28844 | | 41399 |
| 1967 | 31748 | | 44880 |
| 1968 | 36039 | | 53683 |
| 1969 | 30962 | | 56059 |
| 1970 | 35967 | | 68278 |
| 1971 | 41903 | | 72507 |
| 1972 | 44029 | | 77571 |
| 1973 | 59975 | | 106073 |
| 1974 | 63586 | | 118245 |
| 1975 | 70118 | | 123201 |
| 1976 | 74508 | | 128047 |
| 1977 | 87634 | | 128238 |
| 1978 | 86824 | 20714 | 136759 |
| 1979 | 108998 | 28937 | 135713 |
| 1980 | 180707 | 40447 | 174153 |
| 1981 | 226949 | 51440 | 236678 |
| 1982 | 262156 | 67192 | 216040 |
| 1983 | 303130 | 86635 | 236203 |
| 1984 | 388305 | 115766 | 329195 |
| 1985 | 484999 | 159596 | 580180 |
| 1986 | 635514 | 222110 | 769841 |
| 1987 | 776105 | 302762 | 967477 |
| 1988 | 839680 | 351943 | 1145989 |
| 1989 | 1017087 | 501592 | 1338984 |

# 1－19　金融机构存贷款余额(续)

## Deposit and loan balance of financial institutions (continued)

单位:万元　　(10000 Yuan)

| 年　份<br>Year | 各项存款合计<br>Deposits Total | #住户存款<br>Household Deposits | 各项贷款合计<br>Loans Total |
|---|---|---|---|
| 1990 | 1646165 | 697515 | 1803266 |
| 1991 | 2036334 | 904490 | 2136903 |
| 1992 | 2652966 | 1144737 | 2651983 |
| 1993 | 3469954 | 1563328 | 3415527 |
| 1994 | 5061345 | 2394370 | 4450932 |
| 1995 | 7079650 | 3423379 | 5672105 |
| 1996 | 9619291 | 4638458 | 7434243 |
| 1997 | 12251840 | 5583306 | 9388500 |
| 1998 | 14948225 | 6701158 | 11620537 |
| 1999 | 17886717 | 7425967 | 14937506 |
| 2000 | 20884723 | 7885579 | 16866431 |
| 2001 | 26215100 | 9418400 | 20877000 |
| 2002 | 33731500 | 11834000 | 27523800 |
| 2003 | 46527300 | 15899600 | 38187000 |
| 2004 | 57072000 | 18351700 | 48000400 |
| 2005 | 67487200 | 21916600 | 55453000 |
| 2006 | 78555500 | 25552400 | 66038600 |
| 2007 | 93109600 | 26348300 | 84306800 |
| 2008 | 113333500 | 34765900 | 100690500 |
| 2009 | 142842104 | 42869189 | 131133023 |
| 2010 | 170843548 | 49909744 | 150787269 |
| 2011 | 183965719 | 55474824 | 165737441 |
| 2012 | 201487672 | 60899841 | 180908011 |
| 2013 | 221747107 | 64085856 | 193504605 |
| 2014 | 244505093 | 67672009 | 213168315 |
| 2015 | 298638294 | 76177515 | 233279520 |
| 2016 | 333860429 | 84932733 | 261689982 |
| 2017 | 364832373 | 86705977 | 292709406 |
| 2018 | 398104954 | 101985223 | 365982478 |
| 2019 | 452869942 | 119012969 | 422451656 |

# 1-19 新中国成立以来主要指标之八:市区城市供电、供水

## Main indicators since the founding of PRC: Urban Power Supply and Water Supply

| 年 份<br>Year | 供电总量 | | | 供水总量 | | |
|---|---|---|---|---|---|---|
| | 合计(亿千瓦时) | #工业用电 | #生活用电 | 合计(万吨) | #生产用水 | #生活用水 |
| 1949 | 0.24 | 0.15 | 0.08 | 191 | 25 | 166 |
| 1950 | - | - | - | - | - | - |
| 1951 | - | - | - | - | - | - |
| 1952 | 0.43 | 0.35 | 0.06 | 229 | 65 | 164 |
| 1953 | 0.53 | 0.43 | 0.07 | 353 | 109 | 244 |
| 1954 | 0.67 | 0.57 | 0.08 | 452 | 148 | 304 |
| 1955 | 0.66 | 0.55 | 0.08 | 540 | 162 | 378 |
| 1956 | 0.82 | 0.68 | 0.10 | 714 | 249 | 464 |
| 1957 | 0.90 | 0.72 | 0.12 | 845 | 310 | 535 |
| 1958 | 1.47 | 1.27 | 0.13 | 1264 | 622 | 642 |
| 1959 | 2.18 | 1.91 | 0.16 | 2097 | 1259 | 838 |
| 1960 | 2.94 | 2.61 | 0.17 | 2909 | 1834 | 1075 |
| 1961 | 2.73 | 2.37 | 0.18 | 2647 | 1600 | 1047 |
| 1962 | 2.50 | 2.06 | 0.21 | 2556 | 1465 | 1091 |
| 1963 | 2.56 | 2.09 | 0.23 | 2561 | 1440 | 1121 |
| 1964 | 3.00 | 2.50 | 0.25 | 2924 | 1679 | 1244 |
| 1965 | 3.49 | 2.97 | 0.26 | 3164 | 1937 | 1227 |
| 1966 | 4.02 | 3.46 | 0.27 | 3669 | 2392 | 1277 |
| 1967 | 3.74 | 3.11 | 0.51 | 3892 | 2388 | 1504 |
| 1968 | - | - | - | 3891 | 2369 | 1522 |
| 1969 | 4.15 | 3.48 | 0.58 | 4766 | 3100 | 1666 |
| 1970 | 4.68 | 4.00 | 0.59 | 4972 | 3360 | 1578 |
| 1971 | 5.34 | 4.49 | 0.70 | 5978 | 4072 | 1868 |
| 1972 | 5.80 | 4.95 | 0.72 | 6548 | 4440 | 2018 |
| 1973 | 5.94 | 5.05 | 0.77 | 6755 | 4562 | 2193 |
| 1974 | 5.15 | 4.20 | 0.81 | 6725 | 4482 | 2243 |
| 1975 | 4.93 | 3.94 | 0.85 | 7007 | 4707 | 2300 |
| 1976 | 5.40 | 4.33 | 0.92 | 7379 | 4992 | 2387 |
| 1977 | 7.57 | 5.72 | 1.02 | 8140 | 5498 | 2642 |
| 1978 | 8.01 | 6.52 | 1.26 | 9072 | 6116 | 2956 |
| 1979 | 9.04 | 7.23 | 1.54 | 10548 | 6813 | 3388 |
| 1980 | 10.25 | 8.73 | 1.17 | 11199 | 7359 | 3840 |
| 1981 | 10.87 | 8.98 | 1.45 | 12662 | 7943 | 4718 |
| 1982 | 11.62 | 9.41 | 1.70 | 13761 | 8272 | 5380 |
| 1983 | 12.60 | 10.13 | 1.88 | 14226 | 8211 | 6015 |
| 1984 | 13.70 | 10.72 | 2.24 | 15586 | 8713 | 6800 |
| 1985 | 14.94 | 11.18 | 2.34 | 17484 | 8599 | 8144 |
| 1986 | 15.85 | 12.96 | 0.78 | 17894 | 8527 | 9367 |
| 1987 | 16.97 | 13.56 | 1.04 | 18911 | 9424 | 9487 |
| 1988 | 17.95 | 13.96 | 1.30 | 19806 | 10028 | 9764 |
| 1989 | 18.51 | 14.20 | 1.51 | 20733 | 8780 | 11941 |

# 1－19　市区城市供电、供水(续)

# Urban Power Supply and Water Supply (continued)

| 年　　份 Year | 供电总量 | | | 供水总量 | | |
|---|---|---|---|---|---|---|
| | 合计(亿千瓦时) | #工业用电 | #生活用电 | 合计(万吨) | #生产用水 | #生活用水 |
| 1990 | 19.95 | 14.89 | 1.86 | 22290 | 8945 | 13301 |
| 1991 | 21.16 | 15.69 | 1.99 | 22772 | 9223 | 13522 |
| 1992 | 23.34 | 17.04 | 2.31 | 24412 | 10052 | 14338 |
| 1993 | 25.70 | 18.21 | 2.69 | 25333 | 10022 | 15289 |
| 1994 | 29.49 | 19.68 | 3.57 | 25902 | 9707 | 16195 |
| 1995 | 31.41 | 20.89 | 4.07 | 27740 | 9380 | 18336 |
| 1996 | 35.41 | 21.67 | 5.26 | 27216 | 8845 | 18125 |
| 1997 | 42.39 | 25.82 | 6.32 | 26513 | 7593 | 18920 |
| 1998 | 48.46 | 28.58 | 7.67 | 26593 | 8075 | 17838 |
| 1999 | 51.19 | 29.55 | 7.90 | 25504 | 7395 | 18109 |
| 2000 | 60.19 | 33.52 | 9.86 | 33725 | 8100 | 19410 |
| 2001 | 133.12 | 92.99 | 16.79 | 52000 | 18324 | 25710 |
| 2002 | 156.61 | 110.31 | 18.76 | 53372 | 18180 | 31408 |
| 2003 | 190.12 | 131.87 | 23.67 | 59180 | 21796 | 30743 |
| 2004 | 207.75 | 146.56 | 23.89 | 62265 | 23544 | 29187 |
| 2005 | 244.78 | 172.56 | 27.98 | 73331 | 27327 | 35220 |
| 2006 | 279.94 | 197.61 | 32.53 | 64764 | 20258 | 33979 |
| 2007 | 313.47 | 219.92 | 36.86 | 66753 | 19519 | 33682 |
| 2008 | 325.75 | 221.28 | 41.15 | 68178 | 19354 | 35902 |
| 2009 | 346.93 | 230.20 | 45.31 | 69499 | 16671 | 37274 |
| 2010 | 392.64 | 258.35 | 50.74 | 53565 | 11479 | 30978 |
| 2011 | 432.57 | 282.95 | 55.49 | 52660 | 11884 | 22384 |
| 2012 | 444.95 | 278.93 | 63.62 | 58183 | 12478 | 22861 |
| 2013 | 484.05 | 296.08 | 71.52 | 60747 | 13005 | 23733 |
| 2014 | 552.71 | 355.06 | 72.56 | 66172 | 14792 | 26894 |
| 2015 | 559.54 | 345.23 | 78.27 | 66760 | 14902 | 26162 |
| 2016 | 583.96 | 337.04 | 93.03 | 65087 | 14161 | 25078 |
| 2017 | 673.73 | 389.00 | 105.29 | 83192 | 16157 | 33960 |
| 2018 | 724.31 | 397.72 | 117.67 | 88568 | 15866 | 35778 |
| 2019 | 738.88 | 381.96 | 125.83 | 99156 | 21534 | 40117 |

# 1－20 市区分月气象概况(2019 年)

# Monthly Meteorological Conditions in Urban District(2019)

| 月 份 | Month | 平均气温(度) Average Temperature(℃) | 日照时数(小时) Sunshine Hours(hours) | 降雨天数(天) Rainfall Days (day) | 降水量(毫米) Precipitation(mm) |
|---|---|---|---|---|---|
| **全 年** | **Whole Year** | **18.0** | **1657.9** | **160.0** | **1649.9** |
| 1 月 | January | 5.9 | 71.4 | 14 | 96.1 |
| 2 月 | February | 6.1 | 24.3 | 21 | 233.6 |
| 3 月 | March | 12.4 | 127.1 | 18 | 113.2 |
| 4 月 | April | 18.1 | 125.0 | 17 | 77.8 |
| 5 月 | May | 22.1 | 174.7 | 9 | 116.8 |
| 6 月 | June | 25.0 | 118.5 | 16 | 204.0 |
| 7 月 | July | 28.2 | 162.5 | 14 | 207.9 |
| 8 月 | August | 29.4 | 228.5 | 12 | 346.4 |
| 9 月 | September | 25.1 | 189.7 | 9 | 105.4 |
| 10 月 | October | 20.1 | 151.1 | 8 | 27.7 |
| 11 月 | November | 14.5 | 149.2 | 10 | 26.1 |
| 12 月 | December | 9.1 | 135.9 | 12 | 94.9 |

# 1－21 气　象

# Meteorological

| 指　标 |  | Item |  | 市区 Urban District | 萧山区 Xiaoshan |
|---|---|---|---|---|---|
| **一、气　温** |  | **The Atmospheric Temperature** |  |  |  |
| 全年平均气温 | （度） | Annual Average Temperature | （℃） | 18.0 | 17.7 |
| 极端最高气温 | （度） | The Highest Temperature of the Year | （℃） | 38.9 | 38.3 |
| 出现日期 | （日/月） | Date | （d/m） | 7月30日 | 7月26日、7月27日 |
| 极端最低气温 | （度） | The Lowest Temperature of the Year | （℃） | －0.9 | －0.1 |
| 出现日期 | （日/月） | Date | （d/m） | 1月27日 | 1月27日 |
| **二、降　雨** |  | **Rainfall** |  |  |  |
| 本年降雨日数 | （日） | Total Rainy Days | （day） | 160 | 155 |
| 全年降雨总量 | （毫米） | Annual Rainfall | （millimeters） | 1649.9 | 1700.1 |
| 最长连续降雨日数 | （日） | Longest Consecutive Days of Rain | （day） | 16 | 16 |
| 最长连续降雨总量 | （毫米） | Rainfall | （millimeters） | 206.0 | 198.6 |
| 最长连续降雨起止日期 | （日/月） | Start/End | （d/m） | 2月7日－2月22日 | 2月7日－2月22日 |
| 日最大降雨量 | （毫米） | Maximum Daily Rainfall | （millimeters） | 133.3 | 125.8 |
| 出现日期 | （日/月） | Date | （d/m） | 8月10日 | 7月13日 |
| **三、全年日照总时数** | **（小时）** | **Total Sunshine Hours** | **（hours）** | **1657.9** | **1624.7** |
| **四、降　霜** |  | **Frost** |  |  |  |
| 全年降霜日数 | （日） | Annual Frost Days | （day） | 12 | 10 |
| 初霜日期 | （日/月） | Start Date | （d/m） | 2018年12月17日 | 2018年12月3日 |
| 终霜日期 | （日/月） | End Date | （d/m） | 2019年1月27日 | 2019年1月27日 |
| **五、降　雪** |  | **Snow** |  |  |  |
| 全年降雪日数 | （日） | Annual Frost Days | （day） | 8 | 8 |
| 初雪日期 | （日/月） | Start Date | （d/m） | 2018年12月7日 | 2018年12月7日 |
| 终雪日期 | （日/月） | End Date | （d/m） | 2019年2月17日 | 2019年2月17日 |

## 概　　况(2019年)
## Conditions by Region(2019)

| 余杭区 Yuhang | 富阳区 Fuyang | 临安区 Lin'an | 桐庐县 Tonglu | 淳安县 Chun'an | 建德市 Jiande |
|---|---|---|---|---|---|
| 17.8 | 17.8℃ | 16.9 | 17.6 | 18.0 | 17.8 |
| 38.8 | 37.8℃ | 38.5 | 39.4 | 38.3 | 38.7 |
| 7月30日 | 7月31日 | 7月30日 | 8月28日 | 7月27日 | 7月27日、8月28日 |
| -0.4 | -1.9 | -3.7 | -2.0 | 0.1 | -1.8 |
| 1月27日 | 1月27日 | 1月27日 | 1月27日 | 1月27日 | 1月27日 |
| 119 | 164 | 154 | 172天 | 160 | 158 |
| 1492.6 | 1664.8 | 1659.3 | 1781.9 | 1661.6 | 1868.1 |
| 16 | 16 | 11 | 18 | 18 | 18 |
| 185.1 | 182.5 | 161.4 | 196.4 | 191.5 | 193.8 |
| 2月7日-2月22日 | 2月7日-2月22日 | 2月12日-2月22日 | 2月7日-2月24日 | 2月7日-2月24日 | 2月7日-2月24日 |
| 120.6 | 135.9 | 111.2 | 159.1 | 151.6 | 111.3 |
| 8月10日 | 7月13日 | 8月10日 | 6月19日 | 5月15日 | 5月15日 |
| **1657.9** | **1576.6** | **1612.3** | **1632.2** | **1765.0** | **1585.8** |
| 无观测 | 10 | 17 | 8 | 4 | 8 |
| 无观测 | 2018年12月19日 | 2019年1月18日 | 2018年12月3日 | 2018年12月4日 | 2018年12月3日 |
| 无观测 | 2019年1月27日 | 2019年2月1日 | 2019年2月1日 | 2019年1月27日 | 2019年1月27日 |
| 8 | 5 | 6 | 6 | 2 | 2 |
| 2019年1月15日 | 2018年12月7日 | 2018年12月7日 | 2018年12月20日 | 2018年12月8日 | 2018年12月8日 |
| 2019年2月17日 | 2019年2月17日 | 2019年2月17日 | 2019年2月13日 | 2019年2月24日 | 2019年1月2日 |

# 主要统计指标解释

**地区生产总值(GDP)** 指一个国家(或地区)所有常住单位在一定时期内生产活动的最终成果。地区生产总值有三种表现形态,即价值形态、收入形态和产品形态。从价值形态看,它是所有常住单位在一定时期内生产的全部货物和服务价值超过同期投入的全部非固定资产货物和服务价值的差额,即所有常住单位的增加值之和;从收入形态看,它是所有常住单位在一定时期内创造并分配给常住单位和非常住单位的初次收入分配之和;从产品形态看,它是所有常住单位在一定时期内最终使用的货物和服务价值与货物和服务净出口价值之和。在实际核算中,生产总值有三种计算方法,即生产法、收入法和支出法。三种方法分别从不同的方面反映生产总值及其构成。

**三次产业** 是根据社会生产活动历史发展的顺序对产业结构的划分,产品直接取自自然界的部门称为第一产业,对初级产品进行再加工的部门称为第二产业,为生产和消费提供各种服务的部门称为第三产业。它是世界上较为通用的产业结构分类,但各国的划分不尽一致。2012 年前的三次产业划分标准按照当年《统计年鉴》,从 2013 年起,三次产业划分调整为:

第一产业是指农、林、牧、渔业(不含农、林、牧、渔服务业)。

第二产业是指工业[采矿业(不含开采辅助活动),制造业(不含金属制品、机械和设备修理业),电力、热力、燃气及水生产和供应业]和建筑业。

第三产业即服务业,是指除第一产业、第二产业以外的其他行业。

**可比价格** 指在不同时期的价值指标对比时,扣除了价格变动的因素,以确切反映物量的变化。按可比价格计算有两种方法:一种是直接用产品产量乘每一年的不变价格计算;另一种使用价格指数换算。

**不变价格** 指用同类产品的年平均价格作为固定价格,来计算各年产品价值。按不变价格计算的产品价值消除了价格变动因素,不同时期对比可反映出生产的发展速度。新中国成立后,随着工农业产品价格的变化,国家统计局先后五次制定了全国统一的工业产品不变价格和农业产品不变价格,从 1949 年到 1957 年使用 1952 工(农)业产品不变价格,从 1957 年到 1971 年使用 1957 年不变价格,从 1981 年到 1990 年使用 1980 年不变价格,从 1991 年到 2000 年使用 1990 年不变价格,从 2001 年到 2005 年使用 2000 年不变价格,从 2006 年到 2010 年使用 2005 年不变价格,从 2011 年到 2015 年使用 2010 年不变价格,从 2016 年到 2020 年使用 2015 年不变价格。

**数字经济** 按照《国民经济行业分类(2017 版)》新的行业分类目录,界定数字经济核心产业统计分类目录,确定了计算机通信和其他电子设备制造业、电子信息机电制造业、专用电子设备制造业、电信广播电视和卫星传输服务业、互联网及其相关服务业、软件和信息技术服务业、文化数字内容及其服务业等 7 大类 128 个小类行业作为数字经济核心产业统计范围,并确定在全省组织开展数字经济核心产业定期统计监测工作。

**"1+6 产业集群"** 2016 年,杭州在国民经济和社会发展第"十三个"五年规划纲要中,提出:构建以信息经济为引领、现代服务业为主导、先进制造业为支撑、都市现代农业为基础的现代产业新体系,推进产业迈向中高端。确立发展万亿信息产业集群以及文化创意、旅游休闲、金融服务、健康、时尚、高端装备制造等六大千亿产业集群的目标。

**降水量** 从天空降落到地面的液态或固态(经融化后)降水,未经蒸发、渗透、流失而在水平面上积聚的深度。降水量以毫米为单位。

**空气的温度(简称气温)** 表示空气冷热程度的物理量。

**日照时数** 太阳在一地实际照射地面的时数。

# Explanatory Notes on Main Statistical Indicators

**Gross Domestic Product (GDP)** refers to the final products of all resident units in a country (or a region) during a certain period of time. Gross domestic product is expressed in three different forms, i. e. value, income, and products respectively. The form of value refers to the total value of all products and services produced by all resident units during a certain period of time minus total value of input of materials and services of the nature of non – fixed assets or the summation of the value – added of all resident units; the form of income includes all the income created by all resident units and distributed primarily to all resident and non – resident units; the form of products refers to all goods and services for final use by all resident units plus net export of goods and services during a given period of time. In the practice of national accounting, gross domestic product is calculated with three approaches, i. e. production approach, income approach, and expenditure approach, which reflect gross domestic product and its composition from different aspects.

**Three Industries** Industry structure has been classified according to the historical sequence of development. Primary Industry refers to extraction of natural resources; Secondary Industry involves processing of primary products; and Tertiary Industry provides services of various kinds for production and consumption. The above classification is universal although it varies to some extent from country to country. The division standard of three industries was in accordance with Hangzhou Statistical Yearbook of the year before 2012, but since 2013 it has been adjusted as follows.

Primary Industry refers to agriculture, forestry, animal husbandry and fishery industries (excluding their service industries).

Second Industry refers to industry [mining(excluding its support activities), manufacturing( excluding the repair services of metal product, machine and equipment), production and supply of electricity, heat, water and gas] and construction.

Tertiary Industry is the service industry, refers to all other industries other than Primary or Secondary industries.

**Comparable Price** refers to the price deducting the factor of price change when comparing value indicators of different periods to reflect accurately the changes in physical value. There are two methods to calculate comparable price: one is to multiply the output of products by their constant prices of a certain year, and the other is to converse the data by relevant price index.

**Constant Price** refers to the average price of a given production a certain year, which is used to calculate the product value per year. The product value calculated on constant prices eliminates the factor of price changes, so its comparison between different periods may reflect the speed of production development. Since the establishment of new China,, with the changes in general price level, the State Statistical Bureau has issued nationally unified constant prices for five times. The 1952 constant prices had been used from1949 to1957, the 1957 constant prices from1957 to1971, the 1970 constant prices from1971 to1981, the 1980 constant prices from1981 to1990, the 1990 constant prices from 1991 to 2000, the 2000 constant prices from 2001 to 2005, the 2005 constant prices from 2006 to 2010, the 2010 constant prices from 2011 to 2015, and the 2015 constant prices from 2016 to 2020.

**Digital Economy** According to the new industry classification catalogue of national economic industry classification (2017 Edition), define the statistical classification catalogue of core industries of digital economy. The statistical scope of the core industries of digital economy is determined as seven categories and 128 sub industries, including computer communication and other electronic equipment manufacturing industry, electronic information electromechanical manufacturing industry, special electronic equipment manufacturing industry, telecommunication, radio and television and satellite transmission service industry, Internet and its related service industry, software and information technology service industry, cultural digital content and its service industry. The regular statistical monitoring work of digital economy core industry is launched in the whole province.

**"1 +6"Industrial Cluster** In 2016, in the outline of the 13th five – year plan for national economic and social development, Hangzhou suggested to establish a new system of modern industry led by the information economy , dominated by the modern service industry, supported by the advanced manufacturing industry and based on the urban modern agriculture to promote industries to develop towards medium and high end. An aim is established to develop a trillion – scale information industrial cluster, and six hundred – billion – scale industrial cluster of Cultural and Creative Industry, Tourism Leisure Industry, Financial Services Industry, Health Industry, Fashion Industry and High – end Equipment Manufacturing Industry.

**Precipitation** refers to the depth of the water accumulated on the horizontal plane by rainwater, liquid or melt from solid, falling from the sky to the ground without evaporation, infiltration and loss.

It is calculated in the unit of millimeter (mm).

**Air Temperature** refers to the physical quantity indicating the degree of coldness or hotness of the air.

**Duration of sunshine** refers to the number of hours the sun actually shines on the ground in one place.

# 二、人口和就业人员

POPULATION AND EMPLOYMENT

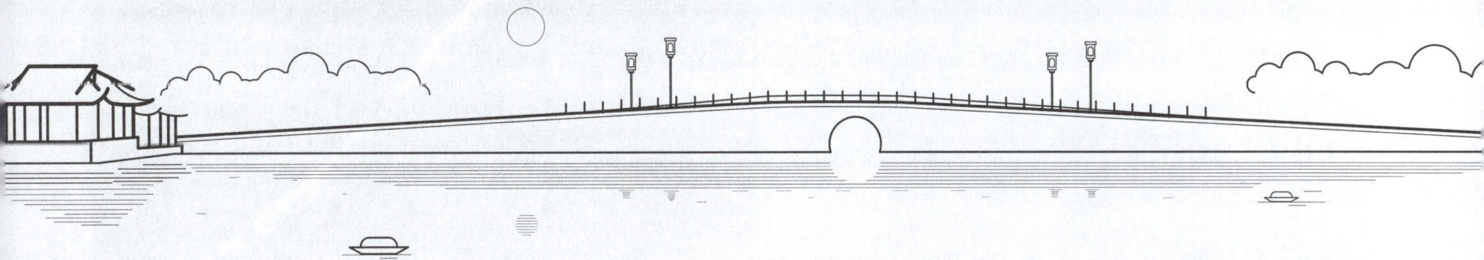

# 2 人口和就业人员
# Population and Employment

## 主要统计指标
## Major Statistical Indicators

| | | | | |
|---|---|---|---|---|
| 年末常住人口 | Long-term Residents(year-end) | 1036 | 万人 | (10, 000 persons) |
| 为上年 | As Compared with the Preceding Year | 105.6 | % | (%) |
| #城镇人口 | Urban Population | 813.30 | 万人 | (10, 000 persons) |
| 年末户籍登记户数 | Total Registration Households(year-end) | 248.14 | 万户 | (10, 000 Subscribers) |
| 为上年 | As Compared with the Preceding Year | 102.6 | % | (%) |
| 年末户籍登记人口 | Total Registration Population(year-end) | 795.37 | 万人 | (10, 000 persons) |
| 为上年 | As Compared with the Preceding Year | 102.7 | % | (%) |
| #男性 | Male | 394.26 | 万人 | (10, 000 persons) |
| 为上年 | As Compared with the Preceding Year | 102.6 | % | (%) |
| 户籍人口自然增长率 | Natural Growth Rate of Household Registered Population | 6.97 | ‰ | (‰) |
| 年末就业人员 | Number of Employed Persons(year-end) | 720.00 | 万人 | (10, 000 persons) |
| 为上年 | As Compared with the Preceding Year | 103.4 | % | (%) |

# 2-01 历次普查常住人口情况

## Long-term Residents in the Past Population Census

单位:万人 （10000 person）

| 地 区 | Region | 第一次人口普查 1953.7.1 the First Population Census (1953.7.1) | 第二次人口普查 1964.7.1 the Second Population Census (1964.7.1) | 第三次人口普查 1982.7.1 the Third Population Census (1982.7.1) | 第四次人口普查 1990.7.1 the Fourth Population Census (1990.7.1) | 第五次人口普查 2000.11.1 the Fifth Population Census (2000.11.1) | 第六次人口普查 2010.11.1 the Sixth Population Census (2010.11.1) |
|---|---|---|---|---|---|---|---|
| **杭州市** | **Hangzhou** | **301.13** | **421.90** | **526.05** | **583.21** | **687.87** | **870.04** |
| 市 区 | Urban District | 227.49 | 318.88 | 405.55 | 454.38 | 564.52 | 752.64 |
| #上城区 | Shangcheng | | | | 21.10 | 33.51 | 34.46 |
| 下城区 | Xiacheng | | | | 25.66 | 41.24 | 52.61 |
| 江干区 | Jianggan | | | | 36.12 | 56.54 | 99.88 |
| 拱墅区 | Gongshu | | | | 29.34 | 42.93 | 55.19 |
| 西湖区 | Xihu | | | | 35.40 | 59.33 | 82.00 |
| 高新(滨江)区 | Hi-Tech(Binjiang) | | | | | 11.59 | 31.90 |
| 萧山区 | Xiaoshan | 56.32 | 82.34 | 106.11 | 113.06 | 123.33 | 151.13 |
| 余杭区 | Yuhang | 52.28 | 64.96 | 80.50 | 86.08 | 81.77 | 117.03 |
| 富阳区 | Fuyang | 29.22 | 39.66 | 54.13 | 58.07 | 62.86 | 71.77 |
| 临安区 | Lin'an | 26.01 | 35.57 | 45.65 | 49.55 | 51.42 | 56.67 |
| 桐庐县 | Tonglu | 19.73 | 26.20 | 34.83 | 37.66 | 37.81 | 40.64 |
| 淳安县 | Chun'an | 27.49 | 38.66 | 42.03 | 43.55 | 38.23 | 33.68 |
| 建德市 | Jiande | 26.42 | 38.15 | 43.64 | 47.63 | 47.31 | 43.08 |

注:历年普查市区口径均已按现行行政辖区调整。

a) The data of the past population censuses in urban district were adjusted according to the current administrative division.

# 2-02 户籍人口和总户数(1978-2019年)

# Household Registered Population and Households(1978-2019)

| 年 份<br>Year | 总户数<br>(万户)<br>Total Households<br>(10000 households) | 总人口数<br>(万人)<br>Total Population<br>(10000 persons) | 城镇人口(万人)<br>Urban Population<br>(10000 persons) | 按性别分 By Sex<br>男(万人)<br>Male<br>(10000 persons) | 按性别分 By Sex<br>女(万人)<br>Female<br>(10000 persons) |
|---|---|---|---|---|---|
| 1978 | 117.89 | 505.55 | 116.06 | 260.74 | 244.81 |
| 1979 | 116.61 | 511.83 | 124.60 | 263.97 | 247.86 |
| 1980 | 119.11 | 515.53 | 128.88 | 266.02 | 249.51 |
| 1981 | 125.96 | 520.73 | 134.56 | 268.69 | 252.04 |
| 1982 | 131.53 | 528.06 | 139.94 | 272.72 | 255.34 |
| 1983 | 135.55 | 533.06 | 143.34 | 275.64 | 257.41 |
| 1984 | 139.24 | 537.49 | 147.46 | 278.04 | 259.45 |
| 1985 | 145.23 | 543.05 | 153.46 | 281.11 | 261.94 |
| 1986 | 151.59 | 549.53 | 157.19 | 284.57 | 264.96 |
| 1987 | 157.66 | 557.63 | 161.12 | 288.70 | 268.93 |
| 1988 | 164.41 | 565.04 | 164.87 | 292.21 | 272.83 |
| 1989 | 169.09 | 570.98 | 167.28 | 295.15 | 275.83 |
| 1990 | 171.94 | 574.78 | 169.00 | 297.02 | 277.76 |
| 1991 | 174.78 | 578.73 | 171.25 | 298.85 | 279.88 |
| 1992 | 177.68 | 582.40 | 174.03 | 300.63 | 281.77 |
| 1993 | 179.17 | 587.10 | 179.11 | 303.03 | 284.07 |
| 1994 | 180.65 | 592.93 | 186.50 | 306.00 | 286.93 |
| 1995 | 182.55 | 597.96 | 191.43 | 308.25 | 289.71 |
| 1996 | 184.33 | 603.22 | 196.68 | 310.76 | 292.46 |
| 1997 | 186.28 | 607.96 | 204.39 | 313.02 | 294.94 |
| 1998 | 187.80 | 611.64 | 210.52 | 314.69 | 296.95 |
| 1999 | 191.60 | 616.05 | 219.05 | 316.63 | 299.42 |
| 2000 | 193.48 | 621.58 | 227.00 | 319.09 | 302.49 |
| 2001 | 195.56 | 629.14 | 237.77 | 322.78 | 306.36 |
| 2002 | 198.27 | 636.81 | 252.02 | 326.62 | 310.19 |
| 2003 | 201.12 | 642.78 | 263.67 | 329.04 | 313.74 |
| 2004 | 204.52 | 651.68 | 282.58 | 332.62 | 319.06 |
| 2005 | 207.42 | 660.45 | 297.54 | 336.12 | 324.33 |
| 2006 | 209.91 | 666.31 | 309.78 | 338.23 | 328.08 |
| 2007 | 211.99 | 672.35 | 323.75 | 340.50 | 331.85 |
| 2008 | 213.74 | 677.64 | 340.76 | 342.45 | 335.19 |
| 2009 | 215.28 | 683.38 | 354.48 | 344.51 | 338.87 |
| 2010 | 216.51 | 689.12 | 365.24 | 346.56 | 342.56 |
| 2011 | 218.26 | 695.71 | 376.03 | 349.09 | 346.62 |
| 2012 | 218.95 | 700.52 | 384.09 | 350.90 | 349.62 |
| 2013 | 220.66 | 706.61 | 393.88 | 353.32 | 353.29 |
| 2014 | 222.35 | 715.76 | 404.27 | 357.26 | 358.50 |
| 2015 | 225.79 | 723.55 | 447.24 | 360.68 | 362.87 |
| 2016 | 229.57 | 736.00 | 463.86 | 366.47 | 369.53 |
| 2017 | 235.26 | 753.88 | 482.55 | 374.75 | 379.12 |
| 2018 | 241.84 | 774.10 | 515.04 | 384.20 | 389.90 |
| 2019 | 248.14 | 795.37 | 535.96 | 394.26 | 401.11 |

注:1. 按公安户籍人口统计。

2. 城镇人口2015年前为非农业人口。

a) Figures in this table are based on the household registered statistics which published by Public Security Bureau.

b) Since 2015, the donotation of Non-agriculture Population has been adjusted to Urban Population.

# 2-03 市区户籍人口和总户数(1978-2019年)

# Household Registered Population and Households of Urban District(1978-2019)

| 年份 Year | 总户数(万户) Total Households (10000 households) | 总人口数(万人) Total Population (10000 persons) | 城镇人口(万人) Urban Population (10000 persons) | 按性别分 By Sex 男(万人) Male (10000 persons) | 女(万人) Female (10000 persons) |
|---|---|---|---|---|---|
| 1978 | 25.52 | 104.53 | 78.73 | 53.95 | 50.58 |
| 1979 | 26.23 | 110.50 | 85.05 | 57.09 | 53.41 |
| 1980 | 27.23 | 113.08 | 87.93 | 58.56 | 54.52 |
| 1981 | 29.88 | 115.59 | 90.53 | 59.96 | 55.63 |
| 1982 | 31.24 | 118.05 | 92.72 | 61.28 | 56.77 |
| 1983 | 32.69 | 120.13 | 94.94 | 62.43 | 57.70 |
| 1984 | 34.07 | 122.29 | 97.34 | 63.63 | 58.66 |
| 1985 | 35.36 | 124.67 | 100.01 | 64.96 | 59.71 |
| 1986 | 37.02 | 127.07 | 102.59 | 66.29 | 60.78 |
| 1987 | 38.70 | 129.16 | 104.09 | 67.38 | 61.78 |
| 1988 | 40.05 | 131.26 | 107.30 | 68.46 | 62.80 |
| 1989 | 41.19 | 132.84 | 108.88 | 69.28 | 63.56 |
| 1990 | 42.26 | 133.89 | 109.97 | 69.75 | 64.14 |
| 1991 | 42.98 | 134.97 | 111.20 | 70.33 | 64.64 |
| 1992 | 43.63 | 136.30 | 112.70 | 71.08 | 65.22 |
| 1993 | 44.55 | 138.33 | 115.13 | 72.22 | 66.11 |
| 1994 | 45.04 | 141.27 | 118.48 | 73.82 | 67.45 |
| 1995 | 46.06 | 143.52 | 121.38 | 74.91 | 68.61 |
| 1996 | 52.39 | 166.73 | 128.76 | 87.15 | 79.58 |
| 1997 | 53.14 | 169.29 | 131.76 | 88.53 | 80.76 |
| 1998 | 53.92 | 171.89 | 134.62 | 89.86 | 82.03 |
| 1999 | 54.64 | 175.27 | 139.29 | 91.65 | 83.62 |
| 2000 | 55.34 | 179.18 | 143.69 | 93.64 | 85.54 |
| 2001 | 115.81 | 379.49 | 193.26 | 194.59 | 184.90 |
| 2002 | 117.11 | 387.01 | 205.98 | 198.47 | 188.54 |
| 2003 | 119.01 | 393.19 | 216.13 | 201.14 | 192.05 |
| 2004 | 120.56 | 401.59 | 233.08 | 204.43 | 197.16 |
| 2005 | 122.02 | 409.52 | 245.56 | 207.70 | 201.82 |
| 2006 | 123.31 | 414.18 | 256.42 | 209.45 | 204.73 |
| 2007 | 124.40 | 419.50 | 269.30 | 211.59 | 207.91 |
| 2008 | 125.56 | 424.30 | 285.11 | 213.54 | 210.76 |
| 2009 | 126.92 | 429.44 | 297.83 | 215.56 | 213.88 |
| 2010 | 128.43 | 434.82 | 307.52 | 217.65 | 217.16 |
| 2011 | 130.14 | 440.34 | 317.63 | 219.86 | 220.48 |
| 2012 | 131.48 | 445.43 | 325.50 | 221.99 | 223.43 |
| 2013 | 133.27 | 450.82 | 334.38 | 224.24 | 226.58 |
| 2014 | 157.11 | 525.07 | 358.56 | 261.17 | 263.90 |
| 2015 | 160.47 | 532.86 | 389.14 | 264.71 | 268.15 |
| 2016 | 164.22 | 544.68 | 403.20 | 270.31 | 274.38 |
| 2017 | 188.48 | 615.23 | 440.61 | 304.86 | 310.37 |
| 2018 | 194.84 | 635.30 | 469.27 | 314.28 | 321.02 |
| 2019 | 201.01 | 656.56 | 488.16 | 324.39 | 332.17 |

注:城镇人口2015年前为非农业人口。

a) Since 2015, the donotation of Non-agriculture Population has been adjusted to Urban Population.

# 2－04 分地区户籍人口和总户数(2019年末)

# Household Registered Population and Households by Region(End of 2019)

| 地 区<br>Region | 总户数<br>(户)<br>Total Households<br>(household) | 总人口数<br>(人)<br>Total Population<br>(person) | 按性别分<br>By Sex | |
|---|---|---|---|---|
| | | | 男(人)<br>Male<br>(person) | 女(人)<br>Female<br>(person) |
| **全 市<br>Whole City** | **2481448** | **7953740** | **3942625** | **4011115** |
| 市 区<br>Urban District | 2010114 | 6565571 | 3243886 | 3321685 |
| #上城区<br>Shangcheng | 111586 | 319039 | 158142 | 160897 |
| 下城区<br>Xiacheng | 132502 | 423678 | 208085 | 215593 |
| 江干区<br>Jianggan | 198458 | 641610 | 317414 | 324196 |
| 拱墅区<br>Gongshu | 139808 | 396799 | 195884 | 200915 |
| 西湖区<br>Xihu | 216430 | 768457 | 383157 | 385300 |
| 西湖风景名胜区<br>The West Lake Scenic Zone | 6179 | 19430 | 9098 | 10332 |
| 高新(滨江)区<br>Hi－Tech(Binjiang) | 76551 | 278241 | 140541 | 137700 |
| 萧山区<br>Xiaoshan | 390685 | 1348413 | 661176 | 687237 |
| 余杭区<br>Yuhang | 337057 | 1161786 | 567602 | 594184 |
| 富阳区<br>Fuyang | 218125 | 688075 | 344408 | 343667 |
| 临安区<br>Lin'an | 188912 | 539473 | 267477 | 271996 |
| 钱塘新区<br>Qiantang | 84073 | 304339 | 151082 | 153257 |
| 桐庐县<br>Tonglu | 149452 | 418803 | 208160 | 210643 |
| 淳安县<br>Chun'an | 146895 | 458669 | 231966 | 226703 |
| 建德市<br>Jiande | 174987 | 510697 | 258613 | 252084 |

注:西湖区包含风景名胜区,江干、萧山含托管在钱塘新区的街道数据。

a) Figures of Xihu include the West Lake Scenic Zone, and Figures of Jianggan and Xiaoshan include districts which under administered by Qiantang New Area.

# 2-05 分地区户籍人口年龄构成(2019年末)

## Age Structure of Household Registered Population by Region(End of 2019)

| 地区<br>Region | 0-17岁<br>0~17 years old | | 18-34岁<br>18~34 years old | | 35-59岁<br>35~59 years old | | 60岁以上<br>over 60 years old | |
|---|---|---|---|---|---|---|---|---|
| | 人数(人)<br>Number of people<br>(person) | 占总人口%<br>of the total population | 人数(人)<br>Number of people<br>(person) | 占总人口%<br>of the total population | 人数(人)<br>Number of people<br>(person) | 占总人口%<br>of the total population | 人数(人)<br>Number of people<br>(person) | 占总人口%<br>of the total population |
| **全 市<br>Whole City** | **1398979** | **17.6** | **1737756** | **21.8** | **3012714** | **37.9** | **1804291** | **22.7** |
| 市 区<br>Urban District | 1194333 | 18.2 | 1445424 | 22.0 | 2454201 | 37.4 | 1471613 | 22.4 |
| #上城区<br>Shangcheng | 39215 | 12.3 | 62371 | 19.5 | 114640 | 35.9 | 102813 | 32.2 |
| 下城区<br>Xiacheng | 55776 | 13.2 | 104330 | 24.6 | 148638 | 35.1 | 114934 | 27.1 |
| 江干区<br>Jianggan | 141949 | 22.1 | 149778 | 23.3 | 231385 | 36.1 | 118498 | 18.5 |
| 拱墅区<br>Gongshu | 71570 | 18.0 | 78645 | 19.8 | 147683 | 37.2 | 98901 | 24.9 |
| 西湖区<br>Xihu | 153149 | 19.9 | 183507 | 23.9 | 292091 | 38.0 | 139710 | 18.2 |
| 西湖风景名胜区<br>The West Lake Scenic Zone | | | | | | | | |
| 高新(滨江)区<br>Hi-Tech(Binjiang) | 64493 | 23.2 | 78252 | 28.1 | 97519 | 35.0 | 37977 | 13.6 |
| 萧山区<br>Xiaoshan | 229552 | 17.0 | 284331 | 21.1 | 498344 | 37.0 | 336186 | 24.9 |
| 余杭区<br>Yuhang | 248422 | 21.4 | 255015 | 22.0 | 424962 | 36.6 | 233387 | 20.1 |
| 富阳区<br>Fuyang | 111375 | 16.2 | 141001 | 20.5 | 280717 | 40.8 | 154982 | 22.5 |
| 临安区<br>Lin'an | 78832 | 14.6 | 108194 | 20.1 | 218222 | 40.5 | 134225 | 24.9 |
| 钱塘新区<br>Qiantang | | | | | | | | |
| 桐庐县<br>Tonglu | 64557 | 15.4 | 88173 | 21.1 | 164750 | 39.3 | 101323 | 24.2 |
| 淳安县<br>Chun'an | 67603 | 14.7 | 94087 | 20.5 | 191411 | 41.7 | 105568 | 23.0 |
| 建德市<br>Jiande | 72486 | 14.2 | 110072 | 21.6 | 202352 | 39.6 | 125787 | 24.6 |

# 2-06 户籍人口自然变动情况(1978-2019年)

# Natural Changes of Household Registered Population(1978-2019)

| 年份 Year | 出生 Birth | | 死亡 Death | | 自然增长 Natural Growth | |
|---|---|---|---|---|---|---|
| | 人数(人) Birth Population (person) | 出生率(‰) Birth Rate(‰) | 人数(人) Death Population (person) | 死亡率(‰) Death Rate(‰) | 人数(人) Natural Growth Population (person) | 自然增长率(‰) Natural Growth Rate(‰) |
| 1978 | 73550 | 14.63 | 29928 | 5.95 | 43622 | 8.68 |
| 1979 | 71442 | 14.04 | 29500 | 5.80 | 41942 | 8.24 |
| 1980 | 52145 | 10.15 | 30727 | 5.98 | 21418 | 4.17 |
| 1981 | 73015 | 14.09 | 31352 | 6.05 | 41663 | 8.04 |
| 1982 | 82910 | 15.81 | 30805 | 5.87 | 52105 | 9.94 |
| 1983 | 69940 | 13.18 | 33598 | 6.33 | 36342 | 6.85 |
| 1984 | 60091 | 11.23 | 33070 | 6.18 | 27021 | 5.05 |
| 1985 | 66757 | 12.36 | 33715 | 6.24 | 33042 | 6.12 |
| 1986 | 84702 | 15.50 | 33576 | 6.15 | 51126 | 9.35 |
| 1987 | 94127 | 17.00 | 33238 | 6.00 | 60889 | 11.00 |
| 1988 | 85472 | 15.23 | 35356 | 6.30 | 50116 | 8.93 |
| 1989 | 81048 | 14.27 | 34031 | 5.99 | 47017 | 8.28 |
| 1990 | 76579 | 13.37 | 34977 | 6.11 | 41602 | 7.26 |
| 1991 | 66144 | 11.47 | 33534 | 5.81 | 32610 | 5.66 |
| 1992 | 61708 | 10.63 | 34681 | 5.97 | 27027 | 4.66 |
| 1993 | 62465 | 10.68 | 34127 | 5.84 | 28338 | 4.84 |
| 1994 | 63580 | 10.78 | 35099 | 5.95 | 28481 | 4.83 |
| 1995 | 62586 | 10.51 | 36186 | 6.08 | 26400 | 4.43 |
| 1996 | 63680 | 10.60 | 35417 | 5.90 | 28263 | 4.70 |
| 1997 | 58471 | 9.65 | 34663 | 5.72 | 23808 | 3.93 |
| 1998 | 53951 | 8.85 | 38302 | 6.28 | 15649 | 2.57 |
| 1999 | 59085 | 9.63 | 36866 | 6.01 | 22219 | 3.62 |
| 2000 | 62300 | 10.07 | 40218 | 6.50 | 22082 | 3.57 |
| 2001 | 52088 | 8.33 | 33827 | 5.41 | 18261 | 2.92 |
| 2002 | 53064 | 8.38 | 35867 | 5.67 | 17197 | 2.72 |
| 2003 | 51420 | 8.04 | 36662 | 5.73 | 14758 | 2.31 |
| 2004 | 59940 | 9.26 | 34078 | 5.27 | 25862 | 3.99 |
| 2005 | 57233 | 8.72 | 35417 | 5.39 | 21816 | 3.33 |
| 2006 | 57790 | 8.71 | 38892 | 5.86 | 18898 | 2.85 |
| 2007 | 60296 | 9.01 | 37833 | 5.65 | 22463 | 3.36 |
| 2008 | 61332 | 9.09 | 42648 | 6.32 | 18684 | 2.77 |
| 2009 | 62441 | 9.18 | 39159 | 5.76 | 23282 | 3.42 |
| 2010 | 69606 | 10.14 | 46193 | 6.73 | 23413 | 3.41 |
| 2011 | 70337 | 10.16 | 38225 | 5.52 | 32112 | 4.64 |
| 2012 | 77349 | 11.08 | 49789 | 7.13 | 27560 | 3.95 |
| 2013 | 70850 | 10.07 | 37544 | 5.34 | 33306 | 4.73 |
| 2014 | 89743 | 12.62 | 40415 | 5.68 | 49328 | 6.94 |
| 2015 | 70617 | 9.81 | 40326 | 5.60 | 30291 | 4.21 |
| 2016 | 90896 | 12.46 | 35614 | 4.88 | 55282 | 7.58 |
| 2017 | 109496 | 14.70 | 63366 | 8.51 | 46130 | 6.19 |
| 2018 | 94713 | 12.40 | 46525 | 6.09 | 48188 | 6.31 |
| 2019 | 91450 | 11.65 | 36774 | 4.68 | 54676 | 6.97 |

注:本表按公安部门统计。

a) Figures in this table are based on the Public Security Bureau.

# 2－07 市区户籍人口自然变动情况(1978－2019年)

## Natural Changes of Household Registered Population of Urban District(1978－2019)

| 年份 Year | 出生 Birth | | 死亡 Death | | 自然增长 Natural Growth | |
|---|---|---|---|---|---|---|
| | 人数(人) Birth Population (person) | 出生率(‰) Birth Rate(‰) | 人数(人) Death Population (person) | 死亡率(‰) Death Rate(‰) | 人数(人) Natural Growth Population (person) | 自然增长率(‰) Natural Growth Rate(‰) |
| 1978 | 11923 | 11.56 | 6449 | 6.25 | 5474 | 5.31 |
| 1979 | 13184 | 12.26 | 5808 | 5.40 | 7376 | 6.86 |
| 1980 | 9708 | 8.68 | 6511 | 5.82 | 3197 | 2.86 |
| 1981 | 14938 | 13.06 | 6599 | 5.77 | 8339 | 7.29 |
| 1982 | 18092 | 15.49 | 6494 | 5.56 | 11598 | 9.93 |
| 1983 | 17107 | 14.36 | 6949 | 5.84 | 10158 | 8.52 |
| 1984 | 16257 | 13.41 | 6892 | 5.69 | 9365 | 7.72 |
| 1985 | 15824 | 12.81 | 7403 | 6.84 | 8421 | 6.82 |
| 1986 | 17120 | 13.60 | 6865 | 5.45 | 10255 | 8.15 |
| 1987 | 18701 | 14.60 | 7070 | 5.52 | 11631 | 9.08 |
| 1988 | 18503 | 14.21 | 7503 | 5.76 | 11000 | 8.45 |
| 1989 | 15868 | 12.02 | 6985 | 5.29 | 8883 | 6.73 |
| 1990 | 14085 | 10.56 | 7490 | 5.62 | 6595 | 4.94 |
| 1991 | 10195 | 7.58 | 7025 | 5.22 | 3170 | 2.36 |
| 1992 | 9994 | 7.37 | 7259 | 5.35 | 2735 | 2.02 |
| 1993 | 10099 | 7.35 | 7196 | 5.24 | 2903 | 2.11 |
| 1994 | 9918 | 7.09 | 7082 | 5.06 | 2836 | 2.03 |
| 1995 | 9806 | 6.89 | 7367 | 5.17 | 2439 | 1.72 |
| 1996 | 12098 | 7.80 | 8221 | 5.30 | 3877 | 2.50 |
| 1997 | 12304 | 7.32 | 8630 | 5.13 | 3674 | 2.19 |
| 1998 | 11714 | 6.87 | 9060 | 5.31 | 2654 | 1.56 |
| 1999 | 13694 | 7.89 | 8148 | 4.69 | 5546 | 3.20 |
| 2000 | 15058 | 8.50 | 10996 | 6.20 | 4062 | 2.30 |
| 2001 | 30902 | 8.22 | 19439 | 5.17 | 11463 | 3.05 |
| 2002 | 33156 | 8.65 | 19922 | 5.20 | 13234 | 3.45 |
| 2003 | 29019 | 7.44 | 21176 | 5.43 | 7843 | 2.01 |
| 2004 | 34858 | 8.77 | 19445 | 4.89 | 15413 | 3.88 |
| 2005 | 34056 | 8.39 | 21310 | 5.25 | 12746 | 3.14 |
| 2006 | 33260 | 8.08 | 21156 | 5.14 | 12104 | 2.94 |
| 2007 | 37029 | 8.88 | 20051 | 4.81 | 16978 | 4.07 |
| 2008 | 38703 | 9.17 | 21428 | 5.08 | 17275 | 4.09 |
| 2009 | 40293 | 9.44 | 22178 | 5.20 | 18115 | 4.24 |
| 2010 | 47052 | 10.89 | 25404 | 5.88 | 21648 | 5.01 |
| 2011 | 47256 | 10.80 | 22140 | 5.06 | 25116 | 5.74 |
| 2012 | 51892 | 11.72 | 27271 | 6.16 | 24621 | 5.56 |
| 2013 | 48107 | 10.74 | 21332 | 4.76 | 26775 | 5.97 |
| 2014 | 69577 | 13.36 | 27249 | 5.23 | 42328 | 8.13 |
| 2015 | 55275 | 10.45 | 26492 | 5.01 | 28783 | 5.44 |
| 2016 | 71427 | 13.26 | 23544 | 4.37 | 47883 | 8.89 |
| 2017 | 92571 | 15.96 | 52817 | 9.11 | 39754 | 6.85 |
| 2018 | 80238 | 12.83 | 36336 | 5.81 | 43902 | 7.02 |
| 2019 | 78168 | 12.10 | 27683 | 4.28 | 50485 | 7.82 |

# 2-08 分地区户籍人口自然变动情况(2019年)
## Natural Changes of Household Registered Population by Region(2019)

| 地区<br>Region | 出生<br>Birth | | 死亡<br>Death | | 自然增长<br>Natural Growth | |
|---|---|---|---|---|---|---|
| | 人数(人)<br>Birth Population<br>(person) | 出生率(‰)<br>Birth<br>Rate(‰) | 人数(人)<br>Death Population<br>(person) | 死亡率(‰)<br>Death<br>Rate(‰) | 人数(人)<br>Natural Growth<br>Population<br>(person) | 自然增长率(‰)<br>Natural Growth<br>Rate(‰) |
| **全市<br>Whole City** | **91450** | **11.65** | **36774** | **4.68** | **54676** | **6.97** |
| 市区<br>Urban District | 78168 | 12.10 | 27683 | 4.28 | 50485 | 7.82 |
| #上城区<br>Shangcheng | 2300 | 7.21 | 1952 | 6.12 | 348 | 1.09 |
| 下城区<br>Xiacheng | 3979 | 9.54 | 1825 | 4.38 | 2154 | 5.16 |
| 江干区<br>Jianggan | 9000 | 14.48 | 1792 | 2.88 | 7208 | 11.60 |
| 拱墅区<br>Gongshu | 4635 | 11.92 | 1688 | 4.34 | 2947 | 7.58 |
| 西湖区<br>Xihu | 8744 | 11.59 | 2285 | 3.03 | 6459 | 8.56 |
| 西湖风景名胜区<br>The West Lake Scenic Zone | | | | | | |
| 高新(滨江)区<br>Hi-Tech(Binjiang) | 4573 | 16.95 | 680 | 2.52 | 3893 | 14.43 |
| 萧山区<br>Xiaoshan | 15205 | 11.39 | 6653 | 4.99 | 8552 | 6.40 |
| 余杭区<br>Yuhang | 17630 | 15.60 | 4464 | 3.95 | 13166 | 11.65 |
| 富阳区<br>Fuyang | 7173 | 10.46 | 3432 | 5.00 | 3741 | 5.46 |
| 临安区<br>Lin'an | 4929 | 9.15 | 2912 | 5.40 | 2017 | 3.75 |
| 钱塘新区<br>Qiantang | | | | | | |
| 桐庐县<br>Tonglu | 4164 | 9.96 | 2727 | 6.52 | 1437 | 3.44 |
| 淳安县<br>Chun'an | 4103 | 8.93 | 2898 | 6.31 | 1205 | 2.62 |
| 建德市<br>Jiande | 5015 | 9.81 | 3466 | 6.78 | 1549 | 3.03 |

# 2-09 分地区户籍人口机械变动情况(2019年)

# Mechanical Changes of Household Registered Population by Region(2019)

单位:人 (person)

| 地　区<br>Region | 本年迁入人数<br>Number of the Persons Moved in(person) | | 本年迁出人数<br>Number of the Persons Moved Out(person) | | 本年净迁入人数<br>Net Persons Moved in |
|---|---|---|---|---|---|
| | 省　内<br>From Zhejiang Province | 省　外<br>From Other Provinces | 省　内<br>To Zhejiang Province | 省　外<br>To Other Provinces | |
| **全　市<br>Whole City** | **71249** | **117333** | **13153** | **16419** | **159010** |
| 市　区<br>Urban District | 69659 | 113569 | 5790 | 14589 | 162849 |
| #上城区<br>Shangcheng | 2720 | 3834 | 237 | 741 | 5576 |
| 下城区<br>Xiacheng | 7443 | 14084 | 501 | 1553 | 19473 |
| 江干区<br>Jianggan | 14886 | 17865 | 1101 | 2453 | 29197 |
| 拱墅区<br>Gongshu | 5981 | 5884 | 392 | 574 | 10899 |
| 西湖区<br>Xihu | 11940 | 16880 | 1344 | 4308 | 23168 |
| 西湖风景名胜区<br>The West Lake Scenic Zone | | | | | |
| 高新(滨江)区<br>Hi-Tech(Binjiang) | 6432 | 7614 | 357 | 976 | 12713 |
| 萧山区<br>Xiaoshan | 5359 | 11670 | 451 | 1079 | 15499 |
| 余杭区<br>Yuhang | 13565 | 31896 | 605 | 1382 | 43474 |
| 富阳区<br>Fuyang | 470 | 1850 | 280 | 588 | 1452 |
| 临安区<br>Lin'an | 863 | 1992 | 522 | 935 | 1398 |
| 钱塘新区<br>Qiantang | | | | | |
| 桐庐县<br>Tonglu | 631 | 1587 | 1572 | 409 | 237 |
| 淳安县<br>Chun'an | 436 | 958 | 2931 | 537 | -2074 |
| 建德市<br>Jiande | 523 | 1219 | 2860 | 884 | -2002 |

# 2－10 婚姻登记情况（2018－2019 年）
## Marriage Registration Situations（2018－2019）

| 地区 Region | 2018 | | | 2019 | | |
|---|---|---|---|---|---|---|
| | 准予登记结婚对数（对） Marriages Legally Registered（couples） | 再婚人数（人） Re－married（person） | 离婚对数（对） Divorces（couples） | 准予登记结婚对数（对） Marriages Legally Registered（couples） | 再婚人数（人） Re－married（person） | 离婚对数（对） Divorces（couples） |
| **全市 Whole City** | **63810** | **20007** | **22330** | **56330** | **18471** | **23172** |
| 市区 Urban District | 53663 | 16168 | 18055 | 47793 | 15106 | 18942 |
| #萧山区 Xiaoshan | 10216 | 2600 | 2427 | 7977 | 2396 | 2577 |
| 余杭区 Yuhang | 8207 | 3110 | 3220 | 7154 | 2773 | 3204 |
| 富阳区 Fuyang | 5362 | 2047 | 1822 | 4519 | 1821 | 1878 |
| 临安区 Lin'an | 4044 | 1644 | 1847 | 3351 | 1491 | 1789 |
| 桐庐县 Tonglu | 3080 | 1246 | 1413 | 2611 | 1085 | 1397 |
| 淳安县 Chun'an | 3281 | 1157 | 1260 | 2808 | 1058 | 1272 |
| 建德市 Jiande | 3786 | 1436 | 1602 | 3118 | 1222 | 1561 |

# 2-11 三次产业就业人员及构成(2012-2019年)
# Number of Employed Persons by Three Industries(2012-2019)

单位:万人 (10000 persons)

| 指标名称 | Item | 2012 | 2013 | 2014 | 2015 | 2016 | 2017 | 2018 | 2019 |
|---|---|---|---|---|---|---|---|---|---|
| **全市总计** | **Total** | **644.43** | **650.51** | **654.92** | **663.03** | **676.95** | **681.06** | **696.10** | **720.00** |
| 第一产业 | Primary Industry | 70.39 | 70.07 | 66.39 | 67.01 | 66.11 | 66.29 | 59.70 | 56.70 |
| 第二产业 | Secondary Industry | 290.01 | 291.51 | 286.99 | 271.90 | 261.78 | 257.60 | 244.30 | 256.60 |
| 第三产业 | Tertiary Industry | 284.03 | 288.93 | 301.54 | 324.12 | 349.06 | 357.17 | 392.10 | 406.70 |
| **全市构成(以合计为100)** | **Composition (Total=100)** | **100** | **100** | **100** | **100** | **100** | **100** | **100** | **100** |
| 第一产业 | Primary Industry | 10.9 | 10.8 | 10.1 | 10.1 | 9.8 | 9.7 | 8.6 | 7.9 |
| 第二产业 | Secondary Industry | 45.0 | 44.8 | 43.9 | 41.0 | 38.7 | 37.8 | 35.1 | 35.6 |
| 第三产业 | Tertiary Industry | 44.1 | 44.4 | 46.0 | 48.9 | 51.5 | 52.5 | 56.3 | 56.5 |

# 2－12 非私营及规上

## Number of Employed Persons of Non－private Units

单位:人

| 地区、行业 | Region, Sector | 就业人员合计<br>Number of Employed Persons | 非私营单位<br>Non－private |
|---|---|---|---|
| **全市** | **Total** | **4603415** | **2865445** |
| 市区 | Urban District | 4350762 | 2737127 |
| #上城区 | Shangcheng District | 240223 | 167965 |
| 下城区 | Xiacheng District | 334706 | 262013 |
| 江干区 | Jianggan District | 498064 | 242698 |
| 拱墅区 | Gongshu District | 338388 | 175718 |
| 西湖区 | Xihu District | 628713 | 483685 |
| 高新(滨江)区 | Hi－Tech(Binjiang) District | 375292 | 280112 |
| 萧山区 | Xiaoshan District | 636571 | 370776 |
| 余杭区 | Yuhang District | 550774 | 279585 |
| 富阳区 | Fuyang District | 255070 | 170552 |
| 临安区 | Lin'an District | 146659 | 76554 |
| 钱塘新区 | Qiantang District | 326573 | 210583 |
| 西湖风景名胜区 | The West Lake Scenic Zone | 19729 | 16886 |
| 桐庐县 | Tonglu County | 115780 | 45406 |
| 淳安县 | Chun'an County | 57389 | 39884 |
| 建德市 | Jiande City | 79484 | 43028 |
| **按国民经济行业分组** | **Grouped by Sector** | | |
| 农、林、牧、渔业 | Farming, Forestry, Animal Husbandry & Fishery | 1078 | 1078 |
| 采矿业 | Mining | 2128 | 1175 |
| 制造业 | Manufacturing | 1007842 | 595579 |
| 电力、热力、燃气及水生产和供应业 | Production & Supply of Electricity, Heat, Gas & Water | 17767 | 16183 |
| 建筑业 | Construction | 1472753 | 673848 |
| 批发和零售业 | Wholesale & Retail Trades | 311750 | 172430 |
| 交通运输、仓储和邮政业 | Transportation, Storage and Posts | 136954 | 101096 |
| 住宿和餐饮业 | Hotels and Catering Services | 120226 | 78082 |
| 信息传输、软件和信息技术服务业 | Information Transmission, Software and Information Technology | 263013 | 180417 |
| 金融业 | Financial Intermediation | 127205 | 126859 |
| 房地产业 | Real Estate | 177033 | 133445 |
| 租赁和商务服务业 | Leasing and Business Services | 207523 | 122018 |
| 科学研究、技术服务业 | Scientific Research, Technical Services | 133823 | 96434 |
| 水利、环境和公共设施管理业 | Management of Water Conservancy, Environment and Public Facilities | 47975 | 33244 |
| 居民服务、修理和其他服务业 | Service to Households, Repair and Other Services | 39112 | 22732 |
| 教育 | Education | 218313 | 210256 |
| 卫生和社会工作业 | Health Care and Social Work | 144733 | 131179 |
| 文化、体育和娱乐业 | Culture, Sports and Entertainment | 29587 | 24790 |
| 公共管理、社会保障和社会组织 | Public Management, Social Security and Social Organizations | 144600 | 144600 |

# 私营单位就业人员数(2019 年末)

## and Private Units Above Designated Size( End of 2019)

(person)

| 女性<br>Female | 非私营单位<br>Non - private | 在岗职工<br>Staff and Workers | 非私营单位<br>Non - private | 其他就业人员<br>Other Employed Persons | 非私营单位<br>Non - private |
|---|---|---|---|---|---|
| **1520001** | **1016333** | **4254622** | **2706604** | **348793** | **158841** |
| 1429996 | 962863 | 4012020 | 2582367 | 338742 | 154760 |
| 95030 | 76216 | 218586 | 157892 | 21637 | 10073 |
| 138158 | 110319 | 274458 | 216807 | 60248 | 45206 |
| 130027 | 79906 | 407670 | 224823 | 90394 | 17875 |
| 91740 | 58979 | 298917 | 158384 | 39471 | 17334 |
| 202877 | 162386 | 596563 | 463233 | 32150 | 20452 |
| 119915 | 90901 | 365672 | 272267 | 9620 | 7845 |
| 201481 | 113269 | 603418 | 358334 | 33153 | 12442 |
| 206152 | 113241 | 521058 | 271470 | 29716 | 8115 |
| 69103 | 41844 | 248915 | 166839 | 6155 | 3713 |
| 51372 | 28033 | 141507 | 72317 | 5152 | 4237 |
| 115044 | 80203 | 316891 | 204277 | 9682 | 6306 |
| 9097 | 7566 | 18365 | 15724 | 1364 | 1162 |
| 37553 | 20131 | 112887 | 44356 | 2893 | 1050 |
| 24180 | 16898 | 53770 | 37960 | 3619 | 1924 |
| 28272 | 16441 | 75945 | 41921 | 3539 | 1107 |
| 282 | 282 | 977 | 977 | 101 | 101 |
| 459 | 258 | 2101 | 1167 | 27 | 8 |
| 386768 | 211377 | 992925 | 586447 | 14917 | 9132 |
| 4599 | 4244 | 17464 | 15899 | 303 | 284 |
| 155960 | 58812 | 1271807 | 639896 | 200946 | 33952 |
| 166707 | 89287 | 301387 | 165318 | 10363 | 7112 |
| 38797 | 28631 | 133713 | 98547 | 3241 | 2549 |
| 66059 | 43823 | 102940 | 62963 | 17286 | 15119 |
| 95823 | 66922 | 260821 | 179116 | 2192 | 1301 |
| 72655 | 72451 | 86415 | 86069 | 40790 | 40790 |
| 76471 | 58738 | 168975 | 127618 | 8058 | 5827 |
| 66590 | 36529 | 196289 | 113552 | 11234 | 8466 |
| 43612 | 32176 | 128776 | 92535 | 5047 | 3899 |
| 17180 | 10932 | 45778 | 32466 | 2197 | 778 |
| 21865 | 12276 | 37172 | 21882 | 1940 | 850 |
| 142816 | 137925 | 205277 | 197660 | 13036 | 12596 |
| 102067 | 92680 | 135979 | 123252 | 8754 | 7927 |
| 15412 | 13111 | 27380 | 22794 | 2207 | 1996 |
| 45879 | 45879 | 138446 | 138446 | 6154 | 6154 |

# 2-13 非私营及规上

## Average Number of Employed Persons of Non-private Units

单位：人

| 地区、行业 | Region, Sector | 就业人员年平均人数 Annual Average Number of Staff and Workers | 非私营单位 Non-private |
|---|---|---|---|
| **全市** | **Total** | **4528889** | **2811114** |
| 市区 | Urban District | 4286121 | 2683427 |
| #上城区 | Shangcheng District | 236469 | 166899 |
| 下城区 | Xiacheng District | 319795 | 248219 |
| 江干区 | Jianggan District | 492918 | 234022 |
| 拱墅区 | Gongshu District | 339444 | 177117 |
| 西湖区 | Xihu District | 612906 | 470473 |
| 高新（滨江）区 | Hi-Tech (Binjiang) District | 370877 | 275629 |
| 萧山区 | Xiaoshan District | 638177 | 367031 |
| 余杭区 | Yuhang District | 537711 | 278359 |
| 富阳区 | Fuyang District | 246576 | 163374 |
| 临安区 | Lin'an Districty | 145234 | 75839 |
| 钱塘新区 | Qiantang District | 326570 | 209795 |
| 西湖风景名胜区 | The West Lake Scenic Zone | 19444 | 16670 |
| 桐庐县 | Tonglu County | 108175 | 45160 |
| 淳安县 | Chun'an County | 56034 | 39701 |
| 建德市 | Jiande City | 78559 | 42826 |
| **按国民经济行业分组** | **Grouped by Sector** | | |
| 农、林、牧、渔业 | Farming, Forestry, Animal Husbandry & Fishery | 1059 | 1059 |
| 采矿业 | Mining | 2082 | 1140 |
| 制造业 | Manufacturing | 1014400 | 599167 |
| 电力、热力、燃气及水生产和供应业 | Production & Supply of Electricity, Heat, Gas & Water | 17627 | 16052 |
| 建筑业 | Construction | 1431943 | 647476 |
| 批发和零售业 | Wholesale & Retail Trades | 311567 | 172876 |
| 交通运输、仓储和邮政业 | Transportation, Storage and Posts | 136963 | 100263 |
| 住宿和餐饮业 | Hotels and Catering Services | 116643 | 76341 |
| 信息传输、软件和信息技术服务业 | Information Transmission, Software and Information Technology | 258415 | 177639 |
| 金融业 | Financial Intermediation | 119710 | 119361 |
| 房地产业 | Real Estate | 172965 | 129445 |
| 租赁和商务服务业 | Leasing and Business Services | 202705 | 120957 |
| 科学研究、技术服务业 | Scientific Research, Technical Services | 131066 | 94543 |
| 水利、环境和公共设施管理业 | Management of Water Conservancy, Environment and Public Facilities | 45374 | 31288 |
| 居民服务、修理和其他服务业 | Service to Households, Repair and Other Services | 37662 | 21092 |
| 教育 | Education | 214624 | 206702 |
| 卫生和社会工作 | Health Care and Social Work | 141559 | 127951 |
| 文化、体育和娱乐业 | Culture, Sports and Entertainment | 29133 | 24370 |
| 公共管理、社会保障和社会组织 | Public Management, Social Security and Social Organizations | 143392 | 143392 |

私营单位平均人员数(2019 年)

and Private Units Above Designated Size(2019)

(person)

| 在岗职工年平均人数 Staff and Workers | 非私营单位 Non - private | 其他就业人员年平均人数 Average Number of Other Employed Persons | 非私营单位 Non - private |
|---|---|---|---|
| **4192497** | **2661592** | **336382** | **149522** |
| 3960311 | 2538587 | 325800 | 144840 |
| 215677 | 157305 | 20792 | 9594 |
| 265221 | 208673 | 54574 | 39546 |
| 404996 | 216053 | 87922 | 17969 |
| 302618 | 160122 | 36826 | 16995 |
| 585473 | 454279 | 27433 | 16194 |
| 361033 | 267939 | 9844 | 7690 |
| 603098 | 354038 | 35079 | 12993 |
| 506447 | 269279 | 31254 | 9080 |
| 240518 | 159849 | 6058 | 3525 |
| 140188 | 71690 | 5046 | 4149 |
| 316905 | 203770 | 9665 | 6025 |
| 18137 | 15590 | 1307 | 1080 |
| 105145 | 44014 | 3030 | 1146 |
| 52129 | 37276 | 3905 | 2425 |
| 74912 | 41715 | 3647 | 1111 |
| | | | |
| 944 | 944 | 115 | 115 |
| 2049 | 1131 | 33 | 9 |
| 998873 | 589885 | 15527 | 9282 |
| 17321 | 15765 | 306 | 287 |
| 1233505 | 612264 | 198438 | 35212 |
| 301235 | 165872 | 10322 | 7004 |
| 133834 | 97925 | 3129 | 2338 |
| 103283 | 65169 | 13360 | 11172 |
| 255712 | 176186 | 2703 | 1453 |
| 85422 | 85073 | 34288 | 34288 |
| 165066 | 123716 | 7899 | 5729 |
| 191831 | 112669 | 10874 | 8288 |
| 125664 | 90295 | 5402 | 4248 |
| 43225 | 30477 | 2149 | 811 |
| 35694 | 20252 | 1968 | 840 |
| 201504 | 193905 | 13120 | 12797 |
| 132939 | 120216 | 8620 | 7735 |
| 27061 | 22513 | 2072 | 1857 |
| 137335 | 137335 | 6057 | 6057 |

# 2－14 分行业非私营单位

## The Education Level of the Staff and Workers in

单位:人

| 行 业 | Sector | 单位就业人员 The Education Level<br>研究生及以上 Graduate of above |
|---|---|---|
| **总 计** | **Total** | **211784** |
| 农、林、牧、渔业 | Farming, Forestry, Animal Husbandry & Fishery | 20 |
| 采矿业 | Mining | 55 |
| 制造业 | Manufacturing | 28365 |
| 电力、热力、燃气及水生产和供应业 | Production & Supply of Electricity, Heat, Gas & Water | 523 |
| 建筑业 | Construction | 4398 |
| 批发和零售业 | Wholesale & Retail Trades | 7202 |
| 交通运输、仓储及邮政业 | Transportation, Storage and Posts | 1228 |
| 住宿和餐饮业 | Hotels and Catering Services | 419 |
| 信息传输、软件和信息技术服务业 | Information Transmission, Software and Information Technology | 40482 |
| 金融业 | Financial Intermediation | 13534 |
| 房地产业 | Real Estate | 3377 |
| 租赁和商务服务业 | Leasing and Business Services | 7732 |
| 科学研究和技术服务业 | Scientific Research, Technical Services | 20620 |
| 水利、环境和公共设施管理业 | Management of Water Conservancy, Environment and Public Facilities | 1008 |
| 居民服务、修理和其他服务业 | Service to Households, Repair and Other Services | 202 |
| 教育 | Education | 47597 |
| 卫生和社会工作 | Health Care and Social Work | 19246 |
| 文化、体育和娱乐业 | Culture, Sports and Entertainment | 2810 |
| 公共管理、社会保障和社会组织 | Public Management, Social Security and Social Organizations | 12966 |

# 职工素质情况(2019 年末)

## Non - private Units by Sector( End of 2019)

(persons)

| 文化程度<br>of the Employed Persons in Onits | | | | 单位就业人员中专业技术人员<br>Professional and Technical Personnel | 单位就业人员中技术工人<br>Skilled Workers |
|---|---|---|---|---|---|
| 大学本科<br>Bachelor' s Degree | 大专<br>College Degree | 中专及高中<br>Technical Secondary School and High School | 初中及以下<br>Junior High School and Below | | |
| **1013561** | **769102** | **1051516** | **1557452** | **1023413** | **1481028** |
| 168 | 216 | 218 | 456 | 177 | 395 |
| 345 | 307 | 439 | 982 | 230 | 681 |
| 156841 | 147562 | 266321 | 408753 | 167595 | 545466 |
| 6272 | 4703 | 4001 | 2268 | 3268 | 8021 |
| 92151 | 161535 | 405562 | 809107 | 195083 | 621852 |
| 78880 | 89422 | 85880 | 50366 | 35617 | 48078 |
| 23236 | 32011 | 43961 | 36518 | 15521 | 40968 |
| 14494 | 28549 | 38424 | 38340 | 5025 | 25445 |
| 146182 | 59871 | 13429 | 3049 | 128988 | 40019 |
| 61143 | 22707 | 27273 | 2548 | 46209 | 4365 |
| 32732 | 36686 | 38942 | 65296 | 16963 | 31873 |
| 48119 | 42506 | 45925 | 63241 | 31208 | 47112 |
| 65142 | 32108 | 11020 | 4933 | 86705 | 10871 |
| 10602 | 10994 | 7025 | 18346 | 6176 | 15481 |
| 4047 | 5739 | 7901 | 21223 | 2839 | 14629 |
| 112475 | 24048 | 19974 | 14219 | 146373 | 11718 |
| 69005 | 31312 | 14149 | 11021 | 107803 | 8388 |
| 14004 | 6076 | 4757 | 1940 | 13325 | 2375 |
| 77723 | 32750 | 16315 | 4846 | 14308 | 3291 |

# 主要统计指标解释

**人口数** 指一定时点、一定地区范围内的有生命的个人的总和。

年度统计的年末人口数是指每年 12 月 31 日 24 时的人口数。

**出生率(又称粗出生率)** 指一定时期内(通常为一年)平均每千人所出生的人数的比率,一般用千分率表示。计算公式:

$$出生率=\frac{年出生人数}{年平均人数}\times 1000‰$$

出生人数是指活产婴儿,即胎儿脱离母体时(不管怀孕月数),有过呼吸或其他生命现象。

年平均人数是年初、年底人口数的平均数,也可用年中人口数代替。

**死亡率(又称粗死亡率)** 指一定时期内(通常为一年)一定地区的死亡人数与同期平均人数(或期中人数)之比,一般用千分率表示。计算公式:

$$死亡率=\frac{年死亡人数}{年平均人数}\times 1000‰$$

**人口自然增长率** 指一定时期内(通常为一年)人口自然增加数(出生人数减死亡人数)与该时期内平均人数(或期中人数)之比,一般用千分率表示。计算公式:

$$人口自然增长率=\frac{本年出生人数-本年死亡人数}{年平均人数}\times 1000‰$$

人口自然增长率 = 人口出生率 - 人口死亡率

**就业人员** 指从事一定社会劳动并取得劳动报酬或经营收入人员,包括各级机关企事业单位就业人员、个体户主、个体就业人员、农村就业人员及其他未包括的就业人员(包括宗教职业者、现役军人等)。

**单位就业人员** 是指在各级国家机关、政党机关、社会团体及企业、事业单位中工作,并取得劳动报酬的全部人员。包括在岗职工、再就业的离退休人员、民办教师、在各单位中工作的外方人员和港、澳、台方人员以及聘用的外单位下岗职工、兼职人员、从事第二职业人员、使用的劳务派遣人员。各单位的就业人员反映了实际参加生产或工作的全部劳动力。

**在岗职工** 指在本单位工作并由单位支付劳动报酬的人员,以及在本单位有工作岗位,但由于学习、病伤产假等原因暂未工作,仍由单位支付劳动报酬的人,包括本单位临时性用工并支付劳动报酬的人员。2012 年开始在岗职工包含劳务派遣人员。

**非私营单位** 包括独立核算的机关、事业单位和国有、集体、股份制、港澳台投资及外商投资企业等。

**非私营单位及规上私营单位** 包括独立核算的非私营单位、规模以上私营工业企业、限额以上私营批发零售住宿餐饮企业、私营房地产开发经营企业、具有资质的私营建筑企业、规模以上私营服务企业、100 人及以上的规模以下私营企业。

# Explanatory Notes on Main Statistical Indicators

**Total Population** refers to the total number of people alive at a certain point of time within a given area.

The annual statistics on total population is taken at midnight on December 31.

**Birth Rate ( or Crude Birth Rate )** refers to the ratio of the number of births to the average population during a certain period of time ( usually a year) , which is often expressed in ‰. The following formula is used:

$$\text{Birth Rate} = \frac{\text{Number of Births}}{\text{Average Number of Population}} \times 1000‰$$

Number of births refers to live births, i. e. the births when babies had showed any vital phenomena regardless of the length of pregnancy.

Annual Average Number of Population is the average of the number of population at the beginning of the year and that at the end of the year. Sometimes it is substituted by the mid – year population.

**Death Rate ( or Crude Death Rate )** refers to the ratio of the number of deaths to the average population ( or mid – year population) during a certain period of time ( usually a year) , which is often expressed in ‰. The following formula is used:

$$\text{Death Rate} = \frac{\text{Number of Deaths}}{\text{Annual Average Number of Population}} \times 1000‰$$

**Natural Growth Rate of Population** refers to the ratio of natural increase in population ( number of births minus number ofdeaths) in a certain period of time ( usually a year) to the average population( or mid – year population) of the same period, which is often expressed in ‰. The following formulas are applied:

$$\text{Natural Growth Rate of Population} = \frac{\text{Number of Births} - \text{Number of Deaths}}{\text{Average Number of Population}} \times 1000‰$$

Natural Growth Rate of Population = Birth Rate – Death Rate

**Employed Persons** refer to persons who are engaged in social labour and receive remuneration payment or earn business income, including all employees of government, enterprises and institutions, self – employed workers, employed persons in the rural areas and other employed workers( including religious professionals, servicemen, etc. ).

**Persons Employed in Various Units** refer to all the persons working in government agencies of various levels, political and party organizations, social organizations, enterprises, institutions, and receiving wages or other forms of payment, which include fully – employed staff and workers, re – employed retirees, teachers in schools run by the local people, foreigners and Chinese compatriots from Hong Kong, Macao, and Taiwan working in various units, hired laid – off workers from other units, part – time employees, employees engaged a second job, dispatched personnels. Persons Employed in various units reflect the total laborers actually engaged in production or work.

**Fully Employed Staff and Workers** refer to persons who work and receive wages from their working units, as well as persons who maintain their posts, are out of commission temporarily for reasons of study, sickness, injury or maternal leave, but still receive wages from their working units, which includes persons who are temporarily employed and receive remuneration payment. After2012, fully employed staff includes dispatched personnels.

**Non – private Units** include independent accounting government organizations and institutions, state – owned, collective – owned and joint stock enterprises, and enterprises with funds from foreign and from Hong Kong, Macao and Taiwan.

**Non – private Units and Private Units Above Designated Size** include independent accounting non – private units , private industrial enterprises above designated size, private enterprises above designated size in wholesale or retail trade, hotels or catering services, private enterprises for real estate development, private construction enterprises with qualification grade, private service enterprises above designated size, private enterprises below designated size of employing at least 100 persons.

# 三、农业

AGRICULTURE

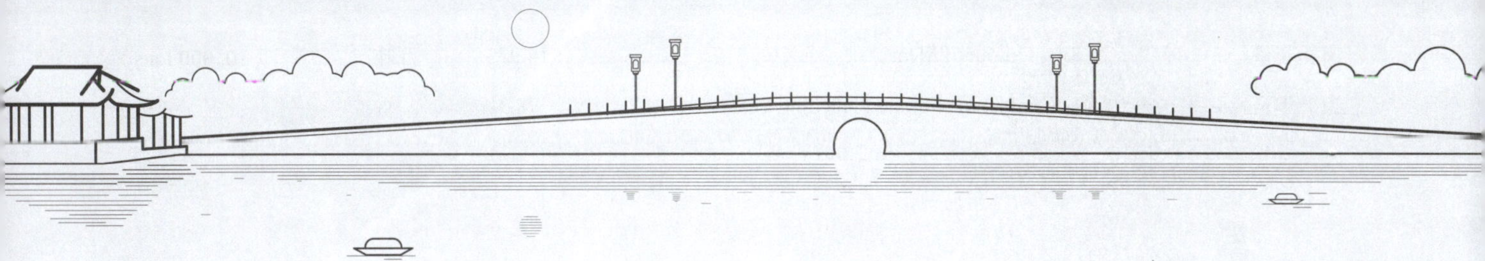

# 3 农　　业
# Agriculture

## 主要统计指标
## Major Statistical Indicators

| | | | | |
|---|---|---|---|---|
| 农村机械总动力 | Total Power of Agricultural Machinery | 214.75 | 万千瓦 | ( 10, 000 kw ) |
| 为上年 | As Compared with the Preceding Year | 90.9 | % | ( % ) |
| 农村从业人员数 | Total Employed Persons in Rural Areas | 264.83 | 万人 | ( 10, 000 persons ) |
| 为上年 | As Compared with the Preceding Year | 97.8 | % | ( % ) |
| 农林牧渔业增加值 | Value-added of Farming,Forestry,Animal Husbandry and Fishery | 332.74 | 亿元 | ( 100 million yuan ) |
| 为上年 | As Compared with the Preceding Year | 106.7 | % | ( % ) |
| 粮食总产量 | Total Output of Grain Crops | 49.64 | 万吨 | ( 10, 000 tons ) |
| 为上年 | As Compared with the Preceding Year | 100.1 | % | ( % ) |
| 肉类产量 | Total Output of Meat | 14.97 | 万吨 | ( 10, 000 tons ) |
| 为上年 | As Compared with the Preceding Year | 78.3 | % | ( % ) |

# 3－01 分地区农林牧渔业增加值(2019 年)

## The added Value of Agriculture, Forestry, Animal Husbandry and Fishery(2019)

单位:万元 (10000 yuan)

| 地区 Region | 农林牧渔业合计 Total | 为上年% | 农业 Agriculture | 为上年% | 林业 Forestry | 为上年% | 畜牧业 Animal Husbandry | 为上年% | 渔业 Fishery | 为上年% | 农、林、牧、渔专业及辅助性活动 Services for Farming, Forestry, Animal Husbandary and Fishery | 为上年% |
|---|---|---|---|---|---|---|---|---|---|---|---|---|
| **全市 Whole City** | **3327369** | **106.7** | **2101139** | **104.5** | **483405** | **108.2** | **369504** | **122.6** | **303120** | **101.9** | **70201** | **111.0** |
| 市区 Urban District | 2323258 | 107.0 | 1406329 | 104.2 | 350221 | 108.8 | 255577 | 129.7 | 257934 | 101.3 | 53197 | 110.3 |
| #江干区 Jianggan | | | | | | | | | | | | |
| 西湖区 Xihu | 27071 | 74.8 | 22496 | 91.2 | 494 | 100.0 | - | - | 3040 | 30.5 | 1040 | 100.1 |
| 高新(滨江)区 Hi－Tech(Binjiang) | 7244 | 92.7 | 6801 | 98.3 | - | - | - | - | 443 | 49.4 | - | - |
| 萧山区 Xiaoshan | 738844 | 109.3 | 513443 | 104.2 | 7999 | 104.3 | 116786 | 147.0 | 78256 | 102.8 | 22360 | 110.6 |
| 余杭区 Yuhang | 554396 | 105.8 | 328323 | 103.3 | 63552 | 112.2 | 22061 | 136.1 | 119169 | 104.7 | 21291 | 109.0 |
| 富阳区 Fuyang | 496160 | 108.9 | 293493 | 106.5 | 110615 | 112.7 | 60963 | 110.9 | 27883 | 115.4 | 3206 | 112.9 |
| 临安区 Lin'an | 463904 | 107.0 | 230463 | 105.3 | 167521 | 105.4 | 54934 | 120.4 | 5686 | 100.0 | 5300 | 116.0 |
| 钱塘新区 Qiantang New Area | 139422 | 109.7 | 92788 | 105.6 | 56 | 37.6 | 25337 | 142.0 | 18115 | 98.1 | 3126 | 110.3 |
| 西湖风景名胜区 The West Lake Scenic Zone | 9491 | 105.8 | 9451 | 105.8 | 40 | 100.0 | - | - | - | - | - | - |
| 桐庐县 Tonglu | 254510 | 106.5 | 163999 | 104.8 | 48523 | 109.0 | 25587 | 111.2 | 12164 | 108.5 | 4237 | 115.4 |
| 淳安县 Chun'an | 386868 | 106.0 | 273911 | 105.2 | 56731 | 106.8 | 32868 | 114.2 | 17920 | 101.1 | 5438 | 109.3 |
| 建德市 Jiande | 362733 | 105.8 | 256900 | 105.8 | 27930 | 102.1 | 55472 | 105.6 | 15102 | 108.5 | 7329 | 114.7 |

# 3－02 农林牧渔业总产值(1978－2019年)

## Gross Output Value of Agriculture, Forestry, Animal Husbandry and Fishery(1978－2019)

单位:万元 (10000 yuan)

| 年份<br>Year | 农林牧渔业<br>Gross Output Value | #农业<br>Farming | 种植业<br>Planting | 林业<br>Forestry | 畜牧业<br>Animal Husbandry | 渔业<br>Fishery | 农、林、牧、渔专业及辅助性活动<br>Services for Farming, Forestry, Animal Husbandary and Fishery |
|---|---|---|---|---|---|---|---|
| 1978 | 85922 | 67365 | 64378 | 3430 | 14474 | 653 | – |
| 1979 | 115649 | 84727 | 81989 | 4629 | 25216 | 1077 | – |
| 1980 | 112377 | 79006 | 76059 | 7262 | 25015 | 1094 | – |
| 1981 | 120792 | 87354 | 81659 | 8309 | 23799 | 1330 | – |
| 1982 | 150606 | 107566 | 103346 | 8912 | 31801 | 2327 | – |
| 1983 | 148878 | 103685 | 96272 | 9800 | 32693 | 2700 | – |
| 1984 | 177029 | 122567 | 115286 | 14769 | 35922 | 3771 | – |
| 1985 | 212961 | 136893 | 126026 | 19095 | 50110 | 6863 | – |
| 1986 | 238285 | 150803 | 138254 | 19990 | 58197 | 9295 | – |
| 1987 | 281326 | 173080 | 155960 | 26427 | 70129 | 11690 | – |
| 1988 | 358500 | 208838 | 187648 | 31434 | 101013 | 17215 | – |
| 1989 | 386805 | 225969 | 201389 | 27857 | 113952 | 19027 | – |
| 1990 | 421045 | 260031 | 233055 | 26962 | 113424 | 20628 | – |
| 1991 | 463578 | 284275 | 254834 | 37763 | 117458 | 24082 | – |
| 1992 | 497915 | 300828 | 256833 | 35589 | 133867 | 27631 | – |
| 1993 | 600760 | 365124 | 300736 | 47476 | 154766 | 33394 | – |
| 1994 | 812473 | 496392 | 415366 | 58627 | 217217 | 40237 | – |
| 1995 | 996440 | 620057 | 526328 | 81321 | 244054 | 51008 | – |
| 1996 | 1173294 | 740202 | 617573 | 95740 | 271652 | 65700 | – |
| 1997 | 1287650 | 797812 | 665172 | 114510 | 294153 | 81175 | – |
| 1998 | 1367578 | 845106 | 701850 | 121197 | 289085 | 112190 | – |
| 1999 | 1414737 | 876685 | 737406 | 126000 | 293495 | 118557 | – |
| 2000 | 1526530 | 903322 | 754311 | 136848 | 331563 | 154797 | – |
| 2001 | 1649978 | 965005 | 816884 | 149264 | 362303 | 173406 | – |
| 2002 | 1685036 | 932995 | 886285 | 162227 | 391844 | 197970 | – |
| 2003 | 1890129 | 991556 | 949138 | 182595 | 417798 | 232599 | 65581 |
| 2004 | 1982683 | 1010947 | 972594 | 206787 | 457619 | 234080 | 73250 |
| 2005 | 2194799 | 1136559 | 1103981 | 233039 | 495900 | 270810 | 58491 |
| 2006 | 2253822 | 1224822 | 1191816 | 267748 | 490448 | 206082 | 64722 |
| 2007 | 2471427 | 1308047 | 1279758 | 294707 | 585536 | 222601 | 60536 |
| 2008 | 2737605 | 1408124 | 1374083 | 320212 | 636633 | 309270 | 63366 |
| 2009 | 2897371 | 1497362 | 1462791 | 362317 | 642892 | 325626 | 69174 |
| 2010 | 3163392 | 1698775 | 1673470 | 329278 | 705596 | 349011 | 80732 |
| 2011 | 3570744 | 1907895 | 1882876 | 348535 | 836532 | 389985 | 87797 |
| 2012 | 3843403 | 2077191 | 2041481 | 381802 | 868504 | 420006 | 95900 |
| 2013 | 3993712 | 2161055 | 2120540 | 408170 | 911324 | 407292 | 105871 |
| 2014 | 4185804 | 2333804 | 2291071 | 470164 | 828184 | 442023 | 111629 |
| 2015 | 4404121 | 2524163 | 2468981 | 498051 | 807001 | 452309 | 122597 |
| 2016 | 4490065 | 2621544 | 2558927 | 530464 | 768795 | 436050 | 133212 |
| 2017 | 4577017 | 2738813 | 2677779 | 549138 | 685811 | 453211 | 150044 |
| 2018 | 4660989 | 2827117 | 2766080 | 572957 | 618513 | 474742 | 167660 |
| 2019 | 5011510 | 2953377 | 2892153 | 618886 | 767683 | 485734 | 185830 |

# 3－03 农林牧渔业总产值构成(1978－2019年)

## Composition of Gross Output Value of Agriculture, Forestry, Animal Husbandry and Fishery(1978－2019)

单位:% (%)

| 年份 Year | 农林牧渔业 Gross Output Value | #农业 Farming | 种植业 Planting | 林业 Forestry | 畜牧业 Animal Husbandry | 渔业 Fishery | 农、林、牧、渔专业及辅助性活动 Services for Farming, Forestry, Animal Husbandary and Fishery |
|---|---|---|---|---|---|---|---|
| 1978 | 100 | 78.4 | 74.9 | 4.0 | 16.8 | 0.8 | – |
| 1979 | 100 | 73.3 | 70.9 | 4.0 | 21.8 | 0.9 | – |
| 1980 | 100 | 70.3 | 67.7 | 6.5 | 22.2 | 1.0 | – |
| 1981 | 100 | 72.3 | 67.6 | 6.9 | 19.7 | 1.1 | – |
| 1982 | 100 | 71.4 | 68.6 | 5.9 | 21.1 | 1.6 | – |
| 1983 | 100 | 69.6 | 64.7 | 6.6 | 22.0 | 1.8 | – |
| 1984 | 100 | 69.2 | 65.1 | 8.3 | 20.3 | 2.2 | – |
| 1985 | 100 | 64.3 | 59.2 | 9.0 | 23.5 | 3.2 | – |
| 1986 | 100 | 63.3 | 58.0 | 8.4 | 24.4 | 3.9 | – |
| 1987 | 100 | 61.5 | 55.4 | 9.4 | 24.9 | 4.2 | – |
| 1988 | 100 | 58.2 | 52.3 | 8.8 | 28.2 | 4.8 | – |
| 1989 | 100 | 58.4 | 52.1 | 7.2 | 29.5 | 4.9 | – |
| 1990 | 100 | 61.8 | 55.4 | 6.4 | 26.9 | 4.9 | – |
| 1991 | 100 | 61.3 | 55.0 | 8.2 | 25.3 | 5.2 | – |
| 1992 | 100 | 60.4 | 51.6 | 7.2 | 26.9 | 5.5 | – |
| 1993 | 100 | 60.8 | 50.1 | 7.9 | 25.8 | 5.5 | – |
| 1994 | 100 | 61.1 | 51.1 | 7.2 | 26.7 | 5.0 | – |
| 1995 | 100 | 62.2 | 52.8 | 8.2 | 24.5 | 5.1 | – |
| 1996 | 100 | 63.1 | 52.6 | 8.2 | 23.1 | 5.6 | – |
| 1997 | 100 | 62.0 | 51.7 | 8.9 | 22.8 | 6.3 | – |
| 1998 | 100 | 61.8 | 51.3 | 8.9 | 21.1 | 8.2 | – |
| 1999 | 100 | 62.0 | 52.1 | 8.9 | 20.7 | 8.4 | – |
| 2000 | 100 | 59.2 | 49.4 | 9.0 | 21.7 | 10.1 | – |
| 2001 | 100 | 58.5 | 52.2 | 9.0 | 22.0 | 10.5 | – |
| 2002 | 100 | 55.4 | 52.6 | 9.6 | 23.3 | 11.7 | – |
| 2003 | 100 | 52.5 | 50.2 | 9.7 | 22.1 | 12.3 | 3.4 |
| 2004 | 100 | 51.0 | 49.1 | 10.4 | 23.1 | 11.8 | 3.7 |
| 2005 | 100 | 51.8 | 50.3 | 10.6 | 22.6 | 12.3 | 2.7 |
| 2006 | 100 | 54.3 | 52.9 | 11.9 | 21.8 | 9.1 | 2.9 |
| 2007 | 100 | 52.9 | 51.8 | 11.9 | 23.7 | 9.0 | 2.5 |
| 2008 | 100 | 51.4 | 50.2 | 11.7 | 23.3 | 11.3 | 2.3 |
| 2009 | 100 | 51.7 | 50.5 | 12.5 | 22.2 | 11.2 | 2.4 |
| 2010 | 100 | 53.7 | 52.9 | 10.4 | 22.3 | 11.0 | 2.6 |
| 2011 | 100 | 53.4 | 52.7 | 9.8 | 23.4 | 10.9 | 2.5 |
| 2012 | 100 | 54.0 | 53.1 | 9.9 | 22.6 | 10.9 | 2.6 |
| 2013 | 100 | 54.1 | 53.1 | 10.2 | 22.8 | 10.2 | 2.7 |
| 2014 | 100 | 55.8 | 54.7 | 11.2 | 19.8 | 10.6 | 2.6 |
| 2015 | 100 | 57.3 | 56.1 | 11.3 | 18.3 | 10.3 | 2.8 |
| 2016 | 100 | 58.4 | 57.0 | 11.8 | 17.1 | 9.7 | 3.0 |
| 2017 | 100 | 59.8 | 58.5 | 12.0 | 15.0 | 9.9 | 3.3 |
| 2018 | 100 | 60.7 | 59.3 | 12.3 | 13.3 | 10.2 | 3.5 |
| 2019 | 100 | 58.9 | 57.7 | 12.3 | 15.3 | 9.7 | 3.8 |

# 3－04 农林牧渔业分项产值（2012－2019年）

## Gross Output Value of Agriculture, Forestry, Animal Husbandry and Fishery by Branch(2012－2019)

单位：万元　　(10000 yuan)

| 指　标 | Item | 2012 | 2013 | 2014 | 2015 | 2016 | 2017 | 2018 | 2019 |
|---|---|---|---|---|---|---|---|---|---|
| **农林牧渔业总产值（现价）** | **Gross Output Value (Current Price)** | **3843403** | **3993712** | **4185804** | **4404121** | **4490065** | **4577017** | **4660989** | **5011510** |
| **一、农业产值** | **Farming** | **2077191** | **2161055** | **2333804** | **2524163** | **2621544** | **2738813** | **2827117** | **2953377** |
| 1.种植业产值 | Planting | 2041481 | 2120540 | 2291071 | 2468981 | 2558927 | 2677779 | 2666080 | 2892153 |
| 粮食 | Grain | 241471 | 248550 | 224164 | 228341 | 171736 | 177764 | 175924 | 179017 |
| 油料 | Oil－bearing Crops | 35482 | 37649 | 37530 | 48373 | 34737 | 37332 | 38607 | 45369 |
| 棉花 | Cotton | 1424 | 1571 | 1152 | 1094 | 467 | 397 | 371 | 451 |
| 麻类 | Fiber Crops | 16 | 25 | 8 | 6 | 5 | 3 | 2 | 2 |
| 甘蔗 | Sugarcane | 18417 | 18496 | 17347 | 16322 | 5770 | 5214 | 5102 | 8426 |
| 烟叶 | Tobacco | 2 | 1 | 1 | 1 | 1 | 1 | － | － |
| 药材类 | Crude Drugs | 60454 | 67623 | 75180 | 86538 | 98954 | 112902 | 122997 | 139832 |
| 蔬菜 | Vegetables | 664937 | 665429 | 686995 | 748644 | 834633 | 829020 | 842779 | 880336 |
| 茶、桑、果、坚果 | Tea, Mulberry & Fruits | 605200 | 630899 | 749516 | 802647 | 828571 | 908024 | 942095 | 985879 |
| 其他 | Others | 414078 | 450297 | 499178 | 537015 | 584053 | 607122 | 638203 | 652841 |
| 2.其他农业产值 | Other Farming | 35710 | 40515 | 42733 | 55182 | 62617 | 61034 | 61037 | 61224 |
| **二、林业产值** | **Forestry** | **381802** | **408170** | **470164** | **498051** | **530464** | **549138** | **572957** | **618886** |
| 人造林木生长 | Artificial Forestry | 32802 | 33734 | 31640 | 32574 | 31490 | 31415 | 32211 | 32962 |
| 林产品 | Forest Products | 214198 | 227962 | 267839 | 294806 | 327864 | 349421 | 373384 | 414016 |
| 竹木采伐 | Lumbering | 93552 | 103425 | 130794 | 127670 | 125112 | 122773 | 121574 | 124431 |
| 采集野生植物 | Wild Plant collected | 41250 | 43049 | 39891 | 43001 | 45998 | 45529 | 45788 | 47477 |
| **三、畜牧业产值** | **Animal Husbandry** | **868504** | **911324** | **828184** | **807001** | **768795** | **685811** | **618513** | **767683** |
| 牲畜 | Livestock Raising | 556742 | 589952 | 522674 | 522001 | 572122 | 498108 | 411261 | 556348 |
| 家禽饲养 | Poultry Raising | 82132 | 77869 | 72333 | 72394 | 36208 | 30122 | 36241 | 43002 |
| 活的畜禽产品 | Livestock Products | 125886 | 132151 | 127075 | 112964 | 92066 | 88831 | 98876 | 98252 |
| 捕猎野兽野禽 | Hunting Wild Beast and Wild Fowl | 5454 | 5126 | 6260 | 5256 | 6032 | 6043 | 5534 | 6777 |
| 其他动物饲养 | Other Animals Raising | 98290 | 106226 | 99842 | 94386 | 62367 | 62707 | 66601 | 63304 |
| **四、渔业产值** | **Fishery** | **420006** | **407292** | **442023** | **452309** | **436050** | **453211** | **474742** | **485734** |
| **五、农、林、牧、渔专业及辅助性活动** | **Services for Farming, Forestry, Animal Husbandary and Fishery** | **95900** | **105871** | **111629** | **122597** | **133212** | **150044** | **167660** | **185830** |

# 3-05 农林牧渔业分项产值构成(2012-2019年)

## Composition of Gross Output Value of Agriculture, Forestry, Animal Husbandry and Fishery by Branch(2012-2019)

单位:% (%)

| 指 标 | Item | 2012 | 2013 | 2014 | 2015 | 2016 | 2017 | 2018 | 2019 |
|---|---|---|---|---|---|---|---|---|---|
| **农林牧渔业总产值(现价)** | **Gross Output Value (Current Price)** | **100** | **100** | **100** | **100** | **100** | **100** | **100** | **100** |
| **一、农业产值** | **Farming** | **54.0** | **54.1** | **55.8** | **57.3** | **58.4** | **59.8** | **60.7** | **58.9** |
| 1. 种植业产值 | Planting | 53.1 | 53.1 | 54.7 | 56.1 | 57.0 | 58.5 | 59.3 | 57.7 |
| 粮食 | Grain | 6.3 | 6.2 | 5.4 | 5.2 | 3.8 | 3.9 | 3.8 | 3.6 |
| 油料 | Oil Plants | 0.9 | 0.9 | 0.9 | 1.1 | 0.8 | 0.8 | 0.8 | 0.9 |
| 棉花 | Cotton | - | - | - | - | - | - | - | - |
| 麻类 | Fiber Crops | - | - | - | - | - | - | - | - |
| 甘蔗 | Sugarcane | 0.6 | 0.5 | 0.4 | 0.4 | 0.1 | 0.1 | 0.1 | 0.2 |
| 烟叶 | Tobacco | - | - | - | - | - | - | - | - |
| 药材类 | Crude Drugs | 1.6 | 1.7 | 1.8 | 2.0 | 2.2 | 2.5 | 2.6 | 2.8 |
| 蔬菜 | Vegetables | 17.3 | 16.7 | 16.4 | 16.9 | 18.6 | 18.1 | 18.1 | 17.6 |
| 茶、桑、果、坚果 | Tea, Mulberry & Fruits | 15.7 | 15.8 | 17.9 | 18.2 | 18.5 | 19.8 | 20.2 | 19.7 |
| 其他 | Others | 10.7 | 11.3 | 11.9 | 12.2 | 13.0 | 13.3 | 13.7 | 13.0 |
| 2. 其他农业产值 | Other Farming | 0.9 | 1.0 | 1.0 | 1.3 | 1.4 | 1.3 | 1.4 | 1.2 |
| **二、林业产值** | **Forestry** | **9.9** | **10.2** | **11.2** | **11.3** | **11.8** | **12.0** | **12.3** | **12.3** |
| 人造林木生长 | Artificial Forestry | 0.8 | 0.8 | 0.8 | 0.7 | 0.7 | 0.7 | 0.7 | 0.6 |
| 林产品 | Forest Products | 5.6 | 5.7 | 6.4 | 6.7 | 7.3 | 7.6 | 8.0 | 8.3 |
| 竹木采伐 | Lumbering | 2.4 | 2.6 | 3.1 | 2.9 | 2.8 | 2.7 | 2.6 | 2.5 |
| 采集野生植物 | Wild Plant collected | 1.1 | 1.1 | 0.9 | 1.0 | 1.0 | 1.0 | 1.0 | 0.9 |
| **三、畜牧业产值** | **Animal Husbandry** | **22.6** | **22.8** | **19.8** | **18.3** | **17.1** | **15.0** | **13.3** | **15.3** |
| 牲畜 | Livestock Raising | 14.5 | 14.8 | 12.5 | 11.9 | 12.7 | 10.9 | 8.9 | 11.1 |
| 家禽饲养 | Poultry Raising | 2.1 | 1.9 | 1.7 | 1.6 | 0.8 | 0.7 | 0.8 | 0.8 |
| 活的畜禽产品 | Livestock Products | 3.3 | 3.3 | 3.0 | 2.6 | 2.1 | 1.9 | 2.1 | 2.0 |
| 捕猎野兽野禽 | Hunting Wild Beast and Wild Fowl | 0.1 | 0.1 | 0.1 | 0.1 | 0.1 | 0.1 | 0.1 | 0.1 |
| 其他动物饲养 | Other Animals Raising | 2.6 | 2.7 | 2.4 | 2.1 | 1.4 | 1.4 | 1.4 | 1.3 |
| **四、渔业产值** | **Fishery** | **10.9** | **10.2** | **10.6** | **10.3** | **9.7** | **9.9** | **10.2** | **9.7** |
| **五、农、林、牧、渔专业及辅助性活动** | **Services for Farming, Forestry, Animal Husbandary and Fishery** | **2.6** | **2.7** | **2.6** | **2.8** | **3.0** | **3.3** | **3.5** | **3.8** |

# 3-06 分地区农林牧

## Gross Output Value of Agriculture, Forestry,

单位:万元

| 指标 | Item | 全市 Whole City | 市区 Urban District | 江干区 Jianggan | 西湖区 Xihu | 高新(滨江)区 Hi-Tech (Binjiang) |
|---|---|---|---|---|---|---|
| **合计** | **Gross Output Value** | **5011510** | **3533379** | | **40037** | **10514** |
| **一、农业产值** | **Farming** | **2953377** | **1975957** | | **28079** | **9750** |
| (一)种植业产值 | Planting | 2892153 | 1952293 | | 28078 | 9750 |
| #副产品产值 | By-products | 9251 | 5621 | | 13 | 2 |
| 1.粮食作物 | Grain | 179017 | 123948 | | - | 45 |
| 谷物 | Cereal | 138349 | 98777 | | - | 45 |
| 豆类 | Beans | 15573 | 9900 | | - | - |
| 薯类 | Tubers | 25095 | 15271 | | - | - |
| 2.油料 | Oil Plants | 45369 | 20514 | | 84 | - |
| 3.棉花 | Cotton | 451 | 236 | | - | - |
| 4.麻类 | Fiber Crops | 2 | - | | - | - |
| 5.甘蔗 | Sugarcane | 8426 | 6845 | | 92 | - |
| 6.烟叶 | Tobacco | - | - | | - | - |
| 7.药材类 | Crude Drugs | 139832 | 44215 | | 37 | - |
| 8.蔬菜 | Vegetables | 880336 | 675962 | | 4922 | 1908 |
| 9.茶、桑、果、坚果 | Tea, Mulberry & Fruits | 985879 | 511597 | | 9579 | 558 |
| 10.其他 | Others | 652841 | 568976 | | 13364 | 7239 |
| (二)其他农业产值 | Other Farming | 61224 | 23664 | | 1 | - |
| **二、林业产值** | **Forestry** | **618886** | **447986** | | **574** | **-** |
| 1.人造林木生长 | Artificial Forestry | 32962 | 19850 | | 573 | - |
| 2.林产品 | Forest Products | 414016 | 306271 | | - | - |
| 3.村及村以下竹木采伐 | Lumbering | 124431 | 92807 | | 1 | - |
| 4.采集野生植物 | Wild Plant collected | 47477 | 29058 | | - | - |
| **三、畜牧业产值** | **Animal Husbandry** | **767683** | **544019** | | **-** | **-** |
| 1.牲畜 | Livestock | 556348 | 447349 | | - | - |
| 2.家禽饲养 | Poultry Raising | 43002 | 30333 | | - | - |
| 3.活的畜禽产品 | Livestock Products | 98252 | 32758 | | - | - |
| 4.捕猎野兽野禽 | Hunting Wild Beast and Wild Fowl | 6777 | 4394 | | - | - |
| 5.其他动物饲养 | Other Animals Raising | 63304 | 29185 | | - | - |
| **四、渔业产值** | **Fishery** | **485734** | **420732** | | **9620** | **764** |
| **五、农、林、牧、渔专业及辅助性活动** | **Services for Farming, Forestry, Animal Husbandary and Fishery** | **185830** | **144685** | | **1764** | **-** |

## 渔业总产值(2019 年)

## Animal Husbandry and Fishery by Region(2019)

(10000 yuan)

| | | | | | | | | |
|---|---|---|---|---|---|---|---|---|
| 萧山区 Xiaoshan | 余杭区 Yuhang | 富阳区 Fuyang | 临安区 Lin'an | 钱塘新区 Qiantang New Area | 西湖风景名胜区 The West Lake Scenic Zone | 桐庐县 Tonglu | 淳安县 Chun'an | 建德市 Jiande |
| **1192965** | **850031** | **698208** | **668463** | **219233** | **15069** | **373740** | **540516** | **563875** |
| 724026 | 460809 | 407790 | 326017 | 135299 | 15001 | 236568 | 363231 | 377621 |
| 723969 | 457260 | 393698 | 320052 | 135299 | 15001 | 231484 | 361909 | 346467 |
| 1770 | 1688 | 1540 | 589 | 577 | – | 932 | 1055 | 1643 |
| 30861 | 40150 | 34627 | 17690 | 7852 | – | 17241 | 15289 | 22539 |
| 21642 | 37956 | 28471 | 10088 | 4794 | – | 14731 | 8176 | 16665 |
| 7245 | 895 | 1373 | 387 | 2873 | – | 1010 | 2386 | 2277 |
| 1974 | 1299 | 4783 | 7215 | 185 | – | 1500 | 4727 | 3597 |
| 7637 | 2324 | 6814 | 3655 | 2417 | – | 6689 | 7635 | 10531 |
| 138 | 98 | – | – | 12 | – | – | 145 | 70 |
| – | – | – | – | – | – | – | 2 | – |
| 5162 | 853 | 708 | 30 | 2063 | – | 992 | 105 | 484 |
| – | – | – | – | – | – | – | – | – |
| 6116 | 10449 | 12321 | 15292 | – | – | 13468 | 44672 | 37477 |
| 333979 | 168511 | 97120 | 66679 | 90858 | – | 67996 | 65036 | 71342 |
| 52602 | 129079 | 138541 | 165170 | 9926 | 15001 | 97587 | 202276 | 174419 |
| 287474 | 105796 | 103567 | 51536 | 22171 | – | 27511 | 26749 | 29605 |
| 57 | 3549 | 14092 | 5965 | – | – | 5084 | 1322 | 31154 |
| **16052** | **87252** | **128572** | **215468** | **71** | **68** | **59140** | **77136** | **34624** |
| 5161 | 13118 | 655 | 275 | 47 | 68 | 2562 | 8936 | 1614 |
| 8963 | 57207 | 81258 | 158843 | 23 | – | 41790 | 45452 | 20503 |
| 1634 | 14976 | 31614 | 44582 | 1 | – | 7516 | 14579 | 9529 |
| 294 | 1951 | 15045 | 11768 | – | – | 7272 | 8169 | 2978 |
| **271652** | **51034** | **116249** | **103748** | **50610** | **–** | **48314** | **63083** | **112267** |
| 249392 | 35656 | 82539 | 79574 | 47214 | – | 26979 | 43994 | 38026 |
| 7834 | 9623 | 10371 | 2505 | 1231 | – | 1928 | 1649 | 9092 |
| 6739 | 3720 | 10919 | 10232 | 1288 | – | 3135 | 5750 | 56609 |
| – | 253 | 2886 | 1255 | – | – | 1400 | 155 | 828 |
| 7687 | 1782 | 9534 | 10182 | 877 | – | 14872 | 11535 | 7712 |
| **120199** | **192789** | **36700** | **8389** | **26660** | **–** | **18002** | **26680** | **20320** |
| **61036** | **58147** | **8897** | **14841** | **6593** | **–** | **11716** | **10386** | **19043** |

# 3－07 主要农作物播种面积及产量(2018－2019年)

## Sown Areas and Yield of Major Farm Crops(2018－2019)

| 指 标 | Item | 2018 | | | 2019 | | |
|---|---|---|---|---|---|---|---|
| | | 播种面积(千公顷) Sown Area (1000 hectares) | 总产量(吨) Total Output (ton) | 公顷产量(公斤) Yield per Hectare (kg/hectare) | 播种面积(千公顷) Sown Area (1000 hectares) | 总产量(吨) Total Output (ton) | 公顷产量(公斤) Yield per Hectare (kg/hectare) |
| **农作物总计** | **Total Farm Crops** | **276.14** | **–** | **–** | **282.21** | **–** | **–** |
| **一、粮 食** | **Grain Crops** | **88.5** | **495951** | **5604** | **88.7** | **496447** | **5595** |
| (一)谷 物 | Cereals | 66.24 | 424743 | 6412 | – | – | – |
| 1.稻谷 | Rice | 43.58 | 333558 | 7654 | – | – | – |
| ①早稻及早中稻 | Early Rice & Semi－late Rice | 1.41 | 9111 | 6462 | – | – | – |
| ②晚稻及迟中稻 | Late Rice & Semi－late Rice | 42.17 | 324447 | 7694 | – | – | – |
| #单季稻 | #Single－crop Rice | 41.55 | 320541 | 7715 | – | – | – |
| 2.小麦 | Wheat | 10.84 | 40402 | 3727 | – | – | – |
| 3.大麦 | Barley | 0.07 | 298 | 4257 | – | – | – |
| 4.玉米 | Corn | 11.62 | 49956 | 4299 | – | – | – |
| 5.其他谷物 | Other Cereals | 0.13 | 528 | 4062 | – | – | – |
| (二)豆 类 | Beans | 14.51 | 38190 | 2632 | – | – | – |
| 1.大豆 | Soybeans | 13.53 | 34709 | 2565 | – | – | – |
| 2.其他小豆类 | | 0.98 | 3481 | 3552 | – | – | – |
| (三)薯 类 | Tubers | 7.75 | 33019 | 4261 | – | – | – |
| **二、油料** | **Oil Plants** | **23.71** | **66139** | **2789** | **26.32** | **70593** | **2682** |
| 1.油菜籽 | Rapeseeds | 20.04 | 55584 | 2774 | 22.55 | 59503 | 2639 |
| 2.花生 | Peanuts | 1.94 | 7548 | 3891 | 2.34 | 8728 | 3724 |
| 3.芝麻 | Sesame | 1.61 | 2785 | 1730 | 1.42 | 2343 | 1645 |
| 4.其他 | Others | 0.12 | 222 | 1850 | 0.01 | 19 | 3167 |
| **三、棉花(皮棉)** | **Cotton** | **0.17** | **240** | **1412** | **0.19** | **292** | **1521** |
| **四、麻类** | **Fiber Cropers** | **0.003** | **6** | **2000** | **0.003** | **5** | **1667** |
| **五、糖类** | **Sugar Crops** | **0.53** | **30833** | **58175** | **0.84** | **49886** | **59177** |
| **六、烟叶** | **Tobacco** | **–** | **–** | **–** | **–** | **–** | **–** |
| **七、药材** | **Crude Drugs** | **7.31** | **42810** | **5856** | **8.47** | **49093** | **5799** |
| **八、蔬菜** | **Vegetables** | **96.68** | **3409063** | **35261** | **98.53** | **3400525** | **34514** |
| **九、果用瓜** | **Melon as Fruit** | **11.30** | **381249** | **33739** | **10.79** | **368848** | **34191** |
| #西瓜 | Watermelon | 7.70 | 283377 | 36802 | 7.29 | 276084 | 37877 |
| 草莓 | Strawberry | 1.55 | 44280 | 28568 | 1.60 | 45015 | 28170 |
| **十、花卉苗木** | **Flower Gardening** | **36.96** | **–** | **–** | **37.53** | **–** | **–** |
| **十一、其他作物** | **Others** | **10.98** | **–** | **–** | **10.84** | **–** | **–** |
| #绿肥 | Green Manure | 1.53 | – | – | 1.46 | – | – |

# 3－08　分地区粮食播种面积及产量(2019 年)
# Sown Areas and Yield of Grain Crops by Region(2019)

| 地　区 | Region | 播种面积总计(公顷)(Sown Area of Grain Crops (hectare) | 总产量(吨) Yield of Grain Crops(ton) | 公顷产量(公斤) Yield per Hectare(kg) |
|---|---|---|---|---|
| **全　市** | **Whole City** | **88730** | **496447** | **5595** |
| 市区 | Urban District | － | － | － |
| #江干区 | Jianggan | － | － | － |
| 西湖区 | Xihu | － | － | － |
| 高新(滨江)区 | Hi－Tech(Binjiang) | － | － | － |
| 萧山区 | Xiaoshan | 12348 | 67800 | 5491 |
| 余杭区 | Yuhang | 17049 | 113071 | 6632 |
| 富阳区 | Fuyang | 15114 | 96944 | 6414 |
| 临安区 | Lin'an | 6780 | 37150 | 5479 |
| 钱塘新区 | Qiantang New Area | － | － | － |
| 西湖风景名胜区 | The West Lake Scenic Zone | － | － | － |
| 桐庐县 | Tonglu | 7875 | 46889 | 5954 |
| 淳安县 | Chun'an | 11161 | 40504 | 3629 |
| 建德市 | Jiande | 12358 | 67435 | 5457 |

# 3－09 分地区油、菜、茶、

## Statistics on Rapeseeds, Vegetables, Tea,

| 指标 | Item | 全市 Whole City | 市区 Urban District | 江干区 Jianggan | 西湖区 Xihu | 高新(滨江)区 Hi－Tech (Binjiang) |
|---|---|---|---|---|---|---|
| **一、油料** | **Oil Plants** | | | | | |
| 播种面积 (公顷) | Sown Area (hectare) | 26321 | 11105 | | 150 | － |
| 每公顷产量 (公斤) | Yield per Hectare (kg) | 2682 | 2733 | | 2626 | － |
| 总产量 (吨) | Total Output (ton) | 70593 | 30345 | | 394 | － |
| **二、蔬菜** | **Vegetables** | | | | | |
| 播种面积 (公顷) | Sown Area (hectare) | 98525 | 73148 | | 780 | 314 |
| 总产量 (吨) | Total Output (ton) | 3400525 | 2659222 | | 15381 | 10555 |
| **三、茶叶** | **Tea** | | | | | |
| (一)茶园面积 (公顷) | Tea Garden Area (hectare) | 35255 | 14544 | | 1072 | 46 |
| (二)总产量 (吨) | Output of Tea (ton) | 31342 | 19543 | | 442 | 18 |
| 春　茶 (吨) | Spring Tea (ton) | 20049 | 12354 | | 305 | 15 |
| 夏　茶 (吨) | Summer Tea (ton) | 7790 | 5471 | | 32 | － |
| 秋　茶 (吨) | Autumn Tea (ton) | 3503 | 1718 | | 105 | 3 |
| **四、桑蚕** | **Silkworm Cocoons & Mulberry** | | | | | |
| (一)桑园总面积 (公顷) | Mulberry Garden Area (hectare) | 6673 | 1257 | | － | － |
| (二)蚕茧总产量 (吨) | Output of Silkworm Cocoons (ton) | 3454 | 920 | | － | － |
| 春　茧 (吨) | Spring Silkworm Cocoons (ton) | 1644 | 526 | | － | － |
| 夏　茧 (吨) | Summer Silkworm Cocoons (ton) | 304 | 33 | | － | － |
| 秋　茧 (吨) | Autumn Silkworm Cocoons (ton) | 1506 | 361 | | － | － |

# 蚕、果生产情况(2019 年)

# Silkworm Cocoons and Fruits Production by Region(2019)

| 萧山区<br>Xiaoshan | 余杭区<br>Yuhang | 富阳区<br>Fuyang | 临安区<br>Lin'an | 钱塘新区<br>Qiantang New Area | 西湖风景名胜区<br>The West Lake Scenic Zone | 桐庐县<br>Tonglu | 淳安县<br>Chun'an | 建德市<br>Jiande |
|---|---|---|---|---|---|---|---|---|
| | | | | | | | | |
| 4024 | 1615 | 3577 | 1739 | 1470 | – | 3119 | 5974 | 6123 |
| 2975 | 2395 | 2719 | 2520 | 3012 | – | 2324 | 1865 | 3570 |
| 11971 | 3869 | 9727 | 4384 | 4427 | – | 7246 | 11142 | 21860 |
| | | | | | | | | |
| 28523 | 23715 | 10511 | 8223 | 9325 | – | 7110 | 9193 | 9074 |
| 1294834 | 712220 | 395413 | 209947 | 404172 | – | 227552 | 255142 | 258609 |
| | | | | | | | | |
| 1249 | 4264 | 3932 | 3618 | – | 363 | 4095 | 12404 | 4212 |
| 619 | 8647 | 7060 | 2633 | – | 124 | 3713 | 4976 | 3110 |
| 525 | 4742 | 4695 | 1964 | – | 108 | 1654 | 4012 | 2029 |
| 39 | 2581 | 2324 | 490 | – | 5 | 1075 | 521 | 723 |
| 55 | 1324 | 41 | 179 | – | 11 | 984 | 443 | 358 |
| | | | | | | | | |
| – | 356 | 150 | 751 | – | – | 579 | 4621 | 216 |
| – | 46 | 251 | 623 | – | – | 669 | 1601 | 264 |
| – | 36 | 174 | 316 | – | – | 345 | 653 | 120 |
| – | 4 | 19 | 10 | – | – | – | 235 | 36 |
| – | 6 | 58 | 297 | – | – | 324 | 713 | 108 |

3-09 续表

| 指标 | Item | 全市 Whole City | 市区 Urban District | 江干区 Jianggan | 西湖区 Xihu | 高新(滨江)区 Hi-Tech (Binjiang) |
|---|---|---|---|---|---|---|
| **五、水果生产** | **Fruits** | | | | | |
| (一)果园面积合计 (公顷) | Area of Orchards (hectare) | 29024 | 11200 | | 62 | 80 |
| 柑桔园 (公顷) | Citrus (hectare) | 6764 | 464 | | 3 | - |
| 梨　园 (公顷) | Pears (hectare) | 3940 | 1892 | | 7 | 30 |
| 桃　园 (公顷) | Peaches (hectare) | 4287 | 1725 | | 21 | - |
| 杨梅园 (公顷) | Red Bayberry (hectare) | 3175 | 1490 | | - | 47 |
| 枇杷园 (公顷) | Loquat (hectare) | 2742 | 1130 | | - | - |
| 柿子园 (公顷) | Persimmons (hectare) | 817 | 255 | | - | - |
| 葡萄园 (公顷) | Grapes (hectare) | 1302 | 1040 | | 13 | 3 |
| 其他果园 (公顷) | Others (hectare) | 4572 | 2521 | | 18 | - |
| (二)水果总产量 (吨) | Yield of Fruits (ton) | 825816 | 381894 | | 1054 | 926 |
| 柑　桔 (吨) | Citrus (ton) | 187752 | 5380 | | 50 | - |
| 梨　头 (吨) | Pears (ton) | 67713 | 34697 | | 86 | 360 |
| 桃　子 (吨) | Peaches (ton) | 78557 | 48126 | | 35 | - |
| 杨　梅 (吨) | Red Bayberry (ton) | 13145 | 6641 | | - | 32 |
| 枇　杷 (吨) | Loquat (ton) | 17371 | 7994 | | - | - |
| 柿　子 (吨) | Persimmons (ton) | 9445 | 3844 | | 1 | - |
| 葡　萄 (吨) | Grapes (ton) | 25022 | 19790 | | 277 | 10 |
| 果用瓜 (吨) | Melon as Fruit (ton) | 368848 | 222267 | | 431 | 524 |
| 其他水果 (吨) | Others (ton) | 41407 | 26239 | | 174 | - |

continued

| 萧山区 Xiaoshan | 余杭区 Yuhang | 富阳区 Fuyang | 临安区 Lin'an | 钱塘新区 Qiantang New Area | 西湖风景名胜区 The West Lake Scenic Zone | 桐庐县 Tonglu | 淳安县 Chun'an | 建德市 Jiande |
|---|---|---|---|---|---|---|---|---|
| 2256 | 3671 | 2927 | 2204 | 17 | – | 3654 | 8613 | 5557 |
| 38 | 61 | 228 | 134 | 2 | – | 119 | 4675 | 1506 |
| 115 | 881 | 768 | 330 | 2 | – | 1142 | 554 | 352 |
| 156 | 449 | 768 | 331 | 3 | – | 831 | 1015 | 716 |
| 638 | 241 | 406 | 158 | – | – | 543 | 438 | 704 |
| 9 | 1043 | 60 | 18 | 1 | – | 136 | 856 | 620 |
| 70 | 27 | 116 | 42 | – | – | 27 | 450 | 85 |
| 112 | 385 | 341 | 186 | – | – | 109 | 97 | 56 |
| 1070 | 451 | 292 | 690 | 7 | – | 478 | 332 | 1241 |
| 126719 | 65272 | 125589 | 59265 | 37334 | – | 90636 | 124743 | 228543 |
| 423 | 1277 | 2349 | 1281 | 82 | – | 2568 | 63277 | 116527 |
| 1451 | 14282 | 14704 | 3814 | 83 | – | 21245 | 5931 | 5840 |
| 1626 | 7980 | 32325 | 6160 | 81 | – | 10029 | 11493 | 8909 |
| 2746 | 1260 | 1610 | 993 | – | – | 1922 | 1902 | 2680 |
| 177 | 7403 | 161 | 253 | 35 | – | 912 | 6065 | 2400 |
| 961 | 658 | 1190 | 1034 | 7 | – | 321 | 3932 | 1348 |
| 2124 | 7956 | 5966 | 3457 | – | – | 1642 | 1083 | 2507 |
| 109945 | 19200 | 63005 | 26093 | 36895 | – | 46807 | 25185 | 74589 |
| 6242 | 3332 | 3261 | 13230 | 111 | – | 2755 | 3224 | 9189 |

# 3－10 分地区畜牧业
## Statistics on Animal Husbanday

| 指 标 | | Item | | 全市 Whole City | | 市区 Urban District | |
|---|---|---|---|---|---|---|---|
| | | | | 2018 年 | 2019 年 | 2018 年 | 2019 年 |
| **一、生猪** | | **Hogs** | | | | | |
| 生猪年末存栏 | （万头） | Being Raised at Year－end | （10000 heads） | 107.02 | 90.34 | 83.19 | 72.04 |
| #能繁殖的母猪 | （万头） | #Reproducible | （10000 heads） | 7.51 | 7.22 | 6.27 | 5.95 |
| 年内肥猪出栏 | （万头） | Slaughtered Hogs of the Year | （10000 heads） | 199.83 | 140.5 | 151.43 | 116.33 |
| 全年饲养量 | （万头） | Number of Hogs Raised in the year | （10000 heads） | | | | |
| **二、牛** | | **Cattle & Buffaloes** | | | | | |
| 牛年末存栏 | （头） | Being Raised at Year－end | （head） | 13856 | 13013 | 9479 | 8884 |
| #良种及改良种乳牛 | （头） | #Improved Milk Cows | （head） | | | | |
| 牛年内出栏 | （头） | Slaughtered Cattle & Buffaloes of the Year | （head） | 13333 | 13928 | 10951 | 11613 |
| **三、羊** | | **Sheep & Goats** | | | | | |
| 羊年末存栏 | （万只） | Being Raised at Year－end | （10000 heads） | 17.7 | 18.75 | 15.49 | 16.48 |
| 羊年内出栏 | （万只） | Slaughtered Sheep & Goats of the Year | （10000 heads） | 25.22 | 23.83 | 23.23 | 21.93 |
| **四、兔** | | **Rabbits** | | | | | |
| 兔年末存栏 | （万只） | Being Raised at Year－end | （10000 heads） | 13.01 | 6.69 | 12.56 | 6.39 |
| 兔年内出栏 | （万只） | Slaughtered Rabbits of the Year | （10000 heads） | 43.9 | 39.62 | 39.95 | 36.48 |
| **五、家禽** | | **Poultry** | | | | | |
| 家禽年末存栏 | （万只） | Being Raised at Year－end | （10000 heads） | 994.76 | 1025.66 | 473.87 | 451.31 |
| 家禽年内出栏 | （万只） | Slaughtered Poultry of the Year | （10000 heads） | 1696.13 | 1836.37 | 1231.65 | 1316.18 |
| **六、年末养蜂箱数** | **（箱）** | **Beehives** | **（case）** | **162005** | **170845** | **42759** | **47345** |
| **七、畜禽产品产量** | | **Output of Livestock Products** | | | | | |
| 1. 肉类产量 | （吨） | Output of Meat | （ton） | 191081 | 149691 | 144887 | 122013 |
| #猪 肉 | （吨） | Pork | （ton） | 156692 | 111811 | 119859 | 93540 |

注：1. 2019 年渔业生产萧山区不含托管在钱塘新区的街道数据。

2. 国家统计局浙江调查总队会同浙江省统计局对 2018、2019 年年度的畜牧业分地区数据进行了核定。

# 渔业生产(2018 - 2019 年)

# and Fishery by Region(2018 - 2019)

| 江干区 Jianggan | | 西湖区 Xihu | | 高新(滨江)区 Hi - Tech(Binjiang) | | 萧山区 Xiaoshan | | 余杭区 Yuhang | |
|---|---|---|---|---|---|---|---|---|---|
| 2018 年 | 2019 年 | 2018 年 | 2019 年 | 2018 年 | 2019 年 | 2018 年 | 2019 年 | 2018 年 | 2019 年 |
| | | | – | | – | 61.26 | 55.02 | 3.55 | 2.9 |
| | | | – | | – | 4.89 | 4.51 | 0.29 | 0.25 |
| | | | – | | – | 78.18 | 76.86 | 7.89 | 6.52 |
| | | | – | | – | 3632 | 3733 | 296 | 87 |
| | | | – | | – | 704 | 433 | 244 | 256 |
| | | | – | | – | 6.69 | 9.27 | 3.27 | 2.46 |
| | | | – | | – | 8.69 | 8.76 | 5.02 | 4.68 |
| – | | – | – | – | | 0.88 | 0.56 | 2.28 | 1.94 |
| – | | – | – | – | – | 3.06 | 1.52 | 8.16 | 9.03 |
| | | | – | | – | 107.7 | 125.72 | 120.08 | 137.34 |
| | | | – | | – | 254.88 | 313.34 | 438.26 | 488.28 |
| – | | – | – | – | – | 12752 | 13965 | 2158 | 2799 |
| | | | – | – | – | 69901 | 70525 | 12881 | 14058 |
| | | | – | – | – | 64800 | 63700 | 4802 | 4927 |

a) Fishery production of Xiaoshan District dont include districts which under administered by Qiantang New Area in 2019.

b) Zhejiang Survey Team of National Bureau of Statistics and Zhejiang Provincial Bureau of Statistics approved the regional data of animal husbandry in 2018 and 2019.

3－10　续表1

| 指　标 | | Item | | 全市 Whole City | | 市区 Urban District | |
|---|---|---|---|---|---|---|---|
| | | | | 2018 年 | 2019 年 | 2018 年 | 2019 年 |
| 牛　肉 | （吨） | Beef | (ton) | 1857 | 2297 | 1460 | 1915 |
| 羊　肉 | （吨） | Mutton | (ton) | 4046 | 4193 | 3697 | 3861 |
| 兔　肉 | （吨） | Rabbit Meat | (ton) | 759 | 669 | 705 | 625 |
| 禽　肉 | （吨） | Poultry Meat | (ton) | 27359 | 30358 | 18863 | 21758 |
| 2. 禽蛋产量 | （吨） | Poultry Eggs | (ton) | 100142 | 91761 | 25268 | 21148 |
| 3. 蜂蜜产量 | （吨） | Honey | (ton) | 19289 | 18367 | 7605 | 6427 |
| 4. 蜂皇浆产量 | （公斤） | Honey Tonic | (kg) | 525229 | 542807 | 211058 | 211888 |
| 5. 牛奶产量 | （吨） | Milk | (ton) | 27328 | 26335 | 23617 | 22821 |
| 6. 兔毛产量 | （吨） | Rabbit Wool | (ton) | 24 | 18 | 24 | 18 |
| **八、渔业生产** | | **Fishery** | | | | | |
| （一）淡水产品产量总计 | （吨） | Total Output of Freshwater Aquatic Products | (ton) | 166947 | 168042 | 136183 | 136508 |
| 其中：养殖产量 | （吨） | Artificially Cultured | (ton) | 154096 | 153981 | 129898 | 128919 |
| 1. 鱼　类 | （吨） | Fish | (ton) | 95799 | 94255 | 73276 | 70989 |
| #鲫　鱼 | （吨） | #Crucians | (ton) | 14594 | 14363 | 10750 | 10829 |
| 鳊　鱼 | （吨） | Breams | (ton) | 7391 | 7071 | 4367 | 4193 |
| 黑　鱼 | （吨） | Snake Heads | (ton) | 506 | 568 | 495 | 501 |
| 2. 虾蟹类 | （吨） | Shrimps, Prawns & Crabs | (ton) | 26377 | 26931 | 26147 | 26667 |
| 3. 贝　类 | （吨） | Shellfish | (ton) | 873 | 848 | 222 | 232 |
| 4. 其　他 | （吨） | Others | (ton) | 759 | 31947 | 665 | 31031 |
| #甲　鱼 | （吨） | Turtles | (ton) | 30291 | 30855 | 29591 | 30113 |
| （二）淡水养殖面积合计 | （公顷） | Freshwater Aquiculture Area | (hectare) | 54804 | 51980 | 10680 | 7916 |

continued 1

| 江干区 Jianggan | | 西湖区 Xihu | | 高新(滨江)区 Hi－Tech(Binjiang) | | 萧山区 Xiaoshan | | 余杭区 Yuhang | |
|---|---|---|---|---|---|---|---|---|---|
| 2018 年 | 2019 年 | 2018 年 | 2019 年 | 2018 年 | 2019 年 | 2018 年 | 2019 年 | 2018 年 | 2019 年 |
| | | | – | | – | 85 | 72 | 43 | 42 |
| | | | – | | – | 1141 | 1541 | 1090 | 824 |
| – | | – | – | – | – | 50 | 32 | 210 | 193 |
| | | | – | | – | 3825 | 5180 | 6736 | 8072 |
| – | | – | – | – | – | 1843 | 2024 | 3542 | 3315 |
| – | | – | – | – | – | 1396 | 1236 | 277 | 326 |
| – | | – | – | – | – | 92128 | 81903 | 6025 | 6100 |
| – | | – | – | – | – | 10912 | 9264 | – | – |
| – | | – | – | – | – | – | – | 22 | 18 |
| | | | | | | | | | |
| 95 | 95 | 9640 | 6340 | 1215 | 748 | 43843 | 36267 | 59652 | 61729 |
| | | 8391 | 5420 | 830 | 386 | 42977 | 35411 | 57643 | 59625 |
| | | 7512 | 5115 | 470 | 256 | 16049 | 13278 | 31364 | 31776 |
| | | 1633 | 950 | 20 | 10 | 50 | 55 | 3281 | 3329 |
| | | 457 | 365 | – | – | 8 | 12 | 2007 | 1841 |
| | | 185 | 204 | – | – | 220 | 210 | 45 | 40 |
| | | 196 | 102 | 190 | 50 | 22927 | 18578 | 1987 | 2139 |
| | | 2 | – | – | – | – | – | – | – |
| | | 1 | 203 | – | 80 | 84 | 3555 | – | 25710 |
| | | 680 | 202 | 170 | 80 | 3920 | 3456 | 24051 | 25246 |
| | | 758 | 432 | 60 | 60 | 2994 | 2005 | 2510 | 2510 |

3－10 续表2

| 指 标 | | Item | | 富阳区 Fuyang | | 临安区 Lin'an | |
|---|---|---|---|---|---|---|---|
| | | | | 2018 年 | 2019 年 | 2018 年 | 2019 年 |
| **一、生猪** | | **Hogs** | | | | | |
| 生猪年末存栏 | （万头） | Being Raised at Year－end | （10000 heads） | 8.42 | 4.25 | 9.96 | 9.87 |
| #能繁殖的母猪 | （万头） | #Reproducible | （10000 heads） | 0.48 | 0.36 | 0.61 | 0.82 |
| 年内肥猪出栏 | （万头） | Slaughtered Hogs of the Year | （10000 heads） | 35.09 | 14.98 | 30.27 | 17.98 |
| 全年饲养量 | （万头） | Number of Hogs Raised in the year | （10000 heads） | | | | |
| **二、牛** | | **Cattle & Buffaloes** | | | | | |
| 牛年末存栏 | （头） | Being Raised at Year－end | （head） | 2921 | 2482 | 2630 | 2582 |
| #良种及改良种乳牛 | （头） | #Improved Milk Cows | （head） | | | | |
| 牛年内出栏 | （头） | Slaughtered Cattle & Buffaloes of the Year | （head） | 7441 | 8642 | 2562 | 2282 |
| **三、羊** | | **Sheep & Goats** | | | | | |
| 羊年末存栏 | （万只） | Being Raised at Year－end | （10000 heads） | 2.35 | 1.45 | 3.18 | 3.31 |
| 羊年内出栏 | （万只） | Slaughtered Sheep & Goats of the Year | （10000 heads） | 4.85 | 3.77 | 4.67 | 4.73 |
| **四、兔** | | **Rabbits** | | | | | |
| 兔年末存栏 | （万只） | Being Raised at Year－end | （10000 heads） | 8.31 | 3.2 | 1.09 | 0.69 |
| 兔年内出栏 | （万只） | Slaughtered Rabbits of the Year | （10000 heads） | 20.23 | 22.84 | 8.5 | 3.09 |
| **五、家禽** | | **Poultry** | | | | | |
| 家禽年末存栏 | （万只） | Being Raised at Year－end | （10000 heads） | 193.12 | 121.04 | 52.97 | 67.21 |
| 家禽年内出栏 | （万只） | Slaughtered Poultry of the Year | （10000 heads） | 443.29 | 419.45 | 95.22 | 95.12 |
| **六、年末养蜂箱数** | **（箱）** | **Beehives** | **（case）** | **18297** | **19134** | **9552** | **11447** |
| **七、畜禽产品产量** | | **Output of Livestock Products** | | | | | |
| 1. 肉类产量 | （吨） | Output of Meat | （ton） | 34620 | 20722 | 27485 | 16708 |
| #猪 肉 | （吨） | Pork | （ton） | 25928 | 11322 | 24329 | 13591 |

continued 2

| 钱塘新区<br>Qiantang New Area | | 西湖风景名胜区<br>The West Lake Scenic Zone | | 桐庐县<br>Tonglu | | 淳安县<br>Chun'an | | 建德市<br>Jiande | |
|---|---|---|---|---|---|---|---|---|---|
| 2018 年 | 2019 年 | 2018 年 | 2019 年 | 2018 年 | 2019 年 | 2018 年 | 2019 年 | 2018 年 | 2019 年 |
| | | | – | 4.61 | 3.2 | 12.5 | 10.28 | 6.72 | 4.82 |
| | | | – | 0.27 | 0.25 | 0.42 | 0.33 | 0.55 | 0.69 |
| | | | – | 11.11 | 5.74 | 20.93 | 11.03 | 16.36 | 7.4 |
| | | | | | | | | | |
| | | | – | 1185 | 1012 | 1333 | 1157 | 1859 | 1960 |
| | | | | | | | | | |
| | | | – | 1017 | 944 | 643 | 635 | 722 | 736 |
| | | | | | | | | | |
| | | | – | 0.63 | 0.58 | 0.49 | 0.45 | 1.09 | 1.24 |
| | | | | 0.54 | 0.54 | 0.43 | 0.45 | 1.01 | 0.91 |
| | | | | | | | | | |
| | 0.32 | – | – | 0.21 | 0.16 | 0.14 | 0.14 | 0.1 | – |
| | 1.23 | – | – | 0.59 | 0.48 | 0.16 | 0.16 | 3.2 | 2.5 |
| | | | | | | | | | |
| | | | – | 45.41 | 53.27 | 61.43 | 57.48 | 414.05 | 463.6 |
| | | | – | 70.57 | 71.17 | 52.24 | 63.51 | 341.67 | 385.51 |
| | 5600 | – | – | 65296 | 67992 | 38379 | 39937 | 15571 | 15571 |
| | | | | | | | | | |
| | | | – | 11210 | 5819 | 16570 | 9579 | 18414 | 12280 |
| | | | – | 9907 | 4340 | 15609 | 8340 | 11317 | 5591 |

3－10 续表3

| 指标 |  | Item |  | 富阳区 Fuyang |  | 临安区 Lin'an |  |
|---|---|---|---|---|---|---|---|
|  |  |  |  | 2018年 | 2019年 | 2018年 | 2019年 |
| 牛肉 | （吨） | Beef | （ton） | 866 | 1425 | 466 | 376 |
| 羊肉 | （吨） | Mutton | （ton） | 615 | 663 | 851 | 833 |
| 兔肉 | （吨） | Rabbit Meat | （ton） | 310 | 344 | 135 | 56 |
| 禽肉 | （吨） | Poultry Meat | （ton） | 6871 | 6934 | 1431 | 1572 |
| 2.禽蛋产量 | （吨） | Poultry Eggs | （ton） | 15124 | 12187 | 4759 | 5622 |
| 3.蜂蜜产量 | （吨） | Honey | （ton） | 3749 | 3064 | 2183 | 1801 |
| 4.蜂皇浆产量 | （公斤） | Honey Tonic | （kg） | 68723 | 79549 | 44182 | 44336 |
| 5.牛奶产量 | （吨） | Milk | （ton） | – | – | 8792 | 8650 |
| 6.兔毛产量 | （吨） | Rabbit Wool | （ton） | – | – | 2 | – |
| **八、渔业生产** |  | **Fishery** |  |  |  |  |  |
| （一）淡水产品产量总计 | （吨） | Total Output of Freshwater Aquatic Products | （ton） | 15748 | 17780 | 5244 | 5246 |
| 其中：养殖产量 | （吨） | Artificially Cultured | （ton） | 14927 | 16860 | 4437 | 2984 |
| 1.鱼类 | （吨） | Fish | （ton） | 13770 | 15609 | 3887 | 2402 |
| #鲫鱼 | （吨） | #Crucians | （ton） | 4894 | 5597 | 822 | 547 |
| 鳊鱼 | （吨） | Breams | （ton） | 1506 | 1735 | 389 | 240 |
| 黑鱼 | （吨） | Snake Heads | （ton） | 45 | 47 |  | – |
| 2.虾蟹类 | （吨） | Shrimps, Prawns & Crabs | （ton） | 340 | 354 | 38 | 69 |
| 3.贝类 | （吨） | Shellfish | （ton） | 220 | 232 |  | – |
| 4.其他 | （吨） | Others | （ton） | 218 | 665 | 121 | 513 |
| #甲鱼 | （吨） | Turtles | （ton） | 379 | 426 | 391 | 398 |
| （二）淡水养殖面积合计 | （公顷） | Freshwater Aquiculture Area | （hectare） | 1503 | 1503 | 2716 | 734 |

continued 3

| 钱塘新区<br>Qiantang New Area | | 西湖风景名胜区<br>The West Lake Scenic Zone | | 桐庐县<br>Tonglu | | 淳安县<br>Chun'an | | 建德市<br>Jiande | |
|---|---|---|---|---|---|---|---|---|---|
| 2018 年 | 2019 年 | 2018 年 | 2019 年 | 2018 年 | 2019 年 | 2018 年 | 2019 年 | 2018 年 | 2019 年 |
| | | | – | 184 | 156 | 54 | 105 | 159 | 121 |
| | | | – | 68 | 94 | 32 | 79 | 249 | 159 |
| | 19 | – | – | 11 | 9 | 5 | 5 | 38 | 30 |
| | | | – | 984 | 1177 | 870 | 1050 | 6642 | 6373 |
| | 138 | – | – | 2307 | 2656 | 6292 | 5933 | 66275 | 62024 |
| | 243 | – | – | 5667 | 5856 | 3978 | 4012 | 2039 | 2072 |
| | 27707 | – | – | 249996 | 266166 | 48469 | 49985 | 15706 | 14768 |
| | 4907 | – | – | – | – | – | – | 3711 | 3514 |
| | – | – | – | – | – | – | – | – | – |
| | | | | | | | | | |
| | 8303 | | – | 8076 | 8720 | 13249 | 13345 | 9439 | 9469 |
| | 8233 | | – | 7656 | 7980 | 10264 | 10625 | 6278 | 6457 |
| | 2553 | | – | 7026 | 7283 | 10085 | 10442 | 5412 | 5541 |
| | 341 | | – | 1610 | 1640 | 1245 | 1259 | 989 | 635 |
| | – | | – | 823 | 906 | 1025 | 1042 | 1176 | 930 |
| | – | | – | 11 | 11 | | – | | 56 |
| | 5375 | | – | 166 | 160 | | – | 64 | 104 |
| | – | | – | | – | | – | 651 | 616 |
| | 305 | | – | | 537 | | 183 | 94 | 196 |
| | 305 | | – | 464 | 483 | 179 | 183 | 57 | 76 |
| | 672 | | – | 1340 | 1340 | 41041 | 41041 | 1743 | 1683 |

# 3-11 分地区林业

## Statistics on Forestry

| 指 标 | Item | 全市 Whole City | 市区 Urban District |
|---|---|---|---|
| **一、营林情况** | **Afforestation** | | |
| 1. 当年造林面积 （公顷） | Afforested Areas (hectare) | 617 | 186 |
| 2. 迹地更新面积 （公顷） | Area of Forest Updating (hectare) | 1559 | 470 |
| 3. 封山育林面积 （公顷） | Area of Afforestation in Enclosed Mountain (hectare) | 648 | 382 |
| 4. 零星（四旁）植树 （万株） | Planting Trees (10000 plant) | 162 | 75 |
| 5. 中、幼龄林抚育面积（公顷） | Area of Grown Forest Cultivated (hectare) | 15389 | 5985 |
| **二、林产品产量** | **Output of Forest Products** | | |
| 1. 油茶籽 （吨） | Camellia Seeds (ton) | 11162 | 192 |
| 2. 竹笋干 （吨） | Dried Bamboo Shoots (ton) | 70762 | 54519 |
| 3. 核 桃 （吨） | Walnuts (ton) | 25528 | 15315 |
| 4. 板 栗 （吨） | Chestnuts (ton) | 12221 | 1343 |
| **三、竹木采伐量** | **Lumbering** | | |
| 1. 木 材 （万立方米） | Timber Cut (10000 cu. m) | 26.33 | 8.46 |
| 2. 竹 材 （万支） | Bamboo Cut (10000 pieces) | 3211.55 | 2420.00 |

注：1. 萧山区不含托管在钱塘新区的街道数据。

2. 2019 年起封山育林面积为当年新增封山育林面积。

生产(2019年)
by Region(2019)

| 萧山区 Xiaoshan | 余杭区 Yuhang | 富阳区 Fuyang | 临安区 Lin'an | 桐庐县 Tonglu | 淳安县 Chun'an | 建德市 Jiande |
|---|---|---|---|---|---|---|
| 27 | 7 | 107 | 45 | 70 | 124 | 237 |
| | 40 | 90 | 340 | 71 | 451 | 567 |
| | | | 382 | | 66 | 200 |
| 32 | | 18 | 25 | 17 | 14 | 56 |
| 866 | 1000 | 1433 | 2550 | 667 | 5060 | 3677 |
| | | 80 | 112 | 390 | 8480 | 2100 |
| 2115 | 11756 | 13080 | 25748 | 7626 | 7734 | 2703 |
| | 6 | 200 | 15109 | 1250 | 8827 | 136 |
| 400 | 136 | 22 | 785 | 450 | 3600 | 2778 |
| 0.01 | 1.45 | 2.11 | 4.89 | 2.09 | 7.16 | 8.62 |
| – | 891.50 | 901.00 | 627.50 | 107.33 | 456.62 | 227.60 |

a) Figures of Xiaoshan District don't include districts which under administered by Qiantang New Area.

b) Area of Afforestation in Enclosed Mountain was newly added in the cument year since 2019.

# 3-12 分地区主要农
## Possession of Major Agricultural

| 指　标 | | Item | | 全市 Whole City | 市区 Urban District |
|---|---|---|---|---|---|
| **一、农业机械总动力** | **(千瓦)** | **Total Power of Agricultural Machinery** | **(kw)** | **2147487** | **1520729** |
| 耕作机械动力 | (千瓦) | Cultivation Machinery | (kw) | 207900 | 155558 |
| 收获机械动力 | (千瓦) | Harvest Machinery | (kw) | 53083 | 39864 |
| 植保机械动力 | (千瓦) | Plant Protection Machinery | (kw) | 50579 | 40169 |
| 排灌机械动力 | (千瓦) | Drainage & Irrigation Machinery | (kw) | 340781 | 248717 |
| 农副产品加工机械动力 | (千瓦) | Processing Machinery of Agricultural Products | (kw) | 243520 | 169190 |
| 运输机械动力 | (千瓦) | Transport Machinery | (kw) | 152492 | 91806 |
| 渔业机械动力 | (千瓦) | Fishery Machinery | (kw) | 126418 | 98323 |
| 其他机械动力 | (千瓦) | Other Machinery | (kw) | 972714 | 677102 |
| **二、主要农机具** | | **Agricultural Machinery and Machinery For Processing Farm Products** | | | |
| 大中型拖拉机 | (台) | Large & Medium Tractors | (unit) | 1265 | 1169 |
| 机引农具 | (台) | Mechanized Farm Implement | (unit) | 8676 | 6878 |
| 农用小型拖拉机 | (台) | Mini - tractors | (unit) | 5982 | 4738 |
| 联合收获机 | (台) | Combine Harvesters | (unit) | 906 | 653 |
| 机动割晒机 | (台) | Motorized Harvesters | (unit) | 6 | 6 |
| 机动脱粒机 | (台) | Motorized Thresher | (unit) | 11616 | 8713 |
| 谷物烘干机 | (台) | Cereal Dryer | (unit) | 719 | 481 |
| 机动喷雾(粉)器 | (架) | Motorized Sprayer | (unit) | 30117 | 24150 |
| 农用水泵 | (台) | Water Pump for Agricultural Use | (unit) | 121542 | 83141 |
| 节水喷灌机械 | (套) | Saving Water and Sprinkling Machinery | (set) | 4235 | 682 |
| 粮食加工机械 | (台) | Grain Processing Machinery | (unit) | 18026 | 7903 |
| 棉花加工机械 | (台) | Cotton Processing Machinery | (unit) | 217 | 133 |
| 油料加工机械 | (台) | Oil Processing Machinery | (unit) | 1478 | 407 |
| 农用运输机械 | (台) | Vehicles for Agricultural Use | (unit) | 7179 | 4988 |

注:萧山区不含托管在钱塘新区的街道数据。

# 机具年末拥有量(2019 年)
## Machinery at the Year - end by Region(2019)

| 萧山区 Xiaosha | 余杭区 Yuhang | 富阳区 Fuyang | 临安区 Lin'an | 桐庐县 Tonglu | 淳安县 Chun'an | 建德市 Jiande |
|---|---|---|---|---|---|---|
| **395082** | **323969** | **276935** | **308887** | **139571** | **311117** | **176070** |
| 41019 | 42229 | 28374 | 29090 | 11252 | 16454 | 24636 |
| 8628 | 9554 | 12366 | 2114 | 6624 | 1559 | 5036 |
| 4197 | 3603 | 2267 | 28104 | 1567 | 4071 | 4771 |
| 75644 | 66518 | 43410 | 44032 | 27860 | 21750 | 42454 |
| 21134 | 13072 | 105921 | 22729 | 11286 | 46463 | 16581 |
| 32824 | 17664 | 16656 | 12752 | 11340 | 25399 | 23947 |
| 71747 | 7429 | 1913 | 137 | 1545 | 24355 | 2196 |
| 139889 | 163900 | 66028 | 169929 | 68097 | 171066 | 56450 |
| | | | | | | |
| 378 | 300 | 162 | 116 | 58 | 27 | 11 |
| 1994 | 1139 | 3205 | 532 | 613 | 105 | 1080 |
| 987 | 1156 | 2129 | 334 | 413 | 176 | 655 |
| 252 | 143 | 161 | 40 | 146 | 32 | 75 |
| – | 4 | 2 | – | – | – | – |
| 202 | 3680 | 4493 | 251 | 1539 | 1312 | 52 |
| 98 | 168 | 106 | 54 | 97 | 25 | 116 |
| 2923 | 623 | 1676 | 15874 | 754 | 3060 | 2153 |
| 15443 | 14282 | 18911 | 31589 | 10822 | 4947 | 22632 |
| 224 | 343 | 8 | 63 | 50 | 556 | 2947 |
| 1105 | 789 | 1106 | 4662 | 1151 | 7335 | 1637 |
| 49 | 8 | 51 | 4 | 13 | 55 | 16 |
| 75 | 41 | 83 | 187 | 224 | 565 | 282 |
| 1967 | 852 | 1050 | 724 | 662 | 481 | 1048 |

a) Figures of Xiaoshan District dont include districts which under administered by Qiantang New Area.

# 3－13 农业物资
# Agricultural Material

| 指　标 | | Item | | 全市 Whole City | 市区 Urban District |
|---|---|---|---|---|---|
| **一、农村用电量** | **（万千瓦时）** | **Electricity Consumed in Rural Area** | **(10000 kwh)** | **1060993** | **951085** |
| **二、农业化肥施用量** | | **Consumption of Chemical Fertilizer** | | | |
| （一）按实物量计算 | （吨） | Physical Quantity Consumption | (ton) | 407001 | 278676 |
| 1. 氮　肥 | （吨） | Nitrogenous Fertilizer | (ton) | 158008 | 97248 |
| 2. 磷　肥 | （吨） | Phosphate Fertilizer | (ton) | 63470 | 45478 |
| 3. 钾　肥 | （吨） | Potash Fertilizer | (ton) | 34922 | 21829 |
| 4. 复合肥 | （吨） | Compound Fertilizer | (ton) | 150601 | 114121 |
| （二）按折纯法计算 | （吨） | Pure Consumption | (ton) | 83773 | 50443 |
| 1. 氮　肥 | （吨） | Nitrogenous Fertilizer | (ton) | 34011 | 19901 |
| 2. 磷　肥 | （吨） | Phosphate Fertilizer | (ton) | 9314 | 5240 |
| 3. 钾　肥 | （吨） | Potash Fertilizer | (ton) | 7001 | 3833 |
| 4. 复合肥 | （吨） | Compound Fertilizer | (ton) | 33447 | 21469 |
| **三、农用塑料薄膜使用量** | **（吨）** | **Use of Plastic Film** | **(ton)** | **8280** | **4138** |
| **四、农用柴油使用量** | **（吨）** | **Consumption of Diesel Oil** | **(ton)** | **24771** | **15010** |
| **五、农药使用量** | **（吨）** | **Consumption of Pesticide** | **(ton)** | **5924** | **3941** |

# 消耗情况（2019 年）
# Consumption（2019）

| 萧山区 Xiaosha | 余杭区 Yuhang | 富阳区 Fuyang | 临安区 Lin'an | 桐庐县 Tonglu | 淳安县 Chun'an | 建德市 Jiande |
|---|---|---|---|---|---|---|
| **160984** | **175987** | **454658** | **134678** | **71822** | **16054** | **22032** |
| | | | | | | |
| 155465 | 38904 | 17530 | 62401 | 33951 | 47695 | 46679 |
| 60289 | 11427 | 7150 | 17057 | 15801 | 25071 | 19888 |
| 30802 | 6970 | 750 | 6361 | 7083 | 5144 | 5765 |
| 10629 | 5424 | 430 | 4864 | 3691 | 4302 | 5100 |
| 53745 | 15083 | 9200 | 34119 | 7376 | 13178 | 15926 |
| 18355 | 10219 | 7537 | 13021 | 9659 | 6750 | 16921 |
| 8462 | 2400 | 3004 | 5458 | 3806 | 2726 | 7578 |
| 2778 | 1045 | 270 | 1082 | 1393 | 675 | 2006 |
| 1277 | 1193 | 215 | 1022 | 1086 | 352 | 1730 |
| 5838 | 5581 | 4048 | 5459 | 3374 | 2997 | 5607 |
| **2151** | **388** | **270** | **1196** | **741** | **1621** | **1780** |
| **5488** | **2005** | **442** | **6793** | **4715** | **1646** | **3400** |
| **1338** | **870** | **652** | **1003** | **654** | **502** | **827** |

# 3－14 乡(镇)

## Statistics on Towns

| 乡镇名称 Town | | 社区(居民委员会) Number of communities (residents committees) | 村民委员会(个) Number of Villagers' Committees (unit) | 乡镇户籍户数(户) Resident Households in Towns (household) |
|---|---|---|---|---|
| **全　市** | **Whole City** | **708** | **2007** | **1768517** |
| **西湖区** | **Xihu District** | **94** | **32** | **96066** |
| 留下街道 | Liuxia Subdistrict | 12 | 1 | 9136 |
| 转塘街道 | Zhuantang Subdistrict | 35 | 8 | 29610 |
| 三墩镇 | Sandun | 38 | 2 | 41551 |
| 双浦镇 | Shuangpu | 9 | 21 | 15769 |
| **高新(滨江)区** | **Hi－Tech(Bingjiang) District** | **61** | **－** | **74800** |
| 西兴街道 | Xixing Subdistrict | 17 | － | 22379 |
| 长河街道 | Changhe Subdistrict | 23 | － | 23177 |
| 浦沿街道 | Puyan Subdistrict | 21 | － | 29244 |
| **西湖风景名胜区** | **The West Lake Scenic Zone** | **6** | **9** | **6179** |
| 西湖街道 | West Lake Subdistrict | 6 | 9 | 6179 |
| **萧山区** | **Xiaoshan District** | **181** | **352** | **339373** |
| 城厢街道 | Chengxiang Subdistrict | 34 | － | 38957 |
| 北干街道 | Beigan Subdistrict | 27 | 6 | 25649 |
| 蜀山街道 | Shushan Subdistrict | 20 | 8 | 11215 |
| 新塘街道 | Xintang Subdistrict | 27 | 17 | 19874 |
| 靖江街道 | Jingjiang Subdistrict | 7 | 10 | 10382 |
| 南阳街道 | Nanyang Subdistrict | 3 | 13 | 10316 |
| 闻堰街道 | Wenyan Subdistrict | 7 | 6 | 10758 |
| 宁围街道 | Ningwei Subdistrict | 11 | 15 | 21616 |

# 基本情况(2019 年)
and Townships(2019)

| 乡镇户籍人口数 (人) Resident Population in Towns (person) | 乡镇常用耕地面积 (公顷) Commonly used cultivated area of township (hectare) | 一般公共预算收入 (万元) General public budget income (10000 yuan) | 一般公共预算支出 (万元) General public budget expenditure (10000 yuan) |
|---:|---:|---:|---:|
| **5745314** | **150023** | **4084799** | **2512117.1** |
| **344772** | **2950.5** | **346354.6** | **81095.6** |
| 33685 | - | 16967 | 16967 |
| 101982 | 406 | 161924.2 | 28368.5 |
| 144297 | 273.5 | 114184.5 | 22528.9 |
| 64808 | 2271 | 53278.9 | 13231.2 |
| **278414** | **547.8** | **122769** | **62727** |
| 85347 | 151.8 | 32606 | 18257 |
| 87522 | 291 | 51100 | 21600 |
| 105545 | 105 | 39063 | 22870 |
| **19434** | **-** | **17377.2** | **17377.2** |
| 19434 | - | 17377.2 | 17377.2 |
| **1164895** | **28637.6** | **1416882.2** | **801110.8** |
| 113145 | - | 27939 | 27845.4 |
| 77752 | 192 | 312939 | 312939 |
| 45414 | 526 | 160028 | 22588.6 |
| 72744 | 682 | 123145 | 26716.3 |
| 36859 | 1303 | 26541 | 26541 |
| 40848 | 1301 | 27480 | 15892 |
| 36799 | 295 | 52872 | 22343 |
| 72206 | 2171 | 130787 | 30500 |

3－14 续表1

| 乡镇名称 | Town | 社区(居民委员会) Number of Communities (residents committees) | 村民委员会(个) Number of Villagers' Committees (unit) | 乡镇户籍户数(户) Resident Households in Towns (household) |
|---|---|---|---|---|
| 新街街道 | Xinjie Subdistrict | 5 | 15 | 17546 |
| 楼塔镇 | Louta | 1 | 12 | 7650 |
| 河上镇 | Heshang | 1 | 15 | 8721 |
| 戴村镇 | Daicun | 1 | 22 | 11033 |
| 浦阳镇 | Puyang | 1 | 18 | 9779 |
| 进化镇 | Jinhua | 1 | 25 | 13671 |
| 临浦镇 | Linpu | 14 | 20 | 16724 |
| 义桥镇 | Yiqiao | 3 | 21 | 16205 |
| 所前镇 | Suoqian | 2 | 19 | 10718 |
| 衙前镇 | Yaqian | 2 | 11 | 6744 |
| 瓜沥镇 | Guali | 12 | 63 | 47189 |
| 益农镇 | Yinong | 1 | 19 | 12377 |
| 党湾镇 | Dangwan | 1 | 17 | 12249 |
| **余杭区** | **Yuhang District** | **190** | **176** | **336958** |
| 临平街道 | Linping Subdistrict | 15 | – | 16472 |
| 南苑街道 | Nanyuan Subdistrict | 26 | – | 26740 |
| 东湖街道 | Donghu Subdistrict | 35 | 4 | 30811 |
| 星桥街道 | Xingqiao Subdistrict | 16 | – | 12957 |
| 五常街道 | Wuchang Subdistrict | 13 | – | 12667 |
| 乔司街道 | Qiaosi Subdistrict | 4 | 11 | 15197 |

| 乡镇户籍人口数（人）Resident Population in Towns (person) | 乡镇常用耕地面积（公顷）Commonly used cultivated area of township (hectare) | 一般公共预算收入（万元）General public budget income (10000 yuan) | 一般公共预算支出（万元）General public budget expenditure (10000 yuan) |
|---|---|---|---|
| 61392 | 1908 | 65104 | 25012 |
| 26498 | 861 | 6124.2 | 7021.3 |
| 28042 | 835.8 | 16821 | 7025 |
| 38902 | 1199.4 | 17775 | 20207 |
| 32731 | 1220.3 | 22137 | 22458 |
| 48104 | 1141 | 14976 | 14886 |
| 56553 | 1048 | 44627 | 32088 |
| 56840 | 1335.4 | 84373 | 26000 |
| 40788 | 794 | 25800 | 9965 |
| 27003 | 520 | 79484 | 41745 |
| 165203 | 6213 | 123257 | 57821 |
| 43757 | 2793 | 25672 | 22754 |
| 43315 | 2298.7 | 29001 | 28763.2 |
| **1161478** | **24666.4** | **1234085.2** | **640007.2** |
| 45371 | 61.4 | 19327.4 | 17679 |
| 88292 | 469 | 46251.3 | 12360.3 |
| 112887 | 791 | 163512 | 163512 |
| 39319 | 147.2 | 12298.4 | 13391.2 |
| 47880 | 21.6 | 166511.3 | 27553.5 |
| 59486 | 805.3 | 26738.4 | 26240.4 |

3－14　续表2

| 乡镇名称 | Town | 社区(居民委员会) Number of Communities (residents committees) | 村民委员会(个) Number of Villagers′ Committees (unit) | 乡镇户籍户数(户) Resident Households in Towns (household) |
|---|---|---|---|---|
| 运河街道 | Yunhe Subdistrict | 5 | 14 | 10437 |
| 崇贤街道 | Chongxian Subdistrict | 4 | 11 | 14409 |
| 仁和街道 | Renhe Subdistrict | 2 | 18 | 17760 |
| 良渚街道 | Liangzhu Subdistrict | 22 | 20 | 39371 |
| 闲林街道 | Xianlin Subdistrict | 8 | 8 | 21229 |
| 仓前街道 | Cangqian Subdistrict | 5 | 6 | 13802 |
| 余杭街道 | Yuhang Subdistrict | 10 | 13 | 29674 |
| 中泰街道 | Zhongtai Subdistrict | 4 | 10 | 10888 |
| 塘栖镇 | Tangqi | 10 | 18 | 22849 |
| 径山镇 | Jingshan | 2 | 13 | 12062 |
| 瓶窑镇 | Pingyao | 6 | 13 | 18456 |
| 鸬鸟镇 | Luniao | 1 | 6 | 3647 |
| 百丈镇 | Baizhang | 1 | 6 | 3283 |
| 黄湖镇 | Huanghu | 1 | 5 | 4247 |
| **富阳区** | **Fuyang District** | **49** | **276** | **217266** |
| 富春街道 | Fuchun Subdistrict | 35 | 12 | 49369 |
| 春江街道 | Chunjiang Subdistrict | - | 9 | 7997 |
| 鹿山街道 | Lushan Subdistrict | 2 | 9 | 8178 |
| 东洲街道 | Dongzhou Subdistrict | 4 | 15 | 12141 |
| 银湖街道 | Yinghu Subdistrict | 1 | 22 | 16342 |
| 万市镇 | Wanshi | 1 | 15 | 7112 |

| 乡镇户籍人口数<br>(人)<br>Resident Population in Towns<br>(person) | 乡镇常用耕地面积<br>(公顷)<br>Commonly used cultivated area of township<br>(hectare) | 一般公共预算收入<br>(万元)<br>General public budget income<br>(10000 yuan) | 一般公共预算支出<br>(万元)<br>General public budget expenditure<br>(10000 yuan) |
|---:|---:|---:|---:|
| 42324 | 1263 | 23366 | 23553 |
| 57279 | 905 | 57649 | 25831 |
| 75092 | 2530 | 20434 | 28218 |
| 140407 | 2800 | 214163 | 69938.3 |
| 61176 | 257.5 | 24684 | 23261 |
| 52296 | 1482.3 | 168211.5 | 30040.9 |
| 86090 | 2747.5 | 83102.4 | 33066.8 |
| 34470 | 1137.3 | 27914.9 | 12126.7 |
| 81729 | 1813 | 34881 | 43022 |
| 39092 | 3175 | 42077.7 | 41899.7 |
| 62085 | 2315 | 89086 | 30371 |
| 11995 | 760 | 1428 | 5096 |
| 10694 | 250.9 | 4403 | 4630 |
| 13514 | 934.4 | 8045.9 | 8216.4 |
| **687358** | **18292.4** | **336556.7** | **278437.4** |
| 134733 | 955 | 73619 | 46329 |
| 30428 | 403 | 11137.9 | 11129.6 |
| 25267 | 756 | 6634 | 6634 |
| 47425 | 1054 | 11536 | 11522 |
| 55646 | 1632 | 17938 | 17357 |
| 22158 | 1184 | 7848 | 7850 |

3-14 续表3

| 乡 镇 名 称<br>Town | | 社区(居民委员会)<br>Number of Communities (residents committees) | 村民委员会(个)<br>Number of Villagers' Committees (unit) | 乡镇户籍户数(户)<br>Resident Households in Towns (household) |
|---|---|---|---|---|
| 洞桥镇 | Dongqiao | – | 11 | 6070 |
| 渌渚镇 | Luzhu | – | 13 | 5263 |
| 永昌镇 | Yongchang | – | 5 | 3449 |
| 里山镇 | Lishan | – | 5 | 2961 |
| 常绿镇 | Changlu | – | 8 | 5143 |
| 场口镇 | Changkou | 1 | 24 | 13615 |
| 常安镇 | Chang'an | – | 16 | 7698 |
| 龙门镇 | Longmen | – | 4 | 2532 |
| 新登镇 | Xindeng | 4 | 28 | 23006 |
| 胥口镇 | Xukou | – | 13 | 6053 |
| 大源镇 | Dayuan | 1 | 15 | 10506 |
| 灵桥镇 | Lingqiao | – | 13 | 7594 |
| 新桐乡 | Xintong | – | 7 | 4500 |
| 上官乡 | Shangguan | – | 5 | 2670 |
| 环山乡 | Huanshan | – | 7 | 3965 |
| 湖源乡 | Huyuan | – | 10 | 4407 |
| 春建乡 | Chunjian | – | 6 | 2951 |
| 渔山乡 | Yushan | – | 4 | 3744 |
| **临安区** | **Lin'an City** | **40** | **270** | **188912** |
| 玲珑街道 | Linlong Subdistrict | 2 | 14 | 8864 |
| 锦南街道 | Jinnan Subdistrict | 3 | 7 | 4345 |
| 锦城街道 | Jincheng Subdistrict | 15 | 4 | 33718 |
| 锦北街道 | Jinbei Subdistrict | 9 | 5 | 13806 |
| 青山湖街道 | Qingshanghu Subdistrict | 7 | 14 | 13275 |

# 基本情况(2019 年)
## and Townships(2019)

| 乡镇户籍人口数(人)<br>Resident Population in Towns (person) | 乡镇常用耕地面积(公顷)<br>Commonly used cultivated area of township (hectare) | 一般公共预算收入(万元)<br>General public budget income (10000 yuan) | 一般公共预算支出(万元)<br>General public budget expenditure (10000 yuan) |
|---|---|---|---|
| 19209 | 1110 | 3070.7 | 3070.7 |
| 16878 | 921 | 43557 | 42651 |
| 11494 | 493 | 2173 | 2173 |
| 10076 | 406 | 3908.2 | 3931.2 |
| 15473 | 198.2 | 2917 | 2258 |
| 43543 | 1522 | 35378.2 | 26442.9 |
| 25196 | 874 | 3707.9 | 3707.9 |
| 6991 | 240 | 6315 | 6315 |
| 68499 | 2259 | 22138.7 | 22110.1 |
| 18343 | 885 | 21490 | 20232 |
| 36085 | 471 | 12888.7 | 12855.9 |
| 26838 | 606 | 8494.3 | 8583.8 |
| 14129 | 705 | 2138 | 2038 |
| 8079 | 257.6 | 4100.1 | 4083.8 |
| 12927 | 387 | 21696 | 4214 |
| 15458 | 268 | 4422.4 | 4417.6 |
| 9275 | 491 | 5086 | 5086 |
| 13208 | 214.6 | 4362.6 | 3444.9 |
| **539473** | **17787.2** | **228990** | **179128.5** |
| 26059 | 650 | 18734 | 6989 |
| 13106 | 114 | 18274 | 5001 |
| 88050 | 322 | 32125.5 | 9246.1 |
| 39488 | 300 | 21417 | 6353 |
| 41237 | 701 | 83877 | 56865 |

3－14　续表4

| 乡镇名称 Town | | 社区(居民委员会) Number of Communities (residents committees) | 村民委员会(个) Number of Villagers' Committees (unit) | 乡镇户籍户数(户) Resident Households in Towns (household) |
|---|---|---|---|---|
| 高虹镇 | Gaohong | – | 9 | 4981 |
| 太湖源镇 | Taihuyuan | – | 20 | 11141 |
| 於潜镇 | Yuqian | 1 | 30 | 17350 |
| 太阳镇 | Taiyang | 2 | 18 | 9270 |
| 潜川镇 | Qianchuan | – | 16 | 8490 |
| 昌化镇 | Changhua | 1 | 14 | 7393 |
| 河桥镇 | Heqiao | – | 11 | 6100 |
| 湍口镇 | Tuankou | – | 13 | 4201 |
| 清凉峰镇 | Qingliangfeng | – | 17 | 9870 |
| 岛石镇 | Daoshi | – | 16 | 8425 |
| 板桥镇 | Banqiao | – | 15 | 8461 |
| 天目山镇 | Tianmushan | – | 23 | 12133 |
| 龙岗镇 | Longgang | – | 24 | 7089 |
| **桐庐县** | **Tonglu County** | **22** | **181** | **153375** |
| 旧县街道 | Jiuxian Subdistrict | – | 5 | 2887 |
| 桐君街道 | Tongjun Subdistrict | 7 | 6 | 19748 |
| 城南街道 | Chengnan Subdistrict | 7 | 13 | 26937 |
| 凤川街道 | Fengchuan Subdistrict | 1 | 13 | 9685 |
| 富春江镇 | Fuchunjiang | 2 | 15 | 9397 |
| 横村镇 | Hengcun | 2 | 24 | 15619 |
| 分水镇 | Fenshui | 2 | 26 | 19160 |
| 瑶琳镇 | Yaolin | – | 16 | 12289 |
| 百江镇 | Baijiang | – | 15 | 6205 |
| 江南镇 | Jiangnan | 1 | 19 | 16843 |

| 乡镇户籍人口数(人) Resident Population in Towns (person) | 乡镇常用耕地面积(公顷) Commonly used cultivated area of township (hectare) | 一般公共预算收入(万元) General public budget income (10000 yuan) | 一般公共预算支出(万元) General public budget expenditure (10000 yuan) |
|---|---|---|---|
| 14536 | 595 | 4742.8 | 7006.8 |
| 31817 | 1967.6 | 7211.8 | 7840.3 |
| 48845 | 2128.8 | 5732 | 8672 |
| 27171 | 1346.4 | 2294.3 | 6536.9 |
| 23745 | 1079.2 | 3134 | 5615 |
| 21526 | 955 | 4137.1 | 11245.3 |
| 17333 | 1191 | 1067 | 4937 |
| 12679 | 564.4 | 7203 | 5700 |
| 28075 | 1282.6 | 2440 | 5793 |
| 25537 | 598.1 | 468.4 | 6002.1 |
| 25412 | 982.6 | 8951 | 7487 |
| 33662 | 1903 | 2315.7 | 9107.7 |
| 21195 | 1106.5 | 4865.4 | 8731.3 |
| **433965** | **14984.2** | **90528.7** | **29691.5** |
| 8365 | 428 | 1981.4 | 1236.4 |
| 47859 | 345.5 | 18282 | 2503 |
| 73616 | 704.6 | 17662.5 | 2136.8 |
| 30003 | 632.3 | 2765 | 1838.4 |
| 24756 | 851 | 10221 | 1456 |
| 43209 | 2738 | 9539 | 2073.9 |
| 52906 | 1835.6 | 8861.5 | 6067.7 |
| 35110 | 1868.3 | 1872 | 1591 |
| 20050 | 899 | 1583 | 1639 |
| 51616 | 1687.5 | 3957.8 | 3957.8 |

3－14 续表5

| 乡镇名称 Town | | 社区(居民委员会) Number of Communities (residents committees) | 村民委员会(个) Number of Villagers' Committees (unit) | 乡镇户籍户数(户) Resident Households in Towns (household) |
|---|---|---|---|---|
| 莪山畲族乡 | Eshan | – | 7 | 2894 |
| 钟山乡 | Zhongshan | – | 11 | 6951 |
| 新合乡 | Xinghe | – | 5 | 1613 |
| 合村乡 | Hecun | – | 6 | 3147 |
| **淳安县** | **Chun'an County** | **16** | **423** | **146895** |
| 千岛湖镇 | Qiandaohu | 12 | 20 | 30480 |
| 文昌镇 | Wenchang | – | 16 | 4258 |
| 石林镇 | Shilin | – | 8 | 1443 |
| 临歧镇 | Linqi | 1 | 17 | 5999 |
| 威坪镇 | Weiping | 1 | 44 | 16151 |
| 姜家镇 | Jiangjia | 1 | 28 | 8481 |
| 梓桐镇 | Zitong | – | 19 | 6023 |
| 汾口镇 | Fenkou | 1 | 51 | 16485 |
| 中洲镇 | Zhongzhou | – | 19 | 5981 |
| 大墅镇 | Dashu | – | 17 | 4438 |
| 枫树岭镇 | Fengshuling | – | 28 | 5748 |
| 里商乡 | Lishang | – | 16 | 3447 |
| 金峰乡 | Jinfeng | – | 11 | 2047 |
| 富文乡 | Fuwen | – | 10 | 2480 |
| 左口乡 | Zuokou | – | 11 | 3306 |
| 屏门乡 | Pingmen | – | 15 | 3890 |
| 瑶山乡 | Yaoshan | – | 11 | 2813 |
| 王阜乡 | Wangfu | – | 18 | 5889 |
| 宋村乡 | Songcun | – | 8 | 2114 |
| 鸠坑乡 | Jiukeng | – | 9 | 2565 |

基本情况(2019 年)

and Townships(2019)

| 乡镇户籍人口数(人) Resident Population in Towns (person) | 乡镇常用耕地面积(公顷) Commonly used cultivated area of township (hectare) | 一般公共预算收入(万元) General public budget income (10000 yuan) | 一般公共预算支出(万元) General public budget expenditure (10000 yuan) |
|---|---|---|---|
| 9205 | 903.4 | 1509.5 | 1849.5 |
| 21762 | 1187 | 10251 | 1393 |
| 5269 | 345 | 698 | 687 |
| 10239 | 559 | 1345 | 1262 |
| **458669** | **17619** | **35113.8** | **192846.7** |
| 84553 | 573.4 | 13425.6 | 14368.1 |
| 14590 | 625.3 | 3704.8 | 8418.4 |
| 5024 | 160.8 | 297.9 | 3341 |
| 20592 | 1026.3 | 1062.2 | 13136 |
| 47428 | 1961.6 | 1654.8 | 20496.3 |
| 26374 | 1456.6 | 3150.2 | 14575.8 |
| 18786 | 779 | 1656.3 | 9261.6 |
| 55392 | 2607.5 | 3703.8 | 21475.6 |
| 20253 | 1118.6 | 264.4 | 9750.2 |
| 14025 | 939.1 | 852.1 | 7481.6 |
| 18484 | 1135.3 | 464.1 | 9062.6 |
| 11363 | 363.6 | 732 | 5904.5 |
| 6070 | 331.9 | 536.9 | 2859.4 |
| 8377 | 231.4 | 219.5 | 4002.4 |
| 11679 | 461.5 | 603.6 | 5480.8 |
| 12423 | 371.3 | 788.9 | 5795.5 |
| 9638 | 297.3 | 356.2 | 4151.9 |
| 17677 | 503.5 | 184.2 | 6880.1 |
| 6962 | 55.1 | 178 | 3305.9 |
| 7608 | 211.2 | 164.1 | 5191.8 |

3－14　续表6

| 乡镇名称 | Town | 社区(居民委员会) Number of Communities (residents committees) | 村民委员会(个) Number of Villagers' Committees (unit) | 乡镇户籍户数(户) Resident Households in Towns (household) |
|---|---|---|---|---|
| 浪川乡 | Langchuan | – | 19 | 6150 |
| 界首乡 | Jieshou | – | 13 | 3042 |
| 安阳乡 | Anyang | – | 15 | 3665 |
| **钱塘新区** | **Qiantang New Area** | **8** | **59** | **41862** |
| 义蓬街道 | Yipeng Subdistrict | 4 | 22 | 17879 |
| 河庄街道 | Hezhuang Subdistrict | 1 | 20 | 13538 |
| 新湾街道 | Xinwan Subdistrict | 1 | 12 | 7139 |
| 临江街道 | Linjiang Subdistrict | 1 | 2 | 1193 |
| 前进街道 | Qianjin Subdistrict | 1 | 3 | 2113 |
| **建德市** | **Jiande City** | **41** | **229** | **166831** |
| 新安江街道 | Xin'anjiang Subdistrict | 11 | 4 | 30682 |
| 洋溪街道 | Yangxi Subdistrict | 4 | 2 | 5089 |
| 更楼街道 | Genglou Subdistrict | 2 | 14 | 8299 |
| 莲花镇 | Lianhua | 1 | 6 | 3306 |
| 乾潭镇 | Qiantan | 1 | 24 | 14729 |
| 梅城镇 | Meicheng | 5 | 13 | 15028 |
| 杨村桥镇 | Yangcunqiao | 1 | 13 | 6224 |
| 下涯镇 | Xiaya | 1 | 11 | 8472 |
| 大洋镇 | Dayang | 3 | 19 | 10489 |
| 三都镇 | Sandu | 1 | 19 | 8711 |
| 寿昌镇 | Shouchang | 4 | 23 | 11752 |
| 航头镇 | Hangtou | 1 | 18 | 11142 |
| 大慈岩镇 | Daciyan | 1 | 12 | 6597 |
| 大同镇 | Datong | 3 | 34 | 17292 |
| 李家镇 | Lijia | 1 | 10 | 6381 |
| 钦堂乡 | Qintang | 1 | 7 | 2638 |

基本情况(2019 年)

and Townships(2019)

| 乡镇户籍人口数(人) Resident Population in Towns (person) | 乡镇常用耕地面积(公顷) Commonly used cultivated area of township (hectare) | 一般公共预算收入(万元) General public budget income (10000 yuan) | 一般公共预算支出(万元) General public budget expenditure (10000 yuan) |
|---|---|---|---|
| 20234 | 1117.4 | 371.8 | 8577.7 |
| 9519 | 517.4 | 203.8 | 4086.4 |
| 11618 | 773.9 | 538.6 | 5243.1 |
| **157034** | **7533.7** | **119500** | **124951** |
| 64598 | 3020 | 44800 | 52882 |
| 54048 | 2370.1 | 29778 | 29778 |
| 25141 | 1196.2 | 22422 | 19791 |
| 4759 | 415.2 | 12500 | 12500 |
| 8488 | 532.2 | 10000 | 10000 |
| **499822** | **17004.2** | **136641.6** | **104744.2** |
| 81823 | 274 | 29042 | 6915 |
| 15369 | 168 | 9351 | 3500 |
| 23611 | 708 | 2997 | 3331 |
| 10653 | 367.7 | 2948.6 | 2948.6 |
| 44834 | 1661.4 | 13859 | 13255 |
| 41056 | 1660 | 7206.9 | 7206.9 |
| 20352 | 838.4 | 5134.1 | 4273.4 |
| 27581 | 944 | 7577.6 | 7577.6 |
| 33860 | 1394.7 | 4242 | 3993.4 |
| 25056 | 1190 | 3845.6 | 3570.2 |
| 36478 | 1280.6 | 17702 | 17058 |
| 34458 | 1589.8 | 6210 | 5420 |
| 20892 | 1195 | 10086.3 | 10017.1 |
| 54374 | 2533 | 5264.5 | 7670 |
| 20614 | 726.8 | 6795 | 5497 |
| 8811 | 472.8 | 4380 | 2511 |

# 3-15 农村基本

## Basic Statistics on

| 指 标 | | Item | |
|---|---|---|---|
| **一、农村人口与从业人员** | | **Rural Population and Employed Persons** | |
| 农村户数 | （万户） | Rural Household | (10000 households) |
| 农村人口 | （万人） | Rural Population | (10000 persons) |
| 男 | | Male | |
| 女 | | Female | |
| 农村劳动力资源数 | （万人） | Rural Laboar Resources | (10000 persons) |
| 男 | | Male | |
| 女 | | Female | |
| 农村从业人员 | （万人） | Jobholders in Rural Areas | (10000 persons) |
| 男 | | Male | |
| #从事农业人员 | | Persons Involved in Agriculture | |
| 女 | | Female | |
| #从事农业人员 | | Persons Involved in Agriculture | |
| **二、农村基础设施** | | **Public Facilities in Rural Areas** | |
| 自来水受益村数 | | Number of Villages with Access to Tap Water | |
| 通有线电视村数 | | Number of Villages Connecting to Cable TV | |
| 通宽带村数 | | Number of Villages Connecting to Prroadband | |
| **三、农林牧渔业增加值** | | **Value - added of Agriculture, Forestry, Animal Husbandry and Fishery** | |
| 农业 | | Farming | |
| 林业 | | Forestry | |
| 畜牧业 | | Animal Husbandry | |
| 渔业 | | Fishery | |
| 农、林、牧、渔专业及辅助性活动 | | Services for Farming, Forestry, Animal Husbandary and Fishery | |

情况(2012－2019年)
Rural Areas(2012－2019)

| 2012 | 2013 | 2014 | 2015 | 2016 | 2017 | 2018 | 2019 |
|---|---|---|---|---|---|---|---|
| 129.29 | 132.18 | 131.96 | 132.15 | 132.00 | 131.53 | 127.60 | 126.39 |
| 425.49 | 469.90 | 480.04 | 482.63 | 482.94 | 488.22 | 471.97 | 467.92 |
| 213.81 | 236.03 | 241.82 | 243.47 | 244.08 | 247.31 | 238.49 | 236.23 |
| 211.68 | 233.87 | 238.22 | 239.16 | 238.86 | 240.91 | 233.48 | 231.69 |
| 276.62 | 304.14 | 314.45 | 313.79 | 314.83 | 317.03 | 304.16 | 300.01 |
| 143.66 | 157.27 | 163.98 | 163.94 | 164.54 | 165.88 | 159.27 | 157.35 |
| 132.96 | 146.87 | 150.47 | 149.85 | 150.29 | 151.15 | 144.89 | 142.66 |
| 257.30 | 279.91 | 286.01 | 284.73 | 281.76 | 282.19 | 270.84 | 264.83 |
| 134.85 | 145.70 | 151.05 | 151.21 | 149.68 | 149.66 | 143.83 | 140.47 |
|  |  | 36.50 | 37.58 | 37.49 | 37.12 | 35.60 | 34.75 |
| 122.45 | 134.21 | 134.96 | 133.52 | 132.08 | 132.53 | 127.01 | 124.36 |
|  |  | 29.75 | 30.22 | 29.74 | 29.17 | 28.51 | 27.84 |
|  |  |  |  |  |  |  |  |
| 2078 | 2058 | 2054 | 2054 | 2053 | 2046 | 2033 | 2021 |
| 2078 | 2058 | 2054 | 2054 | 2053 | 2046 | 2033 | 2021 |
| 2078 | 2058 | 2054 | 2054 | 2053 | 2046 | 2033 | 2021 |
| **2551127** | **2654059** | **2783252** | **2924013** | **2985617** | **3056039** | **3118849** | **3327369** |
| 1510382 | 1571300 | 1685668 | 1806178 | 1866383 | 1951535 | 2009741 | 2101139 |
| 302796 | 324240 | 371932 | 393332 | 415918 | 428898 | 446920 | 483405 |
| 435191 | 458201 | 405348 | 395476 | 377688 | 334289 | 301445 | 369504 |
| 270629 | 262233 | 280544 | 284506 | 276270 | 284845 | 297480 | 303120 |
| 32129 | 38085 | 39760 | 44521 | 49358 | 56472 | 63263 | 70201 |

# 3-16 分地区农村
## Basic Statistics on

| 指标 | Item | 全市 Whole City | 市区 Urban District | 江干区 Jianggan | 西湖区 Xihu |
|---|---|---|---|---|---|
| **一、农村人口与从业人员** | **Rural Population and Employed Persons** | | | | |
| 农村户数 (万户) | Rural Household (10000 households) | 126.39 | 91.46 | | 3.49 |
| 农村人口 (万人) | Rural Population (10000 persons) | 467.92 | 359.93 | | 14.21 |
| 男 | Male | 236.23 | 181.42 | | 7.01 |
| 女 | Female | 231.69 | 178.51 | | 7.2 |
| 农村劳动力资源数 (万人) | Rural Laboar Resources (10000 persons) | 300.01 | 229.56 | | 8.4 |
| 男 | Male | 157.35 | 120.44 | | 4.44 |
| 女 | Female | 142.66 | 109.12 | | 3.96 |
| 农村从业人员 (万人) | Jobholders in Rural Areas (10000 persons) | 264.83 | 201.2 | | 7.66 |
| 男 | Male | 140.47 | 106.33 | | 4.11 |
| #从事农业人员 | Persons Involved in Agriculture | 34.75 | 21.28 | | 0.56 |
| 女 | Female | 124.36 | 94.87 | | 3.55 |
| #从事农业人员 | Persons Involved in Agriculture | 27.84 | 16.65 | | 0.47 |
| **二、农村基础设施** | **Public Facilities in Rural Areas** | | | | |
| 自来水受益村数 | Number of Villages with Access to Tap Water | 2021 | 1188 | | 32 |
| 通有线电视村数 | Number of Villages Connecting to Cable TV | 2021 | 1188 | | 32 |
| 通宽带村数 | Number of Villages Connecting to Broadband | 2021 | 1188 | | 32 |
| **三、农林牧渔业增加值** | **Value - added of Agriculture, Forestry, Animal Husbandry and Fishery** | **3327369** | **2323258** | | **27071** |
| 农业 | Farming | 2101139 | 1406329 | | 22496 |
| 林业 | Forestry | 483405 | 350221 | | 494 |
| 畜牧业 | Animal Husbandry | 369504 | 255577 | | - |
| 渔业 | Fishery | 303120 | 257934 | | 3041 |
| 农、林、牧、渔专业及辅助性活动 | Services for Farming, Forestry, Animal Husbandary and Fishery | 70201 | 53197 | | 1040 |

基本情况（2019 年末）

Rural Areas by Region( End of 2019)

| 高新（滨江）区 Hi - Tech (Binjiang) | 萧山区 Xiaoshan | 余杭区 Yuhang | 富阳区 Fuyang | 临安区 Lin'an | 钱塘新区 Qiantang New Area | 西湖风景名胜区 The West Lake Scenic Zone | 桐庐县 Tonglu | 淳安县 Chun'an | 建德市 Jiande |
|---|---|---|---|---|---|---|---|---|---|
| 2.5 | 33.58 | 21.15 | 16.97 | 13.49 | 4.65 | 0.28 | 10.98 | 10.99 | 12.96 |
| 10.57 | 127.96 | 108.52 | 58 | 40.11 | 18.66 | 0.56 | 32.71 | 34.17 | 41.11 |
| 5.1 | 63.8 | 55.78 | 29.53 | 19.95 | 9.36 | 0.25 | 16.51 | 17.29 | 21.01 |
| 5.47 | 64.16 | 52.74 | 28.47 | 20.16 | 9.3 | 0.31 | 16.2 | 16.88 | 20.1 |
| 6.8 | 78.81 | 70.65 | 37.56 | 27.04 | 12.57 | 0.3 | 21.65 | 23.1 | 25.7 |
| 3.4 | 40.37 | 38.44 | 19.56 | 14.08 | 6.56 | 0.15 | 11.2 | 11.98 | 13.73 |
| 3.4 | 38.44 | 32.21 | 18 | 12.96 | 6.01 | 0.15 | 10.45 | 11.12 | 11.97 |
| 6.17 | 68.84 | 61.27 | 33.15 | 23.83 | 11.49 | 0.28 | 19.25 | 22.07 | 22.31 |
| 3.13 | 35.62 | 33.25 | 17.61 | 12.47 | 6.06 | 0.14 | 10.07 | 11.7 | 12.37 |
| 0.02 | 5.58 | 4.06 | 6.57 | 4.41 | 0.82 | 0.07 | 2.67 | 5.48 | 5.32 |
| 3.04 | 33.22 | 28.02 | 15.54 | 11.36 | 5.43 | 0.14 | 9.18 | 10.37 | 9.94 |
| 0.01 | 4.39 | 2.91 | 4.97 | 3.82 | 0.66 | 0.08 | 2.2 | 4.8 | 4.19 |
| | | | | | | | | | |
| - | 411 | 187 | 279 | 270 | 59 | 9 | 181 | 423 | 229 |
| - | 411 | 187 | 279 | 270 | 59 | 9 | 181 | 423 | 229 |
| - | 411 | 187 | 279 | 270 | 59 | 9 | 181 | 423 | 229 |
| **7244** | **738844** | **554396** | **496160** | **463904** | **139422** | **9491** | **254510** | **386868** | **362733** |
| 6801 | 513443 | 328323 | 293493 | 230463 | 92788 | 9451 | 163999 | 273911 | 256900 |
| - | 7999 | 63552 | 110615 | 167521 | 56 | 40 | 48523 | 56731 | 27930 |
| - | 116786 | 22061 | 60963 | 54934 | 25337 | - | 25587 | 32868 | 55472 |
| 443 | 78256 | 119169 | 27883 | 5686 | 18115 | - | 12164 | 17920 | 15102 |
| - | 22360 | 21291 | 3206 | 5300 | 3126 | - | 4237 | 5438 | 7329 |

# 主要统计指标解释

**农林牧渔业总产值** 是以货币表现的农、林、牧、渔业全部产品的总量和对农林牧渔生产活动进行的各种支持性服务活动的价值。它反映一定时期内农林牧渔业生产的总规模和总成果。

农林牧渔业的统计范围是：

(1)农业 包括农作物种植业和其他农业。

农作物种植业 包括谷类、豆类、薯类、棉花、麻类、烟叶、蔬菜、药材、瓜类和其他农作物的种植以及茶园、桑园、果园的生产经营。

其他农业 包括采集野生植物的果实、纤维、树脂、油料以及柴草、野生药材、菌类等。

(2)林业 包括林木的栽培(不包括茶园、桑园和果园的栽培、管理和收获等活动)、林产品的采集、村及村以下合作经济组织和农户的竹木砍伐。

(3)牧业 包括除渔业养殖以外的一切动物饲养和放牧以及野生动物的捕猎和饲养。

(4)渔业 包括水生动物和海藻类植物的养殖和捕捞。

(5)农林牧渔服务业 包括对农林牧渔生产活动进行的各种支持性服务活动。

**粮食产量** 指全社会的产量,包括国营农场等全民所有制经营、集体统一经营和农民家庭经营的产量,还包括工矿企业家属办的农场和其他生产单位的产量。粮食除包括稻谷、小麦、大麦、玉米、高粱、谷子及其他杂粮外,还包括薯类和豆类。其产量计算方法,豆类按去豆荚后的干豆计算,薯类按5公斤鲜薯折1公斤粮食计算,其他粮食一律按脱粒后的原粮计算。

**猪、牛、羊肉产量** 指当年出栏并已屠宰的猪、牛、羊的肉产量,即屠宰后除去头蹄下水后带骨的(即胴体重)重量。

**水产品产量** 指人工养殖的水产品和天然生长的水产品的捕捞量。包括海水的鱼类、虾蟹类、贝类和藻类以及内陆水域的鱼类、虾蟹类和贝类,不包括淡水生植物。

**有效灌溉面积** 指具有一定水源,地块比较平整,灌溉工程或设备已经配套,在一般年景下当年能够进行正常灌溉的耕地面积。

**农业机械总动力** 指主要用于农、林、牧、渔业的各种动力机械的动力总和。包括耕作机械、排灌机械、收获机械、农用运输机械、植物保护机械、牧业机械、林业机械和其他农业机械[内燃机按引擎马力折成瓦(特)计算,电动机按功率折成瓦(特)计算]。不包括专门用于乡、镇、村、组办工业、基本建设、非农业运输、科学试验和教学等非农业方面的动力机械与作业机械。

**农村用电量** 指本年度内扣除在农村中的全民所有制工业、交通、基建单位的用电量以后的农村生产上和生活上的全年用电总度数(全年累计数),包括国家电网的供电量,也包括农村自办电站的供电量。

**农用化肥施用量** 指本年内实际用于农业生产的化肥数量。包括氮肥、磷肥、钾肥及复合肥。化肥施用量要求按折纯量计算数量。折纯量是指氮肥、磷肥、钾肥分别按含氮、含五氧化二磷、含氧化钾的百分之一百成分进行折算后的数量。复合肥按其所含主要成分折算。

# Explanatory Notes on Main Statistical Indicators

**Gross Output Value of Farming, Forestry, Animal Husbandry and Fishery** refers to the total volume of products of farming, forestry, animal husbandry and fishery in value terms and output value of all kinds of service activities that support farming, forestry, animal husbandry and fishery production. It reflects the total scale and total result of agricultural production during a given period of time.

The statistical scopes for Farming, Forestry, Animal Husbandry and Fishery are as follows:

(1) **Farming** includes crop cultivation and other farming.

Crop cultivation includes planting of cereals, beans, tubers, cotton, fiber crops, tobacco, vegetables, crude drugs, melons and others, as well as production and management of tea, mulberry and fruit plantation.

Other farming includes gathering of wild plant fruits, fiber, gum, oil, firewood, wild crude drugs, fungus.

(2) **Forestry** includes planting of trees (not including planting, management and harvest of tea, mulberry and fruit plantation), collection of forest products, and felling of bamboos and trees by villagers and cooperative organizations of villages and under villages.

(3) **Animal Husbandry** includes raising and grazing of any kind of animals and hunting and raising of wild animals, other than fish breeding.

(4) **Fishery** includes cultivation and catches of aquatic animals and seaweed.

(5) **Service Industry for Farming, Forestry, Animal Husbandry and Fishery** refers to all kinds of service activities that support farming, forestry, animal husbandry and fishery production.

**Grain Yield** refers to the total yield including grains produced by state – owned, collectively operated and family farms as well as grains produced by farms run by family members of industrial and mining enterprises. Grain includes rice, wheat, corn, sorghum, millet and other miscellaneous grains as well as tubers and beans. For the yield of beans, it is to calculated by beans without pods, for tubers is to convert the yield of fresh tubers into that of grain at the ratio 5:1, and for others are all the husked grain.

**Output of Pork, Beef, and Mutton** refers to the meat weight of slaughtered hogs, cattle, sheep and goats, which are full grown, without heads, feets and offal but with bones.

**Output of Aquatic Products** refers to catches of both artificially cultured and naturally grown aquatic products, including fish, shrimps, crabs and shellfish in sea and inland water as well as seaweed. Freshwater plants are not included.

**Irrigated Area** refers to cultivated areas that are flat with water source and complete irrigation projects or equipments to be effectively irrigated under normal conditions. ,

**Total Power of Farm Machinery** refers to total mechanical power of machinery used in farming, forestry, animal husbandry, and fishery, including the machinery of ploughing, irrigation and drainage, harvesting, transport, plant protection, stock breeding, forestry and others. For internal combustion engine is to calculate its engine power in watts and for electric motor is to calculate its power in watts. Machinery employed for non agricultural purposes, such as the machines used in town and village run industries, capital construction, non – agricultural transport, scientific experiments and teaching, is excluded.

**Electricity Consumption in Rural Areas** refers to annual total degree (annual aggregate) of electricity consumption of rural production and living discounting the consumption of industries owned by the whole people, transport and infrastructure units in the rural areas, including the power supply of State Grid and rural run power stations.

**Consumption of Chemical Fertilizers in Agriculture** refers to the quantity of chemical fertilizers applied in agriculture in the year, including nitrogen, phosphorus, potassium and compound fertilizers. The consumption of chemical fertilizers is required to calculate by the purity, i. e. by 100% nitrogen content in nitrogenous fertilizer, 100% phosphorous pent oxide content in phosphorus fertilizer, 100% potassium oxide contents in potassium fertilizer. Compound fertilizer is calculated by its major component.

# 四、工业、能源

INDUSTRY AND ENERGY

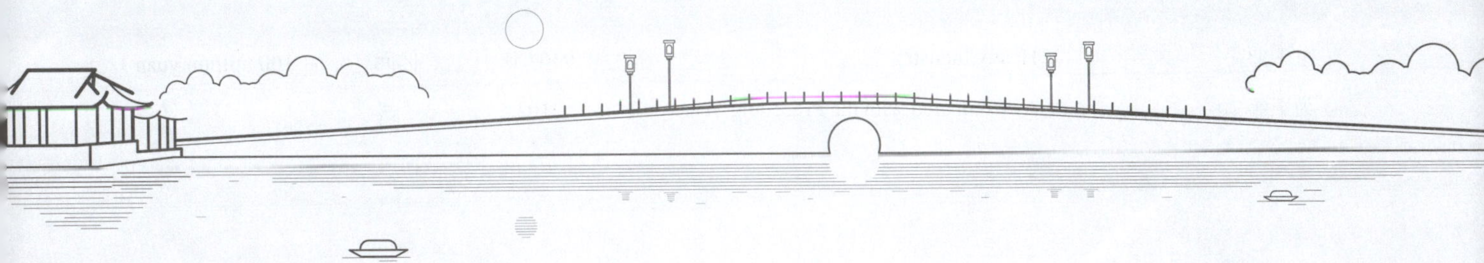

# 4 工业、能源
# Industry and Energy

## 主要统计指标
## Major Statistical Indicators

| | | | | |
|---|---|---|---|---|
| 规模以上工业企业单位数 | Number of Industrial Enterprises above Designated Size | 5698 | 个 | ( unit ) |
| 为上年 | As Compared with the Preceding Year | 104.9 | % | ( % ) |
| 规模以上工业增加值 | Value-added of Industrial Enterprises above Designated Size | 3481.89 | 亿元 | ( 100 million yuan ) |
| 为上年 | As Compared with the Preceding Year | 105.1 | % | ( % ) |
| 规模以上工业总产值 | Gross Output Value of Industrial Enterprises above Designated Size | 14585.45 | 亿元 | ( 100 million yuan ) |
| 为上年 | As Compared with the Preceding Year | 104.1 | % | ( % ) |
| 轻工业 | Light Industry | 5221.27 | 亿元 | ( 100 million yuan ) |
| 为上年 | As Compared with the Preceding Year | 106.9 | % | ( % ) |
| 重工业 | Heavy Industry | 9364.18 | 亿元 | ( 100 million yuan ) |
| 为上年 | As Compared with the Preceding Year | 102.5 | % | ( % ) |

# 4－01 工业企业单位数（主要年份）

## Number of Industrial Enterprises of the Whole City（Main Years）

单位：个 （unit）

| 年 份<br>Year | 规模以上工业合计<br>Industry above Designated Size Total | 国有经济<br>State－owned Enterprises | 集体经济<br>Collective－owned Enterprises | 其他各种经济类型<br>Enterprises of Other Types of Ownership |
|---|---|---|---|---|
| 1978 | 2868 | 680 | 2188 | － |
| 1980 | 3519 | 691 | － | － |
| 1985 | 5800 | 823 | － | － |
| 1990 | 6183 | 921 | 4966 | 11 |
| 1991 | 6234 | 933 | 5219 | 82 |
| 1992 | 6235 | 941 | 5162 | 132 |
| 1995 | 6744 | 1086 | 4722 | 936 |
| 1996 | 6148 | 1011 | 4268 | 869 |
| 1997 | 4980 | 760 | 3250 | 970 |
| 1998 | 2559 | 464 | 815 | 1280 |
| 1999 | 2474 | 396 | 689 | 1389 |
| 2000 | 2715 | 282 | 598 | 1835 |
| 2001 | 3580 | 237 | 252 | 3091 |
| 2002 | 4015 | 172 | 232 | 3611 |
| 2003 | 4689 | 144 | 219 | 4326 |
| 2004 | 7738 | 185 | 192 | 7361 |
| 2005 | 7359 | 124 | 169 | 7066 |
| 2006 | 7826 | 110 | 162 | 7554 |
| 2007 | 8674 | 71 | 131 | 8472 |
| 2008 | 9907 | 73 | 101 | 9733 |
| 2009 | 10032 | 71 | 84 | 9877 |
| 2010 | 10370 | 74 | 68 | 10228 |
| 2011 | 5868 | 52 | 25 | 5791 |
| 2012 | 5927 | 56 | 20 | 5851 |
| 2013 | 6284 | 25 | 11 | 6248 |
| 2014 | 6169 | 22 | 9 | 6138 |
| 2015 | 6073 | 17 | 5 | 6051 |
| 2016 | 5684 | 15 | 4 | 5665 |
| 2017 | 5533 | 10 | 2 | 5521 |
| 2018 | 5431 | 9 | 1 | 5421 |
| 2019 | 5698 | 7 | － | 5691 |

注：规模以上工业口径：1997 年及以前为乡及以上工业；1998－2010 年为主营业务收入 500 万及以上；2011 年为主营业务收入 2000 万及以上（后同）。

a) Industry above Designated Size: Data after 2011 refer to all the industrial enterprises with annual Sales income of over 20 million yuan, data in 1998－2010 refer to all the industrial enterprises with annual sales income of over 5 million yuan, data in 1997 and before refer to enterprises at township and above level.

# 4－02 市区工业企业单位数(主要年份)

## Number of Industrial Enterprises in Urban District(Main Years)

单位:个 (unit)

| 年 份<br>Year | 规模以上工业合计<br>Industry above Designated Size Total | 国有经济<br>State－owned Enterprises | 集体经济<br>Collective－owned Enterprises | 其他各种经济类型<br>Enterprises of Other Types of Ownership |
|---|---|---|---|---|
| 1978 | 787 | 313 | 414 | － |
| 1980 | 894 | 315 | 579 | － |
| 1985 | 1250 | 345 | 859 | 7 |
| 1990 | 1360 | 361 | 971 | 28 |
| 1991 | 1411 | 382 | 990 | 39 |
| 1992 | 1490 | 395 | 1024 | 71 |
| 1995 | 1998 | 440 | 1102 | 456 |
| 1996 | 2043 | 458 | 1109 | 476 |
| 1997 | 1733 | 372 | 951 | 410 |
| 1998 | 1019 | 315 | 315 | 389 |
| 1999 | 959 | 255 | 284 | 420 |
| 2000 | 1005 | 182 | 253 | 570 |
| 2001 | 2645 | 195 | 200 | 2250 |
| 2002 | 2838 | 140 | 178 | 2520 |
| 2003 | 3230 | 115 | 158 | 2957 |
| 2004 | 5527 | 156 | 122 | 5249 |
| 2005 | 4995 | 98 | 104 | 4793 |
| 2006 | 5195 | 85 | 91 | 5019 |
| 2007 | 5726 | 54 | 77 | 5595 |
| 2008 | 6530 | 55 | 64 | 6411 |
| 2009 | 6477 | 52 | 49 | 6376 |
| 2010 | 6478 | 51 | 37 | 6390 |
| 2011 | 3867 | 36 | 10 | 3821 |
| 2012 | 3862 | 37 | 7 | 3818 |
| 2013 | 4145 | 18 | 5 | 4122 |
| 2014 | 4716 | 17 | 5 | 4694 |
| 2015 | 4584 | 12 | 3 | 4569 |
| 2016 | 4235 | 11 | 2 | 4222 |
| 2017 | 4726 | 8 | 1 | 4717 |
| 2018 | 4746 | 8 | 1 | 4737 |
| 2019 | 4984 | 6 | － | 4978 |

# 4－03 工业总产值(主要年份)

## Gross Industrial Output Value of the Whole City(Main Years)

单位:万元 (10000 yuan)

| 年 份<br>Year | 规模以上工业<br>Industry above Designated Size | #轻工业<br>Light Industry | 重工业<br>Heavy Industry | 国有经济<br>State－owned | 集体经济<br>Collective－owned | 其他经济<br>Other Types of Ownership |
|---|---|---|---|---|---|---|
| 1978 | 429624 | － | － | 334799 | 94825 | － |
| 1980 | 617910 | － | － | 451349 | 166561 | － |
| 1985 | 1285888 | 793766 | 492122 | 726172 | 546642 | 13074 |
| 1990 | 2922600 | 1848911 | 1073689 | 1532900 | 1300900 | 88800 |
| 1991 | 3524900 | 2201757 | 1323143 | 1779400 | 1601400 | 144200 |
| 1992 | 4527400 | 2735168 | 1792232 | 2141000 | 2084000 | 302400 |
| 1995 | 10200259 | 5600664 | 4599595 | 3585284 | 3999638 | 2615337 |
| 1996 | 8831167 | 4606720 | 4224447 | 2905614 | 3320757 | 2604796 |
| 1997 | 9114651 | 4871887 | 4242764 | 3185886 | 2971634 | 2957131 |
| 1998 | 11099357 | 5726407 | 5372950 | 3422316 | 2824793 | 4852248 |
| 1999 | 12000796 | 6129963 | 5870833 | 3164602 | 2543981 | 6292213 |
| 2000 | 15435682 | 7623300 | 7812382 | 1860336 | 2698406 | 10876940 |
| 2001 | 19195133 | 9957027 | 9238106 | 1788783 | 1911315 | 15495035 |
| 2002 | 24002972 | 12435498 | 11567474 | 2147066 | 2151485 | 19704421 |
| 2003 | 32025226 | 15652463 | 16372763 | 2484171 | 2444002 | 27097053 |
| 2004 | 44865779 | 19761946 | 25103833 | 3419970 | 558890 | 40886919 |
| 2005 | 54411271 | 24059690 | 30351581 | 6054280 | 603438 | 47753553 |
| 2006 | 69754590 | 29093450 | 40661140 | 6776754 | 667615 | 62310221 |
| 2007 | 83514029 | 35878400 | 47635629 | 7688908 | 517878 | 75307243 |
| 2008 | 93795792 | 38735329 | 55060463 | 7440679 | 386111 | 85969002 |
| 2009 | 93907334 | 40115956 | 53791378 | 7576482 | 354714 | 85976138 |
| 2010 | 110810397 | 45764739 | 65045658 | 9050510 | 300262 | 101459625 |
| 2011 | 123529249 | 48660810 | 74868439 | 10220511 | 171901 | 113136837 |
| 2012 | 129596777 | 51377588 | 78219189 | 11507163 | 167343 | 117922271 |
| 2013 | 124180035 | 48663751 | 75516284 | 7140899 | 39776 | 116999360 |
| 2014 | 128530518 | 49979222 | 78551296 | 6922198 | 32246 | 121576073 |
| 2015 | 124156803 | 48207987 | 75948816 | 2309361 | 14146 | 121833295 |
| 2016 | 124209589 | 46939900 | 77269689 | 5534102 | 12292 | 118663195 |
| 2017 | 129637623 | 47114960 | 82522663 | 1870409 | 5868 | 127761346 |
| 2018 | 140164081 | 48820787 | 91343294 | 1691067 | 2375 | 138470639 |
| 2019 | 145854508 | 52212735 | 93641773 | 1776196 | － | 144078312 |

# 4-04 市区工业总产值(主要年份)

## Gross Industrial Output Value in Urban District(Main Years)

单位:万元 (10000 yuan)

| 年份<br>Year | 规模以上工业<br>Industry above Designated Size | 轻工业<br>Light Industry | 重工业<br>Heavy Industry | 国有经济<br>State - owned | 集体经济<br>Collective - owned | 其他经济<br>Other Types of Ownership |
|---|---|---|---|---|---|---|
| 1978 | 304242 | - | - | 248534 | 55708 | - |
| 1980 | 433623 | - | - | 335789 | 97834 | - |
| 1985 | 812246 | 512767 | 301998 | 536498 | 267613 | 8135 |
| 1990 | 1533000 | 1026764 | 599899 | 1067400 | 416500 | 49100 |
| 1991 | 1814600 | 1140394 | 674072 | 1237600 | 496800 | 80200 |
| 1992 | 2291300 | 1379154 | 917085 | 1497400 | 601200 | 192700 |
| 1995 | 4760900 | 2507752 | 2753196 | 2252300 | 908900 | 1599700 |
| 1996 | 4599778 | 2460319 | 2139459 | 2018768 | 951432 | 1629578 |
| 1997 | 4997257 | 2889406 | 2609217 | 2537740 | 819984 | 1639533 |
| 1998 | 6110192 | 3068600 | 3041592 | 2989467 | 1123013 | 1997712 |
| 1999 | 6280838 | 3178286 | 3102552 | 2668519 | 979070 | 2633249 |
| 2000 | 7804302 | 3635578 | 4168724 | 1498595 | 968509 | 5337198 |
| 2001 | 16156245 | 8377563 | 7778681 | 1695132 | 1792228 | 12668885 |
| 2002 | 20252484 | 10431428 | 9821056 | 2036097 | 2045450 | 16170937 |
| 2003 | 26945006 | 13080771 | 13864235 | 2390424 | 2305431 | 22249151 |
| 2004 | 37564968 | 16361706 | 21203262 | 3097656 | 419720 | 34047592 |
| 2005 | 44775260 | 19601053 | 25174207 | 5592419 | 390555 | 38792286 |
| 2006 | 57255453 | 23722868 | 33532585 | 6305071 | 347788 | 50602594 |
| 2007 | 67565456 | 29452269 | 38113187 | 7123810 | 323842 | 60117804 |
| 2008 | 74564803 | 31236743 | 43328060 | 6812616 | 219140 | 67533047 |
| 2009 | 74059755 | 32178951 | 41880805 | 6880470 | 148937 | 67030348 |
| 2010 | 86653885 | 36440816 | 50213069 | 8155395 | 156026 | 78342464 |
| 2011 | 97800625 | 39467105 | 58333520 | 9253445 | 70299 | 88476881 |
| 2012 | 101396009 | 41428864 | 59967145 | 10452692 | 72743 | 90870574 |
| 2013 | 94197123 | 38407906 | 55789218 | 6332681 | 22398 | 87842044 |
| 2014 | 110230328 | 42840596 | 67389732 | 6463681 | 22354 | 103744292 |
| 2015 | 105641721 | 40775608 | 64866113 | 1841145 | 8633 | 103791944 |
| 2016 | 105688299 | 39331082 | 66357217 | 5061048 | 6629 | 100620622 |
| 2017 | 119823690 | 42792636 | 77031054 | 1689177 | 2846 | 118131668 |
| 2018 | 131259285 | 45433816 | 85825469 | 1570111 | 2375 | 129686799 |
| 2019 | 135952373 | 48734026 | 87218347 | 1649607 | - | 134302766 |

# 4-05 规模以上工业企业主要经济效益指标(2001-2019年)

## Main Economic Indicators of Industrial Enterprises Above Designated Size(2001-2019)

单位:亿元 (100 million yuan)

| 年份 Year | 规模以上工业总产值 Output Value of Industrial Enterprises Above Designated Size | 规模以上工业增加值 Added Value of Industrial Enterprises Above Designated Size | 资产总计 Total Assets | 流动资产合计 Total Current Assets | 主营业务收入 Revenne from Principal Business | 利润总额 Total Profits | 利税总额 Total Profits and Tax |
|---|---|---|---|---|---|---|---|
| 2001 | 1919.51 | 444.91 | 2148.96 | 1122.07 | 1828.28 | 107.56 | 208.54 |
| 2002 | 2400.30 | 597.01 | 2514.19 | 1313.92 | 2288.21 | 145.48 | 274.98 |
| 2003 | 3202.52 | 783.51 | 3258.93 | 1783.50 | 3117.46 | 194.16 | 359.54 |
| 2004 | 4486.58 | 1019.47 | 4118.31 | 2300.84 | 4363.27 | 226.74 | 427.23 |
| 2005 | 5441.13 | 1126.54 | 4781.34 | 2692.73 | 5282.80 | 234.99 | 450.68 |
| 2006 | 6975.46 | 1363.17 | 5564.68 | 3215.19 | 6807.64 | 314.49 | 576.51 |
| 2007 | 8351.40 | 1717.65 | 6573.12 | 3880.23 | 8057.03 | 414.55 | 730.50 |
| 2008 | 9379.58 | 1743.20 | 7506.26 | 4437.50 | 8976.46 | 453.92 | 802.13 |
| 2009 | 9390.73 | 1792.00 | 8405.62 | 4968.21 | 9026.32 | 510.97 | 882.62 |
| 2010 | 11081.04 | 2153.83 | 9937.41 | 6011.68 | 10843.24 | 764.47 | 1224.48 |
| 2011 | 12352.92 | 2369.00 | 10968.69 | 6709.76 | 12022.57 | 795.53 | 1330.48 |
| 2012 | 12959.68 | 2492.00 | 11983.52 | 7215.40 | 12525.39 | 771.68 | 1339.94 |
| 2013 | 12418.00 | 2664.13 | 12680.28 | 7609.51 | 12424.15 | 853.60 | 1450.55 |
| 2014 | 12853.05 | 2813.51 | 13376.72 | 7938.51 | 12833.70 | 904.60 | 1538.07 |
| 2015 | 12415.68 | 2875.05 | 14015.54 | 8306.78 | 12237.39 | 891.12 | 1559.68 |
| 2016 | 12420.96 | 2990.34 | 14467.36 | 8502.92 | 12367.54 | 946.06 | 1655.64 |
| 2017 | 12963.76 | 3184.05 | 15403.30 | 9009.58 | 13209.59 | 998.56 | 1774.52 |
| 2018 | 14016.41 | 3415.45 | 16662.89 | 9885.42 | 14432.89 | 1015.16 | 1800.26 |
| 2019 | 14585.45 | 3481.89 | 18290.37 | 10971.46 | 15212.51 | 1126.17 | 1854.99 |

4-05 续表 continued

| 年份 Year | 资产负债率(%) Ratio of Debts to Assets(%) | 流动资产周转次数(次) Turnover of Current Assets(times) | 成本费用利润率(%) Ratio of Profits to Costs(%) | 全员劳动生产率(元/人) Overall Labor Productivity (Yuan/Person) | 产品销售率(%) Rate of Production Sold (%) |
|---|---|---|---|---|---|
| 2001 | 57.20 | 1.70 | 6.26 | 59518 | 97.40 |
| 2002 | 56.82 | 1.82 | 6.84 | 76402 | 97.76 |
| 2003 | 58.70 | 1.87 | 6.69 | 91284 | 97.68 |
| 2004 | 59.80 | 2.00 | 5.50 | 98809 | 98.10 |
| 2005 | 60.12 | 2.06 | 4.69 | 105786 | 98.25 |
| 2006 | 59.83 | 2.23 | 4.87 | 120289 | 98.36 |
| 2007 | 60.43 | 2.21 | 5.44 | 138016 | 98.17 |
| 2008 | 60.42 | 2.10 | 5.34 | 152070 | 98.14 |
| 2009 | 59.07 | 1.86 | 5.86 | 151002 | 98.63 |
| 2010 | 58.34 | 1.96 | 7.60 | 166516 | 98.83 |
| 2011 | 59.12 | 1.91 | 6.96 | 190110 | 98.61 |
| 2012 | 49.57 | 1.74 | 6.60 | 232587 | 98.63 |
| 2013 | 58.09 | 1.63 | 7.39 | 222570 | 99.18 |
| 2014 | 56.83 | 1.62 | 7.61 | 245726 | 98.48 |
| 2015 | 55.69 | 1.54 | 7.91 | 257020 | 98.50 |
| 2016 | 54.29 | 1.53 | 7.97 | 278384 | 99.43 |
| 2017 | 54.66 | 1.55 | 7.77 | 301608 | 98.45 |
| 2018 | 55.00 | 1.54 | 7.19 | 330206 | 98.28 |
| 2019 | 55.02 | 1.46 | 7.85 | 339577 | - |

# 4-06 分地区工业
## Number of Industrial Enterprises

单位:个

| 项 目 | Item | 全市 Whole City | 市区 Urban District | 上城区 Shangcheng | 下城区 Xiacheng | 江干区 Jianggan | 拱墅区 Gongshu | 西湖区 Xihu |
|---|---|---|---|---|---|---|---|---|
| **规模以上工业合计** | **Industrial above Designated Size** | **5698** | **4984** | **37** | **23** | **46** | **77** | **122** |
| **一、按轻重工业分** | **Grouped by Light & Heavy Industry** | | | | | | | |
| 轻工业 | Light Industry | 2704 | 2350 | 6 | 7 | 15 | 25 | 36 |
| 重工业 | Heavy Industry | 2994 | 2634 | 31 | 16 | 31 | 52 | 86 |
| **二、按所有制分** | **Grouped by Ownership** | | | | | | | |
| 国有企业 | State - owned Enterprises | 7 | 6 | | | | 1 | |
| 集体企业 | Collective - owned Enterprises | - | - | - | - | - | - | - |
| 股份合作企业 | Cooperative Enterprises | 6 | 6 | | 1 | | 1 | |
| 联营企业 | Joint Ownership Enterprises | - | - | - | - | - | - | - |
| 有限责任公司 | Limited Liability Corporations | 562 | 480 | 7 | 9 | 11 | 11 | 25 |
| 股份有限公司 | Share - holding Corporations Ltd. | 227 | 203 | 3 | 1 | 5 | 9 | 14 |
| 私营企业 | Private Enterprises | 4149 | 3592 | 24 | 9 | 26 | 47 | 69 |
| 外商及港澳台投资企业 | Enterprises with Investment from Foreign、Hong Kong、Macao and Taiwan | 747 | 697 | 3 | 3 | 4 | 8 | 14 |
| 其他企业 | Other Enterprises | - | - | - | - | - | - | - |
| 合计中:国有控股企业 | Of the Total:Controlling Share Hold Enterprises | 202 | 177 | 4 | 6 | 2 | 9 | 8 |
| **三、按企业规模分** | **Grouped by Size of Enterprises** | | | | | | | |
| 大型企业 | Large | 124 | 118 | 1 | 1 | 2 | 1 | 3 |
| 中型企业 | Medium - sized | 557 | 512 | 3 | 1 | 8 | 8 | 14 |
| 小微企业 | Small | 5017 | 4354 | 33 | 21 | 36 | 68 | 105 |

## 企业单位数(2019 年末)
## by Region(End of 2019)

(unit)

| 高新(滨江)区 Hi - Tech (Binjiang) | 萧山区 Xiaoshan | 余杭区 Yuhang | 富阳区 Fuyang | 临安区 Lin'an | 钱塘新区 Qiantang New Area | 西湖风景名胜区 The West Lake Scenic Zone | 桐庐县 Tonglu | 淳安县 Chun'an | 建德市 Jiande |
|---|---|---|---|---|---|---|---|---|---|
| **198** | **1429** | **1203** | **632** | **607** | **609** | **1** | **324** | **88** | **302** |
| 44 | 877 | 581 | 250 | 257 | 252 | | 183 | 42 | 129 |
| 154 | 552 | 622 | 382 | 350 | 357 | 1 | 141 | 46 | 173 |
| | 1 | 1 | | | 3 | | 1 | | |
| | 1 | 3 | | | | | | | |
| 35 | 56 | 72 | 52 | 54 | 148 | | 35 | 13 | 35 |
| 25 | 32 | 53 | 21 | 20 | 19 | 1 | 11 | 3 | 10 |
| 93 | 1152 | 931 | 514 | 509 | 218 | | 244 | 64 | 248 |
| 45 | 187 | 143 | 45 | 24 | 221 | | 33 | 8 | 9 |
| 16 | 19 | 30 | 16 | 22 | 44 | 1 | 9 | 4 | 12 |
| 17 | 26 | 18 | 4 | 7 | 38 | | 4 | | 2 |
| 32 | 139 | 119 | 46 | 37 | 105 | | 18 | 7 | 20 |
| 149 | 1264 | 1066 | 582 | 563 | 466 | 1 | 302 | 81 | 280 |

单位:万元

| 项 目 | Item | 全 市 Total | 市 区 Urban District | 上城区 Shangcheng |
|---|---|---|---|---|
| **规模以上工业合计** | **Industrial above Designated Size** | **145854508** | **135952373** | **7655947** |
| **一、按轻重工业分** | **Grouped by Light & Heavy Industry** | | | |
| 轻工业 | Light Industry | 52212735 | 48734026 | 3359023 |
| 重工业 | Heavy Industry | 93641773 | 87218348 | 4296923 |
| **二、按所有制分** | **Grouped by Ownership** | | | |
| 国有企业 | State - owned Enterprises | 1776196 | 1649607 | |
| 集体企业 | Collective - owned Enterprises | | | |
| 股份合作企业 | Cooperative Enterprises | 31742 | 31742 | |
| 联营企业 | Joint Ownership Enterprises | | | |
| 有限责任公司 | Limited Liability Corporations | 38731196 | 35827918 | 7145235 |
| 股份有限公司 | Share - holding Corporations Ltd. | 17322583 | 16404287 | 198507 |
| 私营企业 | Private Enterprises | 52207438 | 47209833 | 291878 |
| 外商及港澳台投资企业 | Enterprises with Investment from Foreign、Hong Kong、Macao and Taiwan | 35785353 | 34828985 | 20326 |
| 其他企业 | Other Enterprises | - | - | - |
| 合计中:国有控股企业 | Of the Total:Controlling Share Hold Enterprises | 27096906 | 25270792 | 7095734 |
| **三、按企业规模分** | **Grouped by Size of Enterprises** | | | |
| 大型企业 | Large | 43959706 | 42051829 | 109284 |
| 中型企业 | Medium - sized | 39911250 | 37514517 | 306393 |
| 小微企业 | Small | 61983552 | 56386027 | 7240269 |

# 总产值(2019 年)

# Output Value by Region(2019)

(10000 yuan)

| 下城区<br>Xiacheng | 江干区<br>Jianggan | 拱墅区<br>Gongshu | 西湖区<br>Xihu | 高新<br>(滨江)区<br>Hi - Tech<br>(Binjiang) | 萧山区<br>Xiaoshan |
|---|---|---|---|---|---|
| **455415** | **1372201** | **2818251** | **2714277** | **22858026** | **27435100** |
| 83774 | 247250 | 1361476 | 789726 | 1976938 | 16359702 |
| 371641 | 1124951 | 1456775 | 1924551 | 20881088 | 11075398 |
| | | 14474 | | | 975997 |
| 7148 | | 1982 | | | 9201 |
| 116546 | 215287 | 502013 | 567193 | 5920368 | 3411451 |
| 16944 | 273356 | 328701 | 346879 | 4204305 | 2579935 |
| 45168 | 276856 | 1774182 | 846692 | 1501371 | 15360019 |
| 269608 | 606703 | 196899 | 953513 | 11231982 | 5098498 |
| | – | – | – | – | – |
| 327937 | 85531 | 504057 | 531110 | 5160600 | 2166660 |
| 237224 | 773320 | 1192258 | 327284 | 12507758 | 6099636 |
| 38020 | 219759 | 704847 | 1279303 | 6000286 | 8786465 |
| 180171 | 379122 | 921145 | 1107690 | 4349982 | 12549000 |

单位:万元　　　　4－07　续表

| 项　目 | Item | 余杭区<br>Yuhang | 富阳区<br>Fuyang |
|---|---|---|---|
| **规模以上工业合计** | **Industrial above Designated Size** | **19258869** | **13343676** |
| **一、按轻重工业分** | **Grouped by Light & Heavy Industry** | | |
| 轻工业 | Light Industry | 7122401 | 2979275 |
| 重工业 | Heavy Industry | 12136468 | 10364401 |
| **二、按所有制分** | **Grouped by Ownership** | | |
| 国有企业 | State－owned Enterprises | 624723 | |
| 集体企业 | Collective－owned Enterprises | | |
| 股份合作企业 | Cooperative Enterprises | 13412 | － |
| 联营企业 | Joint Ownership Enterprises | | |
| 有限责任公司 | Limited Liability Corporations | 2105436 | 3905024 |
| 股份有限公司 | Share－holding Corporations Ltd. | 3335251 | 1560660 |
| 私营企业 | Private Enterprises | 10219245 | 6720266 |
| 外商及港澳台投资企业 | Enterprises with Investment from Foreign、Hong Kong、Macao and Taiwan | 2960802 | 1157726 |
| 其他企业 | Other Enterprises | － | － |
| 合计中:国有控股企业 | Of the Total:Controlling Share Hold Enterprises | 2127463 | 1171762 |
| **三、按企业规模分** | **Grouped by Size of Enterprises** | | |
| 大型企业 | Large | 4073866 | 2503095 |
| 中型企业 | Medium－sized | 5614557 | 3464146 |
| 小微企业 | Small | 9570446 | 7376435 |

continued (10000 yuan)

| 临安区 Lin'an | 钱塘新区 Qiantang New Area | 西湖风景名胜区 The West Lake Scenic Zone | 桐庐县 Tonglu | 淳安县 Chun'an | 建德市 Jiande |
|---|---|---|---|---|---|
| **8868494** | **29168830** | **3288** | **4291999** | **1099047** | **4511089** |
| 2553146 | 11901316 | | 1480115 | 710879 | 1287715 |
| 6315348 | 17267515 | 3288 | 2811884 | 388167 | 3223374 |
| | 34414 | | 126589 | | |
| 1271566 | 10667799 | | 1479577 | 169716 | 1253985 |
| 2642193 | 914268 | 3288 | 60664 | 89984 | 767648 |
| 4559569 | 5614586 | | 2054416 | 771010 | 2172179 |
| 395166 | 11937763 | | 570753 | 68337 | 317278 |
| 853994 | 5242656 | 3288 | 1250980 | 96146 | 478987 |
| 2518983 | 11709122 | | 1229607 | | 678270 |
| 1922013 | 9178727 | | 796941 | 153007 | 1446785 |
| 4427498 | 8280982 | 3288 | 2265451 | 946039 | 2386034 |

# 4－08 规模以上工业

## Main Economic Indicators of Industrial

单位:万元

| 项　目 | Item | 企业单位数（个）Number of Enterprises (unit) | 亏损企业(个) Loss Making Enterprises (unit) | 工业总产值（当年价格）Gross Industrial Output Value (current price) | 新产品产值 Output of New Products |
|---|---|---|---|---|---|
| **总　　计** | **Total** | **5698** | **1034** | **145854508** | **62423222** |
| **按隶属关系分** | **Grouped by Subordination** | | | | |
| 中央 | Central | 40 | 5 | 3454171 | 317362 |
| 地方 | | 79 | 11 | 13294151 | 1628211 |
| 其他 | Other | 5579 | 1018 | 129106186 | 60477650 |
| **按所有制分** | **Grouped by Ownership** | | | | |
| 国有企业 | State－owned Enterprises | 7 | 1 | 1776196 | |
| 集体企业 | Collective－owned Enterprises | | | | |
| 股份合作企业 | Cooperative Enterprises | 6 | 1 | 31742 | 3805 |
| 联营企业 | Joint Ownership Enterprises | | | | |
| 有限责任公司 | Limited Liability Corporations | 563 | 109 | 38731196 | 14493089 |
| 股份有限公司 | Share－holding Corporations Ltd. | 227 | 37 | 17322583 | 11810287 |
| 私营企业 | Private Enterprises | 4148 | 717 | 52207438 | 20042664 |
| 外商及港澳台投资企业 | Enterprises with Investment from Foreign、Hong Kong、Macao and Taiwan | 747 | 169 | 35785353 | 16073377 |
| 其他企业 | Other Enterprises | － | － | － | － |
| **按企业规模分** | **Grouped by Size of Enterprises** | | | | |
| 大型企业 | Large | 124 | 6 | 43959706 | 28242635 |
| 中型企业 | Medium－sized | 557 | 74 | 39911250 | 18367715 |
| 小微企业 | Small | 5017 | 954 | 61983552 | 15812872 |
| **按轻重工业分** | **Grouped by Light & Heavy Industry** | | | | |
| 轻工业 | Light Industry | 2704 | 507 | 52212735 | 18074784 |
| 重工业 | Heavy Industry | 2994 | 527 | 93641773 | 44348438 |

# 企业主要经济指标(2019 年)(一)
# Enterprises Above Designated Size(2019)( Ⅰ )

(10000 yuan)

| 实收资本 Total Capital Hold | 国家资本 State Capital | 个人资本 Personal Capital | 港澳台资本 Hongkong, Macau and TaiWan Capital | 外商资本 Foreign Capital | 就业人员年平均人数(人) Annual Average Number of Staff and Workers (person) |
|---|---|---|---|---|---|
| **35418528** | **4959470** | **7662357** | **2211822** | **3363170** | **1025362** |
| | | | | | |
| 1426201 | 835475 | 5763 | 178760 | 1857 | 9543 |
| 2013556 | 1093768 | 139622 | 34494 | 138131 | 37429 |
| 31978770 | 3030228 | 7516973 | 1998567 | 3223182 | 978390 |
| | | | | | |
| 567105 | 566913 | | | | 2176 |
| | | | | | |
| 4131 | | 4131 | | | 617 |
| | | | | | |
| 8723340 | 2893590 | 338297 | 1677 | 14587 | 156562 |
| 6760299 | 1171234 | 2249903 | 17158 | 750 | 126398 |
| 10983310 | 60914 | 4886043 | 10760 | 7899 | 502326 |
| 8380342 | 266820 | 183984 | 2182226 | 3339934 | 237283 |
| | | | | | |
| 9933974 | 2569103 | 1068587 | 327797 | 829651 | 273773 |
| 9468916 | 1050276 | 1806008 | 756126 | 1025152 | 284585 |
| 16015638 | 1340091 | 4787762 | 1127899 | 1508367 | 467004 |
| | | | | | |
| 11947477 | 481180 | 3085223 | 885794 | 1589720 | 453864 |
| 23471051 | 4478290 | 4577135 | 1326028 | 1773449 | 571498 |

| 项　目 | Item | 企业单位数(个) Number of Enterprises (unit) | 亏损企业(个) Loss Making Enterprises (unit) | 工业总产值(当年价格) Gross Industrial Output Value (current price) | 新产品产值 Output of New Products |
|---|---|---|---|---|---|
| **按市、县分** | **Grouped by County** | | | | |
| 市　区 | Urban District | 4984 | 904 | 135952373 | 57956397 |
| #萧山区 | Xiaoshan | 1429 | 229 | 27435100 | 9941273 |
| 余杭区 | Yuhang | 1203 | 210 | 19258869 | 9510747 |
| 富阳区 | Fuyang | 632 | 141 | 13343676 | 5147481 |
| 临安区 | Lin'an | 607 | 103 | 8868494 | 3934314 |
| 桐庐县 | Tonglu | 324 | 63 | 4291999 | 2223931 |
| 淳安县 | Chun'an | 88 | 25 | 1099047 | 136405 |
| 建德市 | Jiande | 302 | 42 | 4511089 | 2106490 |
| **按国民经济行业分** | **Grouped by Economic Sector** | | | | |
| 采矿业 | Mining and Quarrying | 21 | 2 | 204792 | 24622 |
| 煤炭开采和洗选业 | Coal Mining and Dressing | 1 | | 2599 | |
| 黑色金属矿采选业 | Ferrous Metals Mining and Dressing | | | | |
| 有色金属矿采选业 | Nonferrous Metals Mining and Dressing | 3 | | 29018 | |
| 非金属矿采选业 | Nonmetal Minerals Mining and Dressing | 17 | 2 | 173176 | 24622 |
| 制造业 | Manufacturing Industry | 5579 | 1018 | 133818277 | 61993487 |
| 农副食品加工业 | Agricultural Products Processing | 111 | 18 | 1327882 | 192412 |
| 食品制造业 | Food Manufacturing | 102 | 22 | 1783551 | 248912 |
| 酒、饮料和精制茶制造业 | Wine, Beverage and Tea Manufacturing | 54 | 5 | 2011913 | 552792 |
| 烟草制品业 | Tobacco Processing | 1 | | 3317462 | 209740 |
| 纺织业 | Textile Industry | 644 | 118 | 7232340 | 2453093 |
| 纺织服装、服饰业 | Textile Products and Costune Indnstry | 258 | 76 | 2116856 | 931150 |
| 皮革、毛皮、羽毛及其制品和制鞋业 | Leather. Furs. Downand Related and Shoes Products | 118 | 27 | 1486918 | 543407 |
| 木材加工和木、竹、藤、棕、草制品业 | Timber Processing, Bamboo, Cane, Palm Fiber and Straw Products | 35 | 8 | 217827 | 79125 |
| 家具制造业 | Furniture Manufacturing | 94 | 17 | 1316680 | 710509 |

continued 1 (10000 yuan)

| 实收资本<br>Total Capital Hold | 国家资本<br>State Capital | 个人资本<br>Personal Capital | 港澳台资本<br>Hongkong, Macau and TaiWan Capital | 外商资本<br>Foreign Capital | 就业人员年平均人数(人)<br>Annual Average Number of Staff and Workers (person) |
|---|---|---|---|---|---|
| | | | | | |
| 33103176 | 4619571 | 6905824 | 2119409 | 3210268 | 933945 |
| 8489998 | 504575 | 1934581 | 506479 | 854003 | 228499 |
| 4479992 | 358033 | 1312532 | 369070 | 252367 | 191451 |
| 3070559 | 437960 | 822014 | 28392 | 196401 | 86125 |
| 1880251 | 89090 | 655556 | 93843 | 47909 | 70789 |
| 961198 | 121549 | 262800 | 52691 | 69502 | 42351 |
| 460779 | 90041 | 185889 | 11657 | 3307 | 14332 |
| 893374 | 128309 | 307845 | 28065 | 80093 | 34734 |
| | | | | | |
| 66266 | 3000 | 10266 | | | 1503 |
| 98 | | 98 | | | 15 |
| | | | | | |
| 5568 | | 5568 | | | 462 |
| 60600 | 3000 | 4600 | | | 1026 |
| 32259516 | 2691306 | 7621420 | 2115031 | 3292859 | 1003740 |
| 224369 | 1600 | 83502 | 25442 | 8898 | 8178 |
| 590292 | 27937 | 84691 | 42957 | 250398 | 20667 |
| 594251 | 20919 | 66467 | 113549 | 168375 | 13294 |
| 60424 | | | | | 2573 |
| 1602011 | | 731219 | 92114 | 177242 | 94821 |
| 574807 | 11906 | 121084 | 261126 | 87791 | 43266 |
| 238829 | 179 | 85952 | 21815 | 16202 | 17368 |
| 46416 | 1500 | 22250 | | | 3440 |
| 368273 | | 76134 | 22291 | 77376 | 22181 |

单位:万元　　　　4-08　续表2

| 项　目 | Item | 企业单位数(个) Number of Enterprises (unit) | 亏损企业(个) Loss Making Enterprises (unit) | 工业总产值(当年价格) Gross Industrial Output Value (current price) | 新产品产值 Output of New Products |
|---|---|---|---|---|---|
| 造纸和纸制品业 | Paper Making and Paper Products | 226 | 53 | 3371380 | 932662 |
| 印刷和记录媒介复制业 | Printing and Record Media | 97 | 21 | 775551 | 214109 |
| 文教、工美、体育和娱乐用品制造业 | Cultural, Educational. Industrial Arts. Sports and Entertainment Goods | 95 | 15 | 1295742 | 412520 |
| 石油、煤炭及其他燃料加工业 | Petroleum, Coal and Other Fuel Processing | 14 | 4 | 164124 | 25271 |
| 化学原料和化学制品制造业 | Raw Chemical Materials and Chemical Products | 307 | 38 | 8097733 | 3193881 |
| 医药制造业 | Medical and Pharmaceutical Products | 99 | 12 | 6512571 | 2168828 |
| 化学纤维制造业 | Chemical Fiber | 124 | 23 | 9329144 | 4046020 |
| 橡胶和塑料制品业 | Rubber and Plastic Products | 314 | 44 | 5851354 | 1828273 |
| 非金属矿物制品业 | Nonmetal Minerals Products | 307 | 39 | 6737526 | 1576557 |
| 黑色金属冶炼和压延加工业 | Ferrous Metals Smelting and Processing | 48 | 11 | 823360 | 349870 |
| 有色金属冶炼和压延加工业 | Nonferrous Metals Smelting and Processing | 47 | 16 | 4013880 | 738619 |
| 金属制品业 | Metals Products | 399 | 52 | 5381405 | 2305006 |
| 通用设备制造业 | Ordinary Machinery | 516 | 65 | 10610207 | 5701121 |
| 专用设备制造业 | For Special Purpose Equipment Manufacturing | 257 | 52 | 2566163 | 1164014 |
| 汽车制造业 | Automobile Manufacturing | 231 | 73 | 5959003 | 3729609 |
| 铁路、船舶、航空航天和其他运输设备制造业 | Railway. watercraft. Avigation spaceflight and other Equipment Manufacturing | 49 | 9 | 818156 | 305041 |
| 电气机械和器材制造业 | Electric Equipment and Machinery | 455 | 95 | 12566465 | 7456088 |
| 计算机、通信和其他电子设备制造业 | Computers. Telecommunications and Other Electronic Equipment Manufacturing | 345 | 73 | 23545849 | 17671949 |
| 仪器仪表制造业 | Instruments and Meters Manufacturing | 186 | 25 | 3692155 | 1864790 |
| 其他制造业 | Other Manufacturing | 20 |  | 250945 | 139150 |
| 废弃资源综合利用业 | Multiple Utilization of Waste Resouces | 26 | 7 | 644137 | 248972 |
| 金属制品、机械和设备修理业 | Metal Products, Machinery and Equipment Repair |  |  |  |  |
| 电力、燃气及水的生产和供应业 | Produotion and supply of electricity, gas & water | 98 | 14 | 11831438 | 405113 |
| 电力、热力生产和供应业 | Production and Supply of Electric Power and Hot Water | 56 | 4 | 7511778 | 311614 |
| 燃气生产和供应业 | Production and Supply of Gas | 15 | 4 | 3755434 | 49874 |
| 水的生产和供应业 | Production and Supply of Tap Water | 27 | 6 | 564226 | 43626 |

continued 2 (10000 yuan)

| 实收资本 Total Capital Hold | 国家资本 State Capital | 个人资本 Personal Capital | 港澳台资本 Hongkong, Macau and TaiWan Capital | 外商资本 Foreign Capital | 就业人员年平均人数(人) Annual Average Number of Staff and Workers (person) |
|---|---|---|---|---|---|
| 574343 | 2235 | 229459 | 17014 | 17162 | 28329 |
| 235696 | 23458 | 70303 | 35868 | 2965 | 10389 |
| 235530 | | 64533 | 10622 | 91056 | 14905 |
| 108600 | | 20619 | 353 | | 717 |
| 1881045 | 19772 | 438086 | 49376 | 256063 | 42096 |
| 1394566 | 298562 | 118125 | 15219 | 255567 | 40163 |
| 2259379 | | 475027 | 94773 | 41307 | 34006 |
| 1056228 | 46127 | 331653 | 93720 | 215500 | 50730 |
| 1982738 | 45712 | 373460 | 110989 | 76350 | 33938 |
| 166657 | 5571 | 52507 | 2060 | 6572 | 3526 |
| 380956 | | 22068 | 3026 | 26152 | 6512 |
| 981541 | 43540 | 368242 | 150984 | 33387 | 43958 |
| 2549210 | 78080 | 774322 | 121952 | 310664 | 99308 |
| 964870 | 84708 | 269730 | 107538 | 153114 | 35284 |
| 3742964 | 751057 | 367542 | 287776 | 255936 | 47412 |
| 175501 | 31090 | 47554 | | 24473 | 7308 |
| 3954501 | 130686 | 740986 | 163987 | 356618 | 84945 |
| 4318680 | 1059569 | 1170527 | 245787 | 288587 | 146843 |
| 886023 | 7100 | 369919 | 24693 | 83498 | 41566 |
| 23048 | | 9676 | | 5037 | 3348 |
| 87768 | | 35783 | | 6570 | 2669 |
| | | | | | |
| 3092746 | 2265164 | 30672 | 96791 | 70311 | 20119 |
| 1674177 | 1009251 | 20447 | 62984 | 15966 | 12210 |
| 479605 | 381174 | 1225 | 31308 | 54345 | 2407 |
| 938964 | 874739 | 9000 | 2500 | | 5502 |

# 4-09 规模以上工业

# Main Economic Indicators of Industrial

单位:万元

| 项　目 | Item | 资产合计 Total Assets | 流动资产合　计 Total Circulating Funds | 应收账款 Receivables | 存　货 Stock |
|---|---|---|---|---|---|
| **总　　计** | **Total** | **182903653** | **109714647** | **40145044** | **20860096** |
| **按隶属关系分** | **Grouped by Subordination** | | | | |
| 中央 | Central | 3373949 | 1197011 | 482279 | 151490 |
| 地方 | | 15006924 | 7148536 | 1329579 | 2641002 |
| 其他 | Other | 164522780 | 101369100 | 38333187 | 18067605 |
| **按所有制分** | **Grouped by Ownership** | | | | |
| 国有企业 | State - owned Enterprises | 928297 | 216479 | 8818 | 9554 |
| 集体企业 | Collective - owned Enterprises | | | | |
| 股份合作企业 | Cooperative Enterprises | 46855 | 40513 | 11959 | 3047 |
| 联营企业 | Joint Ownership Enterprises | | | | |
| 有限责任公司 | Limited Liability Corporations | 49995509 | 25390432 | 10688142 | 5224386 |
| 股份有限公司 | Share - holding Corporations Ltd. | 41238841 | 22930613 | 7414384 | 3093106 |
| 私营企业 | Private Enterprises | 52403785 | 34259078 | 11616058 | 6857057 |
| 外商及港澳台投资企业 | Enterprises with Investment from Foreign、Hong Kong、Macao and Taiwan | 38290365 | 26877532 | 10405684 | 5672946 |
| 其他企业 | Other Enterprises | | | | |
| **按企业规模分** | **Grouped by Size of Enterprises** | | | | |
| 大型企业 | Large | 63292878 | 38813460 | 16890139 | 5543434 |
| 中型企业 | Medium - sized | 52525952 | 29608205 | 9878881 | 5968151 |
| 小微企业 | Small | 67084823 | 41292983 | 13376024 | 9348512 |
| **按轻重工业分** | **Grouped by Light & Heavy Industry** | | | | |
| 轻工业 | Light Industry | 61248890 | 35309862 | 8659137 | 8715545 |
| 重工业 | Heavy Industry | 121654763 | 74404785 | 31485908 | 12144551 |

# 企业主要经济指标(2019年)(二)
# Enterprises Above Designated Size(2019)(Ⅱ)

(10000 yuan)

| 产成品 Finished Products | 固定资产净额 Fixed Assets | 累计折旧 Accumulated Depreciation | 本年折旧 Depreciation of the year | 负债合计 Total Liabilities | 流动负债合计 Total Current Liabilities | 非流动负债合计 Total Non-current Liabilities | 所有者权益合计 Creditors´Equity |
|---|---|---|---|---|---|---|---|
| **8273986** | **30657208** | **52750855** | **3843065** | **100634686** | **86070876** | **14563809** | **82175310** |
| 42827 | 1717978 | 2075835 | 222535 | 2128052 | 1351286 | 776765 | 1222781 |
| 510990 | 4535001 | 29077089 | 506225 | 7856218 | 4735290 | 3120928 | 7150705 |
| 7720169 | 24404229 | 21597932 | 3114305 | 90650416 | 79984300 | 10666117 | 73801824 |
| 6216 | 653665 | 887519 | 111918 | 228945 | 147613 | 81332 | 699352 |
| 2386 | 3737 | 6810 | 921 | 16798 | 16798 | | 30057 |
| 1617567 | 11273839 | 34264100 | 1267476 | 32800758 | 26470265 | 6330493 | 17168750 |
| 1218179 | 3441269 | 2745220 | 420210 | 15670280 | 12551641 | 3118639 | 25545443 |
| 3165465 | 9130830 | 7980631 | 1275917 | 30493781 | 27397538 | 3096243 | 21871046 |
| 2264173 | 6153868 | 6866575 | 766624 | 21424123 | 19487021 | 1937102 | 16860663 |
| 2321869 | 7547279 | 6386782 | 891802 | 34152819 | 30373723 | 3779096 | 29140058 |
| 2504775 | 9320009 | 9022692 | 1202704 | 29033805 | 24537756 | 4496050 | 23492145 |
| 3447342 | 13789920 | 37341381 | 1748559 | 37448062 | 31159397 | 6288664 | 29543107 |
| 3493977 | 10812018 | 10018836 | 1382547 | 32224745 | 29198372 | 3026372 | 29010112 |
| 4780009 | 19845190 | 42732020 | 2460518 | 68409941 | 56872504 | 11537437 | 53165198 |

| 项 目 | Item | 资产合计 Total Assets | 流动资产合计 Total Circulating Funds | 应收账款 Receivables | 存 货 Stock |
|---|---|---|---|---|---|
| **按区域分** | **Grouped by County** | | | | |
| 市 区 | Urban District | 172285270 | 104431031 | 38434035 | 19851519 |
| #萧山区 | Xiaoshan | 39835001 | 18647497 | 5257682 | 3649486 |
| 余杭区 | Yuhang | 22994153 | 14736691 | 4737893 | 2928734 |
| 富阳区 | Fuyang | 15828812 | 8908101 | 3069682 | 1695524 |
| 临安区 | Lin'an | 10840819 | 6452927 | 2225813 | 1032282 |
| 桐庐县 | Tonglu | 4245001 | 2359417 | 822474 | 478659 |
| 淳安县 | Chun'an | 1465954 | 716050 | 232537 | 150749 |
| 建德市 | Jiande | 4907428 | 2208149 | 655999 | 379170 |
| **按国民经济行业分** | **Grouped by Economic Sector** | | | | |
| 采矿业 | Mining and Quarrying | 450426 | 268663 | 41778 | 9895 |
| 煤炭开采和洗选业 | Coal Mining and Dressing | 2933 | 1748 | 853 | 294 |
| 黑色金属矿采选业 | Ferrous Metals Mining and Dressing | | | | |
| 有色金属矿采选业 | Nonferrous Metals Mining and Dressing | 62396 | 34509 | 4960 | 1435 |
| 非金属矿采选业 | Nonmetal Minerals Mining and Dressing | 385097 | 232405 | 35965 | 8166 |
| 制造业 | Manufacturing Industry | 170707937 | 106963390 | 39568119 | 20742824 |
| 农副食品加工业 | Agricultural Products Processing | 1116369 | 745458 | 256707 | 246092 |
| 食品制造业 | Food Manufacturing | 2044207 | 1232199 | 405748 | 213960 |
| 酒、饮料和精制茶制造业 | Wine, Beverage and Tea Manufacturing | 2063294 | 1077902 | 304020 | 201292 |
| 烟草制品业 | Tobacco Processing | 3860608 | 3030697 | 250691 | 1901114 |
| 纺织业 | Textile Industry | 7799515 | 4513669 | 1069995 | 1156747 |
| 纺织服装、服饰业 | Textile Products and Costune Indnstry | 2392537 | 1634290 | 348334 | 463005 |
| 皮革、毛皮、羽毛及其制品和制鞋业 | Leather. Furs. Downand Related and Shoes Products | 1253467 | 924140 | 353158 | 302817 |
| 木材加工和木、竹、藤、棕、草制品业 | Timber Processing, Bamboo, Cane, Palm Fiber and Straw Products | 279586 | 151393 | 57189 | 23239 |
| 家具制造业 | Furniture Manufacturing | 2092758 | 1143182 | 200556 | 150507 |

continued 1 (10000 yuan)

| 产成品 Finished Products | 固定资产净额 Fixed Assets | 累计折旧 Accumulated Depreciation | 本年折旧 Depreciation of the year | 负债合计 Total Liabilities | 流动负债合计 Total Current Liabilities | 非流动负债合计 Total Non - current Liabilities | 所有者权益合计 Creditors´Equity |
|---|---|---|---|---|---|---|---|
| | | | | | | | |
| 7850054 | 27720493 | 50323287 | 3465119 | 94812837 | 80979514 | 13833323 | 77384823 |
| 1697950 | 5940051 | 6418702 | 776019 | 22004728 | 19052273 | 2952455 | 17827222 |
| 1250700 | 4114541 | 3391727 | 506199 | 12312816 | 10616163 | 1696653 | 10642822 |
| 772816 | 2979512 | 2194235 | 405563 | 9481854 | 7333428 | 2148426 | 6297219 |
| 429932 | 1731722 | 1317218 | 204238 | 5381445 | 4641012 | 740433 | 5465467 |
| 199938 | 1113281 | 884677 | 141445 | 2522794 | 2307071 | 215723 | 1716165 |
| 66648 | 382125 | 398109 | 73661 | 735994 | 617185 | 118809 | 729959 |
| 157346 | 1441309 | 1144783 | 162840 | 2563061 | 2167107 | 395954 | 2344364 |
| | | | | | | | |
| 4826 | 56589 | 54213 | 11942 | 254733 | 232460 | 22273 | 195692 |
| 287 | 738 | 747 | 169 | 2380 | 2380 | | 553 |
| | | | | | | | |
| 1043 | 9420 | 5702 | 755 | 20083 | 15979 | 4104 | 42313 |
| 3495 | 46431 | 47764 | 11018 | 232270 | 214101 | 18169 | 152827 |
| 8240930 | 23952585 | 21617291 | 3116098 | 93362166 | 82839078 | 10523089 | 77254503 |
| 76630 | 204150 | 124312 | 23498 | 770423 | 752910 | 17513 | 345945 |
| 87935 | 535081 | 436817 | 64076 | 971730 | 951491 | 20238 | 1072476 |
| 76314 | 715033 | 797936 | 104205 | 1110412 | 1061686 | 48725 | 952882 |
| 184246 | 411125 | 471333 | 86848 | 1401656 | 1400400 | 1257 | 2458952 |
| 623725 | 1843155 | 2064957 | 259188 | 4651008 | 4307079 | 343929 | 3150228 |
| 266118 | 404550 | 324186 | 38691 | 1138443 | 996943 | 141500 | 1250478 |
| 62698 | 166649 | 115672 | 16817 | 870338 | 855371 | 14967 | 383129 |
| 10569 | 34567 | 23061 | 5361 | 179316 | 176406 | 2911 | 100269 |
| 32855 | 198812 | 156425 | 26335 | 1199417 | 1015360 | 184057 | 893340 |

单位:万元 4-09 续表2

| 项　目 | Item | 资产合计 Total Assets | 流动资产合计 Total Circulating Funds | 应收账款 Receivables | 存货 Stock |
|---|---|---|---|---|---|
| 造纸和纸制品业 | Paper Making and Paper Products | 3293056 | 2004998 | 520721 | 335620 |
| 印刷和记录媒介复制业 | Printing and Record Media | 907092 | 551135 | 194084 | 95475 |
| 文教、工美、体育和娱乐用品制造业 | Cultural, Educational. Industrial Arts. Sports and Entertainment Goods | 849834 | 591548 | 105079 | 244340 |
| 石油、煤炭及其他燃料加工业 | Petroleum, Coal and Other Fuel Processing | 321472 | 171873 | 71917 | 26118 |
| 化学原料和化学制品制造业 | Raw Chemical Materials and Chemical Products | 10186173 | 4782605 | 1115450 | 853112 |
| 医药制造业 | Medical and Pharmaceutical Products | 7110286 | 4248998 | 1013584 | 1226925 |
| 化学纤维制造业 | Chemical Fiber | 12844387 | 5149069 | 1176350 | 749487 |
| 橡胶和塑料制品业 | Rubber and Plastic Products | 5390437 | 3350475 | 1272134 | 836449 |
| 非金属矿物制品业 | Nonmetal Minerals Products | 6363937 | 4222089 | 2271060 | 519056 |
| 黑色金属冶炼和压延加工业 | Ferrous Metals Smelting and Processing | 635031 | 454979 | 78356 | 133452 |
| 有色金属冶炼和压延加工业 | Nonferrous Metals Smelting and Processing | 2100132 | 1337144 | 192493 | 395127 |
| 金属制品业 | Metals Products | 4100182 | 2758459 | 867444 | 718571 |
| 通用设备制造业 | Ordinary Machinery | 15369430 | 9830684 | 3138109 | 1888008 |
| 专用设备制造业 | For Special Purpose Equipment Manufacturing | 3876017 | 2814345 | 794577 | 610828 |
| 汽车制造业 | Automobile Manufacturing | 18424644 | 9363266 | 5630011 | 940524 |
| 铁路、船舶、航空航天和其他运输设备制造业 | Railway. watercraft. Avigation spaceflight and other Equipment Manufacturing | 847662 | 576203 | 170394 | 100023 |
| 电气机械和器材制造业 | Electric Equipment and Machinery | 19005429 | 12140411 | 4078947 | 2271053 |
| 计算机、通信和其他电子设备制造业 | Computers. Telecommunications and Other Electronic Equipment Manufacturing | 28747686 | 22620629 | 12038041 | 3099501 |
| 仪器仪表制造业 | Instruments and Meters Manufacturing | 6487414 | 4852577 | 1476441 | 903282 |
| 其他制造业 | Other Manufacturing | 291950 | 230610 | 22949 | 45951 |
| 废弃资源综合利用业 | Multiple Utilization of Waste Resouces | 653347 | 458367 | 93580 | 91151 |
| 金属制品、机械和设备修理业 | Metal Products, Machinery and Equipment Repair | | | | |
| 电力、燃气及水的生产和供应业 | Produotion and supply of electricity, gas & water | 11745290 | 2482595 | 535147 | 107378 |
| 电力、热力生产和供应业 | Production and Supply of Electric Power and Hot Water | 6335204 | 1124713 | 381950 | 32019 |
| 燃气生产和供应业 | Production and Supply of Gas | 1617514 | 293218 | 90180 | 25697 |
| 水的生产和供应业 | Production and Supply of Tap Water | 3792572 | 1064665 | 63018 | 49662 |

continued 2 (10000 yuan)

| 产成品 Finished Products | 固定资产净额 Fixed Assets | 累计折旧 Accumulated Depreciation | 本年折旧 Depreciation of the year | 负债合计 Total Liabilities | 流动负债合计 Total Current Liabilities | 非流动负债合计 Total Non - current Liabilities | 所有者权益合计 Creditors´Equity |
|---|---|---|---|---|---|---|---|
| 147671 | 722521 | 595540 | 89729 | 2237622 | 1910661 | 326961 | 1050771 |
| 45787 | 259617 | 330160 | 36497 | 507873 | 444276 | 63596 | 399218 |
| 59616 | 163053 | 187695 | 21364 | 425590 | 403391 | 22199 | 424243 |
| 10872 | 30175 | 17252 | 3439 | 162402 | 146697 | 15705 | 159070 |
| 417299 | 2083023 | 1629461 | 236396 | 4432201 | 3534226 | 897975 | 5751741 |
| 670465 | 1403382 | 801222 | 137509 | 2970782 | 2542691 | 428091 | 4139503 |
| 438172 | 1631555 | 1689141 | 198465 | 7895788 | 7015329 | 880459 | 4945476 |
| 521059 | 1192009 | 1793287 | 190840 | 3003854 | 2734289 | 269565 | 2382612 |
| 289306 | 1016720 | 1005419 | 148507 | 4218290 | 3888144 | 330146 | 2129900 |
| 55091 | 101874 | 176048 | 18892 | 365048 | 299809 | 65239 | 269983 |
| 105773 | 349736 | 270665 | 40005 | 1423007 | 1217809 | 205199 | 632443 |
| 377981 | 860743 | 758463 | 105605 | 2217250 | 2087497 | 129753 | 1879885 |
| 755243 | 1916159 | 1702627 | 227331 | 7841228 | 6963508 | 877719 | 7516315 |
| 208191 | 614219 | 553217 | 74252 | 1718295 | 1572195 | 146100 | 2157719 |
| 417165 | 2298353 | 1731495 | 323574 | 13334589 | 10993819 | 2340770 | 5090053 |
| 38356 | 130428 | 91071 | 15070 | 544049 | 513990 | 30059 | 303613 |
| 1091689 | 2151007 | 1773538 | 264165 | 9407033 | 7845393 | 1561639 | 9598392 |
| 823291 | 1906918 | 1469282 | 279370 | 15101299 | 14207190 | 894108 | 13646384 |
| 292786 | 463867 | 445708 | 61027 | 2699254 | 2509916 | 189338 | 3788159 |
| 11809 | 22772 | 30549 | 3251 | 97514 | 93722 | 3792 | 194436 |
| 42219 | 121333 | 50753 | 15793 | 466457 | 396879 | 69578 | 186890 |
| | | | | | | | |
| 28230 | 6648034 | 31079351 | 715025 | 7017786 | 2999338 | 4018448 | 4725115 |
| 2972 | 4186400 | 29323021 | 535776 | 3843411 | 1440559 | 2402852 | 2489405 |
| 12580 | 1129305 | 544165 | 73682 | 1189131 | 765830 | 423301 | 428384 |
| 12678 | 1332329 | 1212165 | 105567 | 1985245 | 792950 | 1192295 | 1807327 |

# 4－10 规模以上工业

## Main Economic Indicators of Industrial

单位:万元

| 项 目 | Item | 主营业务收入 Revenues in Main Business | 销售费用 Sales Expenses | 管理费用 Management Expenses |
|---|---|---|---|---|
| **总 计** | **Total** | **152125123** | **7891803** | **5717420** |
| **按隶属关系分** | **Grouped by Subordination** | | | |
| 中央 | Central | 3553286 | 27327 | 38727 |
| 地方 | | 13518270 | 295595 | 373992 |
| 其他 | Other | 135053567 | 7568880 | 5304701 |
| **按所有制分** | **Grouped by Ownership** | | | |
| 国有企业 | State－owned Enterprises | 1751404 | 278 | 2253 |
| 集体企业 | Collective－owned Enterprises | | | |
| 股份合作企业 | Cooperative Enterprises | 31161 | 795 | 2297 |
| 联营企业 | Joint Ownership Enterprises | | | |
| 有限责任公司 | Limited Liability Corporations | 42320152 | 1034189 | 1205177 |
| 股份有限公司 | Share－holding Corporations Ltd. | 18134230 | 1394002 | 754100 |
| 私营企业 | Private Enterprises | 52832277 | 2366695 | 2227924 |
| 外商及港澳台投资企业 | Enterprises with Investment from Foreign、Hong Kong、Macao and Taiwan | 37055899 | 3095844 | 1525670 |
| 其他企业 | Other Enterprises | | | |
| **按企业规模分** | **Grouped by Size of Enterprises** | | | |
| 大型企业 | Large | 47853813 | 3790974 | 1266336 |
| 中型企业 | Medium－sized | 40875394 | 2069762 | 1566118 |
| 小微企业 | Small | 63395916 | 2031067 | 2884967 |
| **按轻重工业分** | **Grouped by Light & Heavy Industry** | | | |
| 轻工业 | Light Industry | 55663111 | 3922470 | 2414740 |
| 重工业 | Heavy Industry | 96462012 | 3969332 | 3302681 |

# 企业主要经济指标(2019 年)(三)

# Enterprises Above Designated Size(2019)(Ⅲ)

(10000 yuan)

| 财务费用<br>Financial Expenses | 利息支出<br>Interest Expenditure | 营业利润<br>Business Profits | 利润总额<br>Total Profits | 利税总额<br>Total Pre - tax Profits | 本年应交增值税<br>Value Added Tax Payable |
|---|---|---|---|---|---|
| **1141841** | **1547446** | **10636168** | **11261738** | **18549922** | **4335730** |
| | | | | | |
| 44810 | 35569 | - 106541 | - 78672 | 44766 | 106188 |
| 57171 | 93609 | 944824 | 942360 | 3729334 | 583117 |
| 1039860 | 1418268 | 9797884 | 10398051 | 14775821 | 3646425 |
| | | | | | |
| 2123 | 1590 | 18743 | 20267 | 65507 | 39945 |
| | | | | | |
| 356 | 413 | 1061 | 988 | 2283 | 1143 |
| | | | | | |
| 289000 | 370276 | 2404125 | 2493694 | 6063546 | 1197786 |
| 122300 | 296204 | 3251920 | 3334664 | 4160588 | 699279 |
| 564135 | 638127 | 2653506 | 2940455 | 4762904 | 1564068 |
| 163928 | 240836 | 2306814 | 2471672 | 3495095 | 833509 |
| | | | | | |
| 187789 | 429885 | 4902871 | 5023268 | 6686931 | 1367291 |
| 313450 | 411497 | 2790902 | 2984525 | 4201358 | 1014852 |
| 640602 | 706064 | 2942394 | 3253946 | 7661633 | 1953586 |
| | | | | | |
| 496752 | 644464 | 3575628 | 3841206 | 8234689 | 1939432 |
| 645089 | 902982 | 7060540 | 7420532 | 10315233 | 2396298 |

单位:万元　　　　4-10 续表1

| 项　目 | Item | 主营业务收入 Revenues in Main Business | 销售费用 Sales Expenses | 管理费用 Management Expenses |
|---|---|---|---|---|
| **按市、县分** | **Grouped by County** | | | |
| 市　区 | Urban District | 142334715 | 7435075 | 5313387 |
| #萧山区 | Xiaoshan | 30309088 | 653774 | 977610 |
| 余杭区 | Yuhang | 19506298 | 1119538 | 948366 |
| 富阳区 | Fuyang | 14030574 | 324658 | 444855 |
| 临安区 | Lin'an | 9255215 | 377515 | 415643 |
| 桐庐县 | Tonglu | 4178698 | 154886 | 171125 |
| 淳安县 | Chun'an | 1097377 | 59798 | 48481 |
| 建德市 | Jiande | 4514334 | 242044 | 184427 |
| **按国民经济行业分** | **Grouped by Economic Sector** | | | |
| 采矿业 | Mining and Quarrying | 204432 | 8324 | 21371 |
| 煤炭开采和洗选业 | Coal Mining and Dressing | 2771 | 17 | 320 |
| 黑色金属矿采选业 | Ferrous Metals Mining and Dressing | | | |
| 有色金属矿采选业 | Nonferrous Metals Mining and Dressing | 33376 | 922 | 5889 |
| 非金属矿采选业 | Nonmetal Minerals Mining and Dressing | 168284 | 7386 | 15163 |
| 制造业 | Manufacturing Industry | 140142544 | 7837343 | 5468743 |
| 农副食品加工业 | Agricultural Products Processing | 1382135 | 45701 | 39889 |
| 食品制造业 | Food Manufacturing | 1847077 | 162697 | 110851 |
| 酒、饮料和精制茶制造业 | Wine, Beverage and Tea Manufacturing | 2152804 | 355752 | 73770 |
| 烟草制品业 | Tobacco Processing | 3392065 | 78636 | 119944 |
| 纺织业 | Textile Industry | 7044434 | 143874 | 310402 |
| 纺织服装、服饰业 | Textile Products and Costune Indnstry | 2162402 | 77742 | 197739 |
| 皮革、毛皮、羽毛及其制品和制鞋业 | Leather. Furs. Downand Related and Shoes Products | 1414656 | 39177 | 53514 |
| 木材加工和木、竹、藤、棕、草制品业 | Timber Processing, Bamboo, Cane, Palm Fiber and Straw Products | 241878 | 8708 | 15485 |
| 家具制造业 | Furniture Manufacturing | 1274801 | 134040 | 78224 |

continued 1 (10000 yuan)

| 财务费用<br>Financial Expenses | 利息支出<br>Interest Expenditure | 营业利润<br>Business Profits | 利润总额<br>Total Profits | 利税总额<br>Total Pre - tax Profits | 本年应交增值税<br>Value Added Tax Payable |
|---|---|---|---|---|---|
| | | | | | |
| 1055947 | 1453032 | 9798328 | 10379193 | 17300172 | 4033479 |
| 333190 | 426389 | 1686454 | 1833847 | 2566993 | 616234 |
| 121543 | 189927 | 1230855 | 1331476 | 2067560 | 626069 |
| 262493 | 272446 | 480880 | 572255 | 1163433 | 524390 |
| 63643 | 82047 | 658973 | 704971 | 976410 | 221290 |
| 38158 | 41686 | 287404 | 317524 | 464192 | 123038 |
| 13074 | 12792 | 116072 | 126193 | 175308 | 39174 |
| 34663 | 39936 | 434363 | 438828 | 610250 | 140040 |
| | | | | | |
| 6618 | 6458 | 39389 | 38639 | 57995 | 12048 |
| -1 | | 68 | 60 | 280 | 165 |
| | | | | | |
| 332 | 336 | 5807 | 5772 | 10142 | 3370 |
| 6287 | 6122 | 33513 | 32807 | 47574 | 8514 |
| 1027053 | 1418892 | 10113124 | 10719736 | 17734182 | 4106578 |
| 14289 | 14450 | 34071 | 38697 | 65096 | 22718 |
| 3139 | 10343 | 166782 | 214770 | 299226 | 75297 |
| 7492 | 11190 | 257662 | 258130 | 370233 | 71547 |
| -8246 | 2671 | 345239 | 338159 | 2888848 | 384410 |
| 91372 | 102422 | 210405 | 244089 | 480656 | 204667 |
| 14062 | 19913 | 77193 | 100786 | 196577 | 83051 |
| 13679 | 17711 | 19013 | 28655 | 68233 | 34122 |
| 3648 | 4815 | 16766 | 18006 | 24716 | 5308 |
| 16585 | 18834 | 107461 | 113664 | 166062 | 42885 |

单位:万元　　4-10　续表2

| 项　目 | Item | 主营业务收　入 Revenues in Main Business | 销售费用 Sales Expenses | 管理费用 Management Expenses |
|---|---|---|---|---|
| 造纸和纸制品业 | Paper Making and Paper Products | 3369411 | 103538 | 143082 |
| 印刷和记录媒介复制业 | Printing and Record Media | 773793 | 21729 | 53781 |
| 文教、工美、体育和娱乐用品制造业 | Cultural, Educational. Industrial Arts. Sports and Entertainment Goods | 1248069 | 28568 | 46657 |
| 石油、煤炭及其他燃料加工业 | Petroleum, Coal and Other Fuel Processing | 299716 | 9521 | 8603 |
| 化学原料和化学制品制造业 | Raw Chemical Materials and Chemical Products | 8349567 | 557379 | 477450 |
| 医药制造业 | Medical and Pharmaceutical Products | 5910591 | 1648948 | 380701 |
| 化学纤维制造业 | Chemical Fiber | 12414038 | 35873 | 93546 |
| 橡胶和塑料制品业 | Rubber and Plastic Products | 5924255 | 263973 | 206226 |
| 非金属矿物制品业 | Nonmetal Minerals Products | 6770004 | 332373 | 221125 |
| 黑色金属冶炼和压延加工业 | Ferrous Metals Smelting and Processing | 984092 | 8313 | 18662 |
| 有色金属冶炼和压延加工业 | Nonferrous Metals Smelting and Processing | 4547112 | 22257 | 37481 |
| 金属制品业 | Metals Products | 5461701 | 97088 | 188057 |
| 通用设备制造业 | Ordinary Machinery | 11231792 | 437010 | 539645 |
| 专用设备制造业 | For Special Purpose Equipment Manufacturing | 2566804 | 163637 | 220871 |
| 汽车制造业 | Automobile Manufacturing | 6408637 | 149880 | 353564 |
| 铁路、船舶、航空航天和其他运输设备制造业 | Railway. watercraft. Avigation spaceflight and other Equipment Manufacturing | 917193 | 35582 | 43002 |
| 电气机械和器材制造业 | Electric Equipment and Machinery | 13739114 | 903611 | 525893 |
| 计算机、通信和其他电子设备制造业 | Computers. Telecommunications and Other Electronic Equipment Manufacturing | 23513831 | 1645084 | 628043 |
| 仪器仪表制造业 | Instruments and Meters Manufacturing | 3773468 | 306969 | 256659 |
| 其他制造业 | Other Manufacturing | 355240 | 13876 | 12696 |
| 废弃资源综合利用业 | Multiple Utilization of Waste Resouces | 671865 | 5809 | 13183 |
| 金属制品、机械和设备修理业 | Metal Products, Machinery and Equipment Repair | | | |
| 电力、燃气及水的生产和供应业 | Produotion and supply of electricity, gas & water | 11778148 | 46136 | 227306 |
| 电力、热力生产和供应业 | Production and Supply of Electric Power and Hot Water | 7452051 | 702 | 140582 |
| 燃气生产和供应业 | Production and Supply of Gas | 3760678 | 22795 | 36379 |
| 水的生产和供应业 | Production and Supply of Tap Water | 565419 | 22639 | 50345 |

continued 2 (10000 yuan)

| 财务费用 Financial Expenses | 利息支出 Interest Expenditure | 营业利润 Business Profits | 利润总额 Total Profits | 利税总额 Total Pre - tax Profits | 本年应交增值税 Value Added Tax Payable |
|---|---|---|---|---|---|
| 53457 | 57876 | 112345 | 156257 | 341934 | 161689 |
| 7343 | 7659 | 38294 | 44360 | 72483 | 23846 |
| 10163 | 11606 | 39025 | 44943 | 71537 | 22583 |
| 3401 | 3370 | 13112 | 12577 | 18895 | 5330 |
| 59157 | 96651 | 795855 | 859139 | 1132632 | 231219 |
| 28309 | 46352 | 960604 | 989530 | 1393843 | 350970 |
| 189655 | 227658 | 368644 | 373738 | 516407 | 125426 |
| 62113 | 63008 | 171011 | 174032 | 325530 | 126594 |
| 60197 | 68828 | 582767 | 580192 | 856224 | 238781 |
| 10203 | 10915 | 13861 | 16094 | 29916 | 11771 |
| 31204 | 38066 | 45669 | 53529 | 224612 | 164096 |
| 53006 | 52661 | 161830 | 177211 | 318059 | 119182 |
| 50389 | 91339 | 911728 | 967257 | 1337851 | 314808 |
| 17852 | 23164 | 224945 | 246186 | 365550 | 99914 |
| 62294 | 69257 | 387269 | 426858 | 625725 | 101642 |
| 3217 | 6071 | 29832 | 32339 | 67576 | 25388 |
| 136114 | 170951 | 847295 | 917996 | 1241318 | 256937 |
| 19973 | 126939 | 2583499 | 2657551 | 3372932 | 607066 |
| 3583 | 30647 | 499683 | 530100 | 695971 | 141652 |
| -2188 | 527 | 24008 | 24633 | 37561 | 10608 |
| 11593 | 13001 | 67255 | 80257 | 127980 | 43074 |
| | | | | | |
| 108170 | 122097 | 483656 | 503364 | 757745 | 217104 |
| 52004 | 53819 | 272096 | 287288 | 478062 | 163895 |
| 32184 | 33156 | 130540 | 131481 | 169981 | 33455 |
| 23983 | 35122 | 81020 | 84595 | 109702 | 19754 |

# 4－11 分行业规模以上工业

## Main Economic Beneficial Indicators of Industrial

| 行　业 | Sector |
|---|---|
| 总　　计 | **Total** |
| 煤炭开采和洗选业 | Coal Mining and Dressing |
| 黑色金属矿采选业 | Ferrous Metals Mining and Dressing |
| 有色金属矿采选业 | Nonferrous Metals Mining and Dressing |
| 非金属矿采选业 | Nonmetal Minerals Mining and Dressing |
| 农副食品加工业 | Agricultural Products Processing |
| 食品制造业 | Food Manufacturing |
| 酒、饮料和精制茶制造业 | Wine, Beverage and Tea Manufacturing |
| 烟草制品业 | Tobacco Processing |
| 纺织业 | Textile Industry |
| 纺织服装、服饰业 | Textile Products and Costune Indnstry |
| 皮革、毛皮、羽毛及其制品和制鞋业 | Leather. Furs. Downand Related and Shoes Products |
| 木材加工和木、竹、藤、棕、草制品业 | Timber Processing, Bamboo, Cane, Palm Fiber and Straw Products |
| 家具制造业 | Furniture Manufacturing |
| 造纸和纸制品业 | Paper Making and Paper Products |
| 印刷和记录媒介复制业 | Printing and Record Media |
| 文教、工美、体育和娱乐用品制造业 | Cultural, Educational. Industrial Arts. Sports and Entertainment Goods |
| 石油、煤炭及其他燃料加工业 | Petroleum, Coal and Other Fuel Processing |
| 化学原料和化学制品制造业 | Raw Chemical Materials and Chemical Products |
| 医药制造业 | Medical and Pharmaceutical Products |

# 企业主要经济效益指标(2019 年)

## Enterprises Above Designated Size by Sector(2019)

| 每百元固定资产原值实现利税(元) Pre tax Profits per 100 Yuan Original Value of Fixed Assets (yuan) | 每百元主营业务收入实现利税(元) Pre tax Profits per 100 yuan Revenues in Main Business (yuan) | 新产品产值率(%) New Product ratio (%) |
|---|---|---|
| **30.77** | **11.59** | **42.80** |
| 18.82 | 10.09 | |
| | | |
| 67.07 | 30.29 | |
| 49.78 | 28.27 | 14.22 |
| 19.42 | 4.68 | 14.49 |
| 29.85 | 15.81 | 13.96 |
| 24.05 | 15.31 | 27.48 |
| 327.36 | 49.56 | 6.32 |
| 12.30 | 6.68 | 33.92 |
| 25.98 | 8.98 | 43.99 |
| 24.20 | 4.77 | 36.55 |
| 40.29 | 9.67 | 36.32 |
| 46.56 | 12.43 | 53.96 |
| 25.51 | 9.92 | 27.66 |
| 12.24 | 8.82 | 27.61 |
| 20.43 | 5.71 | 31.84 |
| 39.84 | 6.22 | 15.40 |
| 30.93 | 13.23 | 39.44 |
| 62.91 | 23.13 | 33.30 |

4－11　续表

| 行　业 | Sector |
| --- | --- |
| 化学纤维制造业 | Chemical Fiber |
| 橡胶和塑料制品业 | Rubber and Plastic Products |
| 非金属矿物制品业 | Nonmetal Minerals Products |
| 黑色金属冶炼和压延加工业 | Ferrous Metals Smelting and Processing |
| 有色金属冶炼和压延加工业 | Nonferrous Metals Smelting and Processing |
| 金属制品业 | Metals Products |
| 通用设备制造业 | Ordinary Machinery |
| 专用设备制造业 | For Special Purpose Equipment Manufacturing |
| 汽车制造业 | Automobile Manufacturing |
| 铁路、船舶、航空航天和其他运输设备制造业 | Railway. watercraft. Avigation spaceflight and other Equipment Manufacturing |
| 电气机械和器材制造业 | Electric Equipment and Machinery |
| 计算机、通信和其他电子设备制造业 | Computers. Telecommunications and Other Electronic Equipment Manufacturing |
| 仪器仪表制造业 | Instruments and Meters Manufacturing |
| 其他制造业 | Other Manufacturing |
| 废弃资源综合利用业 | Multiple Utilization of Waste Resouces |
| 金属制品、机械和设备修理业 | Metal Products, Machinery and Equipment Repair |
| 电力、热力生产和供应业 | Production and Supply of Electric Power and Hot Water |
| 燃气生产和供应业 | Production and Supply of Gas |
| 水的生产和供应业 | Production and Supply of Tap Water |

continued

| 每百元固定资产原值实现利税（元）<br>Pre tax Profits per 100 Yuan Original Value of Fixed Assets (yuan) | 每百元主营业务收入实现利税（元）<br>Pre tax Profits per 100 yuan Revenues in Main Business (yuan) | 新产品产值率（%）<br>New Product ratio (%) |
|---|---|---|
| 15.59 | 4.04 | 43.37 |
| 10.87 | 5.03 | 31.25 |
| 41.16 | 12.52 | 23.40 |
| 10.76 | 2.99 | 42.49 |
| 36.20 | 4.71 | 18.40 |
| 19.82 | 5.72 | 42.83 |
| 37.07 | 11.60 | 53.73 |
| 31.25 | 13.91 | 45.36 |
| 15.13 | 9.11 | 62.59 |
| 30.47 | 7.30 | 37.28 |
| 31.85 | 8.46 | 59.33 |
| 89.30 | 13.69 | 75.05 |
| 73.92 | 17.99 | 50.51 |
| 70.44 | 10.52 | 55.45 |
| 73.95 | 18.15 | 38.65 |
| | | |
| 4.90 | 6.39 | 4.15 |
| 10.13 | 4.48 | 1.33 |
| 4.31 | 18.05 | 7.73 |

# 4－12 市区规模以上工业

## Main Economic Indicators of Industrial Enterprises

单位：万元

| 项　目 | Item | 企业单位数（个）Number of Enterprises（unit） | 亏损企业（个）Loss Making Enterprises（unit） | 工业总产值（当年价格）Gross Industrial Output Value（current price） | 新产品产值 Output of New Products |
|---|---|---|---|---|---|
| **总　　计** | **Total** | **4984** | **904** | **135952373** | **57956397** |
| **按隶属关系分** | **Grouped by Subordination** | | | | |
| 中央 | Central | 32 | 4 | 3054680 | 311706 |
| 地方 | | 73 | 10 | 13166832 | 1592349 |
| 其他 | Other | 4879 | 890 | 119730861 | 56052341 |
| **按所有制分** | **Grouped by Ownership** | | | | |
| 国有企业 | State－owned Enterprises | 6 | 1 | 1649607 | |
| 集体企业 | Collective－owned Enterprises | | | | |
| 股份合作企业 | Cooperative Enterprises | 6 | 1 | 31742 | 3805 |
| 联营企业 | Joint Ownership Enterprises | | | | |
| 有限责任公司 | Limited Liability Corporations | 480 | 91 | 35827918 | 12720979 |
| 股份有限公司 | Share－holding Corporations Ltd. | 203 | 28 | 16404287 | 11443454 |
| 私营企业 | Private Enterprises | 3592 | 632 | 47209833 | 18111534 |
| 外商及港澳台投资企业 | Enterprises with Investment from Foreign、Hong Kong、Macao and Taiwan | 697 | 151 | 34828985 | 15676625 |
| 其他企业 | Other Enterprises | | | | |
| **按企业规模分** | **Grouped by Size of Enterprises** | | | | |
| 大型企业 | Large | 118 | 6 | 42051829 | 26794690 |
| 中型企业 | Medium－sized | 512 | 68 | 37514517 | 17055286 |
| 小微企业 | Small | 4354 | 830 | 56386027 | 14106421 |
| **按轻重工业分** | **Grouped by Light & Heavy Industry** | | | | |
| 轻工业 | Light Industry | 2350 | 452 | 48734026 | 16734786 |
| 重工业 | Heavy Industry | 2634 | 452 | 87218348 | 41221611 |

# 企业主要经济指标(2019 年)(一)

## Above Designated Size in Urban District(2019)(Ⅰ)

(10000 yuan)

| 实收资本 Total Capital Hold | 国家资本 State Capital | 个人资本 Personal Capital | 港澳台资本 Hongkong, Macau and TaiWan Capital | 外商资本 Foreign Capital | 就业人员年平均人数(人) Annual Average Number of Staff and Workers (person) |
|---|---|---|---|---|---|
| **33103176** | **4619571** | **6905824** | **2119409** | **3210268** | **933945** |
| | | | | | |
| 1336630 | 753027 | 5717 | 178760 | 1857 | 7942 |
| 1919032 | 1016044 | 139372 | 32964 | 137881 | 36610 |
| 29847514 | 2850500 | 6760735 | 1907684 | 3070530 | 889393 |
| | | | | | |
| 525978 | 525785 | | | | 1903 |
| | | | | | |
| 4131 | | 4131 | | | 617 |
| | | | | | |
| 8214206 | 2623831 | 296330 | 1377 | 14400 | 135772 |
| 6422914 | 1167854 | 2077406 | 17158 | 750 | 119291 |
| 9933692 | 38314 | 4382641 | 10760 | 7899 | 448845 |
| 8002256 | 263786 | 145316 | 2090113 | 3187219 | 227517 |
| | | | | | |
| | | | | | |
| 9742312 | 2530577 | 1055190 | 327797 | 807176 | 257624 |
| 8953152 | 1014819 | 1617946 | 735679 | 1007033 | 259480 |
| 14407712 | 1074175 | 4232688 | 1055932 | 1396059 | 416841 |
| | | | | | |
| 11084067 | 456780 | 2697446 | 841410 | 1501041 | 414712 |
| 22019109 | 4162791 | 4208378 | 1277998 | 1709227 | 519233 |

| 项　目 | Item | 企业单位数(个) Number of Enterprises (unit) | 亏损企业(个) Loss Making Enterprises (unit) | 工业总产值(当年价格) Gross Industrial Output Value (current price) | 新产品产值 Output of New Products |
|---|---|---|---|---|---|
| **按国民经济行业分** | **Grouped by Economic Sector** | | | | |
| 采矿业 | Mining and Quarrying | 11 | 1 | 122312 | 21312 |
| 煤炭开采和洗选业 | Coal Mining and Dressing | | | | |
| 黑色金属矿采选业 | Ferrous Metals Mining and Dressing | | | | |
| 有色金属矿采选业 | Nonferrous Minerals Mining and Dressing | 2 | | 14500 | |
| 非金属矿采选业 | Nonmetal Minerals Mining and Dressing | 9 | 1 | 107811 | 21312 |
| 制造业 | Manufacturing Industry | 4898 | 895 | 124544998 | 57531826 |
| 农副食品加工业 | Agricultural Products Processing | 97 | 14 | 1191021 | 159125 |
| 食品制造业 | Food Manufacturing | 88 | 18 | 1706675 | 215568 |
| 酒、饮料和精制茶制造业 | Wine, Beverage and Tea Manufacturing | 35 | 3 | 1173733 | 272903 |
| 烟草制品业 | Tobacco Processing | 1 | | 3317462 | 209740 |
| 纺织业 | Textile Industry | 570 | 106 | 6821788 | 2312042 |
| 纺织服装、服饰业 | Textile Products and Costume Industry | 196 | 69 | 1833374 | 852098 |
| 皮革、毛皮、羽毛及其制品和制鞋业 | Leather. Furs. Downand Related and Shoes Products | 109 | 25 | 1435962 | 524619 |
| 木材加工和木、竹、藤、棕、草制品业 | Timber Processing, Bamboo, Cane, Palm Fiber and Straw Products | 30 | 6 | 201293 | 72410 |
| 家具制造业 | Furniture Manufacturing | 79 | 15 | 1178753 | 636160 |
| 造纸和纸制品业 | Paper Making and Paper Products | 219 | 51 | 3135191 | 885122 |
| 印刷和记录媒介复制业 | Printing and Record Media | 86 | 18 | 699931 | 198249 |
| 文教、工美、体育和娱乐用品制造业 | Cultural, Educational. Industrial Arts. Sports and Entertainment Goods | 70 | 12 | 1175756 | 346909 |
| 石油、煤炭及其他燃料加工业 | Petroleum, Coal and Other Fuel Processing | 12 | 4 | 155219 | 21934 |
| 化学原料和化学制品制造业 | Raw Chemical Materials and Chemical Products | 261 | 35 | 6697409 | 2694531 |

continued 1　　(10000 yuan)

| 实收资本 Total Capital Hold | 国家资本 State Capital | 个人资本 Personal Capital | 港澳台资本 Hongkong, Macau and TaiWan Capital | 外商资本 Foreign Capital | 就业人员年平均人数(人) Annual Average Number of Staff and Workers (person) |
|---|---|---|---|---|---|
| 47368 | | 6368 | | | 904 |
| 3368 | | 3368 | | | 207 |
| 44000 | | 3000 | | | 697 |
| 30236511 | 2567907 | 6872144 | 2032245 | 3139957 | 915637 |
| 192356 | 1600 | 63340 | 25442 | 8865 | 7241 |
| 552529 | 27937 | 62661 | 42957 | 249470 | 19542 |
| 463621 | 2519 | 34259 | 113549 | 167125 | 9169 |
| 60424 | | | | | 2573 |
| 1546051 | | 707657 | 82747 | 177242 | 89065 |
| 516132 | 11906 | 95202 | 258228 | 84146 | 38879 |
| 231967 | 179 | 83493 | 21774 | 16202 | 16083 |
| 40266 | | 19250 | | | 3221 |
| 324295 | | 61752 | 17925 | 54901 | 19030 |
| 534532 | 2235 | 206370 | 17014 | 5171 | 26844 |
| 222334 | 23458 | 64821 | 35868 | 2965 | 9601 |
| 222785 | | 55313 | 10622 | 91056 | 12502 |
| 106188 | | 19619 | | | 662 |
| 1548785 | 13537 | 378410 | 27826 | 174163 | 35104 |

| 项　目 | Item | 企业单位数(个) Number of Enterprises (unit) | 亏损企业(个) Loss Making Enterprises (unit) | 工业总产值(当年价格) Gross Industrial Output Value (current price) | 新产品产值 Output of New Products |
|---|---|---|---|---|---|
| 医药制造业 | Medical and Pharmaceutical Products | 89 | 12 | 6293041 | 2021903 |
| 化学纤维制造业 | Chemical Fiber | 123 | 23 | 9324420 | 4041343 |
| 橡胶和塑料制品业 | Rubber and Plastic Products | 267 | 36 | 5145336 | 1476244 |
| 非金属矿物制品业 | Nonmetal Mineral Products | 219 | 26 | 5463579 | 1008648 |
| 黑色金属冶炼和压延加工业 | Ferrous Metals Smelting and Processing | 40 | 6 | 753418 | 326049 |
| 有色金属冶炼和压延加工业 | Nonferrous Metals Smelting and Processing | 39 | 11 | 3920065 | 707869 |
| 金属制品业 | Metal Products | 352 | 47 | 5079400 | 2153131 |
| 通用设备制造业 | Ordinary Machinery | 470 | 57 | 10149226 | 5416741 |
| 专用设备制造业 | For Special Purpose Equipment Manufacturing | 236 | 48 | 2414115 | 1062652 |
| 汽车制造业 | Automobile Manufacturing | 218 | 69 | 5857662 | 3680511 |
| 铁路、船舶、航空航天和其他运输设备制造业 | Railway. watercraft. Avigation spaceflight and other Equipment Manufacturing | 42 | 8 | 769124 | 279494 |
| 电气机械和器材制造业 | Electric Equipment and Machinery | 418 | 82 | 12162825 | 7281560 |
| 计算机、通信和其他电子设备制造业 | Computers. Telecommunications and Other Electronic Equipment Manufacturing | 315 | 66 | 22150178 | 16460859 |
| 仪器仪表制造业 | Instruments and Meters Manufacturing | 185 | 25 | 3684783 | 1859016 |
| 其他制造业 | Other Manufacturing | 17 | | 242646 | 138353 |
| 废弃资源综合利用业 | Multiple Utilization of Waste Resouces | 15 | 3 | 411613 | 216046 |
| 金属制品、机械和设备修理业 | Metal Products, Machinery and Equipment Repair | | | | |
| 电力、燃气及水的生产和供应业 | Produotion and supply of electricity, gas & water | 75 | 8 | 11285063 | 403259 |
| 电力、热力生产和供应业 | Production and Supply of Electric Power and Hot Water | 41 | 2 | 7015510 | 309760 |
| 燃气生产和供应业 | Production and Supply of Gas | 11 | 2 | 3723286 | 49874 |
| 水的生产和供应业 | Production and Supply of Tap Water | 23 | 4 | 546267 | 43626 |

continued 2 (10000 yuan)

| 实收资本 Total Capital Hold | 国家资本 State Capital | 个人资本 Personal Capital | 港澳台资本 Hongkong, Macau and TaiWan Capital | 外商资本 Foreign Capital | 就业人员年平均人数(人) Annual Average Number of Staff and Workers (person) |
|---|---|---|---|---|---|
| 1342836 | 295595 | 97717 | 15219 | 255567 | 37551 |
| 2259183 | | 475027 | 94773 | 41307 | 33982 |
| 954882 | 44949 | 296434 | 85122 | 213439 | 38352 |
| 1727216 | 11120 | 244349 | 107724 | 76350 | 26931 |
| 154757 | 5571 | 45970 | 2060 | 6572 | 3127 |
| 375596 | | 19708 | 3026 | 26152 | 6105 |
| 900098 | 43540 | 337574 | 148430 | 33387 | 38813 |
| 2355429 | 78080 | 705509 | 106901 | 306243 | 93669 |
| 882810 | 64708 | 229897 | 94578 | 152927 | 32891 |
| 3695570 | 751057 | 352322 | 287776 | 255936 | 46067 |
| 166241 | 31090 | 40924 | | 24223 | 6207 |
| 3717553 | 130686 | 630512 | 163987 | 339749 | 80076 |
| 4198164 | 1021043 | 1147470 | 244004 | 288266 | 135937 |
| 885023 | 7100 | 368919 | 24693 | 83498 | 41546 |
| 22690 | | 9318 | | 5037 | 3231 |
| 36201 | | 18350 | | | 1636 |
| | | | | | |
| 2819297 | 2051663 | 27312 | 87164 | 70311 | 17404 |
| 1456646 | 842080 | 17087 | 55984 | 15966 | 10013 |
| 454977 | 360134 | 1225 | 28680 | 54345 | 2234 |
| 907675 | 849450 | 9000 | 2500 | | 5157 |

# 4－13 市区规模以上工业

## Main Economic Indicators of Industrial

单位:万元

| 项 目 | Item | 资产合计 Total Assets | 流动资产合计 Total Circulating Funds | 应收账款 Receivables | 存 货 Stock |
|---|---|---|---|---|---|
| **总 计** | **Total** | **172285270** | **104431031** | **38434035** | **19851519** |
| **按隶属关系分** | **Grouped by Subordination** | | | | |
| 中央 | Central | 3050659 | 1149632 | 459063 | 149123 |
| 地方 | | 14824900 | 7116406 | 1323522 | 2634754 |
| 其他 | Other | 154409711 | 96164993 | 36651450 | 17067641 |
| **按所有制分** | **Grouped by Ownership** | | | | |
| 国有企业 | State－owned Enterprises | 845791 | 203472 | 8518 | 9494 |
| 集体企业 | Collective－owned Enterprises | | | | |
| 股份合作企业 | Cooperative Enterprises | 46855 | 40513 | 11959 | 3047 |
| 联营企业 | Joint Ownership Enterprises | | | | |
| 有限责任公司 | Limited Liability Corporations | 47422416 | 24619339 | 10421546 | 5105193 |
| 股份有限公司 | Share－holding Corporations Ltd. | 39429743 | 22058079 | 7283355 | 2923761 |
| 私营企业 | Private Enterprises | 47663587 | 31330432 | 10510445 | 6279440 |
| 外商及港澳台投资企业 | Enterprises with Investment from Foreign、Hong Kong、Macao and Taiwan | 36876878 | 26179196 | 10198213 | 5530584 |
| 其他企业 | Other Enterprises | | | | |
| **按企业规模分** | **Grouped by Size of Enterprises** | | | | |
| 大型企业 | Large | 61891088 | 38345102 | 16791572 | 5469396 |
| 中型企业 | Medium－sized | 49222572 | 27989292 | 9391646 | 5687144 |
| 小微企业 | Small | 61171610 | 38096638 | 12250817 | 8694978 |
| **按轻重工业分** | **Grouped by Light & Heavy Industry** | | | | |
| 轻工业 | Light Industry | 57599454 | 33356280 | 8079428 | 8254385 |
| 重工业 | Heavy Industry | 114685816 | 71074751 | 30354607 | 11597133 |

# 企业主要经济指标（2019 年）（二）

# Enterprises Above Designated Size in Urban District（2019）（Ⅱ）

（10000 yuan）

| 产成品<br>Finished Products | 固定资产净额<br>Fixed Assets | 累计折旧<br>Accumulated Depreciation | 本年折旧<br>Depreciation of the year | 负债合计<br>Total Liabilities | 流动负债合计<br>Total Current Liabilities | 非流动负债合计<br>Total Non - current Liabilities | 所有者权益合计<br>Creditors´Equity |
|---|---|---|---|---|---|---|---|
| **7850054** | **27720493** | **50323287** | **3465119** | **94812837** | **80979514** | **13833323** | **77384823** |
| | | | | | | | |
| 41737 | 1473619 | 1683514 | 188102 | 1922070 | 1216217 | 705853 | 1105472 |
| 508402 | 4427395 | 28964505 | 490289 | 7795408 | 4699443 | 3095965 | 7029491 |
| 7299915 | 21819479 | 19675268 | 2786727 | 85095359 | 75063854 | 10031505 | 69249860 |
| | | | | | | | |
| 6156 | 579467 | 797571 | 100263 | 197605 | 137514 | 60091 | 648186 |
| | | | | | | | |
| 2386 | 3737 | 6810 | 921 | 16798 | 16798 | | 30057 |
| | | | | | | | |
| 1568548 | 10175037 | 33268497 | 1133419 | 31201480 | 25170766 | 6030714 | 16194936 |
| 1123421 | 3150701 | 2541019 | 387984 | 14962572 | 11937434 | 3025139 | 24444052 |
| 2935888 | 8059536 | 7096491 | 1109609 | 27728316 | 24832819 | 2895497 | 19902359 |
| 2213656 | 5752016 | 6612899 | 732923 | 20706066 | 18884183 | 1821883 | 16165233 |
| | | | | | | | |
| | | | | | | | |
| 2288770 | 7036996 | 6073480 | 827491 | 33491142 | 29809183 | 3681958 | 28399946 |
| 2391135 | 8611392 | 8288951 | 1112937 | 27224628 | 22984550 | 4240078 | 21997943 |
| 3170149 | 12072105 | 35960855 | 1524692 | 34097067 | 28185780 | 5911287 | 26986935 |
| | | | | | | | |
| 3300705 | 9835050 | 9319726 | 1244264 | 30098922 | 27214700 | 2884222 | 27490469 |
| 4549348 | 17885443 | 41003561 | 2220855 | 64713915 | 53764814 | 10949101 | 49894353 |

单位:万元　　4－13　续表1

| 项　目 | Item | 资产合计 Total Assets | 流动资产合　计 Total Circulating Funds | 应收账款 Receivables | 存　货 Stock |
|---|---|---|---|---|---|
| **按国民经济行业分** | **Grouped by Economic Sector** | | | | |
| 采矿业 | Mining and Quarrying | 274925 | 204678 | 30140 | 4881 |
| 煤炭开采和洗选业 | Coal Mining and Dressing | | | | |
| 黑色金属矿采选业 | Ferrous Metals Mining and Dressing | | | | |
| 有色金属矿采选业 | Nonferrous Minerals Mining and Dressing | 12825 | 5230 | 126 | 975 |
| 非金属矿采选业 | Nonmetal Minerals Mining and Dressing | 262100 | 199449 | 30014 | 3906 |
| 制造业 | Manufacturing Industry | 161017217 | 101903375 | 37898291 | 19742679 |
| 农副食品加工业 | Agricultural Products Processing | 966313 | 654210 | 214933 | 219575 |
| 食品制造业 | Food Manufacturing | 1937779 | 1175469 | 388936 | 199019 |
| 酒、饮料和精制茶制造业 | Wine, Beverage and Tea Manufacturing | 1382177 | 854911 | 238283 | 139425 |
| 烟草制品业 | Tobacco Processing | 3860608 | 3030697 | 250691 | 1901114 |
| 纺织业 | Textile Industry | 7441984 | 4274500 | 987593 | 1101401 |
| 纺织服装、服饰业 | Textile Products and Costume Industry | 2144529 | 1481540 | 303968 | 436054 |
| 皮革、毛皮、羽毛及其制品和制鞋业 | Leather. Furs. Downand Related and Shoes Products | 1178838 | 895579 | 345738 | 297186 |
| 木材加工和木、竹、藤、棕、草制品业 | Timber Processing, Bamboo, Cane, Palm Fiber and Straw Products | 262478 | 139435 | 50485 | 22579 |
| 家具制造业 | Furniture Manufacturing | 1981190 | 1075186 | 181018 | 132309 |
| 造纸和纸制品业 | Paper Making and Paper Products | 3052408 | 1847143 | 507282 | 305641 |
| 印刷和记录媒介复制业 | Printing and Record Media | 840798 | 501857 | 175314 | 87685 |
| 文教、工美、体育和娱乐用品制造业 | Cultural, Educational. Industrial Arts. Sports and Entertainment Goods | 726246 | 493940 | 90333 | 216410 |
| 石油、煤炭及其他燃料加工业 | Petroleum, Coal and Other Fuel Processing | 315997 | 167016 | 69564 | 24818 |
| 化学原料和化学制品制造业 | Raw Chemical Materials and Chemical Products | 8142550 | 3849510 | 916989 | 707901 |

continued 1 (10000 yuan)

| 产成品 Finished Products | 固定资产净额 Fixed Assets | 累计折旧 Accumulated Depreciation | 本年折旧 Depreciation of the year | 负债合计 Total Liabilities | 流动负债合计 Total Current Liabilities | 非流动负债合计 Total Non－current Liabilities | 所有者权益合计 Creditors´Equity |
|---|---|---|---|---|---|---|---|
| 2618 | 33691 | 44844 | 9679 | 149964 | 149717 | 247 | 124960 |
| 825 | 5525 | 2699 | 216 | 8803 | 8803 | | 4022 |
| 1793 | 28166 | 42145 | 9463 | 141162 | 140915 | 247 | 120938 |
| 7820281 | 21503021 | 19787438 | 2800208 | 88075023 | 78079351 | 9995671 | 72856973 |
| 60794 | 169657 | 109179 | 19867 | 664065 | 648486 | 15580 | 302247 |
| 81043 | 510463 | 418731 | 61323 | 917286 | 903134 | 14152 | 1020493 |
| 60883 | 369922 | 538035 | 43467 | 610230 | 590143 | 20087 | 771947 |
| 184246 | 411125 | 471333 | 86848 | 1401656 | 1400400 | 1257 | 2458952 |
| 598991 | 1757728 | 1973754 | 248096 | 4394935 | 4071022 | 323912 | 3048772 |
| 256711 | 364498 | 280584 | 32242 | 990253 | 862083 | 128170 | 1150661 |
| 59645 | 151697 | 104533 | 15665 | 818457 | 803490 | 14967 | 360380 |
| 10346 | 30365 | 20797 | 5033 | 171035 | 168125 | 2911 | 91442 |
| 29265 | 171604 | 139045 | 23799 | 1157105 | 973047 | 184057 | 824085 |
| 131211 | 655782 | 557297 | 83428 | 2062475 | 1742387 | 320088 | 985271 |
| 41840 | 244844 | 313724 | 34188 | 464791 | 401194 | 63596 | 376006 |
| 52633 | 145437 | 169934 | 18430 | 365683 | 343815 | 21867 | 360563 |
| 10410 | 29579 | 16061 | 3227 | 160121 | 144415 | 15705 | 155876 |
| 332401 | 1614368 | 1364489 | 194505 | 3619211 | 2871611 | 747600 | 4521109 |

单位:万元　　4－13　续表2

| 项　目 | Item | 资产合计 Total Assets | 流动资产合　计 Total Circulating Funds | 应收账款 Receivables | 存　货 Stock |
|---|---|---|---|---|---|
| 医药制造业 | Medical and Pharmaceutical Products | 6873329 | 4142687 | 982779 | 1191047 |
| 化学纤维制造业 | Chemical Fiber | 12842919 | 5148104 | 1175727 | 749426 |
| 橡胶和塑料制品业 | Rubber and Plastic Products | 4875368 | 3146637 | 1200465 | 799989 |
| 非金属矿物制品业 | Nonmetal Mineral Products | 4877946 | 3559772 | 2001794 | 448884 |
| 黑色金属冶炼和压延加工业 | Ferrous Metals Smelting and Processing | 599380 | 428827 | 71110 | 126262 |
| 有色金属冶炼和压延加工业 | Nonferrous Metals Smelting and Processing | 2062478 | 1304953 | 182493 | 389224 |
| 金属制品业 | Metal Products | 3786438 | 2581524 | 787688 | 680973 |
| 通用设备制造业 | Ordinary Machinery | 14696532 | 9338291 | 2843223 | 1833995 |
| 专用设备制造业 | For Special Purpose Equipment Manufacturing | 3652729 | 2639380 | 764349 | 573734 |
| 汽车制造业 | Automobile Manufacturing | 18239190 | 9260338 | 5583474 | 912493 |
| 铁路、船舶、航空航天和其他运输设备制造业 | Railway. watercraft. Avigation spaceflight and other Equipment Manufacturing | 800223 | 544478 | 160367 | 87969 |
| 电气机械和器材制造业 | Electric Equipment and Machinery | 18232614 | 11702923 | 3944646 | 2150076 |
| 计算机、通信和其他电子设备制造业 | Computers. Telecommunications and Other Electronic Equipment Manufacturing | 28114102 | 22336396 | 11906264 | 3028907 |
| 仪器仪表制造业 | Instruments and Meters Manufacturing | 6482967 | 4848313 | 1474720 | 902644 |
| 其他制造业 | Other Manufacturing | 286300 | 227463 | 21457 | 45744 |
| 废弃资源综合利用业 | Multiple Utilization of Waste Resouces | 360806 | 252297 | 76608 | 30197 |
| 金属制品、机械和设备修理业 | Metal Products, Machinery and Equipment Repair | | | | |
| 电力、燃气及水的生产和供应业 | Produotion and supply of electricity, gas & water | 10993128 | 2322978 | 505603 | 103958 |
| 电力、热力生产和供应业 | Production and Supply of Electric Power and Hot Water | 5738736 | 1030935 | 359254 | 29049 |
| 燃气生产和供应业 | Production and Supply of Gas | 1568973 | 284773 | 86848 | 25342 |
| 水的生产和供应业 | Production and Supply of Tap Water | 3685420 | 1007270 | 59502 | 49568 |

continued 2 (10000 yuan)

| 产成品 Finished Products | 固定资产净额 Fixed Assets | 累计折旧 Accumulated Depreciation | 本年折旧 Depreciation of the year | 负债合计 Total Liabilities | 流动负债合计 Total Current Liabilities | 非流动负债合计 Total Non - current Liabilities | 所有者权益合计 Creditors´Equity |
|---|---|---|---|---|---|---|---|
| 657450 | 1343929 | 777572 | 127312 | 2869101 | 2463061 | 406041 | 4004228 |
| 438112 | 1631052 | 1688942 | 198406 | 7894819 | 7014360 | 880459 | 4944977 |
| 508968 | 963407 | 1554185 | 159855 | 2714296 | 2455131 | 259165 | 2161068 |
| 260209 | 714345 | 711094 | 108518 | 3407142 | 3246767 | 160375 | 1455058 |
| 50371 | 95345 | 169917 | 17413 | 340511 | 276896 | 63615 | 258868 |
| 104462 | 342179 | 263667 | 39160 | 1390368 | 1186893 | 203475 | 629501 |
| 355367 | 763498 | 699385 | 95927 | 2035633 | 1910347 | 125286 | 1747758 |
| 737121 | 1811019 | 1585495 | 213169 | 7547225 | 6670599 | 876626 | 7137420 |
| 188957 | 580186 | 528825 | 68886 | 1621555 | 1481350 | 140205 | 2031171 |
| 410823 | 2248703 | 1698729 | 317775 | 13255369 | 10918108 | 2337262 | 4983818 |
| 36340 | 120141 | 79624 | 13106 | 517701 | 487642 | 30059 | 282522 |
| 1045039 | 2064771 | 1667758 | 251034 | 8988825 | 7439371 | 1549455 | 9243785 |
| 800271 | 1640195 | 1388602 | 248080 | 14703251 | 13851038 | 852213 | 13410849 |
| 292475 | 463769 | 445661 | 61013 | 2695932 | 2506593 | 189338 | 3787035 |
| 11776 | 20853 | 29643 | 3114 | 94078 | 90386 | 3692 | 192223 |
| 12124 | 72563 | 20844 | 7323 | 201916 | 157458 | 44458 | 158891 |
| | | | | | | | |
| 27155 | 6183780 | 30491005 | 655232 | 6587850 | 2750445 | 3837405 | 4402890 |
| 2149 | 3770090 | 28772366 | 480433 | 3507682 | 1234267 | 2273415 | 2228665 |
| 12329 | 1113745 | 534242 | 71928 | 1159367 | 740469 | 418898 | 409606 |
| 12677 | 1299946 | 1184397 | 102871 | 1920801 | 775709 | 1145092 | 1764619 |

# 4-14 市区规模以上工业

## Main Economic Indicators of Industrial

单位:万元

| 项　目 | Item | 主营业务收　入 Revenues in Main Business | 销售费用 Sales Expenses | 管理费用 Management Expenses |
|---|---|---|---|---|
| **总　计** | **Total** | **142334715** | **7435075** | **5313387** |
| **按隶属关系分** | **Grouped by Subordination** | | | |
| 中央 | Central | 3148636 | 24927 | 33974 |
| 地方 | | 13392662 | 294262 | 370560 |
| 其他 | Other | 125793417 | 7115886 | 4908853 |
| **按所有制分** | **Grouped by Ownership** | | | |
| 国有企业 | State - owned Enterprises | 1624832 | 178 | 2173 |
| 集体企业 | Collective - owned Enterprises | | | |
| 股份合作企业 | Cooperative Enterprises | 31161 | 795 | 2297 |
| 联营企业 | Joint Ownership Enterprises | | | |
| 有限责任公司 | Limited Liability Corporations | 39481792 | 950983 | 1118463 |
| 股份有限公司 | Share - holding Corporations Ltd. | 17122363 | 1350888 | 707690 |
| 私营企业 | Private Enterprises | 47964959 | 2072877 | 2001720 |
| 外商及港澳台投资企业 | Enterprises with Investment from Foreign、Hong Kong、Macao and Taiwan | 36109608 | 3059355 | 1481044 |
| 其他企业 | Other Enterprises | | | |
| **按企业规模分** | **Grouped by Size of Enterprises** | | | |
| 大型企业 | Large | 45948386 | 3696466 | 1208692 |
| 中型企业 | Medium - sized | 38513019 | 1935763 | 1468465 |
| 小微企业 | Small | 57873311 | 1802846 | 2636231 |
| **按轻重工业分** | **Grouped by Light & Heavy Industry** | | | |
| 轻工业 | Light Industry | 52284957 | 3676271 | 2253231 |
| 重工业 | Heavy Industry | 90049759 | 3758805 | 3060156 |

# 企业主要经济指标(2019 年)(三)

## Enterprises Above Designated Size in Urban District(2019)(Ⅲ)

(10000 yuan)

| 财务费用 Financial Expenses | 利息支出 Interest Expenditure | 营业利润 Business Profits | 利润总额 Total Profits | 利税总额 Total Pre－tax Profits | 本年应交增值税 Value Added Tax Payable |
|---|---|---|---|---|---|
| **1055947** | **1453032** | **9798328** | **10379193** | **17300172** | **4033479** |
| 41235 | 33783 | －137112 | －110228 | －11004 | 85069 |
| 56299 | 92630 | 931044 | 928300 | 3710930 | 579394 |
| 958412 | 1326618 | 9004396 | 9561121 | 13600246 | 3369016 |
| 1197 | 802 | 18127 | 19138 | 59353 | 35471 |
| 356 | 413 | 1061 | 988 | 2283 | 1143 |
| 271685 | 354567 | 2142056 | 2222438 | 5697154 | 1119978 |
| 117124 | 284616 | 3164590 | 3241854 | 4046936 | 683397 |
| 516858 | 589565 | 2295911 | 2557963 | 4171333 | 1388208 |
| 148728 | 223069 | 2176583 | 2336813 | 3323113 | 805281 |
| 185902 | 422530 | 4842410 | 4957744 | 6582138 | 1335197 |
| 294655 | 386806 | 2387885 | 2575377 | 3686260 | 929457 |
| 575390 | 643695 | 2568033 | 2846072 | 7031774 | 1768824 |
| 464367 | 611213 | 3254476 | 3501894 | 7761876 | 1831974 |
| 591579 | 841819 | 6543853 | 6877300 | 9538296 | 2201505 |

单位:万元　　4－14　续表1

| 项　目 | Item | 主营业务收　入 Revenues in Main Business | 销售费用 Sales Expenses | 管理费用 Management Expenses |
|---|---|---|---|---|
| **按国民经济行业分** | **Grouped by Economic Sector** | | | |
| 采矿业 | Mining and Quarrying | 120708 | 6673 | 9981 |
| 煤炭开采和洗选业 | Coal Mining and Dressing | | | |
| 黑色金属矿采选业 | Ferrous Metals Mining and Dressing | | | |
| 有色金属矿采选业 | Nonferrous Minerals Mining and Dressing | 14444 | 727 | 1259 |
| 非金属矿采选业 | Nonmetal Minerals Mining and Dressing | 106263 | 5946 | 8722 |
| 制造业 | Manufacturing Industry | 130973970 | 7385347 | 5084259 |
| 农副食品加工业 | Agricultural Products Processing | 1250466 | 41168 | 35333 |
| 食品制造业 | Food Manufacturing | 1777403 | 158757 | 105150 |
| 酒、饮料和精制茶制造业 | Wine, Beverage and Tea Manufacturing | 1407579 | 268748 | 53545 |
| 烟草制品业 | Tobacco Processing | 3392065 | 78636 | 119944 |
| 纺织业 | Textile Industry | 6636041 | 132999 | 292687 |
| 纺织服装、服饰业 | Textile Products and Costume Industry | 1889359 | 71320 | 183532 |
| 皮革、毛皮、羽毛及其制品和制鞋业 | Leather. Furs. Downand Related and Shoes Products | 1365970 | 38025 | 49387 |
| 木材加工和木、竹、藤、棕、草制品业 | Timber Processing, Bamboo, Cane, Palm Fiber and Straw Products | 225767 | 7894 | 14589 |
| 家具制造业 | Furniture Manufacturing | 1138462 | 126446 | 67812 |
| 造纸和纸制品业 | Paper Making and Paper Products | 3137859 | 78281 | 134900 |
| 印刷和记录媒介复制业 | Printing and Record Media | 694289 | 19065 | 49873 |
| 文教、工美、体育和娱乐用品制造业 | Cultural, Educational. Industrial Arts. Sports and Entertainment Goods | 1137051 | 20302 | 40304 |
| 石油、煤炭及其他燃料加工业 | Petroleum, Coal and Other Fuel Processing | 290703 | 8685 | 8398 |
| 化学原料和化学制品制造业 | Raw Chemical Materials and Chemical Products | 6868780 | 502760 | 419665 |

continued 1 (10000 yuan)

| 财务费用 Financial Expenses | 利息支出 Interest Expenditure | 营业利润 Business Profits | 利润总额 Total Profits | 利税总额 Total Pre－tax Profits | 本年应交增值税 Value Added Tax Payable |
|---|---|---|---|---|---|
| 3306 | 3124 | 18909 | 18190 | 28006 | 5852 |
| 36 | 39 | 831 | 763 | 2594 | 1503 |
| 3270 | 3085 | 18078 | 17427 | 25412 | 4349 |
| 950824 | 1332381 | 9333968 | 9898091 | 16583650 | 3835345 |
| 12460 | 12817 | 31218 | 35334 | 58415 | 19815 |
| 1852 | 9202 | 164746 | 210873 | 293732 | 74051 |
| 4146 | 8474 | 109477 | 110329 | 185002 | 46385 |
| －8246 | 2671 | 345239 | 338159 | 2888848 | 384410 |
| 83803 | 95446 | 204931 | 235127 | 460132 | 194738 |
| 10309 | 16344 | 72269 | 94758 | 181398 | 74972 |
| 12562 | 16500 | 19479 | 28536 | 65760 | 32041 |
| 3511 | 4680 | 16369 | 17401 | 23707 | 4991 |
| 16074 | 18187 | 106619 | 111556 | 157429 | 37192 |
| 53237 | 56399 | 87398 | 129575 | 308202 | 155962 |
| 6742 | 6998 | 36454 | 42378 | 68503 | 22070 |
| 8416 | 9949 | 38305 | 42725 | 65084 | 18879 |
| 3316 | 3283 | 12887 | 12365 | 18327 | 5075 |
| 51987 | 81768 | 609890 | 669938 | 911083 | 204774 |

单位:万元　　4-14 续表2

| 项　目 | Item | 主营业务收　入 Revenues in Main Business | 销售费用 Sales Expenses | 管理费用 Management Expenses |
|---|---|---|---|---|
| 医药制造业 | Medical and Pharmaceutical Products | 5693577 | 1592438 | 367068 |
| 化学纤维制造业 | Chemical Fiber | 12409304 | 35605 | 93321 |
| 橡胶和塑料制品业 | Rubber and Plastic Products | 5201251 | 216808 | 177531 |
| 非金属矿物制品业 | Nonmetal Mineral Products | 5518164 | 278456 | 173651 |
| 黑色金属冶炼和压延加工业 | Ferrous Metals Smelting and Processing | 918254 | 7125 | 16572 |
| 有色金属冶炼和压延加工业 | Nonferrous Metals Smelting and Processing | 4446693 | 21393 | 35632 |
| 金属制品业 | Metal Products | 5163590 | 84407 | 170388 |
| 通用设备制造业 | Ordinary Machinery | 10784411 | 415800 | 513914 |
| 专用设备制造业 | For Special Purpose Equipment Manufacturing | 2414436 | 153867 | 210230 |
| 汽车制造业 | Automobile Manufacturing | 6305000 | 147661 | 345670 |
| 铁路、船舶、航空航天和其他运输设备制造业 | Railway. watercraft. Avigation spaceflight and other Equipment Manufacturing | 868588 | 33091 | 35132 |
| 电气机械和器材制造业 | Electric Equipment and Machinery | 13315877 | 889211 | 500779 |
| 计算机、通信和其他电子设备制造业 | Computers. Telecommunications and Other Electronic Equipment Manufacturing | 22188861 | 1634183 | 592980 |
| 仪器仪表制造业 | Instruments and Meters Manufacturing | 3766193 | 306401 | 256222 |
| 其他制造业 | Other Manufacturing | 347165 | 13676 | 12275 |
| 废弃资源综合利用业 | Multiple Utilization of Waste Resouces | 420811 | 2139 | 7778 |
| 金属制品、机械和设备修理业 | Metal Products, Machinery and Equipment Repair | | | |
| 电力、燃气及水的生产和供应业 | Produotion and supply of electricity, gas & water | 11240038 | 43055 | 219148 |
| 电力、热力生产和供应业 | Production and Supply of Electric Power and Hot Water | 6962483 | 388 | 136920 |
| 燃气生产和供应业 | Production and Supply of Gas | 3728678 | 21272 | 34294 |
| 水的生产和供应业 | Production and Supply of Tap Water | 548877 | 21396 | 47934 |

continued 2 (10000 yuan)

| 财务费用 Financial Expenses | 利息支出 Interest Expenditure | 营业利润 Business Profits | 利润总额 Total Profits | 利税总额 Total Pre - tax Profits | 本年应交增值税 Value Added Tax Payable |
|---|---|---|---|---|---|
| 26515 | 44365 | 932147 | 960276 | 1350839 | 338997 |
| 189653 | 227653 | 368575 | 373638 | 516176 | 125307 |
| 56851 | 58002 | 156569 | 155797 | 280752 | 103852 |
| 48006 | 55391 | 350678 | 347149 | 551893 | 178185 |
| 9733 | 10655 | 16045 | 18853 | 31837 | 11149 |
| 30065 | 36921 | 49489 | 55700 | 221009 | 158907 |
| 48826 | 48862 | 149597 | 163789 | 290718 | 107298 |
| 46686 | 86028 | 895965 | 948179 | 1302792 | 301191 |
| 18111 | 22506 | 181876 | 198989 | 306677 | 89682 |
| 60786 | 67428 | 387553 | 427135 | 622995 | 99374 |
| 2846 | 5700 | 28346 | 30498 | 63542 | 23419 |
| 128915 | 164832 | 830181 | 898612 | 1213876 | 250978 |
| 18618 | 125402 | 2551440 | 2619445 | 3315069 | 591640 |
| 3589 | 30647 | 499662 | 530036 | 695707 | 141466 |
| -2306 | 409 | 23689 | 24209 | 36887 | 10394 |
| 3761 | 4862 | 56879 | 66731 | 97262 | 28155 |
| | | | | | |
| 101817 | 117527 | 445451 | 462913 | 688516 | 192281 |
| 45599 | 49284 | 234705 | 247809 | 411112 | 139934 |
| 32175 | 33121 | 130540 | 131480 | 169616 | 33238 |
| 24043 | 35122 | 80207 | 83625 | 107788 | 19109 |

# 4－15 规模以上工业企业

## Main Economic Indicators of Industrial Enterprises

单位:万元

| 项 目 | Item | 企业单位数(个) Number of Enterprises (unit) | 亏损企业(个) Loss Making Enterprises (unit) | 工业总产值(当年价格) Gross Industrial Output Value (current price) | 新产品产值 Output of New Products |
|---|---|---|---|---|---|
| **按登记注册类型分组** | **Grouped by Status of Registration** | **5698** | **1034** | **145854508** | **62423222** |
| 内资企业 | Domestic－funded Enterprises | 4951 | 865 | 110069154 | 46349845 |
| 国有企业 | State－owned Enterprises | 7 | 1 | 1776196 | |
| 中央企业 | Central Enterprises | 3 | | 1727308 | |
| 地方企业 | Local Enterprises | 4 | 1 | 48888 | |
| 集体企业 | Collective－owned Enterprises | | | | |
| 股份合作企业 | Cooperative Enterprises | 6 | 1 | 31742 | 3805 |
| 联营企业 | Joint Ownership Enterprises | | | | |
| 集体联营企业 | Collective Joint Ownership Enterprises | | | | |
| 有限责任公司 | Limited Liability Corporations | 562 | 109 | 38716889 | 14489512 |
| 国有独资公司 | State－funded Corporations | 32 | 8 | 8145779 | 358100 |
| 其他有限责任公司 | Other Limited Liability Corporations | 530 | 101 | 30571110 | 14131412 |
| 股份有限公司 | Share－holding Corporations Ltd. | 227 | 37 | 17322583 | 11810287 |
| 私营企业 | Private Enterprises | 4149 | 717 | 52221745 | 20046241 |
| 私营独资企业 | Private－funded Enterprises | 87 | 10 | 400546 | 23477 |
| 私营合伙企业 | Private Partnership Enterprises | 13 | 3 | 49057 | 2905 |
| 私营有限责任公司 | Private Limited Liability Corporations | 3939 | 684 | 48877487 | 18359364 |
| 私营股份有限公司 | Private Share－holding Corporations Ltd. | 110 | 20 | 2894655 | 1660495 |
| 港、澳、台商投资公司 | Enterprises with Investment from Hong Kong, Macao and Taiwan | 302 | 90 | 12120728 | 4618882 |
| 内地与港澳台合资经营企业 | Joint－venture Enterprises with funds from Hong Kong, Macao and Taiwan | 160 | 45 | 6239303 | 2511940 |
| 内地与港澳台合作经营企业 | Cooperative Enterprises with funds from Hong Kong, Macao and Taiwan | | | | |
| 港澳台商独资经营企业 | Enterprises with Sole Investment from Hong Kong, Macao and Taiwan | 135 | 44 | 5504742 | 1849147 |
| 港澳台商投资股份有限公司 | Share－holding Corporations Ltd. with Investment from Hong Kong, Macao and Taiwan | 5 | | 356958 | 242689 |
| 其他港澳台商投资 | Other Enterprises with Investment from Hong Kong, Macao and Taiwan | 2 | 1 | 19726 | 15106 |
| 外商投资企业公司 | Enterprises with Foreign Investment | 445 | 79 | 23664625 | 11454495 |
| 中外合资经营企业 | Joint－venture Enterprises | 185 | 29 | 7633831 | 2927453 |
| 中外合作经营企业 | Cooperation Enterprises | 4 | | 85897 | 19772 |
| 外商独资经营企业 | Enterprises with Sole Foreign Investment | 243 | 43 | 15583988 | 8315585 |
| 外商投资股份有限公司 | Share－holding Corporations Ltd. with Foreign Investment | 10 | 5 | 298105 | 191685 |
| 其他外商投资企业 | | 3 | 2 | 62805 | |

# 主要经济指标按登记注册类型分(2019 年)
## Above Designated Size by Status of Registration(2019)

(10000 yuan)

| 实收资本<br>Total Capital Hold | 国家资本<br>State Capital | 个人资本<br>Personal Capital | 港澳台资本<br>Hongkong, Macau and TaiWan Capital | 外商资本<br>Foreign Capital | 就业人员年平均人数(人)<br>Annual Average Number of Staff and Workers (person) |
|---|---|---|---|---|---|
| **35418528** | **4959470** | **7662357** | **2211822** | **3363170** | **102536** |
| 27038186 | 4692651 | 7478373 | 29596 | 23236 | 78808 |
| 567105 | 566913 | | | | 218 |
| 566286 | 566286 | | | | 172 |
| 820 | 627 | | | | 45 |
| | | | | | |
| 4131 | | 4131 | | | 62 |
| | | | | | |
| | | | | | |
| 8718761 | 2893590 | 335143 | 1677 | 14587 | 15645 |
| 984542 | 846927 | | | | 1238 |
| 7734219 | 2046664 | 335143 | 1677 | 14587 | 14407 |
| 6760299 | 1171234 | 2249903 | 17158 | 750 | 12640 |
| 10987889 | 60914 | 4889197 | 10760 | 7899 | 50244 |
| 28172 | | 22509 | | | 517 |
| 6572 | | 6346 | | | 86 |
| 10055342 | 50945 | 4251871 | 10760 | 7899 | 46784 |
| 897804 | 9969 | 608471 | | | 2857 |
| 3314514 | 86635 | 92275 | 2058014 | 143427 | 9301 |
| 1682881 | 26192 | 92275 | 613373 | 109531 | 4627 |
| – | – | – | – | – | – |
| 1523112 | 12460 | | 1432081 | 6177 | 4365 |
| 98518 | 47983 | | 2856 | 27419 | 283 |
| 10004 | | | 9704 | 300 | 27 |
| 5065828 | 180185 | 91710 | 124212 | 3196507 | 14427 |
| 2115892 | 180185 | 72113 | 116122 | 830620 | 5765 |
| 33672 | | | | 20357 | 127 |
| 2742729 | | 1561 | 8090 | 2316259 | 8154 |
| 149429 | | 18036 | | 5776 | 338 |
| 24105 | | | | 23495 | 44 |

# 4-16 分地区规上

## Added Value of Industrial Enterprises Above

单位:亿元

| 年 份 Year | 全 市 Whole City | 市 区 | | | | | |
|---|---|---|---|---|---|---|---|
| | | 上城区 Shangcheng | 下城区 Xiacheng | 江干区 Jianggan | 拱墅区 Gongshu | 西湖区 Xihu | 高新(滨江)区 Hi-Tech (Binjiang) |
| 2000 | 360.97 | | | | | | |
| 2001 | 444.91 | | | | | | |
| 2002 | 597.01 | | | | | | |
| 2003 | 783.51 | | | | | | |
| 2004 | 1019.47 | | | | | | |
| 2005 | 1126.54 | | | | | | |
| 2006 | 1363.17 | | | | | | |
| 2007 | 1717.65 | | | | | | |
| 2008 | 1743.20 | | | | | | |
| 2009 | 1792.00 | | | | | | |
| 2010 | 2153.83 | | | | | | |
| 2011 | 2369.00 | 215.48 | 20.83 | 47.25 | 119.11 | 49.03 | 162.30 |
| 2012 | 2492.00 | 296.64 | 22.05 | 48.00 | 117.08 | 49.07 | 210.02 |
| 2013 | 2664.13 | 318.89 | 23.33 | 53.33 | 104.34 | 49.62 | 278.48 |
| 2014 | 2813.51 | 328.06 | 15.16 | 57.60 | 78.34 | 50.45 | 324.69 |
| 2015 | 2875.05 | 329.70 | 7.13 | 53.79 | 60.64 | 52.30 | 365.67 |
| 2016 | 2990.34 | 349.57 | 9.64 | 47.37 | 65.80 | 57.06 | 374.24 |
| 2017 | 3184.05 | 362.41 | 8.16 | 42.98 | 74.76 | 61.04 | 502.19 |
| 2018 | 3415.45 | 364.56 | 13.36 | 38.46 | 81.84 | 65.07 | 574.95 |
| 2019 | 3481.89 | 374.72 | 14.03 | 42.13 | 93.95 | 68.23 | 623.97 |

注:2019 年萧山区不含托管在钱塘新区的街道数据。

# 工业增加值(2000 - 2019 年)

# Designated Size by Region (2000 - 2019)

(100 million yuan)

| Urban District | | | | | | | | |
|---|---|---|---|---|---|---|---|---|
| 萧山区 Xiaoshan | 余杭区 Yuhang | 富阳区 Fuyang | 临安区 Lin'an | 钱塘新区 Qiantang New Area | 西湖风景名胜区 The West Lake Scenic Zone | 桐庐县 Tonglu | 淳安县 Chun'an | 建德市 Jiande |
| 77.95 | 31.54 | 22.05 | 11.83 | | | 9.29 | 2.24 | 10.13 |
| 106.28 | 38.50 | 31.69 | 14.71 | | | 11.98 | 2.99 | 8.86 |
| 145.26 | 40.29 | 38.87 | 18.55 | | | 14.08 | 3.40 | 13.05 |
| 199.34 | 69.17 | 52.52 | 25.09 | | | 18.98 | 5.46 | 16.82 |
| 245.57 | 86.96 | 63.65 | 32.25 | | | 29.73 | 6.59 | 27.62 |
| 311.61 | 129.16 | 80.22 | 37.84 | | | 31.60 | 9.29 | 28.54 |
| 385.34 | 150.85 | 103.73 | 47.54 | | | 42.10 | 12.70 | 37.88 |
| 401.88 | 195.17 | 136.42 | 62.53 | | | 57.06 | 17.35 | 50.54 |
| 482.29 | 212.97 | 160.31 | 74.51 | | | 68.41 | 20.56 | 61.38 |
| 538.91 | 225.60 | 167.30 | 80.02 | | | 62.17 | 23.48 | 60.03 |
| 606.90 | 297.10 | 182.30 | 98.91 | | | 76.63 | 29.18 | 76.13 |
| 721.27 | 243.41 | 162.41 | 98.20 | | | 71.74 | 32.66 | 68.09 |
| 727.65 | 250.64 | 165.25 | 106.67 | | | 80.02 | 38.69 | 76.19 |
| 704.46 | 275.99 | 198.03 | 115.18 | 380.51 | 0.06 | 81.63 | 43.44 | 81.74 |
| 712.21 | 301.62 | 200.53 | 123.24 | 405.16 | 0.12 | 94.92 | 47.53 | 85.18 |
| 706.49 | 334.30 | 200.89 | 127.85 | 457.66 | 0.76 | 102.26 | 52.06 | 83.67 |
| 742.23 | 349.74 | 201.89 | 136.80 | 541.62 | -1.77 | 99.78 | 49.96 | 85.75 |
| 745.62 | 386.71 | 234.29 | 138.50 | 417.58 | -0.26 | 83.38 | 40.35 | 86.33 |
| 790.64 | 428.65 | 248.45 | 145.71 | 439.27 | 0.06 | 83.09 | 30.36 | 110.96 |
| 531.95 | 462.74 | 231.69 | 168.86 | 632.06 | 0.16 | 86.57 | 34.24 | 116.60 |

a) Figures of Xiaoshan District don't include districts which under administered by Qiantang New Area in 2019.

# 4－17　分地区规上

# Index of Added Value of Industrial

（上年＝100）

| 年　　份<br>Year | 全　市<br>Whole City | 市　区 | | | | | |
|---|---|---|---|---|---|---|---|
| | | 上城区<br>Shangcheng | 下城区<br>Xiacheng | 江干区<br>Jianggan | 拱墅区<br>Gongshu | 西湖区<br>Xihu | 高新（滨江）区<br>Hi－Tech（Binjiang） |
| 2010 | 114.9 | 110.0 | 121.1 | 112.2 | 110.5 | 109.1 | 119.6 |
| 2011 | 112.7 | 112.1 | 104.0 | 109.4 | 112.3 | 111.8 | 118.2 |
| 2012 | 110.9 | 106.6 | 103.5 | 105.5 | 112.2 | 108.8 | 113.7 |
| 2013 | 108.0 | 106.3 | 107.7 | 109.4 | 104.5 | 109.6 | 115.1 |
| 2014 | 108.9 | 108.9 | 91.6 | 115.1 | 105.5 | 104.9 | 118.3 |
| 2015 | 105.4 | 106.0 | 90.1 | 100.5 | 95.2 | 101.0 | 117.8 |
| 2016 | 105.6 | 98.5 | 102.0 | 87.5 | 105.0 | 105.0 | 114.9 |
| 2017 | 107.0 | 108.7 | 105.5 | 95.2 | 111.3 | 105.1 | 118.1 |
| 2018 | 106.3 | 101.7 | 118.9 | 101.3 | 111.2 | 99.2 | 117.3 |
| 2019 | 105.1 | 103.0 | 91.5 | 91.9 | 117.7 | 114.4 | 110.7 |

注:2019 年萧山区不含托管在钱塘新区的街道数据。

# 工业增加值发展指数(2010－2019年)
## Enterprises Above Designated Size by Region(2010－2019)

(Preceding Year＝100)

| Urban District | | | | | | | | |
|---|---|---|---|---|---|---|---|---|
| 萧山区 Xiaoshan | 余杭区 Yuhang | 富阳区 Fuyang | 临安区 Lin'an | 钱塘新区 Qiantang New Area | 西湖风景名胜区 The West Lake Scenic Zone | 桐庐县 Tonglu | 淳安县 Chun'an | 建德市 Jiande |
| 114.3 | 115.0 | 113.1 | 122.7 | 118.5 | | 114.0 | 114.9 | 115.5 |
| 112.9 | 109.2 | 113.3 | 113.1 | 111.2 | | 109.1 | 115.1 | 113.0 |
| 113.5 | 107.2 | 112.1 | 112.4 | 102.4 | | 109.0 | 119.6 | 110.8 |
| 108.1 | 108.0 | 109.3 | 105.5 | 107.3 | | 105.6 | 112.7 | 106.1 |
| 108.1 | 107.0 | 106.2 | 107.2 | 109.3 | | 109.0 | 103.2 | 108.1 |
| 106.2 | 102.6 | 104.1 | 105.1 | 106.9 | 90.9 | 106.9 | 103.4 | 108.2 |
| 106.3 | 105.0 | 103.0 | 109.0 | 110.2 | 100.3 | 108.6 | 110.6 | 107.0 |
| 101.3 | 107.6 | 106.0 | 106.7 | 106.5 | 117.5 | 106.3 | 104.1 | 106.7 |
| 102.6 | 107.0 | 104.5 | 104.5 | 107.0 | | 104.6 | 88.2 | 107.6 |
| 105.1 | 105.3 | 101.1 | 108.8 | 99.7 | | 111.1 | 103.5 | 108.6 |

a) Figures of Xiaoshan District dont include districts which under administered by Qiantang New Area in 2019.

# 4－18 规上工业三大新兴产业发展情况(2013－2019年)
## Statistics on the Three Emerging Industries Above Designated Size(2013－2019)

| 指标<br>Item | 高新技术产业<br>High－tech Industries | | 战略性新兴产业<br>Strategic Emerging Industries | | 装备制造业<br>Equipment Manufacturing Industries | |
|---|---|---|---|---|---|---|
| | 增加值<br>(亿元)<br>Value－added<br>(100 million yuan) | 为上年<br>(%)<br>As Compared with the Preceding Year<br>(%) | 增加值<br>(亿元)<br>Value－added<br>(100 million yuan) | 为上年<br>(%)<br>As Compared with the Preceding Year<br>(%) | 增加值<br>(亿元)<br>Value－added<br>(100 million yuan) | 为上年<br>(%)<br>As Compared with the Preceding Year<br>(%) |
| 2013 | 785.4 | 108.9 | 636.6 | 107.1 | 900.5 | 108.6 |
| 2014 | 1096.6 | 110.5 | 813.1 | 113.0 | 921.4 | 109.3 |
| 2015 | 1212.6 | 109.8 | 877.3 | 109.4 | 1086.1 | 113.5 |
| 2016 | 1372.9 | 112.5 | 812.1 | 111.6 | 1249.6 | 114.6 |
| 2017 | 1605.5 | 113.6 | 979.5 | 115.0 | 1384.2 | 111.0 |
| 2018 | 1948.4 | 110.8 | 1135.3 | 113.1 | 1531.0 | 109.3 |
| 2019 | 2178.4 | 108.5 | 1328.6 | 113.1 | 1640.5 | 107.9 |

# 4－19 主要工业产品生产量(2019年)

## Output of Major Industrial Products(2019)

| 产品名称 | | Item | | 全市 Whole City 2019年 | 全市 Whole City 为上年(%) As Compared with the Preceding Year(%) | 市区 Urban District |
|---|---|---|---|---|---|---|
| 发电量 | (亿千瓦时) | Electricity | (100 million kwh) | 160 | 109.3 | 114 |
| #水力发电 | (亿千瓦时) | of which:Hydropower | (100 million kwh) | 43 | 161.6 | 3.7 |
| 垃圾发电 | (亿千瓦时) | Garbage Power | (100 million kwh) | 13 | 98.1 | 12.8 |
| 罐头 | (万吨) | Canned Food | (10000 tons) | 3 | 104.7 | 3 |
| 乳制品 | (吨) | Dairy Products | (ton) | 180144 | 109.8 | 180144 |
| 啤酒 | (千升) | Beer | (1000 litres) | 996655 | 98.4 | 734698 |
| 软饮料 | (万吨) | Soft Drinks | (10000 tons) | | | |
| 精制茶 | (吨) | Tea | (ton) | 20783 | 94.7 | 14239 |
| 卷烟 | (亿支) | Cigarettes | (100 million) | 514 | 101.4 | 514 |
| 方便面 | (吨) | Instant Noodle | (ton) | 210836 | 103.8 | 210836 |
| 化学纤维 | (吨) | Chemical Fiber | (ton) | 9755530 | 124.8 | 9755530 |
| #合成纤维 | (吨) | Synthetic Fibre | (ton) | 9735477 | 126.7 | 9735477 |
| 纱 | (万吨) | Yarn | (10000 tons) | 39 | 87.6 | 39 |
| 布 | (万米) | Cloth | (10000 m) | 259592 | 93.2 | 257670 |
| 印染布 | (万米) | Printed Fabric | (10000 m) | 556854 | 93.5 | 555984 |
| 蚕丝及交织机织物(含蚕丝≥50%) | (万米) | Silk and Woven Fabrics (Containing Greater than or Equal 50% silk) | (10000 m) | 1204 | 78.0 | 1204 |
| 服装 | (万件) | Garment | (10000 units) | 23672 | 89.7 | 21518 |
| 皮革鞋靴 | (万双) | Leather Footwear | (10000 units) | 1086 | 82.1 | 1086 |
| 家具 | (万件) | Furniture | (10000 units) | 1975 | 50.2 | 1766 |
| 塑料制品 | (吨) | Plastic Membrane | (ton) | 3703573 | 97.4 | 3227772 |
| 机制纸及纸板 | (万吨) | Machine Made Paper and Paperboard | (10000 tons) | 414 | 69.2 | 410 |

4－19 续表1 continued 1

| 产品名称 | Item | 全市 Whole City 2019年 | 全市 Whole City 为上年(%) As Compared with the Preceding Year(%) | 市区 Urban District |
|---|---|---|---|---|
| 盐酸(含量31%以上)(吨) | Mariatic Acid(above 31% percent) (ton) | 75325 | 94.3 | 75325 |
| 氢氧化钠(烧碱)(折100%) (吨) | Caustic Soda (ton) | 246010 | 110.2 | 246010 |
| 碳酸钠(纯碱) (吨) | Soda ash (ton) | 317372 | 94.4 | 317372 |
| 初级形态的塑料(塑料树脂及共聚物)(吨) | Plastics in Primary Form(Plastic Resins and Copolymers) (ton) | 679863 | 107.9 | 670577 |
| 合成氨 (吨) | Synthetic Ammonia (ton) | 235096 | 105.4 | 235096 |
| 农用氮、磷、钾化学肥料总计(折纯)(吨) | Chemical Fertilizer (ton) | 365882 | 118.6 | 365882 |
| 化学农药原药(折有效成分100%)(吨) | Chemical Pesticide (ton) | 106984 | 94.6 | 13640 |
| 涂料(油漆) (吨) | Paint (ton) | 272441 | 206.2 | 126502 |
| 合成洗涤剂 (吨) | Synthetic Detergent (ton) | 166804 | 97.2 | 132427 |
| 化学药品原药(化学原料药) (吨) | Original Drug Chemicals (ton) | 1922 | 74.0 | 1594 |
| 中成药 (吨) | Traditional Chinese Medicine (ton) | 8297 | 99.9 | 6906 |
| 橡胶轮胎外胎(轮胎外胎) (万条) | Rubber Tires (10000 units) | 7167 | 110.5 | 6576 |
| 水泥 (万吨) | Cement (10000 tons) | 1663 | 101.3 | 845 |
| 铁合金 (万吨) | Iron Alloy (10000 tons) | | | |
| 钢材 (万吨) | Steel Products (10000 tons) | 392 | 95.6 | 392 |
| 精炼铜(电解铜) (吨) | Refined Copper (ton) | 434614 | 101.9 | 434614 |
| 工业锅炉 (蒸发量吨) | Industry Boiler (ton) | 7057 | 85.3 | 7057 |
| 金属切削机床 (台) | Metal－cutting Machine Tools (unit) | 9871 | 71.7 | 9402 |

4－19 续表2 continued 2

| 产品名称 | Item | 全市 Whole City 2019年 | 全市 Whole City 为上年(%) As Compared with the Preceding Year(%) | 市区 Urban District |
|---|---|---|---|---|
| 金属成形机床(锻压设备)(台) | Metal Forming Machine(Forge Equipment) (Tai) | 5974 | 85.6 | 5856 |
| 泵(液体泵) (万台) | Pump (10000 sets) | 102 | 96.5 | 101 |
| 滚动轴承(轴承) (万套) | Bearings (10000 units) | 14019 | 79.7 | 14019 |
| 汽车 (辆) | Motor Vehicles (unit) | 158065 | 73.1 | 158045 |
| 叉车 (台) | Forklift (unit) | 151867 | 107.6 | 151867 |
| 两轮自行车(自行车)(万辆) | Bicycles (10000 units) | 95 | 95.0 | 95 |
| 交流电动机 (万千瓦) | AC Motor (10000 kw) | 295 | 94.1 | 295 |
| 钢绞线 (吨) | Strand (ton) | 65491 | 157.7 | 65491 |
| 通信及电子网络用电缆 (万对千米) | Communication Cable (10000 km) | 267 | 94.5 | 267 |
| 光缆(光纤通讯电缆)(万芯千米) | Electric Power Cable (10000 km) | 2069 | 68.8 | 2069 |
| 家用电冰箱 (万台) | Household Refrigerators (10000 units) | 77 | 110.3 | 77 |
| 家用洗衣机 (万台) | Household Washing Machines (10000 units) | 244 | 87.0 | 244 |
| 吸排油烟机 (万台) | Smoke Absorbers (10000 units) | 351 | 99.0 | 351 |
| 移动通信手持机(手机)(万部) | Mobile Telephone Sets (10000 units) | | | |
| 电工仪器仪表 (万台) | Electric Instrument and Apparatus (10000 units) | 4569 | 141.7 | 4569 |
| 工业自动调节仪表与控制系统 (万台) | Industrial Automatic Adjustment Meter and Control System (10000 units) | 376 | 113.2 | 376 |
| 电光源(灯泡) (亿只) | Light Bulbs (100 million units) | 5 | 92.8 | 5 |
| 彩色电视机 (万部) | Color－Television Sets (10000 units) | 2 | － | 2 |
| 微型计算机设备 (万台) | Micro－computer Equipment (10000 units) | 169 | 133.0 | 169 |

# 4-20 分地区单位 GDP 能耗降低情况(2019 年)
## Energy Efficency and Energy Consumption Reduction by Region(2019)

| 地 区 | Region | 单位 GDP 能耗降低率(%) Decrease Rate of Energy Consumption Per Unit of GDP (±%) | 单位 GDP 电耗降低率(%) Decrease Rate of Energy Consumption Per Unit of GDP (±%) | 单位工业增加值能耗降低率 Decrease Rate of Energy Consumption Per Unit of Industriul Value-Added (±%) |
|---|---|---|---|---|
| 杭州市 | Hangzhou | 5.0 | 4.0 | 7.2 |
| 上城区 | Shangcheng | - | 5.9 | 12.4 |
| 下城区 | Xiacheng | - | 4.0 | 1.6 |
| 江干区 | Jianggan | - | 3.3 | -17.8 |
| 拱墅区 | Gongshu | - | 6.1 | 21.0 |
| 西湖区 | Xihu | - | 4.0 | 11.3 |
| 滨江区 | Binjiang | - | 5.0 | 17.7 |
| 萧山区 | Xiaoshan | 5.1 | 3.2 | 8.0 |
| 余杭区 | Yuhang | 5.2 | 2.3 | 9.5 |
| 富阳区 | Fuyang | 12.7 | 13.5 | 16.1 |
| 临安区 | Lin'an | 3.8 | 1.2 | 4.9 |
| 钱塘新区 | Qiantang New Area | - | -0.4 | -1.0 |
| 桐庐县 | Tonglu | -0.6 | -1.0 | -0.6 |
| 淳安县 | Chun'an | -2.2 | -2.8 | -2.4 |
| 建德市 | Jiande | 0.0 | 0.5 | -0.8 |

注:1. 若降低率为负数,说明本期的指标值与去年同期相比没有降低,反而上升。
2. 萧山区不含托管在钱塘新区的街道数据。

a) If the Decrease Rate was a negative number, it means the indicator was increased compared to last year.
b) Figures of Xiaoshan District don't include districts which under administered by Qiantang New Area.

# 4-21 规模以上工业企业主要能源品种购进与消费(2019年)

## Purchasing and Consuming of Major Energy in Industrial Enterprises Above Designated Size(2019)

| 能源名称 | | Item | | 购进量 Purchasing | 消费量合计 Total Consumption | 工业生产消费 Industry |
|---|---|---|---|---|---|---|
| 原煤 | （吨） | Raw Coal | (Ton) | 9899906 | 9909300 | 9900483 |
| 洗精煤 | （吨） | Washing Coal | (Ton) | - | - | - |
| 煤制品 | （吨） | Coal Puoducts | (Ton) | 843151 | 841263 | 841263 |
| 焦炭 | （吨） | Coke | (Ton) | 44736 | 41843 | 41843 |
| 天然气(气态) | （万立方米） | Natural Gas(Gas) | (10000 cu. m) | 191140 | 191081 | 190619 |
| 液化天然气(液态) | （吨） | Liquefied Natural Gas(Liquid) | (Ton) | 87771 | 87125 | 87069 |
| 汽油 | （吨） | Gasoline | (Ton) | 35711 | 35811 | 11411 |
| 煤油 | （吨） | Kerosene | (Ton) | 552 | 566 | 522 |
| 柴油 | （吨） | Diesel Oil | (Ton) | 134753 | 134480 | 120402 |
| 燃料油 | （吨） | Fuel Oil | (Ton) | 27273 | 27080 | 27073 |
| 液化石油气 | （吨） | Liquefied Petroleum Gas | (Ton) | 6675 | 6663 | 6456 |
| 润滑油 | （吨） | Lubricating Oil | (Ton) | 1501 | 1527 | 1527 |
| 溶剂油 | （吨） | Solvent Oil | (Ton) | 357 | 343 | 343 |
| 石油沥青 | （吨） | Petroleum Asphalt | (Ton) | 78881 | 78872 | 78872 |
| 其他石油制品 | （吨） | Other Petroleum Products | (Ton) | 3585 | 3588 | 3588 |
| 热力 | （百万千焦） | Heat | (Million kilo - joule) | 70165993 | 86050190 | 85465595 |
| 电力 | （万千瓦时） | Electricity | (10000 kwh) | 3327601 | 3562235 | 3505209 |
| 煤矸石用于燃料 | （吨） | Coal Gangue For Fuel | (Ton) | 1302 | 1302 | 1302 |
| 城市垃圾用于燃料 | （吨） | Waste For Fuel | (Ton) | 1510820 | 1837874 | 1837874 |
| 生物质废料用于燃料 | （吨标准煤） | Biomass Waste For Fuel | (Ton) | 81797 | 83297 | 83237 |
| 余热余压 | （百万千焦） | Residual Heat and Pressure | (Million kilo - joule) | 4893589 | 10262809 | 10262809 |
| 其它工业废料用于燃料 | （吨） | Other Industrial Wastes Are Used For Fuel | (Ton) | 21575 | 885910 | 885910 |
| 其它燃料 | （吨标准煤） | Other Fuel | | 34376 | 54965 | 54965 |

# 4－22 规模以上工业企业主要能源

## Energy Consumption of Industrial

| 行 业 Sector | 原煤(吨) Raw Coal(Ton) | 洗精煤(吨) Washing Coal(Ton) | 焦炭(吨) Coke(Ton) | 汽油(吨) Gasoline(Ton) | 煤油(吨) Kerosene(Ton) |
|---|---|---|---|---|---|
| **总 计 Total** | **9909300** | **－** | **41843** | **35811** | **566** |
| 煤炭开采和洗选业 Coal Mining and Dressing | － | － | － | － | － |
| 黑色金属矿采选业 Ferrous Metals Mining and Dressing | － | － | － | － | － |
| 有色金属矿采选业 Nonferrous Minerals Mining and Dressing | － | － | － | 8 | － |
| 非金属矿采选业 Nonmetal Minerals Mining and Dressing | 24922 | － | － | 10 | － |
| 农副食品加工业 Agricultural Products Processing | － | － | － | 302 | － |
| 食品制造业 Food Manufacturing | 6545 | － | － | 376 | － |
| 酒、饮料和精制茶制造业 Wine, Beverage and Tea Manufacturing | － | － | － | 60 | － |
| 烟草制品业 Tobacco Processing | － | － | － | 11 | － |
| 纺织业 Textile Processing | 249101 | － | － | 2644 | － |
| 纺织服装、服饰业 Textile Products and Costume Industry | － | － | － | 1235 | － |
| 皮革、毛皮、羽毛及其制品和制鞋业 Leather. Furs. Downand Related and Shoes Products | － | － | － | 708 | － |
| 木材加工和木、竹、藤、棕、草制品业 Timber Processing, Bamboo, Cane, Plam Fiber and Straw Products | － | － | － | 134 | － |
| 家具制造业 Furniture Manufacturing | － | － | － | 541 | － |
| 造纸和纸制品业 Paper Making and Paper Products | 12574 | － | － | 865 | － |
| 印刷和记录媒介复制业 Printing | － | － | － | 542 | － |
| 文教、工美、体育和娱乐用品制造业 Cultural, Educational. Industrial Arts. Sports and Entertainment Goods | － | － | 77 | 558 | － |
| 石油、煤炭和其他燃料加工业 Petroleum, Coal and Other Fuel Processing | 187728 | － | － | 79 | － |

消费量按行业分(2019年)

Enterprises above Designated Size by Sector(2019)

| 柴油(吨) Diesel oil(Ton) | 燃料油(吨) Fuel Oil(Ton) | 液化石油气(吨) Liquefied Petroleum Gas(Ton) | 天然气(万立方米) Natural Gas (10000 cu. m) | 其他石油制品(吨) Other Petroleum Products(Ton) | 热力(百万千焦) Heat(Million kilo - joule) | 电力(万千瓦时) Electricity (10000 kwh) |
|---|---|---|---|---|---|---|
| **134480** | **27080** | **6663** | **191081** | **3588** | **86050190** | **3562235** |
| - | - | - | - | - | - | 208 |
| - | - | - | - | - | - | - |
| 18 | - | 1 | - | - | - | 2167 |
| 4414 | - | - | - | - | - | 7816 |
| 1737 | - | 160 | 1744 | - | 286876 | 14189 |
| 1462 | 811 | 31 | 1696 | - | 1419419 | 30044 |
| 257 | 206 | 6 | 2361 | - | 1468279 | 63527 |
| 189 | - | - | 532 | - | - | 5057 |
| 2855 | 87 | 20 | 11456 | - | 26310066 | 438978 |
| 802 | - | 4 | 718 | - | 495027 | 18799 |
| 467 | - | 5 | 948 | - | 54515 | 12510 |
| 196 | - | - | 25 | - | 27265 | 4834 |
| 534 | - | 14 | 436 | - | 72188 | 13513 |
| 2332 | - | 194 | 3238 | - | 18276579 | 182352 |
| 540 |  | 32 | 313 | - | 71374 | 20223 |
| 307 | - | 1 | 134 | - | 124226 | 14635 |
| 215 | - | - | 28 | - | 29295 | 1249 |

4－22 续表

| 行 业 Sector | 原煤(吨) Raw Coal(Ton) | 洗精煤(吨) Washing Coal(Ton) | 焦炭(吨) Coke(Ton) | 汽油(吨) Gasoline(Ton) | 煤油(吨) Kerosene(Ton) |
|---|---|---|---|---|---|
| 化学原料和化学制品制造业 Raw Chemical Materials and Chemical Products | 1632540 | – | – | 2170 | – |
| 医药制造业 Medical and Pharmaceutical Products | 34754 | – | – | 703 | 1 |
| 化学纤维制造业 Chemical Fiber | 142692 | – | – | 264 | – |
| 橡胶和塑料制品业 Rubber and Plastic Products | 183494 | – | – | 2107 | 10 |
| 非金属矿物制品业 Nonmetal Minerals Products | 2749404 | – | – | 1092 | – |
| 黑色金属冶炼和压延加工业 Smelting and Processing of Ferrous Metals | – | – | 77 | 185 | – |
| 有色金属冶炼和压延加工业 Smelting and Processing of Nonferrous Metals | – | – | 41689 | 178 | – |
| 金属制品业 Metal Products | – | – | – | 1730 | 3 |
| 通用设备制造业 Ordinary Machinery | – | – | – | 4001 | 258 |
| 专用设备制造业 Special Purpose Equipment | – | – | – | 1499 | 1 |
| 汽车制造业 Automobile Manufacturing | – | – | – | 2421 | 275 |
| 铁路、船舶、航空航天和其他运输设备制造业 Railway. watercraft. Avigation spaceflight and other Equipment Manufacturing | – | – | – | 296 | – |
| 电气机械和器材制造业 Electric Equipment and Machinery | – | – | – | 3013 | 17 |
| 计算机、通信和其他电子设备制造业 Computers. Telecommunications and Other Electronic Equipment Manufacturing | – | – | – | 4117 | – |
| 仪器仪表制造业 Instruments and Meters Manufacturing | – | – | – | 1549 | 1 |
| 其他制造业 Other Manufacturing | – | – | – | 143 | – |
| 废弃资源综合利用业 Multiple Utilization of Waste Resouces | 4301 | – | – | 51 | – |
| 金属制品、机械和设备修理业 Metal Products, Machinery and Equipment Repair | – | – | – | – | – |
| 电力、热力生产和供应业 Production and Supply of Electric Power and Hot Water | 4606506 | – | – | 1587 | – |
| 燃气生产和供应业 Production and Supply of Gas | – | – | – | 322 | – |
| 水的生产和供应业 Production and Supply of Tap Water | 74740 | – | – | 309 | – |

continued

| 柴油(吨) Diesel oil(Ton) | 燃料油(吨) Fuel Oil(Ton) | 液化石油气(吨) Liquefied Petroleum Gas(Ton) | 天然气(万立方米) Natural Gas (10000 cu. m) | 其他石油制品(吨) Other Petroleum Products(Ton) | 热力(百万千焦) Heat(Million kilo - joule) | 电力(万千瓦时) Electricity (10000 kwh) |
|---|---|---|---|---|---|---|
| 4922 | 20504 | 105 | 3863 | 2332 | 27828693 | 516257 |
| 1437 | - | 14 | 2726 | - | 1262106 | 77351 |
| 965 | - | 1 | 848 | 190 | 1626881 | 402692 |
| 1776 | 1957 | 3057 | 962 | 3 | 3433569 | 225671 |
| 85765 | 517 | 1 | 5626 | - | 360937 | 235443 |
| 306 | - | 70 | 3319 | 76 | 284250 | 48754 |
| 1060 | 1270 | 258 | 3122 | - | 117690 | 83076 |
| 3407 | 1682 | 555 | 8232 | 14 | 299775 | 112269 |
| 6752 | 15 | 375 | 3079 | 494 | 64397 | 130034 |
| 1013 | - | 231 | 499 | - | 176670 | 28002 |
| 3413 | 31 | 140 | 2025 | 452 | 69424 | 103736 |
| 177 | - | 322 | 475 | 18 | 21253 | 9194 |
| 2233 | - | 537 | 2588 | - | 799055 | 137485 |
| 1528 | - | 522 | 1090 | - | 373205 | 150876 |
| 401 | - | - | 75 | - | 8947 | 22153 |
| 637 | - | 1 | 135 | - | 18396 | 1691 |
| 200 | - | - | 83 | 8 | 84294 | 29430 |
| - | - | - | - | - | - | - |
| 1829 | - | - | 128670 | 2 | 585540 | 339474 |
| 128 | - | - | 31 | - | - | 889 |
| 206 | - | 4 | 6 | - | - | 77658 |

# 4－23　全社会用电情况(2019 年)

## Electricity Consumption In the Whole Society(2019)

单位:万千瓦时　　　　　(10000 kwh)

| 项　目 | Item | 2019 年 | 增长(%) inctease(%) |
|---|---|---|---|
| **总　计** | **Total** | **8167003** | **2.5** |
| #线路损失电量 | #Losses in Transmission | 224432 | -6.1 |
| **全行业用电合计** | **Total Electricy Consumption for the whole industries** | **6791642** | **1.6** |
| 第一产业 | Primary Industry | 35119 | -2.1 |
| 第二产业 | Secondary Industry | 4552610 | -1.7 |
| 第三产业 | Tertiary Industry | 2203913 | 9.2 |
| **全行业用电按行业分** | **Electricity Consumption by Sector** | | |
| 农林牧渔业 | Farming,Forestry,Animal Husbandry and Fishery Conservancy | 49756 | -3.2 |
| 工业 | Industry | 4330353 | -2.9 |
| #采矿业 | #Mining and Quarrying | 27098 | -1.5 |
| 制造业 | Manufacturing Industry | 3853699 | -2.7 |
| 电力、热力、燃气及水的生产和供应业 | Produotion and supply of electricity,gas & water | 449556 | -5.2 |
| 建筑业 | Construction | 222458 | 31.4 |
| 批发和零售业 | Wholesale and Retail Trade | 399987 | 10.1 |
| 交通运输、仓储及邮政业 | Transportation,Storage,Post & Telecommunications | 193589 | 9.7 |
| 住宿和餐饮业 | Lodging and Catering Services | 149485 | 1.3 |
| 信息传输、软件和信息技术服务业 | Information Transmission,Computer Services and Software | 253948 | 9.4 |
| 金融业 | Finance | 39556 | 7.3 |
| 房地产业 | Real Estate | 275433 | 13.8 |
| 租赁和商务服务业 | Renting and Business Service | 277523 | 16.5 |
| 科学研究、技术服务业 | Scientific Researoh and Fechnicla Senice | 37781 | 4.3 |
| 水利环境和公共设施管理业 | Water Conservancy,Environment and Public Utility | 113343 | 10.3 |
| 居民服务、修理和其他服务业 | Service for the Residents,Repair and others | 60653 | 3.7 |
| 教育 | Education | 156743 | 8.3 |
| 卫生和社会工作 | Health Care,Sports Social Welfare | 93735 | 4.6 |
| 文化、体育和娱乐业 | Culture,Sports and Entertainment | 31860 | 5.7 |
| 公共管理、社会保障和社会组织 | Public Administration,Social Security and Social Organization | 105440 | 1.0 |
| **城乡居民生活用电** | **Residential Consumption** | **1375361** | **7.0** |
| #城市 | #Cities | 889165 | 7.8 |
| 乡村 | Rural Areas | 486197 | 5.8 |

# 4－24　水资源量和总用水量(2017－2019 年)

## Total Water Resources and Water Consumption(2017－2019)

单位:亿立方米　　(100 million Cubic Meters)

| 地区 | Region | 水资源量 Water Resources | | | 用水量 Water Consumption | | |
|---|---|---|---|---|---|---|---|
| | | 2017 年 | 2018 年 | 2019 年 | 2017 年 | 2018 年 | 2019 年 |
| 全市 | Whole City | 146.87 | 146.24 | 188.11 | 33.47 | 32.47 | 30.96 |
| 市区 | Urban District | 64.95 | 74.39 | 82.76 | 27.78 | 27.29 | 25.94 |
| 萧山区 | Xiaoshan | 9.15 | 10.94 | 11.06 | 7.92 | 7.72 | 7.45 |
| 余杭区 | Yuhang | 9.80 | 12.22 | 11.54 | 4.93 | 5.08 | 5.3 |
| 富阳区 | Fuyang | 13.99 | 15.61 | 18.37 | 3.84 | 3.78 | 3.59 |
| 临安区 | Lin'an | 26.39 | 28.71 | 35.5 | 3.04 | 2.82 | 2.42 |
| 桐庐县 | Tonglu | 14.67 | 14.05 | 20.55 | 2.15 | 1.89 | 1.73 |
| 淳安县 | Chan'an | 47.21 | 42.42 | 58.3 | 1.30 | 1.26 | 1.96 |
| 建德市 | Jiangde | 20.04 | 15.38 | 26.5 | 2.24 | 2.03 | 1.32 |

# 4－25 规模以下工业主要指标(2016－2019年)
## Main Indicators of Industrial Enterprises Below Designated Size(2016－2019)

| 指标名称 | | Item | | 2016年 | 2017年 | 2018年 | 2019年 |
|---|---|---|---|---|---|---|---|
| 企业数 | (万家) | Number of Enterprises | (10,000 Units) | 3.39 | 3.38 | 3.35 | 3.64 |
| 年末从业人数 | (万人) | Total Number of Employed Persons at Year End | (10,000 persons) | 36.38 | 35.07 | 31.78 | 34.34 |
| 资产总计 | (亿元) | Total Assets | (100 million yuan) | 1940.72 | 2041.22 | 1893.03 | 1892.15 |
| 主营业务收入 | (亿元) | Revenues in Main Business | (100 million yuan) | 1142.00 | 1238.92 | 1293.23 | 1413.05 |
| 主营业务成本 | (亿元) | Costs in Main Business | (100 million yuan) | 948.39 | 1042.97 | 1080.31 | 1203.58 |
| 税金总额 | (亿元) | Total taxes | (100 million yuan) | 41.65 | 50.23 | 49.89 | 47.27 |
| 利润总额 | (亿元) | Total Profits | (100 million yuan) | 17.20 | 15.09 | 30.69 | 20.46 |
| 应付职工薪酬 | (亿元) | Employee benefits Payable | (100 million yuan) | 134.53 | 143.11 | 133.04 | 152.35 |

注:2018年普查年度,规模以下工业抽样推算结果与普查结果存在一定差距。

a) There is a difference between the results of the census in 2018 and that of the below designated size industry sampling.

# 4－26 个体工业主要指标(2018－2019年)
## Industrial Enterprises Below Designated Size(2018－2019)

| 指标名称 | | Item | | 2018年 | 2019年 |
|---|---|---|---|---|---|
| 个体户户数 | (万户) | Number of Enterprises | (10,000 Units) | 4.10 | 3.72 |
| 年末从业人数 | (万人) | Total Number of Employed Persons at Year End | (10,000 persons) | 24.41 | 21.44 |
| 主营业务收入 | (亿元) | Revenues in Main Business | (100 million yuan) | 917.52 | 894.80 |

# 主要统计指标解释

**工业总产值** 是以货币表现的工业企业在报告期内生产的已出售或可供出售工业产品总量，它反映一定时间内工业生产的总规模和总水平，它包括：在本企业内不再进行加工，经检验、包装入库（规定不需包装的产品除外）的成品价值，对外加工费收入，自制半成品，在产品期末初差额价值。工业总产值采用"工厂法"计算，即以工业企业作为一个整体，按企业工业生产活动的最终成果来计算，企业内部不允许重复计算，不能把企业内部各个车间（分厂）生产的成果相加。

**工业增加值** 是指工业行业在报告期内以货币表现的工业生产活动的最终成果。

**固定资产原价** 固定资产原值指企业在建造、购置、安装、改建、扩建、技术改造某项固定资产时所支出的全部货币总额。它一般包括买价、包装费、运杂费和安装费等。

**固定资产净值** 是指固定资产原价减去历年已提折旧额后的净额。

**利税总额** 指企业利润总额、产品销售税金及附加和应交增值税之和。

**主营业务收入** 指企业销售产品的销售收入和提供劳务等主要经营业务取得的收入总额。

**主营业务利润** 指企业销售产品和提供工业性劳务等主要经营业务收入和除其成本、费用、税金后的利润。

**利润总额** 指企业实现的利润。

**应交增值税** 指企业在报告期内应交纳的增值税额。

**总资产** 指企业拥有或控制的全部资产。包括流动资产、长期投资、固定资产、无形及递延资产、其他长期资产、递延税项等，即为企业资产负债表的资产总计项。

（1）流动资产指企业可以在一年内或者超过一年的一个生产周期内变现或耗用的资产合计。包括现金及各种存款、短期投资、应收及预付款项、存货等。

（2）固定资产指企业固定资产净值、固定资产清理、在建工程、待处理固定资产损失所占用的资金合计。

（3）无形资产指企业长期使用而没有实物形态的资产。包括专利权、非专利技术、商标权、著作权、土地使用权、商誉等。

**总负债** 指企业承担并需要偿还的全部债务。包括流动负债和长期负债、递延税项等，即为企业资产负债表的负债合计项。

（1）流动负债指企业在一年内或者超过一年的一个营业周期内需要偿还的债务合计，其中包括短期借款、应付及预收款项、应付工资、应交税金和应交利润等。

（2）长期负债指企业在一年以上或者超过一年的一个生产周期以上需要偿还的债务合计，其中包括长期借款、应付债务、长期应付款项等。

**所有者权益** 指企业投资人对企业净资产的所有权。企业净资产等于企业全部资产减去全部负债后的余额。其中包括投资者对企业的最初投入，以及资本公积金、盈余公积金和未分配利润，对股份制企业即为股东权益。

# Explanatory Notes on Main Statistical Indicators

**Gross Industrial Output Value** is the total volume of industrial products sold or available for sale in value terms which reflects the total achievements and overall scale of industrial production during a given period. It includes the value of the finished products, which are not to be further processed in the enterprises and have been inspected, packed and put in storage, the income from external processing, and the difference of the value of semi – finished products between the beginning and end of the period. The gross industrial output value is calculated with "factory method", which is to consider an industrial enterprise as a whole and calculate by final results of its industrial production activities. It is not allowed to double count or to add up the production results of each workshop (or branch factory) within the enterprise.

**Value Added of Industry** refers to the final results of industrial production in money terms during the reference period.

**Original Value of Fixed Assets** refers to the total amount of the expenditure of industrial enterprises in building, purchasing, installing, reconstructing, expanding or technically transforming a fixed asset, which includes expenses on purchase, package, transportation, and installation, etc.

**Net Value of Fixed Assets** is obtained by deducting depreciation over years from the original value of fixed assets.

**Total Pre – tax Profits** refers to the sum of total profits, products sales tax and surcharges and the value added tax payable.

**Main Business Revenue** refers to the revenue of enterprises from selling products, providing labor services and etc.

**Main Business Profit** refers to the profit gained by the enterprises from the main business income of selling products and providing industrial services after deducting cost, charges and taxes.

**Total Profits** refer to the profits gained by the enterprises.

**Value added Tax Payable** refers to the amount of the value added tax which should be paid by the enterprises in the reporting period.

**Total Assets** refer to all assets which are owned or controlled by enterprises, including circulating assets, long term investment, fixed assets, intangible assets and deferred assets, other long term assets, and deferred taxes, etc. The summation of above items is equal to total assets shown in the balance sheets of the enterprises.

(1) Circulating assets refer to assets which can be cashed in or consumed in an operating cycle of one year or over one year, including cash, all kinds of deposits, short term investment, receivables, advance payment, stock, etc.

(2) Fixed assets refer to the sum of funds occupied by the net value of fixed assets, clearance of fixed assets, project under construction, losses of fixed assets to be processed..

(3) Intangible assets refer to assets without material form used by enterprises over a lone time, such as patents, non – patent technologies, trademarks, copyright, land use right, business reputation, etc.

**Total Liabilities** refer to the debts that enterprises are responsible for repayment, including liquid liabilities, long – term liabilities and deferred taxes, etc. Total liabilities correspond to the summation item of liabilities shown in the balance sheets of the enterprises.

(1) Liquid liabilities refer to enterprises´total debt payable within an operating cycle of one year or over one year, including short term loans, payables and advance payments, payable wages, taxes and profit, etc.

(2) Long term liabilities refers to total debt payable within an operating cycle of over one year, including long – term loans, payable liabilities, long – term payables, etc.

**Creditors´Equity** refers to investors´ownership of net assets of the enterprise. It is equal to the total assets of the enterprise minus its total liabilities, including the primary input from investors, capital accumulation fund, surplus accumulation fund and undistributed profit. It is the shareholder's equity in share – holding companies.

# 五、建筑业

CONSTRUCTION

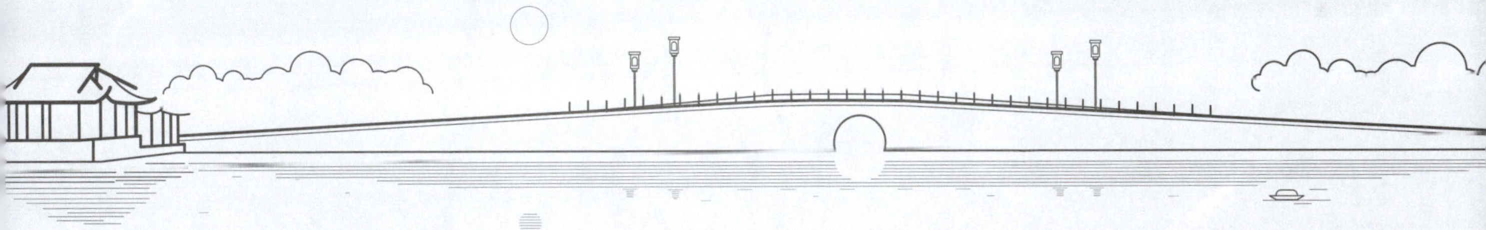

# 5 建筑业 Construction

## 主要统计指标
## Major Statistical Indicators

| | | | | |
|---|---|---|---|---|
| 建筑业总产值 | Gross Output Value of Construction | 4578.21 | 亿元 | ( 100 million yuan ) |
| 为上年 | As Compared with the Preceding Year | 103.3 | % | ( % ) |
| 房屋建筑施工面积 | Floor Space of Buildings Under Construction | 29470 | 万平方米 | ( 10, 000 sq.m ) |
| 为上年 | As Compared with the Preceding Year | 109.8 | % | ( % ) |
| 房屋建筑竣工面积 | Floor Space of Buildings Completed | 6417 | 万平方米 | ( 10, 000 sq.m ) |
| 为上年 | As Compared with the Preceding Year | 94.9 | % | ( % ) |

# 5-01 分地区建筑业总产值(2019年)

## Gross Output Value of Construction by Region(2019)

单位:万元 (10000 yuan)

| 地 区 | Region | 建筑企业单位数(个) Number of Construction Enterprises (unit) | 建筑业总产值 Gross Output Value of Construction | 建筑工程产值 Output Value of Construction Projects | 安装工程产值 Output value of Installation Projects | 其他产值 Other Output Values |
|---|---|---|---|---|---|---|
| **全 市** | **Total** | **1606** | **45782053** | **39495688** | **4916534** | **1369831** |
| 市 区 | Urban District | 1435 | 43807421 | 37729302 | 4745114 | 1333005 |
| #上城区 | Shangcheng | 70 | 3067014 | 1725118 | 1292572 | 49324 |
| 下城区 | Xiacheng | 72 | 2462478 | 2165071 | 195397 | 102010 |
| 江干区 | Jianggan | 113 | 3810493 | 3368539 | 356599 | 85354 |
| 拱墅区 | Gongshu | 148 | 3431740 | 2607110 | 785575 | 39055 |
| 西湖区 | Xihu | 127 | 10806394 | 9747669 | 537107 | 521619 |
| 高新(滨江)区 | Hi-Tech (Binjiang) | 64 | 5499745 | 5334044 | 116351 | 49351 |
| 萧山区 | Xiaoshan | 299 | 7813818 | 6701532 | 725748 | 386538 |
| 余杭区 | Yuhang | 256 | 3751626 | 3379311 | 361248 | 11066 |
| 富阳区 | Fuyang | 128 | 1083579 | 875220 | 171891 | 36468 |
| 临安区 | Lin'an | 85 | 1059894 | 908487 | 131281 | 20127 |
| 钱塘新区 | Qiantang New Area | 70 | 1013075 | 909638 | 71345 | 32093 |
| 西湖风景名胜区 | The West Lake Scenic Zone | 3 | 7565 | 7565 | - | - |
| 桐庐县 | Tonglu | 54 | 1110751 | 1047964 | 61315 | 1471 |
| 淳安县 | Chun'an | 72 | 375114 | 267478 | 72284 | 35351 |
| 建德市 | Jiande | 45 | 488767 | 450943 | 37820 | 4 |

# 5－02 建筑总专包

## Financial Indicators on Construction Enterprises of

单位：万元

| 指标名称 | Item | 年末资产 Asset and Liabilities | | |
|---|---|---|---|---|
| | | 流动资产合计 Circulating Funds | 固定资产原价 Fixed Assets | 资产合计 Total Assets |
| **总计** | **Total** | **33742241** | **3429694** | **41210650** |
| #特、一、二级企业 | of Which: Special Grade, First Grade, Second Grade | 31475320 | 3007113 | 38523468 |
| #国有及国有控股企业 | of Which: State－owned and State Holding Enterprises | 10353276 | 667032 | 13013144 |
| **一、按登记注册类型分组** | **Grouped by Registration Status** | | | |
| 内资企业 | Domestic Funded | 33607993 | 3404818 | 41042412 |
| 国有企业 | State－owned | 187258 | 13843 | 217128 |
| 集体企业 | Collective－owned | 6017 | 2387 | 7334 |
| 股份合作企业 | Share－holding Cooperative Enterprises | 24902 | 23005 | 41017 |
| 联营企业 | Joint Venture | | | |
| 有限责任公司 | Limited Liability Corporations | 14771875 | 998096 | 18057688 |
| 股份有限公司 | Share－holding Corporations Ltd. | 3634524 | 352233 | 4860690 |
| 私营企业 | Private Enterprises | 14983418 | 2015255 | 17858555 |
| 其他企业 | Other Enterprises | | | |
| 港、澳、台商投资企业 | Funded from Hong Kong, Macao and Taiwan | 107692 | 21564 | 138330 |
| 外商投资企业 | Foreign Funded | 26555 | 3312 | 29908 |
| **二、按国民经济行业分组** | **Grouped by Sector** | | | |
| 房屋建筑业 | Housing Construction | 16694333 | 1218186 | 20723310 |
| 土木工程建筑业 | Civil Engineering Construction | 12092020 | 1558632 | 14797201 |
| 建筑安装业 | Installation of Lines, Pipelines and Equipment | 2007534 | 256502 | 2273110 |
| 建筑装饰和其他建筑业 | Fitting、Decoration of Building and Others Construction | 2948355 | 396375 | 3417029 |

# 企业财务指标(2019 年)
# General Contractors and Specialist Contractors(2019)

(10000 yuan)

| 负债<br>at Year - end | | | | |
|---|---|---|---|---|
| 流动负债合计<br>Current Liabilities | 负债合计<br>Total Liabilities | 所有者权益合计<br>Owners´Equity | 实收资本<br>Paid - in Capitals | 个人资本<br>State Capital |
| **27570766** | **29000375** | **12210275** | **6792046** | **2671710** |
| 26132537 | 27497944 | 11025523 | 5878753 | 2243142 |
| 10166312 | 10778859 | 2234285 | 1120013 | 7269 |
| | | | | |
| 27434219 | 28861822 | 12180589 | 6765310 | 2666297 |
| 165629 | 165629 | 51499 | 44910 | |
| 2966 | 3744 | 3589 | 2068 | |
| 26900 | 26900 | 14117 | 10000 | 10000 |
| | | | | |
| 13266548 | 14306864 | 3750824 | 1790784 | 138310 |
| 3057003 | 3209756 | 1650933 | 505268 | 95198 |
| 10915173 | 11148928 | 6709627 | 4412280 | 2422790 |
| | | | | |
| 118854 | 120860 | 17470 | 21245 | 3413 |
| 17693 | 17693 | 12216 | 5490 | 2000 |
| | | | | |
| 13793522 | 14704198 | 6019113 | 3150075 | 1386164 |
| 9801393 | 10241943 | 4555257 | 2680550 | 900777 |
| 1534896 | 1545382 | 727728 | 380742 | 132021 |
| 2440955 | 2508852 | 908177 | 580679 | 252747 |

| 指标名称 | Item | 损益 Expenditure, Income 工程结算收入 Revenue of Project Settlement Accounts | 工程结算成本 Costs of Project Settlement Accounts |
|---|---|---|---|
| **总　计** | **Total** | **44256925** | **41434451** |
| #特、一、二级企业 | of Which: Special Grade, First Grade, Second Grade | 41485379 | 38942326 |
| #国有及国有控股企业 | of Which: State - owned and State Holding Enterprises | 11779456 | 11029897 |
| **一、按登记注册类型分组** | **Grouped by Registration Status** | | |
| 内资企业 | Domestic Funded | 44165879 | 41351022 |
| 国有企业 | State - owned | 286488 | 269214 |
| 集体企业 | Collective - owned | 5590 | 3583 |
| 股份合作企业 | Share - holding Cooperative Enterprises | 15785 | 12135 |
| 联营企业 | Joint Venture | | |
| 有限责任公司 | Limited Liability Corporations | 17968310 | 16898939 |
| 股份有限公司 | Share - holding Corporations Ltd. | 3855651 | 3551160 |
| 私营企业 | Private Enterprises | 22034055 | 20615992 |
| 其他企业 | Other Enterprises | | |
| 港、澳、台商投资企业 | Funded from Hong Kong, Macao and Taiwan | 46884 | 43469 |
| 外商投资企业 | Foreign Funded | 44162 | 39960 |
| **二、按国民经济行业分组** | **Grouped by Sector** | | |
| 房屋建筑业 | Housing Construction | 23172689 | 22072064 |
| 土木工程建筑业 | Civil Engineering Construction | 13840657 | 12767945 |
| 建筑安装业 | Installation of Lines, Pipelines and Equipment | 2780016 | 2522268 |
| 建筑装饰和其他建筑业 | Fitting Decoration of Building and Others Construction | 4463563 | 4072174 |

continued (10000 yuan)

| 及分配<br>and Distribution | | | | | |
|---|---|---|---|---|---|
| 工程结算税金及附加<br>Taxes and Extra Charges Project Settlement Accounts | 销售费用<br>Sales Expenses | 管理费用<br>Management Expenditure | 财务费用<br>Financial Expenditure | 利润总额<br>Total Profits | 应交所得税<br>Income Taxes Payable |
| **139790** | **139520** | **1399064** | **298729** | **977498** | **195466** |
| 128339 | 123404 | 1206847 | 286340 | 928133 | 184324 |
| 27973 | 17431 | 309255 | 84802 | 319564 | 64209 |
| | | | | | |
| 139387 | 138170 | 1392400 | 297595 | 978621 | 195222 |
| 1044 | 781 | 7364 | 623 | 7272 | 1900 |
| 139 | 792 | 860 | 90 | 129 | 53 |
| 210 | 828 | 1816 | 752 | 352 | 88 |
| | | | | | |
| 50040 | 33882 | 515955 | 123665 | 420175 | 81084 |
| 8454 | 7047 | 98005 | 31082 | 161880 | 28211 |
| 79501 | 94839 | 768401 | 141384 | 388813 | 83886 |
| | | | | | |
| 269 | 1000 | 4085 | 855 | -1984 | 28 |
| 134 | 350 | 2580 | 280 | 862 | 215 |
| | | | | | |
| 73361 | 17652 | 470047 | 189238 | 437597 | 86570 |
| 43660 | 40405 | 565695 | 79530 | 378423 | 78135 |
| 8591 | 14150 | 147220 | 12201 | 74760 | 12646 |
| 14178 | 67313 | 216102 | 17759 | 86718 | 18115 |

# 5－03 建筑业企业生产情况(2016－2019年)
## Statistics on Production of Construction Enterprises(2016－2019)

| 指标名称 | | Item | | 2016 | 2017 | 2018 | 2019 |
|---|---|---|---|---|---|---|---|
| **一、建筑业合同情况** | | **Contract of Construction** | | | | | |
| 签订的合同额 | (万元) | Total Value of Contracts | (10000 yuan) | 72311485 | 80872710 | 87772266 | 100912299 |
| 上年结转合同额 | (万元) | Value from Contracts Signed in 2016 | (10000 yuan) | 31413457 | 30503869 | 33731635 | 43492461 |
| 本年新签合同额 | (万元) | Value from New Contracts Signed in 2017 | (10000 yuan) | 40898029 | 50368841 | 54040631 | 57419838 |
| **二、承包工程完成情况** | | **Completion of Contracted Projects** | | | | | |
| 直接从建设单位承揽工程完成的产值 | (万元) | Complete Output Value of Projects Contacted Directly from Investors | (10000 yuan) | 40898836 | 42804635 | 43606124 | 43690527 |
| 自行完成施工产值 | (万元) | Own－completed Output Value | (10000 yuan) | 39270784 | 41202046 | 41057696 | 40837087 |
| 分包出去工程的产值 | (万元) | Output Value of Out－sourced Projects | (10000 yuan) | 1628052 | 1602590 | 2548428 | 2853440 |
| 从建设单位以外承揽工程完成的产值 | (万元) | Completed Output Value of Projects Contacted from Non－investors | (10000 yuan) | 1782188 | 2035210 | 3269828 | 4944966 |
| 建筑业总产值 | (万元) | Gross Output Value | (10000 yuan) | 41052972 | 43237256 | 44327525 | 45782053 |
| #装饰装修产值 | (万元) | of Which: Output Value of Fitting and Decoration of Buildings | (10000 yuan) | 3642482 | 4800059 | 4199587 | 4394782 |
| #在外省完成的产值 | (万元) | of Which: Completed Output Value outside of Zhejiang Province | (10000 yuan) | 11675079 | 12005017 | 12095931 | 12442013 |
| 按构成分 | | by Structure | | | | | |
| 建筑工程产值 | (万元) | Output Value of Construction Projects | (10000 yuan) | 36106015 | 37584752 | 38230682 | 39495688 |
| 安装工程产值 | (万元) | Output value of Installation Projects | (10000 yuan) | 3978388 | 4599347 | 4919966 | 4916534 |
| 其他产值 | (万元) | Other Output Values | (10000 yuan) | 968569 | 1053157 | 1176877 | 1369831 |
| 竣工产值 | (万元) | Output Value of Buildings Completed | (10000 yuan) | 23746502 | 21888828 | 21893653 | 20586072 |
| 房屋建筑施工面积 | (万平方米) | Floor Space of Buildings Under Construction | (10000 sq. m) | 27221 | 25617 | 26842 | 29470 |
| #本年新开工面积 | (万平方米) | of Which: Beginning Projects in this Year | (10000 sq. m) | 8583 | 8869 | 10946 | 10214 |
| #实行投标承包面积 | (万平方米) | of Which: Floor Space of Biding System | (10000 sq. m) | 22615 | | | |
| 房屋建筑竣工面积 | (万平方米) | Floor space of Buildings Completed | (10000 sq. m) | 9754 | 8108 | 6764 | 6417 |
| **三、年末自有施工机械设备** | | **Machinery and Equipment Owned (year－end)** | | | | | |
| 年末自有施工机械设备净值 | (万元) | Net Value of Machinery and Equipment Owned | (10000 yuan) | 782395 | 822402 | 742142 | 669716 |
| 年末自有施工机械设备总台数 | (台) | Number of Machinery and Equipment Owned | (set) | 162491 | 162507 | 149125 | 147904 |
| 年末自有施工机械设备总功率 | (千瓦) | Total Power of Machinery and Equipment Owned | (1000 kw) | 3301850 | 3264229 | 3046124 | 2706236 |
| **四、就业人员情况** | | **Number of Employed Persons** | | | | | |
| 计算劳动生产率的平均人数 | (人) | Average Employed Persons Overall Labor Productivity | (person) | 1237441 | 1239143 | 1221420 | 1230569 |
| 年末就业人员数 | (人) | Employed Persons (year－end) | (person) | 1203999 | 1224693 | 1167509 | 1150807 |

# 5－04 具有资质等级建筑业企业主要生产经营指标(2013－2019 年)

# Major Economic Indicators of Qualified Construction Enterprises(2013－2019)

单位:万元 (10000 yuan)

| 指标名称 Item | 2013 | 2014 | 2015 | 2016 | 2017 | 2018 | 2019 |
|---|---|---|---|---|---|---|---|
| 企业个数(个) Nomber of Enterprises (unit) | 1515 | 1476 | 1480 | 1474 | 1410 | 1541 | 1606 |
| 亏损企业个数(个) Loss Making Enterprises (unit) | 252 | 224 | 236 | 256 | 253 | 329 | 351 |
| 建筑业总产值 Gross Output Value of Construction | 37554704 | 39713876 | 40975734 | 41052972 | 43237256 | 44327525 | 45782053 |
| 竣工产值 Output Value of Buildings Completed | 21021307 | 21665909 | 25994238 | 23746502 | 21888828 | 21893653 | 20586072 |
| 房屋建筑施工面积(万平方米) Floor Space of Buildings Under Construction (10,000 sq. m) | 29538 | 29581 | 28124 | 27221 | 25617 | 26842 | 29470 |
| 房屋建筑竣工面积(万平方米) Floor Space of Buildings Completed (10,000 sq. m) | 9613 | 9514 | 10137 | 9754 | 8108 | 6764 | 6417 |
| 固定资产原价 Orginal Value of Fixed Assets | 3293095 | 3393624 | 3488088 | 3239557 | 3552611 | 3352353 | 3429694 |
| 实收资本合计 Total Capital Hold | 5019389 | 5493120 | 5799067 | 5932301 | 6364527 | 6756936 | 6792046 |
| 流动资产合计 Circulating Funds | 19959672 | 22168981 | 23867659 | 25412440 | 27695056 | 30371728 | 10116084 |
| 其中:存货 Stock | 4934518 | 5900549 | 6360774 | 6751318 | 7530374 | 7823812 | 7414341 |
| 在建工程 Projects wnder Construction | 320533 | 313490 | 211195 | 175075 | 216619 | 262751 | 259028 |
| 固定资产合计 Fixed Assets | 2371260 | 2826312 | 2829483 | 2067226 | 2292476 | 1678207 | - |
| 年末负债合计 Total Liabilities at Year－end | 17591701 | 18186469 | 19365824 | 20274680 | 22067498 | 25107296 | 29000375 |
| 流动负债合计 Circulating Funds | 16473990 | 16894050 | 17964478 | 18752593 | 20579766 | 23735159 | 27570766 |
| 所有者权益合计 Crediors´Equity | 8559878 | 9656533 | 10453107 | 10883382 | 12196061 | 12658441 | 12210275 |
| 营业收入 Revenue of Business | 33709184 | 34704862 | 35568492 | 36069232 | 36965857 | 40293678 | 44677368 |
| 营业成本 Operating Costs | 30614028 | 31501139 | 32365477 | 33270805 | 34248463 | 37687072 | 41764885 |
| 营业税金及附加 Main Sales Tax and Extra Charges | 996370 | 1029405 | 1020437 | 541967 | 199457 | 157132 | 146939 |
| 管理费用 Management Expenditure | 905194 | 918904 | 965161 | 1042943 | 1163505 | 1263222 | 1399064 |
| 财务费用 Financial Expenditure | 318198 | 330680 | 301313 | 258903 | 271466 | 243248 | 298729 |
| 营业利润 Management Profits | 850362 | 888932 | 883320 | 917779 | 1043476 | 912880 | 944590 |
| 利润总额 Total Profits | 883887 | 913117 | 895484 | 950047 | 1075458 | 983741 | 977498 |

# 主要统计指标解释

**建筑业总产值** 建筑业总产值是以货币表现的建筑业企业在一定时期内生产的建筑业产品和服务的总和。建筑业总产值包括建筑工程产值、安装工程产值和其他产值三部分内容。

**房屋建筑施工面积** 指报告期内施过工的全部房屋建筑面积，它包括本期新开工的面积、上期跨入本期继续施工的房屋面积、上期停缓建在本期恢复施工的房屋面积、本期竣工的房屋面积以及本期施工后又停缓建的房屋面积。

**房屋建筑竣工面积** 指在报告期内房屋建筑按照设计要求已全部完工，达到了使用条件，经检查验收鉴定合格的房屋建筑面积。

**工程结算收入（主营业务收入）** 指本企业承包工程实现的工程价款结算收入以及向发包单位收取的除工程价款以外按规定列作营业收入的各种款项，如临时设施费、劳动保险费、施工机构调迁费等以及向发包单位收取的各种索赔款。

**工程结算成本（主营业务成本）** 指在报告期内与发包单位办理工程价款结算的已完工程实际成本。

# Explanatory Notes on Main Statistical Indicators

**Gross Output Value of Construction** refers to the total of construction products and services, expressed in money terms, produced or rendered by construction enterprises in a given period. It includes the output value of construction projects, installation projects and others.

**Floor Space of Buildings Under Construction** refers to the floor space of all buildings under construction during the reference period, including the floor space of buildings those are newly started construction, those were started earlier and continues construction; those were suspended in the previous period but resumed construction in this period, those are completed in this period, and those are under construction but suspended in this period.

**Floor Space of Buildings Completed** refers to the floor space of buildings that are completed in the reference period in accordance with the design requirements, up to the service standard, and qualified after inspection and acceptance.

**Project Settlement Income** refers to the income received by the construction enterprise from the contracted project through settlement procedures, and other charges to the contractee listed as operational costs, such as temporary facility fee, labor insurance premium, moving cost of construction equipment, as well as various types of claims to the contractee.

**Project Settlement Cost** refers to the actual cost of completed projects that have been settled prices with the contractee during the reporting period.

# 六、交通运输邮电

TRANSPORTATION, POST AND TELECOMMUNICATIONS

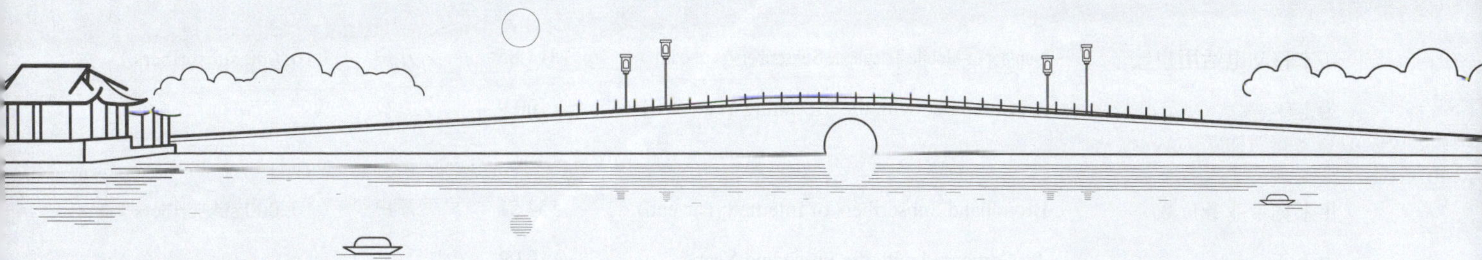

# 6 交通运输、邮电
# Transportation, Post and Telecommunications

## 主要统计指标
## Major Statistical Indicators

| | | | | |
|---|---|---|---|---|
| 客运量 | Passenger Traffic | 20888 | 万人次 | (10, 000 person-times) |
| 为上年 | As Compared with the Preceding Year | 103.8 | % | (%) |
| 货运量 | Freight Traffic | 36384 | 万吨 | (10, 000 tons) |
| 为上年 | As Compared with the Preceding Year | 103.2 | % | (%) |
| 邮电业务收入 | Business Income of Post & Telecommunication Service | 607.78 | 亿元 | (100 million yuan) |
| 为上年 | As Compared with the Preceding Year | 107.9 | % | (%) |
| 年末固定电话用户数 | Number of Local Telephone Subscribers(year-end) | 233.08 | 万户 | (10, 000 subscribers) |
| 为上年 | As Compared with the Preceding Year | 96.4 | % | (%) |
| 年末移动电话用户数 | Number of Mobile Telephone Subscribers(year-end) | 1817.85 | 万户 | (10, 000 subscribers) |
| 为上年 | As Compared with the Preceding Year | 100.9 | % | (%) |
| 年末宽带业务户数 | Broadband Subscribers of Internet(year-end) | 554.51 | 万户 | (10, 000 subscribers) |
| 为上年 | As Compared with the Preceding Year | 103.2 | % | (%) |

# 6－01　客货运输量(2013－2019年)
## Total Passenger and Freight Traffic(2013－2019)

| 项　目<br>Item | 2013 | 2014 | 2015 | 2016 | 2017 | 2018 | 2019 |
|---|---|---|---|---|---|---|---|
| **一、客运量合计(万人次)<br>Passenger Traffic(10000 person－times)** | **36409** | **24070** | **23942** | **20541** | **22289** | **20121** | **20888** |
| 铁路客运量<br>Passenger Railways | 3717 | 4689 | 5282 | 6053 | 6807 | 7535 | 8874 |
| 民航客运量<br>Passenger Civil Aviation | 1151 | 1334 | 1472 | 1622 | 1825 | 1956 | 2044 |
| 公路客运量<br>Passenger Highways | 30994 | 17431 | 16591 | 12282 | 13019 | 10027 | 9360 |
| 水路客运量<br>Passenger Waterways | 547 | 616 | 597 | 584 | 638 | 603 | 610 |
| **二、旅客周转量合计(万人公里)<br>Total Passenger－kilometers(10000 passenger－km)** | **1573289** | **1151642** | **1085769** | **943874** | **905008** | **829027** | **700446** |
| 公路旅客周转量<br>Passenger－kilometers Highways | 1566046 | 1143750 | 1078054 | 936574 | 897116 | 821267 | 689970 |
| 水路旅客周转量<br>Passenger－kilometers Waterways | 7243 | 7892 | 7715 | 7300 | 7892 | 7760 | 10476 |
| **三、货运量合计(万吨)<br>Total Freight Traffic(10000 tons)** | **30734** | **29335** | **29384** | **30170** | **34785** | **35180** | **36384** |
| 铁路货运量<br>Freight Railways | 284 | 312 | 307 | 274 | 328 | 306 | 537 |
| 民航货运量<br>Freight Civil Aviation | 22 | 24 | 25 | 29 | 35 | 38 | 41 |
| 公路货运量<br>Freight Highways | 23884 | 23202 | 23800 | 25194 | 29378 | 30593 | 31732 |
| 水路货运量<br>Freight Waterways | 6545 | 5797 | 5251 | 4673 | 5044 | 4244 | 4073 |
| **四、货运周转量合计(万吨公里)<br>Total Freight Ton－kilometers(10000 ton－km)** | **4724588** | **4550550** | **4629814** | **4796677** | **5304007** | **5440793** | **5534460** |
| 公路货物周转量<br>Freight Ton－kilometers Highways | 2719204 | 2760873 | 3003728 | 3217983 | 3615581 | 3875561 | 3928822 |
| 水路货物周转量<br>Freight Ton－kilometers Waterways | 2005384 | 1789677 | 1626086 | 1578694 | 1688426 | 1565232 | 1605638 |

# 6－02 货运量(1978－2019年)
# Total Freight Traffic (1978－2019)

单位:万吨 (10000 tons)

| 年份<br>Year | 合计<br>Total | 铁路<br>Railways | 公路<br>Highways | 水路<br>Waterways | 民航<br>Civil Aviation |
|---|---|---|---|---|---|
| 1978 | 1706 | 418 | 633 | 655 | |
| 1979 | 1983 | 440 | 771 | 772 | |
| 1980 | 2070 | 444 | 762 | 864 | |
| 1981 | 1972 | 449 | 886 | 637 | |
| 1982 | 2261 | 485 | 795 | 981 | |
| 1983 | 2299 | 488 | 838 | 973 | |
| 1984 | 2385 | 510 | 888 | 987 | |
| 1985 | 2488 | 524 | 890 | 1074 | |
| 1986 | 2558 | 551 | 874 | 1133 | |
| 1987 | 2515 | 574 | 899 | 1041 | 1 |
| 1988 | 2416 | 555 | 823 | 1037 | 1 |
| 1989 | 7377 | 539 | 5095 | 1743 | |
| 1990 | 6522 | 449 | 4479 | 1594 | |
| 1991 | 7017 | 451 | 4891 | 1675 | |
| 1992 | 8434 | 534 | 6063 | 1836 | 1 |
| 1993 | 9082 | 580 | 6353 | 2148 | 1 |
| 1994 | 8962 | 491 | 6563 | 1907 | 1 |
| 1995 | 10347 | 482 | 7021 | 2842 | 2 |
| 1996 | 10962 | 445 | 7735 | 2780 | 2 |
| 1997 | 11015 | 406 | 7932 | 2676 | 1 |
| 1998 | 11329 | 418 | 8196 | 2713 | 2 |
| 1999 | 11684 | 403 | 8037 | 3241 | 3 |
| 2000 | 11459 | 417 | 7865 | 3173 | 4 |
| 2001 | 12443 | 452 | 8588 | 3398 | 5 |
| 2002 | 14347 | 446 | 10391 | 3504 | 6 |
| 2003 | 16815 | 438 | 12118 | 4253 | 6 |
| 2004 | 18895 | 480 | 13117 | 5289 | 9 |
| 2005 | 19909 | 525 | 13539 | 5833 | 12 |
| 2006 | 20924 | 569 | 14588 | 5754 | 13 |
| 2007 | 22569 | 573 | 16484 | 5500 | 12 |
| 2008 | 22550 | 483 | 16822 | 5232 | 13 |
| 2009 | 22372 | 427 | 16536 | 5396 | 13 |
| 2010 | 25915 | 379 | 19148 | 6371 | 17 |
| 2011 | 28831 | 331 | 21755 | 6727 | 18 |
| 2012 | 30089 | 322 | 23243 | 6503 | 20 |
| 2013 | 30734 | 284 | 23884 | 6545 | 22 |
| 2014 | 29335 | 312 | 23202 | 5797 | 24 |
| 2015 | 29384 | 307 | 23800 | 5251 | 25 |
| 2016 | 30170 | 274 | 25194 | 4673 | 29 |
| 2017 | 34785 | 328 | 29378 | 5044 | 35 |
| 2018 | 35180 | 306 | 30593 | 4244 | 38 |
| 2019 | 36384 | 537 | 31732 | 4073 | 41 |

# 6－03　客运量(1978－2019年)

## Total Passenger Traffic (1978－2019)

单位:万人次　　　　(10,000 person－times)

| 年份<br>Year | 合计<br>Total | 铁路<br>Railways | 公路<br>Highways | 水路<br>Waterways | 民航<br>Civil Aviation |
|---|---|---|---|---|---|
| 1978 | 2878 | 485 | － | － | 3 |
| 1979 | 3122 | 560 | 1829 | 729 | 4 |
| 1980 | 3905 | 672 | 2358 | 870 | 5 |
| 1981 | 4484 | 769 | 2857 | 850 | 8 |
| 1982 | 5263 | 813 | 3377 | 1064 | 9 |
| 1983 | 5451 | 878 | 3530 | 1035 | 8 |
| 1984 | 6056 | 983 | 3912 | 1151 | 10 |
| 1985 | 6724 | 1004 | 4595 | 1111 | 14 |
| 1986 | 6765 | 1034 | 4768 | 941 | 22 |
| 1987 | 6905 | 1127 | 4852 | 896 | 30 |
| 1988 | 6593 | 1237 | 4445 | 877 | 34 |
| 1989 | 7493 | 1182 | 5488 | 801 | 22 |
| 1990 | 8119 | 1056 | 6350 | 691 | 22 |
| 1991 | 10701 | 1062 | 8876 | 710 | 53 |
| 1992 | 13358 | 1083 | 11538 | 670 | 67 |
| 1993 | 13070 | 1139 | 11403 | 454 | 74 |
| 1994 | 13373 | 1230 | 11669 | 390 | 84 |
| 1995 | 16620 | 1242 | 14921 | 339 | 118 |
| 1996 | 16714 | 1112 | 15184 | 273 | 145 |
| 1997 | 17034 | 1040 | 15623 | 260 | 111 |
| 1998 | 17395 | 1120 | 15925 | 235 | 115 |
| 1999 | 17882 | 1168 | 16369 | 235 | 110 |
| 2000 | 18607 | 1202 | 17102 | 179 | 124 |
| 2001 | 20342 | 1342 | 18707 | 148 | 145 |
| 2002 | 21089 | 1574 | 19213 | 108 | 194 |
| 2003 | 21348 | 1534 | 19510 | 89 | 215 |
| 2004 | 22833 | 1908 | 20372 | 237 | 316 |
| 2005 | 24124 | 2011 | 21431 | 304 | 378 |
| 2006 | 25810 | 2124 | 22961 | 267 | 458 |
| 2007 | 28026 | 2255 | 24836 | 306 | 629 |
| 2008 | 29084 | 2498 | 25630 | 277 | 679 |
| 2009 | 30116 | 2494 | 26454 | 372 | 796 |
| 2010 | 33772 | 2741 | 29671 | 456 | 904 |
| 2011 | 34778 | 2962 | 30305 | 595 | 916 |
| 2012 | 35819 | 3112 | 31126 | 592 | 989 |
| 2013 | 36409 | 3717 | 30994 | 547 | 1151 |
| 2014 | 24070 | 4689 | 17431 | 616 | 1334 |
| 2015 | 23942 | 5282 | 16591 | 597 | 1472 |
| 2016 | 20541 | 6053 | 12282 | 584 | 1622 |
| 2017 | 22289 | 6807 | 13019 | 638 | 1825 |
| 2018 | 20121 | 7535 | 10027 | 603 | 1956 |
| 2019 | 20888 | 8874 | 9360 | 610 | 2044 |

注:1990年以前为交通系统数,1990年起为全社会数(后同)。2014年起运输量统计方法调整。

a) The data in the table only included transportation department before 1990, while extended to the whole society after 1990 (the same below). The statistical method has been adjusted since 2014.

# 6－04 分地区交通

## Statistics on Traffic and

| 项　目 | | Item | | 全市 Whole City | 市区 Urban District |
|---|---|---|---|---|---|
| 铁路旅客运量 | （万人） | Passenger Railways | (10,000 Persons) | 8874 | 8499 |
| 铁路货物运量 | （万吨） | Freight Railways | (10,000 tons) | 537 | 290 |
| 公路客运量 | （万人） | Passenger Highways | (10,000 Persons) | 9360 | 8466 |
| 公路货运量 | （万吨） | Freight Highways | (10,000 tons) | 31732 | 20358 |
| 民用航空客运量 | （万人） | Passenger Civil Aviation | (10,000 Persons) | 2044 | 2044 |
| 民用航空货邮运量 | （万吨） | Freight Civil Aviation | (10,000 tons) | 41 | 41 |
| 水路客运量 | （万人） | Passenger Waterways | (10,000 Persons) | 610 | 263 |
| 水路货运量 | （万吨） | Freight Waterways | (10,000 tons) | 4073 | 3844 |
| 非营运汽车拥有量 | （辆） | Possession of Non－Business Vehicles(year－end) | (Unit) | 2745840 | 2499716 |
| #私人汽车拥有量 | （辆） | in which:Possession of Private Vehicles | (Unit) | 2441357 | 2211023 |

# 运输情况(2019 年)
# Transport by Region(2019)

| 萧山区 Xiaoshan | 余杭区 Yuhang | 富阳区 Fuyang | 临安区 Lin'an | 桐庐县 Tonglu | 淳安县 Chun'an | 建德市 Jiande |
|---|---|---|---|---|---|---|
| – | 123 | 100 | – | 138 | 148 | 89 |
| 131 | 153 | – | – | – | 91 | 156 |
| 384 | 184 | 211 | 729 | 257 | 421 | 729 |
| 3723 | 1380 | 1459 | 906 | 7934 | 582 | 2857 |
| 2044 | – | – | – | – | – | – |
| 41 | – | – | – | – | – | – |
| 18 | – | – | – | 32 | 285 | 31 |
| 1752 | 526 | 498 | 132 | 91 | 10 | 129 |
| 526882 | 428359 | 163090 | 147169 | 94174 | 63545 | 88405 |
| 471157 | 388876 | 150283 | 135657 | 86443 | 61082 | 82809 |

# 6-05 运输线路长度(2013-2019年)

## Length of Transportation Routes(2013-2019)

单位:公里 (km)

| 项　目 Item | 2013 | 2014 | 2015 | 2016 | 2017 | 2018 | 2019 |
|---|---|---|---|---|---|---|---|
| 公路通车里程 (公里)<br>Length of Highways (km) | 15900 | 16024 | 16210 | 16306 | 16424 | 16520 | 16667 |
| #高速公路 (公里)<br>Expressway (km) | 550 | 582 | 615 | 632 | 632 | 632 | 632 |
| 一级公路 (公里)<br>First Class Highways (km) | 791 | 803 | 836 | 832 | 835 | 840 | 877 |
| 二级公路 (公里)<br>Second Class Highways (km) | 1526 | 1570 | 1616 | 1615 | 1631 | 1634 | 1759 |
| 内河通航里程 (公里)<br>Length of Navigable Inland Waterways (km) | 2006 | 2006 | 2006 | 2006 | 2006 | 2006 | 2006 |
| 民用航空航线 (条)<br>Number of Civil Aviation Routes (line) | 185 | 222 | 235 | 240 | 286 | 292 | 301 |
| 国内航线 (条)<br>Domestic Routes (line) | 156 | 186 | 196 | 195 | 229 | 234 | 232 |
| 国际航线 (条)<br>International Routes (line) | 22 | 28 | 32 | 38 | 49 | 51 | 63 |
| 地区航线 (条)<br>Regional Routes (line) | 7 | 8 | 7 | 7 | 8 | 7 | 6 |
| 民用航空通航城市 (个)<br>Number of Cities Can Arrive by Civil Aviation | 103 | 119 | 129 | 138 | 160 | 172 | 183 |
| 国内城市 (个)<br>Domestic Cities | 82 | 92 | 99 | 103 | 117 | 123 | 126 |
| 港澳台城市 (个)<br>Hongkong, Macau and Taiwan | 6 | 6 | 5 | 5 | 5 | 5 | 5 |
| 国际城市 (个)<br>International Cities | 21 | 27 | 30 | 35 | 43 | 44 | 52 |

# 6-06 民用机动车辆年末拥有量(2013-2019年末)

# Total Number of Motor Vehicles End of the Year(End of 2013-2019)

单位:辆 (unit)

| 项目 | Item | 2013 | 2014 | 2015 | 2016 | 2017 | 2018 | 2019 |
|---|---|---|---|---|---|---|---|---|
| **全市合计** | **Total** | **2542976** | **2696340** | **2733537** | **2633541** | **2793595** | **2880804** | **2975762** |
| 一、汽车 | Vehicles | 2045618 | 2184000 | 2244767 | 2341536 | 2451226 | 2571230 | 2671807 |
| 1. 载客汽车 | Passenger Vehicles | 1860794 | 1992112 | 2056143 | 2127393 | 2210376 | 2310070 | 2399022 |
| 其中:大型 | Large | 17078 | 17485 | 18657 | 20017 | 20880 | 21546 | 20907 |
| 中型 | Medium | 17849 | 14411 | 10797 | 10035 | 9365 | 8499 | 7628 |
| 小型 | Small | 1794017 | 1936836 | 2002730 | 2076098 | 2157089 | 2258635 | 2351862 |
| 微型 | Mini | 31850 | 23380 | 23959 | 21243 | 23042 | 21390 | 18625 |
| 其中:轿车 | Car | 1678453 | 1799442 | 1773864 | 1483128 | 1530805 | 1548328 | 1610070 |
| 2. 载货汽车 | Trucks | 173227 | 180475 | 177674 | 202775 | 229038 | 248614 | 259746 |
| 其中:重型 | Heavy | 35917 | 39998 | 41999 | 49480 | 57794 | 64289 | 71102 |
| 中型 | Medium | 17530 | 14444 | 8851 | 9422 | 9213 | 8147 | 6611 |
| 轻型 | Light | 119205 | 125508 | 126321 | 143441 | 161703 | 175945 | 181872 |
| 微型 | Mini | 575 | 525 | 503 | 432 | 328 | 233 | 161 |
| 3. 其他汽车 | Vehicles | 11597 | 11413 | 10950 | 11368 | 11812 | 12546 | 13039 |
| 其中:三轮汽车 | Vehicles | 385 | 182 | 179 | 139 | 102 | 69 | 44 |
| 低速货车 | Low Speed Trucks | 384 | 416 | 549 | 806 | 792 | 779 | 724 |
| 二、摩托车 | Motorcycles | 490884 | 505360 | 481230 | 282477 | 329905 | 292662 | 281403 |
| 1. 普通 | Genera | 466625 | 481027 | 463722 | 277238 | 324469 | 288562 | 276568 |
| 2. 轻便 | Light | 24259 | 24333 | 17508 | 5239 | 5436 | 4100 | 4835 |
| 三、挂车 | Trailer | 6433 | 6939 | 7464 | 9457 | 12396 | 16846 | 22493 |
| 四、其他类型 | Other | 41 | 41 | 76 | 71 | 68 | 66 | 59 |

# 6-07 邮政、电信主要指标(2013-2019年)

## Main Indicators of Post and Telecommunications(2013-2019)

| 项目 Item | 2013 | 2014 | 2015 | 2016 | 2017 | 2018 | 2019 |
|---|---|---|---|---|---|---|---|
| 邮政业务总收入(万元) Total Business Income of Postal Service (10,000 yuan) | 702664 | 1176704 | 1596884 | 2151732 | 2750911 | 3646724 | 4023039 |
| #快递业务收入(万元) Business Income of Express Mail Service (10,000 yuan) | 563459 | 1022279 | 1437542 | 1956944 | 2510479 | 2966169 | 3267926 |
| 电信业务收入(万元) Total Business Income of Telecommunications Services (10,000 yuan) | 1752286 | 1700825 | 1736600 | 1908315 | 1926800 | 1997000 | 2054800 |
| 函件(万件) Number of Letters (10,000 pcs) | 20133 | 17412 | 13256 | 9634 | 11656 | 8768 | 5508 |
| 订销报纸累计份额(万份) Number of Newspapers (10,000 pcs) | 30694 | 29214 | 29304 | 24067 | 24273 | 23497 | 22342 |
| 订销杂志累计份额(万份) Number of Publications (10,000 pcs) | 1528 | 1437 | 1310 | 1061 | 1010 | 1047 | 895 |
| 包裹(万件) Number of Parcels (10,000 pcs) | 133 | 113 | 81 | 49 | 51 | 50 | 63 |
| 快递(万份) Pieces of Express Mail Service (10,000 copies) | 46852 | 84563 | 125707 | 180473 | 232630 | 258910 | 265666 |
| #国际及港澳台快递(万份) Pieces of Express to overseas and HongKong,macao,Taiwan (10,000 copies) | 738 | 1731 | 2046 | 2495 | 4065 | 11005 | 13741 |
| 纪特邮票(万枚) Stamps for Collettion (10,000 pcs) | 1412 | 1151 | 1231 | 1295 | 969 | 210 | 92860(套) |
| 年末固定电话用户数(万户) Number of Local Telephone Subscribers(year-end) (10,000 subscribers) | 334.87 | 311.14 | 293.44 | 265.70 | 259.37 | 241.84 | 233.08 |
| 年末移动电话用户数(万户) Number of Subscribers of Mobile Telephone(year-end) (10,000 subscribers) | 1546.83 | 1561.71 | 1726.76 | 1734.41 | 1724.17 | 1913.91 | 1817.85 |
| 年末宽带业务户数(万户) Number of Wide Band Subscribers (10,000 subscribers) | 338.63 | 278.78 | 294.96 | 443.57 | 508.69 | 537.73 | 554.51 |

注:邮政业务总收入含规模以上快递企业。

a) The total business income of postal services included the express enterprises above designated sice.

# 主要统计指标解释

**货(客)运量** 指在一定时期内,各种运输工具实际运送的货物(旅客)数量。是反映运输业为国民经济和人民生活服务的数量指标,也是制定和检查运输生产计划、研究运输发展规模和速度的重要指标。货运按吨计算,客运按人计算。货物不论运输距离长短、货物类别,均按实际重量统计。旅客不论行程远近或票价多少,均按一人一次作为客运量统计;半价票、小孩票也按一人统计。

**货物(旅客)周转量** 指在一定时期内,由各种运输工具运送的货物(旅客)数量与其相应运输距离的乘积之总和。是反映运输业生产总成果的重要指标,也是编制和检查运输生产计划,计算运输效率、劳动生产率以及核算运输单位成本的主要基础资料。通常以吨公里和人公里为计算单位。计算货物周转量通常按发出站与到达站之间的最短距离,也就是计费距离计算。

**邮政、电信业务总量** 指以货币形式表示的邮政、电信通信企业为社会提供各类邮政、电信通信服务的总数量。计算方法为各类业务的实物量分别乘以相应的不变单价,求出各类业务的货币量加总求得。没有不变单价的业务按其业务收入直接相加。

**移动电话用户** 指在电信运营企业营业网点办理开户登记手续,通过移动电话交换机进入移动电话网,占用移动电话号码的各类电话用户。包括各类签约用户、智能网预付费用户、无线上网卡用户。

# Explanatory Notes on Main Statistical Indicators

**Freight(passenger) Transport** refers to the volume of freight (passenger) transported with various means in a certain period. It provides a quantitative measure to show how the transport industry serves the national economy and people, and is also an important indicator for working out and checking the transportation plan and studying its development scale and speed. Freight transport is calculated in tons and passenger transport is d in the number of persons. Despite the type of freight and traveling distance, the freight transport is calculated in the actual weight of the goods. Despite the traveling distance and ticket price, the passenger transport is calculated by the principle that one person is counted only once in one travel. The passenger with a half – price ticket or a child ticket is also calculated as one person.

**Freight Ton – kilometers(Passenger – kilometers)** refers to the sum of the products of the volume of transported cargo (passengers) multiplying by the transport distance. It is an important indicator to show the total results of the transport industry, to prepare and examine the transport plan and to measure the efficiency, the labour productivity and the unit cost of transport. Normally, it is calculated using ton – kilometer and passenger – kilometer as calculation units, and by the shortest distance between the departure station and the terminal station (i. e., the payable distance).

**Business Volume of Post and Telecommunication** refers to the total amount of postal and telecommunication services, expressed in value terms, provided by the post and telecommunications departments for society. Business volume of post and telecommunication is the sum of each service in kind multiplying with its correspondent unit price(constant price). Businesses without constant unit price are added directly according to their business income.

**Mobile Telephone Subscribers** refers to persons who have gone through registration procedures in the operation points of enterprises engaged in telecommunications and are hence connected with the mobile telephone communication network through the mobile telephone switchboards and occupy mobile phone numbers. Included are various types of subscriber, prepaid users for intelligent network and wireless network card users.

# 七、固定资产投资

INVESTMENT IN FIXED ASSETS

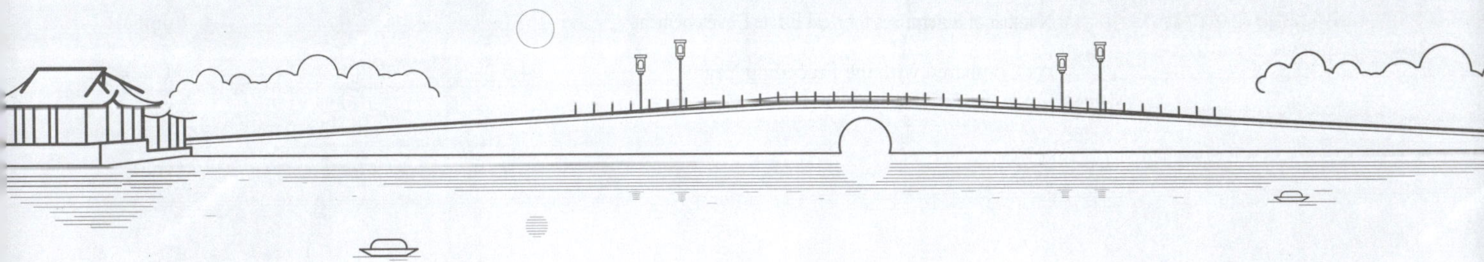

# 7 固定资产投资
# Investment in Fixed Assets

## 主要统计指标
## Major Statistical Indicators

| | | | | |
|---|---|---|---|---|
| 固定资产投资额为上年 | Investment in Fixed Assets As Compared with the Preceding Year | 111.6 | % | (%) |
| 第一产业为上年 | Primary Industry As Compared with the Preceding Year | 61.3 | % | (%) |
| 第二产业为上年 | Secondary Industry As Compared with the Preceding Year | 106.2 | % | (%) |
| 第三产业为上年 | Tertiary Industry As Compared with the Preceding Year | 112.2 | % | (%) |
| 房地产企业营业收入 | Operating Revenue of Real Estate Enterprise | 3032.9 | 亿元 | (100 million yuan) |
| 为上年 | As Compared with the Preceding Year | 102.2 | % | (%) |
| 房地产企业单位数 | Number of Enterprises for Real Estate Developement | 1631 | 个 | (unit) |
| 为上年 | As Compared with the Preceding Year | 94.5 | % | (%) |

# 7-01 固定资产投资总额(1979-2019 年)

## Investment in Fixed Assets (1979-2019)

单位:万元 (10000 yuan)

| 年份<br>Year | 固定资产投资<br>Investment in Fixed Assets | 房地产开发投资<br>Investment in Real Estate Development | 项目投资<br>Projects Investment | 基础设施投资<br>Investment in Infrastructure | 工业投资<br>Industrial Investment | 民间投资<br>Nongovernment Investment |
|---|---|---|---|---|---|---|
| 1979 | 34407 | | | | | |
| 1980 | 45752 | | | | | |
| 1981 | 51538 | | | | | |
| 1982 | 66123 | | | | | |
| 1983 | 68306 | | | | | |
| 1984 | 93244 | | | | | |
| 1985 | 141889 | | | | | |
| 1986 | 182398 | | | | | |
| 1987 | 200516 | | | | | |
| 1988 | 205967 | | | | | |
| 1989 | 202131 | | | | | |
| 1990 | 229214 | 20409 | | | | |
| 1991 | 255696 | 25247 | | | | |
| 1992 | 384136 | 41886 | | | | |
| 1993 | 825382 | 218006 | | | | |
| 1994 | 1059437 | 320532 | | | | |
| 1995 | 1566280 | 527985 | | | | |
| 1996 | 1819333 | 572749 | | | | |
| 1997 | 2139012 | 572686 | | | | |
| 1998 | 2681740 | 666244 | | | | |
| 1999 | 3233609 | 848441 | | | | |
| 2000 | 3766473 | 1015347 | | | | |
| 2001 | 4634929 | 1409132 | | | | |
| 2002 | 5623366 | 1982517 | | | | |
| 2003 | 8952090 | 2588452 | 6363638 | 2907234 | 3194960 | 4192567 |
| 2004 | 11081993 | 3285409 | 7796584 | 3254648 | 4357950 | 5761350 |
| 2005 | 12777972 | 4105706 | 8672266 | 3715525 | 4438723 | 6723758 |
| 2006 | 13734482 | 4426534 | 9307948 | 3871462 | 4640261 | 7551249 |
| 2007 | 15837775 | 5187904 | 10649871 | 4056241 | 5271141 | 8215570 |
| 2008 | 18822936 | 6154060 | 12668876 | 5410313 | 5693385 | 9450542 |
| 2009 | 21951706 | 7046752 | 14904954 | 6018416 | 6091653 | 11127373 |
| 2010 | 26518839 | 9561970 | 16956869 | 6452236 | 6855587 | 13680327 |
| 2011 | 31000218 | 13027234 | 17972984 | 6437025 | 7474806 | 17507040 |
| 2012 | 37227544 | 15973611 | 21253933 | 7785196 | 8518653 | 20595909 |
| 2013 | 42638732 | 18532841 | 24105891 | 8524663 | 9104614 | 22536325 |
| 2014 | 49527010 | 23010823 | 26516187 | 10055306 | 9133973 | 28438054 |
| 2015 | 55563183 | 24720743 | 30842440 | 13551793 | 9300133 | 29768831 |
| 2016 | 58424194 | 26064090 | 32360104 | 16305335 | 8839451 | 30067802 |
| 2017 | 58566453 | 27340047 | 31226406 | 15970399 | 8614761 | 33005389 |
| 2018 比上年增长<br>Increased over the Previous year in 2018 | 10.8 | 12.2 | 9.3 | 26.9 | -11.3 | 10.1 |
| 2019 | 11.6 | 10.7 | 12.6 | 5.2 | 5.6 | 4.8 |

注:1. 2011 年起固定资产投资口径由计划总投资 500 万元以上项目投资及房地产开发投资构成。

2. 项目投资统计口径调整,计划投资 500-5000 万以上项目,由原先形象进度法改为财务支出法统计。2018 年起比上年增长按可比口径计算。

3. 2018 年起基础设施投资口径调整,教育、卫生等剔除并单独设为公共服务投资。

a) Since 2011, the date of investment in fixed Assets was composed by investment projects and investment in Real Estate development of which each is over 5 million yuan.

b) The statistical caliber of project investment was adjusted, the projects which planned to invest 5 million - 50 million ro above, it was changed fron progress method to financial expenditure method. The gronth was calculated at comparable caliber Since 2018.

c) Since 2018, The statistical caliber of infrastructure investment was adjusted, education and health were excluded, and set them as public service investment.

# 7－02 市区固定资产投资总额(1990－2019年)

# Investment in Fixed Assets of Urban District (1990－2019)

单位:万元 (10000 yuan)

| 年份<br>Year | 固定资产投资<br>Investment in Fixed Assets | 房地产开发投资<br>Investment in Real Estate Development | 项目投资<br>Projects Investment | 基础设施投资<br>Investment in Infrastructure | 工业投资<br>Industrial Investment | 民间投资<br>Nongovernment Investment |
|---|---|---|---|---|---|---|
| 1990 | | 12750 | | | | |
| 1991 | | 16509 | | | | |
| 1992 | | 29784 | | | | |
| 1993 | | 115116 | | | | |
| 1994 | | 189357 | | | | |
| 1995 | | 375816 | | | | |
| 1996 | | 439245 | | | | |
| 1997 | | 445316 | | | | |
| 1998 | | 538499 | | | | |
| 1999 | | 636705 | | | | |
| 2000 | | 737950 | | | | |
| 2001 | | 1255605 | | | | |
| 2002 | | 1724128 | | | | |
| 2003 | 7409538 | 2176433 | 5233105 | 2535843 | 2424383 | 3316886 |
| 2004 | 8963515 | 3088508 | 6153009 | 2624214 | 3299235 | 5238005 |
| 2005 | 10358519 | 3485810 | 6872709 | 3071506 | 3247399 | 5802542 |
| 2006 | 10944075 | 3653393 | 7290682 | 3150192 | 3289532 | 5559199 |
| 2007 | 12630099 | 4298687 | 8331412 | 3396807 | 3617512 | 6218211 |
| 2008 | 15184281 | 5269947 | 9914334 | 4726734 | 3676567 | 7076219 |
| 2009 | 17797778 | 6261562 | 11536216 | 5070500 | 3821313 | 8632900 |
| 2010 | 21437496 | 8486495 | 12951001 | 5438685 | 4293707 | 10332997 |
| 2011 | 25202394 | 11409566 | 13792828 | 5451654 | 4801419 | 13302115 |
| 2012 | 30160782 | 13749412 | 16411370 | 6495070 | 5554286 | 15669790 |
| 2013 | 34029665 | 15978470 | 18051195 | 6728552 | 5787728 | 16735292 |
| 2014 | 42572154 | 21128840 | 21443314 | 8010162 | 7100359 | 24220917 |
| 2015 | 47507571 | 22981761 | 24525810 | 10960519 | 6835700 | 25114041 |
| 2016 | 49572744 | 24325359 | 25247385 | 13229143 | 6173050 | 24924679 |
| 2017 | 52395657 | 26449190 | 25946467 | 13447972 | 6718135 | 29402238 |
| 2018 比上年增长<br>Increased over the Previous year in 2018 | 11.5 | 11.7 | 11.4 | 31.1 | －12.6 | 10.2 |
| 2019 | 11.8 | 11.0 | 12.7 | 5.6 | 5.5 | 5.1 |

# 7－03 固定资产投资总额发展指数(2011－2019 年)

# Indices of Investment in Fixed Assets(2011－2019)

(上年＝100)　　(Preceding Year＝100)

| 年份<br>Year | 固定资产投资<br>Investment in Fixed Assets | 第一产业<br>Primary Industry | 第二产业<br>Secondary Industry | 第三产业<br>Primary Industry | 民间投资<br>Nongovernment Investment | 房地产开发投资<br>Investment in Real Estate Development | 基础设施投资<br>Investment in Infrastructure | 工业投资<br>Industrial Investment | 高新技术产业投资<br>High tech industry investment |
|---|---|---|---|---|---|---|---|---|---|
| 2011 | 116.9 | 183.3 | 108.9 | 119.6 | 128.0 | 136.2 | 99.8 | 109.0 | － |
| 2012 | 120.1 | 55.5 | 114.0 | 122.3 | 117.6 | 122.6 | 120.9 | 114.0 | － |
| 2013 | 114.5 | 196.9 | 107.0 | 116.7 | 109.4 | 116.0 | 109.5 | 106.9 | － |
| 2014 | 116.2 | 227.0 | 100.3 | 120.2 | 126.2 | 124.2 | 118.0 | 100.3 | － |
| 2015 | 112.2 | 165.0 | 101.8 | 114.3 | 104.7 | 107.4 | 134.8 | 101.8 | － |
| 2016 | 105.1 | 125.1 | 95.2 | 107.0 | 101.0 | 105.4 | 120.3 | 95.0 | － |
| 2017 | 101.4 | 111.2 | 100.9 | 101.5 | 110.4 | 104.9 | 100.1 | 100.5 | － |
| 2018 | 110.8 | 28.7 | 88.1 | 114.2 | 110.1 | 112.2 | 126.9 | 88.7 | － |
| 2019 | 111.6 | 61.3 | 106.2 | 112.2 | 104.8 | 110.7 | 105.2 | 105.6 | 108.4 |

## 7-04 分地区固定资产投资发展指数(2011-2019年)
## Indices of Investment in Fixed Assets by Region(2011-2019)

(上年=100) (Preceding Year=100)

| 年 份 Year | 全 市 Whole City | 上城区 Shangcheng | 下城区 Xiacheng | 江干区 Jianggan | 拱墅区 Gongshu | 西湖区 Xihu | 高新(滨江)区 Hi-Tech (Binjiang) | 萧山区 Xiaoshan |
|---|---|---|---|---|---|---|---|---|
| 2011 | 116.9 | 67.8 | 101.3 | 119.1 | 135.3 | 120.6 | 115.9 | 115.0 |
| 2012 | 120.1 | 109.4 | 116.6 | 129.8 | 120.7 | 121.5 | 118.9 | 118.9 |
| 2013 | 114.5 | 107.2 | 125.6 | 92.2 | 125.1 | 124.5 | 111.7 | 118.4 |
| 2014 | 116.2 | 121.6 | 66.5 | 118.7 | 124.6 | 118.4 | 118.9 | 116.4 |
| 2015 | 112.2 | 114.1 | 112.5 | 118.5 | 118.9 | 107.2 | 76.5 | 113.2 |
| 2016 | 105.1 | 123.1 | 129.3 | 101.3 | 97.8 | 80.1 | 126.5 | 112.0 |
| 2017 | 101.4 | 111.3 | 102.0 | 87.4 | 75.2 | 120.5 | 79.8 | 104.3 |
| 2018 | 110.8 | 114.3 | 76.9 | 102.1 | 121.2 | 100.0 | 116.8 | 111.7 |
| 2019 | 111.6 | 101.1 | 130.2 | 120.5 | 125.8 | 94.9 | 112.1 | 111.5 |

(上年=100) 7-04 续表 continued (Preceding Year=100)

| 年 份 Year | 余杭区 Yuhang | 富阳区 Fuyang | 临安区 Lin'an | 钱塘新区 Qiantang New Area | 西湖风景名胜区 The West Lake Scenic Zone | 桐庐县 Tonglu | 淳安县 Chun'an | 建德市 Jiande |
|---|---|---|---|---|---|---|---|---|
| 2011 | 118.8 | 106.5 | 118.6 | 116.5 | 46.7 | 115.7 | 118.9 | 120.9 |
| 2012 | 123.9 | 122.5 | 121.6 | 120.7 | 74.2 | 121.9 | 122.0 | 120.8 |
| 2013 | 123.3 | 122.4 | 119.2 | 118.7 | 712.7 | 122.2 | 123.1 | 122.3 |
| 2014 | 124.5 | 122.0 | 120.1 | 106.3 | 125.3 | 121.5 | 121.5 | 121.8 |
| 2015 | 117.0 | 115.3 | 117.1 | 68.2 | 136.9 | 117.9 | 104.3 | 122.7 |
| 2016 | 113.1 | 100.2 | 115.0 | 101.2 | 176.4 | 102.5 | 106.0 | 116.7 |
| 2017 | 108.0 | 87.4 | 109.2 | 111.2 | 28.8 | 89.5 | 108.8 | 115.1 |
| 2018 | 110.0 | 100.5 | 111.2 | 110.6 | 36.2 | 89.3 | 85.4 | 118.6 |
| 2019 | 107.4 | 122.0 | 130.2 | 100.1 | 39.1 | 118.7 | 92.2 | 112.7 |

# 7-05 三次产业固定资产投资(1978-2019年)

# Investment in Fixed Assets Grouped by Three Industries (1978-2019)

单位:万元 (10000 yuan)

| 年份 Year | 绝对数(万元) Absolute Figure(10000 yuan) | | | | 比重(以投资总额为100) Proportion(%) | | |
|---|---|---|---|---|---|---|---|
| | 合计 Total | 第一产业 Primary Industry | 第二产业 Secondary Industry | 第三产业 Tertiary Industry | 第一产业 Primary Industry | 第二产业 Secondary Industry | 第三产业 Tertiary Industry |
| 1978 | 23941 | 2174 | 14455 | 7312 | 9.1 | 60.4 | 30.5 |
| 1979 | 34407 | 2454 | 19927 | 12026 | 7.1 | 57.9 | 35.0 |
| 1980 | 45752 | 1608 | 26211 | 17933 | 3.5 | 57.3 | 39.2 |
| 1981 | 51538 | 850 | 29176 | 21512 | 1.6 | 56.6 | 41.8 |
| 1982 | 66123 | 1352 | 37648 | 27123 | 2.0 | 57.0 | 41.0 |
| 1983 | 68306 | 1297 | 37823 | 29186 | 1.9 | 55.4 | 42.7 |
| 1984 | 93244 | 2831 | 46619 | 43794 | 3.0 | 50.0 | 47.0 |
| 1985 | 141889 | 3207 | 71608 | 67074 | 2.3 | 50.5 | 47.2 |
| 1986 | 182398 | 2265 | 94394 | 85739 | 1.2 | 51.8 | 47.0 |
| 1987 | 200516 | 2994 | 106600 | 90922 | 1.5 | 53.2 | 45.3 |
| 1988 | 205967 | 4746 | 118736 | 82485 | 2.3 | 57.6 | 40.1 |
| 1989 | 202131 | 3038 | 117651 | 81442 | 1.5 | 58.2 | 40.3 |
| 1990 | 229214 | 2181 | 126263 | 100770 | 1.0 | 55.1 | 43.9 |
| 1991 | 255696 | 3204 | 132303 | 120189 | 1.3 | 51.7 | 47.0 |
| 1992 | 384136 | 4424 | 206659 | 173053 | 1.2 | 53.8 | 45.0 |
| 1993 | 825382 | 5650 | 346416 | 473316 | 0.7 | 42.0 | 57.3 |
| 1994 | 1059437 | 3905 | 354672 | 700860 | 0.4 | 33.5 | 66.1 |
| 1995 | 1566280 | 5821 | 534687 | 1025772 | 0.4 | 34.1 | 65.5 |
| 1996 | 1819333 | 3100 | 640273 | 1175960 | 0.2 | 35.2 | 64.6 |
| 1997 | 2139012 | 1712 | 595966 | 1541334 | - | 27.9 | 72.1 |
| 1998 | 2681740 | 4053 | 706948 | 1970739 | 0.2 | 26.4 | 73.4 |
| 1999 | 3233609 | 23546 | 764309 | 2445754 | 0.7 | 23.6 | 75.7 |
| 2000 | 3766473 | 774 | 844334 | 2921365 | - | 22.4 | 77.6 |
| 2001 | 4634929 | 595 | 953494 | 3680840 | - | 20.6 | 79.4 |
| 2002 | 5623366 | 6514 | 1104212 | 4512640 | 0.1 | 19.6 | 80.3 |
| 2003 | 8952090 | 10489 | 3208885 | 5732716 | 0.1 | 35.9 | 64.0 |
| 2004 | 11081993 | 15992 | 4369015 | 6696986 | 0.1 | 39.4 | 60.5 |
| 2005 | 12777972 | 13982 | 4451936 | 8312054 | 0.1 | 34.8 | 65.1 |
| 2006 | 13734482 | 17892 | 4651420 | 9065170 | 0.1 | 33.9 | 66.0 |
| 2007 | 15837775 | 23278 | 5286340 | 10528157 | 0.1 | 33.4 | 66.5 |
| 2008 | 18822936 | 30810 | 5705736 | 13086390 | 0.2 | 30.3 | 69.5 |
| 2009 | 21951706 | 31335 | 6115482 | 15804889 | 0.1 | 27.9 | 72.0 |
| 2010 | 26518839 | 41959 | 6875840 | 19601040 | 0.2 | 25.9 | 73.9 |
| 2011 | 31000218 | 76931 | 7486832 | 23436455 | 0.2 | 24.2 | 75.6 |
| 2012 | 37227544 | 42668 | 8531598 | 28653278 | 0.1 | 22.9 | 77.0 |
| 2013 | 42638732 | 84018 | 9125316 | 33429398 | 0.2 | 21.4 | 78.4 |
| 2014 | 49527010 | 190748 | 9152477 | 40183785 | 0.4 | 18.5 | 81.1 |
| 2015 | 55563183 | 314688 | 9317825 | 45930670 | 0.6 | 16.8 | 82.6 |
| 2016 | 58424194 | 393625 | 8869013 | 49161556 | 0.7 | 15.2 | 84.1 |
| 2017 | 58566453 | 336686 | 8665510 | 49564257 | 0.6 | 14.8 | 84.6 |
| 2018 比上年增长 Increased over the Previous year in 2018 | 10.8 | -71.3 | -11.9 | 14.2 | 0.1 | 9.6 | 90.3 |
| 2019 | 11.6 | -38.7 | 6.2 | 12.2 | 0.0 | 9.2 | 90.8 |

# 7-06 固定资产投资房屋建筑面积及造价(1978-2019年)
# Floor Space of Buildings and Their Cost (1978-2019)

| 年份 Year | 施工面积(万平方米) Floor Space of Buildings Under Construction (10000sq. m) | 住宅 Residential Buildings | 竣工面积(万平方米) Floor Space of Buildings Completed (10000 sq. m) | 住宅 Residential Buildings | 竣工房屋价值(万元) Value of Buildings Completed (10000 yuan) | 住宅 Residential Buildings | 每平方米造价(元) Cost Per Square (yuan) | 住宅 Residential Buildings |
|---|---|---|---|---|---|---|---|---|
| 1978 | | | 101.95 | 39.58 | 8869 | 2810 | 87 | 71 |
| 1979 | | | 150.26 | 68.01 | 13223 | 4965 | 88 | 73 |
| 1980 | 456.54 | | 202.58 | 104.44 | 19448 | 8564 | 96 | 82 |
| 1981 | 507.94 | | 232.25 | 120.35 | 26709 | 12396 | 115 | 103 |
| 1982 | 554.89 | 258.09 | 281.63 | 148.66 | 34095 | 16470 | 121 | 111 |
| 1983 | 531.79 | 244.36 | 247.07 | 125.86 | 33938 | 15494 | 137 | 123 |
| 1984 | 620.71 | 293.21 | 267.85 | 138.71 | 42740 | 18398 | 160 | 133 |
| 1985 | 741.47 | 333.72 | 327.75 | 157.85 | 56561 | 22825 | 173 | 145 |
| 1986 | 674.58 | 278.19 | 338.19 | 160.19 | 50561 | 27338 | 238 | 170 |
| 1987 | 544.64 | 149.07 | 254.73 | 73.16 | 68801 | 14944 | 270 | 204 |
| 1988 | 526.70 | 156.92 | 230.21 | 75.44 | 68407 | 17820 | 297 | 236 |
| 1989 | 420.81 | 116.12 | 202.15 | 64.15 | 69750 | 18200 | 345 | 284 |
| 1990 | 472.59 | 209.50 | 236.44 | 112.77 | 93557 | 34266 | 396 | 304 |
| 1991 | 459.00 | 205.41 | 226.84 | 92.72 | 93158 | 28599 | 411 | 308 |
| 1992 | 604.85 | 301.21 | 262.11 | 114.97 | 116169 | 39834 | 452 | 350 |
| 1993 | 958.91 | 533.01 | 380.29 | 199.96 | 224251 | 105107 | 589 | 525 |
| 1994 | 1069.68 | 613.62 | 460.20 | 274.19 | 375211 | 212705 | 815 | 776 |
| 1995 | 1320.68 | 737.79 | 524.58 | 319.41 | 491705 | 274314 | 937 | 859 |
| 1996 | 1399.70 | 758.00 | 582.70 | 354.50 | 688569 | 370485 | 1182 | 1045 |
| 1997 | 1363.80 | 660.70 | 642.10 | 338.00 | 871361 | 449235 | 1357 | 1329 |
| 1998 | 1456.02 | 743.59 | 515.16 | 271.91 | 709730 | 390624 | 1378 | 1437 |
| 1999 | 1681.71 | 956.15 | 709.10 | 411.44 | 1119141 | 641717 | 1578 | 1560 |
| 2000 | 1721.58 | 949.32 | 744.42 | 419.80 | 1207767 | 709044 | 1622 | 1689 |
| 2001 | 2318.95 | 1251.92 | 830.05 | 402.46 | 1310380 | 679449 | 1579 | 1688 |
| 2002 | 2713.02 | 1586.28 | 890.05 | 492.95 | 1623662 | 956643 | 1820 | 1941 |
| 2003 | 4392.79 | 2083.58 | 1618.01 | 651.58 | 2732763 | 1353422 | 1689 | 2077 |
| 2004 | 5731.48 | 2909.03 | 1865.83 | 717.46 | 2791115 | 1313596 | 1496 | 1831 |
| 2005 | 6671.39 | 3628.34 | 1856.34 | 801.34 | 3265491 | 1865538 | 1759 | 2328 |
| 2006 | 7260.08 | 3747.60 | 1737.51 | 706.13 | 2900836 | 1580689 | 1670 | 2239 |
| 2007 | 7942.07 | 4040.54 | 1849.24 | 858.99 | 3750264 | 2329184 | 2028 | 2712 |
| 2008 | 9471.42 | 4160.27 | 2057.86 | 846.34 | 4113211 | 2171525 | 1999 | 2566 |
| 2009 | 10308.45 | 4441.84 | 2009.90 | 700.63 | 3626421 | 1684092 | 1804 | 2404 |
| 2010 | 12971.81 | 5534.10 | 2695.90 | 902.57 | 5274936 | 2285285 | 1957 | 2532 |
| 2011 | 15982.64 | 6442.52 | 3108.57 | 991.72 | 6209320 | 2498468 | 1997 | 2519 |
| 2012 | 17329.23 | 6938.29 | 2952.06 | 1048.95 | 6015778 | 2485123 | 2038 | 2369 |
| 2013 | 19226.78 | 7392.23 | 3666.67 | 1308.83 | 7744168 | 3530744 | 2112 | 2698 |
| 2014 | 20877.58 | 7757.60 | 4274.87 | 1350.19 | 9613177 | 3951202 | 2249 | 2926 |
| 2015 | 21686.34 | 8163.82 | 4877.76 | 1600.80 | - | - | - | - |
| 2016 | 17896.18 | 7370.57 | 3937.72 | 1443.96 | 12561050 | 5092235 | 3190 | 3527 |
| 2017 | 18807.44 | 6910.48 | 4953.34 | 1470.84 | 15291293 | 6139823 | 3087 | 4174 |
| 2018 | 18880.01 | 7240.20 | 2962.53 | 1110.85 | 12087621 | 5259555 | 4080 | 4735 |
| 2019 | 21556.40 | 7428.54 | 3058.95 | 1032.83 | 12387807 | 4832945 | 4050 | 4679 |

注:2015年竣工房屋价值相关指标取消。

a) Since 2015, the indicators related to floor space of buildings completed have been cancelled.

# 7-07 市区固定资产投资房屋建筑面积及造价(1978-2019年)

## Urban District Floor Space of Buildings and Their Cost (1978-2019)

| 年份 Year | 施工面积(万平方米) Floor Space of Buildings Under Construction (10000 sq. m) | 住宅 Residential Buildings | 竣工面积(万平方米) Floor Space of Buildings Completed (10000sq. m) | 住宅 Residential Buildings | 竣工房屋价值(万元) Value of Buildings Completed (10000 yuan) | 住宅 Residential Buildings | 每平方米造价(元) Cost Per Square (yuan) | 住宅 Residential Buildings |
|---|---|---|---|---|---|---|---|---|
| 1978 | | | 71.56 | 29.06 | 6941 | 2237 | 97 | 77 |
| 1979 | | | 109.23 | 53.37 | 10267 | 4056 | 94 | 76 |
| 1980 | | | 137.11 | 76.73 | 14396 | 6752 | 105 | 88 |
| 1981 | | | 163.36 | 90.12 | 20093 | 9643 | 123 | 107 |
| 1982 | 378.88 | 172.11 | 189.92 | 100.07 | 25200 | 11980 | 133 | 120 |
| 1983 | 376.32 | 169.17 | 157.14 | 81.68 | 24029 | 11045 | 153 | 135 |
| 1984 | 465.27 | 221.72 | 191.13 | 104.55 | 33863 | 14658 | 177 | 140 |
| 1985 | 532.66 | 258.19 | 219.79 | 114.26 | 40344 | 17489 | 184 | 153 |
| 1986 | 465.75 | 203.22 | 219.33 | 116.70 | 58619 | 21149 | 267 | 181 |
| 1987 | 336.85 | 86.05 | 150.59 | 41.72 | 46530 | 9513 | 309 | 228 |
| 1988 | 315.80 | 90.98 | 117.71 | 37.63 | 38501 | 10117 | 330 | 269 |
| 1989 | 253.41 | 56.39 | 99.86 | 28.89 | 38680 | 9087 | 387 | 315 |
| 1990 | 301.82 | 128.50 | 137.88 | 62.47 | 60551 | 20361 | 439 | 326 |
| 1991 | 265.61 | 118.99 | 114.19 | 42.31 | 53819 | 12892 | 471 | 305 |
| 1992 | 329.16 | 190.55 | 115.59 | 57.36 | 55758 | 19706 | 483 | 344 |
| 1993 | 500.08 | 266.80 | 175.22 | 104.83 | 101528 | 53540 | 579 | 511 |
| 1994 | 618.91 | 352.16 | 212.06 | 123.74 | 182730 | 102924 | 862 | 832 |
| 1995 | 821.03 | 463.98 | 244.94 | 152.10 | 250073 | 139666 | 1021 | 918 |
| 1996 | 969.10 | 538.50 | 350.10 | 229.00 | 437239 | 274244 | 1249 | 1196 |
| 1997 | 1017.30 | 485.20 | 442.00 | 232.70 | 675762 | 357624 | 1529 | 1537 |
| 1998 | 1055.24 | 541.41 | 321.17 | 184.18 | 516400 | 317402 | 1608 | 1723 |
| 1999 | 1204.30 | 656.07 | 489.23 | 294.85 | 908844 | 533675 | 1858 | 1810 |
| 2000 | 1176.29 | 617.80 | 497.64 | 269.94 | 916212 | 528385 | 1841 | 1957 |
| 2001 | 2053.02 | 1085.30 | 698.29 | 325.64 | 1193818 | 615802 | 1710 | 1891 |
| 2002 | 2330.97 | 1335.78 | 744.48 | 404.35 | 1483862 | 869969 | 1993 | 2152 |
| 2003 | 3637.82 | 1699.61 | 1325.48 | 516.33 | 2395039 | 1174735 | 1807 | 2275 |
| 2004 | 4740.42 | 2453.87 | 1389.30 | 528.26 | 2257386 | 1068708 | 1625 | 2023 |
| 2005 | 5533.58 | 3039.08 | 1478.07 | 661.56 | 2804402 | 1626514 | 1897 | 2459 |
| 2006 | 5898.15 | 3114.45 | 1327.37 | 580.22 | 2365342 | 1357671 | 1782 | 2340 |
| 2007 | 6496.01 | 3357.18 | 1355.43 | 674.97 | 3063585 | 1992874 | 2260 | 2953 |
| 2008 | 7812.71 | 3466.88 | 1537.69 | 668.13 | 3372465 | 1827426 | 2193 | 2735 |
| 2009 | 8558.17 | 3807.67 | 1398.49 | 537.39 | 2725150 | 1321357 | 1949 | 2459 |
| 2010 | 10738.49 | 4759.75 | 1983.33 | 732.55 | 4255543 | 1927150 | 2146 | 2631 |
| 2011 | 13259.13 | 5451.45 | 2091.12 | 797.96 | 4736356 | 2122126 | 2265 | 2659 |
| 2012 | 14385.57 | 5680.08 | 2169.11 | 889.73 | 4966296 | 2207085 | 2290 | 2481 |
| 2013 | 15693.30 | 5910.71 | 2637.83 | 986.35 | 6074353 | 2822878 | 2303 | 2862 |
| 2014 | 18219.47 | 6591.75 | 3516.92 | 1132.80 | 8406996 | 3536426 | 2390 | 3122 |
| 2015 | 18872.19 | 6972.04 | 3868.26 | 1269.66 | - | - | - | - |
| 2016 | 15655.38 | 6338.80 | 3192.00 | 1205.44 | 10907502 | 4524544 | 3417 | 3753 |
| 2017 | 17404.30 | 6305.16 | 4454.20 | 1332.41 | 14156506 | 5784449 | 3178 | 4341 |
| 2018 | 17812.33 | 6640.67 | 2821.98 | 1056.86 | 12087621 | 5259555 | 4135 | 4810 |
| 2019 | 20365.33 | 6903.07 | 2882.93 | 971.66 | 11911383 | 4618898 | 4132 | 4754 |

# 7-08 分地区
## Investment in Fixed Assets

单位:万元

| 年 份<br>Year | 全 市<br>Whole City | 上城区<br>Shangcheng | 下城区<br>Xiacheng | 江干区<br>Jianggan | 拱墅区<br>Gongshu | 西湖区<br>Xihu | 高新(滨江)区<br>Hi-Tech (Binjiang) |
|---|---|---|---|---|---|---|---|
| 2003 | 8952090 | | | | | | |
| 2004 | 11081993 | | | | | | |
| 2005 | 12777972 | | | | | | |
| 2006 | 13734482 | | | | | | |
| 2007 | 15837775 | | | | | | |
| 2008 | 18822936 | | | | | | |
| 2009 | 21951706 | | | | | | |
| 2010 | 26518839 | 802793 | 1030077 | 2901447 | 1508325 | 2188293 | 1609857 |
| 2011 | 31000218 | 544686 | 1043891 | 3456831 | 2041130 | 2638752 | 1866605 |
| 2012 | 37227544 | 595996 | 1217244 | 4486541 | 2463963 | 3205079 | 2220183 |
| 2013 | 42638732 | 638625 | 1528423 | 4138372 | 3081999 | 3991415 | 2480827 |
| 2014 | 49527010 | 776441 | 1017029 | 4914073 | 3838785 | 4723858 | 2948885 |
| 2015 | 55563183 | 885811 | 1144348 | 5823773 | 4565672 | 5064510 | 2254688 |
| 2016 | 58424194 | 1090808 | 1479399 | 5899757 | 4467059 | 4058658 | 2851746 |
| 2017 | 58566453 | 1214556 | 1509493 | 5158741 | 3327270 | 4889773 | 2274389 |
| 2018 比上年增长<br>Increased over the Previous year in 2018 | 10.8 | 14.3 | -23.1 | 2.1 | 21.2 | 0.0 | 16.8 |
| 2019 | 11.6 | 1.1 | 30.2 | 20.5 | 25.8 | -5.1 | 12.1 |

# 固定资产投资（2003 －2019 年）
# by Region（2003 －2019）

（10000 yuan）

| 萧山区 Xiaoshan | 余杭区 Yuhang | 富阳区 Fuyang | 临安区 Lin'an | 钱塘新区 Qiantang New Area | 西湖风景名胜区 The West Lake Scenic Zone | 桐庐县 Tonglu | 淳安县 Chun'an | 建德市 Jiande |
|---|---|---|---|---|---|---|---|---|
| 1835889 | 1162453 | 563603 | 346980 | | | 250100 | 135275 | 246594 |
| 2246807 | 1478151 | 767880 | 479669 | | | 352987 | 218730 | 299212 |
| 2161067 | 1718028 | 896329 | 525840 | | | 424962 | 275543 | 316779 |
| 2424763 | 1758656 | 1017368 | 600270 | | | 470450 | 324444 | 377875 |
| 2745133 | 1929019 | 1155871 | 673495 | | | 542615 | 403119 | 432576 |
| 3184947 | 2317510 | 1334619 | 665978 | | | 653234 | 475340 | 509484 |
| 3769557 | 2823192 | 1534401 | 763725 | | | 738391 | 542037 | 575374 |
| 4515095 | 3480147 | 1796500 | 956408 | 1732557 | 18393 | 1001737 | 668168 | 658530 |
| 5190805 | 4134743 | 1913712 | 1134746 | 2018316 | 8594 | 1158682 | 794383 | 796301 |
| 6169275 | 5121242 | 2343812 | 1379851 | 2436859 | 6378 | 1412038 | 969471 | 961590 |
| 7307304 | 6312261 | 2868320 | 1644498 | 2891767 | 45458 | 1725986 | 1193796 | 1176467 |
| 8508518 | 7861506 | 3500717 | 1975132 | 3074966 | 56971 | 2096371 | 1450503 | 1432850 |
| 9631238 | 9200016 | 4037889 | 2312053 | 2098220 | 77986 | 2472662 | 1512184 | 1758713 |
| 10783163 | 10403247 | 4043949 | 2659669 | 2123585 | 137576 | 2534994 | 1603624 | 2053163 |
| 11042552 | 11232991 | 3406491 | 2904328 | 2162102 | 39564 | 2133136 | 1744157 | 2293503 |
| 11.7 | 10.0 | 0.5 | 11.2 | 10.6 | -63.8 | -10.7 | -14.6 | 18.6 |
| 11.5 | 7.4 | 22.0 | 30.2 | 0.1 | -60.9 | 18.7 | -7.8 | 12.7 |

# 7-09 分地区分类型固定

## Investment in Fixed Assets

单位:%

| 指标 | Item | 全市 Total | 市区 Urban District |
|---|---|---|---|
| **固定资产投资额** | **Investment in Fixed Assets** | **11.6** | **11.8** |
| #民间投资 | #Private Investment | 4.8 | 5.1 |
| #工业投资 | Industrial Investment | 5.6 | 5.5 |
| #基础设施投资 | Investment in Infrastructure | 5.2 | 5.6 |
| **一、按投资类型分** | **Grouped by Sector** | | |
| 投资项目完成额 | Investment Projects | 12.6 | 12.7 |
| 房地产开发投资完成额 | Real Estate | 10.7 | 11.0 |
| **二、按登记注册类型分** | **Grouped by Status of Registration** | | |
| 内资 | Domestic - funded | 12.4 | 12.6 |
| 国有 | State - owned | -11.0 | -10.9 |
| 集体 | Collective - owned | 82.3 | 87.4 |
| 股份合作 | Cooperative | 31.6 | 47.1 |
| 联营企业 | State Joint Ownership | 1.3 | 1.3 |
| 国有独资公司 | State - owned Corporations | 34.9 | 38.7 |
| 其他有限责任公司 | Other Limited Liability Corporations | 36.0 | 36.4 |
| 股份有限公司 | Share - holding Corporations Ltd. | 17.0 | 25.8 |
| 私营 | Private | -9.1 | -10.2 |
| 其他 | Other | 16.9 | 21.9 |
| 港、澳、台商投资 | Investment from Hong Kong, Macao and Taiwan | -1.3 | 0.2 |
| 外商投资 | Foreign Investment | 11.8 | 11.2 |
| 个体经营 | Individual | -18.8 | - |

## 资产投资(2019 年)
## by Region(2019)

| | | | | 桐庐县 Tonglu | 淳安县 Chun'an | 建德市 Jiande |
|---|---|---|---|---|---|---|
| 萧山区 Xiaoshan | 余杭区 Yuhang | 富阳区 Fuyang | 临安区 Lin'an | | | |
| **11.5** | **7.4** | **22.0** | **30.2** | **18.7** | **-7.8** | **12.7** |
| 8.3 | -7.6 | -2.1 | 38.4 | 18.5 | -30.8 | 2.5 |
| -5.7 | 3.4 | 26.9 | 10.1 | -5.4 | -26.1 | 15.1 |
| 34.1 | -12.5 | 26.0 | -4.6 | 7.0 | 14.0 | -9.7 |
| 20.4 | 8.4 | 43.2 | 8.6 | 13.1 | 2.5 | 14.1 |
| 6.7 | 6.7 | 1.0 | 47.9 | 26.8 | -27.7 | 8.3 |
| 13.0 | 11.5 | 23.5 | 31.2 | 22.6 | -4.8 | 13.0 |
| -42.0 | 27.2 | -40.2 | -47.3 | -23.9 | -25.8 | -0.3 |
| -2.6 | 67.8 | -21.1 | 327.7 | -16.9 | 84.3 | 76.1 |
| – | – | – | – | 182.1 | 64.7 | -80.6 |
| – | – | – | – | – | – | – |
| 59.8 | 12.0 | 110.6 | -18.2 | 8.3 | -47.6 | -15.1 |
| 99.7 | 69.7 | 65.2 | 108.4 | 24.1 | 53.5 | 20.2 |
| 268.8 | -32.4 | 345.2 | 26.1 | 81.9 | -87.2 | -48.6 |
| -12.6 | -26.5 | -25.7 | 29.3 | 28.1 | -44.1 | 14.3 |
| -36.6 | -1.6 | -62.5 | -15.7 | -50.4 | 14.3 | 40.3 |
| 26.5 | -15.3 | -25.5 | 36.0 | -15.6 | -62.0 | -22.4 |
| -36.7 | -0.1 | 7.0 | -57.2 | -23.8 | -53.4 | 90.4 |
| – | – | – | – | – | -87.0 | 43.4 |

单位:%　　7-09 续表

| 指　　标 | Item | 全　　市 Total | 市　　区 Urban District |
|---|---|---|---|
| **三、按行业分** | **Grouped by Sector** | | |
| 农林牧渔业 | Agricultare, Forestry, Animal Husbandry and Fishery | 72.4 | -77.1 |
| 采矿业 | Mining | 129.8 | 44.6 |
| 制造业 | Manufacturing | 3.0 | 3.4 |
| 电力、热力、燃气及水的生产和供应业 | Production and Supply of Electric Power, Heat Power, Gas and Tap Water | 9.5 | 12.9 |
| 建筑业 | Construction | 38.4 | 35.5 |
| 批发和零售业 | Wholesale & Retail Trades | -27.4 | -37.0 |
| 交通运输、仓储和邮政业 | Transportation, Storage and Post | 16.1 | 15.5 |
| 住宿和餐饮业 | Hotels and Catering Services | -39.0 | -52.7 |
| 信息传输、软件和信息技术服务业 | Information Transmission, Softuare and Information Technology | -5.4 | -7.3 |
| 金融业 | Financial Intertnediation | 84.0 | 107.1 |
| 房地产业 | Real Estate | 15.1 | 15.3 |
| 租赁和商务服务业 | Leasing and Business Services | -44.9 | -45.9 |
| 科学研究和技术服务业 | Scientific Research and Technical Service | 263.1 | 294.1 |
| 水利、环境和公共设施管理业 | Management of Water Conservancy, Environment and Public Facilities | -8.7 | -7.9 |
| 居民服务、修理和其他服务业 | Residentid Service, Repairs and Other Service | 314.7 | 282.4 |
| 教育 | Education | 5.3 | 4.7 |
| 卫生和社会工作 | Health Care and Social Welfare | 1.6 | 1.2 |
| 文化、体育和娱乐业 | Culture, Sports and Entertainment | 32.3 | 34.7 |
| 公共管理、社会保障和社会组织 | Public Management, Social Security and Social Organizations | 10.6 | 11.5 |

注:2018 年起采用 2017 版行业代码

continued

| 萧山区 Xiaoshan | 余杭区 Yuhang | 富阳区 Fuyang | 临安区 Lin'an | 桐庐县 Tonglu | 淳安县 Chun'an | 建德市 Jiande |
|---|---|---|---|---|---|---|
| – | – | -87.4 | -64.7 | -31.5 | -66.5 | 992.3 |
| – | – | 96.2 | -11.6 | – | -38.0 | 139.5 |
| -6.8 | 9.4 | 29.0 | 4.1 | -0.9 | -6.4 | 2.5 |
| 22.8 | -29.5 | -12.2 | 134.1 | -69.3 | -49.3 | -9.2 |
| -49.2 | – | – | – | – | – | – |
| – | -71.2 | -71.6 | -10.7 | -35.3 | 28.9 | 361.8 |
| 49.6 | -11.6 | 58.9 | 14.7 | 14.8 | 31.1 | 13.4 |
| -46.1 | -78.9 | – | 64.8 | -14.7 | -71.4 | 14.5 |
| 205.6 | -5.8 | -61.4 | -75.5 | – | -27.4 | -32.2 |
| 268.1 | – | – | – | – | – | -56.0 |
| 10.0 | 12.6 | 8.3 | 49.3 | 32.1 | -25.0 | 19.6 |
| -72.0 | -14.5 | -90.5 | – | -49.1 | 26.8 | -31.4 |
| 1286.1 | 434.0 | 1458.2 | 220.7 | 508.4 | 44.0 | -47.7 |
| 10.8 | -4.4 | 12.8 | -18.0 | 9.7 | -21.2 | -18.8 |
| – | 328.0 | – | -50.4 | – | – | – |
| -10.3 | 20.8 | 232.7 | 262.2 | -6.8 | -3.7 | 114.4 |
| -30.7 | 46.3 | 545.2 | 110.8 | -24.2 | -72.5 | 146.6 |
| 95.8 | -58.6 | 23194.9 | -61.3 | 50.5 | -8.8 | 9.5 |
| 32.5 | 50.0 | 79.2 | -93.2 | -75.7 | 100.6 | 177.4 |

a) Note: The" classification of National Economic Industries 2017" was applied Since 2018.

# 7－10 分地区分类型

## Investment in Industrial

单位:%

| 指标 | Item | 全市 Total | 市区 Urban District 合计 Total |
|---|---|---|---|
| **总计** | **Total** | **5.6** | **5.5** |
| #技术改造投资 | Investment in Technique Innovation | 2.1 | 2.1 |
| **一、按登记注册类型分** | **Grouped by Status of Registration** | | |
| 内资 | Domestic－funded | 4.9 | 4.7 |
| 国有 | State－owned | 6.8 | 7.1 |
| 集体 | Collective－owned | 4086.0 | 5124.8 |
| 股份合作 | Cooperative | － | － |
| 联营企业 | State Joint Ownership | 1.3 | 1.3 |
| 国有独资公司 | State－funded Corporations | －21.4 | －24.8 |
| 其他有限责任公司 | Other Limited Liability Corporations | 2.6 | －1.3 |
| 股份有限公司 | Share－holding Corporations Ltd. | 34.1 | 60.7 |
| 私营 | Private | 2.5 | 2.2 |
| 其他 | Other | 45.9 | －25.7 |
| 港、澳、台商投资 | Investment from Hong Kong, Macao and Taiwan | －8.4 | －5.6 |
| 外商投资 | Foreign Investment | 20.9 | 19.6 |
| 个体经营 | Individual | 9.2 | － |
| **二、按行业分** | **Grouped by Sector** | | |
| 采矿业 | Mining | 129.8 | 44.6 |
| 制造业 | Manufacturing | 3.0 | 3.4 |
| #农副食品加工业 | Processing of Food from Agricultural Products Processing | －34.6 | －49.1 |
| 食品制造业 | Food Manufacturing | 103.0 | 80.9 |
| 酒、饮料和精制茶制造业 | Wine, Beverage and Tea Manufacturing | 22.4 | 23.8 |
| 烟草制品业 | Tobacco Processing | － | － |
| 纺织业 | Textile Processing | －23.2 | －24.3 |
| 纺织服装、服饰业 | Textile Products and Costume Industry | 24.1 | 19.8 |

## 工业投资(2019 年)
## Sector by Region(2019)

| 萧山区 Xiaoshan | 余杭区 Yuhang | 富阳区 Fuyang | 临安区 Lin'an | 桐庐县 Tonglu | 淳安县 Chun'an | 建德市 Jiande |
|---|---|---|---|---|---|---|
| **-5.7** | **3.4** | **26.9** | **10.1** | **-5.4** | **-26.1** | **15.1** |
| 0.1 | -1.9 | 37.6 | 26.8 | -16.9 | -38.5 | 17.5 |
| | | | | | | |
| -11.5 | 11.4 | 26.5 | 8.9 | -4.9 | -12.8 | 14.0 |
| – | -22.1 | – | 78.1 | – | 230.5 | -30.2 |
| – | 857.3 | – | – | – | – | – |
| – | – | – | – | – | – | – |
| – | – | – | – | – | – | – |
| 997.3 | -45.8 | -81.5 | 47.4 | -42.2 | 122.5 | – |
| -52.2 | 37.4 | -9.0 | 122.6 | -28.9 | 61.3 | 64.8 |
| 275.1 | 14.4 | 117.5 | 4.4 | -80.2 | – | -59.5 |
| -10.1 | -0.6 | 76.3 | -17.2 | 27.3 | -52.6 | 5.2 |
| – | – | – | – | – | – | – |
| 26.6 | -32.4 | 338.3 | 216.3 | -5.2 | -79.1 | -15.9 |
| 44.4 | -9.1 | 6.6 | -57.5 | -24.2 | – | 90.4 |
| – | – | – | – | – | – | 43.4 |
| | | | | | | |
| – | – | 96.2 | -11.6 | – | -38.0 | 139.5 |
| -6.8 | 9.4 | 29.0 | 4.1 | -0.9 | -6.4 | 2.5 |
| – | -61.6 | 62.1 | 133.1 | 288.6 | – | 4.4 |
| 197.7 | 431.3 | – | 17.5 | 290.8 | – | 17.9 |
| -50.9 | 201.6 | – | – | 410.1 | -45.0 | 16.4 |
| – | – | – | – | – | – | – |
| -32.7 | 1.2 | -74.0 | -84.8 | – | -65.2 | -7.3 |
| -72.1 | 84.6 | – | -85.8 | 2253.3 | – | 110.6 |

| 指标 | Item | 全市 Total | 市区 Urban District 合计 Total |
|---|---|---|---|
| 皮革、毛皮、羽毛及其制品和制造业 | Leather, Furs, Down and Related Products | -12.9 | -12.4 |
| 木材加工和木、竹、藤、棕、草制品业 | Timber Processing, Bamboo, Cane, Palm Fiber and Straw Products | -11.2 | -53.2 |
| 家具制造业 | Furniture Manufacturing | 151.4 | 125.9 |
| 造纸和纸制品业 | Paper Making and Paper Products | -0.5 | -3.0 |
| 印刷业和记录媒介复制业 | Printing and Reproduction of Recording media | -22.6 | -9.5 |
| 文教、工美、体育和娱乐用品制造业 | Cultural, Educational and Sports Goods | 11.2 | 14.3 |
| 石油加工、炼焦和核燃料加工业 | Petroleum and Nuclear Fuel Processing | -63.5 | 305.9 |
| 化学原料和化学制品制造业 | Raw Chemical Material and Chemical Products | -16.1 | -0.4 |
| 医药制造业 | Medical and Pharmaceutical Products | 12.6 | 28.6 |
| 化学纤维制造业 | Chemical Fiber | -35.8 | -35.9 |
| 橡胶和塑料制品业 | Rubber and Plastic Products | -5.1 | -4.1 |
| 非金属矿物制品业 | Nonmetal Mineral Products | 60.2 | 145.1 |
| 黑色金属冶炼和压延加工业 | Ferrous Metals Smelting and Pressing | 312.3 | 312.3 |
| 有色金属冶炼和压延加工业 | Nonferrous Metal Smelting and Pressing | 113.7 | 78.0 |
| 金属制品业 | Metal Products | -14.5 | -20.9 |
| 通用设备制造业 | General Purpose Machinery | 32.5 | 26.0 |
| 专业设备制造业 | Special Purpose Machinery | 39.0 | 33.6 |
| 汽车制造业 | Automobile Manufacturing | -25.8 | -26.2 |
| 铁路、船舶、航空航天和其他运输设备制造业 | Railway, Watercraft, Avigation Spaceflight and other Equipment Manufacturing | 78.1 | 92.8 |
| 电气机械和器材制造业 | Electric Equipment and Machinery | 23.2 | 21.7 |
| 计算机、通信和其他电子设备制造业 | Computers, Telecommunications and other Electronic Equipment Manufacturing | -12.5 | -7.1 |
| 仪器仪表制造业 | Instruments and Meters Manufacturing | -20.7 | -20.7 |
| 其他制造业 | Other Manufacturing | -13.6 | -57.9 |
| 废弃资源综合利用业 | Multiple Utilization of Waste Resouces | 26.4 | -7.1 |
| 金属制品、机械和设备修理业 | Metal Products, Machinery and Equipment Repair | -65.1 | -46.0 |
| 电力、燃气及水的生产和供应业 | Production and Supply of Electric Power, Heat Power, Gas and Tap Water | 9.5 | 12.9 |

continued

| 萧山区 Xiaoshan | 余杭区 Yuhang | 富阳区 Fuyang | 临安区 Lin'an | 桐庐县 Tonglu | 淳安县 Chun'an | 建德市 Jiande |
|---|---|---|---|---|---|---|
| -52.3 | - | -53.5 | 78.7 | - | 161.8 | 184.4 |
| 343.8 | -53.8 | 115.4 | 657.6 | - | - | 113.5 |
| 134.4 | -39.6 | 67.0 | 4.7 | -17.0 | - | - |
| -53.4 | -12.6 | - | -53.2 | -74.8 | - | - |
| 395.8 | -47.8 | -87.5 | - | 79.6 | - | -76.3 |
| - | - | - | - | - | - | -88.9 |
| -64.8 | -46.8 | 174.0 | 9.9 | 135.6 | -15.8 | -38.9 |
| 217.7 | -25.1 | -65.3 | 265.0 | -29.0 | -91.8 | -34.8 |
| -3.3 | -62.6 | - | - | - | - | - |
| -46.1 | 8.1 | 18.0 | -37.4 | -76.8 | - | 5.1 |
| 257.0 | 5.7 | 245.2 | 706.5 | 51.4 | -48.1 | -37.7 |
| 525.1 | -92.7 | - | - | - | - | - |
| - | 73.1 | - | -30.4 | - | - | 680.2 |
| -30.8 | -19.6 | -26.2 | 74.0 | -88.8 | 74.8 | 158.4 |
| 15.4 | 34.7 | 122.9 | 119.2 | 58.7 | - | 222.0 |
| -8.0 | 32.7 | 921.8 | 378.7 | 30.6 | - | 578.3 |
| -47.6 | 37.0 | 1593.8 | -89.5 | -51.7 | -96.8 | 10.1 |
| 326.2 | 132.7 | 1074.9 | -95.9 | - | - | - |
| 46.4 | 0.4 | 110.4 | -6.8 | 160.6 | 305.3 | -26.8 |
| 112.5 | 38.3 | -25.8 | -44.8 | -57.2 | 272.5 | 86.4 |
| - | -14.2 | 48.6 | -11.9 | - | - | - |
| -59.5 | -61.5 | -72.6 | - | 387.0 | 79.3 | 171.0 |
| -13.6 | 255.1 | -94.7 | -75.4 | - | - | 998.6 |
| -50.5 | -42.5 | - | - | - | - | -95.9 |
| 22.8 | 29.5 | -12.2 | 134.1 | -69.3 | -49.3 | -9.2 |

# 7－11 分地区房地产
# Investment in Real Estate

| 指　标 | Item | 全市 Total | 市区 Urban District 合计 Total |
|---|---|---|---|
| **房地产开发投资额　（万元）** | **Investment in Real Estate Development (10000 yuan)** | **33967460** | **32781983** |
| 住宅　（万元） | Residential Buildings (10000 yuan) | 21987044 | 21045301 |
| 办公楼　（万元） | Office Buildings (10000 yuan) | 2793937 | 2776451 |
| 商业营业用房　（万元） | Buildings for Business Use (10000 yuan) | 2876631 | 2768599 |
| 其他　（万元） | Others (10000 yuan) | 6309848 | 6191632 |
| **房屋建筑面积** | **Floor space of Buildings** | | |
| 施工面积　（万平方米） | Under Construction (10000 sq. m) | 11996 | 11232 |
| #住宅　（万平方米） | #Residential Buildings (10000 sq. m) | 6263 | 5757 |
| 新开工面积　（万平方米） | Started This Year (10000 sq. m) | 2435 | 2326 |
| #住宅　（万平方米） | #Residential Buildings (10000 sq. m) | 1347 | 1282 |
| 竣工面积　（万平方米） | Construction Completed (10000 sq. m) | 1728 | 1642 |
| #住宅　（万平方米） | #Residential Buildings (10000 sq. m) | 964 | 903 |
| **商品房销售情况** | **Selling of Commercialized Buildings** | | |
| 销售金额　（万元） | Total Sales of Buildings (10000 yuan) | 39236384 | 37863461 |
| #住宅　（万元） | #Residential Buildings (10000 yuan) | 34061040 | 32802654 |
| 现房销售额　（万元） | Sales of Completed Buildings (10000 yuan) | 2785181 | 2677680 |
| #住宅　（万元） | #Residential Buildings (10000 yuan) | 1518719 | 1467200 |
| 期房销售金额　（万元） | Sales of Future Buildings (10000 yuan) | 36451203 | 35185781 |
| #住宅　（万元） | #Residential Buildings (10000 yuan) | 32542321 | 31335454 |
| 销售面积　（万平方米） | Floor Space of Buildings Sold (10000 sq. m) | 1514 | 1413 |
| #住宅　（万平方米） | #Residential Buildings (10000 sq. m) | 1284 | 1198 |
| 现房销售面积　（万平方米） | Floor Space of Completed Buildings Sold (10000 sq. m) | 132 | 119 |
| #住宅　（万平方米） | #Residential Buildings (10000 sq. m) | 69 | 65 |
| 期房销售面积　（万平方米） | Floor Space of Futures Buildings Sold (10000 sq. m) | 1381 | 1295 |
| #住宅　（万平方米） | #Residential Buildings (10000 sq. m) | 1215 | 1133 |

# 开发投资(2019 年)
# Development by Region(2019)

| | | | | 桐庐县<br>Tonglu | 淳安县<br>Chun'an | 建德市<br>Jiande |
|---|---|---|---|---|---|---|
| 萧山区<br>Xiaoshan | 余杭区<br>Yuhang | 富阳区<br>Fuyang | 临安区<br>Lin'an | | | |
| **6740100** | **6907475** | **1311502** | **1915331** | **476479** | **257920** | **451078** |
| 4621285 | 4684390 | 1087466 | 1351558 | 415902 | 206461 | 319380 |
| 551981 | 516785 | 82826 | 79419 | 8568 | 2149 | 6769 |
| 405362 | 357350 | 67405 | 150652 | 44587 | 22825 | 40620 |
| 1161472 | 1348950 | 73805 | 333702 | 7422 | 26485 | 84309 |
| | | | | | | |
| 2278 | 2844 | 679 | 1085 | 220 | 229 | 316 |
| 1212 | 1672 | 455 | 692 | 157 | 144 | 204 |
| 449 | 389 | 233 | 458 | 29 | 32 | 48 |
| 267 | 224 | 163 | 269 | 24 | 17 | 24 |
| 451 | 311 | 110 | 165 | 27 | 23 | 35 |
| 264 | 184 | 68 | 123 | 18 | 21 | 21 |
| | | | | | | |
| 8005758 | 8816400 | 2446885 | 3720193 | 575696 | 365120 | 432107 |
| 7281845 | 8204335 | 2159670 | 3560668 | 505150 | 354710 | 398526 |
| 246846 | 792592 | 128738 | 67275 | 73025 | 5848 | 28628 |
| 98241 | 698666 | 67196 | 53718 | 38315 | 5796 | 7408 |
| 7758912 | 8023808 | 2318147 | 3652918 | 502671 | 359272 | 403479 |
| 7183604 | 7505669 | 2092474 | 3506950 | 466835 | 348914 | 391118 |
| 271 | 374 | 131 | 218 | 36 | 25 | 39 |
| 239 | 337 | 114 | 206 | 28 | 24 | 34 |
| 12 | 40 | 9 | 6 | 9 | 1 | 4 |
| 4 | 34 | 4 | 5 | 3 | 1 | 1 |
| 259 | 334 | 122 | 212 | 28 | 25 | 34 |
| 235 | 303 | 109 | 202 | 25 | 24 | 33 |

# 7－12　房屋建筑面积及造价(2019年)

## Floor Space of Buildings and Their Cost(2019)

| 指　　标 | Item | 施工面积(万平方米) Floor Space of Buildings Under Construction (10000 sq. m) | 竣工面积(万平方米) Floor Space of Buildings Completed (10000 sq. m) | 竣工房屋的价值(万元) Value of Buildings Completed (10000 yuan) | 每平方米造价(元) Cost Per Square Meter (yuan) |
|---|---|---|---|---|---|
| **全　　市** | **Total** | | | | |
| **房屋建筑面积合计** | **Floor Space of Buildings** | **21556** | **3059** | **12387807** | **4050** |
| #住宅 | #Residential Buildings | 7429 | 1033 | 4832945 | 4679 |
| 房地产开发 | Real Estate Development | 11996 | 1728 | 8125344 | 4703 |
| #住宅 | #Residential Buildings | 6263 | 964 | 4651713 | 4826 |
| **市　　区** | **Urban District** | | | | |
| **房屋建筑面积合计** | **Floor Space of Buildings** | **20365** | **2883** | **11911383** | **4132** |
| #住宅 | #Residential Buildings | 6903 | 972 | 4618898 | 4754 |
| 房地产开发 | Real Estate Development | 11232 | 1642 | 7844211 | 4776 |
| #住宅 | #Residential Buildings | 5757 | 903 | 4438753 | 4915 |
| **#萧 山 区** | **Xiaoshan** | | | | |
| **房屋建筑面积合计** | **Total Floor Space of Buildings** | **3836** | **667** | **2015103** | **3020** |
| #住宅 | #Residential Buildings | 1510 | 306 | 998454 | 3265 |
| 房地产开发 | Real Estate Development | 2278 | 451 | 1424832 | 3163 |
| #住宅 | #Residential Buildings | 1212 | 264 | 856092 | 3245 |
| **余 杭 区** | **Yuhang** | | | | |
| **房屋建筑面积合计** | **Total Floor Space of Buildings** | **5061** | **672** | **2919028** | **4341** |
| #住宅 | #Residential Buildings | 1847 | 204 | 1329714 | 6523 |
| 房地产开发 | Real Estate Development | 2844 | 311 | 1834985 | 5896 |
| #住宅 | #Residential Buildings | 1672 | 184 | 1320622 | 7168 |

7－12 续表 continued

| 指 标 | Item | 施工面积（万平方米）Floor Space of Buildings Under Construction (10000 sq. m) | 竣工面积（万平方米）Floor Space of Buildings Completed (10000 sq. m) | 竣工房屋的价值（万元）Value of Buildings Completed (10000 yuan) | 每平方米造价（元）Cost Per Square Meter (yuan) |
|---|---|---|---|---|---|
| **富阳区** | **Fuyang** | | | | |
| **房屋建筑面积合计** | **Total Floor Space of Buildings** | **1154** | **171** | **474548** | **2773** |
| #住宅 | #Residential Buildings | 596 | 68 | 283449 | 4160 |
| 房地产开发 | Real Estate Development | 679 | 110 | 367250 | 3331 |
| #住宅 | #Residential Buildings | 455 | 68 | 281750 | 4172 |
| **临安区** | **Lin'an** | | | | |
| **房屋建筑面积合计** | **Total Floor Space of Buildings** | **1465** | **213** | **676851** | **3179** |
| #住宅 | #Residential Buildings | 737 | 123 | 455508 | 3693 |
| 房地产开发 | Real Estate Development | 1085 | 165 | 585210 | 3557 |
| #住宅 | #Residential Buildings | 692 | 123 | 455508 | 3693 |
| **桐庐县** | **Tonglu** | | | | |
| **房屋建筑面积合计** | **Total Floor Space of Buildings** | **445** | **55** | **207665** | **3790** |
| #住宅 | #Residential Buildings | 158 | 19 | 86834 | 4626 |
| 房地产开发 | Real Estate Development | 220 | 27 | 121005 | 4420 |
| #住宅 | #Residential Buildings | 157 | 18 | 83937 | 4653 |
| **淳安县** | **Chun'an** | | | | |
| **房屋建筑面积合计** | **Total Floor Space of Buildings** | **258** | **31** | **113427** | **3718** |
| #住宅 | #Residential Buildings | 146 | 21 | 89950 | 4292 |
| 房地产开发 | Real Estate Development | 229 | 23 | 98979 | 4311 |
| #住宅 | #Residential Buildings | 144 | 21 | 89740 | 4307 |
| **建德市** | **Jiande** | | | | |
| **房屋建筑面积合计** | **Total Floor Space of Buildings** | **488** | **91** | **155332** | **1712** |
| #住宅 | #Residential Buildings | 222 | 21 | 37263 | 1738 |
| 房地产开发 | Real Estate Development | 316 | 35 | 61149 | 1757 |
| #住宅 | #Residential Buildings | 204 | 21 | 37263 | 1738 |

# 7－13 分注册类型和资质等级

## Financial Statistics on Enterprises for Real Estate Development

单位：万元

| 项　　目 | Item | 法人企业数(个) Number of Enterprises (unit) | 年末 Asset and | | |
|---|---|---|---|---|---|
| | | | 流动资产合计 Circulating Funds | 应收账款 Account Receivable | 固定资产合计 Fixed Assets |
| **总计** | **Total** | **1631** | **219720837** | **3865040** | **4214885** |
| **一、按登记注册类型分组** | **Grouped by Registration Status** | | | | |
| 内资企业 | Domestic Funded | 1509 | 190024433 | 3236423 | 2732408 |
| 国有企业 | State－owned | 5 | 532896 | 5584 | 610 |
| 集体企业 | Collective－owned | 1 | | | |
| 股份合作企业 | Share－holding Cooperative Enterprises | | | | |
| 联营企业 | Joint Venture | 1 | 62849 | 209 | 399 |
| 有限责任公司 | Limited Liability Corporations | 825 | 86942386 | 1343623 | 1403215 |
| 股份有限公司 | Share－holding Corporations Ltd. | 23 | 4615721 | 12985 | 36701 |
| 私营企业 | Private Enterprises | 653 | 97870581 | 1874022 | 1291482 |
| 其他企业 | Other Enterprises | | | | |
| 港澳台商投资企业 | Funded from Hong Kong, Macao and Taiwan | 91 | 14496070 | 436466 | 1004449 |
| 外商投资企业 | Foreign Funded | 31 | 15200334 | 192150 | 478029 |
| **二、按企业资质等级分** | **Grouped by Qualification Grade** | | | | |
| 一级 | Grade Ⅰ | 39 | 20487369 | 340083 | 110052 |
| 二级 | Grade Ⅱ | 89 | 9709611 | 325281 | 306290 |
| 三级 | Grade Ⅲ | 132 | 11797750 | 178477 | 394643 |
| 四级 | Grade Ⅳ | 44 | 1366713 | 16250 | 14817 |
| 暂定 | Tentative | 797 | 105082611 | 2149259 | 2043750 |
| 其他 | Others | 530 | 71276782 | 855690 | 1345334 |

# 房地产开发企业财务状况(2019年)

# Grouped by Registration Status and Qualification Grade(2019)

(10000 yuan)

| 资产负债 Liabilities at Year－end | | | | | | 所有者权益合计 Creditors´ Equity | |
|---|---|---|---|---|---|---|---|
| 固定资产原价 Orginal Value of Fixed Assets | 累计折旧 Accumulated Depreciation | #本年折旧 Depreciation This Year | 在建工程 Projects wnder Construction | 资产合计 Total Assets | 负债合计 Total Liabilities | | 实收资本 Capital Hold |
| **5110733** | **895848** | **189322** | **6351359** | **262670925** | **203673872** | **58997052** | **39266675** |
| 3418582 | 686175 | 117404 | 6310445 | 223295173 | 178272798 | 45022375 | 30101495 |
| 1894 | 1284 | 182 | | 542776 | 516616 | 26160 | 13715 |
| 1387 | 988 | 60 | | 93560 | 41666 | 51894 | 1800 |
| 1686217 | 283003 | 50015 | 6123180 | 110049683 | 84909746 | 25139937 | 16558425 |
| 67071 | 30369 | 3208 | 656 | 6516037 | 3786358 | 2729679 | 770621 |
| 1662013 | 370531 | 63940 | 186609 | 106093118 | 89018412 | 17074706 | 12756934 |
| 1151781 | 147332 | 46471 | 582 | 18904158 | 9665483 | 9238674 | 7464247 |
| 540370 | 62341 | 25447 | 40333 | 20471594 | 15735591 | 4736004 | 1700933 |
| 201274 | 91222 | 8638 | 2813 | 31588540 | 22428292 | 9160247 | 2218342 |
| 419570 | 113280 | 14670 | 3936101 | 18250213 | 12718727 | 5531487 | 2122694 |
| 548001 | 153359 | 21899 | 834324 | 14482671 | 11480597 | 3002075 | 1429923 |
| 26782 | 11965 | 1260 | 453297 | 2298624 | 2006334 | 292289 | 127711 |
| 2372371 | 328622 | 93801 | 275513 | 117190755 | 92953683 | 24237071 | 19375444 |
| 1542735 | 197402 | 49054 | 849313 | 78860122 | 62086239 | 16773884 | 13992562 |

| 项　　目 | Item | 营业收入 Revenue of Business | #主营业务收入 Main Revenue of Business | 营业成本 Operating Costs | #主营业务成本 Main Cost of Business |
|---|---|---|---|---|---|
| **总计** | **Total** | **30329029** | **29328447** | **21031826** | **20487245** |
| **一、按登记注册类型分组** | **Grouped by Registration Status** | | | | |
| 内资企业 | Domestic Funded | 27008347 | 26346633 | 19002524 | 18570607 |
| 国有企业 | State－owned | 13722 | 12293 | 9383 | 8814 |
| 集体企业 | Collective－owned | | | | |
| 股份合作企业 | Share－holding Cooperative Enterprises | | | | |
| 联营企业 | Joint Venture | 56 | 56 | 12 | 12 |
| 有限责任公司 | Limited Liability Corporations | 10679545 | 10331034 | 7659220 | 7345915 |
| 股份有限公司 | Share－holding Corporations Ltd. | 88914 | 88914 | 24586 | 24586 |
| 私营企业 | Private Enterprises | 16226111 | 15914337 | 11309323 | 11191280 |
| 其他企业 | Other Enterprises | | | | |
| 港澳台商投资企业 | Funded from Hong Kong, Macao and Taiwan | 2807204 | 2508587 | 1695937 | 1584957 |
| 外商投资企业 | Foreign Funded | 513478 | 473228 | 333365 | 331681 |
| **二、按企业资质等级分** | **Grouped by Qualification Grade** | | | | |
| 一级 | Grade Ⅰ | 889145 | 678935 | 478759 | 276509 |
| 二级 | Grade Ⅱ | 1425992 | 1396610 | 895248 | 891027 |
| 三级 | Grade Ⅲ | 1184334 | 1157177 | 754277 | 744029 |
| 四级 | Grade Ⅳ | 62991 | 62796 | 47800 | 47654 |
| 暂定 | Tentative | 16540584 | 15990345 | 11464255 | 11274974 |
| 其他 | Others | 10225984 | 10042586 | 7391487 | 7253053 |

continued (10000 yuan)

| 营业税金及附加 Main Sales Tax and Extra Charges | 销售费用 Cost of Sales | 管理费用 Administration Cost | 财务费用 Financil Cost | #利息支出 Interest Expenditure | 营业利润 Management Profits | 利润总额 Total Profits | 应交所得税 Income Tax |
|---|---|---|---|---|---|---|---|
| **1709339** | **1195313** | **1244414** | **611201** | **405092** | **5746293** | **5545359** | **1217360** |
| | | | | | | | |
| 1462795 | 1058941 | 1067486 | 600049 | 676837 | 4794266 | 4679117 | 1032705 |
| 344 | 43 | 1691 | | | 2804 | 2973 | 570 |
| | | | | | | | |
| | | | | | | | |
| 31 | 29 | 1416 | | | | | 55 |
| 561771 | 385698 | 460685 | 214707 | 352345 | 2007526 | 2005584 | 324058 |
| 3939 | 2507 | 21563 | 15977 | 50216 | 123776 | 125930 | 21411 |
| 896710 | 670664 | 582132 | 370124 | 274276 | 2660913 | 2545408 | 686611 |
| | | | | | | | |
| 204771 | 80505 | 78383 | 60036 | 71174 | 767837 | 704676 | 170916 |
| 41773 | 55866 | 98545 | | | 184189 | 161566 | 13739 |
| | | | | | | | |
| 21409 | 36353 | 167416 | 2028 | | 812617 | 815427 | 58302 |
| 64825 | 45511 | 96745 | 45721 | 59023 | 301351 | 285193 | 42558 |
| 95490 | 39958 | 90670 | 35652 | 46777 | 262455 | 268255 | 60148 |
| 1883 | 2981 | 5774 | 1857 | 1935 | 3249 | 5815 | 1095 |
| 991513 | 700411 | 578137 | 372913 | 298579 | 2751642 | 2598319 | 595408 |
| 534219 | 370100 | 305672 | 153030 | 166727 | 1614979 | 1572350 | 459849 |

# 7 - 14 分行业基础设施投资(2010 - 2019 年)

## Investment in Infrastructure by Sector(2010 - 2019)

单位:亿元 (100 million yuan)

| 年 份 Year | 基础设施投资 Investment in Infrastructure | 水利、环境和公共设施 Water, Environment and Public Facilities | 电力、燃气及水的生产供应业 Produotion and supply of Electricity, Gas & Water | 交通运输、仓储和邮政业 Transportation, Storage and Post | 电信和其他信息传输服务业 Telecommunications and Other Information Transmission Services | 教育设施 Education Facilities | 卫生设施 Sanitary Facilities |
|---|---|---|---|---|---|---|---|
| 2010 | 6452236 | 2593603 | 682482 | 2415265 | 162166 | 339381 | 165668 |
| 2011 | 6437025 | 2529677 | 809813 | 2193350 | 142099 | 382672 | 167024 |
| 2012 | 7785196 | 2725934 | 1275603 | 2572604 | 162947 | 572350 | 201913 |
| 2013 | 8524663 | 3486809 | 1167072 | 2375342 | 199444 | 643681 | 261722 |
| 2014 | 10055306 | 3940406 | 1131323 | 3129697 | 180788 | 959814 | 241614 |
| 2015 | 13551793 | 5899889 | 1616380 | 3892605 | 201924 | 1234331 | 231015 |
| 2016 | 16305335 | 8101751 | 1696715 | 3887608 | 231813 | 1587853 | 358314 |
| 2017 | 15970399 | 6596611 | 1502546 | 5058477 | 229410 | 1627072 | 396390 |
| 2018 比上年增长 Increased over the Previous year in 2018 | 26.9 | 4.0 | -12.9 | 63.3 | 19.9 | 11.5 | -24.4 |
| 2019 | 5.2 | -8.7 | 9.5 | 16.9 | -11.6 | 5.3 | 16.5 |

注:2018 年起基础设施投资口径调整,教育、卫生等剔除并单独设为公共服务投资。

a) Since 2018, The statistical caliber of infrastructure investment was adjusted, education and health were excluded, and set them as public service investment.

## 7-15 分地区房地产开发企业商品房屋销售面积和销售额(2016-2019年)
## Sales Area and Sales Volume of Commercial Housing of Real Estate Development Enterprises by Region(2016-2019)

| 城市 | City | 销售面积(万平方米) Sales Area(10,000 sq. m) | | | | 销售额(亿元) Sales Volume(100 million yuan) | | | |
|---|---|---|---|---|---|---|---|---|---|
| | | 2016年 | 2017年 | 2018年 | 2019年 | 2016年 | 2017年 | 2018年 | 2019年 |
| **全市** | **Total** | **2326.69** | **2053.67** | **1675.50** | **1513.62** | **3665** | **4180** | **4008** | **3924** |
| #上城区 | Shangcheng | 17.42 | 4.17 | 22.40 | 20.70 | 71 | 21 | 152 | 125 |
| 下城区 | Xiacheng | 35.66 | 30.62 | 18.00 | 4.54 | 82 | 102 | 86 | 22 |
| 江干区 | Jianggan | 331.72 | 214.76 | 130.23 | 128.40 | 728 | 615 | 437 | 483 |
| 拱墅区 | Gongshu | 149.62 | 163.69 | 79.65 | 97.59 | 391 | 509 | 287 | 361 |
| 西湖区 | Xihu | 176.82 | 143.74 | 102.66 | 54.66 | 358 | 365 | 294 | 183 |
| 高新(滨江)区 | Hi-Tech (Binjiang) | 91.77 | 52.37 | 42.76 | 35.55 | 209 | 153 | 174 | 153 |
| 萧山区 | Xiaoshan | 393.01 | 438.70 | 400.85 | 270.90 | 584 | 992 | 988 | 801 |
| 余杭区 | Yuhang | 679.87 | 525.23 | 443.92 | 373.52 | 805 | 895 | 949 | 882 |
| 富阳区 | Fuyang | 110.62 | 110.69 | 129.66 | 131.03 | 128 | 147 | 225 | 245 |
| 临安区 | Lin'an | 127.14 | 139.37 | 141.81 | 218.00 | 106 | 162 | 201 | 372 |
| 钱塘新区 | Qiantang New Area | 72.16 | 51.06 | 11.65 | 78.23 | 86 | 70 | 26 | 160 |
| 西湖风景名胜区 | The West Lake Scenic Zone | - | - | - | - | - | - | - | - |
| 桐庐县 | Tonglu | 63.85 | 81.80 | 40.76 | 36.30 | 48 | 61 | 49 | 58 |
| 淳安县 | Chun'an | 43.14 | 44.22 | 52.66 | 25.33 | 37 | 38 | 73 | 37 |
| 建德市 | Jiande | 33.89 | 53.26 | 58.51 | 38.86 | 31 | 49 | 69 | 43 |

# 7－16　分地区房地产开发企业住宅销售面积和销售额(2016－2019年)

## Sales Area and Sales Volume of Residence of Real Estate Development Enterprises by Region(2016－2019)

| 城市 | City | 销售面积(万平方米) Sales Area(10,000 sq. m) | | | | 销售额(亿元) Sales Volume(100 million yuan) | | | |
|---|---|---|---|---|---|---|---|---|---|
| | | 2016年 | 2017年 | 2018年 | 2019年 | 2016年 | 2017年 | 2018年 | 2019年 |
| **全　市** | **Total** | **1887.11** | **1519.73** | **1328.92** | **1284.27** | **3060** | **3226** | **3238** | **3406** |
| #上城区 | Shangcheng | 11.06 | 2.42 | 22.11 | 15.21 | 53 | 15 | 150 | 107 |
| 下城区 | Xiacheng | 15.81 | 13.71 | 12.27 | 2.02 | 50 | 62 | 71 | 15 |
| 江干区 | Jianggan | 247.53 | 146.19 | 76.04 | 93.97 | 588 | 447 | 288 | 376 |
| 拱墅区 | Gongshu | 121.78 | 99.10 | 46.61 | 68.71 | 344 | 371 | 201 | 290 |
| 西湖区 | Xihu | 139.27 | 84.56 | 62.48 | 29.68 | 304 | 249 | 202 | 109 |
| 高新(滨江)区 | Hi－Tech (Binjiang) | 43.70 | 17.86 | 19.64 | 29.48 | 117 | 70 | 96 | 130 |
| 萧山区 | Xiaoshan | 313.44 | 351.62 | 320.32 | 238.79 | 493 | 834 | 796 | 728 |
| 余杭区 | Yuhang | 590.16 | 402.05 | 394.17 | 336.73 | 724 | 743 | 869 | 820 |
| 富阳区 | Fuyang | 104.81 | 83.71 | 110.92 | 113.65 | 121 | 111 | 198 | 216 |
| 临安区 | Lin'an | 119.40 | 128.08 | 130.82 | 206.31 | 102 | 151 | 188 | 356 |
| 钱塘新区 | Qiantang New Area | 48.57 | 28.27 | 4.40 | 63.25 | 59 | 41 | 11 | 134 |
| 西湖风景名胜区 | The West Lake Scenic Zone | | | | | | | | |
| 桐庐县 | Tonglu | 59.50 | 72.41 | 24.77 | 27.68 | 44 | 52 | 33 | 51 |
| 淳安县 | Chun'an | 42.11 | 41.20 | 50.54 | 24.48 | 35 | 35 | 71 | 35 |
| 建德市 | Jiande | 29.97 | 48.55 | 53.82 | 34.30 | 25 | 44 | 63 | 40 |

# 主要统计指标解释

**固定资产投资额**　固定资产投资完成额是以货币表现的建造和购置固定资产的工作量以及与此有关的费用的总称。它是反映固定资产投资规模、速度、比例关系和使用方向的综合性指标。

**房地产开发投资**　包括各种经济类型的房地产开发公司、商品房建设公司及其他房地产开发单位统一开发的包括统代建、拆迁还建的住宅、厂房、仓库、饭店、宾馆、度假村、写字楼、办公楼等房屋建筑物和配套的服务设施、土地开发工程,如道路、给水、排水、供电、供热、通讯、平整场地等基础设施工程的投资。不包括单纯的土地交易活动。

**施工和竣工房屋建筑面积**　房屋建筑面积是从房屋外墙线算起的各层平面面积的总和,包括房屋结构(如柱、墙)占用的面积和地下室面积。多层建筑按各自然层面积总和计算,包括房屋内的楼隔层,突出墙面的眺望间、门斗、有柱雨罩的面积。不包括突出墙面结构的构件、艺术装饰等所占的面积,如台阶等。凹阳台、挑阳台按其水平投影面积一半计算建筑面积。

**房屋新开工面积**　指在报告期内新开工建设的房屋面积。不包括上期跨入报告期继续施工的房屋面积和上期停缓建而在本期恢复施工的房屋面积。房屋的开工应以房屋正式开始破土刨槽(地基处理或打永久桩)的日期为准。

**商品房销售面积**　指报告期内出售商品房屋的合同总面积(即双方签署的正式买卖合同中所确定的建筑面积)。由现房销售建筑面积和期房销售建筑面积两部分组成。

(1)现房销售面积:是指在报告期内正式签订买卖合同、已经竣工达到入住条件的商品房屋建筑面积。包括以一次性付款方式和分期付款方式销售的现房建筑面积。

(2)期房销售面积:是指在报告期内正式签订买卖合同、正在建设尚未竣工交付使用的商品房屋建筑面积。包括以一次性付款方式和分期付款方式销售的商品房屋建筑面积。期房销售建筑面积竣工后不再转为现房销售建筑面积。

**新增固定资产**　指通过投资活动所形成的新的固定资产价值。包括已经建成投入生产或交付使用的工程价值和达到固定资产标准的设备、工具、器具的价值及有关应摊入的费用。它是以价值形式表示的固定资产投资成果的综合性指标,可以综合反映不同时期、不同部门、不同地区的固定资产投资成果。

# Explanatory Notes on Main Statistical Indicators

**Investment in Fixed Assets** refer to the volume of activities in construction and purchases of fixed assets in monetary terms and other relative expenses. It is a comprehensive indicator which shows the size, pace, proportional relations and use orientation of investment in fixed assets.

**Investment in Real Estate Development** include the investment by the real estate development companies, commercial buildings construction companies and other real estate development units of various types of ownership on the construction of house buildings, such as residential buildings, factory buildings, warehouses, hotels, guesthouses, Resorts and office buildings, and supporting service facilities and land development projects, and infrastructure projects like roads, water supply, water drainage, power supply, heating, telecommunications and land leveling. The simple activities of land transaction are excluded.

**Floor space of Building Under Construction and Completed** refer to total floor space of each story of buildings calculated from the exterior wall line of buildings, including the area occupied by construction like pillars or walls and basement area. The floor space of multi – story building includes the total floor space of each story, including area occupied by separating walls inside the house, watching rooms protruding from walls, anterooms, and rain covers with pillars, but excluding protruding wall structures, artistic decoration, etc. ( for example, steps) . The floor space of recessed veranda and cantilevered balcony is counted by half of the projection area.

**New Construction Floor Space of Building** refer to the area space which constructed in report period, not including the floor whose construction lasted to report period and which stopped in the last period to continue construction in the report period. The new construction should be subjected to the date of breaking the earth( foundation treatment or permanent pile driving).

**Sales Area of the Commercial Building** refer to the total area in contracts for sale of commercial housing( i. e. the floor space confirmed in contracts signed by two parties), which is composed by the floor area of existing house sales and that of future house sales.

(1) Floor Space of Existing House: refer to the floor area of commercial houses that have been completed and reached the condition of living, and whose formal sale contracts have been signed in report period, including houses sold in one – off payment and installment payment.

(2) Floor Space of Future House: refer to the floor area of commercial houses still under constructing but whose formal sale contracts have been signed in report period, including houses sold in one – off payment and installment payment. It cannot be turned into the floor space of existing house when these houses are completed.

**Newly Increased Fixed Assets** refer to the value of new fixed assets through investment, including the value of projects completed and put into production, the value of equipment, tools, and vessels considered as fixed assets, as well as the relevant expenses. It is a comprehensive indicator of investment in fixed assets, reflecting the achievements of investment in fixed assets in different periods, sectors and regions.

# 八、批发、零售贸易和住宿餐饮业

## WHOLESALE AND RETAIL TRADE AND HOTEL AND CATERING TRADE

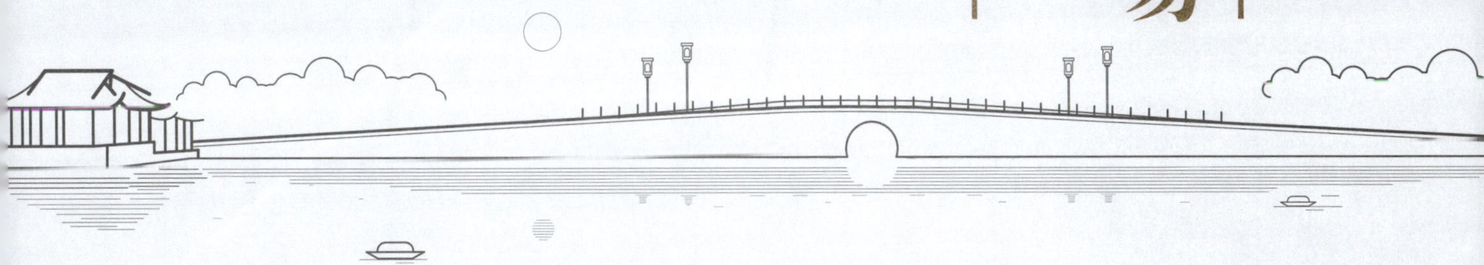

# 8 批发、零售贸易和住宿餐饮业
# Wholesale and Retail Trade and Hotel and Catering Trade

## 主 要 统 计 指 标
## Major Statistical Indicators

| | | | | |
|---|---|---|---|---|
| 社会消费品零售总额 | Total Retail Sales of Consumer Goods | 6187.70 | 亿元 | (100 million yuan) |
| 为上年 | As Compared with the Preceding Year | 108.8 | % | (%) |
| 商品零售 | Commodity Retail | 5110.24 | 亿元 | (100 million yuan) |
| 为上年 | As Compared with the Preceding Year | 108.8 | % | (%) |
| 餐饮收入 | Catering Revenue | 1077.46 | 亿元 | (100 million yuan) |
| 为上年 | As Compared with the Preceding Year | 108.6 | % | (%) |

# 8-01 社会消费品零售总额(2001-2019年)
## Total Retail Sale of Consumer Goods(2001-2019)

单位:万元 (10,000 yuan)

| 年 份<br>Year | 全 市<br>Total | 为上年(%)<br>As Compared with the Preceding Year(%) |
|---|---|---|
| 2001年 | 6156771 | 113.6 |
| 2002年 | 7024876 | 114.1 |
| 2003年 | 7895960 | 112.4 |
| 2004年 | 9096146 | 115.2 |
| 2005年 | 10369607 | 114.0 |
| 2006年 | 11821352 | 114.0 |
| 2007年 | 13771875 | 116.5 |
| 2008年 | 16553794 | 120.2 |
| 2009年 | 18937540 | 114.4 |
| 2010年 | 22706111 | 119.9 |
| 2011年 | 26962354 | 118.7 |
| 2012年 | 31154966 | 115.5 |
| 2013年 | 35220534 | 113.0 |
| 2014年 | 38288159 | 108.7 |
| 2015年 | 42806146 | 111.8 |
| 2016年 | 47279732 | 110.5 |
| 2017年 | 52223306 | 110.5 |
| 2018年 | 56898168 | 109.0 |
| 2019年 | 61876990 | 108.8 |

注:根据国家统计制度规定,2018年经济普查后对各年度数据作了相应调整。

a) According to the national statistical regulations, the annual data of previous years has been adjusted accordingly after the Economic Census in 2018.

# 8-02 分地区社会消费品零售总额(2018-2019年)
# Total Retail Sale of Consumer Goods by Region(2018-2019)

单位:万元 (10000 yuan)

| 地 区 | Region | 2018年 | 为上年(%) As Compared with the Preceding Year (%) | 2019年 | 为上年(%) As Compared with the Preceding Year (%) |
|---|---|---|---|---|---|
| **全 市** | **Total** | **56898168** | **109.0** | **61876990** | **108.8** |
| 市 区 | Urban District | 53726755 | 108.9 | 58430625 | 108.8 |
| #上城区 | Shangcheng | 3059516 | 109.4 | 3319582 | 108.5 |
| 下城区 | Xiacheng | 4929667 | 109.0 | 5348700 | 108.5 |
| 江干区 | Jianggan | 5293171 | 109.0 | 5751030 | 108.7 |
| 拱墅区 | Gongshu | 5733382 | 108.7 | 6207274 | 108.3 |
| 西湖区 | Xihu | 6551890 | 109.0 | 7117271 | 108.6 |
| 高新(滨江)区 | Hi-Tech(Binjiang) | 3767533 | 110.0 | 4143613 | 110.0 |
| 萧山区 | Xiaoshan | 7614394 | 109.6 | 8371880 | 109.9 |
| 余杭区 | Yuhang | 6928796 | 110.4 | 7578201 | 109.4 |
| 富阳区 | Fuyang | 3389581 | 110.1 | 3686169 | 108.8 |
| 临安区 | Lin'an | 1883083 | 110.0 | 2052324 | 109.0 |
| 钱塘新区 | Qiantang New Area | 2871755 | 110.3 | 3116726 | 108.5 |
| 西湖风景名胜区 | The West Lake Scenic Zone | 416621 | 109.6 | 452035 | 108.5 |
| 桐庐县 | Tonglu | 1337984 | 109.3 | 1457817 | 109.0 |
| 淳安县 | Chun'an | 776184 | 109.6 | 839928 | 108.2 |
| 建德市 | Jiande | 1057245 | 110.2 | 1148620 | 108.6 |

## 8－03 按登记注册类型分限额以上批发零售贸易企业商品销售总额(2019 年)

## Sales of Wholesale and Retail Trades Above Designated Size by Status of Registration(2019)

单位:万元 (10000 yuan)

| 项目 | Item | 法人企业(个) Number of Enterprises (unit) | 销售总额 Total Sales | 批发额 Wholesale | 零售额 Retail |
|---|---|---|---|---|---|
| **总计** | **Total** | **5373** | **271366505** | **236376536** | **34989969** |
| **1. 内资企业** | **Domestic－funded Enterprises** | **5153** | **238169127** | **212597831** | **25571296** |
| 国有企业 | State－owned Enterprises | 16 | 2320208 | 2254778 | 65429 |
| 集体企业 | Collective－owned Enterprises | 4 | 22962 | 7023 | 15939 |
| 股份合作企业 | Cooperative Enterprises | 2 | 7002 | － | 7002 |
| 联营企业 | Joint Ownership Enterprises | 5 | 35523 | 2255 | 33269 |
| 国有联营企业 | State Joint Ownership Enterprises | 1 | － | － | － |
| 集体联营企业 | Collective Joint Ownership Enterprises | － | － | － | － |
| 国有与集体联营企业 | Joint State－collective Enterprises | 4 | 23493 | 1777 | 21716 |
| 其他联营企业 | Other Joint Ownership Enterprises | － | － | － | － |
| 有限责任公司 | Limited Liability Corporations | 934 | 96125972 | 86379236 | 9746736 |
| 国有独资公司 | State－funded Corporations | 52 | 11112452 | 10831245 | 281208 |
| 其他有限责任公司 | Other Limited Liability Corporations | 882 | 85013520 | 75547991 | 9465529 |
| 股份有限公司 | Share－holding Corporations Ltd. | 85 | 26820294 | 25853518 | 966776 |
| 私营企业 | Private Enterprises | 4090 | 112781569 | 98061637 | 14719933 |
| 私营独资企业 | Private－funded Enterprises | 19 | 53985 | 25814 | 28171 |
| 私营合伙企业 | Private Partnership Enterprises | 1 | － | － | － |
| 私营有限责任公司 | Private Limited Liability Corporations | 4044 | 112040840 | 97544974 | 14495867 |
| 私营股份有限公司 | Private Share－holding Corporations Ltd. | 26 | 667223 | 471328 | 195895 |
| 其他企业 | Other Enterprises | 17 | 55598 | 39386 | 16212 |
| **2. 港、澳、台商投资企业** | **Enterprises With Investment from Hong Kong, Macao and Taiwan** | **77** | **5985654** | **2853302** | **3132352** |
| 合资经营企业(港或澳、台资) | Joint－venture Enterprises(With Funds from Hong Kong, Macao and Taiwan) | 17 | 967902 | 178666 | 789236 |
| 合作经营企业(港或澳、台资) | Coorperative Enterprises (With Funds from Hong Kong, Macao and Taiwan) | 2 | 42338 | 15790 | 26548 |
| 港、澳、台商独资经营企业 | Enterprises With Sole Investment from Hong Kong, Macao and Taiwan | 55 | 4744028 | 2427640 | 2316387 |
| 港、澳、台商投资股份有限公司 | Share－holding Corporations Ltd. With Investment from Hong Kong, Macao and Taiwan | 1 | － | － | － |
| 其他港澳台投资企业 | Other Enterprises With Investment from Hong Kong, Macao and Taiwan | 2 | 223011 | 223011 | － |
| **3. 外商投资企业** | **Enterprises With Foreign Investment** | **143** | **27211724** | **20925402** | **6286322** |
| 中外合资经营企业 | Joint－venture Enterprises | 41 | 12982039 | 10983429 | 1998610 |
| 中外合作经营企业 | Cooperation Enterprises | 4 | 158737 | 31611 | 127126 |
| 外资企业 | Enterprises With Sole Foreign Investment | 91 | 10960549 | 6801118 | 4159432 |
| 外商投资股份有限公司 | Share－holding Corporations Ltd. With Foreign Investment | 6 | 382043 | 380890 | 1154 |
| 其他外商投资企业 | Other Share－holding Corporations Enterprises | 1 | － | － | － |

# 8-04 按国民经济行业分限额以上批发零售

## Total Sales of Wholesale and Retail Trades

单位:万元

| 项 目 | Item |
|---|---|
| **总 计** | **Total** |
| **一、批发业** | **Wholesale** |
| 农、林、牧产品批发 | Wholesale of Farm, Forestry and Animal Husbandry Products |
| 食品、饮料及烟草制品批发 | Wholesale of Food, Beverages and Tobaccos |
| 纺织、服装及家庭用品批发 | Wholesale of Textile Products, Garments and Household Articles |
| 文化、体育用品及器材批发 | Wholesale of Cultural and Sports Goods |
| 医药及医疗器材批发 | Wholesale of Medicines and Medical Appliances |
| 矿产品、建材及化工产品批发 | Wholesale of Mineral Products, Building and Chemical Materials |
| 机械设备、五金产品及电子产品批发 | Wholesale of Machinery, Hardware and Electronic Products |
| #汽车、摩托车及零配件批发 | Wholesale of Automobiles, Motorcycle and Parts |
| 贸易经纪与代理 | Trade Broker and agent |
| 其他批发业 | Other |
| **二、零售业** | **Retail Trade** |
| 综合零售 | Comprehensive Retail Trade |
| 食品、饮料及烟草制品专门零售 | Specialism Retail of Food, Beverages and Tobaccos |
| 纺织、服装及日用品专门零售 | Specialism Retail of Textile Products, Garments, Shoes and Caps |
| 文化、体育用品及器材专门零售 | Specialism Retail of Cultural and Sports Goods |
| 医药及医疗器材专门零售 | Specialism Retail of Medicines and Medical Appliances |
| 汽车、摩托车、燃料及零配件专门零售 | Specialism Retail of Automobiles, Motorcycle, Fuels and Parts |
| #汽车零售 | Specialism Retail of Automobiles |
| 家用电器及电子产品专门零售 | Specialism Retail of Household Electric Applianes, and Electronic Products |
| 五金、家具及室内装饰材料专门零售 | Specialism Retail of Hardware and Upholstery Materials |
| 货摊、无店铺及其他零售业 | Stall, Non-shop and Other Retails |

# 贸易企业商品销售总额(2019 年)

## Above Designated Size by Sector(2019)

(10000 yuan)

| 法人企业(个) Number of Enterprises(unit) | 销售总额 Total Sales | 批发额 Wholesale | 零售额 Retail |
|---|---|---|---|
| **5373** | **271366505** | **236376536** | **34989969** |
| **3849** | **234256034** | **231654814** | **2601221** |
| 44 | 980797 | 970286 | 10511 |
| 333 | 15576202 | 15357328 | 218873 |
| 884 | 29406720 | 28968733 | 437987 |
| 155 | 4495833 | 4426587 | 69246 |
| 251 | 12128253 | 12055311 | 72943 |
| 1474 | 137471381 | 136711782 | 759599 |
| 632 | 28723123 | 28178028 | 545094 |
| 152 | 12571994 | 12154484 | 417510 |
| 1 | – | – | – |
| 75 | 5472798 | 4985830 | 486968 |
| **1524** | **37110470** | **4721722** | **32388748** |
| 124 | 6564463 | 701747 | 5862716 |
| 117 | 512435 | 36342 | 476093 |
| 121 | 1442692 | 134378 | 1308314 |
| 60 | 600720 | 171464 | 429255 |
| 90 | 825145 | 72392 | 752753 |
| 543 | 15707605 | 2201551 | 13506054 |
| 361 | 10432316 | 842100 | 9590216 |
| 129 | 1665140 | 338677 | 1326463 |
| 52 | 283039 | 23713 | 259326 |
| 288 | 9509233 | 1041459 | 8467775 |

# 8－05 按登记注册类型分限额以上

## Main Financial Indicators of Enterprises Above Designated Size of

单位:万元

| 项　目 | Item | 法人企业数(个) Number of Enterprises (unit) | 年末资产负债 Assets and Liabilities 流动资产合计 Circulating Funds | 存　货 Inventory | 固定资产原价 Orginal Value of Fixed Assets |
|---|---|---|---|---|---|
| **批发零售贸易业企业合计** | **Total** | **5373** | **82661967** | **13200566** | **6366749** |
| **1. 内资企业** | **Domestic－funded Enterprises** | **5153** | **73089524** | **11701092** | **5645345** |
| 国有企业 | State－owned Enterprises | 16 | 886342 | 78786 | 116342 |
| 集体企业 | Collective－owned Enterprises | 4 | 6789 | 1056 | 900 |
| 股份合作企业 | Cooperative Enterprises | 2 | 13455 | 2941 | 3780 |
| 联营企业 | Joint Ownership Enterprises | 5 | 5289 | 241 | 1428 |
| 国有联营企业 | State Joint Ownership Enterprises | 1 | － | － | － |
| 国有与集体联营企业 | Joint State－collective Enterprises | 4 | 4069 | 192 | 1243 |
| 有限责任公司 | Limited Liability Corporations | 934 | 25958670 | 5050007 | 1584756 |
| 国有独资公司 | State－funded Corporations | 52 | 2610591 | 887693 | 145445 |
| 其他有限责任公司 | Other Limited Liability Corporations | 882 | 23348079 | 4162314 | 1439311 |
| 股份有限公司 | Share－holding Corporations Ltd. | 85 | 10638270 | 1731875 | 1415522 |
| 私营企业 | Private Enterprises | 4090 | 35562582 | 4835711 | 2519388 |
| 私营独资企业 | Private－funded Enterprises | 19 | 20577 | 1600 | 2884 |
| 私营合伙企业 | Private Partnership Enterprises | 1 | － | － | － |
| 私营有限责任公司 | Private Limited Liability Corporations | 4044 | 35161695 | 4735547 | 2460722 |
| 私营股份有限公司 | Private Share－holding Corporations Ltd. | 26 | 364945 | 97500 | 55695 |
| 其他企业 | Other Enterprises | 17 | 18128 | 474 | 3229 |
| **2. 港、澳、台商投资企业** | **Enterprises With Investment from Hong Kong, Macao and Taiwan** | **77** | **2270888** | **462842** | **232956** |
| 合资经营企业(港或澳、台资) | Joint－venture Enterprises (With Funds from Hong Kong, Macao and Taiwan) | 17 | 511547 | 26505 | 118944 |
| 合作经营企业(港或澳、台资) | Coorperative Enterprises (With Funds from Hong Kong, Macao and Taiwan) | 2 | 25836 | － | 13894 |
| 港、澳、台商独资经营企业 | Enterprises With Sole Investment from Hong Kong, Macao and Taiwan | 55 | 1715302 | 434156 | 98990 |
| 港、澳、台商投资股份有限公司 | Share－holding Corporations Ltd. With Investment from Hong Kong, Macao and Taiwan | 1 | － | － | － |
| 其他港澳台投资企业 | Other Enterprises With Investment from Hong Kong, Macao and Taiwan | 2 | 15364 | 11 | 1101 |
| **3. 外商投资企业** | **Enterprises With Foreign Investment** | **143** | **7301555** | **1036632** | **488448** |
| 中外合资经营企业 | Joint－venture Enterprises | 41 | 1940639 | 275483 | 161794 |
| 中外合作经营企业 | Cooperation Enterprises | 4 | 380632 | 7477 | 16429 |
| 外资企业 | Enterprises With Sole Foreign Investment | 91 | 4380876 | 747527 | 297692 |
| 外商投资股份有限公司 | Share－holding Corporations Ltd. With Foreign Investment | 6 | 126595 | 6145 | 12226 |

# 批发零售贸易企业财务状况(2019 年)
# Wholesale and Retail Trades by Status of Registration(2019)

(10000 yuan)

| 累计折旧<br>Accumulated Depreciation | 本年折旧<br>Depreciation | 资产总计<br>Total Assets | 负债合计<br>Total Liabilities | 所有者权益合计<br>Creditors´ Equity |
|---|---|---|---|---|
| **2637464** | **353573** | **116016833** | **85953980** | **32069791** |
| **2307957** | **299609** | **104465081** | **77194194** | **29301898** |
| 79912 | 5821 | 1008777 | 225272 | 783244 |
| 631 | 43 | 7058 | 2371 | 4686 |
| 650 | 14 | 22461 | 18356 | 4105 |
| 631 | 116 | 6321 | 2815 | 3506 |
| – | – | – | – | – |
| 525 | 84 | 5021 | 2446 | 2575 |
| 662438 | 79550 | 38023362 | 26664082 | 11344881 |
| 52198 | 4903 | 3627426 | 2566045 | 1061381 |
| 610240 | 74647 | 34395936 | 24098038 | 10283500 |
| 625958 | 61235 | 18135221 | 12363396 | 7861676 |
| 937256 | 152731 | 47239333 | 37905329 | 9293345 |
| 1045 | 188 | 23668 | 20697 | 2995 |
| – | – | – | – | – |
| 915870 | 150265 | 46708907 | 37516081 | 9152643 |
| 20259 | 2274 | 490966 | 367083 | 123383 |
| 482 | 99 | 22549 | 12573 | 6456 |
| **114571** | **13451** | **3273876** | **2244646** | **1029251** |
| 63677 | 4497 | 735862 | 306489 | 429373 |
| 9149 | 228 | 63685 | 22812 | 40873 |
| 41262 | 8649 | 2455157 | 1910128 | 545049 |
| – | – | – | – | – |
| 478 | 72 | 16163 | 3523 | 12640 |
| **214935** | **40513** | **8277876** | **6515140** | **1738642** |
| 80763 | 22665 | 2322375 | 1665941 | 624777 |
| 4418 | 997 | 409820 | 372913 | 36907 |
| 126651 | 15920 | 4902473 | 4001124 | 908913 |
| 3020 | 873 | 170166 | 73282 | 96884 |

| 项　目 | Item | 营业收入 Revenue of Business | 主营业务收入 Main Revenue of Business | 营业成本 Cost of Business | 税金及附加 Sales Tax and Extra Charges |
|---|---|---|---|---|---|
| **批发零售贸易业企业合计** | **Total** | **254523279** | **252136892** | **240481686** | **503235** |
| **1. 内资企业** | **Domestic－funded Enterprises** | **226100087** | **223942295** | **214211411** | **444231** |
| 国有企业 | State－owned Enterprises | 2063981 | 2055032 | 1478807 | 240546 |
| 集体企业 | Collective－owned Enterprises | 20137 | 20137 | 16367 | 66 |
| 股份合作企业 | Cooperative Enterprises | 6607 | 6607 | 5203 | 41 |
| 联营企业 | Joint Ownership Enterprises | 31247 | 31247 | 24743 | 103 |
| 国有联营企业 | State Joint Ownership Enterprises | – | – | – | – |
| 国有与集体联营企业 | Joint State－collective Enterprises | 20678 | 20678 | 16839 | 59 |
| 有限责任公司 | Limited Liability Corporations | 86449187 | 85706912 | 83083335 | 65249 |
| 国有独资公司 | State－funded Corporations | 9871593 | 9850878 | 9715979 | 4276 |
| 其他有限责任公司 | Other Limited Liability Corporations | 76577594 | 75856034 | 73367356 | 60973 |
| 股份有限公司 | Share－holding Corporations Ltd. | 33764986 | 33001843 | 31843239 | 34536 |
| 私营企业 | Private Enterprises | 103710724 | 103067300 | 97708935 | 103663 |
| 私营独资企业 | Private－funded Enterprises | 37531 | 37498 | 34323 | 131 |
| 私营合伙企业 | Private Partnership Enterprises | – | – | – | – |
| 私营有限责任公司 | Private Limited Liability Corporations | 103035040 | 102396900 | 97104919 | 102683 |
| 私营股份有限公司 | Private Share－holding Corporations Ltd. | 621094 | 616069 | 556079 | 779 |
| 其他企业 | Other Enterprises | 53219 | 53218 | 50783 | 27 |
| **2. 港、澳、台商投资企业** | **Enterprises With Investment from Hong Kong, Macao and Taiwan** | **5486084** | **5389309** | **4773627** | **19790** |
| 合资经营企业(港或澳、台资) | Joint－venture Enterprises (With Funds from Hong Kong, Macao and Taiwan) | 909263 | 878082 | 748095 | 7868 |
| 合作经营企业(港或澳、台资) | Coorperative Enterprises (With Funds from Hong Kong, Macao and Taiwan) | 38354 | 38354 | 31737 | 423 |
| 港、澳、台商独资经营企业 | Enterprises With Sole Investment from Hong Kong, Macao and Taiwan | 4334012 | 4268481 | 3800367 | 11059 |
| 港、澳、台商投资股份有限公司 | Share－holding Corporations Ltd. With Investment from Hong Kong, Macao and Taiwan | – | – | – | – |
| 其他港澳台投资企业 | Other Enterprises With Investment from Hong Kong, Macao and Taiwan | 196981 | 196980 | 189318 | 437 |
| **3. 外商投资企业** | **Enterprises With Foreign Investment** | **22937108** | **22805288** | **21496649** | **39215** |
| 中外合资经营企业 | Joint－venture Enterprises | 11514130 | 11460973 | 10858904 | 7486 |
| 中外合作经营企业 | Cooperation Enterprises | 152015 | 145462 | 131551 | 463 |
| 外资企业 | Enterprises With Sole Foreign Investment | 8540313 | 8469504 | 7871202 | 28033 |
| 外商投资股份有限公司 | Share－holding Corporations Ltd. With Foreign Investment | 333172 | 331872 | 313587 | 461 |

continued (10000 yuan)

| 销售费用 Cost of Sales | 管理费用 Administration Cost | 财务费用 Financil Cost | 营业利润 Management Profits | 利润总额 Total Profits | 应交所得税 Income Tax | 从事批发和零售业活动的从业人员平均人数(人) Average Number of Employees (person) engaged in wholesale and retail activities |
|---|---|---|---|---|---|---|
| **7714340** | **3201534** | **1045304** | **4740818** | **4898769** | **736854** | **303351** |
| **6352828** | **2804869** | **1011921** | **4351713** | **4494207** | **612115** | **265893** |
| 29956 | 44545 | -26777 | 299983 | 299370 | 75281 | 1487 |
| 598 | 359 | -50 | 2797 | 2796 | 661 | 54 |
| 132 | 1663 | 121 | -553 | 160 | 16 | 82 |
| 1609 | 127 | -103 | 4711 | 4718 | 1201 | 71 |
| - | - | - | - | - | - | - |
| 1258 | 102 | -100 | 2463 | 2469 | 638 | 50 |
| 1808164 | 747665 | 311533 | 1309904 | 1387457 | 211496 | 76680 |
| 80480 | 48777 | 30296 | 64080 | 93106 | 13980 | 2786 |
| 1727684 | 698889 | 281237 | 1245824 | 1294351 | 197516 | 73894 |
| 1028099 | 326959 | 174080 | 1765572 | 1772274 | 109027 | 27844 |
| 3484003 | 1683001 | 553118 | 968341 | 1026317 | 214424 | 159520 |
| 1213 | 1258 | 173 | 440 | 458 | 96 | 323 |
| - | - | - | - | - | - | - |
| 3447052 | 1661251 | 543837 | 959841 | 1017414 | 211519 | 155282 |
| 35135 | 20266 | 9072 | 5681 | 6065 | 2190 | 3871 |
| 267 | 548 | - | 959 | 1115 | 9 | 155 |
| **503233** | **191040** | **24988** | **215** | **6183** | **39475** | **13339** |
| 42574 | 45145 | -5640 | 87335 | 90307 | 17232 | 2392 |
| 1750 | 3096 | -23 | 1405 | 1384 | 341 | 249 |
| 454703 | 137007 | 30831 | -89298 | -86497 | 21613 | 10487 |
| - | - | - | - | - | - | - |
| 1465 | 5258 | -161 | 666 | 884 | 266 | 185 |
| **858279** | **205626** | **8395** | **388890** | **398379** | **85264** | **24119** |
| 493426 | 62805 | -1781 | 141117 | 146922 | 24715 | 11360 |
| 9511 | 3066 | 2809 | 4255 | 4310 | 1517 | 527 |
| 349138 | 132144 | 6750 | 150607 | 153202 | 38486 | 11930 |
| 5439 | 5919 | 632 | 19938 | 20972 | 2302 | 278 |

# 8－06 按国民经济行业分限额以上

## Main Financial Indicators of Enterprises Above Designated

单位:万元

| 项目 | Item | 法人企业数(个) Number of Enterprises (unit) | 年末资产负债 Assets and Liabilities 流动资产合计 Circulating Funds | 存货 Inventory | 固定资产原价 Orginal Value of Fixed Assets |
|---|---|---|---|---|---|
| **总计** | **Total** | **5373** | **82661967** | **13200566** | **6366749** |
| **一、批发业** | **Wholesale** | **3849** | **71195959** | **10468698** | **4161402** |
| 农、林、牧产品批发 | Wholesale of Farm, Forestry and Animal Husbandry Products | 44 | 452220 | 88439 | 49355 |
| 食品、饮料及烟草制品批发 | Wholesale of Food, Beverages and Tobaccos | 333 | 7473803 | 1360390 | 513886 |
| 纺织、服装及家庭用品批发 | Wholesale of Textile Products, Garments and Household Articles | 884 | 9535303 | 1213005 | 494222 |
| 文化、体育用品及器材批发 | Wholesale of Cultural and Sports Goods | 155 | 1879305 | 567194 | 113100 |
| 医药及医疗器材批发 | Wholesale of Medicines and Medical Appliances | 251 | 5088055 | 990547 | 300159 |
| 矿产品、建材及化工产品批发 | Wholesale of Mineral Products, Building and Chemical Materials | 1474 | 35624596 | 4608702 | 2264961 |
| 机械设备、五金产品及电子产品批发 | Wholesale of Machinery, Hardware and Electronic Products | 632 | 9662926 | 1472923 | 404660 |
| #汽车、摩托车及零配件批发 | Wholesale of Automobiles, Motorcycle and Parts | 152 | 3078676 | 425190 | 104991 |
| 其他批发业 | Other | 76 | 1479752 | 167498 | 21059 |
| **二、零售业** | **Retail Trade** | **1524** | **11466008** | **2731869** | **2205348** |
| 综合零售 | Comprehensive Retail Trade | 124 | 3493340 | 397275 | 973900 |
| 食品、饮料及烟草制品专门零售 | Specialism Retail of Food, Beverages and Tobaccos | 117 | 290841 | 32389 | 34399 |
| 纺织、服装及日用品专门零售 | Specialism Retail of Textile Products, Garments, Shoes and Caps | 121 | 636347 | 235098 | 89649 |
| 文化、体育用品及器材专门零售 | Specialism Retail of Cultural and Sports Goods | 60 | 408645 | 183822 | 91436 |
| 医药及医疗器材专门零售 | Specialism Retail of Medicines and Medical Appliances | 60 | 408645 | 183822 | 91436 |
| 汽车、摩托车、燃料及零配件专门零售 | Specialism Retail of Automobiles, Motorcycle, Fuels and Parts | 543 | 3000589 | 843991 | 700915 |
| #汽车零售 | Specialism Retail of Automobiles | 361 | 2508801 | 784592 | 435838 |
| 家用电器及电子产品专门零售 | Specialism Retail of Household Electric Appliances, and Electronic Products | 129 | 745626 | 183593 | 53587 |
| 五金、家具及室内装饰材料专门零售 | Specialism Retail of Hardware and Upholstery Materials | 52 | 115809 | 29130 | 73554 |
| 货摊、无店铺及其他零售业 | Stall, Non－shop and Other Retails | 288 | 2499150 | 742679 | 162936 |

# 批发零售贸易企业财务状况(2019 年)

# Size in Wholesale and Retail Trades by Sector(2019)

(10000 yuan)

| 累计折旧 Accumulated Depreciation | 本年折旧 Depreciation | 资产总计 Total Assets | 负债合计 Total Liabilities | 所有者权益合计 Creditors´ Equity |
|---|---|---|---|---|
| **2637464** | **353573** | **116016833** | **85953980** | **32069791** |
| **1782983** | **221055** | **101083522** | **73008558** | **27980117** |
| 19063 | 2898 | 787761 | 563331 | 222177 |
| 246356 | 29856 | 9541073 | 6132056 | 3405003 |
| 210312 | 25817 | 11555085 | 8934948 | 2593262 |
| 47977 | 5051 | 2356749 | 1695584 | 659946 |
| 121279 | 24847 | 6954804 | 4400433 | 2553265 |
| 946846 | 96481 | 55764485 | 40330486 | 15388042 |
| 181979 | 33647 | 12353692 | 9386735 | 2953818 |
| 49586 | 9288 | 3516467 | 3048380 | 467699 |
| 9171 | 2457 | 1769874 | 1564985 | 204605 |
| **854480** | **132518** | **14933312** | **12945422** | **4089674** |
| 416242 | 58433 | 4947082 | 3463891 | 1487328 |
| 13996 | 2992 | 359856 | 214792 | 144496 |
| 39668 | 7608 | 785192 | 636549 | 159222 |
| 37695 | 4107 | 489166 | 388810 | 98315 |
| 37695 | 4107 | 489166 | 388810 | 98315 |
| 246218 | 42521 | 4206034 | 4858822 | 1432301 |
| 175842 | 32772 | 3148064 | 2432619 | 713533 |
| 29354 | 3558 | 878711 | 621223 | 257488 |
| 23151 | 3779 | 186091 | 134405 | 52738 |
| 34232 | 8898 | 2769121 | 2395189 | 377469 |

单位:万元 8－06 续表

| 项　目 | Item | 营业收入 Revenue of Business | 主营业务收入 Main Revenue of Business | 营业成本 Cost of Business | 税金及附加 Sales Tax and Extra Charges |
|---|---|---|---|---|---|
| **总　计** | **Total** | **254523279** | **252136892** | **240481686** | **503235** |
| **一、批发业** | **Wholesale** | **222160674** | **220423351** | **212778726** | **401009** |
| 农、林、牧产品批发业 | Wholesale of Farm , Forestry and Animal Husbandry Products | 930752 | 912993 | 882072 | 499 |
| 食品、饮料、烟草制品批发 | Wholesale of Food, Beverages and Tobaccos | 14062003 | 13608308 | 12043050 | 261642 |
| 纺织、服装及家庭用品批发 | Wholesale of Textile Products, Garments and Household Articles | 26718709 | 26597045 | 24952762 | 21613 |
| 文化、体育用品及器材批发 | Wholesale of Cultural and Sports Goods | 4104345 | 4088057 | 3867400 | 4764 |
| 医药及医疗器材批发 | Wholesale of Medicines and Medical Appliances | 10942000 | 10887237 | 9978780 | 17065 |
| 矿产品、建材及化工产品批发 | Wholesale of Mineral Products, Building and Chemical Materials | 134106532 | 133162476 | 131523661 | 69949 |
| 机械设备、五金产品及电子产品批发 | Wholesale of Machinery, Hardware and Electronic Products | 26007732 | 25900962 | 24485866 | 20214 |
| #汽车、摩托车及零配件批发 | Wholesale of Automobiles, Motorcycle and Parts | 11179819 | 11140758 | 10702782 | 5009 |
| 其他批发业 | Other | 5288602 | 5266274 | 5045136 | 5264 |
| **二、零售业** | **Retail Trade** | **32362605** | **31713541** | **27702961** | **102226** |
| 综合零售 | Comprehensive Retail Trade | 6271200 | 5935623 | 5188863 | 27521 |
| 食品、饮料及烟草制品专门零售 | Specialism Retail of Food, Beverages and Tobaccos | 468153 | 462789 | 374196 | 1248 |
| 纺织、服装及日用品专门零售 | Specialism Retail of Textile Products, Garments, Shoes and Caps | 1295471 | 1273403 | 804165 | 6080 |
| 文化、体育用品及器材专门零售 | Specialism Retail of Cultural and Sports Goods | 548838 | 543437 | 458590 | 5185 |
| 医药及医疗器材专门零售 | Specialism Retail of Medicines and Medical Appliances | 548838 | 543437 | 458590 | 5185 |
| 汽车、摩托车、燃料及零配件专门零售 | Specialism Retail of Automobiles, Motorcycle, Fuels and Parts | 12459626 | 12272776 | 11469131 | 37958 |
| #汽车零售 | Specialism Retail of Automobiles | 9526175 | 9400653 | 8876615 | 33138 |
| 家用电器及电子产品专门零售 | Specialism Retail of Household Electric Applianes, and Electronic Products | 1512390 | 1491495 | 1352275 | 2198 |
| 五金、家具及室内装饰材料专门零售 | Specialism Retail of Hardware and Upholstery Materials | 259690 | 251407 | 179239 | 1628 |
| 货摊、无店铺及其他零售业 | Stall, Non - shop and Other Retails | 8790863 | 8730715 | 7278270 | 18319 |

continued (10000 yuan)

| 销售费用 Cost of Sales | 管理费用 Administration Cost | 财务费用 Financil Cost | 营业利润 Management Profits | 利润总额 Total Profits | 应交所得税 Income Tax | 从事批发和零售业活动的从业人员平均人数(人) Average Number of Employees (person) engaged in wholesale and retail activities |
|---|---|---|---|---|---|---|
| **7714340** | **3201534** | **1045304** | **4740818** | **4898769** | **736854** | **303351** |
| **4651141** | **2265451** | **983976** | **4168234** | **4294313** | **550125** | **170044** |
| 12276 | 18958 | 17071 | 7903 | 12005 | 1922 | 1631 |
| 977578 | 252734 | -16944 | 1361996 | 1385259 | 145099 | 34979 |
| 832035 | 475857 | 83012 | 419366 | 427972 | 92312 | 41459 |
| 91085 | 67165 | 19437 | 59983 | 62660 | 12736 | 5438 |
| 460183 | 237542 | 56034 | 373970 | 375444 | 62684 | 18635 |
| 1216616 | 780558 | 752511 | 1719707 | 1790644 | 157113 | 37072 |
| 913284 | 386650 | 51199 | 178979 | 191820 | 68093 | 27991 |
| 443959 | 107921 | 20749 | -100436 | -97123 | 2878 | 8574 |
| 148084 | 45987 | 21656 | 46330 | 48509 | 10167 | 2839 |
| **3063199** | **936083** | **61328** | **572584** | **604456** | **186730** | **133307** |
| 718490 | 211812 | -12223 | 200307 | 220229 | 56076 | 42648 |
| 59942 | 29661 | 3590 | 2258 | 3050 | 1562 | 4492 |
| 333717 | 87554 | 6056 | 61766 | 64815 | 18001 | 14563 |
| 50993 | 26083 | 3909 | 4363 | 4519 | 680 | 4137 |
| 50993 | 26083 | 3909 | 4363 | 4519 | 680 | 4137 |
| 482869 | 236108 | 39720 | 198998 | 220007 | 64298 | 28207 |
| 298961 | 188920 | 36297 | 90239 | 102415 | 34252 | 22388 |
| 100639 | 50792 | 9382 | 1395 | 1472 | 1989 | 9862 |
| 49595 | 26546 | 1759 | 906 | 1387 | 906 | 2171 |
| 1165482 | 229798 | 7558 | 82429 | 68974 | 38951 | 18487 |

# 8－07 分地区限额以上

## Main Indicators of Wholesale

单位:万元

| 地 区 | Region | 企业法人数(个) Number of Enterprises (unit) | 商品销售总额 Total Sales of Commodities | 主营业务收入 Main Revenue of Business | 营业成本 Cost of Business | 税金及附加 Sales Tax and Extra Charges |
|---|---|---|---|---|---|---|
| **全 市** | **Total** | **5373** | **271366505** | **252136892** | **240481686** | **503235** |
| 市 区 | Urban District | 5086 | 267730067 | 248858405 | 237545030 | 498343 |
| #上城区 | Shangcheng | 477 | 30367203 | 36609801 | 34993060 | 275457 |
| 下城区 | Xiacheng | 547 | 49410717 | 44315530 | 42657270 | 41287 |
| 江干区 | Jianggan | 482 | 34862821 | 33018559 | 31555860 | 27712 |
| 拱墅区 | Gongshu | 408 | 23696055 | 21090960 | 20154423 | 24291 |
| 西湖区 | Xihu | 372 | 15507324 | 11878618 | 10740094 | 24017 |
| 高新(滨江)区 | Hi－Tech(Binjiang) | 356 | 26714229 | 23853585 | 22663989 | 23806 |
| 萧山区 | Xiaoshan | 924 | 43751441 | 38924915 | 37566863 | 35455 |
| 萧山本级 | Xiaoshan | 812 | 40313022 | 35876114 | 34729959 | 32416 |
| 余杭区 | Yuhang | 764 | 24421572 | 22099011 | 21216141 | 24840 |
| 富阳区 | Fuyang | 325 | 10081247 | 8949620 | 8617467 | 8742 |
| 临安区 | Lin'an | 187 | 2134600 | 1896492 | 1815804 | 1956 |
| 钱塘新区 | Qiantang New Area | 340 | 10154649 | 9211349 | 8354280 | 13586 |
| 西湖风景名胜区 | The West Lake Scenic Zone | 16 | 66628 | 58768 | 46683 | 234 |
| 桐庐县 | Tonglu | 136 | 1254785 | 1130317 | 996455 | 1915 |
| 淳安县 | Chun'an | 74 | 1663923 | 1478083 | 1331213 | 1724 |
| 建德市 | Jiande | 77 | 717730 | 670086 | 608989 | 1253 |

# 批发零售业主要指标(2019 年)
## and Retail Trades by Region(2019)

(10000 yuan)

| 销售费用<br>Cost of Sales | 管理费用<br>Administration Cost | 财务费用<br>Financil Cost | 利润总额<br>Total Profits | 本年应交增值税<br>Value Added Tax Payable | 从事批发和零售业活动从业人员平均人数(人)<br>Average Number of Employees (person) engaged in wholesale and retail activities |
|---|---|---|---|---|---|
| **7714340** | **3201534** | **1045304** | **4898769** | **1424526** | **303351** |
| 7515231 | 3143939 | 1028339 | 4788559 | 1332621 | 294027 |
| 820884 | 405278 | 92010 | 926344 | 2811843 | 28438 |
| 962591 | 493961 | 144322 | 725801 | 1454427 | 39095 |
| 915173 | 360959 | 48828 | 338344 | 1447571 | 38004 |
| 534431 | 314019 | 181037 | 232744 | 945474 | 27899 |
| 931889 | 253053 | 56158 | 1123206 | 1340091 | 36618 |
| 948896 | 272450 | 59375 | 447442 | 1056445 | 26672 |
| 832098 | 340951 | 183494 | 458945 | 187885 | 32388 |
| 681201 | 305431 | 172923 | 389382 | 1684655 | 29516 |
| 764631 | 369396 | 142942 | 467141 | 995181 | 35627 |
| 230682 | 89381 | 51677 | 27668 | 572648 | 8451 |
| 35744 | 30788 | 11110 | 19814 | 69686 | 4252 |
| 684927 | 243330 | 67875 | 85272 | 925515 | 18934 |
| 4184 | 5893 | 83 | 5400 | 22672 | 521 |
| 76925 | 27399 | 11071 | 34161 | 148605 | 3080 |
| 84647 | 18039 | 3149 | 63792 | 705153 | 4515 |
| 37537 | 12158 | 2745 | 12257 | 65293 | 1729 |

# 8-08 按注册类型、行业分限额以上

## Main Financial Indicators of Hotels and Catering Services

单位：万元

| 项目 | Item | 法人企业数(个) Number of Enterprises (unit) | 年末资产负债 Assets and Liabilities 流动资产合计 Circulating Funds | 存货 Inventory | 固定资产原价 Orginal Value of Fixed Assets |
|---|---|---|---|---|---|
| **总计** | **Total** | **1125** | **2339352** | **148038** | **3036597** |
| **(一)按登记注册类型分组** | **Grouped By Registered Type** | | | | |
| **1. 内资企业** | **Domestic - funded Enterprises** | **1083** | **1789309** | **109913** | **2464676** |
| 国有企业 | State - owned Enterprises | 34 | 103013 | 3250 | 351754 |
| 集体企业 | Collective - owned Enterprises | 8 | 11877 | 437 | 36261 |
| 股份合作企业 | Cooperative Enterprises | 1 | - | - | - |
| 联营企业 | Joint Ownership Enterprises | 1 | - | - | - |
| 有限责任公司 | Limited Liability Corporations | 172 | 432048 | 11780 | 914928 |
| 股份有限公司 | Share - holding Corporations Ltd. | 7 | 26517 | 775 | 60863 |
| 私营企业 | Private Enterprises | 860 | 1210460 | 93621 | 1092146 |
| 其他企业 | Other Enterprises | - | - | - | - |
| **2. 港、澳、台商投资企业** | **Enterprises With Investment from Hong Kong, Macao and Taiwan** | **18** | **237982** | **15453** | **303842** |
| **3. 外商投资企业** | **Enterprises With Foreign Investment** | **24** | **312062** | **22672** | **268080** |
| **(二)按国民经济行业分组** | **Grouped By Sector** | | | | |
| **1. 住宿业** | **Lodging** | **531** | **1652346** | **113822** | **2349129** |
| 旅游饭店 | Restaurants for Junketing | 285 | 1476236 | 110490 | 2235545 |
| 一般旅馆 | General Hotel | 240 | 173611 | 3305 | 112242 |
| 民宿服务 | Homestay Service | 6 | 2499 | 27 | 1343 |
| 露营地服务 | Campgralad Service | - | - | - | - |
| 其他住宿业 | Others Lodging | - | - | - | - |
| **2. 餐饮业** | **Catering Services** | **594** | **687006** | **34216** | **687467** |
| 正餐服务 | Dinner Services | 520 | 548013 | 24537 | 534703 |
| 快餐服务 | Short Order Services | 30 | 83701 | 7398 | 134871 |
| 饮料及冷饮服务 | Beverages and Services | 24 | 17896 | 1771 | 4198 |
| 餐饮配送及外卖送餐服务 | Catering Distribution and Delivery Service | 13 | 14401 | 156 | 8533 |
| 其他餐饮业 | Others Catering Services | 7 | 22995 | 354 | 5162 |

# 住宿业和餐饮业财务状况(2019 年)

## Enterprises Above Designated Size by Status of Registration and Sector(2019)

(10000 yuan)

| 累计折旧<br>Accumulated Depreciation | 本年折旧<br>Depreciation | 资产总计<br>Total Assets | 负债合计<br>Total Liabilities | 所有者权益合计<br>Creditors´ Equity |
|---|---|---|---|---|
| **1376363** | **147519** | **5428001** | **3984797** | **1446374** |
| | | | | |
| **1094918** | **122336** | **4351753** | **3233465** | **1122331** |
| 152053 | 19293 | 318984 | 70328 | 248656 |
| 28234 | 687 | 33574 | 24018 | 7165 |
| – | – | – | – | – |
| – | – | – | – | – |
| 406711 | 46967 | 1558614 | 1121881 | 436362 |
| 38640 | 2800 | 111660 | 18294 | 93366 |
| 463439 | 52323 | 2320103 | 1996769 | 330139 |
| – | – | – | – | – |
| **138258** | **12245** | **495958** | **426781** | **69177** |
| **143186** | **12939** | **580291** | **324550** | **254866** |
| | | | | |
| **1114896** | **113972** | **3964033** | **2842419** | **1125300** |
| 1053264 | 106549 | 3628486 | 2573800 | 1056941 |
| 61291 | 7316 | 326587 | 262246 | 65773 |
| 341 | 107 | 8960 | 6373 | 2587 |
| – | – | – | – | – |
| – | – | – | – | – |
| **261467** | **33547** | **1463968** | **1142378** | **321074** |
| 183320 | 26033 | 1108260 | 870084 | 237078 |
| 67955 | 5915 | 280445 | 214972 | 65486 |
| 2262 | 511 | 25511 | 33475 | –7339 |
| 4782 | 511 | 18628 | 8048 | 10526 |
| 3149 | 578 | 31124 | 15800 | 15324 |

| 项　目 | Item | 营业收入 Revenue of Business | 主营业务收入 Main Revenue of Business | 税金及附加 Sales Tax and Extra Charges |
|---|---|---|---|---|
| **总　计** | **Total** | **3510852** | **3438260** | **18745** |
| **(一)按登记注册类型分组** | **Grouped By Registered Type** | | | |
| **1. 内资企业** | **Domestic - funded Enterprises** | **2442354** | **2388791** | **15666** |
| 国有企业 | State - owned Enterprises | 154139 | 147766 | 1532 |
| 集体企业 | Collective - owned Enterprises | 13054 | 12859 | 145 |
| 股份合作企业 | Cooperative Enterprises | - | - | - |
| 联营企业 | Joint Ownership Enterprises | - | - | - |
| 有限责任公司 | Limited Liability Corporations | 616889 | 605550 | 6358 |
| 股份有限公司 | Share - holding Corporations Ltd. | 46714 | 46178 | 859 |
| 私营企业 | Private Enterprises | 1606884 | 1571764 | 6730 |
| 其他企业 | Other Enterprises | - | - | - |
| **2. 港、澳、台商投资企业** | **Enterprises With Investment from Hong Kong, Macao and Taiwan** | **268908** | **263809** | **1006** |
| **3. 外商投资企业** | **Enterprises With Foreign Investment** | **799590** | **785660** | **2073** |
| **(二)按国民经济行业分组** | **Grouped By Sector** | | | |
| **1. 住宿业** | **Lodging** | **1393742** | **1332595** | **14586** |
| 旅游饭店 | Restaurants for Junketing | 1131470 | 1078569 | 13099 |
| 一般旅馆 | General Hotel | 259679 | 251433 | 1480 |
| 民宿服务 | Homestay Service | 2593 | 2593 | 7 |
| 露营地服务 | Campgralad Service | - | - | - |
| 其他住宿业 | Others Lodging | - | - | - |
| **2. 餐饮** | **Catering Services** | **2117109** | **2105665** | **4159** |
| 正餐服务 | Dinner Services | 1174923 | 1167726 | 3544 |
| 快餐服务 | Short Order Services | 769557 | 765390 | 306 |
| 饮料及冷饮服务 | Beverages and Services | 79482 | 79402 | 91 |
| 餐饮配送及外卖送餐服务 | Catering Distribution and Delivery Service | 41780 | 41780 | 176 |
| 其他餐饮业 | Others Catering Services | 51367 | 51367 | 42 |

continued (10000 yuan)

| 销售费用 Cost of Sales | 管理费用 Administration Cost | 财务费用 Financial Cost | 营业利润 Management Profits | 利润总额 Total Profits | 应交所得税 Income Tax | 从事住宿和餐饮业活动的从业人员平均人数(人) Average Number of Employees (person) engaged in hotel and catering activities |
|---|---|---|---|---|---|---|
| **1190496** | **681815** | **78932** | **139547** | **151090** | **70151** | **114999** |
| | | | | | | |
| **815572** | **559688** | **62991** | **20882** | **33438** | **39264** | **76620** |
| 53157 | 51884 | -520 | 8177 | 10695 | 2929 | 4524 |
| 6162 | 3440 | -14 | -326 | -276 | 35 | 594 |
| - | - | - | - | - | - | - |
| - | - | - | - | - | - | - |
| 224506 | 149736 | 20160 | 28119 | 30857 | 5454 | 21799 |
| 17075 | 12931 | 88 | 1263 | 1455 | 479 | 1403 |
| 513973 | 338750 | 43310 | -16487 | -9542 | 30347 | 48267 |
| - | - | - | - | - | - | - |
| **134082** | **31060** | **16896** | **1865** | **392** | **937** | **13673** |
| **240842** | **91067** | **-955** | **116800** | **117259** | **29950** | **24706** |
| | | | | | | |
| **527883** | **438698** | **61125** | **-13338** | **-4661** | **16599** | **45274** |
| 451387 | 350690 | 58247 | -5682 | 764 | 14897 | 37591 |
| 75368 | 87269 | 2836 | -7415 | -5264 | 1690 | 7561 |
| 1128 | 739 | 42 | -241 | -162 | 12 | 122 |
| - | - | - | - | - | - | - |
| - | - | - | - | - | - | - |
| **662613** | **243116** | **17807** | **152885** | **155751** | **53552** | **69725** |
| 382281 | 157190 | 15032 | 57760 | 60479 | 28955 | 36198 |
| 237912 | 66794 | 2741 | 95864 | 95740 | 23739 | 28802 |
| 18814 | 10264 | 72 | -3381 | -3211 | 976 | 2204 |
| 3464 | 4958 | -57 | 1982 | 2052 | 416 | 1036 |
| 20142 | 3911 | 19 | 660 | 691 | -534 | 1485 |

# 8-09 按登记注册类型和国民经济行业分限额以上住宿业和餐饮业经营情况(2019年)

## Management Conditions of Hotels and Catering Services Enterprises Above Designated Size by Status of Registration and Sector(2019)

单位:万元 (10000 yuan)

| 项　目 | Item | 法人企业(个) Number of Enterprises (unit) | 营业额 Revenue of Business | 客房收入 Revenue of Guest Rooms | 餐费收入 Revenue of Catering Services | 商品销售额 Revenue of Goods Sales |
|---|---|---|---|---|---|---|
| **一、按登记注册类型分** | **Grouped By Registered Type** | | | | | |
| **总　计** | **Total** | **1125** | **3657188** | **803703** | **2578752** | **52273** |
| **1. 内资企业** | **Domestic-funded Enterprises** | **1083** | **2544692** | **686899** | **1644736** | **48595** |
| 国有企业 | State-owned Enterprises | 34 | 162278 | 69689 | 70936 | 1562 |
| 集体企业 | Collective-owned Enterprises | 8 | 13834 | 8281 | 3262 | 49 |
| 股份合作企业 | Cooperative Enterprises | 1 | - | - | - | - |
| 联营企业 | Joint Ownership Enterprises | 1 | - | - | - | - |
| 国有联营企业 | State owned jointly operated enterprises | - | - | - | - | - |
| 集体联营企业 | Collective owned jointly operated enterprises | - | - | - | - | - |
| 国有与集体联营企业 | Joint State-collective Enterprises | 1 | - | - | - | - |
| 其他联营企业 | Other jointly operated enterprises | - | - | - | - | - |
| 有限责任公司 | Limited Liability Corporations | 172 | 639662 | 201067 | 351443 | 6214 |
| 国有独资公司 | State-funded Corporations | 17 | 69929 | 17833 | 37963 | 295 |
| 其他有限责任公司 | Other Limited Liability Corporations | 155 | 569732 | 183234 | 313479 | 5919 |
| 股份有限公司 | Share-holding Corporations Ltd. | 7 | 48822 | 14618 | 30845 | 1362 |
| 私营企业 | Private Enterprises | 860 | 1675143 | 390459 | 1186433 | 39351 |
| 私营独资企业 | Private-funded Enterprises | 10 | 10449 | 225 | 10130 | 93 |
| 私营合伙企业 | Private Partnership Enterprises | 2 | 2575 | - | 2453 | - |
| 私营有限责任公司 | Private Limited Liability Corporations | 844 | 1636981 | 389158 | 1149844 | 39255 |
| 私营股份有限公司 | Private Share-holding Corporations Ltd. | 4 | 25138 | 1076 | 24006 | 4 |
| 其他企业 | Other Enterprises | - | - | - | - | - |

单位:万元 8-09 续表 continued (10000 yuan)

| 项 目 | Item | 法人企业(个) Number of Enterprises (unit) | 营业额 Revenue of Business | 客房收入 Revenue of Guest Rooms | 餐费收入 Revenue of Catering Services | 商品销售额 Revenue of Goods Sales |
|---|---|---|---|---|---|---|
| **2. 港、澳、台商投资企业** | **Enterprises With Investment from Hong Kong, Macao and Taiwan** | **18** | **277179** | **35056** | **236535** | **245** |
| 合资经营企业(港或澳、台资) | Joint-venture Enterprises (With Funds from Hong Kong, Macao and Taiwan) | 10 | 91380 | 30159 | 57181 | 245 |
| 合作经营企业(港或澳、台资) | Coorperative Enterprises (With Funds from Hong Kong, Macao and Taiwan) | - | - | - | - | - |
| 港、澳、台商独资经营企业 | Enterprises With Sole Investment from Hong Kong, Macao and Taiwan | 7 | 184879 | 4489 | 178874 | - |
| 港、澳、台商投资股份有限公司 | Share-holding Corporations Ltd. With Investment from Hong Kong, Macao and Taiwan | 1 | - | - | - | - |
| **3. 外商投资企业** | **Enterprises With Foreign Investment** | **24** | **835317** | **81747** | **697481** | **3433** |
| 中外合资经营企业 | Joint-venture Enterprises | 6 | 615111 | 9802 | 603726 | - |
| 中外合作经营企业 | Cooperation Enterprises | - | - | - | - | - |
| 外资企业 | Enterprises With Sole Foreign Investment | 17 | 80109 | 20357 | 46342 | 302 |
| 外商投资股份有限公司 | Share-holding Corporations Ltd. With Foreign Investment | 1 | - | - | - | - |
| **二、按国民经济行业分** | **Grouped By Sector** | | | | | |
| **总 计** | **Total** | **1125** | **3657188** | **803703** | **2578752** | **52273** |
| **1. 住宿业** | **Lodging** | **531** | **1423765** | **765225** | **467021** | **11394** |
| 旅游饭店 | Restaurants for Junketing | 285 | 1150880 | 554587 | 429586 | 10512 |
| 一般旅馆 | General Hotel | 240 | 270166 | 208851 | 36528 | 882 |
| 民宿服务 | Homestay Service | 6 | 2719 | 1787 | 907 | - |
| 露营地服务 | Campground Service | - | - | - | - | - |
| 其他住宿业 | Others Lodging | - | - | - | - | - |
| **2. 餐饮业** | **Catering Services** | **594** | **2233422** | **38478** | **2111731** | **40879** |
| 正餐服务 | Dinner Services | 520 | 1243903 | 38478 | 1135965 | 35914 |
| 快餐服务 | Short Order Services | 30 | 808907 | - | 804494 | 1507 |
| 饮料及冷饮服务 | Beverages and Services | 24 | 83891 | - | 77885 | 3352 |
| 餐饮配送及外卖送餐服务 | Catering Distribution and Delivery Service | 13 | 42866 | - | 40482 | 105 |
| 其他餐饮业 | Others Catering Services | 7 | 53857 | - | 52906 | - |

# 8－10 分地区限额以上
## Main Indicators of Lodging

单位:万元

| 地　区　Region | | 企业法人数(个) Number of Enterprises (unit) | 营业额 Revenue of Business | 客房收入 Revenue of Guest Rooms | 餐费收入 Revenue of Catering Services | 主营业务收入 Main Revenue of Business |
|---|---|---|---|---|---|---|
| **全　市** | **Total** | **1125** | **3657188** | **803703** | **2578752** | **3438260** |
| 市　区 | Urban District | 1017 | 3506856 | 727517 | 2515174 | 3302568 |
| #上城区 | Shangcheng | 183 | 630607 | 132644 | 468860 | 593270 |
| 下城区 | Xiacheng | 99 | 448509 | 77999 | 338547 | 418287 |
| 江干区 | Jianggan | 108 | 219595 | 63603 | 138420 | 210418 |
| 拱墅区 | Gongshu | 78 | 203309 | 40345 | 134209 | 188686 |
| 西湖区 | Xihu | 146 | 944316 | 85715 | 803119 | 897825 |
| 高新(滨江)区 | Hi－Tech(Binjiang) | 41 | 87055 | 27083 | 58591 | 83785 |
| 萧山区 | Xiaoshan | 91 | 426767 | 141440 | 225126 | 397119 |
| 萧山本级 | Xiaoshan | 85 | 414536 | 137495 | 217406 | 385495 |
| 余杭区 | Yuhang | 78 | 146153 | 40695 | 88986 | 139583 |
| 富阳区 | Fuyang | 35 | 35998 | 12369 | 21849 | 33518 |
| 临安区 | Lin'an | 32 | 38531 | 12439 | 22137 | 33714 |
| 钱塘新区 | Qiantang New Area | 65 | 96548 | 19212 | 73714 | 89601 |
| 西湖风景名胜区 | The West Lake Scenic Zone | 67 | 241701 | 77919 | 149337 | 228388 |
| 桐庐县 | Tonglu | 29 | 31482 | 12620 | 16185 | 27098 |
| 淳安县 | Chun'an | 58 | 96433 | 53681 | 35461 | 87445 |
| 建德市 | Jiande | 21 | 22417 | 9885 | 11932 | 21148 |

# 住宿餐饮业主要指标(2019 年)

# and Catering by Region(2019)

(10000 yuan)

| 税金及附加<br>Sales Tax and Extra Charges | 销售费用<br>Cost of Sales | 管理费用<br>Administration Cost | 财务费用<br>Financil Cost | 利润总额<br>Total Profits | 从事住宿和餐饮业活动从业人员平均人数(人)<br>Average Number of Employees (person) engaged in hotel and catering activities |
|---|---|---|---|---|---|
| **18745** | **1190496** | **681815** | **78932** | **151090** | **114999** |
| 17098 | 1133791 | 635367 | 72755 | 155767 | 108456 |
| 4136 | 227816 | 104623 | 20188 | 61433 | 16957 |
| 1707 | 173147 | 60203 | 12557 | 822 | 16752 |
| 755 | 69703 | 49566 | 1802 | 2440 | 6107 |
| 1053 | 68176 | 40995 | 1582 | 557 | 5736 |
| 2410 | 235489 | 123083 | 4661 | 98480 | 29379 |
| 377 | 20905 | 26684 | 1778 | -4425 | 2596 |
| 1885 | 177110 | 72189 | 19961 | 11561 | 14104 |
| 1866 | 173352 | 68929 | 19000 | 12975 | 13688 |
| 465 | 34552 | 42374 | 3448 | -4963 | 4893 |
| 628 | 10177 | 11780 | 3034 | -6122 | 1831 |
| 572 | 11157 | 9095 | 2369 | -3435 | 1650 |
| 129 | 30119 | 18447 | 1978 | -3782 | 2525 |
| 2999 | 79200 | 79588 | 359 | 1787 | 6342 |
| 66 | 8710 | 11274 | 1749 | -4614 | 1338 |
| 1343 | 39570 | 29064 | 3799 | 1315 | 4067 |
| 238 | 8426 | 6111 | 629 | -1378 | 1138 |

# 8－11　个体工商业登记注册情况（2019年末）

## Statistics on Individual Business Registration（End of 2019）

| 项　目 | Item | 全市 Whole City 合计 Total | 全市 Whole City #城镇 Urban | 市区 Urban District 合计 Total | 市区 Urban District #城镇 Urban |
|---|---|---|---|---|---|
| **户数（户）** | **Number of Households（household）** | **610074** | **405386** | **525907** | **361821** |
| 农、林、牧、渔业 | Farming, Forestry, Animal Husbandry and Fishery | 9549 | 3610 | 6909 | 2946 |
| 农、林、牧、渔专业及辅助性活动 | Service for Farming, Forestry, Animal Husbandry and Fishery | 794 | 382 | 662 | 333 |
| 采矿业 | Mining and Quarrying | 44 | 21 | 25 | 8 |
| 开采专业及辅助性活动 | Support Activity for Mining and Quarrying | – | – | – | – |
| 制造业 | Manufacturing | 23481 | 9477 | 16283 | 6954 |
| 金属制品、机械和设备修理业 | Metal Products, Machinery and Equipment Repair | 245 | 132 | 192 | 108 |
| 电力、热力、燃气及水的生产和供应业 | Production and Supply of Electricity, Gas and Water | 50 | 25 | 37 | 23 |
| 建筑业 | Construction | 5994 | 4125 | 5336 | 3784 |
| 批发和零售业 | Wholesale and Retail Trade & Catering Services | 386988 | 245367 | 342036 | 222317 |
| 交通运输、仓储和邮政业 | Transportation, Storage and Post | 7854 | 4858 | 5845 | 3782 |
| 住宿和餐饮业 | Lodging and Catering | 87457 | 70362 | 74834 | 62850 |
| 信息传输、软件和信息技术服务业 | Information Transmission, Computer Services and Software | 3076 | 1951 | 2650 | 1656 |
| 金融业 | Banking and Insurance | 32 | 25 | 27 | 22 |
| 房地产业 | Real Estate | 228 | 190 | 96 | 84 |
| 租赁和商务服务业 | Renting and Business Service | 18098 | 13062 | 14485 | 11041 |
| 科学研究和技术服务业 | Scientific Research and Technical Service | 1467 | 1106 | 1134 | 915 |
| 水利、环境和公共设施管理业 | Water Conservancy, Environment and Public Utility | 117 | 79 | 104 | 72 |
| 居民服务、修理和其他服务业 | Service for the Residents and Other Service Sector | 59623 | 46100 | 50985 | 40931 |
| 教育 | Education | 417 | 332 | 378 | 308 |
| 卫生和社会工作 | Health Care, Sports & Social Welfare | 678 | 511 | 525 | 418 |
| 文化、体育和娱乐业 | Culture, Sports and Entertainment | 4616 | 3910 | 3952 | 3466 |
| 其他 | Others | 305 | 275 | 266 | 244 |

8-11 续表1 continued 1

| 项目 | Item | 全市 Whole City 合计 Total | 全市 Whole City #城镇 Urban | 市区 Urban District 合计 Total | 市区 Urban District #城镇 Urban |
|---|---|---|---|---|---|
| **从业人员(人)** | **Employed Persons(person)** | **1063243** | **731593** | **881598** | **637782** |
| 农、林、牧、渔业 | Farming, Forestry, Animal Husbandry and Fishery | 23052 | 7723 | 15040 | 5700 |
| 农、林、牧、渔专业及辅助性活动 | Service for Farming, Forestry, Animal Husbandry and Fishery | 1609 | 805 | 1165 | 597 |
| 采矿业 | Mining and Quarrying | 155 | 63 | 99 | 31 |
| 开采专业及辅助性活动 | Support Activity for Mining and Quarrying | - | - | - | - |
| 制造业 | Manufacturing | 79184 | 27634 | 43818 | 17259 |
| 金属制品、机械和设备修理业 | Metal Products, Machinery and Equipment Repair | 503 | 249 | 377 | 195 |
| 电力、热力、燃气及水的生产和供应业 | Production and Supply of Electricity, Gas and Water | 86 | 51 | 63 | 47 |
| 建筑业 | Construction | 12794 | 7587 | 10022 | 6400 |
| 批发和零售业 | Wholesale and Retail Trade & Catering Services | 566411 | 385391 | 493489 | 344953 |
| 交通运输、仓储和邮政业 | Transportation, Storage and Post | 12519 | 7749 | 9066 | 5894 |
| 住宿和餐饮业 | Lodging and Catering | 189673 | 156213 | 161523 | 138187 |
| 信息传输、软件和信息技术服务业 | Information Transmission, Computer Services and Software | 4200 | 2973 | 3440 | 2429 |
| 金融业 | Banking and Insurance | 46 | 32 | 38 | 28 |
| 房地产业 | Real Estate | 332 | 290 | 150 | 135 |
| 租赁和商务服务业 | Renting and Business Service | 28990 | 21504 | 21984 | 17300 |
| 科学研究和技术服务业 | Scientific Research and Technical Service | 2250 | 1815 | 1745 | 1508 |
| 水利、环境和公共设施管理业 | Water Conservancy, Environment and Public Utility | 291 | 158 | 252 | 127 |
| 居民服务、修理和其他服务业 | Service for the Residents and Other Service Sector | 130714 | 102086 | 110687 | 89092 |
| 教育 | Education | 1116 | 852 | 1035 | 798 |
| 卫生和社会工作 | Health Care, Sports & Social Welfare | 1609 | 1221 | 1243 | 986 |
| 文化、体育和娱乐业 | Culture, Sports and Entertainment | 9367 | 7843 | 7524 | 6555 |
| 其他 | Others | 454 | 408 | 380 | 353 |

8－11　续表2　continued 2

| 项　目 | Item | 全市 Whole City 合计 Total | 全市 Whole City #城镇 Urban | 市区 Urban District 合计 Total | 市区 Urban District #城镇 Urban |
|---|---|---|---|---|---|
| **注册资金(万元)** | **Capital Registered(10000 yuan)** | **7517273** | **4426775** | **6040076** | **3610216** |
| 农、林、牧、渔业 | Farming, Forestry, Animal Husbandry and Fishery | 341854 | 131646 | 210963 | 94081 |
| 农、林、牧、渔专业及辅助性活动 | Service for Farming, Forestry, Animal Husbandry and Fishery | 26439 | 12571 | 21811 | 10575 |
| 采矿业 | Mining and Quarrying | 3272 | 2036 | 1012 | 194 |
| 开采专业及辅助性活动 | Support Activity for Mining and Quarrying | – | – | – | – |
| 制造业 | Manufacturing | 320397 | 133134 | 187561 | 86144 |
| 金属制品、机械和设备修理业 | Metal Products, Machinery and Equipment Repair | 2741 | 1696 | 1974 | 1201 |
| 电力、热力、燃气及水的生产和供应业 | Production and Supply of Electricity, Gas and Water | 407 | 122 | 234 | 117 |
| 建筑业 | Construction | 146470 | 94028 | 126308 | 84069 |
| 批发和零售业 | Wholesale and Retail Trade & Catering Services | 4123307 | 2216286 | 3543219 | 1871128 |
| 交通运输、仓储和邮政业 | Transportation, Storage and Post | 114813 | 66207 | 86220 | 53525 |
| 住宿和餐饮业 | Lodging and Catering | 1282676 | 949197 | 989519 | 759330 |
| 信息传输、软件和信息技术服务业 | Information Transmission, Computer Services and Software | 48318 | 22029 | 40547 | 17284 |
| 金融业 | Banking and Insurance | 446 | 345 | 401 | 320 |
| 房地产业 | Real Estate | 2015 | 1589 | 661 | 501 |
| 租赁和商务服务业 | Renting and Business Service | 362566 | 225589 | 217254 | 154188 |
| 科学研究和技术服务业 | Scientific Research and Technical Service | 18500 | 14186 | 12424 | 10621 |
| 水利、环境和公共设施管理业 | Water Conservancy, Environment and Public Utility | 3028 | 1340 | 2456 | 1180 |
| 居民服务、修理和其他服务业 | Service for the Residents and Other Service Sector | 655168 | 488022 | 546260 | 411618 |
| 教育 | Education | 4756 | 3043 | 4254 | 2731 |
| 卫生和社会工作 | Health Care, Sports & Social Welfare | 12771 | 10411 | 8991 | 7667 |
| 文化、体育和娱乐业 | Culture, Sports and Entertainment | 72402 | 64098 | 58488 | 52652 |
| 其他 | Others | 4107 | 3467 | 3304 | 2866 |

# 8-12 私营企业登记注册情况(2019年末)

# Statistics on Private Enterprises Registration(End of 2019)

| 项目 | Item | 全市 Whole City | | 市区 Urban District | |
|---|---|---|---|---|---|
| | | 合计 Total | #城镇 Urban | 合计 Total | #城镇 Urban |
| **户数(户)** | **Number of Households (household)** | **632298** | **530632** | **583524** | **498888** |
| 农、林、牧、渔业 | Farming, Forestry, Animal Husbandry and Fishery | 7380 | 3531 | 5335 | 2803 |
| 农、林、牧、渔专业及辅助性活动 | Service for Farming, Forestry, Animal Husbandry and Fishery | 1123 | 706 | 871 | 587 |
| 采矿业 | Mining and Quarrying | 164 | 49 | 97 | 33 |
| 开采专业及辅助性活动 | Support Activity for Mining and Quarrying | 7 | 4 | 7 | 4 |
| 制造业 | Manufacturing | 54242 | 24143 | 46926 | 21579 |
| 金属制品、机械和设备修理业 | Metal Products, Machinery and Equipment Repair | 420 | 324 | 396 | 307 |
| 电力、热力、燃气及水的生产和供应业 | Production and Supply of Electricity, Gas and Water | 886 | 527 | 583 | 431 |
| 建筑业 | Construction | 30842 | 25277 | 28723 | 23888 |
| 批发和零售业 | Wholesale and Retail Trade & Catering Services | 208015 | 179902 | 191042 | 167711 |
| 交通运输、仓储和邮政业 | Transportation, Storage and Post | 8644 | 6605 | 6948 | 5447 |
| 住宿和餐饮业 | Lodging and Catering | 12133 | 9920 | 11261 | 9371 |
| 信息传输、软件和信息技术服务业 | Information Transmission, Computer Services and Software | 77005 | 71754 | 73054 | 68629 |
| 金融业 | Banking and Insurance | 6213 | 5499 | 5830 | 5244 |
| 房地产业 | Real Estate | 15122 | 12836 | 13883 | 11941 |
| 租赁和商务服务业 | Renting and Business Service | 97410 | 89237 | 91709 | 84836 |
| 科学研究和技术服务业 | Scientific Research and Technical Service | 59121 | 53958 | 56629 | 52293 |
| 水利、环境和公共设施管理业 | Water Conservancy, Environment and Public Utility | 2227 | 1762 | 1919 | 1566 |
| 居民服务、修理和其他服务业 | Service for the Residents and Other Service Sector | 21643 | 17646 | 20066 | 16463 |
| 教育 | Education | 4916 | 4417 | 4652 | 4195 |
| 卫生和社会工作 | Health Care, Sports & Social Welfare | 2535 | 1501 | 2368 | 1398 |
| 文化、体育和娱乐业 | Culture, Sports and Entertainment | 23378 | 21672 | 22120 | 20699 |
| 其他 | Others | 422 | 396 | 379 | 361 |

8－12 续表1 continued 1

| 项 目 | Item | 全 市 Whole City | | 市 区 Urban District | |
|---|---|---|---|---|---|
| | | 合 计 Total | #城 镇 Urban | 合 计 Total | #城 镇 Urban |
| **从业人员(人)** | **Employed Persons(person)** | **2420288** | **1694153** | **2171434** | **1556713** |
| 农、林、牧、渔业 | Farming,Forestry,Animal Husbandry and Fishery | 28812 | 13240 | 18347 | 9687 |
| 农、林、牧、渔专业及辅助性活动 | Service for Farming,Forestry,Animal Husbandry and Fishery | 4105 | 2595 | 2859 | 2000 |
| 采矿业 | Mining and Quarrying | 2018 | 416 | 1274 | 134 |
| 开采专业及辅助性活动 | Support Activity for Mining and Quarrying | 8 | 5 | 8 | 5 |
| 制造业 | Manufacturing | 353944 | 122839 | 270857 | 100478 |
| 金属制品、机械和设备修理业 | Metal Products,Machinery and Equipment Repair | 1635 | 1102 | 1495 | 996 |
| 电力、热力、燃气及水的生产和供应业 | Production and Supply of Electricity,Gas and Water | 4107 | 2047 | 2759 | 1637 |
| 建筑业 | Construction | 125045 | 88578 | 111051 | 79185 |
| 批发和零售业 | Wholesale and Retail Trade & Catering Services | 679192 | 492078 | 627800 | 454246 |
| 交通运输、仓储和邮政业 | Transportation,Storage and Post | 33915 | 22618 | 26011 | 17188 |
| 住宿和餐饮业 | Lodging and Catering | 52384 | 42188 | 46853 | 38322 |
| 信息传输、软件和信息技术服务业 | Information Transmission,Computer Services and Software | 261555 | 225293 | 247865 | 214154 |
| 金融业 | Banking and Insurance | 29129 | 23581 | 26520 | 22039 |
| 房地产业 | Real Estate | 54073 | 43174 | 47365 | 37749 |
| 租赁和商务服务业 | Renting and Business Service | 401664 | 305005 | 379004 | 287832 |
| 科学研究和技术服务业 | Scientific Research and Technical Service | 206583 | 165345 | 193622 | 157814 |
| 水利、环境和公共设施管理业 | Water Conservancy,Environment and Public Utility | 8408 | 6337 | 7000 | 5391 |
| 居民服务、修理和其他服务业 | Service for the Residents and Other Service Sector | 77492 | 54965 | 71105 | 50563 |
| 教育 | Education | 17461 | 14803 | 16149 | 13662 |
| 卫生和社会工作 | Health Care,Sports & Social Welfare | 10222 | 6939 | 9390 | 6359 |
| 文化、体育和娱乐业 | Culture,Sports and Entertainment | 73213 | 63795 | 67522 | 59474 |
| 其他 | Others | 1071 | 912 | 940 | 799 |

8－12　续表2　continued 2

| 项　　目 | Item | 全市 Whole City 合计 Total | 全市 Whole City #城镇 Urban | 市区 Urban District 合计 Total | 市区 Urban District #城镇 Urban |
|---|---|---|---|---|---|
| **注册资金(万元)** | **Capital Registered(10000 yuan)** | **548095350** | **493902108** | **521002480** | **474812187** |
| 农、林、牧、渔业 | Farming, Forestry, Animal Husbandry and Fishery | 3522123 | 2104395 | 2515253 | 1693852 |
| 农、林、牧、渔专业及辅助性活动 | Service for Farming, Forestry, Animal Husbandry and Fishery | 876234 | 648681 | 678419 | 548835 |
| 采矿业 | Mining and Quarrying | 215801 | 100680 | 158865 | 81893 |
| 开采专业及辅助性活动 | Support Activity for Mining and Quarrying | 27700 | 27100 | 27700 | 27100 |
| 制造业 | Manufacturing | 27760353 | 13658312 | 24924246 | 12350432 |
| 金属制品、机械和设备修理业 | Metal Products, Machinery and Equipment Repair | 162379 | 135198 | 156839 | 131088 |
| 电力、热力、燃气及水的生产和供应业 | Production and Supply of Electricity, Gas and Water | 1237005 | 1008608 | 1050375 | 909186 |
| 建筑业 | Construction | 29736446 | 25488785 | 27663557 | 23976406 |
| 批发和零售业 | Wholesale and Retail Trade & Catering Services | 71224197 | 64466874 | 66720995 | 61048176 |
| 交通运输、仓储和邮政业 | Transportation, Storage and Post | 4325793 | 3516207 | 3457165 | 2851350 |
| 住宿和餐饮业 | Lodging and Catering | 2763418 | 2351771 | 2432421 | 2136783 |
| 信息传输、软件和信息技术服务业 | Information Transmission, Computer Services and Software | 40928646 | 38651973 | 39516766 | 37504370 |
| 金融业 | Banking and Insurance | 24068180 | 22175118 | 22011881 | 20707011 |
| 房地产业 | Real Estate | 20075845 | 17149329 | 19033802 | 16282178 |
| 租赁和商务服务业 | Renting and Business Service | 259628320 | 245358534 | 251993038 | 239800112 |
| 科学研究和技术服务业 | Scientific Research and Technical Service | 39104072 | 36187447 | 37585457 | 35071052 |
| 水利、环境和公共设施管理业 | Water Conservancy, Environment and Public Utility | 1978999 | 1757458 | 1695061 | 1550284 |
| 居民服务、修理和其他服务业 | Service for the Residents and Other Service Sector | 8085229 | 7131060 | 7677748 | 6806472 |
| 教育 | Education | 1040643 | 974915 | 973757 | 921843 |
| 卫生和社会工作 | Health Care, Sports & Social Welfare | 1056290 | 1014928 | 805617 | 773241 |
| 文化、体育和娱乐业 | Culture, Sports and Entertainment | 10279710 | 9749936 | 9793008 | 9356478 |
| 其他 | Others | 1064280 | 1055778 | 993468 | 991068 |

# 8－13 分行业、类型规模以上

## Main Indicators of Service Enterprises

单位:亿元

| 项　目 | Item | 单位数(个) Number of Enterprise (Unit) | 资产总计 Total Assets | 固定资产原价 Orginal Value of Fixed Assets |
|---|---|---|---|---|
| **总　计** | **Total** | **4303** | **29337** | **4915** |
| **按登记注册类型分** | **Grouped By Registered Type** | | | |
| 国有企业 | State－owned Enterprises | 62 | 998 | 251 |
| 集体企业 | Collective－owned Enterprises | 73 | 501 | 180 |
| 股份合作企业 | Cooperative Enterprises | 11 | 94 | 49 |
| 其他联营企业 | Other Joint Ownership Enterprises | 1 | 1 | － |
| 其他有限责任公司 | Other Limited Liability Corporations | 826 | 6806 | 1461 |
| 股份有限公司 | Share－holding Corporations Ltd. | 192 | 2809 | 354 |
| 私营企业 | Private Enterprises | 2718 | 3880 | 642 |
| 其他企业 | Other Enterprises | 24 | 19 | 3 |
| 港澳台商投资企业 | Enterprises With Investment from Hong Kong, Macao and Taiwan | 106 | 6234 | 836 |
| 外商投资企业 | Enterprises With Foreign Investment | 125 | 1138 | 333 |
| **按国民经济行业分** | **Grouped by Sector** | | | |
| 交通运输、仓储和邮政业 | Transportation, Storage and Post | 712 | 2299 | 1301 |
| 信息传输、软件和信息技术服务业 | Information Transmission, Softuare and Information Technology | 903 | 9562 | 1458 |
| 房地产业 | Real Estate | 447 | 1850 | 363 |
| 租赁和商务服务业 | Leasing and Business Services | 928 | 7913 | 1107 |
| 科学研究和技术服务业 | Scientific Research and Technical Service | 607 | 1680 | 178 |
| 水利、环境和公共设施管理业 | Water Conservancy, Environment and Public Utility | 129 | 5061 | 367 |
| 居民服务、修理和其他服务业 | Service for the Residents and Other Service Sector | 141 | 49 | 11 |
| 教育 | Education | 58 | 49 | 10 |
| 卫生和社会工作 | Health Care and Social Welfare | 155 | 86 | 20 |
| 文化、体育和娱乐业 | Culture, Sports and Entertainment | 223 | 787 | 100 |

# 服务业企业主要经济指标(2019年)

# Above Designated Size by Sector and Type(2019)

(100 million yuan)

| 其中:本年折旧 Depreciation | 负债合计 Total Liabilities | 所有者权益合计 Total Owners´ Equities | 营业收入 Revenue of Business | 营业成本 Operating Costs | 营业税金及附加 Sales Taxes and Extra Charges in Main Business |
|---:|---:|---:|---:|---:|---:|
| **396** | **15205** | **14132** | **12866** | **8102** | **61** |
| 7 | 210 | 788 | 334 | 254 | 1 |
| 5 | 181 | 321 | 36 | 19 | 3 |
| 1 | 21 | 73 | 8 | 1 | 1 |
| – | 1 | – | 1 | | – |
| 69 | 4031 | 2775 | 1984 | 1564 | 10 |
| 23 | 1070 | 1739 | 459 | 301 | 3 |
| 76 | 2684 | 1196 | 3965 | 2752 | 16 |
| – | 14 | 4 | 29 | 18 | – |
| 153 | 2957 | 3277 | 3494 | 860 | 20 |
| 29 | 596 | 543 | 2007 | 1929 | 4 |
| 75 | 1429 | 871 | 1594 | 1502 | 5 |
| 223 | 4765 | 4798 | 7516 | 3676 | 27 |
| 15 | 1093 | 758 | 354 | 233 | 11 |
| 50 | 3721 | 4193 | 1464 | 1188 | 10 |
| 13 | 935 | 746 | 1115 | 883 | 4 |
| 9 | 2935 | 2127 | 391 | 320 | 1 |
| 1 | 31 | 18 | 64 | 42 | – |
| 1 | 36 | 13 | 51 | 30 | – |
| 2 | 56 | 30 | 112 | 71 | – |
| 6 | 207 | 580 | 203 | 157 | 2 |

| 项　　目 | Item | 销售费用 Cost of Sales | 管理费用 Administration Cost | 财务费用 Financil Cost |
|---|---|---|---|---|
| **总　计** | **Total** | **724** | **2064** | **58** |
| **按登记注册类型分** | **Grouped By Registered Type** | | | |
| 国有企业 | State－owned Enterprises | 14 | 23 | －12 |
| 集体企业 | Collective－owned Enterprises | 1 | 11 | －2 |
| 股份合作企业 | Cooperative Enterprises | – | 2 | – |
| 其他联营企业 | Other Joint Ownership Enterprises | – | – | – |
| 其他有限责任公司 | Other Limited Liability Corporations | 81 | 191 | 38 |
| 股份有限公司 | Share－holding Corporations Ltd. | 35 | 46 | 7 |
| 私营企业 | Private Enterprises | 247 | 581 | 32 |
| 其他企业 | Other Enterprises | 3 | 6 | – |
| 港澳台商投资企业 | Enterprises With Investment from Hong Kong, Macao and Taiwan | 291 | 1109 | －62 |
| 外商投资企业 | Enterprises With Foreign Investment | 36 | 56 | －4 |
| **按国民经济行业分** | **Grouped by Sector** | | | |
| 交通运输、仓储和邮政业 | Transportation, Storage and Post | 25 | 63 | 27 |
| 信息传输、软件和信息技术服务业 | Information Transmission, Softuare and Information Technology | 554 | 1661 | －67 |
| 房地产业 | Real Estate | 20 | 46 | 20 |
| 租赁和商务服务业 | Leasing and Business Services | 57 | 120 | 35 |
| 科学研究和技术服务业 | Scientific Research and Technical Service | 22 | 96 | 5 |
| 水利、环境和公共设施管理业 | Water Conservancy, Environment and Public Utility | 3 | 16 | 42 |
| 居民服务、修理和其他服务业 | Service for the Residents and Other Service Sector | 9 | 10 | – |
| 教育 | Education | 7 | 9 | – |
| 卫生和社会工作 | Health Care and Social Welfare | 13 | 19 | 1 |
| 文化、体育和娱乐业 | Culture, Sports and Entertainment | 14 | 24 | －5 |

continued (100 million yuan)

| 营业利润 Management Profits | 利润总额 Total Profits | 所得税费用 Income Tax | 应付职工薪酬 Payroll Payable | 应交增值税 Value Added Tax Payable | 平均用工人数(万人) Average Number of Employed Persons(10000 Persons) |
|---|---|---|---|---|---|
| **1994** | **2073** | **240** | **1599** | **253** | **85** |
| | | | | | |
| 180 | 181 | 2 | 52 | 9 | 3 |
| 7 | 7 | – | 5 | 2 | – |
| 4 | 3 | – | 1 | – | – |
| – | – | – | – | – | – |
| 143 | 151 | 28 | 368 | 39 | 21 |
| 117 | 118 | 14 | 96 | 11 | 6 |
| 270 | 283 | 24 | 427 | 73 | 36 |
| 2 | 2 | – | 10 | 1 | 1 |
| 1187 | 1200 | 128 | 467 | 101 | 7 |
| -15 | -11 | 38 | 86 | 9 | 5 |
| | | | | | |
| 26 | 34 | 24 | 163 | 20 | 13 |
| 1479 | 1502 | 166 | 854 | 154 | 23 |
| 51 | 64 | 14 | 90 | 14 | 12 |
| 295 | 298 | 17 | 162 | 26 | 16 |
| 77 | 79 | 11 | 197 | 23 | 10 |
| 11 | 41 | 3 | 33 | 4 | 3 |
| 3 | 3 | 1 | 20 | 2 | 3 |
| 4 | 4 | 1 | 19 | 1 | 1 |
| 8 | 8 | 2 | 28 | – | 2 |
| 39 | 40 | 2 | 34 | 8 | 2 |

# 8－14 规模以上服务业企业主要经济指标(2013－2019 年)

## Main Indicators of Service Enterprises Above Designated Size(2013－2019)

单位:亿元 (100 million yuan)

| 项　目 | Item | 2013 | 2014 | 2015 | 2016 | 2017 | 2018 | 2019 |
|---|---|---|---|---|---|---|---|---|
| 单位数(个) | Number of Enterprises(Unit) | 4770 | 4393 | 3238 | 3486 | 3744 | 4145 | 4303 |
| 资产总计 | Total Assets | 13208 | 14340 | 15412 | 18951 | 20198 | 27522 | 29337 |
| 固定资产原价 | Orginal Value of Fixed Assets | 2399 | 2716 | 2847 | 3129 | 3657 | 4319 | 4915 |
| 本年折旧 | Depreciation | 138 | 156 | 177 | 207 | 234 | 303 | 396 |
| 负债合计 | Total Liabilities | 6789 | 7181 | 7463 | 9134 | 10063 | 14317 | 15205 |
| 所有者权益合计 | Total Owners´Equities | 6418 | 7160 | 7949 | 9816 | 10135 | 13235 | 14132 |
| 营业收入 | Revenue of Business | 3719 | 4353 | 5236 | 6639 | 8557 | 11158 | 12866 |
| 营业成本 | Main Cost of Business | 2335 | 2650 | 3215 | 4111 | 5410 | 7280 | 8102 |
| 营业税金及附加 | Sales Taxes and Extra Charges in Main Business | 59 | 58 | 59 | 47 | 47 | 54 | 61 |
| 销售费用 | Cost of Sales | 221 | 257 | 314 | 341 | 457 | 651 | 724 |
| 管理费用 | Administration Cost | 468 | 621 | 765 | 932 | 1223 | 1747 | 2064 |
| 财务费用 | Financil Cost | 70 | 62 | 65 | 43 | 53 | 37 | 58 |
| 营业利润 | Management Profits | 725 | 858 | 1020 | 1352 | 1636 | 1812 | 1994 |
| 利润总额 | Total Profits | 795 | 934 | 1110 | 1443 | 1689 | 1853 | 2073 |
| 所得税费用 | Income Tax Costs | 76 | 123 | 110 | 174 | 196 | 192 | 240 |
| 应付职工薪酬 | Employee benefits Payable | 486 | 588 | 718 | 904 | 1123 | 1344 | 1599 |
| 应交增值税 | Value Added Tax Payable | 61 | 107 | 106 | 153 | 194 | 216 | 253 |
| 平均用工人数(万人) | Average Number of Employed Persons | 57.74 | 60.29 | 63.22 | 68.92 | 76.24 | 81.15 | 85.43 |

# 主要统计指标解释

**社会消费品零售总额** 指各种经济类型的批发零售贸易业、住宿餐饮业对城乡居民和社会集团的消费品零售额总和。这个指标反映通过各种商品流通渠道向居民和社会集团供应的生活消费品来满足他们生活需要，是研究人民生活、社会消费品购买力、货币流通等问题的重要指标。社会消费品零售额包括:(1)售给城乡居民作为生活用的商品和修建房屋用的建筑材料;(2)售给机关、团体、学校、部队、企业、事业单位的职工食堂各种食品、燃料;(3)售给部队干部、战士生活用的粮食、副食品、衣着品、日用品、燃料;(4)售给来华的外国人、华侨、港澳台同胞的消费品;(5)售给社会集团的办公用品、纸张、帐册、文印用品、计算工具、书刊杂志和奖品;公共用品和纺织品、针织品;学校用的教学用具;文体用品;非专用的劳动保护用品，如工作服、套袖、围裙、手套、毛巾、肥皂等;日用百货和杂品，包括职工食堂用的餐具、炊具、设备和清洁卫生工具等;家具、设备、日用电器、电讯设备、电影器材和照相器材等;取暖用的设备和燃料、防暑、降温的饮料;非生产经营用的交通工具，如小轿车、面包车、工具车、卡车和油料;零星修理的各种零配件、材料、工具、建筑材料等;举办各种招待会、茶话会、宴会用的烟酒茶和各种食品及馈赠的礼品;从公费医疗经费中开支的中、西药品、中药材和医疗器材以及其他非生产性设备和用品。

**限额以上批发零售业** 指批发业年主营业务收入在2000万元及以上，零售业年主营业务收入在500万元及以上的各种经济类型商贸企业。

**商品销售总额** 指对本企业(单位)以外的单位和个人出售(包括对国(境)外直接出口)的商品金额。这个指标反映批发零售贸易业在国内市场上销售商品以及出口商品的总量。商品销售总额包括:(1)售给城乡居民和社会集团消费用的商品;(2)售给工业、农业、建筑业、运输邮电业、批发零售贸易业、餐饮业、服务业等作为生产、经营使用的商品;(3)售给批发零售贸易业作为转卖或加工后转卖的商品;(4)对国(境)外直接出口的商品，不包括:出售本企业(单位)自用的废旧包装用品，未通过买卖行为付出的商品，经本单位介绍，由买卖双方直接结算，本单位只收取手续费的业务，购货退出的商品以及商品损耗和损失等。

# Explanatory Notes on Main Statistical Indicators

**Total Retail Sales of Consumer Goods** refer to the sum of retail sales of consumer goods sold by wholesale and retail trade, catering and lodging industry of various economic types to urban and rural residents and social groups. This indicator is used to show the supply of consumer goods through various channels to residents and social groups to meet their needs in life, and is very important for the study on people's livelihood, on the purchasing power of consumer goods and on the circulation of money. The total retail sales of consumer goods include: (1) commodities sold to urban and rural residents for their daily use and building materials sold to them for the construction or repair of houses; (2) food and fuels sold to canteens of government organs, organizations, schools, troops, enterprises and institutions; (3) grains, non – staple food, clothing, daily articles and fuels sold to military, personnel for their daily use; (4) consumer goods sold to foreigners, overseas Chinese, and Chinese compatriots form Taiwan, Hong Kong and Macao during their stay in the mainland of China; (5) commodities sold to social groups, including office appliances, paper, account books, printing articles, calculators, newspapers, magazines and prizes; public articles, textiles and knit goods; school teaching equipment; cultural and sports articles; non special labor protection articles like working clothes, sleeves, aprons, gloves, towel sand soaps; commodities and miscellaneous goods for daily use including tableware, cooking utensils, equipment and cleaning articles for canteens; furnishings, appliances, household electrical appliances, communications facilities, film and photograph equipment; heating facilities, fuels and cooling beverages preventing heatstroke; vehicles ( not for business use ) such as cars, vans, tool cars, trucks and oils; parts, fittings, materials, instruments and building materials in ordinary repair, tobaccos, alcohols, teas, foods and presents for all kinds of reception meetings and banquets; Chinese and Western medicines, herbs and medical facilities and other non – production goods and equipment paid by public medical fund.

**Wholesale and Retail Trade Above Designated Size** refer to business enterprises of various economic types engaged in wholesale trade with year main business revenue over 20 million Yuan, and in retail sale trade with year main business revenue over 5 million Yuan.

**Total Sales of Commodities** refer to the amount of commodities sold by enterprises to other units and individuals (including direct export). This indictor is used to show the total value of commodities sold at domestic markets and exported. It includes: (1) commodities sold to urban and rural residents and social groups for consumption; (2) commodities sold for production and management of industry, agriculture, construction, transportation, post and telecommunications, wholesale and retail trades, catering trade and service industry; (3) commodities sold to wholesale and retail establishment for re – selling, with or without further processing; (4) commodities for direct export, excluding waste packaging materials used by the establishments (units) themselves, commodities transferred without buying or selling procedures, businesses directly settled by both parties through introduction of units who only charge commission, rejected commodities in the purchase, loss in commodities, etc.

# 九、对外经济旅游

FOREIGN ECONOMIC COOPERATION AND TOURISM

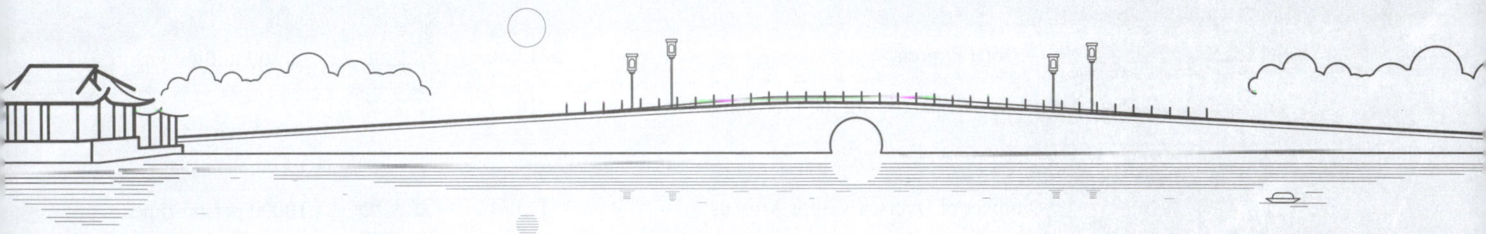

# 9 对外经济、旅游
# Foreign Economic Cooperation and Tourism

## 主要统计指标
## Major Statistical Indicators

| | | | | |
|---|---|---|---|---|
| 实际利用外资金额 | Foreign Investments Actually Utilized | 61.28 | 亿美元 | ( USD 100 million ) |
| 为上年 | As Compared with the Preceding Year | 114.0 | % | ( % ) |
| 进出口总额 | Total Imports and Exports | 811.54 | 亿美元 | ( USD 100 million ) |
| 为上年 | As Compared with the Preceding Year | 102.0 | % | ( % ) |
| # 出口总额 | Total Exports | 523.83 | 亿美元 | ( USD 100 million ) |
| 为上年 | As Compared with the Preceding Year | 101.1 | % | ( % ) |
| 进出口总额 | Total Imports and Exports | 5596.81 | 亿元 | ( 100 million yuan ) |
| 为上年 | As Compared with the Preceding Year | 106.7 | % | ( % ) |
| # 出口总额 | Total Exports | 3612.66 | 亿元 | ( 100 million yuan ) |
| 为上年 | As Compared with the Preceding Year | 105.7 | % | ( % ) |
| 入境过夜游客 | Number of Oversea Visitor Arrivals | 113.31 | 万人次 | ( 10000 person-times ) |
| 为上年 | As Compared with the Preceding Year | 105.7 | % | ( % ) |
| 旅游外汇收入 | Total Foreign Exchange Earnings from International Tourism | 7.37 | 亿美元 | ( USD 100 million ) |
| 为上年 | As Compared with the Preceding Year | 99.4 | % | ( % ) |

# 9-01 外商直接投资情况(1978-2019年)
# Foreign Direct Investment(1978-2019)

单位:万美元 (USD 10000)

| 年 份 Year | 项目个数(个) Number of Projects (unit) | 协议总投资额 Total Investments of Agreements | 协议利用外资金额 Contracted Foreign Investment | 实际利用外资金额 Foreign Investments Actually Utilized |
|---|---|---|---|---|
| 1978 | | | | |
| 1979 | | | | |
| 1980 | 3 | 153 | 128 | |
| 1981 | | | | |
| 1982 | | | | |
| 1983 | 2 | 356 | 100 | |
| 1984 | 9 | 6932 | 2697 | |
| 1985 | 21 | 6638 | 1731 | 907 |
| 1986 | 9 | 5722 | 2017 | 683 |
| 1987 | 10 | 2685 | 1256 | 1470 |
| 1988 | 23 | 6781 | 2734 | 696 |
| 1989 | 34 | 3897 | 1569 | 1860 |
| 1990 | 68 | 7817 | 3951 | 751 |
| 1991 | 121 | 11107 | 5551 | 2129 |
| 1992 | 583 | 125224 | 60915 | 9678 |
| 1993 | 1078 | 222325 | 121947 | 35713 |
| 1994 | 624 | 174406 | 110541 | 41098 |
| 1995 | 427 | 136662 | 90207 | 42659 |
| 1996 | 221 | 108150 | 70982 | 53651 |
| 1997 | 174 | 51682 | 27888 | 41187 |
| 1998 | 216 | 98219 | 51400 | 38425 |
| 1999 | 212 | 83416 | 56742 | 42025 |
| 2000 | 315 | 89781 | 64548 | 43093 |
| 2001 | 483 | 154447 | 103023 | 50324 |
| 2002 | 587 | 247888 | 96720 | 52186 |
| 2003 | 869 | 432660 | 200104 | 100850 |
| 2004 | 802 | 629727 | 307746 | 140982 |
| 2005 | 756 | 770941 | 400503 | 171274 |
| 2006 | 747 | 1080602 | 537986 | 225536 |
| 2007 | 574 | 854907 | 558059 | 280181 |
| 2008 | 483 | 862523 | 622788 | 331154 |
| 2009 | 554 | 948323 | 696486 | 401370 |
| 2010 | 545 | 1188055 | 770911 | 435627 |
| 2011 | 500 | 1291015 | 817108 | 472230 |
| 2012 | 510 | 1342616 | 826516 | 496061 |
| 2013 | 415 | 1419926 | 913144 | 527633 |
| 2014 | 408 | 1329217 | 723838 | 633460 |
| 2015 | 475 | 1649709 | 1038042 | 711253 |
| 2016 | 462 | 1503411 | 847841 | 720915 |
| 2017 | 575 | 1877119 | 1069651 | 661001 |
| 2018 | 744 | 2545689 | 1565483 | 682658 |
| 2019 | 735 | 3066139 | 1321928 | 612818 |

# 9－02 分行业外商直接投资情况(2019年)

## Foreign Direct Investment by Sector(2019)

单位:万美元 (USD 10,000)

| 行　业<br>Sector | 项目数(个)<br>Projects(unit) | 占总数%<br>Proportion(%) | 实际利用外资金额<br>Foreign Investments Actually Utilized | 占总数(%)<br>Proportion(%) |
|---|---|---|---|---|
| **合　计<br>Total** | **735** | **100** | **612818** | **100** |
| **第一产业** | **3** | **0.41** | **30** | **-** |
| 农、林、牧、渔业<br>Agriculture | 3 | 0.41 | 30 | - |
| **第二产业** | **70** | **9.52** | **72999** | **11.91** |
| 制造业<br>Manufacturing | 60 | 8.16 | 59617 | 9.73 |
| 电力、燃气及水生产和供应业<br>Production & Supply of Electricity, Gas & Water | 4 | 0.54 | 3337 | 0.54 |
| 建筑业<br>Construction | 6 | 0.82 | 10045 | 1.64 |
| **第三产业** | **662** | **90.05** | **539789** | **88.09** |
| 批发和零售业 | 190 | 25.85 | 35043 | 5.72 |
| 交通运输、仓储和邮政业<br>Transportation, Storage and Post | 3 | 0.41 | 28233 | 4.61 |
| 住宿和餐饮业 | 14 | 1.9 | 85 | 0.01 |
| 信息传输、软件和信息技术服务业<br>Information Transmission, Softuare and Information Technology | 218 | 29.66 | 156753 | 25.58 |
| 金融业<br>Banking and Insuranc | 2 | 0.27 | 30740 | 5.02 |
| 房地产业<br>Real Estat | 17 | 2.31 | 210139 | 34.29 |
| 租赁和商务服务业<br>Leasing and Business Services | 73 | 9.93 | 51536 | 8.41 |
| 科学研究和技术服务业<br>Scientific Research and Technical Service | 111 | 15.1 | 23852 | 3.89 |
| 其他行业<br>Others | 34 | 4.62 | 3408 | 0.56 |

# 9-03 分国别(地区)外商直接投资情况(2019年)
## Foreign Direct Investment by Region or Territory(2019)

单位:万美元 (USD 10000)

| 国别(地区) | Country (territory) | 历年累计 Accumulated | | | 2019年 In Year 2019 | | | |
|---|---|---|---|---|---|---|---|---|
| | | 项目(个) Projects (unit) | 总投资额 Total Investments | 协议外资金额 Total Contracted Foreign Investments | 项目(个) Projects (unit) | 总投资额 Total Investments | 协议外资金额 Total Contracted Foreign Investments | 实际利用外资 Foreign Investments Actually Utilized |
| **合计** | **Total** | **15405** | **24343379** | **14098046** | **735** | **3066139** | **1321928** | **612818** |
| #香港 | #Hong Kong | 6721 | 17253965 | 9880504 | 279 | 2614119 | 1155615 | 506408 |
| 澳门 | Macao | 82 | 83981 | 49412 | 1 | 29 | 29 | 100 |
| 台湾 | Taiwan | 1680 | 489495 | 262021 | 65 | 9475 | 4928 | 387 |
| 日本 | Japan | 824 | 644117 | 278459 | 29 | 37857 | 9854 | 8703 |
| 泰国 | Thailand | 45 | 13416 | 3708 | - | - | - | 22 |
| 马来西亚 | Malaysia | 99 | 51341 | 34481 | 4 | 73 | 63 | 16 |
| 新加坡 | Singapore | 382 | 673555 | 393780 | 21 | 44236 | 22289 | 11343 |
| 印度 | India | 46 | 6199 | 5549 | 11 | 134 | 96 | 1 |
| 韩国 | Republic of Korea | 422 | 175673 | 87063 | 29 | 3565 | 1984 | 182 |
| 德国 | Germany | 239 | 146072 | 83536 | 6 | 26413 | 13722 | 5927 |
| 法国 | France | 155 | 77534 | 47082 | 14 | 1302 | 240 | 32 |
| 意大利 | Italy | 237 | 157609 | 76042 | 4 | 175 | 127 | 68 |
| 荷兰 | Netherlands | 99 | 113561 | 27530 | 4 | 268 | 1065 | - |
| 英国 | Britain | 248 | 270038 | 166221 | 19 | 62621 | 20787 | 5623 |
| 西班牙 | Spain | 79 | 70331 | 27447 | 2 | 921 | -469 | 74 |
| 奥地利 | Austria | 28 | 43206 | 33069 | 2 | 6170 | 6084 | 5159 |
| 俄罗斯联邦 | The Russion Federation | 22 | 3494 | 1642 | 3 | 184 | 70 | - |
| 英属维尔京群岛 | The British Virgin Islands | 603 | 1636979 | 806763 | 15 | 66675 | 31301 | 42349 |
| 加拿大 | Canada | 281 | 113947 | 75467 | 17 | 556 | -107 | 62 |
| 美国 | U.S.A | 1931 | 1381223 | 654533 | 88 | 144149 | 34861 | 9237 |
| 澳大利亚 | Australia | 241 | 108891 | 84751 | 21 | 2300 | 1864 | 369 |
| 新西兰 | New Zealand | 47 | 13772 | 9534 | 3 | 222 | 121 | - |

# 9－04 分地区外商直接投资情况(2019年)

## Foreign Direct Investment by Region(2019)

单位:万美元 (USD 10000)

| 区 域 Region | 批准项目个数(个) Number of Projects(unit) | | 实际利用外资金额 Foreign Investments Actually Utilized | |
|---|---|---|---|---|
| | 2019年 In Year 2019 | 历年累计 Accumulated Until the End of 2019 | 2019年 In Year 2019 | 历年累计 Accumulated Until the End of 2019 |
| **全 市 Total** | **735** | **15405** | **612818** | **8063799** |
| 市 区 Urban District | 712 | 14315 | 544089 | 7599850 |
| #上城区 Shangcheng | 31 | 831 | 38579 | 335359 |
| 下城区 Xiacheng | 47 | 886 | 67025 | 227981 |
| 江干区 Jianggan | 66 | 901 | 46554 | 391088 |
| 拱墅区 Gongshu | 45 | 1072 | 38124 | 496289 |
| 西湖区 Xihu | 92 | 1326 | 70232 | 668177 |
| 高新(滨江)区 Hi－Tech(Binjiang) | 132 | 1437 | 64744 | 954503 |
| 萧山区 Xiaoshan | 65 | 2082 | 83516 | 1287269 |
| 余杭区 Yuhang | 115 | 1878 | 89560 | 922177 |
| 富阳区 Fuyang | 23 | 787 | 29747 | 349062 |
| 临安区 Lin'an | 20 | 472 | 16008 | 225728 |
| 钱塘新区 Qiantang New Area | 76 | 197 | 38119 | 240265 |
| 桐庐县 Tonglu | 6 | 578 | 17000 | 199973 |
| 淳安县 Chun'an | 5 | 226 | 2003 | 101729 |
| 建德市 Jiande | 12 | 286 | 11607 | 124128 |

# 9-05 省级产业集聚区建设发展情况(2016-2019年末)

## Statistics on Provincial-level Industry Cluster Districts Development (End of 2016-2019)

| 项　目 | Item | 城西科创产业集聚区 Chengxi Technological and Creative Industry Cluster District | | | |
|---|---|---|---|---|---|
| | | 2019年末 End of 2019 | 2018年末 End of 2018 | 2017年末 End of 2017 | 2016年末 End of 2016 |
| 入区企业数(个) Proposed Enterprises | (unit) | 18103 | 15103 | 13956 | 12506 |
| 投产企业数(个) Operating Enterprises | (unit) | 1117 | 622 | 594 | 543 |
| 已开发建设面积(平方千米) Land Space under Construction | (sq. km) | *41.94 | 36.70 | 36.70 | 36.70 |
| 已建成投产面积(平方千米) Land Space Completed | (sq. km) | *37.51 | 34.20 | 34.20 | 34.20 |
| 当年产业增加值(亿元) Current year's Value-added | (100 million yuan) | 1879.40 | 1582.90 | 1341.31 | 1013.70 |
| #工业增加值(亿元) Value-added of Industry | (100 million yuan) | 200.40 | 155.50 | 130.00 | 111.06 |
| #服务业增加值(亿元) Value-added of the Tertiary Industry | (100 million yuan) | 1679.00 | 1427.40 | 1211.34 | 902.64 |
| 当年实际引进内资(亿元) Current Year's Amount of Domestic Investment | (100 million yuan) | - | 82.70 | 51.70 | 44.80 |
| 当年实际利用外资(亿美元) Current Year's Amount of Foreign Investment Actually Utilized | (100 million USD) | - | 5.20 | 2.90 | 2.40 |
| 当年科技活动经费支出(亿元) Current Year's S & T Expenditure | (100 million yuan) | *282.56 | 233.10 | 179.07 | 164.74 |
| 科技活动人员数(人) S & T Personnel | (person) | *34119 | 24678 | 20316 | 16261 |
| 当年财政预算总收入(亿元) Current Year's Total Financial Revenue | (100 million yuan) | 431.00 | 320.60 | 233.70 | 169.10 |
| 当年固定资产投资完成额(亿元) Current Year's Investment in Fixed Assets | (100 million yuan) | *568.5 | - | 430.72 | 366.90 |
| 当年工业总产值(亿元) Current Year's Gross Industrial Output Value | (100 million yuan) | *726.39 | 678.40 | 588.25 | 494.78 |
| 当年服务业营业收入(亿元) Current Year's Operating Revenue of the Tertiary Industry | (100 million yuan) | 7599.90 | 4728.40 | 3307.80 | 2226.81 |
| 当年出口交货值(亿元) Current Year's Export Delivery Value | (100 million yuan) | - | 91.10 | 94.00 | 83.08 |
| 当年利税总额(亿元) Current Year's Total Taxes and Profits | (100 million yuan) | 1499.80 | 1212.50 | 1107.27 | 811.90 |
| #利润总额(亿元) Total Profits | (100 million yuan) | 1346.10 | 1110.40 | 1016.08 | 732.80 |

注:2019年加*数据为城西科创产业集聚区数据,其它为城西科创大走廊数据;2017年城西科创产业集聚区统计口径有调整,2016年数据已调整成同口径;城西科创产业集聚区的财政预算总收入为企业税收收入。

a) Data with * in 2019 is the data of science and innovation industry cluster area in the west of the city, and the other is the data of science and innovation corridor in the west of the city. The statistical method of Chengxi Technological and Creative Industry Cluster District was adjusted in 2017, and the data of 2016 were adjusted by the same way. The total financial revenue of Chengxi Technological and Creative Industry Cluster District refers to enterperises'tax revenue.

# 9-06 国家级开发区

## The Construction of National -

| 项 目 | Item |
|---|---|
| 规划面积 （平方公里） | Area of planning (sq. km) |
| 已开发面积 （平方公里） | Area of Development (sq. km) |
| 历年累计基础设施投资额 （亿元） | Accumulative Total Investments in Infrastructure (100 million yuan) |
| 历年累计批准进区企业 （个） | Accumulative Number of Enterprises Approved (unit) |
| #三资企业 （个） | Foreign Investments Enter-prises (unit) |
| 历年累计协议利用外资 （亿美元） | Accumulative Total Foreign Investments of Agreements (USD 100 million) |
| 历年累计实际利用外资 （亿美元） | Accumulative Total Foreign Investments Actually Used (USD 100 million) |
| 年末实有投产企业个数 （个） | Number of Enterprises in Production or Operation at the Year-end (unit) |
| #三资企业 （个） | Foreign Investments Enter-prises (unit) |
| 当年规模以上工业总产值 （亿元） | Gross Industrial Output Value of the Year (100 million yuan) |
| 当年规模以上企业主营业务收入 （亿元） | Fulfilled Profits and Tax of the Year (100 million yuan) |
| 当年规模以上企业实现利润 （亿元） | Fulfilled Profits of the Enterprises above the Designated Size of the Year (100 million yuan) |
| 当年出口创汇 （亿美元） | Foreign Exchange Earnings of Export of the Year (USD 100 million) |
| 当年财政总收入 （亿元） | Total Financial Revenue of the Year (100 million yuan) |
| # 税收收入 （亿元） | Tax Revenue (unit) |

## 建设发展情况(2019 年)
## Class Development Zones(2019)

| 合计<br>Total | 杭州高新技术开发区<br>Hangzhou High - tech Development Zone | 萧山经济技术开发区<br>Xiaoshan Economic and Technological Development Zone | 富阳经济技术开发区<br>Fuyang Economic and Technological Development Zone | 余杭经济技术开发区<br>Yuhang Economic and Technological Development Zone | 临江国家高新区<br>Linjiang Nationd High - Tech Zone |
|---|---|---|---|---|---|
| 817.53 | 12.12 | 58.41 | 106.04 | 109.26 | 531.70 |
| 250.66 | 12.12 | 45.40 | 41.14 | 46.20 | 105.80 |
| 3155.87 | 440.83 | 380.68 | 818.47 | 535.52 | 980.37 |
| 180454 | 64748 | 10262 | 21646 | 37713 | 46085 |
| 3721 | 775 | 585 | 565 | 510 | 1286 |
| 447.66 | – | 115.48 | 37.75 | 43.94 | 250.49 |
| 354.70 | 92.35 | 63.21 | 28.84 | 32.43 | 137.87 |
| 122552 | 26804 | 10097 | 7229 | 37713 | 40709 |
| 2804 | 775 | 402 | 207 | 510 | 910 |
| 8495.98 | 2285.80 | 828.29 | 1030.48 | 1434.53 | 2916.88 |
| 20030.69 | 7772.51 | 3399.92 | 2166.95 | 3231.11 | 3460.20 |
| 1263.38 | 593.08 | 146.53 | 120.20 | 214.37 | 189.20 |
| 233.08 | 70.35 | 34.55 | 14.92 | 45.67 | 67.59 |
| 1034.95 | 341.90 | 216.48 | 106.86 | 168.51 | 201.20 |
| 975.65 | 332.60 | 209.40 | 73.04 | 168.51 | 192.10 |

# 9-07 特色小镇发展情况(2019年)
## Statistics on Characteristic Towns(2019)

| | 企业数(家) Number of Enterprises (unit) | 本年新入驻企业数(家) Number of new Enterprises to enter this year (unit) | "新四军"人数(个) Number of XinSiJun (unit) | 固定资产投资(不包括商业住宅和商业综合体项目)(亿元) Investment in Fixed Assets (Excluding commercial housing and commercial complex projects) (100 million yuan) |
|---|---|---|---|---|
| **合　计 Total** | **44997** | **9510** | **18923** | **364** |
| 省级特色小镇创建对象 Provincial Characteristic Towns to Create Objects | 36082 | 8042 | 16971 | 267 |
| 省级特色小镇培育对象 Provincial Characteristic Towns to Cultivate Objects | 8915 | 1468 | 1952 | 97 |

注:"新四军"创业人员数:包括大学生创业者、大企业高管及其他连续创业者、科技人员创业者、留学归国人员创业者等创业人员数。包括个体工商户和企业中有技术、资本入股的人员。

a)"XinSiJun" Entrepreneurs: including college student entrepreneurs, big business executives and other serial entrepreneurs, tech entrepreneurs, overseas returnees entrepreneurs and so on. Also including people with technical capital and equity of individual industrial and commercial businesses or enterprises.

9-07 续表 continued

| | 特色产业投资(亿元) Characteristic Industry Investment (100 million yuan) | 工业企业营业收入(亿元) Industrial Enterprise Revenues in Main Business (100 million yuan) | 服务业营业收入(亿元) Service Revenues (100 million yuan) | 税收收入(亿元) Tax Revenues (100 million yuan) |
|---|---|---|---|---|
| **合　计 Total** | **284** | **2557** | **7873** | **708** |
| 省级特色小镇创建对象 Provincial Characteristic Towns to Create Objects | 211 | 2359 | 3254 | 413 |
| 省级特色小镇培育对象 Provincial Characteristic Towns to Cultivate Objects | 73 | 198 | 4619 | 295 |

# 9-08 进出口情况(1990-2019年)
# Imports and Exports (1990-2019)

| 年份 Year | 亿美元 USD 100 million | | | | | | 亿元 100 million yuan | | | | | |
|---|---|---|---|---|---|---|---|---|---|---|---|---|
| | 进出口 Exports And Imports | | 出口 Exports | | 进口 Imports | | 进出口 Exports And Imports | | 出口 Exports | | 进口 Imports | |
| | 总值 Total Value | 为上年% As Compared with the Preceding Year(%) | 总值 Total Value | 为上年% As Compared with the Preceding Year(%) | 总值 Total Value | 为上年% As Compared with the Preceding Year(%) | 总值 Total Value | 为上年% As Compared with the Preceding Year(%) | 总值 Total Value | 为上年% As Compared with the Preceding Year(%) | 总值 Total Value | 为上年% As Compared with the Preceding Year(%) |
| 1990 | 1.45 | 172.6 | 0.99 | 198.0 | 0.46 | 135.3 | | | | | | |
| 1991 | 2.18 | 150.3 | 1.48 | 149.5 | 0.70 | 152.2 | | | | | | |
| 1992 | 3.42 | 156.9 | 2.16 | 146.0 | 1.26 | 180.0 | | | | | | |
| 1993 | 8.73 | 255.3 | 4.92 | 227.8 | 3.81 | 302.4 | | | | | | |
| 1994 | 34.96 | 400.5 | 26.11 | 530.7 | 8.85 | 232.3 | | | | | | |
| 1995 | 45.18 | 129.2 | 33.18 | 127.1 | 12.00 | 135.6 | | | | | | |
| 1996 | 43.52 | 96.3 | 31.11 | 93.8 | 12.41 | 103.4 | | | | | | |
| 1997 | 48.83 | 112.2 | 37.43 | 120.3 | 11.40 | 91.8 | | | | | | |
| 1998 | 59.73 | 122.3 | 44.16 | 118.0 | 15.57 | 136.6 | | | | | | |
| 1999 | 73.40 | 122.9 | 50.79 | 115.0 | 22.61 | 145.3 | | | | | | |
| 2000 | 104.76 | 142.7 | 69.65 | 137.1 | 35.11 | 155.3 | | | | | | |
| 2001 | 112.98 | 107.9 | 72.84 | 104.6 | 40.14 | 114.3 | | | | | | |
| 2002 | 131.07 | 116.0 | 84.81 | 116.4 | 46.26 | 115.3 | | | | | | |
| 2003 | 182.38 | 139.2 | 109.55 | 129.2 | 72.83 | 157.4 | | | | | | |
| 2004 | 244.96 | 134.3 | 151.75 | 138.6 | 93.21 | 128.0 | | | | | | |
| 2005 | 298.70 | 121.9 | 198.04 | 130.5 | 100.66 | 108.0 | | | | | | |
| 2006 | 389.09 | 130.3 | 262.28 | 132.4 | 126.81 | 126.0 | | | | | | |
| 2007 | 434.26 | 111.7 | 299.66 | 114.3 | 134.60 | 106.2 | | | | | | |
| 2008 | 480.65 | 110.7 | 336.14 | 112.2 | 144.51 | 107.4 | | | | | | |
| 2009 | 404.20 | 84.1 | 271.80 | 80.9 | 132.40 | 91.6 | | | | | | |
| 2010 | 523.55 | 129.5 | 353.37 | 130.0 | 170.18 | 128.6 | 3551.87 | | 2397.67 | | 1154.20 | |
| 2011 | 639.72 | 122.2 | 415.21 | 117.5 | 224.50 | 131.9 | 4152.76 | 116.9 | 2696.47 | 112.5 | 1456.28 | 126.2 |
| 2012 | 616.83 | 96.4 | 412.62 | 99.4 | 204.22 | 91.0 | 3893.23 | 93.8 | 2604.88 | 96.6 | 1288.35 | 88.5 |
| 2013 | 650.71 | 105.5 | 447.66 | 108.5 | 203.05 | 99.5 | 4037.01 | 103.7 | 2777.31 | 106.6 | 1259.70 | 97.8 |
| 2014 | 679.98 | 104.5 | 491.66 | 109.8 | 188.32 | 92.8 | 4177.24 | 103.5 | 3020.29 | 108.7 | 1156.95 | 91.8 |
| 2015 | 665.66 | 97.9 | 500.67 | 101.8 | 165.00 | 87.7 | 4132.43 | 99.0 | 3108.03 | 102.9 | 1024.40 | 88.7 |
| 2016 | 679.92 | 102.2 | 502.59 | 100.5 | 177.34 | 107.6 | 4485.97 | 108.7 | 3313.80 | 106.7 | 1172.17 | 114.6 |
| 2017 | 750.65 | 110.4 | 509.95 | 101.5 | 240.70 | 135.7 | 5085.08 | 113.3 | 3455.61 | 104.3 | 1629.46 | 138.8 |
| 2018 | 795.56 | 106.0 | 518.23 | 101.8 | 277.33 | 114.8 | 5245.28 | 103.1 | 3417.11 | 99.0 | 1828.17 | 111.8 |
| 2019 | 811.54 | 102.0 | 523.83 | 101.1 | 287.71 | 103.7 | 5596.81 | 106.7 | 3612.66 | 105.7 | 1984.14 | 108.5 |

# 9－09　分经济类型进出口情况(2018－2019 年)

## Statistics on Imports and Exports by Econimic Type(2018－2019)

单位:亿美元　　(USD 100 million)

| 项　　目 | Item | 2019 年<br>In Year 2019 | 2018 年<br>In Year 2018 | 为上年(%)<br>As Compared with the Preceding Year(%) |
|---|---|---|---|---|
| 全市进出口总值(海关口径) | Total Exports And Imports | 811.54 | 795.56 | 102.0 |
| 一、出口总额 | Exports | 523.83 | 518.23 | 101.1 |
| 1. 国有企业 | State－owned Enterprises | 58.68 | 63.30 | 92.7 |
| 2. 三资企业 | Foreign Investment Enterprises | 105.49 | 107.84 | 97.8 |
| (1)中外合作企业 | Cooperation Enterprises | 0.40 | 0.81 | 49.1 |
| (2)中外合资企业 | Joint－Venture Enterprises | 46.94 | 49.35 | 95.1 |
| (3)外商独资企业 | Enterprises With Sole Foreign Investment | 58.16 | 57.68 | 100.8 |
| 3. 集体企业 | Collective－owned Enterprises | 15.62 | 17.43 | 89.6 |
| 4. 私营企业 | Private Enterprises | 338.76 | 329.34 | 102.9 |
| 二、进口总额 | Imports | 287.71 | 277.33 | 103.7 |

# 9-10 分地区外贸进出口情况(2019年)

## Imports and Exports by Region(2019)

单位:万美元 (USD 10000)

| 区域 Region | | 进出口总值 Total Imports and Exports | 为上年(%) As Compared with the Preceding Year(%) | 出口总值 Exports of This Year | 为上年(%) As Compared with the Preceding Year(%) | 进口总值 Imports of This Year | 为上年(%) As Compared with the Preceding Year(%) |
|---|---|---|---|---|---|---|---|
| **全市合计** | **Total** | **8115399** | **102.0** | **5238273** | **101.1** | **2877126** | **103.7** |
| #不含省属 | #Non-provincial | 7528513 | 102.4 | 4861172 | 101.8 | 2667341 | 103.5 |
| #上城区 | Shangcheng | 299853 | 104.7 | 154899 | 110.4 | 144954 | 99.2 |
| 下城区 | Xiacheng | 501481 | 94.1 | 272625 | 98.5 | 228857 | 89.4 |
| 江干区 | Jianggan | 353758 | 105.7 | 231078 | 96.2 | 122679 | 129.7 |
| 拱墅区 | Gongshu | 187133 | 104.9 | 156158 | 105.3 | 30975 | 102.8 |
| 西湖区 | Xihu | 468866 | 105.9 | 339381 | 100.3 | 129484 | 124.1 |
| 高新(滨江)区 | Hi-Tech(Binjiang) | 1112607 | 107.7 | 707978 | 102.6 | 404629 | 118.1 |
| 萧山区 | Xiaoshan | 1214129 | 101.0 | 927039 | 101.9 | 287090 | 98.4 |
| 余杭区 | Yuhang | 694110 | 98.9 | 639888 | 101.8 | 54221 | 73.8 |
| 富阳区 | Fuyang | 429135 | 101.4 | 191832 | 98.5 | 237304 | 103.9 |
| 临安区 | Lin'an | 246122 | 103.2 | 180699 | 99.8 | 65423 | 113.9 |
| 钱塘新区 | Qiantang New Area | 1228664 | 99.4 | 675880 | 102.7 | 552784 | 95.7 |
| 桐庐县 | Tonglu | 108729 | 91.9 | 99951 | 93.8 | 8779 | 75.0 |
| 淳安县 | Chun'an | 19382 | 101.3 | 15740 | 92.7 | 3643 | 168.9 |
| 建德市 | Jiande | 97860 | 91.1 | 90720 | 92.5 | 7140 | 77.0 |

# 9－11　分地区外贸进出口总值(2004－2019 年)

## Total Value of Imports and Exports by Region(2004－2019)

单位:万美元　　　　(USD 10000)

| 年份 Year | 全市 Whole City | 市区 Urban District 合计 Total | #萧山区 Xiaoshan | 余杭区 Yuhang | 富阳区 Fuyang | 临安区 Lin'an | 桐庐县 Tonglu | 淳安县 Chun'an | 建德市 Jiande |
|---|---|---|---|---|---|---|---|---|---|
| 2004 | 2449671 | 2364434 | 414374 | 88538 | 52399 | 28918 | 32333 | 4461 | 19525 |
| 2005 | 2986993 | 2892191 | 510950 | 128999 | 72357 | 33262 | 30489 | 5211 | 25841 |
| 2006 | 3890853 | 3769910 | 610201 | 183930 | 81616 | 41492 | 38522 | 6797 | 34132 |
| 2007 | 4342666 | 4181699 | 795487 | 255534 | 105765 | 55542 | 48811 | 8319 | 48295 |
| 2008 | 4806503 | 4545719 | 953377 | 324421 | 126829 | 74862 | 71753 | 12478 | 101692 |
| 2009 | 4041991 | 3821965 | 829827 | 285496 | 116158 | 70454 | 60064 | 12039 | 77470 |
| 2010 | 5235549 | 4946409 | 1135326 | 385736 | 166652 | 101387 | 73919 | 17183 | 96651 |
| 2011 | 6397180 | 6044765 | 1432742 | 484903 | 216575 | 132729 | 93464 | 20459 | 105763 |
| 2012 | 6168325 | 5814547 | 1367290 | 512531 | 224446 | 142340 | 103153 | 21604 | 86681 |
| 2013 | 6507102 | 6115754 | 1408929 | 555640 | 265788 | 165094 | 119539 | 19692 | 87023 |
| 2014 | 6799775 | 6355378 | 1384823 | 601220 | 284980 | 193001 | 133392 | 23802 | 94202 |
| 2015 | 6656636 | 6178381 | 1189039 | 537405 | 285540 | 209150 | 147326 | 20814 | 100965 |
| 2016 | 6799241 | 6313076 | 1120689 | 520195 | 273306 | 223014 | 139150 | 18377 | 105623 |
| 2017 | 7506524 | 7295048 | 1079155 | 577771 | 372442 | 274535 | 110464 | 16843 | 84169 |
| 2018 | 7352678 | 7108994 | 1199436 | 701156 | 426099 | 238136 | 118296 | 18005 | 107382 |
| 2019 | 8115399 | 7889427 | 1214129 | 694110 | 429135 | 246122 | 108729 | 19382 | 97860 |

# 9－12　外贸出口分国别(地区)情况(2018－2019年)

## Export by Country or Region(2018－2019)

单位:万美元　　(USD 10000)

| 国　别<br>(地区) | Country<br>(territory) | 2019年<br>In Year 2019 | 2018年<br>In Year 2018 | 为上年(%)<br>As Compared with the Preceding Year(%) |
|---|---|---|---|---|
| **合　计** | **Total** | **5238273** | **5182140** | **101.1** |
| #中国香港 | Hong Kong China | 87561 | 67456 | 129.8 |
| 中国台湾 | Taiwan China | 63456 | 53603 | 118.4 |
| 美国 | U. S. A | 923736 | 1031125 | 89.6 |
| 日本 | Japan | 341524 | 332392 | 102.7 |
| 德国 | Germany | 207175 | 203465 | 101.8 |
| 英国 | Britain | 197114 | 178365 | 110.5 |
| 印度 | India | 215388 | 226471 | 95.1 |
| 越南 | Vietnam | 197833 | 169613 | 116.6 |
| 韩国 | Republic of Korea | 166631 | 155215 | 107.4 |
| 荷兰 | Netherlands | 143475 | 152728 | 93.9 |
| 意大利 | Italy | 109177 | 111375 | 98.0 |
| 法国 | France | 116000 | 116014 | 100.0 |
| 俄罗斯 | Russia | 125397 | 117073 | 107.1 |
| 澳大利亚 | Australia | 113114 | 108501 | 104.3 |
| 印度尼西亚 | Indonesia | 115189 | 119505 | 96.4 |
| 西班牙 | Spain | 88637 | 86586 | 102.4 |
| 加拿大 | Canada | 94488 | 95863 | 98.6 |
| 巴西 | Brazil | 113500 | 111165 | 102.1 |
| 墨西哥 | Mexico | 105148 | 96243 | 109.3 |
| 泰国 | Thailand | 95330 | 89064 | 107.0 |
| "一带一路"国家(地区) | Countries along the Belt and Road | 1705822 | 1625984 | 104.9 |

# 9-13 进出口货物分贸易方式总值表(2018-2019年)

# Total Value Table of Import and Export Goods by Trade Mode(2018-2019)

单位:万美元 (USD 10,000)

| 贸易方式 Trade Mode | 出口 Export | | 进口 Import | |
|---|---|---|---|---|
| | 2018 | 2019 | 2018 | 2019 |
| **总值 Total Value** | **5182139.85** | **5238272.54** | **2775228.75** | **2877126.27** |
| 一般贸易 General Trade | 4462488.69 | 4475445.54 | 2424798.44 | 2445132.33 |
| 来料加工装配贸易 Processing and Assembling Trade with Supplied Materials | 31519.92 | 32201.54 | 24997.35 | 26731.77 |
| 进料加工贸易 Imported Materials Processing | 620764.00 | 609862.95 | 239946.67 | 251414.84 |
| 外商投资企业作为投资进口的设备物品 Equipments and Goods Imported by Foreign-invested Enterprises as Investment | - | - | 1173.04 | 731.37 |
| 保税监管场所进出境货物 Import and Export Cargos at Bonded Supervision Place | 472.34 | 300.83 | 47884.34 | 51683.07 |
| 海关特殊监管区域物流货物 Logistics Goods in Areas under Customs Special Supervision | 22274.01 | 10810.16 | 31289.00 | 81576.58 |
| 海关特殊监管区域进口设备 Import Equipments in Areas under Customs Special Supervision | - | - | 893.01 | 1319.27 |
| 华侨、港澳台同胞、外籍华人捐赠物资 Materials Donated by Overseas Chinese, Compatriots from Hong Kong, Macao and Taiwan, and Foreign Nationality Overseas | - | - | 41.58 | 15.44 |
| 对外承包工程出口货物 Export Goods of Foreign Contracted Projects | 27400.05 | 39763.37 | - | - |
| 其他贸易 Other Trade | 15760.71 | 69795.18 | 2596.81 | 18516.54 |

# 9-14 旅游发展情况(1995-2019年)
## Statistics on Tourism(1995-2019)

| 年份 Year | 旅游总收入(亿元) Total Tourism Revenue (100 million yuan) | 国内旅游收入(亿元) Domestic Earnings (100 million yuan) | 旅游外汇收入(亿美元) Foreign Exchange Earnings from International Tourism (USD 100 million) | 旅游总人数(万人次) Total Tourists (10000 person-times) | 国内游客人数(万人次) Domestic Tourists (10000 person-times) |
|---|---|---|---|---|---|
| 1995 | 106.0 | 94.3 | 1.45 | 2148 | 2104 |
| 1996 | 136.5 | 122.6 | 1.67 | 2055 | 2009 |
| 1997 | 158.8 | 142.1 | 2.01 | 2150 | 2100 |
| 1998 | 163.4 | 146.0 | 2.10 | 2172 | 2121 |
| 1999 | 186.0 | 166.7 | 2.37 | 2266 | 2207 |
| 2000 | 214.3 | 190.0 | 2.92 | 2376 | 2305 |
| 2001 | 249.7 | 218.9 | 3.37 | 2592 | 2510 |
| 2002 | 294.4 | 254.8 | 4.77 | 2758 | 2652 |
| 2003 | 325.9 | 290.9 | 4.22 | 2862 | 2776 |
| 2004 | 410.1 | 361.2 | 5.97 | 3139 | 3016 |
| 2005 | 465.1 | 403.6 | 7.58 | 3417 | 3266 |
| 2006 | 543.7 | 471.2 | 9.09 | 3864 | 3682 |
| 2007 | 630.1 | 548.6 | 11.19 | 4320 | 4112 |
| 2008 | 707.2 | 617.2 | 12.96 | 4773 | 4552 |
| 2009 | 803.1 | 708.9 | 13.80 | 5324 | 5094 |
| 2010 | 1025.7 | 910.9 | 16.90 | 6581 | 6305 |
| 2011 | 1191.0 | 1063.8 | 19.60 | 7487 | 7181 |
| 2012 | 1392.3 | 1253.2 | 22.02 | 8568 | 8237 |
| 2013 | 1603.7 | 1469.9 | 21.60 | 9725 | 9409 |
| 2014 | 1886.3 | 1743.9 | 23.18 | 10933 | 10606 |
| 2015 | 2200.7 | 2019.7 | 29.31 | 12382 | 12040 |
| 2016 | 2571.8 | 2362.6 | 31.49 | 14059 | 13696 |
| 2017 | 3041.3 | 2802.1 | 35.43 | 16287 | 15884 |
| 2018 | 3589.1 | 3335.6 | 38.31 | 18403 | 17983 |
| *2019 | 4004.5 | 3953.7 | 7.37 | 20814 | 20700 |

注:自2019年开始,入境旅游口径调整为"入境过夜游客",2018年以前为"境外旅游者人数"。

a) Since 2019, the caliber of inbound tourism has been adjusted to "inbound overnight tourists", which was "the number of overseas tourists" before 2018.

# 9－15 境外旅游者人数(1978－2019年)
## Number of International Tourists (1978－2019)

单位:人次　　　　(person－times)

| 年　份 Year | 合　计 Total | #外国人 Foreigners | 港澳台同胞 Compatriots from Hong Kong, Macao and Taiwan | 平均逗留天数 Average days of Staying |
|---|---|---|---|---|
| 1978 | 53475 | 728 | 26648 | |
| 1979 | 84914 | 44714 | 39131 | 2.59 |
| 1980 | 124960 | 61710 | 61382 | 2.70 |
| 1981 | 154745 | 87727 | 65014 | 2.71 |
| 1982 | 152897 | 89100 | 61314 | 2.49 |
| 1983 | 160564 | 97803 | 59625 | 2.18 |
| 1984 | 179200 | 105771 | 70915 | 2.12 |
| 1985 | 238385 | 156311 | 75063 | 2.18 |
| 1986 | 266370 | 170960 | 87092 | 2.38 |
| 1987 | 300603 | 183477 | 100078 | 2.38 |
| 1988 | 349246 | 149512 | 159745 | 2.08 |
| 1989 | 248502 | 66094 | 163589 | 2.08 |
| 1990 | 388345 | 86621 | 268131 | 2.09 |
| 1991 | 390197 | 136809 | 229690 | 2.00 |
| 1992 | 489578 | 183781 | 267256 | 2.03 |
| 1993 | 459620 | 199796 | 234640 | 2.06 |
| 1994 | 337362 | 201692 | 124346 | 2.10 |
| 1995 | 441262 | 249418 | 177236 | 2.06 |
| 1996 | 462313 | 273477 | 178845 | 2.07 |
| 1997 | 504276 | 288949 | 205267 | 2.20 |
| 1998 | 507243 | 261353 | 231609 | 2.20 |
| 1999 | 591853 | 324625 | 257978 | 2.09 |
| 2000 | 707148 | 400906 | 306242 | 2.15 |
| 2001 | 819438 | 447689 | 371749 | 2.41 |
| 2002 | 1056266 | 631576 | 424690 | 2.50 |
| 2003 | 861163 | 482073 | 379090 | 2.72 |
| 2004 | 1234063 | 791616 | 442447 | 2.59 |
| 2005 | 1513585 | 1020840 | 492745 | 2.63 |
| 2006 | 1820171 | 1236792 | 583379 | 2.57 |
| 2007 | 2085997 | 1453650 | 632347 | 2.67 |
| 2008 | 2213329 | 1543665 | 669654 | 2.73 |
| 2009 | 2304045 | 1572838 | 731207 | 2.87 |
| 2010 | 2757147 | 1878528 | 878619 | 2.94 |
| 2011 | 3063140 | 2108263 | 954877 | 2.96 |
| 2012 | 3311225 | 2298763 | 1012462 | 2.95 |
| 2013 | 3160058 | 2198187 | 961871 | 2.93 |
| 2014 | 3261337 | 2254866 | 1006471 | 2.93 |
| 2015 | 3415619 | 2378461 | 1037158 | 2.99 |
| 2016 | 3632252 | 2556247 | 1076005 | 3.14 |
| 2017 | 4022309 | 2849993 | 1172316 | 3.25 |
| 2018 | 4205063 | 2990183 | 1214056 | 2.80 |
| 2019 | 1133143 | 839504 | 293639 | 3.20 |

注:从1995年起为全市数。自2019年开始,全省入境旅游统计口径调整为"入境过夜游客",根据省文旅厅数据,我市2018年接待入境旅游者人次为107.23万人次。2018年以前为"境外旅游者人数"。

a) Data in this table has included the tourists of whole municipality since 1995. Since 2019, the statistical caliber of inbound tourism in the whole province has been adjusted to "inbound overnight tourists". According to the data from the Zhejiang Provincial Department of Culture and Tourism, Hangzhou received 1.0723 million person/times inbound tourists in 2018. which was "the number of overseas tourists" before 2018.

# 9-16 接待境外游客及居民出境旅游情况(2016-2019年)
## Number of International Tourists and Outbound Tourists(2016-2019)

| 项目 | Item | 2016年<br>In Year 2016 | 2017年<br>In Year 2017 | 2018年<br>In Year 2018 | 2019年<br>In Year 2019 |
|---|---|---|---|---|---|
| **一、接待境外游客** | **International Tourists** | | | | |
| **全年接待人数(人次)** | **Number of Foreign Tourists(person-times)** | **3632252** | **4022309** | **4205063** | **1133143** |
| #外国人 | #Foreigners | 2556247 | 2849993 | 2990183 | 839504 |
| 港澳台同胞 | Compatriots From Hong Kong, Macao and Taiwan | 1076005 | 1172316 | 1214056 | 293639 |
| **全年接待人天数(人天)** | **Total Person-days (person-days)** | **11414114** | **13092273** | **14694611** | **2991120** |
| #外国人 | #Foreigners | 8409339 | 9545816 | 10727681 | 2312566 |
| 港澳台同胞 | Compatriots From Hong Kong, Macao and Taiwan | 3004775 | 3545457 | 3966930 | 678553 |
| **平均逗留天数(天)** | **Average Days of Staying (days)** | **3.14** | **3.25** | **2.8** | **3.2** |
| #外国人 | #Foreigners | 3.29 | 3.35 | 2.8 | 3.2 |
| 港澳台同胞 | Compatriots From Hong Kong, Macao and Taiwan | 2.79 | 3.02 | 2.6 | 2.8 |
| **旅游外汇总收入(万美元)** | **Total Foreign Exchange Earnings From International Tourism (USD 10000)** | **314944** | **354286** | **383063** | **73660** |
| **二、居民出境旅游** | **Outbound Tourism** | | | | |
| **居民出境旅游人数(人次)** | **Outbound Tourists(Person-time)** | **1598969** | **1730474** | **2125332** | **2186500** |

注:自2019年开始,全省入境旅游统计口径调整为“入境过夜游客”,根据省文旅厅数据,我市2018年接待入境旅游者人次为107.23万人次。2018年以前为“境外旅游者人数”。

a) Since 2019, the statistical caliber of inbound tourism in the whole province has been adjusted to "inbound overnight tourists". According to the data from the Zhejiang Provincial Department of Culture and Tourism, Hangzhou received 1.0723 million person/times inbound tourists in 2018. which was "the number of overseas tourists" before 2018.

# 9-17 接待境外游客分国别(地区)情况(2018-2019年)
# Number of International Tourists by Country or Territory(2018-2019)

单位:人次 (person-times)

| 国别(地区) | Country (territory) | 2019年 In Year 2019 | 2018年 In Year 2018 | 为上年(%) As Compared with the Preceding Year(%) |
|---|---|---|---|---|
| **合计** | **Total** | **1133143** | **1072266** | **105.68** |
| #中国香港 | #Hong Kong China | 106739 | 105311 | 101.36 |
| 中国澳门 | Macao China | 11269 | 11233 | 100.32 |
| 中国台湾 | Taiwan China | 175631 | 182886 | 96.03 |
| 日本 | Japan | 62631 | 61697 | 101.51 |
| 美国 | U.S.A | 140771 | 120225 | 117.09 |
| 新加坡 | Singapore | 31601 | 29927 | 105.59 |
| 澳大利亚 | Australia | 29094 | 25020 | 116.28 |
| 泰国 | Thailand | 17756 | 14926 | 118.96 |
| 意大利 | Italy | 12513 | 13048 | 95.90 |
| 荷兰 | Netherlands | 13008 | 10962 | 118.66 |
| 西班牙 | Spain | 9160 | 7856 | 116.60 |
| 马来西亚 | Malaysia | 36486 | 30284 | 120.48 |
| 韩国 | Republic of Korea | 111195 | 97444 | 114.12 |
| 法国 | France | 17003 | 16224 | 104.80 |
| 德国 | Germany | 28429 | 25735 | 110.47 |
| 加拿大 | Canada | 27422 | 28524 | 96.14 |
| 英国 | Britain | 23608 | 21184 | 111.44 |
| 印度尼西亚 | Indonesia | 11185 | 11200 | 99.87 |
| 印度 | India | 17434 | 14582 | 119.56 |
| 菲律宾 | Filipine | 4821 | 4080 | 118.16 |

注:自2019年开始,全省入境旅游统计口径调整为"入境过夜游客",该表2018年数据已调整为同口径。

a) Since 2019, the statistical caliber of inbound tourism in the whole province has been adjusted to "inbound overnight tourists", The data of 2018 in the table has been adjusted to the same caliber.

# 主要统计指标解释

**利用外资** 指我市政府部门，企业和其他经济组织通过对外借款，吸收外商直接投资以及用其他方式筹措的境外现汇、设备、技术等。

**外商直接投资** 是指外国企业和经济组织或个人（包括华侨、港澳台胞以及我国在境外注册的企业）按我国有关政策、法规，用现汇、实物、技术等在我市境内开办外商独资企业、与我市境内的企业或经济组织共同举办中外合资经营企业、合作经营企业或者合作开发资源的投资（包括外商投资收益的再投资）以及经政府有关部门批准的项目投资总额内，企业从境外借入的资金。

**进出口总额** 海关进出口总额指实际进出我国国境的货物总金额。包括对外贸易实际进出口货物，来料加工装配进出口货物，国家间、联合国及国际组织无偿援助物资和赠送品，华侨、港澳台同胞和外籍华人捐赠品，租赁期满归承租人所有的租赁货物，进料加工进出口货物，边境地方贸易及边境地区小额贸易进出口货物（边民互市贸易除外），中外合资经营企业、中外合作经营企业、外商独资经营企业进出口货物和公用物品，到、离岸价格在规定限额以上的进出口货样和广告品（无商业价值、无使用价值和免费提供出口的除外），从保税仓库提取在中国境内销售的进口货物，以及其他进出口货物。进出口总额以观察一个国家在对外贸易方面的总规模。我国规定出口货物按离岸价格统计，进口货物按到岸价格统计。

**境外旅游者人数** 指来我市参观、访问、旅行、探亲、访友、休养、考察、参加会议和从事经济、科技、文化、教育、体育、宗教等活动的外国人、华侨、港澳和台湾同胞的人数。不包括外国在我市的常驻机构，如使领馆、通讯社、企业办事处的工作人员；来我市常住的外国专家、留学生以及在岸逗留不过夜人员。

**境外旅游（外汇）收入** 指入境旅游的外国人、华侨、港澳台同胞在杭州旅游过程中发生的一切旅游支出，对我市来说就是境外旅游（外汇）收入。

# Explanatory Notes on Main Statistical Indicators

**Utilization of Foreign Capital** refers to foreign spot exchange, equipment and technology financed by foreign loans, foreign direct investment and other forms undertaken by Hangzhou government, enterprises and other economic units.

**Foreign Direct Investment** refers to the investments inside China by foreign enterprises and economic organizations or individuals ( including overseas Chinese, compatriots from Hong Kong, Macao and Taiwan, and Chinese enterprises registered abroad) , following the relevant policies and laws of China, to establish wholly foreign owned enterprises, Sino foreign joint ventures and cooperative enterprises, or to explore resources jointly with enterprises or economic organizations in Hangzhou with spot exchange, material objects and technology. It also includes the re – investment of the foreign entrepreneurs with the profits gained from the investment and funds that enterprises borrow from abroad in the total investment of projects approved by the relevant department of the government.

**Total Imports and Exports** refer to the value of commodities imported into and exported from the boundary of China. It includes the actual imports and exports through foreign trades, imported and exported goods processed and assembled with supplied materials, supplies and gifts as aid given gratis between countries and by the United Nations and other international organizations, and contributions donated by overseas Chinese, compatriots in Hong Kong, Macao and Chinese foreign citizenship, leasing commodities belong to tenants at the end of leasing period, the imported and exported commodities processed with imported materials, commodities trading in border areas (excluding mutual exchange goods), the imported and exported commodities and articles for public use of the Sino – foreign joint ventures, cooperative enterprises and wholly foreign owned enterprises. It also includes imported or exported samples and advertising goods whose CIF or FOB value are beyond the permitted ceiling (excluding goods without trading or use value and exported free), imported goods sold in China from bonded warehouses and other imported or exported goods. This indicator is used to observe the total size of external trade in a country. In accordance with the stipulation of Chinese government, imports are calculated at CIF, while exports are calculated at FOB.

**Number of International Tourists** refers to foreigners, overseas Chinese and compatriots from Hong Kong, Macao and Taiwan, who come to Hangzhou for sightseeing, visits, tours, family reunions, vacations, study tours, conferences and other activities of business, scientific and technological, cultural, educational and religious natures. It does not include employees of permanent offices of foreign countries in our city such as embassies, consulates, news agencies and offices of foreign companies, or long – term foreign experts or students residing in Hangzhou, or persons in transition without spending a night in Hangzhou.

**Foreign Exchange Earnings from Overseas Tourism** refer to the total expenditures of foreigners, overseas Chinese, Chinese compatriots from Hong Kong, Macao and Taiwan during their stay in Hangzhou, which are, for Hangzhou, foreign exchange earnings from overseas tourism.

# 十、财政、金融保险

FINANCE,BANKING AND INSURANCE

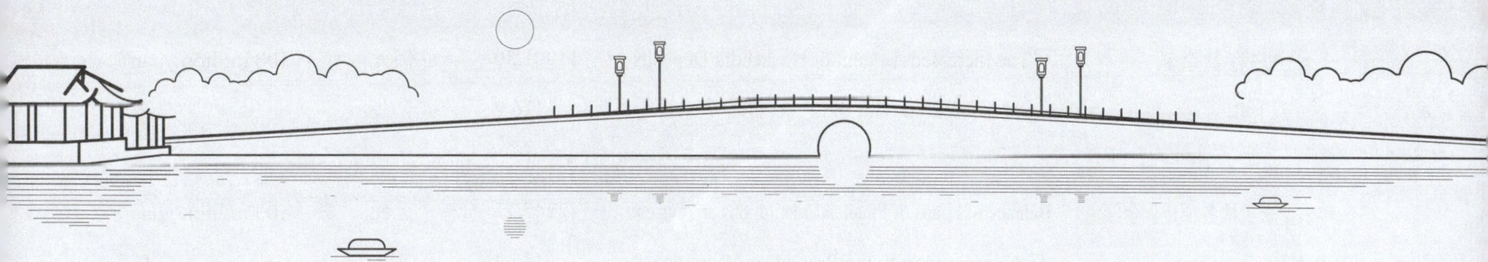

# 10 财政、金融、保险
# Finance, Banking and Insurance

## 主要统计指标
## Major Statistical Indicators

| | | | | |
|---|---|---|---|---|
| 财政总收入 | Total Financial Revenue | 3650.04 | 亿元 | ( 100 million yuan ) |
| 为上年 | As Compared with the Preceding Year | 105.6 | % | ( % ) |
| 一般公共预算收入 | General Public Budget Revenue | 1965.97 | 亿元 | ( 100 million yuan ) |
| 为上年 | As Compared with the Preceding Year | 107.7 | % | ( % ) |
| 一般公共预算支出 | General Public Financial Budgetary Expenditure | 1952.85 | 亿元 | ( 100 million yuan ) |
| 为上年 | As Compared with the Preceding Year | 113.7 | % | ( % ) |
| 年末金融机构各项存款余额 | Balance of Deposits of Financial Institutions at Year-end | 45286.99 | 亿元 | ( 100 million yuan ) |
| 为上年 | As Compared with the Preceding Year | 113.8 | % | ( % ) |
| # 住户存款余额 | The Increased Amount of Household Deposits | 11901.30 | 亿元 | ( 100 million yuan ) |
| 为上年 | As Compared with the Preceding Year | 116.7 | % | ( % ) |
| 年末金融机构各项贷款余额 | Balance of Loans of Financial Institutions at Year-end | 42245.17 | 亿元 | ( 100 million yuan ) |
| 为上年 | As Compared with the Preceding Year | 115.4 | % | ( % ) |

# 10－01 财政收入及支出(1978－2019年)

## Financial Revenue and Expenditure (1978－2019)

单位:万元 (10000 yuan)

| 年份 Year | 财政总收入 Financial Revenue | | 一般公共预算收入 General Public Budget Revenue | | 一般公共预算支出 General Public Budget Expenditure | |
|---|---|---|---|---|---|---|
| | 全市 Total | 市区 Urban District | 全市 Total | 市区 Urban District | 全市 Total | 市区 Urban District |
| 1978 | 94102 | 73396 | – | – | 16170 | 7779 |
| 1979 | 103259 | 81885 | – | – | 20334 | 11289 |
| 1980 | 118529 | 94015 | – | – | 21726 | 11867 |
| 1981 | 128564 | 100645 | – | – | 23964 | 13891 |
| 1982 | 140510 | 107298 | – | – | 24945 | 13687 |
| 1983 | 153941 | 116559 | – | – | 32765 | 17822 |
| 1984 | 172996 | 130757 | – | – | 46937 | 28710 |
| 1985 | 186472 | 131923 | – | – | 57710 | 35435 |
| 1986 | 205952 | 141943 | – | – | 73213 | 43959 |
| 1987 | 226262 | 152268 | – | – | 70717 | 41011 |
| 1988 | 246961 | 161208 | – | – | 95655 | 53031 |
| 1989 | 255003 | 156649 | – | – | 113571 | 61534 |
| 1990 | 252503 | 149904 | – | – | 118167 | 62587 |
| 1991 | 267597 | 158130 | – | – | 123134 | 62403 |
| 1992 | 286394 | 168341 | – | – | 132814 | 65984 |
| 1993 | 394946 | 233670 | – | – | 185168 | 90545 |
| 1994 | 484597 | 300014 | 197292 | 116733 | 215415 | 102430 |
| 1995 | 551262 | 339828 | 230431 | 135041 | 249050 | 120084 |
| 1996 | 635334 | 414557 | 268438 | 169987 | 302390 | 151016 |
| 1997 | 740725 | 485650 | 312797 | 196885 | 363834 | 197054 |
| 1998 | 869824 | 585615 | 368484 | 236269 | 424478 | 237221 |
| 1999 | 1026577 | 689394 | 449593 | 288002 | 563524 | 335243 |
| 2000 | 1428519 | 970937 | 691891 | 599910 | 734328 | 445698 |
| 2001 | 1884608 | 1612225 | 1042789 | 884738 | 1049330 | 849479 |
| 2002 | 2571408 | 2235021 | 1183153 | 1022964 | 1410199 | 1166298 |
| 2003 | 3297091 | 2861459 | 1503888 | 1290778 | 1635948 | 1340463 |
| 2004 | 3957516 | 3488744 | 1974523 | 1712813 | 1956282 | 1602303 |
| 2005 | 5207930 | 4584112 | 2504565 | 2172575 | 2383344 | 1957619 |
| 2006 | 6244906 | 5484645 | 3013888 | 2616084 | 2754809 | 2254347 |
| 2007 | 7884237 | 6929667 | 3916195 | 3421403 | 3357153 | 2747060 |
| 2008 | 9105489 | 7991043 | 4553531 | 3972842 | 4196674 | 3454599 |
| 2009 | 10194264 | 8965758 | 5207899 | 4535191 | 4903983 | 4000324 |
| 2010 | 12454323 | 10988265 | 6713413 | 5894414 | 6165836 | 4988197 |
| 2011 | 14889206 | 13009046 | 7851524 | 6822765 | 7475004 | 5971740 |
| 2012 | 16278879 | 14244888 | 8599875 | 7475989 | 7862800 | 6222930 |
| 2013 | 17349750 | 15157584 | 9452020 | 8207264 | 8557370 | 6662314 |
| 2014 | 19201076 | 17750305 | 10273169 | 9426504 | 9611771 | 8077961 |
| 2015 | 22387456 | 20738698 | 12338820 | 11360166 | 12054777 | 10235061 |
| 2016 | 25584128 | 23844189 | 14023826 | 12988095 | 14043065 | 12019355 |
| 2017 | 29212996 | 28010839 | 15674169 | 14979182 | 15409156 | 13968866 |
| 2018 | 34574596 | 33198717 | 18250616 | 17466268 | 17170834 | 15573258 |
| 2019 | 36500413 | 35006136 | 19659731 | 18800198 | 19528530 | 17796386 |

单位:万元

| 指标 | Item | 全市 Total | 市区 Urban District | 上城区 Shangcheng |
|---|---|---|---|---|
| **财政总收入合计** | **Total** | **36500413** | **35006136** | **1659306** |
| 一、一般公共预算收入 | General Public Budget Revenue | 19659731 | 18800198 | 851296 |
| (一)税收收入 | Tax Revenue | 17911758 | 17129242 | 814791 |
| 1. 国内增值税 | Domestic Value－added Tax | 6464435 | 6136868 | 275316 |
| #改征增值税 | Newly Changed Value－added Tax | 3293607 | 3163158 | 175430 |
| 2. 企业所得税 | Corporate Income Tax | 3762660 | 3613849 | 227427 |
| 3. 个人所得税 | Individual Income Tax | 1813506 | 1762274 | 123448 |
| 4. 城市维护建设税 | City Construction and Maintenance Tax | 1117782 | 1079269 | 39825 |
| 5. 房产税 | Real Estate Tax | 589684 | 555916 | 42548 |
| 6. 城镇土地使用税 | Urban Land Use Tax | 116652 | 92603 | 1737 |
| 7. 土地增值税 | Land Appreciation Tax | 1639773 | 1593486 | 86428 |
| 8. 耕地占用税 | Tax on the Use of Arable Land | 119847 | 112683 | － |
| 9. 契税 | Contract Tax | 1839509 | 1775405 | － |
| 10. 其他税收 | Others Tax | 447910 | 406889 | 18062 |
| (二)非税收入 | Non－tax Revenue | 1747973 | 1670956 | 36505 |
| 1. 专项收入 | Special Revenue | 1173121 | 1124980 | 33825 |
| #教育费附加 | Revenue from Extra－Charges for Education | 422634 | 402857 | 14367 |
| 地方教育附加收入 | Local Education Additional Revenue | 281309 | 268115 | 9604 |
| 残疾人就业保障金收入 | Employment Security for The Disabled Revenue | 179677 | 173355 | 9850 |
| 教育资金收入 | Educational Fund Revenue | 170651 | 168152 | － |
| 农田水利建设资金收入 | Fund in The Farmland Irrigation Construction Revenue | 104225 | 102626 | － |
| 2. 行政事业性收费收入 | Income from Administrative Fees | 101292 | 94977 | － |
| 3. 罚没收入 | Penalty and Confiscatory Income | 279899 | 257972 | 2410 |
| 4. 国有资本经营收入 | Revenue of state－owned capital | －198006 | －193306 | － |
| #国有企业计划亏损补贴 | Subsides to Loss－making of state－owned Enterprises | －198299 | －193599 | － |
| 5. 国有资源(资产)有偿使用收入 | Compensation for the Use of Seate－owned Assets Income | 292317 | 287887 | 270 |
| 6. 政府住房基金收入 | Government Housing Fund Income | 92493 | 91648 | － |
| 7. 其他收入 | Others Revenue | 6857 | 6798 | － |
| 二、上划中央"六税"小计 | Subtotal Revenue of Central Government | 16840682 | 16205938 | 808010 |
| 1. 消费税 | Consumption Tax | 2011991 | 2004879 | 6381 |
| 2. 增值税 | Domestic Value－added Tax | 6464435 | 6136868 | 275316 |
| 3. 企业所得税 | Corporate Income Tax | 5643993 | 5420776 | 341141 |
| 4. 个人所得税 | Individual Income Tax | 2720263 | 2643415 | 185172 |

# 总收入(2019年)

# Revenue by Region(2019)

(10000 yuan)

| 下城区 Xiacheng | 江干区 Jianggan | 拱墅区 Gongshu | 西湖区 Xihu | 高新(滨江)区 Hi-Tech (Binjiang) | 萧山区 Xiaoshan |
|---|---|---|---|---|---|
| **1751194** | **1909707** | **1619966** | **2944057** | **3419438** | **4304418** |
| 965861 | 1036818 | 911928 | 1506362 | 1755863 | 2676630 |
| 869823 | 1010955 | 859427 | 1415741 | 1662371 | 2443038 |
| 302943 | 381405 | 363644 | 535761 | 697954 | 772920 |
| 152325 | 251756 | 192555 | 366059 | 270039 | 346818 |
| 229368 | 259774 | 187651 | 366245 | 353110 | 453318 |
| 87563 | 65502 | 37370 | 232739 | 289913 | 108426 |
| 51746 | 61078 | 54604 | 78228 | 116586 | 131317 |
| 63026 | 72159 | 43400 | 50910 | 58175 | 64837 |
| 2743 | 3319 | 5192 | 4231 | 1934 | 22866 |
| 47368 | 147363 | 146226 | 118345 | 118605 | 317680 |
| - | - | - | - | - | 67811 |
| - | - | - | - | - | 445120 |
| 85066 | 20355 | 21340 | 29282 | 26094 | 58743 |
| 96038 | 25863 | 52501 | 90621 | 93492 | 233592 |
| 45552 | 48922 | 42506 | 67762 | 90686 | 153717 |
| 18667 | 22379 | 18814 | 28970 | 43937 | 50549 |
| 12424 | 14948 | 12635 | 19314 | 28985 | 33868 |
| 14457 | 11583 | 11044 | 19405 | 17764 | 19857 |
| - | - | - | - | - | 29927 |
| - | - | - | - | - | 19154 |
| 5088 | - | 1854 | 4724 | - | 15003 |
| 44973 | 7988 | 7613 | 7305 | 2127 | 37209 |
| 20 | -31415 | - | - | - | -15000 |
| - | -31415 | - | - | - | -15000 |
| 405 | 355 | 525 | 10830 | 679 | 12641 |
| - | - | - | - | - | 30008 |
| - | 13 | 3 | - | - | 14 |
| 785333 | 872889 | 708038 | 1437695 | 1663575 | 1627788 |
| 6993 | 3570 | 6862 | 3457 | 1086 | 12252 |
| 302943 | 381405 | 363644 | 535761 | 697954 | 772920 |
| 344052 | 389661 | 281477 | 549368 | 529665 | 679977 |
| 131345 | 98253 | 56055 | 349109 | 434870 | 162639 |

| 指　　标 | Item | 余杭区 Yuhang | 富阳区 Fuyang |
|---|---|---|---|
| **财政总收入合计** | **Total** | **7264729** | **1312560** |
| 一、一般公共预算收入 | General Public Budget Revenue | 3914479 | 800008 |
| (一)税收收入 | Tax Revenue | 3737627 | 721045 |
| 1. 国内增值税 | Domestic Value - added Tax | 1052057 | 277515 |
| #改征增值税 | Newly Changed Value - added Tax | 578719 | 88004 |
| 2. 企业所得税 | Corporate Income Tax | 880817 | 119306 |
| 3. 个人所得税 | Individual Income Tax | 642090 | 36717 |
| 4. 城市维护建设税 | City Construction and Maintenance Tax | 156291 | 46589 |
| 5. 房产税 | Real Estate Tax | 77386 | 17026 |
| 6. 城镇土地使用税 | Urban Land Use Tax | 17224 | 15851 |
| 7. 土地增值税 | Land Appreciation Tax | 394156 | 79829 |
| 8. 耕地占用税 | Tax on the Use of Arable Land | 4624 | 16674 |
| 9. 契税 | Contract Tax | 455420 | 85381 |
| 10. 其他税收 | Others Tax | 57562 | 26157 |
| (二)非税收入 | Non - tax Revenue | 176852 | 78963 |
| 1. 专项收入 | Special Revenue | 114872 | 41030 |
| #教育费附加 | Revenue from Extra - Charges for Education | 57769 | 21428 |
| 地方教育附加收入 | Local Education Additional Revenue | 38025 | 14274 |
| 残疾人就业保障金收入 | Employment Security for The Disabled Revenue | 18950 | 4881 |
| 教育资金收入 | Educational Fund Revenue | - | - |
| 农田水利建设资金收入 | Fund in The Farmland Irrigation Construction Revenue | - | - |
| 2. 行政事业性收费收入 | Income from Administrative Fees | 137 | 9177 |
| 3. 罚没收入 | Penalty and Confiscatory Income | 41870 | 15959 |
| 4. 国有资本经营收入 | Revenue of state - owned capital | -7000 | -5000 |
| #国有企业计划亏损补贴 | Subsides to Loss - making of state - owned Enterprises | -7000 | -5000 |
| 5. 国有资源(资产)有偿使用收入 | Compensation for the Use of Seate - owned Assets Income | 26904 | 15735 |
| 6. 政府住房基金收入 | Government Housing Fund Income | 69 | 2062 |
| 7. 其他收入 | Others Revenue | - | - |
| 二、上划中央"六税"小计 | Subtotal Revenue of Central Government | 3350250 | 512552 |
| 1. 消费税 | Consumption Tax | 13832 | 1002 |
| 2. 国内增值税 | Domestic Value - added Tax | 1052057 | 277515 |
| 3. 企业所得税 | Corporate Income Tax | 1321226 | 178959 |
| 4. 个人所得税 | Individual Income Tax | 963135 | 55076 |

continued (10000 yuan)

| 临安区 Lin'an | 钱塘新区 Qiantang New Area | 西湖风景名胜区 The West Lake Scenic Zone | 桐庐县 Tonglu | 淳安县 Chun'an | 建德市 Jiande |
|---|---|---|---|---|---|
| **1019314** | **2012001** | **162743** | **580877** | **372220** | **541180** |
| 611600 | 1057592 | 84209 | 337654 | 210871 | 311008 |
| 541553 | 967118 | 80210 | 304820 | 194859 | 282837 |
| 203395 | 516794 | 24284 | 131729 | 78192 | 117646 |
| 90156 | 94619 | 18267 | 49655 | 48279 | 32515 |
| 108131 | 199897 | 28410 | 52562 | 37015 | 59234 |
| 24607 | 44971 | 7755 | 21726 | 15833 | 13673 |
| 32574 | 84205 | 4112 | 15148 | 8050 | 15315 |
| 11160 | 37347 | 13329 | 15036 | 8789 | 9943 |
| 9599 | 6155 | 1466 | 13482 | 2811 | 7756 |
| 58340 | 56347 | - | 15889 | 17383 | 13015 |
| 18221 | - | - | 4415 | 1734 | 1015 |
| 61484 | - | - | 22743 | 19314 | 22047 |
| 14042 | 21402 | 854 | 12090 | 5738 | 23193 |
| 70047 | 90474 | 3999 | 32834 | 16012 | 28171 |
| 39155 | 63000 | 3523 | 18174 | 8831 | 21136 |
| 13048 | 31117 | 1469 | 8174 | 4422 | 7181 |
| 8753 | 20741 | 980 | 5450 | 2949 | 4795 |
| 6322 | 11120 | 1074 | 2347 | 1312 | 2663 |
| 7800 | - | - | - | - | 2499 |
| - | - | - | - | - | 1599 |
| 3546 | 16886 | 51 | 1969 | 1886 | 2460 |
| 10577 | 8084 | 399 | 11611 | 2707 | 7609 |
| -14911 | - | - | - | - | -4700 |
| -15184 | - | - | - | - | -4700 |
| 28482 | 2504 | 26 | 1021 | 1946 | 1463 |
| - | - | - | - | 642 | 203 |
| 3198 | - | - | 59 | - | - |
| 407714 | 954409 | 78534 | 243223 | 161349 | 230172 |
| 5211 | 70312 | 2 | 62 | 3885 | 3165 |
| 203395 | 516794 | 24284 | 131729 | 78192 | 117646 |
| 162197 | 299846 | 42615 | 78843 | 55523 | 88851 |
| 36911 | 67457 | 11633 | 32589 | 23749 | 20510 |

# 10－03 分地区一般公共

## General Public

单位：万元

| 指标 |  Item | 全市 Total | 市区 Urban District | 上城区 Shangcheng |
|---|---|---|---|---|
| **一般公共预算支出** | **General Public Budget Expenditure** | **19528530** | **17796386** | **525476** |
| 一、一般公共服务 | Expenditure for General Public Services | 1708207 | 1546219 | 57651 |
| 二、国防 | Expenditure for National Defense | 10731 | 9435 | 24 |
| 三、公共安全 | Expenditure for Public Security | 1190269 | 1100968 | 47238 |
| 四、教育 | Expenditure for Education | 3635648 | 3327779 | 106146 |
| #教育费附加支出 | Expenditure on Extra－Charges for Educations | 243694 | 233493 | 10672 |
| 五、科学技术 | Expenditure for Science and Technology | 1481879 | 1417913 | 16043 |
| 六、文化旅游体育与传媒 | Expenditure for Culture, Sports and Media | 389757 | 353701 | 6472 |
| 七、社会保障和就业 | Expenditure for Social Safety Net and Employment Effort | 2292860 | 2104157 | 87961 |
| 八、卫生健康 | Expenditure for Medical and Health Care and Birth Control | 1300003 | 1118496 | 21678 |
| 九、节能环保 | Expenditure for Energy Conservation Environmental Protection | 471506 | 429717 | 3368 |
| 十、城乡社区 | Expenditure for Urban and Rural Community | 3308192 | 3186113 | 70986 |
| 十一、农林水 | Expenditure for Agriculture, Forestry and Water Conservancy | 1053876 | 844681 | 3970 |
| 十二、交通运输 | Expenditure for Trarssportation | 743181 | 602972 | 60090 |
| 十三、资源勘探信息等 | Resources Exploration Information, etc | 540280 | 525538 | 4718 |
| 十四、商业服务业等 | Expenditure for Commercial Service Industry | 353291 | 342773 | 6779 |
| 十五、金融 | Expenditure for Financial Supervision | 15875 | 15820 | 13087 |
| 十六、援助其他地区 | Expenditure for Aiding Other Territories | 130475 | 124381 | 13647 |
| 十七、自然资源海洋气象等 | Expenditure for Land, Ocean and Meteorological Services | 180117 | 122497 | 949 |
| 十八、住房保障 | Expenditure on Housing Support | 229186 | 193303 | 83 |
| 十九、粮油物资储备 | Expenditure for Grain and Oil Reservation and other Materials Services | 22207 | 18508 | － |
| 二十、债务付息和发行费用 | Expenditure for Interest Payment and issue costs of Government debt | 360625 | 307296 | 2529 |
| 二十一、其他 | Other Expenditure | 110365 | 104119 | 2057 |

预算支出(2019 年)
Expenditure by Region(2019)

(10000 yuan)

| 下城区 Xiacheng | 江干区 Jianggan | 拱墅区 Gongshu | 西湖区 Xihu | 高新(滨江)区 Hi - Tech (Binjiang) | 萧山区 Xiaoshan |
|---|---|---|---|---|---|
| **444493** | **762888** | **510072** | **930128** | **1236919** | **2754342** |
| 50808 | 74415 | 65457 | 89122 | 42636 | 235390 |
| 343 | 63 | 25 | 1175 | - | 2993 |
| 53018 | 58317 | 57709 | 70881 | 44875 | 125780 |
| 109393 | 157111 | 129918 | 203602 | 247272 | 519056 |
| 2069 | 15111 | 13391 | 16158 | 43838 | 45083 |
| 16107 | 71140 | 29996 | 73820 | 233220 | 99666 |
| 9460 | 11145 | 4562 | 13833 | 32640 | 38221 |
| 81990 | 103140 | 55497 | 128258 | 155204 | 163990 |
| 23441 | 39015 | 25770 | 76652 | 34453 | 223620 |
| 25 | 10120 | 6825 | 555 | 6919 | 65726 |
| 67599 | 169731 | 121423 | 161484 | 285653 | 629634 |
| 1507 | 14742 | 1370 | 19719 | 10919 | 239401 |
| 20 | 120 | 75 | 55 | 105 | 70768 |
| 2452 | 529 | 426 | 46912 | 55491 | 91363 |
| 8889 | 3482 | 4050 | 4155 | 9958 | 75242 |
| 98 | - | 81 | - | - | 732 |
| - | - | 1565 | 8600 | 18160 | 12749 |
| 1245 | 2039 | 1474 | 3503 | 2313 | 40062 |
| 12235 | 3104 | 3351 | 20014 | 26610 | 58449 |
| - | - | - | - | - | 177 |
| 5074 | 10892 | 489 | 3762 | 21100 | 52549 |
| 789 | 33783 | 9 | 4026 | 9391 | 8774 |

| 指　　标 | Item | 余杭区 Yuhang | 富阳区 Fuyang |
|---|---|---|---|
| **一般公共预算支出** | **General Public Budget Expenditure** | **3767331** | **1055038** |
| 一、一般公共服务 | Expenditure for General Public Services | 308966 | 96061 |
| 二、国防 | Expenditure for National Defense | 2184 | 38 |
| 三、公共安全 | Expenditure for Public Security | 132895 | 50704 |
| 四、教育 | Expenditure for Education | 696375 | 218846 |
| #教育费附加支出 | Expenditure on Extra－Charges for Educations | 58136 | 4142 |
| 五、科学技术 | Expenditure for Science and Technology | 283115 | 56338 |
| 六、文化旅游体育与传媒 | Expenditure for Culture,Sports and Media | 60823 | 17870 |
| 七、社会保障和就业 | Expenditure for Social Safety Net and Employment Effort | 313320 | 36790 |
| 八、卫生健康 | Expenditure for Medical and Health Care and Birth Control | 228371 | 57003 |
| 九、节能环保 | Expenditure for Energy Conservation Environmental Protection | 106470 | 58139 |
| 十、城乡社区 | Expenditure for Urban and Rural Community | 942917 | 87772 |
| 十一、农林水 | Expenditure for Agriculture,Forestry and Water Conservancy | 154451 | 79358 |
| 十二、交通运输 | Expenditure for Trarssportation | 45150 | 201856 |
| 十三、资源勘探信息等 | Resources Exploration Information,etc | 157211 | 13623 |
| 十四、商业服务业等 | Expenditure for Commercial Service Industry | 194559 | 6688 |
| 十五、金融 | Expenditure for Financial Supervision | 182 | 236 |
| 十六、援助其他地区 | Expenditure for Aiding Other Territories | 25003 | 7293 |
| 十七、自然资源海洋气象等 | Expenditure for Land, Ocean and Meteorological Services | 24159 | 10837 |
| 十八、住房保障 | Expenditure on Housing Support | 13228 | 21102 |
| 十九、粮油物资储备 | Expenditure for Grain and Oil Reservation and other Materials Services | 4875 | 40 |
| 二十、债务付息和发行费用 | Expenditure for Interest Payment and issue costs of Government debt | 61657 | 31351 |
| 二十一、其他 | Other Expenditure | 11420 | 3093 |

continued (10000 yuan)

| 临安区 Lin'an | 钱塘新区 Qiantang New Area | 西湖风景名胜区 The West Lake Scenic Zone | 桐庐县 Tonglu | 淳安县 Chun'an | 建德市 Jiande |
|---|---|---|---|---|---|
| **856154** | **938381** | **161529** | **501985** | **688654** | **541505** |
| 78283 | 93811 | 8552 | 38368 | 72373 | 51247 |
| 445 | 150 | – | 479 | 287 | 530 |
| 45293 | 61201 | 18308 | 29703 | 29166 | 30432 |
| 168709 | 183936 | 4525 | 130365 | 81190 | 96314 |
| 1062 | 1493 | 556 | 5011 | 4991 | 199 |
| 50557 | 64423 | 85 | 26710 | 10952 | 26304 |
| 15755 | 3145 | 12115 | 14378 | 11114 | 10564 |
| 135080 | 34487 | 17696 | 48549 | 77784 | 62370 |
| 70156 | 70715 | 2750 | 76784 | 61328 | 43395 |
| 15891 | 66945 | 126 | 6424 | 25903 | 9462 |
| 77663 | 143182 | 79476 | 25243 | 48511 | 48325 |
| 74818 | 25113 | 17115 | 44858 | 89522 | 74815 |
| 37405 | 4898 | – | 24088 | 96223 | 19898 |
| 15327 | 122797 |  | 2124 | 11045 | 1573 |
| 7417 | 7891 | 299 | 1579 | 5292 | 3647 |
| 35 | – | – | 30 | 25 | – |
| 1848 | 2841 | 214 | 4977 | – | 1117 |
| 6639 | 4677 | 267 | 8646 | 24069 | 24905 |
| 27658 | 7469 | – | 8819 | 15229 | 11835 |
| 27 | 2107 | – | 1587 | 2112 | – |
| 17992 | 33042 | – | 7295 | 25002 | 21032 |
| 9156 | 5551 | 1 | 979 | 1527 | 3740 |

## 10－04 分税种、支出科目财政收支情况(2013－2019 年)

## Local Public Financial Budgetary Expenditure by Tax and Expenditure Account(2013－2019)

单位:万元 (10000 yuan)

| 指标 Item | 2013 | 2014 | 2015 | 2016 | 2017 | 2018 | 2019 |
|---|---|---|---|---|---|---|---|
| **财政总收入合计 Total** | **17349750** | **19201076** | **22387456** | **25584128** | **29212996** | **34574596** | **36500413** |
| 一、一般公共预算收入 General Public Budget Revenue | 9452020 | 10273169 | 12338820 | 14023826 | 15674169 | 18250616 | 19659731 |
| (一)税收收入 Tax Revenue | 9106690 | 9952111 | 11259532 | 12892210 | 14171594 | 16512101 | 17911758 |
| 1. 国内增值税 Domestic Value－added Tax | 1122297 | 1224336 | 1301043 | 2097640 | 2969672 | 3222118 | 6464435 |
| 改征增值税 Newly Changed Value－added Tax | 593744 | 837724 | 1000427 | 1705813 | 2693559 | 3354083 | 3293607 |
| 2. 营业税 Business Tax | 2670660 | 2650471 | 3094627 | 1988053 | 5288 | 16053 | |
| 3. 企业所得税 Corporate Income Tax | 1518112 | 1723639 | 1928567 | 2215439 | 2702212 | 3230360 | 3762660 |
| 4. 个人所得税 Individual Income Tax | 573227 | 681449 | 920917 | 1155176 | 1461998 | 1863436 | 1813506 |
| 5. 城市维护建设税 City Construction and Maintenance Tax | 658593 | 693932 | 792815 | 890160 | 984315 | 1133495 | 1117782 |
| 6. 房产税 Real Estate Tax | 323897 | 378171 | 398528 | 443407 | 557952 | 663805 | 589684 |
| 7. 城镇土地使用税 Urban Land Use Tax | | | 155914 | 147437 | 205548 | 172024 | 116652 |
| 8. 土地增值税 Land Appreciation Tax | | | 551468 | 851760 | 975587 | 931792 | 1639773 |
| 9. 耕地占用税 Tax on the Use of Arable Land | 91622 | 72117 | 64426 | 40610 | 37784 | 31261 | 119847 |
| 10. 契税 Contract Tax | 674188 | 805656 | 761861 | 1056441 | 1205784 | 1474897 | 1839509 |
| 11. 其他税收 Others Tax | 880350 | 884616 | 288939 | 300274 | 371895 | 418777 | 447910 |
| (二)非税收入 Non－tax Revenue | 345330 | 321058 | 1079288 | 1131616 | 1502575 | 1738515 | 1747973 |
| 1. 专项收入 Special Revenue | 267287 | 278423 | 1073893 | 1102959 | 1180199 | 1293351 | 1173121 |
| 2. 行政事业性收费收入 Income from Administrative Fees | 19738 | 13988 | 12213 | 10968 | 48079 | 111730 | 101292 |

| 指　　标<br>Item | 2013 | 2014 | 2015 | 2016 | 2017 | 2018 | 2019 |
|---|---|---|---|---|---|---|---|
| 3. 罚没收入<br>Penalty and Confiscatory Income | 148738 | 148190 | 149897 | 160147 | 218482 | 328202 | 279899 |
| 4. 国有资本经营收入<br>Revenue of state－owned capital | | | | | | | －198006 |
| #国有企业计划亏损补贴<br>Subsides to Loss－making of state－owned Enterprises | －105699 | －147887 | －197823 | －250873 | －174529 | －230413 | －198299 |
| 5. 国有资源(资产)有偿使用收入<br>Compensation for the Use of Seate－owned Assets Income | 14314 | 27927 | 38904 | 58175 | 101288 | 146357 | 292317 |
| 6. 政府住房基金收入<br>Government Housing Fund Income | － | － | － | 47.46 | 128247 | 79003 | 92493 |
| 7. 其他收入<br>Others Revenue | 952 | 417 | 2204 | 47146 | 809 | 10285 | 6857 |
| 二、一般公共预算支出<br>General Public Budget Expenditure | 8557370 | 9611771 | 12054777 | 14043065 | 15409156 | 17170834 | 19528530 |
| 1. 一般公共服务<br>Expenditure for General Public Services | 915881 | 892027 | 1011605 | 1125425 | 1311829 | 1503663 | 1708207 |
| 2. 教育<br>Expenditure for Education | 1624445 | 1826924 | 2234425 | 2530114 | 2792968 | 3154350 | 3635648 |
| 3. 科学技术<br>Expenditure for Science and Technology | 462600 | 524082 | 701490 | 749190 | 923236 | 1182090 | 1481879 |
| 4. 文化旅游体育与传媒<br>Expenditure for Culture, Sports and Media | 223604 | 242375 | 449192 | 283936 | 309282 | 332192 | 389757 |
| 5. 社会保障和就业<br>Expenditure for Social Safety Net and Employment Effort | 946033 | 1082564 | 1309862 | 1492895 | 1731704 | 2043585 | 2292860 |
| 6. 卫生健康<br>Expenditure for Medical and Health Care and Birth Control | 621518 | 716754 | 766328 | 970504 | 1123291 | 1107731 | 1300003 |
| 7. 节能环保<br>Expenditure for Energy Conservation Environmental Protection | 197392 | 300159 | 445749 | 408576 | 377904 | 360033 | 471506 |
| 8. 城乡社区<br>Expenditure for Urban and Rural Community | 1064358 | 1143602 | 1586419 | 2338331 | 2736428 | 2930114 | 3308192 |
| 9. 农林水<br>Expenditure for Agriculture, Forestry and Water Conservancy | 506246 | 562286 | 880440 | 914373 | 896205 | 942335 | 1053876 |
| 10. 交通运输<br>Expenditure for Trassportation | 305919 | 306032 | 389625 | 518178 | 515070 | 754753 | 743181 |
| 11. 住房保障<br>Expenditure on Housing Support | 77290 | 93521 | 122825 | 219590 | 286287 | 227453 | 229186 |

# 10－05 金融机构存、贷款余额（1978－2019 年）

## Balance of Deposits and Loans of Financial Institutions（1978－2019）

单位：万元 （10000 yuan）

| 年份 Year \ 项目 Item | 各项存款 Deposits | 住户存款 Household Deposits | 城镇住户存款 Urban Household Deposits | 各项贷款 Loans |
|---|---|---|---|---|
| 1978 | 86824 | 20714 | 17056 | 136759 |
| 1979 | 108998 | 28937 | 22640 | 135713 |
| 1980 | 180707 | 40447 | 30896 | 174153 |
| 1981 | 226949 | 51440 | 38889 | 236678 |
| 1982 | 262156 | 67192 | 50113 | 216040 |
| 1983 | 303130 | 86635 | 64736 | 236203 |
| 1984 | 388305 | 115766 | 85439 | 329195 |
| 1985 | 484999 | 159596 | 115592 | 580180 |
| 1986 | 635514 | 222110 | 153572 | 769841 |
| 1987 | 776105 | 302762 | 207505 | 967477 |
| 1988 | 839680 | 351943 | 241839 | 1145989 |
| 1989 | 1017087 | 501592 | 346318 | 1338984 |
| 1990 | 1646165 | 697515 | 479031 | 1803266 |
| 1991 | 2036334 | 904490 | 616308 | 2136903 |
| 1992 | 2652966 | 1144737 | 763309 | 2651983 |
| 1993 | 3469954 | 1563328 | 1048413 | 3415527 |
| 1994 | 5061345 | 2394370 | 1642498 | 4450932 |
| 1995 | 7079650 | 3423379 | 2448787 | 5672105 |
| 1996 | 9619291 | 4638458 | 3459439 | 7434243 |
| 1997 | 12251840 | 5583306 | 4229591 | 9388500 |
| 1998 | 14948225 | 6701158 | 5155548 | 11620537 |
| 1999 | 17886717 | 7425967 | 5760527 | 14937506 |
| 2000 | 20884723 | 7885579 | 6151084 | 16866431 |
| 2001 | 26215100 | 9418400 | 7396800 | 20877000 |
| 2002 | 33731500 | 11834000 | 9492300 | 27523800 |
| 2003 | 46527300 | 15899600 | 13079600 | 38187000 |
| 2004 | 57072000 | 18351700 | 15016100 | 48000400 |
| 2005 | 67487200 | 21916600 | 17960100 | 55453000 |
| 2006 | 78555500 | 25552400 | 20789600 | 66038600 |
| 2007 | 93109600 | 26348300 | 21154300 | 84306800 |
| 2008 | 113333500 | 34765900 | 27584600 | 100690500 |
| 2009 | 142842104 | 42869189 | 34027871 | 131133023 |
| 2010 | 170843548 | 49909744 | 39352353 | 150787269 |
| 2011 | 183965719 | 55474824 | 43464332 | 165737441 |
| 2012 | 201487672 | 60899841 | 46965391 | 180908011 |
| 2013 | 221747107 | 64085856 | 47733077 | 193504605 |
| 2014 | 244505093 | 67672009 | 49107745 | 213168315 |
| 2015 | 298638294 | 76177515 | 55659016 | 233279520 |
| 2016 | 333860429 | 84932733 | 62521938 | 261689982 |
| 2017 | 364832373 | 86705977 | 63076960 | 292709406 |
| 2018 | 398104954 | 101985223 | 75755331 | 365982478 |
| 2019 | 452869942 | 119012969 | – | 422451656 |

注：1. 1989 年以前数据均为银行机构存贷款，1990 年及以后年份数据为调整后金融机构存贷款。2003 年起金融机构存贷款为本外币合并数据。

2. 2015 年起，各项存款和各项贷款分类调整。

3. 2019 年起，不再区分城镇住户和农村住户。

a) Data before 1989 belonged to banking system, data after 1990 adjusted for deposits and loans of financial institutions, data of 2003 included both RMB and foreign currency.

b) Since 2015, the classification in deposits and Loans has been adjusted.

c) Since 2019, no distinction are made between urban and rural households.

# 10－06 市区金融机构存、贷款余额(1978－2019年)

## Balance of Deposits and Loans of Financial Institutions of Urban District(1978－2019)

单位:万元 (10000 yuan)

| 年份 Year \ 项目 Item | 各项存款 Deposits | 住户存款 Household Deposits | 城镇住户存款 Urban Household Deposits | 各项贷款 Loans |
|---|---|---|---|---|
| 1978 | 58372 | 13774 | 13246 | 101144 |
| 1979 | 73720 | 18055 | 17241 | 98792 |
| 1980 | 134275 | 24702 | 23282 | 121231 |
| 1981 | 172721 | 31358 | 29345 | 170539 |
| 1982 | 198350 | 39756 | 37047 | 142091 |
| 1983 | 226160 | 50439 | 46833 | 155297 |
| 1984 | 293145 | 66108 | 61934 | 194977 |
| 1985 | 359825 | 89114 | 82868 | 418214 |
| 1986 | 458142 | 115818 | 106703 | 557763 |
| 1987 | 565429 | 156704 | 142642 | 714313 |
| 1988 | 610601 | 180341 | 163466 | 846998 |
| 1989 | 737388 | 256238 | 229518 | 1000731 |
| 1990 | 1062574 | 354316 | 297390 | 1271779 |
| 1991 | 1309462 | 451756 | 397322 | 1469671 |
| 1992 | 1695011 | 572660 | 479248 | 1774158 |
| 1993 | 2263969 | 762234 | 662234 | 2298124 |
| 1994 | 3383877 | 1242379 | 1085363 | 3033010 |
| 1995 | 4851774 | 1853512 | 1639875 | 3907199 |
| 1996 | 6828786 | 2734904 | 2371657 | 5350499 |
| 1997 | 8831147 | 3287475 | 2873638 | 6772221 |
| 1998 | 10785066 | 3905602 | 3440607 | 8615412 |
| 1999 | 13051806 | 4336058 | 3835542 | 11462505 |
| 2000 | 15436286 | 4620235 | 4101716 | 13105849 |
| 2001 | 23765400 | 7976400 | 6460200 | 19237800 |
| 2002 | 30638400 | 10139800 | 8370100 | 25476700 |
| 2003 | 42522000 | 13834200 | 11693000 | 30297500 |
| 2004 | 52542100 | 16014700 | 13479900 | 44517600 |
| 2005 | 62249500 | 19231800 | 16208400 | 51455900 |
| 2006 | 72269600 | 22391800 | 18737800 | 61190700 |
| 2007 | 86197300 | 23124600 | 19132300 | 78456200 |
| 2008 | 104930100 | 30665200 | 24996500 | 93838100 |
| 2009 | 131800234 | 37837816 | 30801878 | 121473548 |
| 2010 | 156776515 | 43676938 | 35370599 | 138671334 |
| 2011 | 168052916 | 48263525 | 38996516 | 151756838 |
| 2012 | 183719227 | 52347969 | 41789531 | 156426086 |
| 2013 | 201596137 | 54488059 | 42142666 | 175670366 |
| 2014 | 222558892 | 57202595 | 43243610 | 191888081 |
| 2015 | 284321331 | 68516344 | 51360093 | 222078475 |
| 2016 | 317723682 | 76306727 | 57718389 | 249684325 |
| 2017 | 345461303 | 77416526 | 57941703 | 278049912 |
| 2018 | 385383821 | 94991531 | 71808820 | 354926592 |
| 2019 | 437946336 | 110826488 | － | 409258262 |

注:1. 2018年起,市区数据包含临安区

2. 2019年起,不再区分城镇住户和农村住户。

a) Since 2018, data of urban District Includes Lin'an district.

b) Since 2019, no distinction are made between urban and rural households.

# 10－07 全市金融机构本外币

# Balance of Deposits and Loans(RMB and Foreign Currency)

单位:万元

| 指 标 | Item | 全 市 Total 绝对值 Absolute Value | 全 市 Total 为上年(%) As Compared with the Preceding Year(%) | 市 区 Urban District 小计 Subtotal |
|---|---|---|---|---|
| **一、各项存款** | **Deposits** | **452869942** | **113.76** | **437946336** |
| (一)境内存款 | Domestic Deposits | 446205803 | 112.82 | 431318503 |
| 1.住户存款 | Household Deposits | 119012969 | 116.70 | 110826488 |
| (1)活期存款 | Current Deposits | 50828963 | 114.28 | 47814565 |
| (2)定期及其他存款 | Term and Other Deposits | 68184006 | 118.57 | 63011923 |
| 2.非金融企业存款 | Non－financial Enterprise Deposits | 202802755 | 116.49 | 198313199 |
| (1)活期存款 | Current Deposits | 76279501 | 111.40 | 73367188 |
| (2)定期及其他存款 | Term and Other Deposits | 126523255 | 119.79 | 124946010 |
| 3.广义政府存款 | General Government Deposits | 93435481 | 110.67 | 91235595 |
| (1)财政性存款 | Treasury Deposits | 18501265 | 99.58 | 18132864 |
| (2)机关团体存款 | Organization Deposits | 74934217 | 113.80 | 73102731 |
| 4.非银行业金融机构存款 | Non－banking Financial Institutions Deposits | 30954597 | 88.46 | 30943221 |
| (二)境外存款 | Overseas Deposits | 6664139 | 256.55 | 6627833 |
| **二、各项贷款** | **Loans** | **422451656** | **115.43** | **409258262** |
| (一)境内贷款 | Domestic Loans | 419099994 | 115.50 | 405906804 |
| 1.住户贷款 | Household Loans | 165180005 | 118.45 | 158711760 |
| (1)短期贷款 | Short－term Loans | 59267605 | 111.03 | 57711758 |
| (2)中长期贷款 | Medium and Long term Loans | 105912400 | 123.05 | 101000002 |
| 2.非金融企业及机关团体贷款 | Non－financial Enterprise and Organization Loans | 253754944 | 113.62 | 247030000 |
| (1)短期贷款 | Short－term Loans | 81137176 | 105.69 | 78951548 |
| (2)中长期贷款 | Medium and Long term Loans | 146832401 | 116.42 | 142453000 |
| (3)票据融资 | Note Financing | 16272930 | 144.47 | 16113110 |
| (4)融资租赁 | Finance lease | 9313274 | 106.41 | 9313274 |
| (5)各项垫款 | Advance Money | 199163 | 45.80 | 199067 |
| 3.非银行业金融机构贷款 | Non－banking Financial Institutions Loans | 165044 | 342.35 | 165044 |
| (二)境外贷款 | Overseas Loans | 3351663 | 106.95 | 3351458 |

# 存、贷款余额(2019年末)
# of Financial Institutions(End of 2019)

(10000 yuan)

| 萧山区 Xiaoshan | 余杭区 Yuhang | 富阳区 Fuyang | 临安区 Lin′an | 桐庐县 Tonglu | 淳安县 Chun′an | 建德市 Jiande |
|---|---|---|---|---|---|---|
| **48720506** | **37997915** | **13396796** | **9806328** | **5755521** | **3795092** | **5372993** |
| 48509855 | 37938217 | 13369235 | 9802305 | 5725092 | 3794357 | 5367851 |
| 20010664 | 14772692 | 5879562 | 3981041 | 3186764 | 1956247 | 3043471 |
| 6653368 | 5346418 | 2601106 | 1754290 | 1151661 | 773233 | 1089504 |
| 13357296 | 9426274 | 3278456 | 2226751 | 2035102 | 1183013 | 1953967 |
| 18390950 | 13147898 | 5446650 | 3652146 | 1830420 | 1051599 | 1607538 |
| 7742620 | 6248247 | 2787583 | 1973848 | 1163888 | 630656 | 1117768 |
| 10648330 | 6899651 | 2659067 | 1678298 | 666531 | 420942 | 489770 |
| 9868453 | 9960605 | 1889907 | 2169050 | 706751 | 786473 | 706663 |
| 1494225 | 2235386 | 138389 | 347202 | 79133 | 139880 | 149388 |
| 8374229 | 7725219 | 1751517 | 1821849 | 627618 | 646593 | 557275 |
| 239788 | 57023 | 153116 | 66 | 1158 | 39 | 10179 |
| 210651 | 59697 | 27561 | 4023 | 30429 | 735 | 5142 |
| 44287658 | 26292408 | 14899948 | 8031955 | 5558189 | 3118729 | 4516477 |
| 44242013 | 26289963 | 14899833 | 8031433 | 5558189 | 3118652 | 4516348 |
| 15049345 | 12135674 | 5606220 | 3832290 | 2553807 | 1811109 | 2103330 |
| 3480805 | 2208145 | 1111297 | 1009638 | 564799 | 352358 | 638690 |
| 11568540 | 9927528 | 4494924 | 2822651 | 1989008 | 1458751 | 1464639 |
| 29077668 | 14154290 | 9293613 | 4199143 | 3004381 | 1307544 | 2413019 |
| 13084212 | 5396989 | 4458183 | 1119039 | 1067875 | 358354 | 759398 |
| 14983009 | 7985838 | 4544437 | 2897609 | 1882636 | 910552 | 1586213 |
| 956191 | 771463 | 289882 | 181139 | 53870 | 38637 | 67312 |
| | | | | | | |
| 54257 | – | 1110 | 1356 | | | 95 |
| 115000 | | | | | | |
| 45645 | 2445 | 115 | 522 | | 77 | 128 |

# 10－08 金融机构人民币

# Balance of RMB Deposits and Loans

单位:万元

| 指 标 | Item | 全 市 Total 绝对值 Absolute Value | 全 市 Total 为上年(%) As Compared with the Preceding Year(%) | 市 区 Urban District 小计 Subtotal |
|---|---|---|---|---|
| **一、各项存款** | **Deposits** | **439320152** | **113.20** | **424690429** |
| (一)境内存款 | Domestic Deposits | 438541055 | 113.27 | 423919325 |
| 1.住户存款 | Household Deposits | 117018626 | 117.24 | 108946945 |
| (1)活期存款 | Current Deposits | 49922951 | 115.20 | 46922670 |
| (2)定期及其他存款 | Term and Other Deposits | 67095675 | 118.80 | 62024275 |
| 2.非金融企业存款 | Non－financial Enterprise Deposits | 197285694 | 117.30 | 192942112 |
| (1)活期存款 | Current Deposits | 72522933 | 111.61 | 69736116 |
| (2)定期及其他存款 | Term and Other Deposits | 124762761 | 120.89 | 123205997 |
| 3.广义政府存款 | General Government Deposits | 93386015 | 110.63 | 91190842 |
| (1)财政性存款 | Treasury Deposits | 18501265 | 99.58 | 18132864 |
| (2)机关团体存款 | Organization Deposits | 74884750 | 113.74 | 73057978 |
| 4.非银行业金融机构存款 | Non－banking Financial Institutions Deposits | 30850720 | 88.74 | 30839426 |
| (二)境外存款 | Overseas Deposits | 779097 | 84.61 | 771104 |
| **二、各项贷款** | **Loans** | **415457647** | **115.80** | **402272776** |
| (一)境内贷款 | Domestic Loans | 414644051 | 115.78 | 401459384 |
| 1.住户贷款 | Household Loans | 165164918 | 118.44 | 158696887 |
| (1)短期贷款 | Short－term Loans | 59252672 | 111.01 | 57697039 |
| (2)中长期贷款 | Medium and Long term Loans | 105912246 | 123.05 | 100999847 |
| 2.非金融企业及机关团体贷款 | Non－financial Enterprise and Organization Loans | 249314089 | 114.04 | 242597453 |
| (1)短期贷款 | Short－term Loans | 78732786 | 105.82 | 76555467 |
| (2)中长期贷款 | Medium and Long term Loans | 144819546 | 116.91 | 140440145 |
| (3)票据融资 | Note Financing | 16272930 | 144.47 | 16113110 |
| (4)融资租赁 | Finance lease | 9313274 | 106.41 | 9313274 |
| (5)各项垫款 | Advance Money | 175553 | 54.40 | 175457 |
| 3.非银行业金融机构贷款 | Non－banking Financial Institutions Loans | 165044 | 342.35 | 165044 |
| (二)境外贷款 | Overseas Loans | 813596 | 123.42 | 813391 |

# 存、贷款余额(2019 年末)

## of Financial Institutions(End of 2019)

(10000 yuan)

| 萧山区 Xiaoshan | 余杭区 Yuhang | 富阳区 Fuyang | 临安区 Lin'an | 桐庐县 Tonglu | 淳安县 Chun'an | 建德市 Jiande |
|---|---|---|---|---|---|---|
| **47787635** | **37658568** | **13248838** | **9724002** | **5581509** | **3778143** | **5270071** |
| 47731451 | 37608785 | 13245833 | 9720179 | 5575629 | 3777428 | 5268673 |
| 19904272 | 14711845 | 5853339 | 3966379 | 3085097 | 1952557 | 3034026 |
| 6602202 | 5307974 | 2585077 | 1746458 | 1144871 | 770675 | 1084735 |
| 13302070 | 9403871 | 3268262 | 2219921 | 1940226 | 1181882 | 1949292 |
| 17719569 | 12900348 | 5349619 | 3584923 | 1782623 | 1041661 | 1519298 |
| 7361116 | 6039390 | 2707693 | 1909337 | 1132895 | 621029 | 1032893 |
| 10358453 | 6860957 | 2641926 | 1675586 | 649728 | 420632 | 486405 |
| 9868213 | 9939571 | 1889758 | 2168810 | 706751 | 783171 | 705252 |
| 1494225 | 2235386 | 138389 | 347202 | 79133 | 139880 | 149388 |
| 8373988 | 7704185 | 1751368 | 1821609 | 627618 | 643291 | 555863 |
| 239397 | 57022 | 153116 | 66 | 1158 | 39 | 10097 |
| 56184 | 49783 | 3006 | 3823 | 5880 | 715 | 1398 |
| 44024393 | 26166666 | 14887626 | 8029577 | 5558106 | 3118614 | 4508151 |
| 44021389 | 26164221 | 14887511 | 8029056 | 5558106 | 3118537 | 4508023 |
| 15048772 | 12135358 | 5606016 | 3832168 | 2553732 | 1811078 | 2103221 |
| 3480233 | 2207830 | 1111150 | 1009517 | 564723 | 352328 | 638582 |
| 11568540 | 9927528 | 4494866 | 2822651 | 1989008 | 1458751 | 1464639 |
| 28857617 | 14028863 | 9281495 | 4196888 | 3004374 | 1307459 | 2404802 |
| 12864161 | 5280160 | 4446066 | 1116784 | 1067868 | 358269 | 751182 |
| 14983009 | 7977240 | 4544437 | 2897609 | 1882636 | 910552 | 1586213 |
| 956191 | 771463 | 289882 | 181139 | 53870 | 38637 | 67312 |
| 54257 | – | 1110 | 1356 | | | 95 |
| 115000 | | | | | | |
| 3003 | 2445 | 115 | 522 | | 77 | 128 |

# 10－09 住户（本外币）存款余额（2019 年末）

## Balance of Savings Deposits(RMB and Foreign Currency) of Rural and Urban Residents(End of 2019)

单位：万元 (10000 yuan)

| 地区 | Region | 总计 Total 2019 年末 At the End of Year 2019 | 总计 Total 为上年(%) As Compared with the Preceding Year(%) |
|---|---|---|---|
| **全 市** | **Total** | **119012969** | **116.70** |
| 市 区 | Urban District | 110826488 | 116.67 |
| #萧山区 | Xiaoshan | 20010664 | 116.11 |
| 余杭区 | Yuhang | 14772692 | 119.28 |
| 富阳区 | Fuyang | 5879562 | 118.40 |
| 临安区 | Lin'an | 3981041 | 116.66 |
| 桐庐县 | Tonglu | 3186764 | 118.75 |
| 淳安县 | Chun'an | 1956247 | 116.09 |
| 建德市 | Jiande | 3043471 | 115.94 |

# 10－10　金融机构人民币信贷收支表(资金来源,2013－2019年)

## Credit Funds Balance Sheet of Financial Institutions (RMB,Sources of Funds,2013－2019)

单位:亿元　　(100 million yuan)

| 项　目 | Item | 2013 | 2014 | 2015 | 2016 | 2017 | 2018 | 2019 |
|---|---|---|---|---|---|---|---|---|
| **资金来源合计** | **All Sources** | **22028.95** | **25403.81** | **30190.21** | **36881.85** | **38680.06** | **42616.04** | **48921.91** |
| 一、各项存款 | Deposits | 22386.39 | 25721.84 | 29003.07 | 32514.64 | 35321.94 | 38810.05 | 43932.02 |
| (一)境内存款 | Domestic Deposits | 22322.27 | 25642.26 | 28945.99 | 32440.97 | 35270.79 | 38717.97 | 43854.11 |
| 1.住户存款 | Household Deposits | 6831.58 | 7223.78 | 7507.09 | 8313.13 | 8502.96 | 9981.24 | 11701.86 |
| 2.非金融企业存款 | Non－financial Enterprise Deposits | 10733.60 | 11508.67 | 12437.24 | 13853.66 | 15556.61 | 16818.70 | 19728.57 |
| 3.广义政府存款 | General Government Deposits | 3476.44 | 4218.53 | 4674.92 | 5788.91 | 7161.81 | 8441.52 | 9338.60 |
| 4.非银行业金融机构存款 | Non－banking Financial Institutions Deposits | 1280.64 | 2691.28 | 4326.75 | 4485.28 | 4049.41 | 3476.51 | 3085.07 |
| (二)境外存款 | Overseas Deposits | 64.12 | 79.58 | 57.08 | 73.67 | 51.15 | 92.08 | 77.91 |
| 二、金融债券 | Bonds | 130.65 | 168.43 | 239.84 | 342.64 | 439.42 | 378.36 | 541.95 |
| 三、卖出回购资产 | Sell Repurchase Assets | 27.11 | | | | 4.72 | 0.95 | 0.00 |
| 四、借款及非银行业金融机构拆入 | Borrowing and Non Banking Financial Institutions Borrowing | 216.25 | 258.90 | 0.30 | 15.35 | 3.00 | 21.52 | 44.14 |
| 五、联行往来(净) | Interbank Transactions (net) | | | | | | 906.44 | 1382.55 |
| 六、应付及暂收款 | Accounts Payable and Temporary Collection of Money | 699.24 | 907.61 | 935.16 | 1008.12 | 1101.74 | 1138.08 | 1281.64 |
| 七、各项准备 | All Reserves | 399.37 | 480.22 | 600.05 | 733.19 | 850.04 | 1020.51 | 1165.55 |
| 八、所有者权益 | Creditor's Equity | 828.71 | 929.92 | 967.10 | 1104.44 | 1491.11 | 1831.24 | 2103.47 |
| 其中:实收资本 | Paid－in Capital | 180.29 | 201.14 | 283.48 | 315.27 | 475.22 | 524.60 | 572.79 |
| 九、其他 | Others | －2658.76 | －3063.11 | －1555.31 | 1163.46 | －531.90 | －1491.11 | －1529.39 |

# 10－11　金融机构人民币信贷收支表(资金运用,2014－2019年)

## Credit Funds Balance Sheet of Financial Institutions (RMB,Use of Funds,2014－2019)

单位:亿元　　(100 million yuan)

| 项　目 | Item | 2014 | 2015 | 2016 | 2017 | 2018 | 2019 |
|---|---|---|---|---|---|---|---|
| **资金运用合计** | | **25403.81** | **30190.21** | **36881.85** | **38680.06** | **42616.04** | **48921.91** |
| **一、各项存款** | **Deposits** | **20388.37** | **22395.29** | **25464.83** | **28573.63** | **35877.56** | **41545.76** |
| **(一)境内贷款** | **Domestic Loans** | **20382.37** | **22373.03** | **25431.25** | **28552.46** | **35811.64** | **41464.41** |
| **1.住户贷款** | **Household Loans** | **4918.01** | **5858.42** | **7799.69** | **9653.02** | **13945.02** | **16516.49** |
| (1)短期贷款 | Short－term Loans | 1770.03 | 1874.03 | 1998.31 | 2350.55 | 5337.55 | 5925.27 |
| (2)中长期贷款 | Medium and Long term Loans | 3147.99 | 3984.39 | 5801.38 | 7302.47 | 8607.47 | 10591.22 |
| **2.非金融企业及机关团体贷款** | **Non－financial Enterprise and Organization Loans** | **15432.16** | **16502.18** | **17613.23** | **18867.79** | **21861.79** | **24931.41** |
| (1)短期贷款 | Short－term Loans | 6909.51 | 6943.84 | 7082.51 | 7182.69 | 7440.18 | 7873.28 |
| (2)中长期贷款 | Medium and Long term Loans | 7145.36 | 7539.38 | 8023.23 | 9969.89 | 12387.74 | 14481.95 |
| (3)票据融资 | Note Financing | 731.55 | 1311.28 | 1678.99 | 818.90 | 1126.38 | 1627.29 |
| (4)融资租赁 | Finance lease | 589.24 | 663.57 | 783.39 | 865.12 | 875.23 | 931.33 |
| (5)各项垫款 | Advance Money | 56.49 | 44.11 | 45.11 | 31.18 | 32.27 | 17.56 |
| **3.非银行业金融机构贷款** | **Non－banking Financial Institutions Deposits** | **32.20** | **12.44** | **18.34** | **31.65** | **4.82** | **16.50** |
| **(二)境外贷款** | **Overseas Loans** | **6.00** | **22.26** | **33.58** | **21.17** | **65.92** | **81.36** |
| **二、债券投资** | **Bond Investment** | **1667.86** | **2005.65** | **2032.81** | **2694.21** | **3239.73** | **4020.00** |
| **三、股权及其他投资** | **Equity and other Investment** | **1076.84** | **1738.10** | **2642.37** | **2804.86** | **2494.60** | **2321.37** |
| **四、买入返售资产** | **Bug Assets Repurchased** | **336.63** | **62.63** | **48.35** | **87.36** | **348.01** | **254.43** |
| **五、存放非银行业金融机构款项** | **Deposit of non Banking Financial Institutions** | **0.27** | **0.97** | **1.11** | **1.36** | **0.54** | **1.40** |
| **六、联行往来(净)** | **Interbank Transactions (net)** | **1315.59** | **3374.29** | **5960.97** | **3831.49** | | **－** |
| **七、金银占款** | **Funds Outstanding for Gold and Silver** | | | | | | |
| **八、外汇买卖** | **Foreign Exchange Trading** | **－33.91** | **－7.34** | | | | **－** |
| **九、应收及预付款** | **Collectable Account and Advance Payment** | **420.79** | **391.61** | **488.74** | **430.88** | **404.93** | **500.91** |
| **十、投资性房地产** | **Investment Property** | **2.75** | **2.63** | **5.74** | **6.49** | **7.73** | **7.47** |
| **十一、固定资产** | **Fitness Assets** | **228.62** | **226.38** | **236.93** | **249.78** | **242.95** | **270.57** |

# 10－12 保险业务情况（2017－2019年）

## Statistics on Insurance Business（2017－2019）

单位：万元 （10000 yuan）

| 指 标 | Item | 保险费收入 Premium | | | 赔付金额 Indemnity Expenditure | | |
|---|---|---|---|---|---|---|---|
| | | 2017 | 2018 | 2019 | 2017 | 2018 | 2019 |
| **全市总计** | **Total** | **6337034** | **6636184** | **8462670** | **1696079** | **2028187** | **2430755** |
| 为上年% | As Compared with the Preceding Year（%） | 122.2 | 104.7 | 127.5 | 106.8 | 119.6 | 119.9 |
| 一、财产保险 | Property Insurance | 1939978 | 2171005 | 2479772 | 1059642 | 1274718 | 1526217 |
| 企业财产险 | Enterprise Property Insurance | 93949 | 102228 | 115355 | 37715 | 43599 | 68244 |
| 家庭财产险 | Family Property Insurance | 9003 | 16095 | 24345 | 4668 | 4445 | 6808 |
| 机动车辆险 | Transportation Equipment Insurance | 1330482 | 1421091 | 1427142 | 762543 | 886742 | 917104 |
| 工程险 | Project Insurance | 21736 | 45065 | 45007 | 8251 | 6234 | 12625 |
| 责任险 | Responsibilihty Insurance | 91555 | 134739 | 275356 | 43768 | 55074 | 136641 |
| 信用险 | Export Credit Insurance | 162086 | 147775 | 147038 | 89346 | 109388 | 98022 |
| 保证险 | Guarantee Insurance | 70729 | 121959 | 192314 | 12146 | 39312 | 73051 |
| 船舶险 | Shipping Insurance | 4474 | 5223 | 6814 | 4238 | 5434 | 3570 |
| 货运险 | Cargo Insurance | 72197 | 102036 | 96766 | 45655 | 76928 | 69951 |
| 特殊风险保险 | Special Pisks Insurance | 7184 | 10717 | 7718 | 2183 | 234 | 22085 |
| 农业保险 | Agriculture Insurance | 21903 | 25425 | 26714 | 13793 | 19569 | 25432 |
| 其他险 | Other | 54679 | 38650 | 115202 | 35337 | 27761 | 92682 |
| 二、人身险 | Personal Insurance | 4397056 | 4465179 | 5982897 | 636437 | 753469 | 904538 |
| 寿险 | Life Insurance | 3291187 | 3420019 | 4711382 | 471473 | 520054 | 588620 |
| 意外伤害险 | Accidental Insurance | 204765 | 235145 | 259426 | 44147 | 56872 | 66799 |
| 健康险 | Health Insurance | 901104 | 810016 | 1012089 | 120817 | 176543 | 249119 |

# 主要统计指标解释

**财政收入**　包括:(1)各项税收。主要有增值税、营业税、土地增值税、城市维护建设税、资源税、城市土地使用税、印花税、个人所得税、企业所得税、关税和耕地占用税等。

(2)专项收入包括征收排污费、征收城市水资源费收入,教育费附加收入等。

**存款**　企业、机关、团体或居民根据可以收回的原则,把货币资金存入银行或其他信用机构保管并取得一定利息的一种信用活动形式。根据存款对象的不同可划分为企业存款、财政存款、机关团体存款、基本建设存款、城镇储蓄存款、农村存款等科目。它是银行信贷资金的主要来源。

**贷款**　银行或其他信用机构根据必须归还的原则,按一定利率,为企业、个人等提供资金的一种信用活动形式。我国银行贷款分为流动资金贷款、固定资产贷款、城乡个体工商户贷款、城乡个体工商户贷款以及农业贷款等科目。

# Explanatory Notes on Main Statistical Indicators

**Financial Revenue** includes: (1) various tax revenues, mainly including value added tax, business tax, land value added tax, tax on city maintenance and construction, resources tax, tax on use of urban land, stamp tax, personal income tax, enterprise income tax, tariff and tax on occupancy of cultivated land, etc. (2) Special revenues, including revenue collected from imposing fee on sewage treatment and on urban water resources, and extra charges for education, etc.

**Deposit** is a form of credit activity that enterprises, institutions, organizations or residents deposit money into banks or other credit institutions for safekeeping and interest earning under the recoverable principle. According to different depositors, deposits are divided into enterprise deposits, treasury deposits, deposits of institutions and groups, capital construction deposits, urban savings deposits, rural deposits and other deposits. It is the major source of bank credit funds.

**Loan** is a form of credit activity that banks or other credit institutions provide funds at certain interest rate to enterprises and individuals in the light of the principle of unconditional repayment. Loans from Chinese banks include circulating capital loans, fixed assets loans, loans to urban and rural individuals engaged in industrial and commercial business and agricultural loans.

# 十二、城市建设环境保护

URBAN CONSTRUCTION AND ENVIRONMENTAL PROTECTION

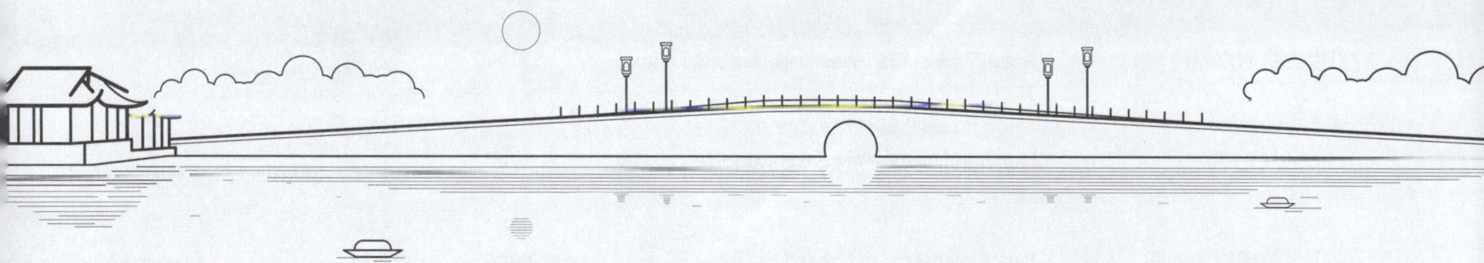

# 11 城市建设、环境保护
# Urban Construction and Environmental Protection

## 主要统计指标
## Major Statistical Indicators

| | | | | |
|---|---|---|---|---|
| 市区建成区面积 | Developed Area in Urban District | 648.46 | 平方千米 | ( sq.km ) |
| 市区实有道路面积 | Area of Roads in Urban District at Year-end | 9341 | 万平方米 | ( 10, 000 sq.m ) |
| 市区用电量 | Electricity Consumption of Urban District | 738.88 | 亿千瓦时 | ( 100 million kw/h ) |
| # 工业用电 | Industrial Electricity Consumption | 381.96 | 亿千瓦时 | ( 100 million kw/h ) |
| 生活用电 | Electricity Consumption for Residential Use | 125.83 | 亿千瓦时 | ( 100 million kw/h ) |
| 市区供水能力 | Water-supply Capacity of Urban District | 459 | 万吨/日 | ( 10, 000 tons/day ) |
| 市区供水总量 | Annual Volume of Tap Water Supplied in Urban District | 99156 | 万吨 | ( 10, 000 tons ) |
| 市区气化率 | Percentage of Population with Access to Gas in Urban District | 100 | % | ( % ) |
| 市区公园绿地面积 | Park Green Area in Urban District | 9246 | 公顷 | ( hectare ) |
| 市区空气质量达标(AQI＜100)天数 | The Number of Days of Air Quality Reaching(AQI＜100) the Standards | 287 | 天 | ( day ) |

# 11－01　市区公共交通情况（2012－2019年）

# Public Transportation in Urban Districts（2012－2019）

| 指　标 | Item | 2012 | 2013 | 2014 | 2015 | 2016 | 2017 | 2018 | 2019 |
|---|---|---|---|---|---|---|---|---|---|
| **一、轨道交通** | **Rail Transit** | | | | | | | | |
| 年末运营线路总长度（千米） | Length of Operating Routes (year－end) (km) | 47.97 | 47.97 | 66.30 | 81.50 | 81.50 | 117.60 | 117.60 | 135.40 |
| 客运总量　（万人次） | Passenger Traffic (10,000 person－times) | 561 | 9237 | 14521 | 22348 | 26877 | 33986 | 52985 | 63202 |
| **二、公共汽车** | **Bus** | | | | | | | | |
| 年末运营线路条数（条） | Number of Operating Routes (year－end) (unit) | 620 | 645 | 703 | 756 | 758 | 937 | 1152 | 1140 |
| 年末运营线路总长度（千米） | Length of Operating Routes (year－end) (km) | 11351 | 11445 | 12032 | 12791 | 13866 | 16819 | 21460 | 18547 |
| #BRT线路长度（千米） | BRT line length (km) | | 122 | 113 | 128 | 151 | 151 | 132 | 289 |
| 年末运营公共汽车（辆） | Number of Public Transportation Vehicles(year－end) (unit) | 7450 | 8249 | 8656 | 8555 | 8770 | 9672 | 11272 | 10708 |
| #无轨电车　（辆） | Number of Operating Trolleys (unit) | 51 | 101 | 115 | 150 | 150 | 150 | 150 | 85 |
| 客运总量　（万人次） | Passenger Traffic (10,000 person－times) | 131901 | 132221 | 140928 | 142312 | 141441 | 151263 | 158753 | 155496 |
| **三、出租汽车** | **Tax** | | | | | | | | |
| 年末实有出租汽车数（辆） | Number of Taxis(year－end) (unit) | 10344 | 10904 | 11913 | 11963 | 12209 | 13233 | 14125 | 14133 |

# 11－02 市区城市供电、供水情况（2012－2019 年）
# Electricity and Water Supply in Urban Districts（2012－2019）

| 指　标 | Item | 2012 | 2013 | 2014 | 2015 | 2016 | 2017 | 2018 | 2019 |
|---|---|---|---|---|---|---|---|---|---|
| **一、城市供电** | **Urban Electricity Supply** | | | | | | | | |
| 全年用电总量（亿千瓦时） | Total Electricity Consumption（100 million kwh） | 444.95 | 484.05 | 552.71 | 559.54 | 583.96 | 673.73 | 724.31 | 738.88 |
| #工业（亿千瓦时） | Industrial Electricity Consumption（100 million kwh） | 278.93 | 296.08 | 355.06 | 345.23 | 337.04 | 389.00 | 397.72 | 381.96 |
| 生活（亿千瓦时） | Electricity Consumption for Residential Use（100 million kwh） | 63.62 | 71.52 | 72.56 | 78.27 | 93.03 | 105.29 | 117.67 | 125.83 |
| **二、城市供水（自来水）** | **Urban Water Supply** | | | | | | | | |
| 总售水量（万吨） | Total Annual Volume of Tap Water Saled（10,000 tons） | 49549 | 51709 | 56401 | 56478 | 55566 | 71076 | 76667 | － |
| 平均日供水（万吨） | Per Capita Daily Consumption of Tap Water（10,000 tons） | 159 | 166 | 181 | 183 | 178 | 228 | 243 | 272 |
| 供水能力（万吨/日） | Capacity of Water Supply（10,000 tons/day） | 320 | 350 | 380 | 380 | 384 | 421 | 437 | 459 |
| 供水总量（万吨） | Total Annual Volume of Tap Water Supplied（10,000 tons） | 58183 | 60747 | 66172 | 66760 | 65087 | 83192 | 88568 | 99156 |
| #生产用水（万吨） | For Productive Use（10,000 tons） | 12478 | 13005 | 14792 | 14902 | 14161 | 16157 | 15866 | 21534 |
| 生活用水（万吨） | For Residential Use（10,000 tons） | 22861 | 23733 | 26894 | 26162 | 25078 | 33960 | 35778 | 40117 |
| 用水普及率（%） | Percentage of Population with Access to Tap Water（%） | 100 | 100 | 100 | 100 | 100 | 100 | 100 | 100 |

# 11－03　市区市政建设情况(2012－2019年)

# Public Utilities in Urban Districts(2012－2019)

| 指　标 | Item | 2012 | 2013 | 2014 | 2015 | 2016 | 2017 | 2018 | 2019 |
|---|---|---|---|---|---|---|---|---|---|
| **一、市政建设** | **Urban Infrastructure** | | | | | | | | |
| 建成区面积（平方公里） | Constructed Area (sq. m) | 452.62 | 462.48 | 495.22 | 506.09 | 541.38 | 591.08 | 615.22 | 648.46 |
| 年末实有道路面积（万平方米） | Area of Roads (year－end) (10,000 sq. m) | 5284 | 5426 | 6145 | 6540 | 6932 | 8291 | 8840 | 9341 |
| 年末实有道路长度（公里） | Length of Roads(year－end) (km) | 2458 | 2479 | 2748 | 2991 | 3075 | 3550 | 3783 | 3990 |
| 年末实有桥梁数(座) | Number of Bridges(year－end) (unit) | 1129 | 1165 | 1235 | 1337 | 1353 | 1443 | 1473 | 1545 |
| 排水管道长度(公里) | Length of Drainage Pipelines (km) | 4280 | 4455 | 5012 | 5370 | 5944 | 8614 | 8924 | 9125 |
| 城市污水排放量（万立方米） | Volume of Sewage Drained (10,000 cu. m) | 47330 | 48432 | 53111 | 56974 | 57916 | 69834 | 74438 | 80447 |
| 城市污水处理总量（万立方米） | the Total Volume of Urban Sewage Treatment (10,000 cu. m) | 45197 | 46251 | 50318 | 54137 | 55061 | 66516 | 71364 | 77245 |
| **二、城市液化气** | **Urban Liquefied Petroleum Gas** | | | | | | | | |
| 供气总量 (万吨) | Total Volume of Liquefied Petroleum Gas Supply (10,000 tons) | 11.17 | 11.92 | 9.87 | 12.38 | 13.14 | 12.86 | 13.28 | 12.24 |
| #家庭用气(万吨) | Supply for Residential Use (10,000 tons) | 5.90 | 4.70 | 5.08 | 6.08 | 5.90 | 6.48 | 5.81 | 5.15 |
| **三、人工煤气及天然气** | **Coal Gas and Natural Gas** | | | | | | | | |
| 家庭用气总量（万立方米） | Total Volume of Coal Gas Consumed (10,000 cu. m) | 13397 | 13869 | 18019 | 20659 | 21878 | 23614 | 26506 | 32907 |
| 家庭用气户数(万户) | Residential Households with Access to Gas (10,000 households) | 81.72 | 91.08 | 111.30 | 130.69 | 139.03 | 153.17 | 172.81 | 187.85 |
| **四、全社会气化率 %** | **Percentage of Population with Access to Gas** (%) | **100** | **100** | **100** | **100** | **100** | **100** | **100** | **100** |

# 11－04　市区园林绿化情况(2012－2019 年)

## Urban Forestation(2012－2019)

| 指　标 | Item | 2012 | 2013 | 2014 | 2015 | 2016 | 2017 | 2018 | 2019 |
|---|---|---|---|---|---|---|---|---|---|
| 建城区绿化覆盖面积(公顷) | The Green Areas Coveraged in Constructed Areas (hectare) | 18135 | 18606 | 20031 | 20464 | 22035 | 23620 | 24999 | 26312 |
| 建城区园林绿地面积(公顷) | Total Area of Parks, Gardens and Green Areas in Constructed Areas (hectare) | 16647 | 17071 | 18386 | 18949 | 20118 | 21726 | 22886 | 23986 |
| #公园绿地(公顷) | Public Green Area (hectare) | 5635 | 5820 | 6304 | 7640 | 8118 | 8770 | 8976 | 9246 |
| 建城区绿化覆盖率(%) | Rate of the Green Areas Coveraged in Constructed Areas (%) | 40.07 | 40.23 | 40.57 | 40.43 | 40.70 | 39.96 | 40.63 | 40.58 |
| 公园景点个数(个) | Number of Parks and Scenic Resorts (unit) | 185 | 190 | 207 | 217 | 222 | 245 | 251 | 260 |
| 公园景点面积(公顷) | Area of Parks and Scenic Resorts (hectare) | 2065 | 2094 | 2298 | 2488 | 2754 | 3074 | 3150 | 3208 |

# 11－05 环境保护情况(2019年)

## Statistics on Environmental Protection(2019)

| 指标名称 | | Item | | 全 市 Whole City | 市 区 Urban District |
|---|---|---|---|---|---|
| 工业废水排放量 | (万吨) | Industrial Wastewater Emissions | (10,000 tons) | 20346 | 19042 |
| 工业废水中COD排放量 | (吨) | COD Emissions in Industrial Wastewater | (tons) | 7634 | 7117 |
| 工业废水中氨氮排放量 | (吨) | Ammonia emissions in Industrial wastewater | (tons) | 243 | 214 |
| 工业二氧化硫产生量 | (吨) | Industrial Sulfur Dioxide Produced | (tons) | 96939 | 68707 |
| 工业二氧化硫排放量 | (吨) | Industrial Emissions of Sulfur Dioxide | (tons) | 8177 | 4913 |
| 工业氮氧化物排放量 | (吨) | Industrial Nitrogen Oxide Emissions | (tons) | 21088 | 12736 |
| 工业烟(粉)产生量 | (吨) | Industrial Smoke (Powder) Production | (tons) | 3256074 | 1528723 |
| 工业烟(粉)尘排放量 | (吨) | Industrial Smoke, Powder and Dust Emissions | (tons) | 12022 | 6057 |
| 一般工业固体废物综合利用率 | (%) | Comprehensive Utilization Rate of General Industrial Solid Waste | (%) | 97.52 | 97.34 |
| 城市污水集中处理率 | (%) | Centralized Treatment Rate of Urban Sewage | (%) | 95.96 | 96.02 |
| 城市生活垃圾无害化处理率 | (%) | Harmless Treatment Rate of City's Living Garbage | (%) | 100 | 100 |
| 空气质量优良天数 | (天) | Air Quality Days | (days) | – | 287 |
| 集中式饮用水源地水质达标率 | (%) | Compliance Rate of Centralized Sources of Drinking Water | (%) | 100 | 100 |

# 主要统计指标解释

**自来水生产能力** 指年底城建部门管理的自来水厂实际生产能力。

**生活用水量** 指居民日常生活与公共福利设施的用水量。包括居民、饮食店、旅馆、医院、理发店、浴池、洗衣店、游泳池、商店、学校、机关、部队等单位的用水量。

**供气总量** 指全年售给各类用户的全部煤气量。包括工业用量、家庭用量和其他用量。

**年末实有道路长度** 指除土路外,路面经过铺装宽度在3.5米以上的道路,包括高级、次高级道路和普通道路。

**城市桥梁** 指城市范围内,修建在河道上的桥梁和道路与道路立交、道路跨越铁路的立交桥,以及人行天桥。包括永久性桥和半永久性桥,不包括临时性桥、铁路桥、涵洞。

**营运线路长度** 指设置的固定营运线路的长度,包括郊区营运线路长度。不包括临时行驶的线路长度。

**用水普及率** 指城市用水的非农业人口数(不包括临时人口和流动人口)与城市非农业人口总数之比。计算公式为:

$$用水普及率 = \frac{城市用水非农业人口数}{城市非农业人口数} \times 100\%$$

**城市园林绿地面积** 指城市公共绿地、专用绿地、生产绿地、防护绿地、郊区风景名胜区的全部面积。

**公园绿地面积** 指供游览休息的各种公园、动物园、植物园、陵园以及花园、游园和供游览休息用的林荫道绿地、广场绿地。不包括一般栽植的行道树及林荫道的面积。

# Explanatory Notes on Main Statistical Indicators

**Production Capacity of Tap Water** refers to the actual production capacity of the waterworks administered by the urban construction department at the year end.

**Domestic water consumption** refers to the water consumption of residents daily life and public welfare facilities, including the consumption of residents, restaurants, hotels, hospitals, barber shops, public bathhouses, laundries, swimming pools, shops, schools, institutions, army and other units.

**Total Gas Supply** refers to the total volume of gas sold to users in a year, including the gas for industrial use, family use and others.

**Length of Roads at the Year End** refers to the length of roads with pavement width more than 3.5 meters except unsurfaced roads, including high quality, medium quality and ordinary roads.

**Urban Bridges** refer to bridges over river courses, overpasses crossing roads or railways and passenger footbridge sin urban areas. Permanent and semi – permanent bridges are included. Temporary bridges, railway bridges and culverts are excluded.

**Length of Operation Line** refers to the length of the roads in fixed operation, including the suburb one, but excluding the temporary one.

**Urban Water Popularity rate** refers to the ratio of the urban non – agricultural population (excluding temporary and floating population) using tap water to the total urban non – agricultural population. The formula is as follows:

$$\text{Urban Water Popularity rate} = \frac{\text{Urban Non – agricultural Population Using Tap Water}}{\text{Urban Non – agricultural Population}} \times 100\%$$

**Area of Urban Gardens and Green Lands** refers to the total area of urban public green land, special green land, production green land, protection green land and suburban scenic spots.

**Park Green Area** refers to the area of various parks, zoos, botanical gardens, cemeteries, gardens, and boulevard and square green land for sightseeing and rest. Areas of street trees and boulevards are excluded.

# 十二、科技、教育 文化、卫生、体育

SCIENCE AND TECHNOLOGY,EDUCATION,
CULTUREPUBLIC HEALTHAND SPORTS

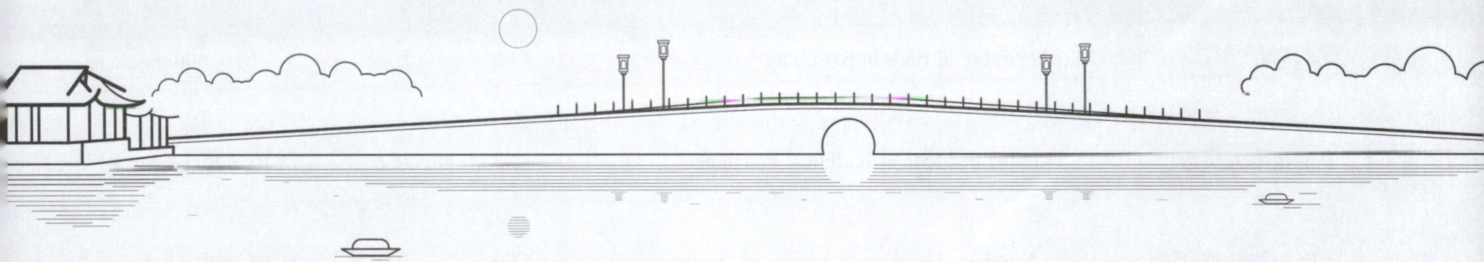

12

# 科技、教育、文化、卫生、体育
# Science and Technology, Education, Culture, Public Health and Sports

## 主要统计指标
## Major Statistical Indicators

| | | | | |
|---|---|---|---|---|
| 高等学校数 | Number of Regular Institution of Higher Education | 40 | 个 | (unit) |
| 高等学校在校学生数 | Number of Students in Regular Institution of Higher Education | 51.83 | 万人 | (10, 000 person) |
| 高中在校学生数 | Number of Students in Senior High Schools | 11.80 | 万人 | (10, 000 person) |
| 初中在校学生数 | Number of Students in Junior High Schools | 24.41 | 万人 | (10, 000 person) |
| 小学在校学生数 | Number of Students in Primary Schools | 61.69 | 万人 | (10, 000 person) |
| 医疗病床数 | Number of Beds in Health Institutions | 8.57 | 万张 | (10, 000 bed) |
| # 医院 | Number of Beds in Hospitals | 8.00 | 万张 | (10, 000 bed) |
| 卫生技术人员数 | Number of Medical Technical Personnel | 12.7 | 万人 | (10, 000 person) |
| # 执业(助理)医师 | Number of Licensed (Assistant) Doctors | 4.90 | 万人 | (10, 000 person) |
| 公共图书馆 | Public Library | 16 | 个 | (unit) |

# 12－01 科技活动情况(2014－2019年)
## Statistics on Scientific and Technological Activities(2014－2019)

| 指标 Item | 2014 | 2015 | 2016 | 2017 | 2018 | 2019 |
|---|---|---|---|---|---|---|
| **一、全社会科技活动**<br>**The Scientific and Technological Activities in Whole Society** | | | | | | |
| 研究与试验发展活动折合全时人员 (人年)<br>Full－time Equivalent of R&D Personnel | 90193 | 94323 | 94696 | 103245 | 109507 | 126275 |
| 研究与试验发展经费支出 (亿元)<br>R&D Expenditure (0.1 billion Yuan) | 274.00 | 302.19 | 346.36 | 396.82 | 464.25 | 530.42 |
| 研究与试验发展经费支出与GDP之比 (%)<br>The Proportion of R&D Expenditure in GDP (%) | 2.98 | 3.01 | 3.06 | 3.15 | 3.25 | 3.45 |
| **二、规模以上工业科技活动**<br>**The Scientific and Technological Activities of Industrial Enterprises Above Designated Size** | | | | | | |
| 有研究与试验发展活动企业数 (个)<br>The Number of Enterprises with R&D Activities (Unit) | 1518 | 1671 | 1753 | 1819 | 1784 | 2075 |
| 研究与试验发展项目数 (个)<br>The Number of R&D Projects (Unit) | 7383 | 8265 | 8943 | 10000 | 10102 | 12430 |
| 企业有科技机构 (个)<br>Scientific and Technological Institutions of Enterprises (Unit) | 1346 | 1354 | 1410 | 1611 | 1567 | 1904 |
| 科技机构仪器和设备原价 (亿元)<br>Original Value of Equipment in Scientific and Technological Institutions (0.1 billion Yuan) | 99.61 | 100.73 | 126.23 | 142.78 | 156 | 172.41 |
| 研究与试验发展人员 (万人)<br>R&D Personnel (10,000) | 7.41 | 8.01 | 7.92 | 8.39 | 9.29 | 9.68 |
| 每万名从业人员中研究与试验发展活动人员数 (人)<br>The Number of R&D Personnel per 10,000 Employees (Person) | 644 | 724 | 743 | 794 | 906 | 961 |
| 研究与试验发展经费支出 (亿元)<br>R&D Expenditure (0.1 billion Yuan) | 177.39 | 198.06 | 215.03 | 241.93 | 268.28 | 296.90 |
| 研究与试验发展经费支出占营业收入的比例 (%)<br>The Proportion of R&D Expenditure in Business Income (%) | 1.33 | 1.55 | 1.70 | 1.78 | 1.77 | 1.86 |

# 12-02 全社会R&D经费投入情况(2012-2019年)
## R&D Investment of the Whole Society(2012-2019)

单位:亿元 (100 million yuan)

| 年份<br>Year | 总计<br>Total | 按执行部门分 By Sector | | | |
|---|---|---|---|---|---|
| | | 研究机构<br>Research and Development Institutions | 高等院校<br>Colleges and Universties | 规模以上工业企业<br>Industrial Enterprises above Designated Size | 其他<br>Others |
| 2012 | 228.00 | 14.96 | 38.12 | 143.47 | 31.44 |
| 2013 | 248.73 | 15.91 | 39.78 | 160.21 | 32.83 |
| 2014 | 274.00 | 17.34 | 42.06 | 177.39 | 37.21 |
| 2015 | 302.19 | 20.88 | 46.04 | 198.06 | 37.21 |
| 2016 | 346.36 | 16.55 | 40.79 | 215.03 | 73.99 |
| 2017 | 396.82 | 18.04 | 44.56 | 241.93 | 92.29 |
| 2018 | 464.25 | 26.35 | 49.93 | 268.28 | 119.69 |
| 2019 | 530.42 | 29.17 | 62.60 | 296.90 | 141.75 |

## 12-03 规模以上工业企业 R&D 经费投入情况(2012-2019年)

## Basic Statistics on R&D Investment of Industrial Enterprises above Designated Size(2012-2019)

单位:亿元 (100 million yuan)

| 年份<br>Year | 总计<br>Total | 按经费来源分 By Source | | | |
|---|---|---|---|---|---|
| | | 政府资金<br>Government Funds | 企业资金<br>Self-raised Funds by Enterprise | 境外资金<br>Overseas Funds | 其他资金<br>Other |
| 2012 | 143.47 | 4.63 | 137.73 | 0.41 | 0.70 |
| 2013 | 160.21 | 4.35 | 154.42 | 0.26 | 1.19 |
| 2014 | 177.39 | 5.24 | 171.18 | 0.10 | 0.89 |
| 2015 | 198.06 | 5.35 | 191.03 | 0.24 | 1.43 |
| 2016 | 215.03 | 3.88 | 209.98 | 0.08 | 1.09 |
| 2017 | 241.93 | 7.73 | 233.04 | 0.22 | 0.94 |
| 2018 | 268.28 | 6.31 | 261.25 | 0.41 | 0.21 |
| 2019 | 296.90 | 5.65 | 291.25 | 0 | - |

# 12-04 规模以上工业企业R&D经费投入情况(2019年)

## Basic Statistics on R&D Investment of Industrial Enterprises above Designated Size(2019)

| 项目 | Item | 有R&D活动的企业数（个） | 企业办研发机构（个） | 企业办机构仪器和设备原价（亿元） | R&D人员（万人） | R&D经费支出（亿元） |
|---|---|---|---|---|---|---|
| **总　计** | **Total** | **2075** | **1904** | **172.41** | **9.68** | **296.90** |
| **按企业规模分** | **Grouped by Size of Enterprises** | | | | | |
| 大型企业 | Large | 101 | 133 | 60.14 | 3.70 | 144.88 |
| 中型企业 | Medium - sized | 367 | 384 | 54.63 | 2.49 | 72.36 |
| 小微企业 | Small | 1607 | 1387 | 57.64 | 3.49 | 79.66 |
| **按登记注册类型分** | **Grouped by Status of Registration** | | | | | |
| 国有企业 | State - owned Enterprises | | | | | |
| 集体企业 | Collective - owned Enterprises | | | | | |
| 股份合作企业 | Cooperative Enterprises | 2 | 3 | 0.04 | 0.01 | 0.07 |
| 联营企业 | Joint Ownership Enterprises | | | | | |
| 有限责任公司 | Limited Liability Corporations | 250 | 236 | 29.00 | 1.29 | 39.40 |
| 股份有限公司 | Share - holding Corporations Ltd. | 174 | 243 | 36.69 | 2.63 | 99.46 |
| 私营企业 | Private Enterprises | 1378 | 1191 | 63.33 | 3.99 | 97.44 |
| 外商及港澳台投资企业 | Enterprises with Investment from Foreign、Hong Kong、Macao and Taiwan | 271 | 231 | 43.35 | 1.76 | 60.53 |
| 其他企业 | Other Enterprises | | | | | |

# 12－05 分地区、行业非私营及规上私营单位年末人才资源(2019年)

## Trained Personnel Resource of Non－Private and Private Units above Designated Size by Region(2019)

单位:人 (person)

| 项目 | Item | 合计 Total | 非私营单位 Non－Private | #专业技术人员 Technical Personnel | 非私营单位 Non－Private | #技术工人 Technical Workers | 非私营单位 Non－Private |
|---|---|---|---|---|---|---|---|
| **全市** | **Whole City** | **3113381** | **1936109** | **1023413** | **760472** | **1481028** | **781619** |
| 市区 | Urban District | 2920611 | 1838505 | 973117 | 726243 | 1377191 | 743513 |
| #上城区 | Shangcheng | 153331 | 106023 | 66715 | 56462 | 49390 | 20441 |
| 下城区 | Xiacheng | 204813 | 167074 | 84492 | 73091 | 69953 | 55486 |
| 江干区 | Jianggan | 317291 | 159731 | 92361 | 62849 | 164952 | 58576 |
| 拱墅区 | Gongshu | 189747 | 99465 | 58844 | 35961 | 93991 | 42680 |
| 西湖区 | Xihu | 387344 | 286154 | 140621 | 107797 | 181481 | 132422 |
| 高新(滨江)区 | Hi－Tech(Binjiang) | 274539 | 211136 | 156076 | 128890 | 61460 | 42486 |
| 萧山区 | Xiaoshan | 462346 | 269270 | 115007 | 78698 | 270711 | 146071 |
| 余杭区 | Yuhang | 408543 | 207758 | 113737 | 74733 | 210855 | 89335 |
| 富阳区 | Fuyang | 163233 | 100501 | 49573 | 34586 | 83482 | 47950 |
| 临安区 | Lin'an | 108652 | 58029 | 31111 | 21385 | 51519 | 20451 |
| 钱塘新区 | Qiantang New Area | 238424 | 162358 | 60162 | 47698 | 134727 | 83632 |
| 西湖风景名胜区 | The West Lake Scenic Zone | 12348 | 11006 | 4418 | 4093 | 4670 | 3983 |
| 桐庐县 | Tonglu | 93371 | 37490 | 19894 | 11804 | 56385 | 15688 |
| 淳安县 | Chun'an | 41231 | 29250 | 12658 | 10225 | 19046 | 11400 |
| 建德市 | Jiande | 58168 | 30864 | 17744 | 12200 | 28406 | 11018 |

注:因经普,指标有调整。

单位:人 12-05 续表 continued (person)

| 项目 | Item | 合计 Total | 非私营单位 Non-Private | #专业技术人员 Technical Personnel | 非私营单位 Non-Private | #技术工人 Technical Workers | 非私营单位 Non-Private |
|---|---|---|---|---|---|---|---|
| **按国民经济行业分组** | **Total** | | | | | | |
| 农、林、牧、渔业 | Farming, Forestry, Animal Husbandry and Fishery | 866 | 866 | 177 | 177 | 395 | 395 |
| 采矿业 | Mining | 1372 | 781 | 230 | 167 | 681 | 352 |
| 制造业 | Manufacturing | 838284 | 488777 | 167595 | 119511 | 545466 | 298350 |
| 电力、热力、燃气及水生产和供应业 | Production & Supply of Electricity, Heat, Gas & Water | 14367 | 13068 | 3268 | 3026 | 8021 | 7212 |
| 建筑业 | Construction | 893009 | 381727 | 195083 | 94800 | 621852 | 258500 |
| 批发和零售业 | Wholesale & Retail Trades | 161893 | 85738 | 35617 | 20897 | 48078 | 28971 |
| 交通运输、仓储和邮政业 | Transportation, Storage and Posts | 76323 | 56790 | 15521 | 10966 | 40968 | 31858 |
| 住宿和餐饮业 | Hotels and Catering Services | 44950 | 29423 | 5025 | 2658 | 25445 | 18823 |
| 信息传输、软件和信息技术服务业 | Information Transmission, Software and Information Technology | 206545 | 141992 | 128988 | 91468 | 40019 | 28568 |
| 金融业 | Financial Intermediation | 71920 | 71836 | 46209 | 46192 | 4365 | 4346 |
| 房地产业 | Real Estate | 83207 | 60173 | 16963 | 12253 | 31873 | 24984 |
| 租赁和商务服务业 | Leasing and Business Services | 115741 | 65709 | 31208 | 16688 | 47112 | 26313 |
| 科学研究、技术服务业 | Scientific Research, Technical Services | 121253 | 87885 | 86705 | 65221 | 10871 | 6560 |
| 水利、环境和公共设施管理业 | Management of Water Conservancy, Environment and Public Facilities | 28635 | 22953 | 6176 | 4640 | 15481 | 13042 |
| 居民服务、修理和其他服务业 | Service to Honseholds, Repair and Other Services | 22128 | 13866 | 2839 | 1315 | 14629 | 9795 |
| 教育 | Education | 185228 | 180637 | 146373 | 143477 | 11718 | 11214 |
| 卫生和社会工作 | Health Care and Social Work | 128962 | 117593 | 107803 | 100282 | 8388 | 7027 |
| 文化、体育和娱乐业 | Culture, Sports and Entertainment | 21816 | 19413 | 13325 | 12426 | 2375 | 2018 |
| 公共管理、社会保障和社会组织 | Public Management, Social Security and Social Organizations | 96882 | 96882 | 14308 | 14308 | 3291 | 3291 |

Note: The indicators were adjusted becouse of Economic census.

# 12-06 专利申请与授权情况(2007-2019年)

# Patent Application and Authorization(2007-2019)

单位:件 (item)

| 年份 Year | 专利申请合计 Patent Applications | 发明 Inventions | 实用新型 Utility Models | 外观设计 Designs | 专利授权合计 Patent Applications Granted | 发明 Inventions | 实用新型 Utility Models | 外观设计 Designs |
|---|---|---|---|---|---|---|---|---|
| 2007 | 13295 | 4592 | 4332 | 4371 | 7563 | 1320 | 3638 | 2605 |
| 2008 | 18549 | 5130 | 5796 | 7623 | 9831 | 1923 | 4637 | 3271 |
| 2009 | 26077 | 6703 | 9806 | 9568 | 15507 | 2535 | 5806 | 7166 |
| 2010 | 29732 | 7766 | 13108 | 8858 | 26483 | 3238 | 11888 | 11357 |
| 2011 | 40890 | 9717 | 18783 | 12390 | 29249 | 4511 | 14556 | 10182 |
| 2012 | 53785 | 11960 | 25313 | 16512 | 40651 | 5526 | 20400 | 14725 |
| 2013 | 58280 | 14031 | 25523 | 18726 | 41518 | 4903 | 23159 | 13456 |
| 2014 | 48569 | 14779 | 21711 | 12079 | 33548 | 5552 | 18147 | 9849 |
| 2015 | 60839 | 17777 | 29048 | 14014 | 46245 | 8296 | 24764 | 13185 |
| 2016 | 73546 | 24951 | 32187 | 16408 | 41052 | 8647 | 21763 | 10642 |
| 2017 | 75709 | 25578 | 35096 | 15035 | 42227 | 9872 | 21282 | 11073 |
| 2018 | 98396 | 36539 | 44963 | 16894 | 55379 | 10267 | 30891 | 14221 |
| 2019 | 113562 | 43357 | 53957 | 16248 | 61568 | 11748 | 36326 | 13494 |

# 12－07 分地区专利申请与授权情况(2019年)

## Patent Application and Authorization by Region(2019)

单位:件 (item)

| 地 区 | Region | 专利申请合计 Patent Applications | 发明 Inventions | 实用新型 Utility Models | 外观设计 Designs | 专利授权合计 Patent Applications Granted | 发明 Inventions | 实用新型 Utility Models | 外观设计 Designs |
|---|---|---|---|---|---|---|---|---|---|
| **全市** | **Whole City** | **113562** | **43357** | **53957** | **16248** | **61568** | **11748** | **36326** | **13494** |
| 市区 | Urban District | 108395 | 42534 | 51487 | 14374 | 58560 | 11618 | 34974 | 11968 |
| #上城区 | Shangcheng | 3055 | 1081 | 1432 | 542 | 1631 | 177 | 947 | 507 |
| 下城区 | Xiacheng | 6672 | 3805 | 2429 | 438 | 3470 | 1115 | 1753 | 602 |
| 江干区 | Jianggan | 4637 | 1371 | 2145 | 1121 | 2165 | 264 | 1135 | 766 |
| 拱墅区 | Gongshu | 3590 | 1055 | 1968 | 567 | 1975 | 182 | 1190 | 603 |
| 西湖区 | Xihu | 16108 | 9318 | 5193 | 1597 | 7732 | 3178 | 3361 | 1193 |
| 高新(滨江)区 | Hi－Tech(Binjiang) | 18330 | 9309 | 6022 | 2999 | 10341 | 2939 | 4612 | 2790 |
| 萧山区 | Xiaoshan | 12853 | 2775 | 8823 | 1255 | 7459 | 545 | 6028 | 886 |
| 余杭区 | Yuhang | 21315 | 5671 | 12212 | 3432 | 12509 | 982 | 8904 | 2623 |
| 富阳区 | Fuyang | 4934 | 1467 | 2987 | 480 | 2744 | 395 | 1997 | 352 |
| 临安区 | Lin'an | 5122 | 922 | 3536 | 664 | 2955 | 219 | 2239 | 497 |
| 钱塘新区 | Qiantang New Area | 13272 | 6096 | 5806 | 1370 | 6569 | 1694 | 3656 | 1219 |
| 西湖风景名胜区 | The West Lake Scenic Zone | | | | | | | | |
| 桐庐县 | Tonglu | 2589 | 371 | 1337 | 881 | 1855 | 61 | 724 | 1070 |
| 淳安县 | Chun'an | 915 | 216 | 501 | 198 | 531 | 24 | 338 | 169 |
| 建德市 | Jiande | 1663 | 236 | 632 | 795 | 622 | 45 | 290 | 287 |

注:西湖区含风景名胜区;萧山区不含托管在钱塘新区的街道数据。

a) Figures of Xihu include the West Lake Scenic Zone; Figures of Xiaoshan District don't include districts which under administered by Qiantang New Area.

# 12－08　文化事业单位数（2000－2019年）

## Number of Culture Institutions（2000－2019）

单位：个　　　　(unit)

| 年份 Year | 电影院 Cinemas | 剧场 Theaters | 剧团 Opera Troupes | 文化馆 Cultural Centers | 文化站 Cultural Stations | 图书馆 Libraries | 博物馆 Museums | 展览馆 Exhibition Buildings |
|---|---|---|---|---|---|---|---|---|
| 2000 | 16 | 9 | 18 | 13 | 268 | 10 | 9 | 1 |
| 2001 | 16 | 15 | 18 | 13 | 226 | 10 | 11 | 1 |
| 2002 | 18 | 13 | 18 | 13 | 221 | 10 | 11 | 1 |
| 2003 | 20 | 11 | 18 | 13 | 220 | 10 | 11 | 1 |
| 2004 | 18 | 16 | 18 | 13 | 165 | 10 | 12 | 1 |
| 2005 | 22 | 12 | 19 | 13 | 204 | 12 | 12 | 1 |
| 2006 | 22 | 12 | 19 | 13 | 197 | 13 | 12 | 1 |
| 2007 | 22 | 12 | 19 | 13 | 195 | 14 | 12 | 1 |
| 2008 | 23 | 12 | 19 | 13 | 195 | 14 | 13 | 1 |
| 2009 | 22 | 12 | 20 | 13 | 198 | 16 | 35 | 1 |
| 2010 | 31 | 12 | 21 | 13 | 199 | 16 | 65 | 1 |
| 2011 | 30 | 11 | 21 | 15 | 190 | 15 | 65 | 1 |
| 2012 | 40 | 11 | 21 | 15 | 192 | 15 | 65 | 1 |
| 2013 | 48 | 11 | 21 | 15 | 189 | 15 | 65 | 1 |
| 2014 | 66 | 12 | 21 | 15 | 189 | 15 | 65 | 1 |
| 2015 | 90 | 11 | 20 | 15 | 189 | 15 | 67 | 1 |
| 2016 | 90 | 11 | 20 | 15 | 189 | 15 | 68 | 1 |
| 2017 | 158 | 11 | 20 | 15 | 189 | 15 | 68 | 1 |
| 2018 | 158 | 11 | 20 | 15 | 189 | 16 | 76 | 1 |
| 2019 | 193 | 9 | 20 | 15 | 189 | 16 | 79 | 1 |

# 12－09　分地区文化部门机构数(2019年末)

# Number of Culture Institutions by Region(End of 2019)

单位:个　　　　(unit)

| 指　标 | Item | 剧场 Theaters | 剧团 Opera Troupes | 文化馆 Cultural Centers | 文化站 Cultural Stations | 图书馆 Libraries | 博物馆 Museums | 展览馆 Exhibition Buildings |
|---|---|---|---|---|---|---|---|---|
| **全市** | **Total** | **9** | **20** | **15** | **189** | **16** | **79** | **1** |
| 市区 | Urban District | 9 | 18 | 12 | 136 | 13 | 74 | 1 |
| #萧山区 | Xiaoshan | – | 1 | 1 | 22 | 1 | 9 | – |
| 余杭区 | Yuhang | 1 | 1 | 1 | 19 | 1 | 5 | – |
| 富阳区 | Fuyang | – | 1 | 1 | 24 | 1 | 2 | – |
| 临安区 | Lin'an | – | – | 1 | 18 | 1 | 2 | – |
| 桐庐县 | Tonglu | – | 1 | 1 | 14 | 1 | 2 | – |
| 淳安县 | Chun'an | – | – | 1 | 23 | 1 | 2 | – |
| 建德市 | Jiande | – | 1 | 1 | 16 | 1 | – | – |

# 12－10 市区文化事业单位数(1978－2019年)

# Culture Institutions of Urban District (1978－2019)

单位:个 (unit)

| 年 份<br>Year | 电影院<br>Cinemas | 剧 团<br>Opera Troupes | 剧 场<br>Theaters | 文化馆<br>Cultural Centers | 文化站<br>Cultural Stations | 图书馆<br>Libraries | 博物馆<br>Museums |
|---|---|---|---|---|---|---|---|
| 1978 | 7 | 13 | 6 | 5 | – | 2 | 1 |
| 1979 | 8 | 14 | 7 | 5 | 27 | 2 | 1 |
| 1980 | 8 | 15 | 7 | 5 | 37 | 2 | 1 |
| 1981 | 8 | 17 | 7 | 6 | 40 | 2 | 1 |
| 1982 | 9 | 17 | 7 | 6 | 45 | 3 | 1 |
| 1983 | 9 | 15 | 3 | 6 | 46 | 3 | 1 |
| 1984 | 9 | 15 | 4 | 6 | 49 | 3 | 1 |
| 1985 | 8 | 16 | 9 | 6 | 47 | 3 | 2 |
| 1986 | 8 | 15 | 8 | 6 | 48 | 3 | 2 |
| 1987 | 8 | 15 | 9 | 6 | 38 | 3 | 2 |
| 1988 | 7 | 14 | 9 | 6 | 50 | 3 | 2 |
| 1989 | 7 | 14 | 9 | 6 | 48 | 2 | 2 |
| 1990 | 9 | 14 | 9 | 5 | 48 | 3 | 2 |
| 1991 | 10 | 14 | 8 | 5 | 48 | 3 | 2 |
| 1992 | 11 | 14 | 8 | 5 | 48 | 3 | 6 |
| 1993 | 10 | 14 | 9 | 5 | 42 | 3 | 6 |
| 1994 | 11 | 13 | 9 | 5 | 48 | 3 | 6 |
| 1995 | 11 | 13 | 9 | 5 | 67 | 3 | 6 |
| 1996 | 10 | 13 | 8 | 5 | 55 | 3 | 6 |
| 1997 | 10 | 13 | 8 | 5 | 52 | 3 | 6 |
| 1998 | 9 | 13 | 8 | 6 | 55 | 3 | 7 |
| 1999 | 9 | 13 | 6 | 6 | 52 | 3 | 8 |
| 2000 | 8 | 12 | 6 | 6 | 52 | 3 | 9 |
| 2001 | 49 | 14 | 11 | 8 | 89 | 5 | 11 |
| 2002 | – | 14 | 10 | 8 | 90 | 4 | 11 |
| 2003 | 19 | 14 | 11 | 13 | 92 | 4 | 11 |
| 2004 | 18 | 14 | 14 | 8 | 93 | 5 | 12 |
| 2005 | 16 | 15 | 10 | 8 | 94 | 7 | 12 |
| 2006 | 16 | 15 | 10 | 8 | 94 | 8 | 12 |
| 2007 | 16 | 15 | 10 | 8 | 92 | 9 | 12 |
| 2008 | 18 | 15 | 11 | 8 | 92 | 9 | 13 |
| 2009 | 15 | 16 | 11 | 8 | 95 | 11 | 34 |
| 2010 | 25 | 17 | 11 | 8 | 96 | 11 | 54 |
| 2011 | 23 | 17 | 10 | 10 | 94 | 10 | 54 |
| 2012 | 31 | 17 | 10 | 10 | 96 | 10 | 54 |
| 2013 | 31 | 17 | 11 | 10 | 94 | 10 | 54 |
| 2014 | 55 | 18 | 11 | 11 | 118 | 11 | 57 |
| 2015 | 78 | 18 | 11 | 11 | 118 | 11 | 59 |
| 2016 | 78 | 18 | 11 | 11 | 118 | 11 | 60 |
| 2017 | 146 | 18 | 11 | 12 | 136 | 12 | 61 |
| 2018 | 146 | 18 | 11 | 12 | 136 | 13 | 72 |
| 2019 | 178 | 18 | 9 | 12 | 136 | 13 | 74 |

# 12－11 分地区艺术表演团体演出情况(2019 年)

## Basic Statistics on Performance of Art Troupes by Region(2019)

| 指标 | Item | 艺术表演场所演出场次(场) Number of Performances in Artistic Performance Place (scene) | 艺术表演场所演出收入(万元) Income of Performances in Artistic Performance Place (10000 yuan) | 剧团演出场次(场) Number of Performances of Opera Troupes (scene) | 农村(场) Rural Areas (scene) | 剧团演出观众人数(万人次) Number of Spectators of Opera Troupes (10000 person－times) | 剧团演出收入(万元) Income of Performances of Opera Troupes (10000 yuan) |
|---|---|---|---|---|---|---|---|
| **全市** | **Total** | **1385** | **5284.2** | **5617** | **2539** | **501.1** | **13683.9** |
| 为上年(%) | As Compared with the Preceding Year (%) | 122.1 | 113.6 | 98.0 | 100.8 | 86.5 | 99.7 |
| 市区 | Urban District | 1385 | 5284.2 | 5077 | 2189 | 371.1 | 13288.6 |
| #萧山区 | Xiaoshan | – | – | 110 | 100 | 9.21 | – |
| 余杭区 | Yuhang | 50 | 83.8 | 220 | 200 | 47 | – |
| 富阳区 | Fuyang | – | – | 140 | 130 | 28.2 | 222 |
| 临安区 | Lin'an | – | – | – | – | – | – |
| 桐庐县 | Tonglu | – | – | 260 | 180 | 50 | 275.3 |
| 淳安县 | Chun'an | – | – | – | – | – | – |
| 建德市 | Jiande | – | – | 280 | 170 | 80 | 120 |

# 12－12　图书出版数量(2018－2019年)
# Number of Books Published(2018－2019)

| 项　目　Item | 本版图书种数(种) Number of Publications (kind) | | 租型图书种数(种) Number of Publications for Lease (kind) | | 总印数(万册、万份) Total Printed Copies (1000 copies) | | 总印张(千印张) Total Printed Sheets (1000 sheets) | |
|---|---|---|---|---|---|---|---|---|
| | 2018 | 2019 | 2018 | 2019 | 2018 | 2019 | 2018 | 2019 |
| **图书总计 Total** | **14422** | **15352** | **420** | **386** | **41114.80** | **44287.50** | **3002967.11** | **3317561.33** |
| 使用《中国标准书号》部分合计 Publication wirh "China Standard Book Number" | 14394 | 15237 | 420 | 386 | 41088.78 | 44235.00 | 3000801.82 | 3312682.45 |
| #哲学 Philosophy | 155 | 198 | － | － | 149.03 | 197.38 | 19679.21 | 25673.33 |
| 社会科学总论 General Social Science | 230 | 212 | － | － | 164.93 | 155.73 | 22387.65 | 21313.83 |
| 文化、科学、教育、体育 Culture, Science, Education and Sports | 6861 | 7909 | 411 | － | 30464.97 | 35506.53 | 2005329.64 | 2472666.18 |
| 文学 Literature | 2158 | 2067 | － | － | 5293.58 | 4208.31 | 487859.16 | 384326.52 |
| 艺术 Arts | 1989 | 2054 | － | － | 903.86 | 885.88 | 83574.18 | 104747.78 |
| 自然科学总论 General Natural Science | 16 | 21 | － | － | 17.50 | 18.29 | 3790.29 | 3395.10 |
| 不使用《中国标准书号》部分合计 Publications without "China Standard Book Number" | 28 | 115 | － | － | 26.02 | 52.50 | 2165.29 | 4878.88 |

# 12－13　幼儿园基本情况(1978－2019年)

## Basic Statistics on Kindergartens(1978－2019)

单位:人　　　　(person)

| 年　份<br>Year | 园　数(个)<br>Kindergartens(unit) | 在园幼儿数<br>Number of Children | 教职员工数<br>Teachers and Staff | 教　师<br>Number of Full－time Teachers |
|---|---|---|---|---|
| 1978 | 266 | 37597 | 2570 | 1439 |
| 1979 | 216 | 59245 | 3731 | 2201 |
| 1980 | 518 | 82182 | 4763 | 3398 |
| 1981 | 676 | 82808 | 5275 | 3691 |
| 1982 | 853 | 95733 | 6357 | 4269 |
| 1983 | 1034 | 95676 | 6271 | 4135 |
| 1984 | 1749 | 112095 | 7238 | 4900 |
| 1985 | 1743 | 115766 | 7360 | 5278 |
| 1986 | 1607 | 118792 | 7898 | 5659 |
| 1987 | 1678 | 133773 | 8622 | 6335 |
| 1988 | 1541 | 139883 | 9221 | 6608 |
| 1989 | 1397 | 132947 | 9595 | 6849 |
| 1990 | 1526 | 136277 | 9808 | 7167 |
| 1991 | 1422 | 150982 | 10472 | 7388 |
| 1992 | 1431 | 133773 | 9240 | 6487 |
| 1993 | 1328 | 171005 | 10779 | 7886 |
| 1994 | 1470 | 165860 | 10718 | 7891 |
| 1995 | 1493 | 149497 | 10102 | 7943 |
| 1996 | 1437 | 150587 | 10203 | 7625 |
| 1997 | 1504 | 146530 | 10480 | 7743 |
| 1998 | 1695 | 153035 | 10691 | 7956 |
| 1999 | 1787 | 156372 | 10719 | 8107 |
| 2000 | 2037 | 168414 | 11740 | 8770 |
| 2001 | 1249 | 174204 | 11447 | 7880 |
| 2002 | 1268 | 175891 | 11988 | 8086 |
| 2003 | 1285 | 176862 | 13702 | 9076 |
| 2004 | 1098 | 186472 | 14991 | 9544 |
| 2005 | 1188 | 188991 | 16161 | 10288 |
| 2006 | 1188 | 195552 | 17550 | 11053 |
| 2007 | 1071 | 212754 | 19330 | 12168 |
| 2008 | 1037 | 235867 | 21193 | 12917 |
| 2009 | 972 | 246336 | 22970 | 14211 |
| 2010 | 969 | 267352 | 25525 | 15203 |
| 2011 | 970 | 271128 | 27458 | 16023 |
| 2012 | 914 | 283421 | 29843 | 17811 |
| 2013 | 860 | 285406 | 32037 | 18945 |
| 2014 | 881 | 295036 | 35212 | 20088 |
| 2015 | 910 | 313385 | 38238 | 21404 |
| 2016 | 930 | 325495 | 40833 | 22955 |
| 2017 | 960 | 336343 | 43692 | 24628 |
| 2018 | 991 | 343646 | 47635 | 26326 |
| 2019 | 1020 | 350261 | 50352 | 27685 |

# 12－14　小学基本情况(1978－2019年)

## Basic Statistics on Primary Schools(1978－2019)

单位:人　　(person)

| 年　份<br>Year | 学校数(个)<br>Number of Schools<br>(unit) | 在校学生数<br>Enrollment | 毕业生数<br>Graduates | 教职员工数<br>Number of<br>Teachers and Staff | 专职教师数<br>Number of Full－time<br>Teachers |
|---|---|---|---|---|---|
| 1978 | 4959 | 605137 | – | 24103 | 22291 |
| 1979 | 4850 | 577811 | – | 25089 | 23220 |
| 1980 | 4781 | 560244 | – | 25388 | 22902 |
| 1981 | 4668 | 525503 | – | 22468 | 20832 |
| 1982 | 4528 | 479264 | – | 22213 | 20289 |
| 1983 | 4417 | 444301 | – | 20842 | 18945 |
| 1984 | 4345 | 427763 | – | 20496 | 18500 |
| 1985 | 4286 | 414839 | – | 20945 | 18415 |
| 1986 | 4250 | 413507 | – | 20796 | 18464 |
| 1987 | 4205 | 405856 | – | 21067 | 18751 |
| 1988 | 4137 | 426842 | – | 21658 | 19236 |
| 1989 | 4106 | 459162 | – | 22660 | 20177 |
| 1990 | 4077 | 460514 | – | 20542 | 18099 |
| 1991 | 3972 | 453055 | – | 20781 | 18369 |
| 1992 | 3654 | 450496 | – | 21452 | 19067 |
| 1993 | 3473 | 477026 | – | 22141 | 19775 |
| 1994 | 3352 | 504867 | – | 22751 | 20462 |
| 1995 | 3172 | 513988 | – | 23743 | 21380 |
| 1996 | 3006 | 525674 | – | 24553 | 22197 |
| 1997 | 2762 | 538390 | – | 25269 | 23022 |
| 1998 | 2395 | 532845 | – | 25718 | 23499 |
| 1999 | 1996 | 512874 | – | 26350 | 24120 |
| 2000 | 1659 | 485679 | 100405 | 25938 | 23876 |
| 2001 | 1354 | 467982 | 93365 | 25535 | 23179 |
| 2002 | 1197 | 456535 | 89752 | 25425 | 23138 |
| 2003 | 1044 | 448969 | 84051 | 25304 | 22955 |
| 2004 | 897 | 447971 | 74872 | 25396 | 23066 |
| 2005 | 791 | 458942 | 75337 | 25793 | 23541 |
| 2006 | 605 | 459529 | 79070 | 26040 | 23848 |
| 2007 | 437 | 456152 | 81767 | 26455 | 24251 |
| 2008 | 418 | 452143 | 82620 | 26894 | 24743 |
| 2009 | 417 | 445132 | 80441 | 27445 | 25424 |
| 2010 | 408 | 453897 | 76126 | 27881 | 25709 |
| 2011 | 409 | 465289 | 73465 | 27862 | 26395 |
| 2012 | 415 | 472613 | 74547 | 25620 | 27777 |
| 2013 | 419 | 483489 | 73682 | 30373 | 28949 |
| 2014 | 421 | 502688 | 73244 | 31490 | 30139 |
| 2015 | 443 | 524513 | 71398 | 32815 | 31280 |
| 2016 | 447 | 543038 | 77726 | 33873 | 32549 |
| 2017 | 458 | 560411 | 84615 | 35510 | 34150 |
| 2018 | 478 | 590491 | 78951 | 37316 | 35793 |
| 2019 | 489 | 616929 | 85564 | 39297 | 37708 |

# 12－15 初中基本情况(1978－2019年)

## Basic Statistics on Junior Middle Schools(1978－2019)

单位:人 (person)

| 年份<br>Year | 学校数(个)<br>Number of Schools<br>(unit) | 在校学生数<br>Enrollment | 毕业生数<br>Graduates | 专职教师数<br>Number of Full－time Teachers |
|---|---|---|---|---|
| 1978 | 254 | 247209 | － | 11978 |
| 1979 | 363 | 208484 | － | 11020 |
| 1980 | 369 | 204073 | － | 10695 |
| 1981 | 359 | 194024 | － | 10015 |
| 1982 | 367 | 193135 | － | 10107 |
| 1983 | 370 | 190221 | － | 9948 |
| 1984 | 368 | 192971 | － | 9679 |
| 1985 | 361 | 196889 | － | 9799 |
| 1986 | 376 | 199638 | － | 9821 |
| 1987 | 385 | 195426 | － | 10264 |
| 1988 | 380 | 170079 | － | 10055 |
| 1989 | 376 | 151223 | － | 9825 |
| 1990 | 382 | 160111 | － | 9564 |
| 1991 | 387 | 185590 | － | 10020 |
| 1992 | 367 | 212022 | － | 10603 |
| 1993 | 365 | 203896 | － | 10876 |
| 1994 | 371 | 205388 | － | 11495 |
| 1995 | 373 | 216300 | － | 12058 |
| 1996 | 374 | 229466 | － | 12810 |
| 1997 | 368 | 227809 | － | 13370 |
| 1998 | 359 | 222191 | － | 13493 |
| 1999 | 339 | 239174 | － | 13723 |
| 2000 | 330 | 269484 | 68347 | 14529 |
| 2001 | 314 | 285203 | 75722 | 15685 |
| 2002 | 315 | 282951 | 91056 | 15758 |
| 2003 | 316 | 268824 | 98412 | 15836 |
| 2004 | 303 | 252291 | 93042 | 16042 |
| 2005 | 289 | 241374 | 90094 | 16205 |
| 2006 | 263 | 235527 | 85436 | 16374 |
| 2007 | 262 | 238252 | 76194 | 16591 |
| 2008 | 260 | 244464 | 74827 | 16965 |
| 2009 | 252 | 241899 | 77268 | 17317 |
| 2010 | 245 | 236014 | 78379 | 17795 |
| 2011 | 246 | 223545 | 78431 | 17652 |
| 2012 | 244 | 215701 | 75489 | 17992 |
| 2013 | 241 | 213452 | 71006 | 18260 |
| 2014 | 241 | 213936 | 67988 | 18671 |
| 2015 | 243 | 211323 | 69200 | 18909 |
| 2016 | 249 | 215756 | 69674 | 19469 |
| 2017 | 251 | 224797 | 69084 | 20144 |
| 2018 | 264 | 235003 | 66949 | 20800 |
| 2019 | 269 | 244070 | 73657 | 21691 |

# 12－16 高中基本情况(1978－2019年)

## Basic Statistics on Senior High Schools(1978－2019)

单位:人 (person)

| 年 份<br>Year | 学校数(个)<br>Number of Schools<br>(unit) | 在校学生数<br>Enrollment | 毕业生数<br>Graduates | 专职教师数<br>Number of Full－time Teachers |
|---|---|---|---|---|
| 1978 | 352 | 102815 | － | 5235 |
| 1979 | 182 | 58866 | － | 3471 |
| 1980 | 151 | 43661 | － | 3173 |
| 1981 | 118 | 34606 | － | 2825 |
| 1982 | 113 | 35136 | － | 2740 |
| 1983 | 111 | 38580 | － | 2740 |
| 1984 | 105 | 43167 | － | 2781 |
| 1985 | 104 | 47510 | － | 3016 |
| 1986 | 95 | 46379 | － | 2972 |
| 1987 | 92 | 44697 | － | 3006 |
| 1988 | 89 | 42196 | － | 2947 |
| 1989 | 88 | 39994 | － | 2898 |
| 1990 | 86 | 39829 | － | 2922 |
| 1991 | 82 | 37809 | － | 2896 |
| 1992 | 74 | 34620 | － | 2791 |
| 1993 | 72 | 32483 | － | 2641 |
| 1994 | 75 | 35720 | － | 2673 |
| 1995 | 72 | 40771 | － | 2880 |
| 1996 | 70 | 43692 | － | 3135 |
| 1997 | 69 | 47975 | － | 3388 |
| 1998 | 75 | 55688 | － | 3693 |
| 1999 | 82 | 64459 | － | 4172 |
| 2000 | 85 | 73049 | 17484 | 4745 |
| 2001 | 88 | 79632 | 22012 | 5262 |
| 2002 | 81 | 91635 | 22630 | 6126 |
| 2003 | 77 | 108116 | 25429 | 6879 |
| 2004 | 81 | 115303 | 30630 | 7510 |
| 2005 | 80 | 120883 | 34486 | 8041 |
| 2006 | 82 | 124177 | 39484 | 8421 |
| 2007 | 80 | 122939 | 39805 | 8542 |
| 2008 | 76 | 120294 | 40551 | 8646 |
| 2009 | 75 | 118057 | 41408 | 8751 |
| 2010 | 72 | 116983 | 39319 | 8871 |
| 2011 | 71 | 117089 | 38579 | 9061 |
| 2012 | 70 | 115652 | 38623 | 9069 |
| 2013 | 70 | 113894 | 37810 | 9125 |
| 2014 | 72 | 110478 | 38489 | 9378 |
| 2015 | 75 | 109983 | 37303 | 9630 |
| 2016 | 77 | 110431 | 36022 | 10016 |
| 2017 | 80 | 113054 | 34860 | 10430 |
| 2018 | 87 | 114324 | 36460 | 10825 |
| 2019 | 87 | 118039 | 36865 | 11161 |

# 12－17 中等专业学校基本情况(1978－2019年)

## Basic Statistics on Specialized Secondary Schools(1978－2019)

单位:人 (person)

| 年 份 Year | 学校数(个) Number of Schools (unit) | 在校学生数 Enrollment | 毕业生数 Graduates | 教职员工数 Teachers and Staff | 专职教师数 Number of Full－time Teachers |
|---|---|---|---|---|---|
| 1978 | 26 | 8711 | － | 3044 | 1080 |
| 1979 | 27 | 11093 | － | 2601 | 1124 |
| 1980 | 26 | 9453 | － | 2450 | 1101 |
| 1981 | 35 | 7309 | － | 3122 | 1276 |
| 1982 | 37 | 8284 | － | 3694 | 1529 |
| 1983 | 37 | 10516 | － | 3716 | 1604 |
| 1984 | 42 | 13419 | － | 4194 | 1758 |
| 1985 | 46 | 16527 | － | 5095 | 1959 |
| 1986 | 50 | 19114 | － | 5641 | 2336 |
| 1987 | 52 | 20929 | － | 6081 | 2623 |
| 1988 | 51 | 22117 | － | 6144 | 2741 |
| 1989 | 54 | 23302 | － | 6602 | 2888 |
| 1990 | 55 | 23564 | － | 6679 | 2948 |
| 1991 | 55 | 23331 | － | 6584 | 2770 |
| 1992 | 55 | 26373 | － | 6786 | 2825 |
| 1993 | 56 | 30336 | － | 6732 | 2780 |
| 1994 | 57 | 36079 | － | 6881 | 2840 |
| 1995 | 57 | 42784 | － | 6851 | 2888 |
| 1996 | 58 | 49593 | － | 6789 | 2904 |
| 1997 | 57 | 51752 | － | 6731 | 2896 |
| 1998 | 56 | 55796 | － | 6554 | 2746 |
| 1999 | 50 | 52272 | － | 5023 | 2272 |
| 2000 | 28 | 45238 | 15674 | 2950 | 1421 |
| 2001 | 26 | 32763 | 15202 | 2053 | 1051 |
| 2002 | 14 | 26255 | 13355 | 1251 | 566 |
| 2003 | 13 | 21735 | 11866 | 1058 | 457 |
| 2004 | 11 | 21262 | 6399 | 869 | 416 |
| 2005 | 10 | 20344 | 6661 | 893 | 443 |
| 2006 | 8 | 12540 | 5830 | 410 | 184 |
| 2007 | 8 | 8927 | 4849 | 414 | 194 |
| 2008 | 8 | 5514 | 4130 | 345 | 152 |
| 2009 | 8 | 4016 | 2025 | 233 | 65 |
| 2010 | 6 | 3999 | 1092 | 348 | 151 |
| 2011 | 5 | 4071 | 934 | 369 | 154 |
| 2012 | 5 | 3909 | 1252 | 376 | 150 |
| 2013 | 5 | 3656 | 1215 | 390 | 158 |
| 2014 | 7 | 3974 | 1077 | 469 | 226 |
| 2015 | 7 | 3968 | 1134 | 494 | 244 |
| 2016 | 7 | 4402 | 982 | 504 | 262 |
| 2017 | 7 | 4566 | 1348 | 386 | 177 |
| 2018 | 6 | 4448 | 1457 | 381 | 172 |
| 2019 | 7 | 4535 | 1385 | 372 | 173 |

# 12－18 高等学校基本情况(1978－2019年)

## Basic Statistics on Regular Institutions of Higher Education(1978－2019)

单位:人 (person)

| 年份 Year | 学校数(个) Number of Schools (unit) | 招生数 Entrants | 在校学生数 Enrollment | 毕业生数 Graduates | 教职员工数 Teachers and Staff | 专职教师数 Number of Full－time Teachers |
|---|---|---|---|---|---|---|
| 1978 | 9 | – | 13319 | – | 8966 | 3946 |
| 1979 | 12 | – | 17518 | – | 10182 | 4458 |
| 1980 | 13 | – | 23545 | – | 12400 | 5278 |
| 1981 | 13 | – | 28936 | – | 13090 | 5359 |
| 1982 | 13 | – | 25821 | – | 14363 | 6067 |
| 1983 | 14 | – | 27443 | – | 15267 | 6172 |
| 1984 | 16 | – | 31384 | – | 15889 | 6387 |
| 1985 | 20 | – | 36996 | – | 17507 | 7247 |
| 1986 | 22 | – | 40051 | – | 18968 | 7845 |
| 1987 | 21 | – | 39922 | – | 18965 | 7876 |
| 1988 | 21 | – | 40787 | – | 19582 | 8133 |
| 1989 | 21 | – | 40330 | – | 19680 | 8107 |
| 1990 | 21 | – | 39866 | – | 19495 | 8075 |
| 1991 | 21 | – | 42192 | – | 19489 | 7737 |
| 1992 | 19 | – | 43787 | – | 19841 | 7561 |
| 1993 | 19 | – | 51063 | – | 19787 | 7561 |
| 1994 | 19 | – | 59109 | – | 19903 | 7703 |
| 1995 | 20 | – | 63124 | – | 19883 | 7799 |
| 1996 | 20 | – | 66023 | – | 19693 | 7824 |
| 1997 | 20 | – | 69391 | – | 19540 | 7793 |
| 1998 | 17 | – | 76546 | – | 19320 | 7723 |
| 1999 | 18 | – | 89109 | – | 20136 | 8135 |
| 2000 | 32 | 46070 | 122386 | 17004 | 23791 | 10477 |
| 2001 | 33 | 63001 | 174894 | 22756 | 25805 | 11866 |
| 2002 | 34 | 74656 | 224048 | 27213 | 27307 | 13605 |
| 2003 | 35 | 85865 | 269798 | 41192 | 34508 | 18141 |
| 2004 | 36 | 96810 | 313599 | 53288 | 33325 | 18445 |
| 2005 | 36 | 101374 | 351918 | 63989 | 34816 | 19583 |
| 2006 | 36 | 103885 | 373563 | 80069 | 36929 | 21375 |
| 2007 | 36 | 110371 | 392770 | 90944 | 38843 | 23197 |
| 2008 | 36 | 114714 | 409559 | 97778 | 39762 | 24017 |
| 2009 | 36 | 114568 | 429774 | 96101 | 40420 | 24765 |
| 2010 | 37 | 113529 | 434811 | 101681 | 41582 | 25003 |
| 2011 | 38 | 117892 | 446721 | 104486 | 42222 | 25735 |
| 2012 | 38 | 121331 | 459181 | 107484 | 43216 | 26689 |
| 2013 | 38 | 123046 | 471820 | 108688 | 43992 | 27544 |
| 2014 | 38 | 122099 | 474652 | 110512 | 44710 | 28265 |
| 2015 | 39 | 139002 | 475558 | 125013 | 44825 | 28868 |
| 2016 | 39 | 138819 | 480953 | 128434 | 45512 | 29222 |
| 2017 | 39 | 143784 | 484070 | 128880 | 46337 | 29843 |
| 2018 | 40 | 149848 | 496383 | 131823 | 47124 | 30247 |
| 2019 | 40 | 160426 | 518325 | 132048 | 49020 | 31448 |

# 12-19 小学、幼儿园及特殊

## Basic Statistics on Primary Schools,

单位：人

| 指标 | Item | 全市 Total | 市区 Urban District | 萧山区 Xiaoshan |
|---|---|---|---|---|
| **小学** | **Primary Schools** | | | |
| 学校数(所) | Number of Schools(unit) | 489 | 390 | 79 |
| 班数(班) | Number of Classes(unit) | 16195 | 14362 | 2558 |
| 在校学生数 | Number of Students | 616929 | 554279 | 100047 |
| 本年招生数 | Number of New Students Enrollment | 115666 | 104449 | 18913 |
| 本年毕业生数 | Number of Graduates | 85564 | 75382 | 13842 |
| 专职教师数 | Full - time Teachers | 37708 | 33275 | 5593 |
| 2020年预计毕业生数 | Number of Students Will Graduate in 2020 | 89428 | 79504 | 14221 |
| **幼儿园** | **Kindergartens** | | | |
| 园数(个) | Number of Kindergartens(unit) | 1020 | 892 | 196 |
| 班数(班) | Number of Classes(unit) | 12457 | 11183 | 1946 |
| 在园幼儿数 | Number of Children | 350261 | 314930 | 56014 |
| 教师数 | Full - time Teachers | 27685 | 25125 | 4284 |
| **盲聋哑学校** | **Schools for the Blind, Deaf and Deaf - mute** | | | |
| 学校数(个) | Number of Schools(unit) | 2 | 2 | - |
| 在校学生数 | Number of Students | 350 | 350 | - |
| 本年招生数 | Number of New Students Enrollment | 46 | 46 | - |
| 本年毕业生数 | Number of Graduates | 72 | 72 | - |
| 专职教师数 | Number of Full - time Teachers | 159 | 159 | - |
| **弱智学校** | **Schools for Weaken in Intelligence** | | | |
| 学校数(个) | Number of Schools(unit) | 12 | 9 | 1 |
| 在校学生数 | Number of Students | 1290 | 1154 | 267 |
| 本年招生数 | Number of New Students Enrollment | 208 | 199 | 72 |
| 本年毕业生数 | Number of Graduates | 169 | 153 | 46 |
| 专职教师数 | Number of Full - time Teachers | 408 | 377 | 71 |
| **工读学校** | **Reformatory Schools** | | | |
| 学校数(个) | Number of Schools(unit) | 1 | 1 | - |
| 在校学生数 | Number of Students | 401 | 401 | - |
| 本年招生数 | Number of New Students Enrollment | 209 | 209 | - |
| 本年毕业生数 | Number of Graduates | 129 | 129 | - |
| 专任教师数 | Number of Full - time Teachers | 65 | 65 | - |

# 教育基本情况(2019 年)

# Kindergartens and Special Education(2019)

(person)

| 余杭区<br>Yuhang | 富阳区<br>Fuyang | 临安区<br>Lin'an | 桐庐县<br>Tonglu | 淳安县<br>Chun'an | 建德市<br>Jiande |
|---|---|---|---|---|---|
| | | | | | |
| 59 | 43 | 40 | 32 | 38 | 29 |
| 2851 | 1252 | 885 | 660 | 586 | 587 |
| 114476 | 44996 | 32354 | 25118 | 15451 | 22081 |
| 23143 | 7533 | 5888 | 4543 | 2813 | 3861 |
| 13983 | 7316 | 5010 | 3953 | 2756 | 3473 |
| 6306 | 2811 | 1925 | 1492 | 1610 | 1331 |
| 15157 | 7228 | 5000 | 3927 | 2491 | 3506 |
| | | | | | |
| 144 | 76 | 75 | 48 | 40 | 40 |
| 2298 | 884 | 643 | 455 | 339 | 480 |
| 64830 | 24817 | 17365 | 13974 | 8453 | 12904 |
| 5265 | 1866 | 1418 | 894 | 657 | 1009 |
| | | | | | |
| – | – | – | – | – | – |
| – | – | – | – | – | – |
| – | – | – | – | – | – |
| – | – | – | – | – | – |
| – | – | – | – | – | – |
| | | | | | |
| 1 | 1 | 1 | 1 | 1 | 1 |
| 137 | 72 | 99 | 34 | 34 | 68 |
| 16 | 5 | 14 | 2 | – | 7 |
| 28 | 7 | 10 | 11 | 5 | – |
| 36 | 28 | 33 | 11 | 8 | 12 |
| | | | | | |
| – | – | – | – | – | – |
| – | – | – | – | – | – |
| – | – | – | – | – | – |
| – | – | – | – | – | – |
| – | – | – | – | – | – |

# 12－20 普通中学、职业中学

## Basic Statistics on Senior, Junior High

单位：人

| 指 标 | Item | 全 市<br>Total | 市 区<br>Urban District | 萧山区<br>Xiaoshan |
|---|---|---|---|---|
| **高 中** | **Senior High Schools** | | | |
| 学校数(所) | Number of Schools(unit) | 87 | 71 | 11 |
| 在校学生数 | Number of Students | 118039 | 100005 | 20016 |
| 本年招生数 | Number of New Students Enrollment | 41385 | 35224 | 7009 |
| 本年毕业生数 | Number of Graduates | 36865 | 30856 | 6353 |
| 专职教师数 | Full－time Teachers | 11161 | 9283 | 1782 |
| 2020 年预计毕业生数 | Number of Students Will Graduate in 2020 | 37880 | 31824 | 6477 |
| **初 中** | **Junior High Schools** | | | |
| 学校数(所) | Number of Schools(unit) | 269 | 225 | 45 |
| 在校学生数 | Number of Students | 244070 | 213709 | 39583 |
| 本年招生数 | Number of New Students Enrollment | 84090 | 73985 | 13231 |
| 本年毕业生数 | Number of Graduates | 73657 | 63795 | 12984 |
| 专职教师数 | Full－time Teachers | 21691 | 18730 | 3335 |
| 2020 年预计毕业生数 | Number of Students Will Graduate in 2020 | 80627 | 70430 | 13780 |
| **职业中学** | **Vocational Schools** | | | |
| 学校数(所) | Number of Schools(unit) | 30 | 25 | 4 |
| 在校学生数 | Number of Students | 56711 | 50271 | 10040 |
| 本年招生数 | Number of New Students Enrollment | 20379 | 18067 | 3616 |
| 本年毕业生数 | Number of Graduates | 19307 | 16947 | 3385 |
| 专职教师数 | Full－time Teachers | 4659 | 4144 | 863 |
| 2020 年预计毕业生数 | Number of Students Will Graduate in 2020 | 18579 | 16445 | 3322 |
| **技工学校** | **Technical Schools** | | | |
| 学校数(所) | Number of schools(unit) | 19 | 18 | 1 |
| 在校学生数 | Number of Students | 27261 | 25689 | 2110 |
| 专职教师数 | Full－time Teachers | 1527 | 1432 | 203 |

和技工学校基本情况(2019 年)

Schools and Vacational,Technical Schools(2019)

(person)

| 余杭区 Yuhang | 富阳区 Fuyang | 临安区 Lin'an | 桐庐县 Tonglu | 淳安县 Chun'an | 建德市 Jiande |
|---|---|---|---|---|---|
| | | | | | |
| 15 | 7 | 5 | 5 | 5 | 6 |
| 14679 | 12357 | 7077 | 5369 | 5510 | 7155 |
| 5174 | 4255 | 2482 | 1905 | 1925 | 2331 |
| 4514 | 3929 | 2211 | 1651 | 1842 | 2516 |
| 1355 | 1115 | 648 | 576 | 558 | 744 |
| 4688 | 4058 | 2301 | 1718 | 1802 | 2536 |
| | | | | | |
| 37 | 17 | 17 | 12 | 14 | 18 |
| 40625 | 22014 | 13905 | 11405 | 8763 | 10193 |
| 13974 | 7368 | 4853 | 3774 | 2896 | 3435 |
| 12254 | 7028 | 4326 | 3387 | 3081 | 3394 |
| 3262 | 1737 | 1057 | 929 | 959 | 1073 |
| 13294 | 7496 | 4609 | 3711 | 3064 | 3422 |
| | | | | | |
| 5 | 2 | 2 | 2 | 2 | 1 |
| 10533 | 6789 | 3535 | 2051 | 2931 | 1458 |
| 3761 | 2591 | 1260 | 729 | 1064 | 519 |
| 3486 | 2322 | 1201 | 868 | 1109 | 383 |
| 755 | 633 | 331 | 157 | 249 | 109 |
| 3499 | 2143 | 1108 | 777 | 960 | 397 |
| | | | | | |
| – | 1 | 1 | – | – | 1 |
| – | 439 | 699 | – | – | 1572 |
| – | 35 | 55 | – | – | 95 |

# 12－21 各高等学校

## Basic Statistics on Regular

单位：人

| 单位名称 | Item | 在校学生数 Number of students 2019 | 为上年(%) As Compared with the Preceding Year(%) | 其中研究生 Graduate Student |
|---|---|---|---|---|
| **全　　市** | **Total** | **518325** | **104.50** | **71642** |
| **#市　　区** | **Urban District** | **509824** | **104.44** | **71642** |
| 浙江大学 | Zhejiang University | 59062 | 106.93 | 33138 |
| 杭州电子科技大学 | Hangzhou Dianzi University | 20502 | 103.84 | 4504 |
| 浙江工业大学 | Zhejiang Univesity of Technology | 28621 | 104.13 | 9442 |
| 浙江理工大学 | Zhejiang Sci－Tech University | 22095 | 102.36 | 4226 |
| 浙江农林大学 | Zhejiang Forestry University | 17304 | 103.87 | 2534 |
| 浙江中医药大学 | Zhejiang University of Traditional Chinese Medicine | 11847 | 107.34 | 2447 |
| 杭州师范大学 | Hangzhou Normal University | 20085 | 102.77 | 3164 |
| 浙江工商大学 | Zhejiang Gongshang University | 20250 | 104.11 | 4606 |
| 中国美术学院 | China Academy of Art | 9169 | 104.79 | 2038 |
| 中国计量大学 | China JiLiang University | 17485 | 102.31 | 2084 |
| 浙江科技学院 | Hangzhou Application Engineering and TechnologyCollege | 17656 | 100.91 | 810 |
| 浙江广播电视大学 | Zhejiang Radio & TV University | 8984 | 99.90 | － |
| 浙江水利水电专科学校 | Zhejiang Water Conservancy and Hydroelectricity College | 9443 | 100.10 | － |
| 浙江财经大学 | Zhejiang University of Finance and Economics | 16293 | 103.68 | 2143 |
| 浙江警察学院 | Zhejiang Police College | 3603 | 89.83 | － |
| 浙江传媒学院 | Zhejiang Institute of Media and Communications | 14032 | 99.84 | 220 |
| 浙江树人大学 | Zhejiang Shuren University | 16887 | 105.99 | － |
| 浙江大学城市学院 | Zhejiang University City College | 11625 | 93.63 | － |

## 基本情况(2019年)
## Institutions of Higher Education(2019)

(person)

| 本年招生数 Entrants | 其中研究生 Graduate Student | 本年毕业生数 Graduates | 其中研究生 Graduate Student | 教职员工数 Number of Teachers and Staff 合计 Total | 专职教师 Full - time Teachers |
|---|---|---|---|---|---|
| **160426** | **24009** | **132048** | **15463** | **49020** | **31448** |
| **157765** | **24009** | **130085** | **15463** | **48523** | **31021** |
| 16771 | 10523 | 11943 | 6405 | 9204 | 3856 |
| 5735 | 1584 | 4666 | 1092 | 2273 | 1658 |
| 7886 | 3116 | 6381 | 2015 | 3115 | 2214 |
| 6081 | 1455 | 5377 | 1063 | 2160 | 1553 |
| 4761 | 935 | 4014 | 565 | 1646 | 1143 |
| 3429 | 864 | 2586 | 661 | 1289 | 842 |
| 5427 | 1169 | 4789 | 839 | 2451 | 1578 |
| 5769 | 1625 | 4818 | 1189 | 1935 | 1488 |
| 2479 | 689 | 2047 | 377 | 1109 | 677 |
| 4678 | 745 | 4110 | 519 | 1687 | 1202 |
| 4223 | 348 | 3603 | 116 | 1446 | 1166 |
| 3725 | - | 3446 | - | 256 | 73 |
| 2843 | - | 2763 | - | 736 | 490 |
| 4435 | 717 | 3767 | 472 | 1626 | 1140 |
| 873 | - | 1271 | - | 476 | 246 |
| 3548 | 121 | 3187 | 79 | 1446 | 939 |
| 5159 | - | 4163 | - | 891 | 683 |
| 2751 | - | 3162 | - | 1051 | 714 |

# 12－22　各级成人教育

## Basic Statistics on

单位:人

| 指　标 | Item | 成人高等学历教育 Higher Education for Adults | 成人高校 Adult Institutions of Higher Education | 普通高校成人高等学历教育 Adult Higher Education in Ordinary Universities |
|---|---|---|---|---|
| **全　市** | **Total** | | | |
| 学校数(所) | Number of Schools(unit) | 3 | 3 | – |
| 在校学生数 | Number of Students | 123317 | 8984 | 114333 |
| 本年招生数 | Number of New Students Enrollment | 64722 | 3725 | 60997 |
| 本年毕业生数 | Number of Graduates | 41078 | 4106 | 36972 |
| 教职员工数 | Number of Teachers and Staff | 415 | 415 | – |
| #专职教师 | #Full－time Teachers | 160 | 160 | – |
| **市　区** | **Urban District** | | | |
| 学校数(所) | Number of Schools(unit) | 3 | 3 | – |
| 在校学生数 | Number of Students | 123317 | 8984 | 114333 |
| 本年招生数 | Number of New Students Enrollment | 64722 | 3725 | 60997 |
| 本年毕业生数 | Number of Graduates | 41078 | 4106 | 36972 |
| 教职员工数 | Number of Teachers and Staff | 415 | 415 | – |
| #专职教师 | #Full－time Teachers | 160 | 160 | – |

# 基本情况(2019 年)
# Various Adult Education(2019)

(person)

| 成人中等学历教育 Adult Secondary Education | 成人中等专业 Adult Secondary Specialized | 成人中学 Secondary Schools for Adults |
|---|---|---|
| 7 | 5 | 2 |
| 15635 | 15523 | 112 |
| 7999 | 7999 | – |
| 7066 | 6957 | 109 |
| 689 | 670 | 19 |
| 332 | 322 | 10 |
| | | |
| 7 | 5 | 2 |
| 15635 | 15523 | 112 |
| 7999 | 7999 | – |
| 7066 | 6957 | 109 |
| 689 | 670 | 19 |
| 332 | 322 | 10 |

# 12-23 医疗卫生机构数(1978-2019年)

## Number of Health Institutions(1978-2019)

单位:个 (unit)

| 年 份<br>Year | 全市合计<br>Total | 医 院<br>Hospitals | 市区合计<br>Urban District | 医 院<br>Hospitals |
|---|---|---|---|---|
| 1978 | 1361 | 421 | 689 | 45 |
| 1979 | 1390 | 426 | 696 | 50 |
| 1980 | 1381 | 425 | 675 | 51 |
| 1981 | 1476 | 424 | 749 | 51 |
| 1982 | 1540 | 432 | 798 | 56 |
| 1983 | 1540 | 435 | 800 | 58 |
| 1984 | 1574 | 437 | 807 | 54 |
| 1985 | 1582 | 404 | 787 | 47 |
| 1986 | 1636 | 407 | 826 | 53 |
| 1987 | 1693 | 420 | 865 | 55 |
| 1988 | 1710 | 438 | 878 | 55 |
| 1989 | 1721 | 443 | 882 | 57 |
| 1990 | 1738 | 440 | 890 | 58 |
| 1991 | 1789 | 441 | 889 | 58 |
| 1992 | 1767 | 436 | 885 | 58 |
| 1993 | 1730 | 403 | 882 | 68 |
| 1994 | 1717 | 416 | 882 | 72 |
| 1995 | 1712 | 414 | 883 | 72 |
| 1996 | 1712 | 416 | 893 | 83 |
| 1997 | 1711 | 411 | 891 | 81 |
| 1998 | 1491 | 419 | 757 | 89 |
| 1999 | 1530 | 400 | 789 | 85 |
| 2000 | 1599 | 396 | 853 | 85 |
| 2001 | 1496 | 391 | 1072 | 191 |
| 2002 | 1817 | 116 | 1277 | 88 |
| 2003 | 1901 | 99 | 1323 | 73 |
| 2004 | 1985 | 114 | 1396 | 87 |
| 2005 | 2196 | 127 | 1604 | 97 |
| 2006 | 2570 | 134 | 1886 | 107 |
| 2007 | 2607 | 138 | 1872 | 104 |
| 2008 | 2544 | 141 | 1813 | 108 |
| 2009 | 2687 | 144 | 1887 | 111 |
| 2010 | 2819 | 151 | 1906 | 113 |
| 2011 | 2958 | 167 | 1992 | 122 |
| 2012 | 3017 | 198 | 2004 | 146 |
| 2013 | 4139 | 208 | 2233 | 156 |
| 2014 | 4198 | 218 | 2763 | 173 |
| 2015 | 4428 | 244 | 2982 | 198 |
| 2016 | 4691 | 277 | 3214 | 226 |
| 2017 | 4933 | 302 | 3906 | 273 |
| 2018 | 5377 | 316 | 4338 | 282 |
| 2019 | 5925 | 343 | 4857 | 304 |

# 12－24　医疗病床数(1978－2019年)

# Number of Beds in Health Institutions(1978－2019)

单位:张　　　　(bed)

| 年份<br>Year | 全市<br>Total | 医院<br>Hospitals | 市区<br>Urban District | 医院<br>Hospitals |
|---|---|---|---|---|
| 1978 | 14042 | 11704 | 6588 | 5789 |
| 1979 | 15124 | 12682 | 7335 | 6282 |
| 1980 | 16317 | 13478 | 8244 | 6940 |
| 1981 | 17408 | 13576 | 9646 | 7185 |
| 1982 | 17179 | 14350 | 9194 | 7580 |
| 1983 | 17338 | 14584 | 9411 | 7833 |
| 1984 | 17694 | 14691 | 9536 | 7867 |
| 1985 | 19637 | 15010 | 11095 | 7933 |
| 1986 | 20555 | 16035 | 11657 | 8448 |
| 1987 | 21465 | 16770 | 12203 | 8863 |
| 1988 | 23394 | 17954 | 13204 | 9651 |
| 1989 | 24111 | 18363 | 13581 | 9773 |
| 1990 | 24121 | 18879 | 13219 | 10041 |
| 1991 | 24966 | 19444 | 13968 | 10437 |
| 1992 | 25606 | 20243 | 14206 | 10821 |
| 1993 | 25653 | 20884 | 14058 | 10982 |
| 1994 | 25984 | 20870 | 14231 | 11045 |
| 1995 | 26684 | 21360 | 14731 | 11336 |
| 1996 | 28141 | 22217 | 15427 | 12132 |
| 1997 | 26616 | 22341 | 15076 | 12190 |
| 1998 | 27327 | 23110 | 15530 | 12766 |
| 1999 | 26713 | 22952 | 14988 | 12691 |
| 2000 | 27166 | 23303 | 15496 | 13068 |
| 2001 | 27063 | 23520 | 20523 | 17770 |
| 2002 | 27609 | 22797 | 21200 | 18667 |
| 2003 | 29144 | 22036 | 22641 | 18205 |
| 2004 | 31738 | 24444 | 25008 | 20338 |
| 2005 | 33251 | 25907 | 26732 | 21931 |
| 2006 | 33972 | 27186 | 27172 | 23184 |
| 2007 | 36928 | 29987 | 29884 | 25664 |
| 2008 | 38114 | 31416 | 30663 | 26882 |
| 2009 | 40226 | 33094 | 32412 | 28031 |
| 2010 | 42828 | 36148 | 34693 | 30639 |
| 2011 | 45291 | 39363 | 36633 | 33291 |
| 2012 | 49471 | 44019 | 40534 | 37383 |
| 2013 | 52056 | 46636 | 42506 | 39489 |
| 2014 | 55779 | 50805 | 48406 | 44639 |
| 2015 | 63632 | 58400 | 55540 | 51672 |
| 2016 | 69452 | 63994 | 60666 | 56522 |
| 2017 | 75948 | 70187 | 69057 | 64524 |
| 2018 | 81215 | 75186 | 73481 | 68765 |
| 2019 | 85708 | 79957 | 77680 | 73202 |

# 12-25 分种类分地区

# Number of

单位:个

| 指标 | Item | 全市 Total | 市区 Urban District |
|---|---|---|---|
| **总计** | **Total** | **5925** | **4857** |
| **一、医院** | **Number of Hospitals** | **343** | **304** |
| 1. 综合医院 | General Hospitals | 163 | 144 |
| 2. 中医医院 | Hospitals of Chinese Medicine | 41 | 34 |
| 3. 中西医结合医院 | Chinese Therapeutics with Western | 8 | 7 |
| 4. 专科医院 | Specialized Hospitals | 112 | 100 |
| #口腔医院 | Hospitals for Mouth | 22 | 21 |
| 眼科医院 | Hospitals for Eye | 11 | 8 |
| 耳鼻喉科医院 | ENT Hospitals | – | – |
| 肿瘤医院 | Tumor Hospitals | 2 | 2 |
| 心血管病医院 | Cardiovascular Hospitals | 2 | 2 |
| 胸科医院 | Chest Hospitals | – | – |
| 血液病医院 | Blood Diseases Hospitals | – | – |
| 妇产(科)医院 | Hospitals for Pregnant Woman | 10 | 10 |
| 儿童医院 | Children Hospitals | 5 | 5 |
| 精神病医院 | Mental Hospitals | 9 | 6 |
| 传染病医院 | Hospitals for Infectious Diseases | 1 | 1 |
| 皮肤病医院 | Dermatology Hospital | 5 | 5 |
| 结核病医院 | Tuberculosis Hospitals | – | – |
| 麻疯病医院 | Leprosy Hospitals | – | – |
| 职业病医院 | Occupational Disease Hospitals | – | – |
| 骨科医院 | Orthopaedics Hospitals | 7 | 6 |
| 康复医院 | Healing Hospitals | 15 | 13 |
| 整型外科医院 | Plastic Hospitals | 2 | 2 |
| 美容医院 | Beauty Hospitals | 12 | 12 |
| 其他专科医院 | Other Special Hospitals | 9 | 7 |
| 5. 护理院 | Nursing Centers | 19 | 19 |
| **二、基层医疗卫生机构** | **Community Medical Institutions** | **5474** | **4466** |
| 1. 社区卫生服务中心(站) | Health Service Centers for Community | 1313 | 1140 |
| #社区卫生服务中心 | Health Service Centers | 133 | 126 |
| 社区卫生服务站 | Health Service Stations | 1180 | 1014 |
| 2. 卫生院 | Health Service Centers | 81 | 30 |
| #街道卫生院 | Rural Township Hospitals in Subdistrict | – | – |
| 乡镇卫生院 | Rural Township Hospitals in Country | 81 | 30 |
| 3. 村卫生室 | Health Offices in Village | 871 | 355 |
| 4. 门诊部 | Clinics | 769 | 717 |
| 5. 诊所、卫生所、医务室、护理站 | Other Health Care Institutions | 2440 | 2224 |
| **三、专业公共卫生机构** | **Professional Public Health Institutions** | **58** | **41** |
| 疾病预防控制中心 | Centers for Disease Prevention and Control | 14 | 11 |
| 专科疾病防治所(所、站) | Specialized Centers for Disease Prevention and Control(stations) | 2 | – |
| 健康教育所(站、中心) | Education Center for Health(stations) | – | – |
| 妇幼保健院(所、站) | Maternity and Child Care Centers(stations) | 10 | 7 |
| 急救中心(站) | First-aid Centers(stations) | 10 | 6 |
| 采供血机构 | Blood Supplying Agencies | 3 | 2 |
| 卫生监督所 | Institutions of Public Health Inspection | 15 | 12 |
| 计划生育服务机构 | Family Planning Service Institutions | 4 | 3 |
| **四、其他卫生机构** | **Other Health Care Institutions** | **50** | **46** |
| 疗养院 | Sanatoriums | 8 | 8 |
| 医学科学研究机构 | Research Institutions of Medical Science | – | – |
| 医学在职培训机构 | Medical Training Organization for Incumbent | 4 | 2 |
| 临床检验中心(所、站) | Clinical Laboratory Center | 22 | 21 |
| 统计信息中心 | Statistical Information Centers | 1 | 1 |
| 其他 | Other | 15 | 14 |

# 医疗卫生机构数(2019年末)

# Health Institutions(End of 2019)

(unit)

| 萧山区 Xiaoshan | 余杭区 Yuhang | 富阳区 Fuyang | 临安区 Lin'an | 桐庐县 Tonglu | 淳安县 Chun'an | 建德市 Jiande |
|---|---|---|---|---|---|---|
| **848** | **794** | **445** | **492** | **343** | **329** | **396** |
| **57** | **33** | **15** | **29** | **17** | **12** | **10** |
| 45 | 14 | 6 | 14 | 10 | 5 | 4 |
| 5 | 3 | 4 | 8 | 3 | 2 | 2 |
| – | 1 | 1 | – | – | – | 1 |
| 7 | 11 | 4 | 6 | 4 | 5 | 3 |
| 2 | 3 | 1 | 1 | – | 1 | – |
| – | 1 | 1 | – | 1 | 1 | 1 |
| – | – | – | – | – | – | – |
| – | – | – | – | – | – | – |
| – | – | – | – | – | – | – |
| – | – | – | – | – | – | – |
| – | – | – | – | – | – | – |
| – | 1 | – | – | – | – | – |
| – | 1 | – | – | – | – | – |
| – | 3 | 1 | 1 | 1 | 1 | 1 |
| – | – | – | – | – | – | – |
| 1 | – | – | – | – | – | – |
| – | – | – | – | – | – | – |
| – | – | – | – | – | – | – |
| – | – | – | – | – | – | – |
| – | 2 | – | 2 | 1 | – | – |
| 1 | – | 1 | – | – | 1 | 1 |
| – | – | – | – | – | – | – |
| – | – | – | 1 | – | – | – |
| 3 | – | – | 1 | 1 | 1 | – |
| – | 4 | – | 1 | – | – | – |
| **782** | **745** | **422** | **459** | **321** | **308** | **379** |
| 328 | 194 | 169 | 83 | 106 | 48 | 19 |
| 29 | 20 | 25 | 5 | 3 | 2 | 2 |
| 299 | 174 | 144 | 78 | 103 | 46 | 17 |
| – | – | 10 | 20 | 10 | 21 | 20 |
| – | – | – | – | – | – | – |
| – | – | 10 | 20 | 10 | 21 | 20 |
| 102 | – | 105 | 148 | 118 | 170 | 228 |
| 74 | 107 | 25 | 18 | 27 | 8 | 17 |
| 278 | 444 | 113 | 190 | 60 | 61 | 95 |
| **6** | **5** | **4** | **4** | **3** | **8** | **6** |
| 1 | 1 | 1 | 1 | 1 | 1 | 1 |
| – | – | – | – | – | 1 | 1 |
| – | – | – | – | – | – | – |
| – | 1 | 1 | 1 | 1 | 1 | 1 |
| 2 | 1 | 1 | 1 | – | 3 | 1 |
| 1 | – | – | – | – | – | 1 |
| 1 | 1 | 1 | 1 | 1 | 1 | 1 |
| 1 | 1 | – | – | – | 1 | – |
| **3** | **11** | **4** | **–** | **2** | **1** | **1** |
| 1 | 1 | 4 | – | – | – | – |
| – | – | – | – | – | – | – |
| – | 1 | – | – | – | 1 | 1 |
| 2 | 9 | – | – | 1 | – | – |
| – | – |  | – | – | – | – |
| – | – | – | – | 1 | – | – |

# 12-26 分种类分地区

# Total Number of

单位:张

| 指标 | Item | 全市 Total | 市区 Urban District |
|---|---|---|---|
| **总计** | **Total** | **85708** | **77680** |
| **一、医院** | **Number of Hospitals** | **79957** | **73202** |
| 1.综合医院 | General Hospitals | 42594 | 38864 |
| 2.中医医院 | Hospitals of Chinese Medicine | 11225 | 9478 |
| 3.中西医结合医院 | Chinese Therapeutics with Western | 5486 | 5223 |
| 4.专科医院 | Specialized Hospitals | 17554 | 16539 |
| #口腔医院 | Stomatology Hospitals | 339 | 324 |
| 眼科医院 | Ophthalmology Hospitals | 435 | 311 |
| 耳鼻喉科医院 | ENT Hospitals | – | – |
| 肿瘤医院 | Tumor Hospitals | 2675 | 2675 |
| 心血管病医院 | Cardiovascular Hospitals | 1051 | 1051 |
| 胸科医院 | Chest Hospitals | – | – |
| 血液病医院 | Blood Diseases Hospitals | – | – |
| 妇产(科)医院 | Hospitals for Pregnant Woman | 1931 | 1931 |
| 儿童医院 | Children Hospitals | 1793 | 1793 |
| 精神病医院 | Mental Hospitals | 2734 | 2244 |
| 传染病医院 | Hospitals for Infectious Diseases | 700 | 700 |
| 皮肤病医院 | Dermatology Hospital | 197 | 197 |
| 结核病医院 | Tuberculosis Hospitals | – | – |
| 麻疯病医院 | Leprosy Hospitals | – | – |
| 职业病医院 | Occupational Disease Hospitals | – | – |
| 骨科医院 | Orthopaedics Hospitals | 934 | 894 |
| 康复医院 | Healing Hospitals | 3439 | 3164 |
| 整型外科医院 | Plastic Hospitals | 136 | 136 |
| 美容医院 | Beauty Hospitals | 235 | 235 |
| 其他专科医院 | Other Special Hospitals | 955 | 884 |
| 5.护理院 | Nursing Centers | 3098 | 3098 |
| **二、基层医疗卫生机构** | **Community Medical Institutions** | **3608** | **2888** |
| 1.社区卫生服务中心(站) | Health Service Centers for Community | 2765 | 2715 |
| #社区卫生服务中心 | Health Service Centers | 2765 | 2715 |
| 社区卫生服务站 | Health Service Stations | – | – |
| 2.卫生院 | Health Service Centers | 802 | 136 |
| #街道卫生院 | Rural Township Hospitals in Subdistrict | – | – |
| 乡镇卫生院 | Rural Township Hospitals in Country | 802 | 136 |
| 3.村卫生室 | Health Offices in Village | – | – |
| 4.门诊部 | Clinics | 41 | 37 |
| 5.诊所、卫生所、医务室、护理站 | Other Health Care Institutions | – | – |
| **三、专业公共卫生机构** | **Professional Public Health Institutions** | **1230** | **677** |
| 疾病预防控制中心 | Centers for Disease Prevention and Control | – | – |
| 专科疾病防治所(所、站) | Specialized Centers for Disease Prevention and Control(stations) | 200 | – |
| 健康教育所(站、中心) | Education Center for Health(stations) | – | – |
| 妇幼保健院(所、站) | Maternity and Child Care Centers(stations) | 1006 | 663 |
| 急救中心(站) | First-aid Centers(stations) | 24 | 14 |
| 采供血机构 | Blood Supplying Agencies | – | – |
| 卫生监督所(中心) | Institutions of Public Health Inspection | – | – |
| 计划生育服务机构 | Family Planning Service Institutions | – | – |
| **四、其他卫生机构** | **Other Health Care Institutions** | **913** | **913** |
| #疗养院 | Sanatoriums | 913 | 913 |
| 医学科学研究机构 | Research Institutions of Medical Science | – | – |
| 医学在职培训机构 | Medical Training Organization for Incumbent | – | – |
| 临床检验中心(所、站) | Clinical Laboratory Center | – | – |
| 统计信息中心 | Statistical Information Centers | – | – |
| 其他 | Other | – | – |

# 医疗病床数（2019 年末）

# Beds in Health Institutions( End of 2019)

（bed）

| 萧山区 Xiaoshan | 余杭区 Yuhang | 富阳区 Fuyang | 临安区 Lin'an | 桐庐县 Tonglu | 淳安县 Chun'an | 建德市 Jiande |
|---|---|---|---|---|---|---|
| **10465** | **6819** | **4107** | **3202** | **2437** | **2543** | **3048** |
| **10100** | **5510** | **3107** | **3088** | **2120** | **2276** | **2359** |
| 7579 | 2883 | 1489 | 1906 | 1503 | 1135 | 1092 |
| 1795 | 550 | 1091 | 553 | 506 | 801 | 440 |
| – | 330 | 72 | – | – | – | 263 |
| 726 | 1203 | 455 | 603 | 111 | 340 | 564 |
| 30 | 30 | 15 | 25 | – | 15 | – |
| – | 30 | 20 | – | 20 | 25 | 79 |
| – | – | – | – | – | – | – |
| – | – | – | – | – | – | – |
| – | – | – | – | – | – | – |
| – | – | – | – | – | – | – |
| – | – | – | – | – | – | – |
| – | 35 | – | – | – | – | – |
| – | 50 | – | – | – | – | – |
| – | 670 | 320 | 200 | – | 120 | 370 |
| – | – | – | – | – | – | – |
| 40 | – | – | – | – | – | – |
| – | – | – | – | – | – | – |
| – | – | – | – | – | – | – |
| – | – | – | – | – | – | – |
| – | 388 | – | 336 | 40 | – | – |
| 152 | – | 100 | – | – | 160 | 115 |
| – | – | – | – | – | – | – |
| – | – | – | 22 | – | – | – |
| 504 | – | – | 20 | 51 | 20 | – |
| – | 544 | – | 26 | – | – | – |
| **305** | **779** | **346** | **70** | **214** | **117** | **389** |
| 295 | 779 | 244 | 36 | 22 | – | 28 |
| 295 | 779 | 244 | 36 | 22 | – | 28 |
| – | – | – | – | – | – | – |
| – | – | 102 | 34 | 188 | 117 | 361 |
| – | – | – | – | – | – | – |
| – | – | 102 | 34 | 188 | 117 | 361 |
| – | – | – | – | – | – | – |
| 10 | – | – | – | 4 | – | – |
| – | – | – | – | – | – | – |
| **–** | **310** | **320** | **44** | **103** | **150** | **300** |
| – | – | – | – | – | – | – |
| – | – | – | – | – | – | 200 |
| – | – | – | – | – | – | – |
| – | 310 | 320 | 30 | 103 | 150 | 90 |
| – | – | – | 14 | – | – | 10 |
| – | – | – | – | – | – | – |
| – | – | – | – | – | – | – |
| – | – | – | – | – | – | – |
| **60** | **220** | **334** | **–** | **–** | **–** | **–** |
| 60 | 220 | 334 | – |  | – | – |
| – | – | – | – | – | – | – |
| – | – | – | – | – | – | – |
| – | – | – | – | – | – | – |
| – | – | – | – | – | – | – |
| – | – | – | – | – | – | – |

# 12－27 医院诊疗

Number of

| 指　　标 | Item | 机构数(个) Number of Institutions (unit) | 诊疗人次数(万人次) Total Number of Patients Treate (10000 person－times) |
|---|---|---|---|
| **总　　计** | **Total** | **5925** | **14639.24** |
| **一、医院** | **Number of Hospitals** | **343** | **7857.36** |
| 1.综合医院 | General Hospitals | 163 | 4679.41 |
| 2.中医医院 | Hospitals of Chinese Medicine | 41 | 1218.84 |
| 3.中西医结合医院 | Chinese Therapeutics with Western | 8 | 613.14 |
| 4.专科医院 | Specialized Hospitals | 112 | 1340.50 |
| #口腔医院 | Stomatology Hospitals | 22 | 194.61 |
| 眼科医院 | Ophthalmology Hospitals | 11 | 36.49 |
| 耳鼻喉科医院 | ENT Hospitals | － | － |
| 肿瘤医院 | Tumor Hospitals | 2 | 75.68 |
| 心血管病医院 | Cardiovascular Hospitals | 2 | 47.47 |
| 胸科医院 | Chest Hospitals | － | － |
| 血液病医院 | Blood Diseases Hospitals | － | － |
| 妇产(科)医院 | Hospitals for Pregnant Woman | 10 | 251.75 |
| 儿童医院 | Children Hospitals | 5 | 415.56 |
| 精神病医院 | Mental Hospitals | 9 | 59.35 |
| 传染病医院 | Hospitals for Infectious Diseases | 1 | 91.57 |
| 皮肤病医院 | Dermatology Hospital | 5 | 23.17 |
| 结核病医院 | Tuberculosis Hospitals | － | － |
| 麻风病医院 | Leprosy Hospitals | － | － |
| 职业病医院 | Occupational Disease Hospitals | － | － |
| 骨科医院 | Orthopaedics Hospitals | 7 | 40.89 |
| 康复医院 | Healing Hospitals | 15 | 17.72 |
| 整型外科医院 | Plastic Hospitals | 2 | 5.08 |
| 美容医院 | Beauty Hospitals | 12 | 66.07 |
| 其他专科医院 | Other Special Hospitals | 9 | 15.08 |
| 5.护理院 | Nursing Centers | 19 | 5.46 |
| **二、基层医疗卫生机构** | **Community Medical Institutions** | **5474** | **6503.50** |
| 1.社区卫生服务中心(站) | Health Service Centers for Community | 1313 | 4055.10 |
| #社区卫生服务中心 | Health Service Centers | 133 | 3971.36 |
| 社区卫生服务站 | Health Service Stations | 1180 | 83.74 |
| 2.卫生院 | Health Service Centers | 81 | 542.65 |
| #乡镇卫生院 | Rural Township Hospitals in Country | 81 | 542.65 |
| 3.村卫生室 | Health Offices in Village | 871 | 118.91 |
| 4.门诊部 | Clinics | 769 | 1058.39 |
| 5.诊所、卫生所、医务室 | Other Health Care Institutions | 2440 | 728.46 |
| **三、专业公共卫生机构** | **Professional Public Health Institutions** | **58** | **259.98** |
| 专科疾病防治院(所、站) | Specialized Centers for Disease Prevention and Control(stations) | 2 | 7.70 |
| 妇幼保健院(所、站) | Maternity and Child Care Centers(stations) | 10 | 238.30 |
| **四、其他机构** | **Other Institutions** | **50** | **18.40** |
| 疗养院 | Sanatoriums | 8 | 18.40 |

次数和入院人数（2019 年）

Hospital Patients(2019)

| 门、急诊人次数(万人次) Out - Patients and Emergency Patients (10000 person - times) | 入院人数 (人) Hospital Admissions(person) | 每百门急诊次入院人数(人) Hospital Admissions Per 100 Patient - time (person) |
|---|---|---|
| **14231.26** | **2751401** | **2.18** |
| **7826.60** | **2635894** | **3.37** |
| 4670.06 | 1592194 | 3.41 |
| 1214.52 | 334687 | 2.76 |
| 608.35 | 166931 | 2.74 |
| 1328.67 | 523082 | 3.94 |
| 190.38 | 1994 | 0.10 |
| 36.05 | 15564 | 4.32 |
| - | - | - |
| 75.68 | 149958 | 19.82 |
| 44.31 | 8585 | 1.94 |
| - | - | - |
| - | - | - |
| 250.08 | 121339 | 4.85 |
| 415.56 | 99051 | 2.38 |
| 58.80 | 29095 | 4.95 |
| 90.77 | 25103 | 2.77 |
| 23.16 | 1548 | 0.67 |
| - | - | - |
| - | - | - |
| - | - | - |
| 40.89 | 22529 | 5.51 |
| 17.36 | 19295 | 11.11 |
| 5.08 | 4332 | 8.52 |
| 66.06 | 13090 | 1.98 |
| 14.49 | 11599 | 8.00 |
| 5.00 | 19000 | 38.03 |
| **6136.17** | **24159** | **0.05** |
| 3933.98 | 13338 | 0.03 |
| 3850.24 | 13338 | 0.03 |
| 83.74 | - | - |
| 523.16 | 10413 | 0.20 |
| 523.16 | 10413 | 0.20 |
| 116.64 | - | - |
| 849.72 | 408 | - |
| 712.66 | - | - |
| **254.97** | **72030** | **2.99** |
| 7.70 | 968 | 1.26 |
| 233.28 | 71062 | 3.05 |
| **13.52** | **19318** | **14.29** |
| 13.52 | 19318 | 14.29 |

# 12-28 卫生事业

## Total Number of

单位：人

| 指 标 | Item | 全 市 Total | 市 区 Urban District |
|---|---|---|---|
| **总 计** | **Total** | **156349** | **143066** |
| 一、卫生技术人员 | Number of Medical Technical Personnel | 126995 | 115959 |
| 1. 执业(助理)医师 | Licensed (Assistant) Doctor | 48962 | 44842 |
| #执业医师 | Licensed Doctor | 45339 | 41885 |
| 2. 注册护士 | Registered Nurse | 55004 | 50639 |
| 3. 药剂师 | Druggist | 7610 | 6749 |
| 4. 技师人员 | Checking Member | 6847 | 6257 |
| #检验师 | Docimaster | 4783 | 4356 |
| 5. 其他 | Others | 8572 | 7472 |
| 二、其他技术人员 | Other Medical Technical Personnel | 8546 | 8113 |
| 三、管理人员 | Managerial Personnel | 6639 | 6181 |
| 四、工勤人员 | Logistics Worker | 13581 | 12546 |

# 人员数(2019年末)

# Medical Technical Personnel( End of 2019 )

(person)

| 萧山区 Xiaoshan | 余杭区 Yuhang | 富阳区 Fuyang | 临安区 Lin'an | 桐庐县 Tonglu | 淳安县 Chun'an | 建德市 Jiande |
|---|---|---|---|---|---|---|
| **18448** | **13806** | **7102** | **5704** | **4997** | **3636** | **4650** |
| 15024 | 11315 | 5857 | 4708 | 4149 | 3017 | 3870 |
| 5526 | 4502 | 2397 | 1948 | 1602 | 1179 | 1339 |
| 4895 | 4038 | 2042 | 1671 | 1353 | 993 | 1108 |
| 6361 | 4454 | 2221 | 1710 | 1566 | 1180 | 1619 |
| 1055 | 686 | 296 | 347 | 327 | 233 | 301 |
| 660 | 676 | 264 | 262 | 205 | 172 | 213 |
| 473 | 501 | 174 | 178 | 151 | 121 | 155 |
| 1422 | 997 | 679 | 441 | 449 | 253 | 398 |
| 751 | 438 | 369 | 351 | 170 | 136 | 127 |
| 872 | 576 | 299 | 212 | 221 | 74 | 163 |
| 1694 | 1477 | 508 | 342 | 445 | 256 | 334 |

# 12-29 卫生技术人员(1978-2019年)
## Number of Medical Technical Personnel(1978-2019)

单位:人 (person)

| 年份 Year | 全市 Total | 执业(助理)医师 Number of Licensed (Assistant) Doctors | 注册护士 Registered Nurses | 市区 Urban District | 执业(助理)医师 Number of Licensed (Assistant) Doctors | 注册护士 Registered Nurses |
|---|---|---|---|---|---|---|
| 1978 | 19059 | 7375 | 3483 | 10867 | 4346 | 2510 |
| 1979 | 20060 | 7539 | 3536 | 11779 | 4733 | 2632 |
| 1980 | 21110 | 8311 | 3885 | 12376 | 5179 | 2804 |
| 1981 | 22737 | 9284 | 4139 | 13697 | 5946 | 3032 |
| 1982 | 23558 | 9883 | 4369 | 14221 | 6204 | 3193 |
| 1983 | 24914 | 10833 | 4562 | 15213 | 6990 | 3352 |
| 1984 | 25648 | 11291 | 4817 | 15807 | 7393 | 3487 |
| 1985 | 25593 | 11503 | 5071 | 15840 | 7644 | 3705 |
| 1986 | 26489 | 12623 | 5391 | 16543 | 8239 | 3940 |
| 1987 | 27663 | 12369 | 5805 | 17361 | 8329 | 4156 |
| 1988 | 28676 | 13674 | 6938 | 18022 | 8710 | 4801 |
| 1989 | 29791 | 14177 | 7348 | 18619 | 9146 | 5085 |
| 1990 | 30990 | 14483 | 7822 | 19231 | 9374 | 5397 |
| 1991 | 32169 | 14858 | 8153 | 19630 | 9494 | 5610 |
| 1992 | 32628 | 14842 | 8417 | 19690 | 9373 | 5736 |
| 1993 | 33172 | 15181 | 8643 | 19708 | 9499 | 5797 |
| 1994 | 33964 | 15465 | 8979 | 19907 | 9472 | 5940 |
| 1995 | 34245 | 16465 | 9531 | 19943 | 9607 | 6249 |
| 1996 | 34946 | 16789 | 9794 | 20695 | 9889 | 6508 |
| 1997 | 35423 | 17112 | 10019 | 20728 | 9902 | 6571 |
| 1998 | 35857 | 16022 | 10577 | 21035 | 9452 | 6788 |
| 1999 | 35256 | 16668 | 10587 | 20519 | 9610 | 6856 |
| 2000 | 35487 | 16317 | 11186 | 20344 | 9050 | 7300 |
| 2001 | 36643 | 16994 | 11576 | 28293 | 12968 | 9343 |
| 2002 | 37193 | 16092 | 11922 | 28818 | 12332 | 9653 |
| 2003 | 39019 | 16614 | 12460 | 30299 | 12731 | 10161 |
| 2004 | 39816 | 16770 | 13248 | 30886 | 12894 | 10840 |
| 2005 | 42353 | 17833 | 14514 | 33206 | 13802 | 12034 |
| 2006 | 45375 | 18831 | 15557 | 35904 | 14689 | 12986 |
| 2007 | 49780 | 20701 | 17455 | 39860 | 16290 | 14601 |
| 2008 | 52379 | 21223 | 18702 | 42015 | 16747 | 15556 |
| 2009 | 56270 | 22753 | 20997 | 45219 | 17996 | 17530 |
| 2010 | 61117 | 24345 | 23418 | 49232 | 19414 | 19481 |
| 2011 | 65869 | 25773 | 25231 | 53008 | 20566 | 20949 |
| 2012 | 71618 | 27369 | 28382 | 57971 | 22004 | 23760 |
| 2013 | 78340 | 29686 | 30996 | 63359 | 23886 | 25808 |
| 2014 | 85614 | 31977 | 34724 | 74064 | 27675 | 30528 |
| 2015 | 93036 | 34832 | 38182 | 80799 | 30316 | 33672 |
| 2016 | 101194 | 38172 | 42011 | 88076 | 33344 | 37154 |
| 2017 | 110395 | 41833 | 46343 | 100478 | 38333 | 42580 |
| 2018 | 117425 | 44896 | 49911 | 106923 | 41105 | 45838 |
| 2019 | 126995 | 48962 | 55004 | 115959 | 44842 | 50639 |

# 12-30 体育运动情况(2015-2019年)

# Basic Statistics on Sports Activities(2015-2019)

单位:人 (person)

| 指 标 | Item | 2015年 | 2016年 | 2017年 | 2018年 | 2019年 |
|---|---|---|---|---|---|---|
| **一、年末体委工作人员数** | **Workers in Sports Commissions at Year-end** | **695** | **705** | **696** | **687** | **615** |
| #教练员 | #Full-time Coaches | 151 | 152 | 157 | 163 | 153 |
| **二、等级裁判员发展人数** | **Number of Referees in Grades** | **266** | **78** | **110** | **-** | **-** |
| #女 | #Female | 66 | 44 | 60 | - | - |
| 一级裁判员 | First Grade Referees | 34 | 28 | - | - | - |
| 二级裁判员 | Second Grade Referees | 232 | 50 | 110 | - | - |
| 三级裁判员 | Third Grade Referees | - | - | - | - | - |
| **三、等级运动员发展人数** | **Number of Athletes in Grades** | **349** | **469** | **509** | **364** | **478** |
| #女 | #Female | 149 | 182 | 223 | 139 | 179 |
| 一级运动员 | First Grade Athlete | 64 | 78 | 113 | - | - |
| 二级运动员 | Second Grade Athlete | 285 | 391 | 396 | 364 | 478 |
| 三级运动员 | Third Grade Athlete | - | - | - | - | - |

# 主要统计指标解释

**文化事业机构** 指从事专业文化工作和为专业文化工作服务的独立建制的单独核算的单位。不包括这些单位另外举办独立核算的其他机构和各部门的业余文化组织。

**艺术表演团体** 指从事戏曲、音乐、舞蹈、杂技等专业艺术表演,有独立帐户,实行单独核算的团体。不包括半工半艺、半农半艺和民间职业剧团。

**普通高等学校** 指按照国家规定的设置标准和审批程序批准举办,通过国家统一招生考试,招收高中毕业生为主要培养对象,实施高等教育的全日制大学、独立设置的学院和高等专科学校、短期职业大学。

**成人高等学校** 指按照国家有关规定审批,招收通过全国成人高教统一招生考试的具有高中毕业或同等学历的在职从业人员利用脱产、半脱产、业余或函授等多种形式对其实施高等学历教育,培养高等教育专科或本科毕业水平的专门人才,修业年限、课程设置和总学时数均按高等学历教育要求付诸实施的学校。包括广播电视大学、职工高等学校、农民高等学校、管理干部学院、教育学院、独立设置的函授学院等。

**小学学龄儿童入学率** 指调查范围内已入小学学习的学龄儿童占校内外学龄儿童总数(包括弱智儿童在内,但不包括盲聋哑儿童)的比重。计算公式:

$$\text{小学学龄儿童入学率}=\frac{\text{已入学的小学学龄儿童数}}{\text{校内外小学学龄儿童总数}}*100\%$$

**等级运动员人数** 指经考核正式批准授予等级运动员称号的人数。运动员等级分为国际级运动健将、运动健将、一级运动员、二级运动员、三级运动员、少年级运动员。

**等级裁判员人数** 指经考核正式批准授予等级裁判员称号的人数。裁判员等级分为国际裁判、国家级裁判、一级裁判、二级裁判、三级裁判。

**卫生机构** 卫生机构是指从卫生行政部门取得《医疗机构执业许可证》,或从民政、工商行政、机构编制管理部门取得法人单位登记证书,为社会提供医疗保健、疾病控制、卫生监督等服务或从事医学科研、医学教育等卫生单位和卫生社会团体。不包括卫生行政机构、香港和澳门特别行政区以及台湾所属卫生机构。

**卫生技术人员** 卫生技术人员包括执业(助理)医师、注册护士、药剂人员、检验和影像技师(士、员)等卫生专业人员。

**执业(助理)医师、执业(中)药师和注册护士** 执业(助理)医师、执业(中)药师和注册护士是指领取医师、药师执业证书和注册护士证书的人员。不包括从事管理工作的医师、药师和护士。

# Explanatory Notes on Main Statistical Indicators

**Culture Institutions** refer to units specialized in cultural development or service, which have independent organizational system and accounting system, excluding other self - accounting establishments run by these units and amateur cultural groups established by various departments.

**Art Troupe** refers to the troupe engaged in drama, music, dance, acrobatics or other art performance with independent accounts in banks and self accounting system, excluding the troupes which are engaged partly in industrial or agricultural activities and partly in art performance, and folk professional troupes.

**Regular Institutions of Higher Education** refer to full - time universities, independent colleges, high professional schools and short - term professional universities which are set up according to the government evaluation and approval procedures, recruit high school graduates as main training objects through the national unified entrance examination and, provide higher education courses.

**Adult Higher Education Institutions** refer to educational establishments, which are set up in line with government relevant rules and approval, enroll staff and workers with senior secondary school or equivalent education through the national unified entrance examination of adult higher education, provide higher education courses in many forms, such as full - time, part - time, spare - time, or correspondence to cultivate specialized talents with the graduation level of junior college or undergraduate, and implement the length of schooling, curriculum and total class hours according to the requirements of higher education. It includes Radio and TV universities, high education schools for staff and workers and for peasants, colleges for management cadres, pedagogical colleges, and independent correspondence colleges.

**Enrollment Rate of Primary School - age Children** refer to the proportion of primary school - age children enrolled at primary schools to primary school - age children both in and outside schools within the scope of investigation (including retarded children, but excluding blind, deaf and mute children). The formula is:

$$\text{Enrollment Rate of Primary School - age Children} = \frac{\text{Number of primary School - age Children at Primary Schools}}{\text{Total Number of Primary School - age Children Both in and Outside schools}} \times 100\%$$

**Number of Grade Athletes** refers to the number of athletes who have been given titles through examination. They are classified as international masters of sports, masters of sports, first - grade, second - grade and third - grade sportsmen and young athletes.

**Number of Grade Referees** refers to the number of referees who have been given titles after examination. They are classified as international referees, national referees and referees of the first, second and third grades.

**Health Institutions** refer to health institutions and society organization that get the practice license of medical institution from the health administration department, or get registration certificate of legal entity from civil administration, industry and business administration or organization management department, and offer medical treatment, disease control, supervision of sanitation for society or are engaged in medical research and medical education. It excludes health administration department and Institutions of Hong Kong, Macao, and Taiwan.

**Medical Technical Personnel** include licensed (assistant) doctor, registered nurse, druggist, checking members and photo artificer.

**Licensed(Assistant) Doctor, Licensed Druggist and Registered Nurse** refers to the doctor, druggist and nurse who get the practice certificate. Those engaged in management are excluded.

# 十三、人民生活 物价、民政

PEOPLE' S LIVELIHOOD, PRICE INDICES AND CIVIL ADMINISTRATION

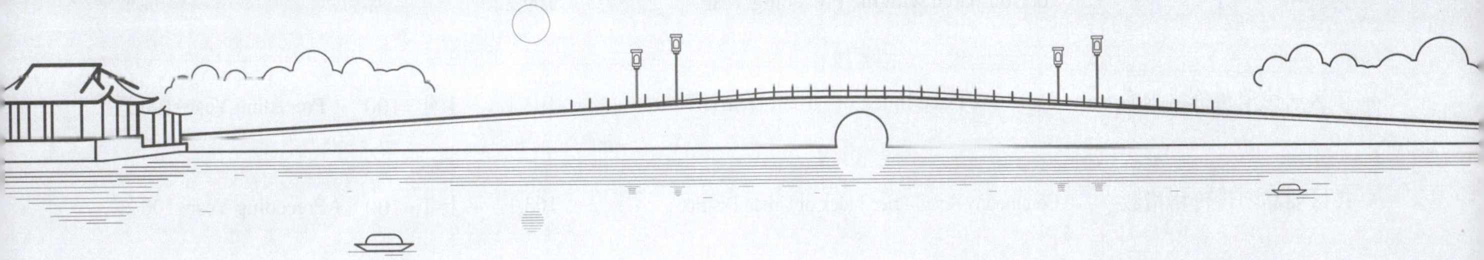

# 13 人民生活、物价、民政
# People's Livelihood, Price Indices and Civil Administration

## 主要统计指标
## Major Statistical Indicators

| | | | | |
|---|---|---|---|---|
| 非私营单位就业人员工资总额 | Total Wages of Employed Persons of Non-private Units | 3298.52 | 亿元 | (100 million yuan) |
| 非私营单位就业人员平均工资 | Annual Average Wages of Employed Persons of Non-private Units | 117339 | 元 | (yuan) |
| 全体居民人均可支配收入 | Per Capita Disposable Income of Urban and Rural Residents | 59261 | 元 | (yuan) |
| 为上年 | As Compared with the Preceding Year | 109.0 | % | (%) |
| 城镇常住居民人均可支配收入 | Per Capita Disposable Income of Permanent Urban Residents | 66068 | 元 | (yuan) |
| 为上年 | As Compared with the Preceding Year | 108.0 | % | (%) |
| 农村常住居民人均可支配收入 | Per Capita Disposable Income of Permanent Rural Residents | 36255 | 元 | (yuan) |
| 为上年 | As Compared with the Preceding Year | 109.2 | % | (%) |
| 市区居民消费价格指数 | Consume Price Index of Urban District | 103.1 | 上年=100 | (Preceding Year=100) |
| 市区商品零售价格指数 | Commodity Retail Price Index of Urban District | 103.1 | 上年=100 | (Preceding Year=100) |
| 工业生产者出厂价格指数 | Producer Price Indices for Industrial Products | 99.0 | 上年=100 | (Preceding Year=100) |

# 13－01　居民家庭人均收入支出(2017－2019年)

## Per Capita Income and Expenditure of Households(2017－2019)

单位:元　　　　(yuan)

| 项　　目<br>Item | 全体居民<br>Urban and Rural Residents | | | 城镇常住居民<br>Permanent Urban Residents | | | 农村常住居民<br>Permanent Rural Residents | | |
|---|---|---|---|---|---|---|---|---|---|
| | 2017 | 2018 | 2019 | 2017 | 2018 | 2019 | 2017 | 2018 | 2019 |
| 一、可支配收入<br>Disposable Income | 49832 | 54348 | 59261 | 56276 | 61172 | 66068 | 30397 | 33193 | 36255 |
| 工资性收入<br>Icome from Wages and salaries | 28680 | 31355 | 34136 | 32144 | 35084 | 37845 | 18232 | 19796 | 21601 |
| 经营净收入<br>Net Buisness Income | 5609 | 6084 | 6584 | 4893 | 5298 | 5849 | 7770 | 8521 | 9067 |
| 财产净收入<br>Net Income from Property | 6574 | 7202 | 8111 | 8329 | 9080 | 10045 | 1280 | 1380 | 1574 |
| 转移净收入<br>Net Income from Transfer | 8969 | 9707 | 10430 | 10910 | 11710 | 12329 | 3115 | 3496 | 4013 |
| 二、消费支出<br>Expenditure | 34146 | 37369 | 40016 | 38179 | 41615 | 44076 | 21983 | 24203 | 26296 |
| 食品烟酒<br>Food,Tobacco and Liquor | 9336 | 9278 | 9833 | 10412 | 10160 | 10651 | 6092 | 6542 | 7067 |
| 衣着<br>Clothing | 1983 | 2185 | 2182 | 2233 | 2470 | 2432 | 1231 | 1301 | 1339 |
| 居住<br>Residence | 9576 | 9939 | 10204 | 10710 | 10971 | 11081 | 6154 | 6739 | 7242 |
| 生活用品及服务<br>Daily Necessities and Services | 1765 | 2195 | 2089 | 1963 | 2468 | 2300 | 1170 | 1351 | 1375 |
| 交通通信<br>Transportation and Communication | 4855 | 6140 | 6761 | 5267 | 6743 | 7446 | 3612 | 4269 | 4444 |
| 教育文化娱乐<br>Education, Cultural and Recreation Service | 3735 | 3625 | 4149 | 4346 | 4196 | 4765 | 1894 | 1856 | 2070 |
| 医疗保健<br>Medicine and Medical Service | 2119 | 2929 | 3636 | 2332 | 3335 | 4057 | 1474 | 1670 | 2210 |
| 其他用品及服务<br>Other Supplies and Services | 777 | 1078 | 1162 | 916 | 1272 | 1344 | 356 | 475 | 549 |

# 13-02 城镇住户调查情况(1978-2019年)

## Basic Conditions of Urban Households (1978-2019)

| 年 份<br>Year | 调查户数<br>(户)<br>Number of Households Surveyed (household) | 平均每户人口<br>(人)<br>Average Household Size (person) | 平均每户就业人数(人)<br>Average Number of Employed Persons Per Household(person) | 年人均可支配收入(元)<br>Per Capita Annual Disposable Income (yuan) | 年人均消费支出(元)<br>Per Capita Annual Consumption Expenditure(yuan) | 人均住房建筑面积<br>(平方米)<br>Per Capita Living Space in City Areas (sq. m) |
|---|---|---|---|---|---|---|
| 1978 | 28 | 4.20 | 2.89 | 338 | 301 | |
| 1979 | 28 | 4.19 | 2.77 | 396 | 365 | |
| 1980 | 28 | 4.18 | 2.79 | 521 | 491 | |
| 1981 | 100 | 3.97 | 2.37 | 540 | 513 | |
| 1982 | 100 | 3.90 | 2.35 | 532 | 532 | |
| 1983 | 100 | 3.90 | 2.42 | 578 | 535 | 11.7 |
| 1984 | 100 | 3.90 | 2.36 | 729 | 679 | 12.4 |
| 1985 | 150 | 3.53 | 2.26 | 1026 | 908 | 12.9 |
| 1986 | 150 | 3.49 | 2.27 | 1169 | 1072 | 13.2 |
| 1987 | 150 | 3.42 | 2.25 | 1260 | 1118 | 14.1 |
| 1988 | 200 | 3.41 | 2.16 | 1565 | 1515 | 14.1 |
| 1989 | 200 | 3.40 | 2.15 | 1764 | 1615 | 14.1 |
| 1990 | 200 | 3.37 | 2.15 | 1985 | 1685 | 14.5 |
| 1991 | 200 | 3.40 | 2.20 | 2128 | 1894 | 14.4 |
| 1992 | 200 | 3.28 | 2.14 | 2580 | 2296 | 14.8 |
| 1993 | 200 | 3.21 | 2.10 | 3525 | 3183 | 14.9 |
| 1994 | 200 | 3.31 | 2.10 | 5249 | 4559 | 15.9 |
| 1995 | 200 | 3.20 | 2.05 | 6301 | 5559 | 15.6 |
| 1996 | 200 | 3.20 | 2.00 | 7206 | 6095 | 15.9 |
| 1997 | 200 | 3.14 | 1.99 | 7896 | 6766 | 16.5 |
| 1998 | 300 | 3.12 | 1.93 | 8465 | 7235 | 18.8 |
| 1999 | 300 | 3.11 | 1.92 | 9085 | 7424 | 19.5 |
| 2000 | 300 | 3.10 | 1.83 | 9668 | 7790 | 19.9 |
| 2001 | 440 | 2.98 | 1.72 | 10896 | 8968 | 20.7 |
| 2002 | 500 | 2.93 | 1.53 | 11778 | 9215 | 21.7 |
| 2003 | 500 | 2.92 | 1.51 | 12898 | 9950 | 22.9 |
| 2004 | 500 | 2.92 | 1.48 | 14565 | 11213 | 23.7 |
| 2005 | 600 | 2.84 | 1.42 | 16601 | 13438 | 27.6 |
| 2006 | 600 | 2.81 | 1.44 | 19027 | 14472 | 28.0 |
| 2007 | 600 | 2.72 | 1.45 | 21689 | 14896 | 28.8 |
| 2008 | 600 | 2.75 | 1.29 | 24104 | 16719 | 29.9 |
| 2009 | 600 | 2.68 | 1.25 | 26864 | 18595 | 30.8 |
| 2010 | 600 | 2.70 | 1.25 | 30035 | 20219 | 30.9 |
| 2011 | 600 | 2.71 | 1.32 | 34065 | 22642 | 33.7 |
| 2012 | 600 | 2.69 | 1.31 | 37511 | 22800 | 34.4 |
| 2013 | 1920 | 2.79 | 1.51 | 40925 | 30659 | 34.9 |
| 2014 | 1920 | 2.79 | 1.53 | 44632 | 32165 | 35.1 |
| 2015 | 1920 | 2.79 | 1.48 | 48316 | 33818 | 35.5 |
| 2016 | 1920 | 2.80 | 1.49 | 52185 | 35686 | 35.8 |
| 2017 | 1920 | 2.91 | 1.48 | 56276 | 38179 | 36.4 |
| 2018 | 2250 | 2.93 | 1.50 | 61172 | 41615 | 37.3 |
| 2019 | 2250 | 2.96 | 1.53 | 66068 | 44076 | 38.2 |

注:2000年及以前为主城区数据;2001-2012年为包括萧山区和余杭区在内的市区数据;2013-2019年为包括所有区、县(市)城乡住户一体化改革后新口径数据。

a) The data on the table include the main urban districts before 2000; The data include Xiaoshan district and Yuhang district in 2001-2012; The date include all districts and counties since 2013; The data in this table are calculated at new rage by the results of integrated survey of urban households and rural households sine 2013.

# 13-03 城镇居民家庭平均每百户耐用消费品拥有量(2011-2019年)

## Number of Major Durable Consumer Goods Owned Per 100 Urban Households(2011-2019)

| 项目 Item | | 2011 | 2012 | 2013 | 2014 | 2015 | 2016 | 2017 | 2018 | 2019 |
|---|---|---|---|---|---|---|---|---|---|---|
| 家用汽车 Family Car | (辆) (unit) | 31.2 | 34.3 | 40.2 | 45.4 | 48.7 | 52.3 | 55.8 | 59.7 | 62.6 |
| 摩托车 Motorcycle | (辆) (unit) | 4.1 | 4.0 | 6.6 | 6.8 | 5.4 | 5.0 | 4.8 | 7.0 | 6.2 |
| 电冰箱 Refrigerator | (台) (unit) | 102.5 | 102.5 | 88.0 | 92.3 | 92.2 | 97.6 | 99.9 | 107.0 | 110.0 |
| 洗衣机 Washing Machine | (台) (unit) | 96.3 | 96.6 | 82.6 | 86.8 | 86.9 | 92.6 | 94.6 | 98.5 | 102.3 |
| 热水器 Water Heater | (台) (unit) | 103.4 | 105.4 | 89.4 | 93.7 | 95.5 | 101.4 | 105.2 | 109.2 | 114.0 |
| 空调器 Air Conditioner | (台) (unit) | 212.0 | 214.7 | 189.6 | 201.5 | 207.3 | 226.6 | 235.3 | 243.2 | 250.2 |
| 彩色电视机 Color TV Set | (台) (unit) | 176.9 | 178.4 | 166.4 | 174.0 | 174.1 | 183.1 | 187.3 | 187.9 | 193.8 |
| 摄像机 | (架) (unit) | 11.6 | 12.4 | 10.0 | 10.5 | 10.5 | 10.3 | - | - | - |
| 照相机 Camera | (架) (unit) | 62.1 | 63.5 | 50.6 | 54.4 | 51.5 | 48.4 | 49.9 | 34.9 | 28.9 |
| 计算机 Computer | (台) (unit) | 109.7 | 112.2 | 103.7 | 110.6 | 110.1 | 112.0 | 115.1 | 100.5 | 89.8 |
| #接入互联网的计算机 of which: Internet - connected computer | (台) (unit) | 92.3 | 98.6 | 92.5 | 100.2 | 99.8 | 100.8 | 104.9 | 92.9 | 86.0 |
| 固定电话 Telephone | (部) (set) | 84.7 | 83.6 | 51.6 | 54.2 | 50.7 | 47.3 | 45.9 | 28.9 | 19.8 |
| 移动电话 Mobile Phone | (部) (set) | 211.0 | 213.1 | 217.4 | 227.9 | 229.9 | 242.1 | 245.4 | 258.3 | 259.0 |
| #接入互联网的移动电话 of which: Internet - connected Mobile Phone | (部) (set) | - | - | 125.1 | 140.8 | 155.8 | 175.3 | 191.4 | 212.9 | 223.6 |

注:2011-2012年为包括萧山区和余杭区在内的市区数据;2013-2019年为包括所有区、县(市)城乡住户一体化改革后新口径数据。

a) The data include Xiaoshan district and Yuhang district in 2011-2012; The date include all districts and counties since 2013; The data in this table are calculated at new rage by the results of integrated survey of urban households and rural households sine 2013.

# 13-04 农村住户调查情况(1978-2019年)
## Basic Conditions of Rural Households(1978-2019)

| 年 份<br>Year | 调查户数(户)<br>Number of Households Surveyed (household) | 平均每户人口(人)<br>Average Number of Residents per Household (person) | 平均每户就业人数(人)<br>Average Number of Employed Persons Per Household (person) | 人均可支配收入(元)<br>Per Capita Annual Disposable Income of Rural Households (yuan) | 人均消费支出(元)<br>Per Capita Annual Consumption Expenditure (yuan) | 人均住房建筑面积(平方米)<br>Per Capita Floor Space (sq. m) |
|---|---|---|---|---|---|---|
| 1978 | | | | 162 | | |
| 1979 | | | | 204 | | |
| 1980 | 60 | 4.72 | 2.93 | 250 | 287 | 23.3 |
| 1981 | 60 | 4.60 | 2.70 | 333 | 294 | 25.2 |
| 1982 | 60 | 4.43 | 2.73 | 405 | 328 | 26.3 |
| 1983 | 170 | 4.55 | 2.85 | 395 | 355 | 29.9 |
| 1984 | 170 | 4.44 | 2.81 | 510 | 416 | 31.7 |
| 1985 | 420 | 4.40 | 2.88 | 624 | 542 | 29.9 |
| 1986 | 620 | 4.39 | 2.88 | 675 | 601 | 31.3 |
| 1987 | 620 | 4.34 | 2.86 | 820 | 714 | 33.1 |
| 1988 | 620 | 4.26 | 2.87 | 996 | 925 | 35.5 |
| 1989 | 620 | 4.17 | 2.85 | 1117 | 1011 | 36.8 |
| 1990 | 620 | 4.16 | 2.89 | 1171 | 923 | 39.6 |
| 1991 | 620 | 4.03 | 2.81 | 1308 | 1018 | 38.0 |
| 1992 | 620 | 4.01 | 2.81 | 1493 | 1129 | 37.5 |
| 1993 | 540 | 3.91 | 2.76 | 1748 | 1276 | 37.1 |
| 1994 | 630 | 3.85 | 2.35 | 2267 | 1884 | 37.8 |
| 1995 | 630 | 3.87 | 2.30 | 3012 | 2373 | 40.5 |
| 1996 | 630 | 3.81 | 2.77 | 3482 | 2772 | 42.2 |
| 1997 | 630 | 3.87 | 2.86 | 3785 | 2762 | 42.0 |
| 1998 | 630 | 3.87 | 2.88 | 4006 | 2858 | 46.2 |
| 1999 | 630 | 3.80 | 2.80 | 4209 | 2851 | 48.0 |
| 2000 | 630 | 3.61 | 2.59 | 4894 | 3393 | 49.0 |
| 2001 | 630 | 3.57 | 2.53 | 5330 | 3909 | 52.0 |
| 2002 | 630 | 3.53 | 2.53 | 5708 | 4444 | 52.7 |
| 2003 | 670 | 3.48 | 2.53 | 6250 | 5142 | 54.7 |
| 2004 | 670 | 3.48 | 2.54 | 6950 | 5608 | 58.9 |
| 2005 | 1100 | 3.34 | 2.34 | 7655 | 6004 | 66.0 |
| 2006 | 1100 | 3.63 | 2.52 | 8515 | 6901 | 66.5 |
| 2007 | 1100 | 3.60 | 2.61 | 9549 | 7568 | 68.0 |
| 2008 | 1100 | 3.56 | 2.58 | 10692 | 8446 | 69.7 |
| 2009 | 1100 | 3.57 | 2.59 | 11822 | 9065 | 70.7 |
| 2010 | 1100 | 3.58 | 2.59 | 13186 | 10267 | 71.2 |
| 2011 | 1100 | 3.46 | 2.49 | 15245 | 12125 | 72.5 |
| 2012 | 1100 | 3.45 | 2.50 | 17017 | 13612 | 71.0 |
| 2013 | 1280 | 3.38 | 2.03 | 21208 | 16021 | 66.9 |
| 2014 | 1280 | 3.35 | 2.05 | 23555 | 17816 | 67.9 |
| 2015 | 1280 | 3.36 | 2.02 | 25719 | 19334 | 68.8 |
| 2016 | 1280 | 3.38 | 2.04 | 27908 | 20563 | 69.9 |
| 2017 | 1280 | 3.38 | 2.03 | 30397 | 21983 | 70.9 |
| 2018 | 950 | 3.40 | 2.05 | 33193 | 24203 | 72.5 |
| 2019 | 950 | 3.42 | 2.01 | 36255 | 26296 | 74.1 |

注:2013-2019年为城乡住户一体化改革后新口径数据。

a) The data in this table are calculated at new rage by the results of integrated survey of urban households and rural households sine 2013.

# 13-05 农村居民家庭平均每百户耐用消费品拥有量(2011-2019年)
# Number of Major Durable Consumer Goods Owned Per 100 Rural Households(2011-2019)

| 项　目 | Item | 2011 | 2012 | 2013 | 2014 | 2015 | 2016 | 2017 | 2018 | 2019 |
|---|---|---|---|---|---|---|---|---|---|---|
| 家用汽车　(辆) | Family Car (Unit) | 21.6 | 27.5 | 28.8 | 34.3 | 38.2 | 42.4 | 46.5 | 50.9 | 52.7 |
| 摩托车　(辆) | Motorcycle (Unit) | 40.8 | 42.6 | 33.5 | 32.7 | 30.7 | 26.0 | 24.5 | 20.4 | 18.8 |
| 电冰箱　(台) | Refrigerator (Unit) | 93.3 | 101.8 | 93.8 | 99.5 | 103.9 | 109.0 | 112.0 | 121.8 | 124.4 |
| 洗衣机　(台) | Washing Machine (Unit) | 78.2 | 87.8 | 78.3 | 82.7 | 86.4 | 92.5 | 96.0 | 100.6 | 103.4 |
| 热水器　(台) | Water Heater (Unit) | 80.7 | 90.9 | 79.3 | 85.9 | 93.2 | 103.2 | 109.9 | 121.1 | 124.0 |
| 空调机　(台) | Air Conditioner (Unit) | 120.3 | 143.3 | 122.9 | 135.9 | 147.6 | 168.2 | 186.7 | 206.4 | 211.4 |
| 彩色电视机　(台) | Color TV Set (Unit) | 192.5 | 210.6 | 186.0 | 196.1 | 202.0 | 213.5 | 220.3 | 223.5 | 217.0 |
| 摄像机　(架) | (unit) | 1.3 | 1.8 | 2.3 | 2.5 | 2.9 | 2.4 | - | - | - |
| 照相机　(架) | Camera (Unit) | 21.7 | 26.5 | 21.1 | 21.1 | 19.6 | 19.8 | 17.4 | 10.5 | 9.7 |
| 计算机　(台) | Personal Computer (Unit) | 51.3 | 60.4 | 59.3 | 67.3 | 69.6 | 75.0 | 76.4 | 70.4 | 60.2 |
| #接入互联网的计算机　(台) | of which: Internet - connected computer (Unit) | 44.6 | 51.8 | 51.5 | 59.8 | 64.2 | 68.5 | 70.2 | 65.0 | 57.4 |
| 固定电话　(部) | Telephone (Set) | - | - | 49.6 | 52.7 | 46.4 | 35.0 | 31.8 | 23.0 | 16.1 |
| 移动电话　(部) | Mobile Phone (Set) | 230.4 | 253.1 | 235.5 | 244.6 | 253.8 | 265.2 | 274.5 | 286.4 | 267.9 |
| #接入互联网的移动电话　(部) | of which: Internet - connected Mobile Phone (Set) | - | - | 106.0 | 121.2 | 141.7 | 172.2 | 200.8 | 214.7 | 209.6 |

注:2013-2019年为城乡住户一体化改革后新口径数据。

a) The data in this table are calculated at new rage by the results of integrated survey of urban households and rural households since 2013.

# 13-06 就业人员工资总额(1978-2019年)

## Total Wages of Employed Persons(1978-2019)

单位:万元 (10000 yuan)

| 年 份 Year | 全市(非私营及规上私营) Total (includes Non-private Units and private units above designated size) | 非私营单位 Non-private | 市区(非私营及规上私营) Urban District(includes Non-private Units and private units above designated size) | 非私营单位 Non-private |
|---|---|---|---|---|
| 1978 | | 43775 | | 28256 |
| 1979 | | 52127 | | 34318 |
| 1980 | | 67918 | | 45574 |
| 1981 | | 72896 | | 48809 |
| 1982 | | 75584 | | 50959 |
| 1983 | | 78336 | | 52909 |
| 1984 | | 102223 | | 69135 |
| 1985 | | 130114 | | 87774 |
| 1986 | | 157471 | | 105995 |
| 1987 | | 180077 | | 121003 |
| 1988 | | 230868 | | 152859 |
| 1989 | | 253956 | | 167055 |
| 1990 | | 277910 | | 182985 |
| 1991 | | 313906 | | 209052 |
| 1992 | | 377614 | | 253653 |
| 1993 | | 534537 | | 359041 |
| 1994 | | 772236 | | 521669 |
| 1995 | | 890488 | | 615450 |
| 1996 | | 973592 | | 683244 |
| 1997 | | 1073862 | | 762957 |
| 1998 | | 1112718 | | 803264 |
| 1999 | | 1180947 | | 864418 |
| 2000 | | 1267524 | | 949872 |
| 2001 | | 1481659 | | 1279749 |
| 2002 | | 1614676 | | 1398222 |
| 2003 | | 1867776 | | 1617504 |
| 2004 | 2844691 | 2188159 | 2313930 | 1859164 |
| 2005 | 3711915 | 2970200 | 3112937 | 2584779 |
| 2006 | 4526841 | 3811735 | 3830043 | 3338568 |
| 2007 | 6233799 | 4954813 | 5256791 | 4317965 |
| 2008 | 8592198 | 6416424 | 7338932 | 5679543 |
| 2009 | 9909330 | 7549145 | 8475547 | 6665279 |
| 2010 | 12305726 | 9330552 | 10531483 | 8238017 |
| 2011 | 15012179 | 11222834 | 12934215 | 9954506 |
| 2012 | 19540005 | 14839012 | 17115217 | 13217453 |
| 2013 | 23604682 | 17582336 | 20762852 | 15820468 |
| 2014 | 26630950 | 19822713 | 24629017 | 18551986 |
| 2015 | 28884146 | 21523984 | 26718242 | 20179320 |
| 2016 | 32370091 | 24176045 | 29918514 | 22617274 |
| 2017 | 35985206 | 26467155 | 34266225 | 25422943 |
| 2018 | 39952564 | 28646933 | 38177817 | 27526523 |
| 2019 | 45772971 | 32985194 | 43842112 | 31754987 |

注:口径范围,1997年及以前为全市全部职工,1998-2012为在岗职工,2013年起为就业人员。2004年起包含规模以上私营单位。

a) Data on this table refer to wages of all employees before 1997, that refer to all staff and workers in 1998-2012, and refer to employed persons since 2013. Data on this bill includes Private units above designated size since 2004.

# 13－07 就业人员年平均工资(1978－2019年)

# Average Annual Wages of Employed Persons(1978－2019)

单位:元 (yuan)

| 年 份<br>Year | 全市(非私营及规上私营)<br>Total (includes Non－private Units and private units above designated size) | 非私营单位<br>Non－private | 市区(非私营及规上私营)<br>Urban District(includes Non－private Units and private units above designated size) | 非私营单位<br>Non－private | 市区全社会在岗职工<br>The Fully Employed Persons in Urban Districts | 全社会就业人员 |
|---|---|---|---|---|---|---|
| 1978 | | 597 | | 642 | | |
| 1979 | | 643 | | 692 | | |
| 1980 | | 777 | | 814 | | |
| 1981 | | 783 | | 810 | | |
| 1982 | | 791 | | 809 | | |
| 1983 | | 813 | | 835 | | |
| 1984 | | 1036 | | 1071 | | |
| 1985 | | 1266 | | 1316 | | |
| 1986 | | 1469 | | 1536 | | |
| 1987 | | 1616 | | 1690 | | |
| 1988 | | 1986 | | 2073 | | |
| 1989 | | 2173 | | 2261 | | |
| 1990 | | 2382 | | 2486 | | |
| 1991 | | 2586 | | 2706 | | |
| 1992 | | 3071 | | 3233 | | |
| 1993 | | 4220 | | 4561 | | |
| 1994 | | 6118 | | 6597 | | |
| 1995 | | 7156 | | 7786 | | |
| 1996 | | 7966 | | 7851 | | |
| 1997 | | 9108 | | 10048 | | |
| 1998 | | 10555 | | 11512 | | |
| 1999 | | 12187 | | 13225 | | |
| 2000 | | 14257 | | 15454 | | |
| 2001 | | 18319 | | 18962 | 18205 | |
| 2002 | | 21418 | | 22091 | 19749 | |
| 2003 | | 24668 | | 25535 | 20113 | |
| 2004 | 21879 | 28891 | 24204 | 30719 | 22235 | |
| 2005 | 24685 | 31069 | 26366 | 32166 | 22645 | |
| 2006 | 27620 | 32791 | 29397 | 33967 | 23581 | |
| 2007 | 29864 | 36496 | 31625 | 37991 | 25489 | |
| 2008 | 32513 | 40193 | 34107 | 41501 | 27863 | |
| 2009 | 35638 | 43947 | 37270 | 45149 | 30480 | |
| 2010 | 39772 | 48772 | 41303 | 49938 | 34330 | |
| 2011 | 45775 | 54408 | 47695 | 55958 | 38837 | |
| 2012 | 51077 | 56417 | 52610 | 57548 | 42493 | |
| 2013 | 55124 | 63664 | 56857 | 64941 | 46831 | |
| 2014 | 60904 | 69209 | 61924 | 70034 | 51449 | |
| 2015 | 66322 | 76073 | 67569 | 77061 | 55908 | |
| 2016 | 73390 | 85022 | 74589 | 85767 | 61174 | |
| 2017 | 80482 | 93891 | 81440 | 94430 | 67047 | |
| 2018 | 88752 | 103798 | 89762 | 104479 | － | 72951 |
| 2019 | 101069 | 117339 | 102289 | 118337 | － | 80817 |

注:口径范围,1997年及以前为全市全部职工,1998－2012为在岗职工,2013年起为就业人员。2004年起包含规模以上私营单位。2015年富阳纳入市区统计范围;2017年临安纳入市区统计范围。

a) Data on this table refer to wages of all employees before 1997, that refer to all staff and workers in 1998－2012, and refer to employed persons since 2013. Data on this bill includes Private units above designated size since 2004. Fuyang was included in urban statistics since 2015, Lin'an was included in ruban statistics since2017.

# 13－08　非私营及规上私营单位就业人员工资总额(2019 年)

## Total Wages of Employed Persons of Non－private Units and Private Units Above Designated Size(2019)

单位：万元　　　　(10000 yuan)

| 项　目 | Item | 就业人员工资总额 Total Wages of Employed Persons | 非私营 Non－private | 在岗职工工资总额 Total Wages of Fully Employed Staff and Workers | 非私营 Non－private | 其他就业人员工资总额 Total Wages of Other Employed Persons | 非私营 Non－private |
|---|---|---|---|---|---|---|---|
| **全市总计** | **Whole city Total** | **45772971** | **32985194** | **43644872** | **32021037** | **2128100** | **964156** |
| 市区总计 | Urban District | 43842112 | 31754987 | 41767232 | 30817833 | 2074880 | 937153 |
| #上城区 | Shangcheng | 3076009 | 2513862 | 2873814 | 2419025 | 202195 | 94837 |
| 下城区 | Xiacheng | 3748862 | 3233744 | 3425461 | 3001265 | 323401 | 232479 |
| 江干区 | Jianggan | 4709862 | 2811921 | 4078511 | 2699415 | 631351 | 112506 |
| 拱墅区 | Gongshu | 2929136 | 1698251 | 2742078 | 1613950 | 187058 | 84301 |
| 西湖区 | Xihu | 6499662 | 5100023 | 6345822 | 4999113 | 153840 | 100910 |
| 高新(滨江)区 | Hi－Tech(Binjiang) | 5617633 | 4604836 | 5538071 | 4544192 | 79563 | 60644 |
| 萧山区 | Xiaoshan | 5192762 | 3325505 | 5004983 | 3241253 | 187779 | 84251 |
| 余杭区 | Yuhang | 5622090 | 3840277 | 5470214 | 3787101 | 151876 | 53176 |
| 富阳区 | Fuyang | 1892153 | 1378211 | 1860411 | 1360351 | 31742 | 17860 |
| 临安区 | Lin'an | 1224183 | 776009 | 1193699 | 750315 | 30484 | 25694 |
| 钱塘新区 | Qiantang New Area | 3101959 | 2261227 | 3015620 | 2198667 | 86340 | 62560 |
| 西湖风景名胜区 | The West Lake Scenic Zone | 227800 | 211121 | 218549 | 203186 | 9251 | 7935 |
| 桐庐县 | Tonglu | 858424 | 452676 | 841103 | 444816 | 17322 | 7860 |
| 淳安县 | Chun'an | 470512 | 370439 | 449108 | 356102 | 21404 | 14338 |
| 建德市 | Jiande | 601923 | 407092 | 587429 | 402287 | 14494 | 4806 |

单位:万元　　13－08　续表　continued　　(10000 yuan)

| 项　目<br>Item | 就业人员工资总额<br>Total Wages of Employed Persons | 非私营<br>Non－private | 在岗职工工资总额<br>Total Wages of Fully Employed Staff and Workers | 非私营<br>Non－private | 其他就业人员工资总额<br>Total Wages of Other Employed Persons | 非私营<br>Non－private |
|---|---|---|---|---|---|---|
| **按国民经济行业分组**<br>**Grouped by Sector** | | | | | | |
| 农、林、牧、渔业<br>Farming, Forestry, Animal Husbandry & Fishery | 6919 | 6919 | 6493 | 6493 | 426 | 426 |
| 采矿业<br>Mining | 20386 | 14078 | 20222 | 14041 | 164 | 38 |
| 制造业<br>Manufacturing | 8857104 | 6008475 | 8725986 | 5914730 | 131119 | 93745 |
| 电力、热力、燃气及水生产和供应业<br>Production & Supply of Electricity, Heat, Gas & Water | 238376 | 224584 | 236425 | 222741 | 1952 | 1843 |
| 建筑业<br>Construction | 9178687 | 4221020 | 7965521 | 4027185 | 1213166 | 193835 |
| 批发和零售业<br>Wholesale & Retail Trades | 2963441 | 1876267 | 2903714 | 1834504 | 59727 | 41763 |
| 交通运输、仓储和邮政业<br>Transportation, Storage and Post | 1345504 | 998981 | 1325702 | 985822 | 19802 | 13159 |
| 住宿和餐饮业<br>Hotels and Catering Services | 644200 | 416924 | 603972 | 387599 | 40228 | 29325 |
| 信息传输、软件和信息技术服务业<br>Information Transmission, Software and Information Technology | 5879900 | 4545652 | 5857024 | 4534006 | 22876 | 11646 |
| 金融业<br>Financial Intermediation | 2334660 | 2331538 | 2111836 | 2108714 | 222824 | 222824 |
| 房地产业<br>Real Estate | 1571290 | 1135944 | 1526406 | 1102107 | 44884 | 33837 |
| 租赁和商务服务业<br>Leasing and Business Services | 1850741 | 1129233 | 1776506 | 1071880 | 74235 | 57354 |
| 科学研究、技术服务业<br>Scientific Research, Technical Services | 1917221 | 1527559 | 1869654 | 1489267 | 47567 | 38292 |
| 水利、环境和公共设施管理业<br>Management of Water Conservancy, Environment and Public Facilities | 399587 | 322499 | 391758 | 318562 | 7829 | 3936 |
| 居民服务、修理和其他服务业<br>Service to Honseholds, Repair and Other Services | 244457 | 145583 | 230194 | 140424 | 14263 | 5158 |
| 教育<br>Education | 2974515 | 2892622 | 2898455 | 2818232 | 76060 | 74390 |
| 卫生和社会工作<br>Health Care and Social Work | 2464287 | 2344256 | 2369378 | 2256869 | 94908 | 87387 |
| 文化、体育和娱乐业<br>Culture, Sports and Entertainment | 402266 | 363628 | 386717 | 348950 | 15549 | 14678 |
| 公共管理、社会保障和社会组织<br>Public Management, Social Security and Social Organizations | 2479432 | 2479432 | 2438911 | 2438911 | 40522 | 40522 |

# 13－09 非私营及规上私营单位就业人员平均工资(2019 年)

## Average Annual Wages of Employed Persons of Non－private Units and Private Units Above Designated Size(2019)

单位:元 (yuan)

| 项目 |  Item | 就业人员 Total employment | 非私营单位 Non－private | 在岗职工 Staff and Workers | 非私营单位 Non－private |
|---|---|---|---|---|---|
| **全市** | **Total** | **101069** | **117339** | **104102** | **120308** |
| 市区 | Urban District | 102289 | 118337 | 105465 | 121398 |
| #上城区 | Shangcheng | 130081 | 150622 | 133246 | 153779 |
| 下城区 | Xiacheng | 117227 | 130278 | 129155 | 143826 |
| 江干区 | Jianggan | 95551 | 120156 | 100705 | 124942 |
| 拱墅区 | Gongshu | 86292 | 95883 | 90612 | 100795 |
| 西湖区 | Xihu | 106047 | 108402 | 108388 | 110045 |
| 高新(滨江)区 | Hi－Tech(Binjiang) | 151469 | 167066 | 153395 | 169598 |
| 萧山区 | Xiaoshan | 81369 | 90606 | 82988 | 91551 |
| 余杭区 | Yuhang | 104556 | 137961 | 108012 | 140639 |
| 富阳区 | Fuyang | 76737 | 84359 | 77350 | 85102 |
| 临安区 | Lin'an | 84290 | 102323 | 85150 | 104661 |
| 钱塘新区 | Qiantang New Area | 94986 | 107783 | 95158 | 107899 |
| 西湖风景名胜区 | The West Lake Scenic Zone | 117157 | 126647 | 120499 | 130331 |
| 桐庐县 | Tonglu | 79355 | 100238 | 79995 | 101062 |
| 淳安县 | Chun'an | 83969 | 93307 | 86153 | 95531 |
| 建德市 | Jiande | 76620 | 95057 | 78416 | 96437 |

| 项目<br>Item | 就业人员<br>Total employment | 非私营单位<br>Non-private | 在岗职工<br>Staff and Workers | 非私营单位<br>Non-private |
|---|---|---|---|---|
| **按国民经济行业分组**<br>**Grouped by Sector** | | | | |
| 农、林、牧、渔业<br>Farming, Forestry, Animal Husbandry & Fishery | 65332 | 65332 | 68781 | 68781 |
| 采矿业<br>Mining | 97913 | 123494 | 98690 | 124143 |
| 制造业<br>Manufacturing | 87314 | 100280 | 87358 | 100269 |
| 电力、热力、燃气及水生产和供应业<br>Production & Supply of Electricity, Heat, Gas & Water | 135234 | 139910 | 136496 | 141289 |
| 建筑业<br>Construction | 64100 | 65192 | 64576 | 65775 |
| 批发和零售业<br>Wholesale & Retail Trades | 95114 | 108533 | 96394 | 110598 |
| 交通运输、仓储和邮政业<br>Transportation, Storage and Post | 98238 | 99636 | 99056 | 100671 |
| 住宿和餐饮业<br>Hotels and Catering Services | 55228 | 54613 | 58477 | 59476 |
| 信息传输、软件和信息技术服务业<br>Information Transmission, Software and Information Technology | 227537 | 255893 | 229048 | 257342 |
| 金融业<br>Financial Intermediation | 195026 | 195335 | 247224 | 247871 |
| 房地产业<br>Real Estate | 90844 | 87755 | 92472 | 89084 |
| 租赁和商务服务业<br>Leasing and Business Services | 91302 | 93358 | 92608 | 95135 |
| 科学研究、技术服务业<br>Scientific Research, Technical Services | 146279 | 161573 | 148782 | 164934 |
| 水利、环境和公共设施管理业<br>Management of Water Conservancy, Environment and Public Facilities | 88065 | 103074 | 90632 | 104526 |
| 居民服务、修理和其他服务业<br>Service to Honseholds, Repair and Other Services | 64908 | 69023 | 64491 | 69339 |
| 教育<br>Education | 138592 | 139942 | 143841 | 145341 |
| 卫生和社会工业<br>Health Care and Social Work | 174082 | 183215 | 178230 | 187735 |
| 文化、体育和娱乐业<br>Culture, Sports and Entertainment | 138079 | 149211 | 142906 | 154999 |
| 公共管理、社会保障和社会组织<br>Public Management, Social Security and Social Organizations | 172913 | 172913 | 177588 | 177588 |

# 13－10 市区消费价格指数(1978－2019年)

## Consumer Price Indices in Urban District(1978－2019)

(上年=100) (Preceding Year=100)

| 年 份<br>Year | 居民消费价格指数<br>Consumer Price Index | 商品零售价格指数<br>Retail Price Index |
|---|---|---|
| 1978 | 100.1 | 100.1 |
| 1979 | 100.4 | 100.9 |
| 1980 | 100.8 | 109.3 |
| 1981 | 102.0 | 102.0 |
| 1982 | 102.0 | 102.3 |
| 1983 | 102.1 | 102.3 |
| 1984 | 103.1 | 103.1 |
| 1985 | 117.2 | 117.5 |
| 1986 | 106.0 | 106.1 |
| 1987 | 110.5 | 111.3 |
| 1988 | 121.9 | 123.4 |
| 1989 | 117.8 | 118.2 |
| 1990 | 104.6 | 104.4 |
| 1991 | 107.5 | 106.9 |
| 1992 | 110.4 | 110.2 |
| 1993 | 121.4 | 117.3 |
| 1994 | 121.5 | 118.8 |
| 1995 | 116.5 | 113.3 |
| 1996 | 110.5 | 107.2 |
| 1997 | 106.7 | 102.4 |
| 1998 | 101.8 | 99.8 |
| 1999 | 100.4 | 98.2 |
| 2000 | 100.8 | 98.3 |
| 2001 | 99.5 | 95.3 |
| 2002 | 98.8 | 97.9 |
| 2003 | 99.5 | 98.1 |
| 2004 | 102.5 | 101.6 |
| 2005 | 101.7 | 100.3 |
| 2006 | 101.2 | 100.2 |
| 2007 | 103.5 | 103.1 |
| 2008 | 104.9 | 106.0 |
| 2009 | 98.6 | 98.6 |
| 2010 | 103.9 | 103.7 |
| 2011 | 104.8 | 104.4 |
| 2012 | 102.5 | 101.9 |
| 2013 | 102.5 | 101.5 |
| 2014 | 102.0 | 100.8 |
| 2015 | 101.8 | 100.2 |
| 2016 | 102.6 | 101.5 |
| 2017 | 102.5 | 101.0 |
| 2018 | 102.3 | 102.0 |
| 2019 | 103.1 | 103.1 |

# 13－11 市区居民消费价格分类指数(2019 年)
# Consumer Price Indices by Category in Urban District(2019)

(上年＝100) (Preceding Year＝100)

| 项目 | Item | 2019 |
|---|---|---|
| **居民消费价格总指数** | **Consumer Price Index** | **103.1** |
| **一、食品烟酒** | **Food, Tobacco and Liquor** | **106.3** |
| 1.食品 | Food | 107.9 |
| (1)粮食 | Grain | 101.1 |
| (2)薯类 | Tubers | 106.1 |
| (3)豆类 | Beans | 109.9 |
| (4)食用油 | Edible Oil and Fats | 102.6 |
| (5)菜 | Vegetables | 103.1 |
| (6)畜肉类 | Meat of Livestock | 123.1 |
| (7)禽肉类 | Meat of Poultry | 108.2 |
| (8)水产品 | Aquatic Products | 99.1 |
| (9)蛋类 | Eggs | 105.6 |
| (10)奶类 | Milk | 104.1 |
| (11)干鲜瓜果类 | Dried and Fresh Melons and Fruits | 112.8 |
| (12)糖果糕点类 | Candy and Cake | 101.2 |
| (13)调味品 | Flavoring | 105.7 |
| (14)其他食品类 | Other Foods | 101.9 |
| 2.茶及饮料 | Tea and Beverages | 104.6 |
| 3.烟酒 | Tobacco and Liquor | 100.8 |
| 4.在外餐饮 | Dining Out | 104.8 |
| **二、衣着** | **Clothing** | **101.3** |
| 1.服装 | Garments | 101.8 |
| 2.服装材料 | Garments Material | 100.0 |
| 3.其他衣着及配件 | Other Clothing and Parts | 99.4 |
| 4.衣着加工服务费 | Clothing Manufacturing Services | 103.7 |

| 项　目 | Item | 2019 |
|---|---|---|
| 5. 鞋类 | Footwear | 99.0 |
| **三、居住** | **Residence** | **100.9** |
| 1. 租赁房房租 | Rent of Rental Housing | 101.9 |
| 2. 住房保养维修及管理 | Housing Maintenance and Management | 100.3 |
| 3. 水电燃料 | Water, Electricity and Fuels | 100.7 |
| 4. 自有住房 | Private Housing | 101.0 |
| **四、生活用品及服务** | **Articles for Daily Use and Services** | **103.0** |
| 1. 家具及室内装饰品 | Furniture and Interior Decorations | 102.3 |
| 2. 家用器具 | Home Appliances | 99.4 |
| 3. 家用纺织品 | Home Textiles | 102.2 |
| 4. 家庭日用杂品 | Daily Use Household Articles | 105.4 |
| 5. 个人护理用品 | Personal - care Supplies | 106.0 |
| 6. 家庭服务 | Household Services | 103.7 |
| **五、交通和通信** | **Transport and Communications** | **99.0** |
| 1. 交通 | Transport | 98.6 |
| 2. 通信 | Communications | 100.0 |
| **六、教育文化和娱乐** | **Education, Culture and Recreation** | **104.3** |
| 1. 教育 | Education | 103.5 |
| 2. 文化娱乐 | Cultural and Recreation | 105.4 |
| **七、医疗保健** | **Health Care** | **107.0** |
| 1. 药品及医疗器具 | Medicine and Medical Instrument | 111.3 |
| 2. 医疗服务 | Medical Services | 104.1 |
| **八、其他用品和服务** | **Other Articles and Services** | **102.8** |
| 1. 其他用品类 | Other Articles | 104.7 |
| 2. 其他服务类 | Other Services | 101.6 |

# 13－12　市区零售价格分类指数(2019 年)

## Retail Price Indices by Category in Urban District(2019)

(上年＝100)　　(Preceding Year＝100)

| 项　　目 | Item | 2019 |
|---|---|---|
| **商品零售价格指数** | **Retail Price Index** | **103.1** |
| **一、食品** | **Food** | **106.8** |
| 1.粮食 | Grain | 101.1 |
| 2.薯类 | Tubers | 106.1 |
| 3.豆类 | Beans | 109.9 |
| 4.食用油 | Edible Oil and Fats | 102.6 |
| 5.菜 | Vegetables | 103.1 |
| 6.畜肉类 | Meat of Livestock | 123.1 |
| 7.禽肉类 | Meat of Poultry | 108.2 |
| 8.水产品 | Aquatic Products | 99.1 |
| 9.蛋类 | Eggs | 105.6 |
| 10.奶类 | Milk | 104.1 |
| 11.干鲜瓜果类 | Dried and Fresh Melons and Fruits | 112.8 |
| 12.糖果糕点类 | Candy and Cake | 101.2 |
| 13.调味品 | Flavoring | 105.4 |
| 14.其他食品类 | Other Foods | 101.9 |
| 15.在外餐饮 | Dining out | 104.8 |
| **二、饮料、烟酒** | **Beverages,Tobacco and Liquor** | **101.8** |
| 1.茶及饮料 | Tea and Beverages | 104.6 |
| 2.烟草 | Tobacco | 100.0 |
| 3.酒类 | Liquor | 102.6 |
| **三、服装、鞋帽** | **Garments,Shoes and Hats** | **101.2** |
| 1.服装 | Garments | 101.8 |
| 2.鞋帽袜 | Footgear and Hat | 99.4 |
| 3.其他衣着配件 | Other Clothing and Parts | 95.2 |
| **四、纺织品** | **Textiles** | **101.6** |
| 1 服装材料 | Garments Material | 100.0 |
| 2.床上用品 | Bedding | 102.5 |
| **五、家用电器及音像器材** | **Household Appliances,Music and Video Equipment** | **98.6** |
| 1.家庭设备 | Household Equipment | 99.8 |
| 2.文娱用耐用消费品 | Durable Consumer Goods for Entertainment | 97.2 |

| 项　　目 | Item | 2019 |
| --- | --- | --- |
| 3. 专业音像器材 | Audio and Video Equipment | 93.9 |
| **六、文化办公用品** | **Cultural and office Appliances** | **100.9** |
| **七、日用品** | **Articles for Daily Use** | **104.6** |
| 1. 日用百货 | General Merchandise for Daily Use | 107.0 |
| 2. 厨具餐具茶具 | Kitchen Ware, Table Ware, Tea Set | 107.1 |
| 3. 清洗用品 | Cleaning Supplies | 103.0 |
| 4. 其他日用品 | Other Articles for Daily Use | 100.0 |
| **八、体育娱乐用品** | **Sports and Recreation Articles** | **102.7** |
| 1. 体育户外用品 | Sports Outdoor Products | 97.7 |
| 2. 娱乐用品 | Recreation Articles | 104.7 |
| **九、交通、通信用品** | **Transportation and Communication Appliances** | **100.1** |
| 1. 交通运输机械 | Transportation Vehicles | 100.0 |
| 2. 通信器材 | Equipment of Communication | 101.0 |
| **十、家具** | **Furniture** | **103.2** |
| **十一、化妆品** | **Cosmetics** | **106.7** |
| **十二、金银饰品** | **Gold and Silver Ornaments** | **107.3** |
| **十三、中西药品及医疗保健用品** | **Traditional Chinese and Western Medicine and Health Care Articles** | **111.2** |
| 1. 医疗卫生器具 | Medical Instruments and Articles | 103.2 |
| 2. 中药 | Traditional Chinese Medicines | 103.4 |
| 3. 西药 | Western Medicines | 109.2 |
| 4. 保健器具及用品 | Articles for Health Care | 122.0 |
| **十四、书报杂志及电子出版物** | **Books, Newspapers, Magazines and Electronic Publications** | **104.7** |
| 1. 教材及参考书 | Teaching Materials and Reference Books | 103.5 |
| 2. 书报杂志 | Books, Newspapers and Magazines | 110.1 |
| 3. 计算机办公软件 | Computer Office Software | 96.2 |
| **十五、燃料** | **Fuels** | **97.0** |
| 1. 煤炭及制品 | Coal and Coal Products | 99.0 |
| 2. 石油及制品 | Oil and Oil Products | 96.8 |
| **十六、建筑材料及五金电料** | **Building Materials and Hardware** | **100.7** |
| 1. 建筑装璜材料 | Building Decoration Materials | 100.3 |
| 2. 五金水暖 | Hardware | 102.0 |

# 13-13 工业生产者出厂价格指数(2012-2019年)

# Producer Price Indices for Industrial Products(2012-2019)

(上年=100) (Preceding Year=100)

| 项目 Item | 2012 | 2013 | 2014 | 2015 | 2016 | 2017 | 2018 | 2019 |
|---|---|---|---|---|---|---|---|---|
| **工业生产者出厂价格总指数 Total Producer Price Indices for Industrial Products** | **97.2** | **98.5** | **98.6** | **96.5** | **99.2** | **104.4** | **102.4** | **99.0** |
| **一、按轻重工业分 Grouped by Industries** | | | | | | | | |
| **轻工业 Light Industry** | **98.1** | **99.9** | **99.2** | **97.4** | **99.8** | **104.0** | **102.0** | **98.1** |
| 以农产品为原料 Made from Agricultural Products | 99.4 | 100.8 | 99.9 | 98.5 | 99.8 | 102.6 | 101.6 | 98.6 |
| 以非农产品为原料 Made from Non-agricultural Products | 96.1 | 98.4 | 98.2 | 95.8 | 99.8 | 106.1 | 102.5 | 97.2 |
| **重工业 Heavy Industry** | **96.5** | **97.5** | **98.2** | **95.8** | **98.7** | **104.6** | **102.6** | **99.6** |
| 采掘 Mining & Quarrying Industry | 101.3 | 101.0 | 104.2 | 94.9 | 97.3 | 100.6 | 101.7 | 96.9 |
| 原料 Raw Materials Industry | 96.9 | 97.5 | 96.7 | 92.5 | 96.4 | 106.7 | 102.3 | 100.0 |
| 加工 Manufacturing Industry | 96.4 | 97.5 | 98.5 | 96.7 | 99.4 | 104.1 | 102.7 | 99.5 |
| **二、按二大部类分 Grouped by Means of Producting and Consumer Goods** | | | | | | | | |
| **生产资料 Means of Production** | **95.5** | **97.8** | **98.0** | **95.3** | **98.8** | **105.8** | **103.0** | **98.4** |
| 采掘 Mining | 101.3 | 101.0 | 104.2 | 94.9 | 97.3 | 100.6 | 101.7 | 96.9 |
| 原料 Raw Materials | 92.6 | 96.5 | 95.7 | 91.0 | 96.1 | 109.9 | 103.2 | 95.8 |
| 加工 Manufacture | 96.4 | 98.2 | 98.7 | 96.6 | 99.6 | 104.7 | 103.0 | 99.2 |
| **生活资料 Consumer Goods** | **102.6** | **100.6** | **100.6** | **100.1** | **100.1** | **99.9** | **100.3** | **100.8** |
| 食品 Foods | 101.8 | 101.0 | 101.1 | 100.9 | 100.0 | 99.4 | 100.2 | 101.1 |
| 衣着 Clothing | 104.6 | 102.0 | 100.1 | 100.1 | 101.1 | 99.9 | 101.3 | 99.6 |
| 一般日用品 Articles for Daily Use | 102.3 | 99.8 | 100.7 | 99.9 | 100.5 | 100.4 | 99.7 | 101.1 |
| 耐用消费品 Durable Consumer Goods | 102.0 | 99.6 | 100.0 | 99.2 | 99.1 | 99.7 | 100.7 | 100.6 |

| 项　　目<br>Item | 2012 | 2013 | 2014 | 2015 | 2016 | 2017 | 2018 | 2019 |
|---|---|---|---|---|---|---|---|---|
| **三、按工业部门分<br>Grouped by Industrial Sector** | | | | | | | | |
| 冶金工业<br>Metallurgical Industry | 93.3 | 95.4 | 96.2 | 93.2 | 101.7 | 115.0 | 103.9 | 97.7 |
| 电力工业<br>Power Industry | 101.7 | 99.1 | 99.6 | 98.2 | 97.8 | 100.2 | 100.9 | 100.9 |
| 煤炭及炼焦工业<br>Coal and Coking Industry | | | | | | | | |
| 石油工业<br>Petroleum Industry | 103.0 | 100.5 | 100.5 | 92.4 | 87.7 | 97.9 | 101.6 | 111.1 |
| 化学工业<br>Chemical Industry | 93.8 | 97.3 | 95.8 | 92.7 | 97.3 | 107.8 | 103.4 | 96.2 |
| 机械工业<br>Machine Building Industry | 97.6 | 98.1 | 98.9 | 97.6 | 99.4 | 101.4 | 100.2 | 99.3 |
| 建材材料工业<br>Building Materials Industry | 94.0 | 97.3 | 103.0 | 94.0 | 96.3 | 111.5 | 123.1 | 105.4 |
| 森林工业<br>Timber Industry | 100.7 | 101.0 | 101.3 | 99.9 | 98.9 | 100.9 | 100.5 | 100.0 |
| 食品工业<br>Food Industry | 102.0 | 101.2 | 100.5 | 100.2 | 100.2 | 99.6 | 100.4 | 101.2 |
| 纺织工业<br>Textile Industry | 95.5 | 101.1 | 98.9 | 96.3 | 100.1 | 103.5 | 101.7 | 97.8 |
| 缝纫工业<br>Tailoring Industry | 104.6 | 102.6 | 100.5 | 99.8 | 99.6 | 99.6 | 101.2 | 99.6 |
| 皮革工业<br>Leather Industry | 103.4 | 101.1 | 101.0 | 100.4 | 100.5 | 101.3 | 101.4 | 100.2 |
| 造纸工业<br>Paper Industry | 96.7 | 96.3 | 99.7 | 98.5 | 98.9 | 109.8 | 103.0 | 93.2 |
| 文教艺术用品工业<br>Cultural,Educational & Handicrafts Articles | 100.1 | 100.0 | 98.8 | 98.9 | 99.5 | 99.7 | 97.9 | 98.0 |
| 其它工业<br>Others | 103.9 | 101.3 | 104.6 | 102.9 | 105.5 | 102.5 | 103.0 | 105.4 |

# 13－14　工业生产者购进价格指数(2012－2019年)

# Purchasing Price Indices for Industrial Producers(2012－2019)

(上年＝100)　　(Preceding Year＝100)

| 项　　目<br>Item | 2012 | 2013 | 2014 | 2015 | 2016 | 2017 | 2018 | 2019 |
|---|---|---|---|---|---|---|---|---|
| **工业生产者购进价格指数<br>Purchasing Price Index for Industrial Producers** | **94.6** | **97.3** | **97.3** | **92.9** | **98.9** | **108.4** | **103.7** | **96.8** |
| 燃料动力类<br>Fuel and Power | 98.2 | 96.9 | 99.0 | 95.1 | 93.6 | 105.7 | 103.1 | 99.3 |
| 黑色金属材料类<br>Ferrous and Metals | 88.7 | 95.0 | 92.4 | 85.9 | 100.9 | 115.5 | 106.8 | 97.6 |
| 1. 钢材<br>Rolled－steel | 88.5 | 95.4 | 92.5 | 86.3 | 101.0 | 115.9 | 106.8 | 97.4 |
| 2. 其他<br>Other | 91.2 | 90.1 | 90.3 | 80.5 | 98.2 | 106.8 | 105.1 | 100.7 |
| 有色金属材料及电线类<br>Non－ferrous Metals and Electric Wire | 93.1 | 93.7 | 94.5 | 92.2 | 101.3 | 114.7 | 101.3 | 99.8 |
| 化工原料类<br>Chemical Raw Materials | 94.2 | 97.0 | 97.7 | 91.7 | 100.8 | 110.9 | 105.4 | 91.9 |
| 木材及纸浆类<br>Wood and Paper Pulps | 97.7 | 98.8 | 98.5 | 98.5 | 99.8 | 111.6 | 104.4 | 92.9 |
| 建筑材料及非金属类<br>Building Materials | 99.5 | 99.4 | 105.7 | 96.9 | 99.0 | 117.1 | 120.9 | 102.7 |
| 其他工业原材料及半成品类<br>Other Industrial Raw Materials and Semi－products | 99.1 | 97.8 | 98.9 | 96.7 | 98.8 | 102.7 | 101.1 | 98.0 |
| 农副产品类<br>Farm and Sideline Products | 97.2 | 98.4 | 100.4 | 99.3 | 99.3 | 106.9 | 96.5 | 97.4 |
| 纺织原料类<br>Textile Raw Materials | 96.3 | 101.9 | 99.9 | 97.1 | 98.8 | 104.8 | 101.9 | 98.6 |

# 13-15 住宅销售价格指数(2019 年)
# Residential Sales Price Indices(2019)

| 月份 | Month | 新建商品住宅 New Residential Commodities Building | | 二手住宅 The Second - hand Residence | |
|---|---|---|---|---|---|
| | | 上月=100 Lost month=100 | 上年同期=100 Preceding Year =100 | 上月=100 Lost month=100 | 上年同期=100 Preceding Year =100 |
| 一月 | January | 100.4 | 106.0 | 100.1 | 104.5 |
| 二月 | February | 100.5 | 106.6 | 100.0 | 104.0 |
| 三月 | March | 100.4 | 106.6 | 100.7 | 104.0 |
| 四月 | April | 101.0 | 107.7 | 100.9 | 104.1 |
| 五月 | May | 100.8 | 108.5 | 101.3 | 104.5 |
| 六月 | June | 101.1 | 109.1 | 100.4 | 104.1 |
| 七月 | July | 100.5 | 108.8 | 100.1 | 103.2 |
| 八月 | August | 100.0 | 108.2 | 99.9 | 102.4 |
| 九月 | September | 100.2 | 108.2 | 99.8 | 102.1 |
| 十月 | October | 99.8 | 106.7 | 99.9 | 102.4 |
| 十一月 | November | 99.9 | 105.8 | 100.0 | 102.9 |
| 十二月 | December | 100.3 | 105.0 | 100.2 | 103.0 |

## 13－16　分地区社会办福利院情况(2019 年末)
## Basic Statistics on Welfare Homes by Region(End of 2019)

| 地区 Region | 单位(个) Homes (unit) | 职工(人) Staff and Workers (person) | 床位数(张) Beds (bed) | 在院人数(人) Persons Housed (person) | 老人(人) Seniors(person) |
|---|---|---|---|---|---|
| **全市 Total** | **328** | **6898** | **74685** | **35542** | **35083** |
| 市区 Urban District | 234 | 6003 | 64916 | 31468 | 31035 |
| #萧山区 Xiaoshan | 41 | 1552 | 8879 | 4342 | 4299 |
| 余杭区 Yuhang | 23 | 271 | 10149 | 6066 | 6019 |
| 富阳区 Fuyang | 33 | 540 | 6011 | 2094 | 2078 |
| 临安区 Lin'an | 38 | 222 | 5520 | 1383 | 1364 |
| 桐庐县 Tonglu | 35 | 420 | 3252 | 930 | 915 |
| 淳安县 Chun'an | 32 | 280 | 3062 | 1323 | 1320 |
| 建德市 Jiande | 24 | 195 | 3455 | 1821 | 1813 |

注:萧山区不含托管在钱塘新区的街道数据。

a) Figures of Xiaoshan District don't include districts which under administered by Qiantang New Area.

# 13－17 分地区优抚对象

## Number of Persons Receiving

单位:人

| 指标<br>Item | 全市<br>Total | 市区<br>Urban District | 上城区<br>Shangcheng | 下城区<br>Xiacheng | 江干区<br>Jianggan |
|---|---|---|---|---|---|
| 享受定期抚恤金人数<br>Number of Persons Receiving Periodical Commiseration | 4770 | 3519 | 244 | 227 | 215 |
| 烈属遗属<br>Number of Martyr Kinsfolk | 186 | 92 | 3 | 1 | 2 |
| 牺牲军人遗属<br>Number of the Sacrifice Soldiers | 94 | 66 | 1 | 1 | － |
| 病故军人遗属<br>Number of Kinsfolks of the Illness－died Soldiers | 161 | 112 | 4 | － | 6 |
| 残疾军人 | 4329 | 3249 | 236 | 225 | 207 |
| 享受定期补助人数<br>Number of Persons Enjoying Regular Subsidies | 44829 | 29144 | 306 | 298 | 884 |
| 在乡复员军人<br>Rural Demobilized Soldier | 1170 | 764 | 4 | 8 | 7 |
| 优待优抚对象带病回乡退伍军人<br>Number of Rural Veterans with Illness Receiving Subsiders | 2688 | 1498 | 2 | 3 | 14 |
| 优待优抚对象人数 | 40971 | 26882 | 300 | 287 | 863 |

## 人员情况(2019年)

## Public Subsidies by Region(2019)

(person)

| 拱墅区 Gongshu | 西湖区 Xihu | 高新(滨江)区 Hi-Tech (Binjiang) | 萧山区 Xiaoshan | 余杭区 Yuhang | 富阳区 Fuyang | 临安区 Lin'an | 桐庐县 Tonglu | 淳安县 Chun'an | 建德市 Jiande |
|---|---|---|---|---|---|---|---|---|---|
| 208 | 498 | 83 | 612 | 485 | 591 | 356 | 371 | 363 | 517 |
| 1 | 8 | 3 | 11 | 10 | 27 | 26 | 25 | 34 | 35 |
| - | 7 | - | 7 | 10 | 36 | 4 | 15 | 5 | 8 |
| 2 | 7 | 1 | 22 | 19 | 38 | 13 | 17 | 19 | 13 |
| 205 | 476 | 79 | 572 | 446 | 490 | 313 | 314 | 305 | 461 |
| 346 | 2004 | 735 | 9885 | 5789 | 7535 | 1362 | 5875 | 4212 | 5598 |
| 10 | 21 | 16 | 120 | 186 | 216 | 176 | 131 | 125 | 150 |
| - | 18 | 12 | 300 | 190 | 801 | 158 | 658 | 167 | 365 |
| 336 | 1965 | 707 | 9465 | 5413 | 6518 | 1028 | 5086 | 3920 | 5083 |

单位:个

| 指　　标 | Item | 全　市 Total | 市　区 Urban District | 萧山区 Xiaoshan |
|---|---|---|---|---|
| **合　　计** | **Total** | **3394** | **2542** | **323** |
| **按活动区域分** | **Grouped by Region** | | | |
| 地级社团 | City - level Societies | 770 | 770 | - |
| 县级社团 | County - level Societies | 2624 | 1772 | 323 |
| **按性质分** | **Grouped by Category** | | | |
| 科技与研究 | Technology and Research | 85 | 76 | 5 |
| 生态环境 | Ecological Envirenment | 24 | 19 | 7 |
| 教育 | Education | 52 | 42 | 7 |
| 卫生 | Health | 84 | 68 | 10 |
| 社会服务 | Social Services | 722 | 432 | 82 |
| 文化 | Culture | 442 | 367 | 44 |
| 体育 | Sport | 334 | 263 | 32 |
| 法律 | Law | 20 | 16 | 5 |
| 工商业服务 | Industry and Business Services | 809 | 744 | 39 |
| 宗教 | Religion | 43 | 31 | 8 |
| 农业及农村发展 | Agricure and Rural Development | 254 | 153 | 56 |
| 职业及从业组织 | Vocational and Business Organizations | 152 | 143 | 17 |
| 国际及涉外组织 | International and Foreign Organizations | 4 | 4 | - |
| 其他 | Other | 369 | 184 | 11 |

# 团体机构情况(2019 年)
# Organizations at County Level(2019)

(unit)

| | | | 桐庐县<br>Tonglu | 淳安县<br>Chun'an | 建德市<br>Jiande |
|---|---|---|---|---|---|
| 余杭区<br>Yuhang | 富阳区<br>Fuyang | 临安区<br>Lin'an | | | |
| **236** | **230** | **251** | **244** | **370** | **238** |
| 236 | 230 | 251 | 244 | 370 | 238 |
| 18 | 9 | – | – | 5 | 4 |
| 1 | 2 | | 1 | 3 | 1 |
| 1 | 2 | 3 | 2 | 4 | 4 |
| 11 | 7 | 5 | 6 | 5 | 5 |
| 10 | 52 | 106 | 20 | 260 | 10 |
| 24 | 39 | 27 | 31 | 20 | 24 |
| 24 | 18 | 21 | 27 | 10 | 34 |
| – | 3 | – | 1 | 1 | 2 |
| 74 | 55 | 37 | 17 | 26 | 22 |
| 4 | 4 | 4 | 5 | 3 | 4 |
| 22 | 23 | 38 | 43 | 24 | 34 |
| 8 | 14 | 10 | – | 9 | – |
| – | 2 | – | – | – | – |
| 39 | – | – | 91 | – | 94 |

# 13 – 19 社会保障情况(2012 – 2019 年)

## Social Security(2012 – 2019)

单位:万人 (10000 persons)

| 项 目<br>Item | 2012 | 2013 | 2014 | 2015 | 2016 | 2017 | 2018 | 2019 |
|---|---|---|---|---|---|---|---|---|
| 城镇登记失业人员<br>Number of the Registered Unemployed Persons in Urban | 3.97 | 4.60 | 4.03 | 3.67 | 3.72 | 3.76 | 4.27 | 5.32 |
| 城镇登记失业率(%)<br>The Registered Rate of Unemployment in Urban (%) | 1.63 | 1.85 | 1.84 | 1.74 | 1.72 | 1.70 | 1.60 | 1.80 |
| 失业人员再就业<br>The Re – employed Persons of Unemployment | 13.29 | 13.13 | 13.50 | 14.22 | 11.48 | 11.04 | 11.31 | 6.37 |
| 职工基本养老保险参保人数<br>Number of Persons in the Basic Pension Program in Urban | 492.62 | 530.70 | 559.48 | 569.09 | 575.98 | 628.32 | 671.07 | 704.69 |
| 失业保险参保人数<br>Number of Persons in the Unemployment Insurance Program | 299.78 | 316.36 | 331.83 | 349.42 | 374.16 | 413.20 | 459.37 | 486.65 |
| 职工基本医疗保险参保人数<br>Number of Persons in the Basic Medical Insurance Program | 425.82 | 448.35 | 469.40 | 500.21 | 529.32 | 580.50 | 632.66 | 671.12 |
| 工伤保险参保人数<br>Number of Persons in the Work – injure Insurance Program | 382.21 | 394.82 | 406.65 | 418.17 | 428.41 | 462.44 | 520.12 | 556.67 |
| 生育保险参保人数<br>Number of Persons in the Bear Insurance Program | 277.11 | 292.01 | 309.23 | 324.59 | 349.33 | 390.73 | 430.43 | 457.01 |
| 城乡居民养老保险(障)人数<br>Number of Persons in the Urban and Rural old – age Security | 112.98 | 106.40 | 103.97 | 99.45 | 95.51 | 88.68 | 85.09 | 83.61 |
| 城乡居民参加医疗保险人数<br>Number of urban and rural residents participated in medical insurance | 378.99 | 373.93 | 370.81 | 370.50 | 368.21 | 373.93 | 359.74 | 364.75 |

# 13－20 分地区社会保障情况(2019 年末)

# Social Security by Region(End of 2019)

单位:人 (persons)

| 指标<br>Item | 职工基本养老保险参保人数<br>Number of Employed Persons in the Basic Pension Program | 职工基本医疗保险参保人数<br>Number of Persons in the Basic Medical Insurance Program | 工伤保险参保人数<br>Number of Persons in the Work－injure Insurance Program | 生育保险参保人数<br>Number of Persons in the Bear Insurance Program | 失业保险参保人数<br>Number of Persons in the Unemployment Insurance Program |
|---|---|---|---|---|---|
| **全 市<br>Total** | **7046901** | **6711227** | **5566719** | **4570087** | **4866498** |
| 市 区<br>Urban District | 6519268 | 6281649 | 5233217 | 4333397 | 4626187 |
| 桐庐县<br>Tonglu | 212460 | 171377 | 120157 | 103892 | 103185 |
| 淳安县<br>Chun'an | 104727 | 104072 | 92685 | 51195 | 52243 |
| 建德市<br>Jiande | 210446 | 154129 | 120660 | 81603 | 84883 |

# 主要统计指标解释

**就业人员劳动报酬**　指各单位在一定时期内直接支付给本单位全部就业人员的劳动报酬总额。

**在岗职工工资总额**　指各单位在一定时期内直接支付给本单位全部在岗职工的劳动报酬总额。

工资总额的计算原则应以直接支付给职工的全部劳动报酬为根据。各单位支付给本单位全部职工的劳动报酬，不论是计入成本的还是不计入成本的，不论是以货币形式支付还是以实物形式支付的，不论是单位自筹的资金还是上级（或政府财政部门）下拨的资金，不论是厂级单位筹集的资金还是下属车间（科室）及附属经营单位筹集的资金，均应列入工资总额计算的范围。

**在岗职工平均工资**　指各单位的在岗职工在一定时期内平均每人所得的工资额。它表明一定时期内在岗职工工资收入的高低程度，是反映在岗职工工资水平的主要指标。计算公式为：

$$在岗职工平均工资=\frac{报告期实际支付的全部在岗职工工资总额}{报告期全部在岗职工平均人数}$$

**全社会单位**　包括独立核算的机关、事业单位，非私营企业和私营企业，但不含个体工商户。

**离休、退休、退职人员**　指正式办理了离休、退休、退职手续，并享受相应的离休、退休、退职待遇的人员。

**保险福利费用**　指企业、事业、机关单位在工资以外实际支付给职工和离休、退休、退职人员个人以及用于集体的劳动保险和福利费用。

**社会福利事业单位**　指集中收养社会孤、老、残、幼的机构。包括由民政部门管理的社会福利院、儿童福利院、精神病人福利院和城镇集体办的福利院，以及农村集体举办的敬老院。

**社会福利事业单位收养人数**　包括民政部门管理和城镇及农村集体举办的社会福利事业单位中收养的老人，少年儿童，缺乏生活自理能力的残疾人员和精神病人。

**商品零售价格指数**　是反映城乡商品零售价格变动趋势的一种经济指数。零售物价的调整变动直接影响到城乡居民的生活支出和国家的财政收入，影响居民购买力和市场供需平衡，影响消费与积累的比例。因此，计算零售价格指数，可以从一个侧面对上述经济活动进行观察和分析。

**居民消费价格指数**　是反映一定时期内城乡居民所购买的生活消费品价格和服务项目价格变动趋势和程度的相对数。是综合了城市居民消费价格指数和农民消费价格指数计算取得。利用居民消费价格指数，可以观察和分析消费品的零售价格和服务价格变动对城乡居民实际生活支出的影响程度。

**工业生产者出厂价格指数**　是反映全部工业产品出厂价格总水平的变动趋势和程度的相对数。其中除包括工业企业售给商业、外贸、物资部门的产品外，还包括售给工业和其他部门的生产资料以及直接售给居民的生活消费品。通过工业生产价格指数能观察出厂价格变动对工业总产值的影响。

# Explanatory Notes on Main Statistical Indicators

**Labour Remuneration of Employees** refers to total remuneration payment by various units to all their employees during a certain period of time.

**Total Wages of On – the – job Staff and Workers** refer to the total remuneration payment by various units to all their on – the – job staff and workers during a certain period of time.

The calculation of total wages should be based on the total remuneration payment directly paid to staff and workers. All wages and salaries and other payments to staff and workers should be calculated in, whether they are include in cost or not, paid in money or in kind, raised by the unit itself or allocated by the superior ( or the financial department of the government), raised by the factory level units or by subordinate workshops ( departments) and affiliated business units.

**Average Wage of On – the – job Staff and Workers** refers to the average wage per person during a certain period of time for on – the – job staff and workers in all units, which is a main indicator to reflect the general level of wage income of on – the – job staff and workers during a certain period of time. It is calculated as follows:

$$\text{Average Wage of On – the – job Staff and Workers} = \frac{\text{Total wages of on – the – job staff and workers actually paid in Reference Period}}{\text{Number of on – the – job Staff and workers in Reference period}}$$

**Units of Whole Society** includes independent accounting units of government organizations and institutions, non – private and private enterprises, but excludes individual business.

**Retired and Resigned Person** refers to persons who have formally gone through the formalities for their retirement or quitting from work and enjoy the corresponding treatments.

**Insurance and Welfare Funds** refers to labour insurance and welfare funds paid by enterprises, organizations and institutions to their staff and workers as well as retired and resigned persons individually in addition to their wages and salaries, and for collective use.

**Social Welfare Institutions** refer to institutions for centralized adoption of orphans, the elderly, the disabled and the young. It includes social welfare institutions run by civil affairs department, children welfare institutions, welfare institutions for mental patients, collective – owned welfare institutions and old people´s home in rural areas.

**Number of People Taken in by Social Welfare Institutions** refers to the number of old people, children, disabled persons and mental patients who lack self – care ability taken in by social welfare institutions run by civil affairs departments and collective units in urban and rural areas.

**Retail Price Index** reflects the general change in retail prices of commodities. The change and adjustment in retail prices directly affect the living expenditure of urban and rural residents, government revenue, purchasing power of residents and the equilibrium of market supply and demand, and the ratio of consumption to accumulation. Therefore, the calculation of retail price index is useful in observing and analyzing the above economic activities from one aspect.

**Consumer Price Index** reflects the trend and degree of changes in prices of consumer goods and services purchased by urban and rural residents in a certain period, and is a composite index derived from the urban consumer price index and the rural consumer price index. Consumer price index can be used to observe and analyze the impact of the change of consumer price and service price on actual expenditure for living cost of urban and rural residents.

**Ex – factory Price Index of Industrial Products** reflects the trend and degree of changes in general ex – factory prices of all industrial products, including products sold by industrial enterprise to commerce, foreign trade and materials departments, means of production sold to industry and other sectors, as well as consumer goods sold to residents. It can be used to analyze the impact of ex – factory prices on gross industrial output value.

# 中国统计出版社有限公司最新图书简目

（仅供参考，以实际出版为准）

**统计资料**

中国统计年鉴　中国统计摘要　中国第三产业统计年鉴
中国第三次全国农业普查综合资料　国际统计年鉴　金砖国家联合统计手册
中国－东盟国家统计手册　中国农村统计年鉴　中国县域统计年鉴
中国农产品价格调查年鉴　中国城市统计年鉴　中国价格统计年鉴
中国贸易外经统计年鉴　中国零售和餐饮连锁企业统计年鉴　中国商品交易市场统计年鉴
大中型批发零售和住宿餐饮企业统计年鉴　中国住户调查年鉴　中国工业统计年鉴
中国环境统计年鉴　中国能源统计年鉴　中国建筑业统计年鉴
中国房地产统计年鉴　投资领域统计年鉴　中国对外直接投资统计公报
中国人口和就业统计年鉴　中国劳动统计年鉴　中国社会统计年鉴
中国科技统计年鉴　中国高技术产业统计年鉴　全国企业创新调查年鉴
中国文化及相关产业统计年鉴　2018 年时间利用调查资料　中国妇女儿童状况统计资料
中国基本单位统计年鉴　中国教育统计年鉴　中国教育经费统计年鉴
中国民族统计年鉴　中国残疾人事业统计年鉴　长江经济带发展统计年鉴

**省级综合统计年鉴系列**

北京　天津　河北　山西　内蒙古　辽宁　吉林　黑龙江　上海　江苏　浙江　安徽　福建　江西　山东　河南　湖北　湖南　广东　广西　海南　重庆　四川　贵州　云南　西藏　陕西　甘肃　青海　宁夏　新疆　新疆生产建设兵团

**市（县）级综合统计年鉴系列**

滨海新区　石家庄　唐山　邯郸　保定　沧州　邢台　廊坊　承德　衡水　秦皇岛　张家口　太原　大同　阳泉　长治　晋城　朔州　晋中　运城　忻州　临汾　吕梁　呼和浩特　鄂尔多斯　包头　沈阳　大连　长春　延吉　四平　白山　通化　哈尔滨　齐齐哈尔　黑龙江垦区　上海浦东新区　南京　无锡　徐州　常州　苏州　南通　连云港　淮安　盐城　扬州　镇江　泰州　宿迁　江阴　丹阳　海门　张家港　杭州　宁波　温州　嘉兴　湖州　绍兴　金华　衢州　舟山　台州　丽水　合肥　安庆　福州　厦门　宁德　漳州　龙岩　莆田　泉州　三明　南平　南昌　九江　上饶　新余　抚州　赣州　景德镇　济南　青岛　枣庄　潍坊　聊城　郑州　洛阳　平顶山　三门峡　南阳　商丘　信阳　济源　汝州　武汉　十堰　荆州　宜昌　荆门　咸宁　黄冈　长沙　鹰潭　广州　深圳　惠州　东莞　汕尾　湛江　肇庆　南宁　柳州　桂林　贵港　梧州　来宾　河池　防城港　海口　三亚　儋州　成都　内江　贵阳　黔南　毕节　昆明　文山　德宏　西安　延安　安康　铜川　汉中　商洛　银川　兰州　庆阳　乌鲁木齐　昌吉　阿勒泰　兵团一师、二师、三师、四师、六师、七师、八师、十师、十三师、十四师

**调查年鉴系列**

天津　内蒙古　上海　河南　湖北　湖南　广东　广西　重庆　四川　云南　甘肃　宁夏　南宁　贵港　昆明

**统计方法应用/实用手册**

Python 数据分析基础（第二版）　非参数统计（第五版）　现代金融投资统计分析（第四版）
国民经济核算初级教程（第二版）　国民经济核算教程（第五版）　概率统计基础
全国统计专业技术资格考试系列考试用书：统计业务知识（第四版修订版）　统计业务知识学习指导与习题
全国统计专业技术资格考试系列考试用书：统计相关知识（第四版）　统计相关知识学习指导与习题

**统计通俗读物/统计科普图书**

领导干部统计知识问答　统计公文写作及会议办理实用手册　大数据在统计工作中的应用案例汇编
中国国民经济核算知识问答（修订版）　地区生产总值核算国际比较研究　新中国统计制度方法的发展与改革

**重点图书**

中国农业统计资料 1949－2019　第四次全国经济普查地图集　中国经济普查年鉴 2018
新编英汉汉英统计大词典　中国国民经济核算体系 2016　国民经济行业分类注释
挑大学选专业 2020—考研择校指南　挑大学选专业 2020—高考志愿填报指南　中华医学统计百科全书

发行部电话：（010）63376907　63376908　63376909　同槓行书店电话：（010）68783171　68783172
地址：北京市丰台区西三环南路甲 6 号　邮政编码：100073　网址：http://www.zgtjcbs.com

HANGZHOU

STATISTICAL YEARBOOK

杭州统计年鉴